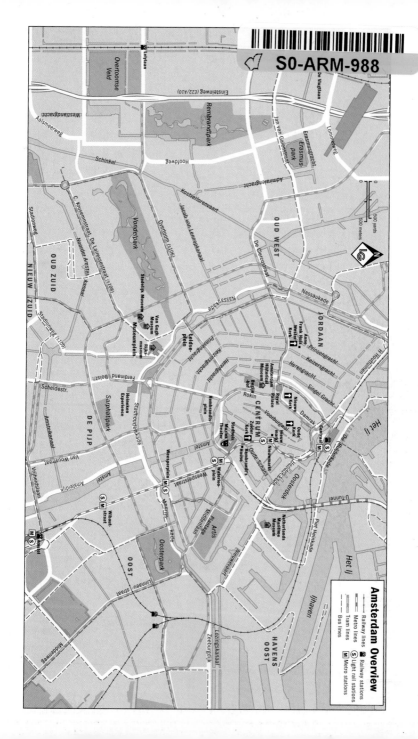

S0-ARM-988

Amsterdam Overview

Railway lines
🚆 Railway stations
Ⓢ Light rail stations
Ⓜ Metro stations
Metro lines
Ⓢ Light rail lines
Tram lines
Bus lines

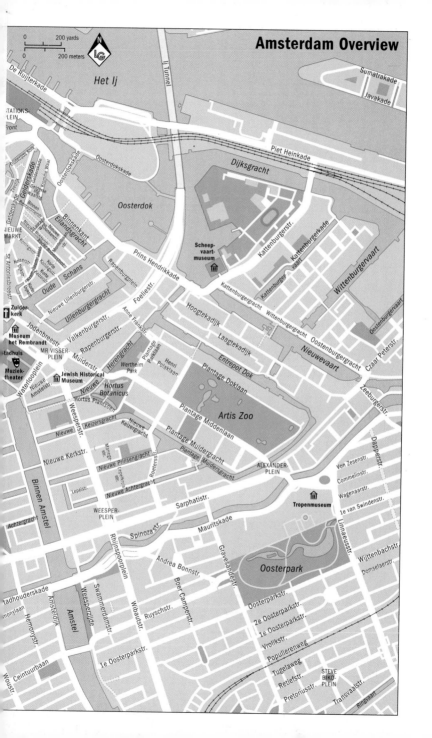

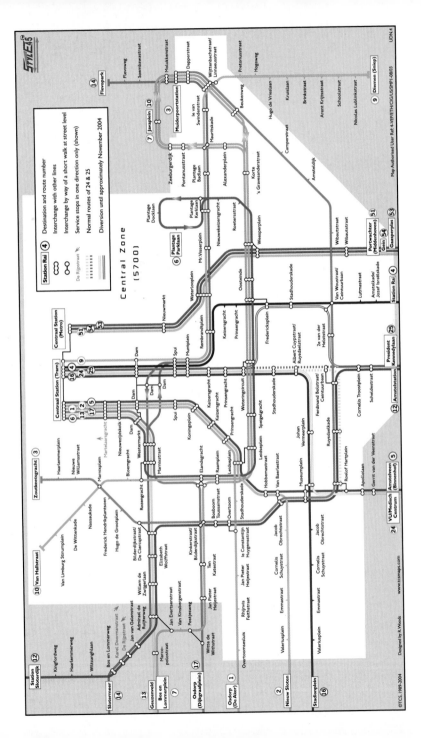

unknown country com

LET'S GO

■ THE RESOURCE FOR THE INDEPENDENT TRAVELER

"The guides are aimed not only at young budget travelers but at the indepedent traveler; a sort of streetwise cookbook for traveling alone."

—The New York Times

"Unbeatable; good sight-seeing advice; up-to-date info on restaurants, hotels, and inns; a commitment to money-saving travel; and a wry style that brightens nearly every page."

—The Washington Post

"Lighthearted and sophisticated, informative and fun to read. [Let's Go] helps the novice traveler navigate like a knowledgeable old hand."

—Atlanta Journal-Constitution

"A world-wise traveling companion—always ready with friendly advice and helpful hints, all sprinkled with a bit of wit."

—The Philadelphia Inquirer

■ THE BEST TRAVEL BARGAINS IN YOUR PRICE RANGE

"All the dirt, dirt cheap."

—People

"Anything you need to know about budget traveling is detailed in this book."

—The Chicago Sun-Times

"Let's Go follows the creed that you don't have to toss your life's savings to the wind to travel—unless you want to."

—The Salt Lake Tribune

■ REAL ADVICE FOR REAL EXPERIENCES

"The writers seem to have experienced every rooster-packed bus and lunar-surfaced mattress about which they write."

—The New York Times

"A guide should tell you what to expect from a destination. Here Let's Go shines."

—The Chicago Tribune

"[Let's Go's] devoted updaters really walk the walk (and thumb the ride, and trek the trail). Learn how to fish, haggle, find work—anywhere."

—Food & Wine

LET'S GO PUBLICATIONS

TRAVEL GUIDES

Alaska 1st edition **NEW TITLE**
Australia 2004
Austria & Switzerland 2004
Brazil 1st edition **NEW TITLE**
Britain & Ireland 2004
California 2004
Central America 8th edition
Chile 1st edition
China 4th edition
Costa Rica 1st edition
Eastern Europe 2004
Egypt 2nd edition
Europe 2004
France 2004
Germany 2004
Greece 2004
Hawaii 2004
India & Nepal 8th edition
Ireland 2004
Israel 4th edition
Italy 2004
Japan 1st edition **NEW TITLE**
Mexico 20th edition
Middle East 4th edition
New Zealand 6th edition
Pacific Northwest 1st edition **NEW TITLE**
Peru, Ecuador & Bolivia 3rd edition
Puerto Rico 1st edition **NEW TITLE**
South Africa 5th edition
Southeast Asia 8th edition
Southwest USA 3rd edition
Spain & Portugal 2004
Thailand 1st edition
Turkey 5th edition
USA 2004
Western Europe 2004

CITY GUIDES

Amsterdam 3rd edition
Barcelona 3rd edition
Boston 4th edition
London 2004
New York City 2004
Paris 2004
Rome 12th edition
San Francisco 4th edition
Washington, D.C. 13th edition

MAP GUIDES

Amsterdam
Berlin
Boston
Chicago
Dublin
Florence
Hong Kong
London
Los Angeles
Madrid
New Orleans
New York City
Paris
Prague
Rome
San Francisco
Seattle
Sydney
Venice
Washington, D.C.

COMING SOON:
Road Trip USA

LET'S GO

AMSTERDAM

JAMES A. M. CRAWFORD EDITOR
MIRANDA I. LASH ASSOCIATE EDITOR

RESEARCHER-WRITERS
IRIN CARMON
JOHN HULSEY
LINDA LI

BRIAN J. EMEOTT MAP EDITOR
EMMA NOTHMANN MANAGING EDITOR

ST. MARTIN'S PRESS ✣ NEW YORK

Maps by David Lindroth copyright © 2004 by St. Martin's Press.

Distributed outside the USA and Canada by Macmillan.

ISBN: 0-312-31976-2

First edition
10 9 8 7 6 5 4 3 2 1

Let's Go: Amsterdam is written by Let's Go Publications, 67 Mount Auburn Street, Cambridge, MA 02138, USA.

Let's Go® and the LG logo are trademarks of Let's Go, Inc.
Printed in the USA.

HOW TO USE THIS BOOK

PRICE RANGES & RANKINGS. Within every neighborhood, our researchers rank all lists in order of descending quality. Those places particularly worthy of praise get a Let's Go thumbs up (🔲). Each food and accommodation listing is followed by an icon indicating its price range and giving a general indication of the cost of goods and services offered. For more information on these, see p. xii.

ORGANIZATION. The coverage in this book, like the city of Amsterdam, is divided into neighborhoods. The **Discover** chapter is organized roughly as the city is laid out; the **Sights, Museums & Galleries, Food & Drink, Nightlife,** and **Accommodations** are broken down into neighborhood groupings. The **Shopping** and **Arts & Entertainment** chapters are organized alphabetical according to establishment type.

FEATURES & ARTICLES. Unique to this book is **Only in Amsterdam,** a chapter that lists the city's best coffeeshops and gives information on health and safety. Throughout this book, you'll find sidebars in black boxes. You can get **The Local Story** from Amsterdammers themselves, learn what's been going on **In Recent News,** delve into fine paintings with **Get Smart,** learn historical tidbits with **In the Know,** hear about some of the The Netherlands' **Local Legends,** discover **Hidden Deals** and the best ways to blow your budget on **Big Splurges,** and get to do **No Work All Play** with The Netherlands' coolest festivals. Don't miss the book's **Articles:** a history of The Netherlands' soft drugs culture and politics (p. 48) and an exploration of the paintings by Dutch master Joahnnes Vermeer (p. 95).

WHEN TO USE IT

1-2 MONTHS BEFORE YOU GO. Our book is filled with practical information to help you before you go. **Planning Your Trip** has advice about passports, plane tickets, insurance, and more. The **Accommodations** section can help you with booking a room from home.

2 WEEKS BEFORE YOU GO. Start thinking about your ideal trip. **Discover Amsterdam** lists the city's top 25 sights, along with suggested itineraries, walking tours, Let's Go Picks (the best and most bizarre in the city), and the dirt on neighborhoods. Read up on Dutch history and culture in the **Life & Times** chapter.

ON THE ROAD. Once in Amsterdam (p. 25) will be your best friend once you've arrived, with all the practical information you'll need alongside the listings in the various chapters (see above). When you feel like striking out, the **Daytripping** chapter will help; it provides options for short trips away from Amsterdam. The **Service Directory** contains a list of local services. Should you decide that you want to do more than just tour, turn to **Alternatives to Tourism** for information on volunteering, studying, and working in Amsterdam. Finally, just remember to put down this guide once in a while and go exploring on your own; you'll be glad you did**.**

CONTENTS

arts & entertainment 163

shopping 173

accommodations 183

daytripping 207

planning your trip 283

alternatives to tourism 303

service directory 319

index 325

map appendix 335

bold denotes maps

RESEARCHER-WRITERS

Irin Carmon   *CCR, DP, J, JP, LP, OW, Groningen, Wadden Islands*

With her *Boston Globe* travel column and past stint as a Let's Go editor, Irin was a well-established travel writer before she brought her urbane, cultured sensibilities to the 'Dam. Though turned away from men-only haunts, she breezed through nightlife and classy coffeeshops, saw De Pijp's gentrification, and delved into her cultural history in the Jodenbuurt. An urban sophisticate at heart, Irin still braved the Waddens and made friends in Groningen. Her polished, professional writing was as elegant as her Bohemian sense of style.

John Hulsey   *MV, NZ, SQ, Arnhem, Delft, The Hague,*
De Hoge Veluwe, Maastricht, Rotterdam, Utrecht

Ever dapper in his blue crushed-velvet jacket, this dauntless daytripper, art aficionado, and doggedly budget-minded traveler biked everywhere—from Museumplein symphonies to Nieuwe Zijd tourist hordes—before heading out to cover the country's painted treasures with passion and insight (finding one of the country's best museums in a national park). Writing lucidly and stripped of hyperbole, John gave a brutally honest, uncompromising view of the city.

Linda Li   *CRW, OZ, RLD, RP, GA, Aalsmeer, Haarlem,*
Leiden, Lisse, Zansee Schans, Zaandvoort-aan-Zee

Both in print and in person, Linda exudes boundless energy—which served her well as she ran through Red Lights, (almost) kicked pigeons in The Dam (see p. 29), got a Cannabis College Ph.D. for delving in to the *intellectual* side of coffeeshop culture, and conquered Rembrandtplein's hottest clubs. Plucky enough to play dumb tourist, she clog-hopped from Zansee Schans to Tulip Country with a refreshing approach to travel—a worldly ingenue, without the naivete.

CONTRIBUTING WRITERS

Stefan Atkinson ("From the Road: Queen of Hearts?") is a graduate of Harvard University with a degree in European history. He was also a Researcher-Writer (in the Canal Ring West, Jodenbuurt, Nieuwe Zijd, and Plantage neighborhoods) for the 2003 edition of this *Let's Go* guide. See **Sights,** p. 61.

Sasha Polakow-Suransky ("Soft Drugs & Rock 'n' Roll: The Changing, Controversial History of Tolerance") is currently a writer for the magazine *The American Prospect*. See **Life & Times,** p. 48.

Dr. Ivan Gaskell ("On the Trail of Vermeer") is the Margaret S. Winthrop Curator in the Department of Paintings, Sculpture, and Decorative Arts at the Fogg Art Museum at Harvard University. He is a respected scholar and commentator on the works of Dutch master painter Johannes Vermeer. He is also the co-editor of *Vermeer Studies*. See **Museums,** p. 95.

ABOUT LET'S GO

GUIDES FOR THE INDEPENDENT TRAVELER

Budget travel is more than a vacation. At *Let's Go*, we see every trip as the chance of a lifetime. If your dream is to grab a knapsack and a machete and forge through the jungles of Brazil, we can take you there. Or, if you'd rather enjoy the Riviera sun at a beachside cafe, we'll set you a table. If you know what you're doing, you can have any experience you want—whether it's camping among lions or sampling Tuscan desserts—without maxing out your credit card. We'll show you just how far your coins can go, and prove that the greatest limitation on your adventure is not your wallet, but your imagination. That said, we understand that you may want the occasional indulgence after a week of hostels and kebab stands, so we've added "Big Splurges" to let you know which establishments are worth those extra euros, as well as price ranges to help you quickly determine whether an accommodation or restaurant will break the bank. While we may have diversified, our emphasis will always be on finding the best values for your budget, giving you all the info you need to spend six days in London or six months in Tasmania.

BEYOND THE TOURIST EXPERIENCE

We write for travelers who know there's more to a vacation than riding double-deckers with tourists. Our researchers give you the heads-up on both world-renowned and lesser-known attractions, on the best local eats and the hottest nightclub beats. In our travels, we talk to everybody; we provide a snapshot of real life in the places you visit with our sidebars on topics like regional cuisine, local festivals, and hot political issues. We've opened our pages to respected writers and scholars to show you their take on a given destination, and turned to lifelong residents to learn the little things that make their city worth calling home. And we've even given you Alternatives to Tourism—ideas for how to give back to local communities through responsible travel and volunteering.

OVER FORTY YEARS OF WISDOM

When we started, way back in 1960, Let's Go consisted of a small group of well-traveled friends who compiled their budget travel tips into a 20-page packet for students on charter flights to Europe. Since then, we've expanded to suit all kinds of travelers, now publishing guides to six continents, including our newest guides: *Let's Go: Japan* and *Let's Go: Brazil*. Our guides are still annually researched and written entirely by students on shoe-string budgets, adventurous travelers who know that train strikes, stolen luggage, food poisoning, and marriage proposals are all part of a day's work. Even as you read this, work on next year's editions is well underway. Whether you're reading one of our new titles, like *Let's Go: Puerto Rico* or *Let's Go Adventure Guide: Alaska*, or our original best-seller, *Let's Go: Europe*, you'll find the same spirit of adventure that has made *Let's Go* the guide of choice for travelers the world over since 1960.

GETTING IN TOUCH

The best discoveries are often those you make yourself; on the road, when you find something worth sharing, please drop us a line. We're Let's Go Publications, 67 Mt. Auburn St., Cambridge, MA 02138, USA (feedback@letsgo.com).

For more info, visit our website: www.letsgo.com.

PRICE RANGES >> AMSTERDAM

Our researchers rank all establishments in this guide by value, in descending order of quality; their favorite places get the Let's Go thumbs-up (🖐). Since the best value isn't always the cheapest price, we have a system of price ranges for quick reference. For **accommodations,** we base the range on the cheapest per night rate for a solo traveler. For **food,** we base it on the average price of a main course. Below we list what you'll *typically* find at the corresponding price range.

ACCOMMODATIONS	RANGE	WHAT YOU'RE LIKELY TO FIND
❶	under €30	Mostly hostels and really cheap hotels; expect a basic dorm-style room and shared bathrooms. There may be lockout and/or curfew. Breakfast is sometimes included.
❷	€31-49	Smaller hotels. Expect basic but clean, comfortable rooms, sometimes private bathrooms. Breakfast included.
❸	€50-69	Small hotels in more central areas, potentially on more frequently traveled streets and with more amenities or better decor. Most rooms with private bath, TV, and phone.
❹	€70-99	Nicer hotels in convenient areas; away from noisy touristed streets. Well-decorated rooms, and smarter service.
❺	above €100	Larger hotels or upscale chains. If you're paying this much, your room should cater to all your needs, and have all the amenities you want. Decor and service should be especially charming and comfortable.

FOOD	RANGE	WHAT YOU'RE LIKELY TO FIND
❶	under €7	Mostly take-out food, like sandwiches, falafel or shwarma. Bakeries, desserts, and soup shops; some *eetcafes*.
❷	€7-10	Small restaurants, standard *eetcafes*, and cheaper ethnic food. Appetizers at a bar, low-priced entrees and *tapas*.
❸	€11-14	Mid-priced entrees, cheaper seafood and exotic pasta dishes; more upscale ethnic food. Tip will bump you up a couple of Euros because you'll have a waiter or waitress.
❹	€15-19	Upscale restaurants with a decent wine list, tasteful decor, and good service. Pricier seafood, and high-end ethnic cuisine. Few places with dress code, but avoid t-shirt and jeans.
❺	above €20	Beautifully appointed surroundings, extensive wine list and epicurean food that matches the decor—dress nicely. Exotic dishes and ingredients; no *tostis* here.

ACKNOWLEDGMENTS

LET'S GO

James thanks: Special thanks go out to my RWs—Irin, John, and Linda for agreeing to tackle this daunting, incredible city, and to one-fifth of my AE, Miranda, for tolerating my outlandish—and decidedly non-Harrison-like—behaviour in the office. Emma, my patient ME, thank you for trusting me with this resurrection project, and Scrobins, our caring cityguide matron, thanks for always being there to avert a crisis. Great affection for the cityguide crew: Abigail, Daparker, Dunia, Mike, Megan M-G, and Mrsmith, but especially for Matt and Steph—I'd have gone even more squirrelly without nipple pinching, the honourary Dirrrty Canuck, and, em, trips next door. Thomas, my man with Beatles and breakfast, and the ever-tolerant roommates Mac and Lauren—thank you. And most importantly, but in alphabetical (i.e. non-heirarchical) order: love to ▉Dad, ▉Jess, ▉Mum, and ▉Si for the infinite support they have shown through frequently difficult times. Hello NYU.

Miranda thanks: Dear James, you crazy Canuck, thank you for sing-alongs and spontaneous dance routines, oh yes, and for drooling with me over good art and great write-ups. A big thanks to our RWs John, Linda and Irin, you really went the extra mile for us. Thanks to Sarah, our faithful Manager for smiles and scorpion bowls. Of course, lots of love to my crazy City Guide buds. A big hug to Cristina, who brightened my summer with her silliness and charm. I was so happy to have you. Thanks to Becky for making life a little more fun. A million thanks to my parents for their love and support. Finally, thanks to Danny, for your friendship and affection. You put up with my ranting and gave me an extra boost when I needed it most. Texas here I come!

Brian thanks: The impossible Dutch language for being so hard to spell, yet so fun to pronounce. David A., who suffered through AMS with me last summer so I could picture the city as I mapped it. Christine Y. for allowing me to think I was talking to her all summer when I was really talking to myself or inanimate objects (and for giving in to proofing these maps).

Editor James A. M. Crawford
Associate Editor Miranda I. Lash
Managing Editor Emma Nothmann
Map Editor Brian J. Emeott
Typesetter Ankur Ghosh
Photographer Vanessa Bertozzi

Publishing Director
Julie A. Stephens
Editor-in-Chief
Jeffrey Dubner
Production Manager
Dusty Lewis
Cartography Manager
Nathaniel Brooks
Design Manager
Caleb Beyers
Editorial Managers
Lauren Bonner, Ariel Fox,
Matthew K. Hudson, Emma Nothmann,
Joanna Shawn Brigid O'Leary,
Sarah Robinson
Financial Manager
Suzanne Siu
Marketing & Publicity Managers
Megan Brumagim, Nitin Shah
Personnel Manager
Jesse Reid Andrews
Researcher Manager
Jennifer O'Brien
Web Manager
Jesse Tov
Web Content Director
Abigail Burger
Production Associates
Thomas Bechtold, Jeffrey Hoffman Yip
IT Directors
Travis Good, E. Peyton Sherwood
Financial Assistant
R. Kirkie Maswoswe
Associate Web Manager
Robert Dubbin
Office Coordinators
Abigail Burger, Angelina L. Fryer,
Liz Glynn

Director of Advertising Sales
Daniel Ramsey
Senior Advertising Associates
Sara Barnett, Daniella Boston
Advertising Artwork Editors
Julia Davidson, Sandy Liu

President
Abhishek Gupta
General Manager
Robert B. Rombauer
Assistant General Manager
Anne E. Chisholm

Discover Amsterdam

Amsterdam is not merely the city of garish sin, of anything-goes libertinism. A history of tolerance that permits institutions offensive to conservative sensibilities—soft drug use and a legalized sex trade—also includes a pervasive, progressive tradition of a different sort. Long before coffeeshops dotted the cityscape, Amsterdam in particular, and The Netherlands in general, was a haven for refugees seeking asylum from varied persecution. From Portuguese Jews in the early 17th century to Surinamese escaping military dictatorship in the 1980s, Amsterdam has welcomed and respected many immigrant communities, giving the country a cultural richness that offests the sometime seediness of pervasive drug tourism. The same culture of openness has allowed the gay and lesbian community to flourish, giving a certain dose of vibrancy that might otherwise remain absent in this supremely amiable city.

Yet as easy and free as its liberal policies seem, Amsterdam has seen its fair share of struggles. In years past, Amsterdammers fought for their city, saving it from sinking into the swamps and succumbing under the tides by sheer stubbornness. The 16th-century Alteration denied Catholics the right to practice their religion. During World War II tolerance was quite literally attacked on Dutch home soil, as Nazi forces occupied the city and deported its Jewish citizens to concentration camps. Accordingly, the city has sometimes doubted its openness, but it still patiently receives temporary guests: eagerly experimenting youth, pot pilgrims, businesspeople, drunken stag parties, art aficionados, and history buffs. And though Amsterdam cannot be reduced to the description of rampant liberal tolerance, it *is* partially a place for indulging desires, a place with limitless possibilities, where anything goes. Just remember that a Golden Age of art flourished here, and here art remains in many forms—Rembrandt's shadowy portraiture and Vermeer's luminous women, the post-Impressionist swirls of van Gogh's brush and the clean, sharp lines of Mondrian's squares. They serve as a reminder that the best trip to Amsterdam isn't necessarily the one you won't remember.

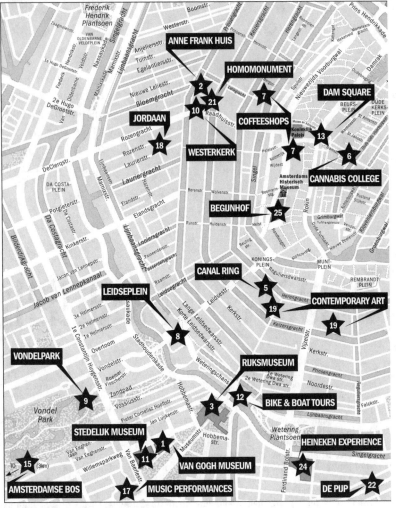

ANNE FRANK HUIS

HOMOMONUMENT

DAM SQUARE

JORDAAN

COFFEESHOPS

WESTERKERK

CANNABIS COLLEGE

BEGIJNHOF

CANAL RING

LEIDSEPLEIN

CONTEMPORARY ART

VONDELPARK

RIJKSMUSEUM

BIKE & BOAT TOURS

STEDELIJK MUSEUM

HEINEKEN EXPERIENCE

AMSTERDAMSE BOS

VAN GOGH MUSEUM

MUSIC PERFORMANCES

DE PIJP

TOP 25 SIGHTS

Unlike many other European cities, Amsterdam tends to shy away from grandiose regalia. Expect to find few "monuments" in Amsterdam: the following "sights" are really suggestions for how to spend a shorter visit to the city on the Amstel.

25. BEGIJNHOF. This serene courtyard provides early-risers a space for secluded contemplation. Peaceful rose-lined gardens and beautifully manicured lawns afford much-needed respite from the bustling, tourist-filled excesses of the Nieuwe Zijd neighborhood (see p. 60).

24. HEINEKEN EXPERIENCE. It's touristy and commercial, but nonetheless, the Experience provides some goofy fun with video exhibits and interactive displays. Three beers and a souvenir glass are well worth the price of admission (see p. 69).

Het Ij

Centraal Station
STATIONS-PLEIN
Open Haven Front

Javakade

Piet Heinkade

0   200 yards
0   200 meters

MUSEUM AMSTELKRING

Dijksgracht

Oosterdoksskade
Oosterdoksskade

16
4

Oosterdok

Scheep-vaart-museum

NIEUW-MARKT
St Antoniesbreestr.
RED LIGHT DISTRICT

Prins Hendrikkade

Oude Schans

Kattenburgerstr.
Kattenburgervaart
Kattenburgerkade

Wittenburgervaart

MUSEUM HET REMBRANDT

Jodenbreestr.
Uilenburgergracht
Foeliestr.

Kattenburgergracht
Kattenburger
Wittenburgergracht Oostenburgergracht Nieuwevaart

Czaar Peterstr.

PORTUGEES-ISRAELIETISCHE SYNAGOGE

23
Stadhuis
Muziektheater
Waterlooplein
MR VISSER-PLEIN
14
Muiderstr.
Rapenburgerstr.
Herengracht
Plantage Pekslaan
Henri Polaklaan
Wertheim Park

Hoogtekadijk

Entrepot Dok

Plantage Doklaan

Nieuwe Amstelstr.
Nieuwe
20
Hortus Plantsoen
Keizersgracht

HORTUS BOTANICUS

Artis Zoo

Plantage Middenlaan

Zeeburgerstr.
Dappertstr.

Weesperstr.
Nieuwe Kerkstr.
Nieuwe Prinsengracht

Plantage Muidergracht
Plantage Muidergracht

ALEXANDER-PLEIN

Von Zesenstr.
Commelinstr.
Wagenaarstr.
Eerste van Swindenstr.

Utrechtstr.
Utrechtsedwarsstr.
Achtergracht
Binnen Amstel
Lepelstr.
Nieuwe Achtergracht
Roeterstr.

WEESPER-PLEIN
Sarphatistr.

Linnaeusstr.

FREDERIKS-PLEIN

Rhijnspoorplein
Spinozastr.
Mauritskade

Andrea Bonnstr.
Boerhaavestr.

Ooster Park

Stadhouderskade
Hemonylaan
Hemonystr.
Amstel
Amsteldijk
Weesperzijde
Swammerdamstr.
Wibautstr.
Ruyschstr.
Eerste Oosterparkstr.

Top ★25★ Sights

23. MUSEUM HET REMBRANDT. Step into Rembrandt's former house, now home to the artist's collection of over 250 etchings. Watch where the master ate and slept, and learn his painting and color-mixing techniques from skilled artisans (see p. 97).

22. DE PIJP. Have dinner in one of this up-and-coming neighborhood's peerless assemblage of stellar ethnic restaurants (see p. 119).

21. HOMOMONUMENT & PINK POINT. Get all the information you need about gay, lesbian, and bisexual life in Amsterdam at this site that also commemorates persecution of gays throughout the ages (see p. 67).

20. HORTUS BOTANICUS. One of the oldest medicinal gardens in the world, the Hortus Botanics has a host of rare or exotic plants, making for a quite relaxing afternoon detour (see p. 71).

amsterdam by the numbers

Age: 729 years old in 2004

Population: 735,500

Total Area: 212 sq. km

Land Area: 159 sq. km

Visitors per year: 6,500,000

Cars: 234,000

Bikes: 400,000

Trams: 260

Houseboats: 2500

Bulb flowers in public gardens & parks: 600,000

Canals: 165

Bridges: 1281

Wooden bridges: 8

Skinny bridges: 1

Markets: 28

Chinese temples: 1

Coffeeshops in 1960: 5

Coffeeshops today: 281

Grams of pot you can legally buy & carry at one time: 5

Marijuana smokers: 420

Rembrandts: 22

*Night Watch*es: 1

Attacks on *Night Watch*: 2

Van Goghs: 206

Diamond Factories: 26

Wax statues at Madame Tussaud's: 115

Windmills: 6

Cinemas: 40

Giant Chess Pieces: 32

Giant Marble Penises: 1

19. CONTEMPORARY ART. Amsterdam is brimming with work by both established and up-and-coming artists. Check out the **FOAM Photography Museum** (see p. 88), **De Appel** (see p. 88), **The Netherlands Media Art Institute** (see p. 88), or **W 139** (see p. 101) for the best work. Be sure to visit **galleries** in the Jordaan (see p. 90) or Canal Ring West (see p. 85).

18. JORDAAN. This peaceful yet fashionable neighborhood is arguably one of the Amsterdam's most beautiful, with restored gabled houses and flower-filled terraces. Low-key and cozy, with a bevy of excellent museums (see p. 90) and dining (see p. 116), The Jordaan is a perfect escape from frenetic Centrum.

17. MUSIC PERFORMANCES. Take in a performance at one of Amsterdam's premier classical, contemporary or pop music concert venues, such as the **Concertgebouw** (see p. 164), **Bimhuis** (see p. 164), or **Paradiso** (see p. 166).

16. MUSEUM AMSTELKRING. Visit one of the few remaining hidden churches, built into the attic of a canal house during the Alteration, when Catholics were forbidden to practice their religion (see p. 81).

15. AMSTERDAMSE BOS. Go beyond the touristed areas of Amsterdam to its "woods" in the south. The park is full of lush greenery and bike paths (see p. 74).

14. PORTUGEES-ISRAELIETISCHE SYNAGOGE. The Portuguese Synagogue miraculously escaped destruction during Amsterdam's Nazi occupation during WWII. The 1675 structure is one of the few remaining monuments to the **Jodenbuurt's** once-thriving Jewish community. The nearby **Joods Historisch Museum (Jewish Historical Museum)** celebrates and commemorates Jewish culture (see p. 97).

13. DAM SQUARE. Nieuwe Kerk, with some of the city's prettiest stained glass, has risen from the flames time after time to throw its shadow upon Dam Square. Aside from being a superb people-watching venue, and the city's best meeting place, the Dam also houses the **Koninklijk Paleis,** the **Royal Palace** (see p. 61).

12. BIKE & BOAT TOURS. See the city as the locals do by renting a bike; it's the most pleasant way to while away a morning or an afternoon. Tour through the city's winding canals on a relaxing boat tour; though they skim low on the surface of the water, boats promise the best views of the city (see p. 76).

11. STEDELIJK MUSEUM OF MODERN & CONTEMPORARY ART. The best collection of modern painting and sculpture in all of The Netherlands, with a great selection of works by such greats as Malevich, Mondrian, plus several contemporary artists (see p. 93).

10. WESTERKERK. You'll find the best views of the city from the **Westerkerktoren,** (see p. 63), and because The Netherlands is extraordinarily flat, on a clear day, you'll be able to see for kilometers in every direction. Rembrandt is buried here, and the music played by the church bell tower is the most lovely in Amsterdam.

9. VONDELPARK OUTDOOR EVENTS. Spend a late afternoon in this especially in this luminously green expanse and catch an outdoor concert or movie here on a languid summer's evening (see p. 68).

Winding Residential Canal

8. LEIDSEPLEIN. Day or night, this area is always bustling with activity, with locals and tourists alike. Your head will spin with all the restaurants, bars, and clubs all clamor for attention (see p. 113 and p. 152).

7. COFFEESHOPS. The other half to Amsterdam's partnered culture of liberalism, coffeeshops peddle marijuana and hashish (decriminalized in The Netherlands) as well as any number of foodstuffs laced with the hallucinogens. For some of the city's best that blaze the brightest, see **Cream of the Shop,** p. 126.

Bloemenmarkt

6.CANNABIS COLLEGE. A heady experience of a different sort, the "College" will help you get the facts—physiological, political, and criminal—straight before toking up in the city. Exceptionally friendly staff, willing to answer any question, no matter how outlandish, make the trip even more worthwhile (see p. 80).

5. CANAL RING. Whether you're in Amsterdam for the gallery scene, soft drug culture, or historic sights, the Canal Ring—Western and Central—is an obligatory stop. Elegant canal houses perch on winding waterways as they have since the Golden Age. Check out the opulent homes along the **Golden Bend** (p. 65), on Herengracht between Leidsestraat and Vijzelstraat.

4. RED LIGHT DISTRICT. Gaudy, slick, and unimaginably professional, the Red Light District is a must-see. Enjoying the outlandish spectacle does not necessarily mean touching: watch the tourists watching the prostitutes or step into the Casa Rosso for a live **sex show,** but be sure to always watch your wallet (see p. 58).

BGL Solidarity

✎ let's go picks

Most perplexing Dutch "delicacy": *bitterballen.*

Best place for a three-way collision between a bus, a car, and a tram: Muntplein.

Grooviest (really) museum owner: Nick Padalino of Electric Ladyland (p. 90).

Best place to check your mate: playing chess at Max Euweplein (p. 66).

Classiest Sex Shop: Stout (p. 126).

Most painful stomach cramp: All you can eat in 1hr. at Taste of Culture (p. 105).

Highest elevation & best view: Westerkerktoren (p. 63).

Best place to unleash your inner tourist: Zaanse Schans (p. 221).

Fruitiest space shakes: Abraxas (p. 131).

Most embarrassing museum to visit with your family: Sex Museum (p. 81).

Best place to kick pigeons: Dam Square (p. 61).

Headiest Dutch brew: Wieckse Witte from Maastricht.

Best converted churches now devoted to sacrilege: Paradiso (p. 152), De Engel (p. 159).

Biggest rotating balls: Outside Casa Rosso (p. 125).

Greatest escape: Wadden Islands (p. 274).

Best Pastries: Lanskroon (p. 112).

Best Coffeeshop: See "Cream of the Shop," p. 126.

3. RIJKSMUSEUM. Containing the country's best collection of Golden Age art, the museum houses two monumental paintings—Rembrandt's *Night Watch* and Vermeer's *Milkmaid*—as well as works by Jan Steen and Frans Hals. (see p. 94).

2. ANNE FRANK HUIS. This museum poignantly preserves the memory of Anne Frank. Walk behind the secret false bookcase to enter the rooms that sheltered the Frank family from 1942 to 1944 during the invasion of Nazi Germany (see p. 85).

1. VAN GOGH MUSEUM. Even if you're not a Van Gogh fan, you'll enjoy this polished modern home to over 200 paintings and drawings by the painter of *Sunflowers*, *The Courtesan*, and *Bedroom at Arles*. The collection also houses an assemblage of works by the master's contemporaries (see p. 91).

SUGGESTED ITINERARIES

THREE DAYS

DAY 1: MAJOR MUSEUMS

Spend your first morning in Amsterdam at the **Museumplein,** at the **Rijksmuseum** (p. 94) and the **Van Gogh Museum** (p. 91); after museum-hopping stop into the **Vondelpark** (p. 68) for a picnic lunch. In the afternoon, orient yourself by taking a **boat tour** (p. 76). A night out—dinner and clubbing in **Leidseplein** (p. 113)—will get you to the city's vibrant after-hours scene.

DAY 2: CANAL RING & NIEUWE ZIJD

If you're an early-riser, check out the organic produce at the **Noordermarkt** (p. 179), the most touristed but arguably most important stop in the city. Move down Prinsengracht to explore the canal houses on the rest of the beautiful Canal Ring. Begin your afternoon at the **Begijnhof** (p. 60), then work your way north to **Dam Square** (p. 61) for the **National Monument, Nieuwe Kerk** (p. 82), and the **Royal Palace**. Head up to the **Sex Museum** (p. 80) for fetishist thrills and then in the early evening, stroll through the **Red Light District** (p. 58) for a glimpse of the real thing—a must-see, however touristy and bizarrely sanitized. End your evening at one of the many high-quality Nieuwe Zijd **coffeeshops** (p. 131).

DAY 3:
JODENBUURT, PLANTAGE, & REMBRANDTPLEIN

Begin with the **Museum Het Rembrandt** (p. 97) and the **Zuiderkerk** (p. 72). Head south towards the **Jewish Historical Museum** (p. 97) and the **Portugees-Israelietische Synagoge** (p. 70). To explore greener pastures, visit the **Hortus Botanicus** (p. 71). In the late afternoon, backtrack over to the northern part of De Pijp to visit the **Heineken Experience** (p. 69), and once you're slightly loaded, ramble on up to **Rembrandtplein** (p. 154) and surroundings; the hottest streets for clubbing the night away. For a more sedate evening, go a bit south for one of **De Pijp's** ethnic eateries (p. 119) and relaxed, elegant bars (p. 159).

In de Waag

FIVE DAYS

DAY 4: THE ARTS

Start in the Shipping Quarter, a tiny neighborhood but one filled with some of the city's best shopping. Have breakfast any time of the day at **Barney's** (p. 135), everybody's favorite coffeeshop, and travel over to **Electric Ladyland** (p. 90) for fluorescent art that will blow your befuddled mind. Traipse through cutting-edge contemporary **art galleries** (p. 100) and now that you've awoken your intellectual spirit, head down to the **Stedelijk Museum of Modern and Contemporary Art** (p. 93). Spend the afternoon at the city's photography centers: **Amsterdams Centrum voor Fotografie** (p. 80), **Foam Photography Museum** (p. 88), and **Huis Marseille** (p. 86). Once evening comes, it's time to visit the **Stadhuis-het-Muziektheater** (p. 164) to watch an opera or the ballet; alternatively, head to the **Concertgebouw** (p. 164) for first-rate classical music.

The Netherlands in Miniature, The Hague

DAY 5: OUDE ZIJD

Exploring the city's periphery, head back to the "Old Side." Stroll into the Oude Zijd to visit the **Museum Amstlekring (Our Lord in the Attic)** (p. 81), one of the city's former hidden churches and then amble down to the city's oldest Church, **Oude Kerk** (p. 59). Have a meal in or just glance at the **Waag** (p. 58), the city's old weighing house on **Nieuwmarkt,** and walk down Zeedijk through Amsterdam's Chinatown for all-you-can-eat chow. Stop at **Cannabis College** (p. 80) the intellectual side of hemp culture, and then down to **Leidseplein** for **Melkweg** (p. 152), one of the city's hottest clubs and art centers.

Amsterdam by Little Boat

Crooked Canal House

Oost Indisch Huis

Artis

SEVEN DAYS

DAY 6: EDGE OF TOWN

Some of Amsterdam's best sights are actually on the periphery of this compact city. Hop on the tram or take your **bike** down to **Amsterdamse Bos** (p. 74), the city's forest. Here you can explore eveything from duck ponds to tree-lined pathways to your heart's content. Still on the edge of town, you can learn to appreciate The Netherlands' fanatical passion for football (soccer) at **ArenA Amsterdam** (p. 75). On the way back to the heart of Amsterdam, you can explore one of country's great modern art movements at **CoBrA Museum** (p. 100).

DAY 7: GET OUT OF TOWN

There are so many excellent daytrips to choose from on your last day. Spend a day at nearby **Haarlem** (p. 211) for churches and other architectural delights, as well as the brilliant **Frans Hals Museum**. Explore **Rotterdam** (p. 244), a city full of modern art and architecture. Or go to **The Hague** (p. 231), The Netherlands' seat of government, politics in action, and the home of the Royal Family. An hour train ride will take you to **De Hoge Veluwe National Park** for extensive parklands and one of The Netherlands' best museums (p. 263) or to the glorious desolation of **The Wadden Islands** (p. 274). For The Netherlands' top five daytrip destinations, see p. 210.

AMSTERDAM BY SEASON

FESTIVALS

Amsterdams Uit Buro (AUB), Leidseplein 26 (☎621 13 11; www.uitlijn.nl; open daily 9am-9pm), has tickets and info for most events.

SPRING

Koninginnedag (Queen's Day; Apr. 30), nominally the celebration of Queen Beatrix's mum's birthday, turns the city into a huge carnival of food and free-flowing drinks served amid the deafening sounds of countless outdoor concerts. Also in celebration of Queen's Day is the year's largest flea market, where such oddities as parrots, skulls, and glue sticks are bought and sold with equal fervor. The **National Museum Weekend** (☎670 11 11) opens up museums for free or discounted fares in mid-April, making for a weekend of culture. At the May **Oosterpark Festival,** the park fills with people celebrating international cultural ties through music, food, and games.

SUMMER

The **Holland Festival** (☎530 71 10; www.holland-festival.nl) in June, features an international arts celebration, including over 30 theater Dutch theater productions. Also in June, the **Amsterdam Roots Festival** (☎531 81 22; www.amsterdam-roots.nl) pays tribute to world music and culture in clubs throughout the city, while the **Drum and Rhythm Festival** celebrates, somewhat predictably, drums and rhythms. The **ITs Festival** (International Theatre School Festival) features performances by students at the end of June.

Almost Infinite Canals

July and August see the start of the summer concert series at Amsterdam's Concertgebouw, with the world-famous orchestra and the Nederlandse Opera (see p. 164) and the **Grachtenfestival** (www.grachtenfestival.nl) in August converts the whole of Amsterdam into a venue for over 70 concert performances. **Julidans** (www.julidans.com) brings many international dance acts to Amsterdam primarily to the Stadsschouwburg, Melkweg, and Vondelpark theaters.

On the first weekend in August, gay pride comes out in street parties along Warmoesstraat, the Amstel, Kerkstraat, and Reguliersdwarsstraat, and in the outrageously fun **Gay Pride Boat Parade** (www.amsterdampride.nl), when floats, boats, queens, and queers take over the Prinsengracht. During **Uitmarkt** weekend at the end of August (www.uitmarkt.nl), a preview of cultural events means there are free concerts at Dam Square, Leidseplein, and Museumplein.

Rembrandt Statue

There are a number of other festivals that run from June through September in other parts of The Netherlands, including: **Pinkpop** (Landgraaf; June); **Oerol** (Terschelling; June), **Mysteryland** (Floriade Park; June), **Parkpop** (The Hague; June), **Dance Valley** (Velsen; Aug.), and **The Netherlands Film Festival** (Utrecht; Sept.).

FALL

On the first Saturday in September, the **Bloemen Corso** (Flower Parade; www.bloemencorsoaalsmeer.nl) runs from Aalsmeer to Amsterdam. Many historic houses and windmills open to the public for **National Monument Day** (www.openmonumentendag.nl) in September. The **Cannabis Cup** (Nov. 24-27, 2004; www.hightimes.com) celebrates the magical mystery weed that brings millions of visitors to Amsterdam every year.

Stepped Gable

WINTER

The Dutch don't celebrate as much in winter (aside from Christmas and a raging New Year's Eve), but the upside is that you might get to go **ice-skating** on the canals.

NATIONAL HOLIDAYS

The Netherlands' major 2004 holidays are: **New Year's Day** (Jan. 1); **Good Friday** (Apr. 9); **Easter Sunday** (Apr. 11); **Liberation Day** (May 5); **Ascension Day** (May 20); **Whit Sunday and Whit Monday** (May 30-31); **Christmas Day** (Dec. 25); and **Boxing Day** (Dec. 26).

LAY OF THE LAND & WATER

Welcome to Amsterdam, the "Venice of the North," whose confusing neighborhoods can be easily explored through its guiding canals. In Amsterdam, water runs in concentric circles, radiating from Centraal Station, every visitor's starting point. The **Singel** runs around the **Centrum**, which includes the **Oude Zijd,** the infamous **Red Light District,** the **Nieuwe Zijd.** In a space not even a kilometer in diameter, brothels, bars, clubs, and tourists abound under wafting marijuana smoke. The next three canals are the **Herengracht,** the **Keizersgracht,** and the **Prinsengracht.** The land around them is known as the **Canal Ring,** home to beautiful canal houses and classy nightlife—bars and traditional *bruin cafes.* Just over the Singelgracht, **Museumplein** is home to the city's most deservedly famous art museums as well as the sprawling **Vondelpark.** Farther out lie the more residential Amsterdam neighborhoods: the **Jordaan, Oud-West, Westerpark,** to the West, **Plantage** and the **Jodenbuurt** to the east, and **De Pijp** to the south. Though these districts are populated by dense housing, they still boast excellent eateries and brilliant museums. South of Leidseplein, a few sights can be found in what we call **Greater Amsterdam,** including **Amsterdamse Bos (Forest).**

NEIGHBORHOODS

OUDE ZIJD

see map p. 344

One of two wobbly halves that make up Amsterdam's historic Centrum, the Oude Zijd (Old Side) is ironically the newer side of the city center, infamously celebrated for its enclosure of the **Red Light District.** But any visitor intent on merely experimenting with the area's legalized trappings will be sorely deprived. While **Warmoesstraat** and **Oudezijds Achterburgwal** boast wall-to-wall brothels and coffeeshops, the Oude Zijd extends to include the southern end of **Oudezijds Voorburgwal** and **Kloveniersburgwal,** two streets as serene and picturesque as any in Amsterdam. **Nieuwmarkt,** the base of Amsterdam's **Chinatown,** remains a pleasant refuge, offering up a large marketplace amidst the shrouds of coffeeshops, restaurants, and local bars. Nieuwmarkt sits just east of the Red Light District, centering on the formidable **Waag,** whose mere presence throws any tourist into the tumultuous centuries of history past.

RED LIGHT DISTRICT

see map p. 344

The Red Light District—bordered by **Warmoesstraat** to the west, **Zeedijk** to the north, **Damstraat** to the south, and **Kloveniersburgwaal** to the east—has existed in its sexual glorification since the 13th century. It was then that Amsterdam was the seat of European maritime trade, and with the frequent travels of so many lonely sailors and increasingly wealthy men, the "world's oldest profession" soon set down roots here. Today the Dutch themselves avoid the District like the plague, as it has become indecently overrun with tourists often too excited at being set loose in such liberated surroundings. Feel free to indulge fully in all the tantalizing and titillating thrills that the Red Light District has in store, but be advised that if you decide to eat, shop, or smoke up between Warmoesstraat and Oudezijds Acterburgwal, you'll be paying twice the price for half the value. Bring an open, respectful mind, but leave your wallet at home.

NIEUWE ZIJD

The Nieuwe Zijd (New Side) gets its name from the **Nieuwe Kerk,** in the southern part of the neighborhood. This side of the Centrum is technically older than the

see map p. 344

Oude Zijd, but its church, built in the early 15th century, is younger than the Oude Zijd's Oude Kerk—one of the earliest structures in the city. The Nieuwe Zijd is bordered on the east by Damrak, which turns into Rokin as it crosses **Dam Square,** Amsterdam's enormous plaza lined by Nieuwe Kerk, the **Koninklijk Paleis** and **Nationaal Monument.** The messy tourist schmaltz closer to the Dam fades with each successive street to the west: **Nieuwezijds Voorburgwal,** originally constructed as a bulwark against attack just outside the city center, is now a haven for nightlife; **Spuistraat** has its share of trendy cafes; **Kalverstraat** reigns as Amsterdam's premier shopping district; and **Singelgracht,** is a mixed bag where hoity-toity restaurants lie not far from prostitutes beckoning from behind red-lit windows.

SCHEEPVAART BUURT

Amsterdam's Shipping Quarter—**Scheepvaartbuurt,** for those brave enough to attempt multiple vowels—

see map p. 342

occupies a spit north of the Jordaan and Canal Ring. Centered on **Haarlemmerstraat,** this increasingly gentrified area has hip restaurants and smokeries, just outside the tourist crush of Nieuwendijk. It's worth the trip for some of the city's best establishments and nicest people. Venture south to photogenic **Brouwersgracht,** at the top of the Canal Ring. At the **Korte Prisengracht,** Haarlemmerstraat becomes **Haarlemmerdijk,** and the district becomes considerably more residential.

Westerkerk Organ

Prinsengracht at Night

Inside the Royal Palace

in recent news

concrete pancakes

"Amsterdam, that great big city, has been built on poles, and if it ever tumbled down, who would pay the bill?"

–Dutch nursery rhyme

The canal houses intrinsic to Amsterdam's charm are under something of a threat as work proceeds on a north-south Metro line designed to supplement their limited underground system. The potential shifts caused by tunnel digging could cause building supports to give way completely. But what to do about the 17th-century buildings that threatened to collapse when excavations began?

Golden Age engineers dealt with waterlogged earth by digging canals and erecting buildings on 12m poles stuck into the ground. Inheritors of the Dutch insistence to make this land livable weren't discouraged. They designed elaborate measurement systems to detect pole shifts as small as 0.1mm; should the foundations move, engineers will pump a cement mixture through a perforated pipe that will create a "concrete pancake" to hold the buildings up. This proposal has already been successfully tested near Rotterdam with a model house built to 17th-century standards on similarly marshy ground. With luck, and perhaps some help from *pannekoeken*, Amsterdam won't come tumbling down any time soon.

CANAL RING

If the Centrum is at the head of spectacular Amsterdam, the Canal Ring is the city's genteel heart. Collectively, **Prinsengracht** (Prince's canal), **Keizersgracht** (Emperor's canal), and **Herengracht** (Gentlemen's canal) are known as the *grachtengordel* ("canal girdle"). In the early 17th century these water bodies were carved out of the marshy landscape, and on the remaining plots sprung up some some of Amsterdam's most important architecture. Narrow canal houses, their width dictated by the dearth of available space, were built in the pioneering Amsterdam Renaissance style by Hendrick de Keyser and his followers. That mode of building combined Classical elements with gables, the triangular fronts of rooftops, which were disguised with a variety of ornamented mantles. Behind these facades lived the city's wealthiest inhabitants, drawn by proximity to—and seclusion from—the bustling trade found in the city center. Later architects rebelled against de Keyser and pushed for a type of "citizen's architecture," one that would replace his Renaissance—vertical accents and religious overtones included—with Dutch Classicism, a classicist variation on international Baroque architecture.

Today this is one of the most beautiful spots in Amsterdam, with rents—the highest per square foot in the world—to match. The four main waterways, **Singelgracht,** the **River Amstel,** the **Singel,** and **Brouwersgracht,** bear most of the tourist traffic and noise. The Ring's inner reaches are quieter and more picturesque. In this book the Canal Ring is split into two parts—the **Canal Ring West** and the **Central Canal Ring.** The split is at **Leidsegracht,** just northwest of Leidseplein.

see map p. 342

CANAL RING WEST

The Western Canal Ring is quick, busy, and bustling during the day, but lies tame at night, as clubs and bars have yet to settle down in this area. **Prinsengracht,** the busiest of the four canals, tends to pull in the most visitors with its numerous cafes serving traditional Dutch cuisine; proximity to the popular **Anne Frank Huis** attracts visitors wandering in from the historic house. Small boutiques line the neighborhood's streets; these shops typically specialize in homemade jewelry, candles, or soaps. The scenery throughout the area is bedecked with narrow houses and cozy restaurants lining serene canals. Keep an eye out for the **Westerkerkstoren,** Amsterdam's tallest tower, which sits atop the famed **Westerkerk,** at the corner of Raadhuisstraat and Prinsengracht. The Westerkerk church marks the exact center of the Canal Ring West.

CENTRAL CANAL RING

The succession of canals that makes up the Central Ring is an underrated treasure of tranquil historic homes and quirky neighborhood hangouts. This area is also home to a stretch on the **Herengracht** known as the **Golden Bend,** so called because of the wealth of the 17th-century merchants who built these especially wide and lavish canal houses. **Keizersgracht** and

see map p. 340

Prinsengracht south of Herengracht, as well as the **Singelgracht** to the north, features canal houses that are not as spectacular as their wealthy neighbors, but ones that are no less important—historically or architecturally. These buildings date back as early as 1600 and are topped by many types of gables, among them the notable Dutch stylings of step-gables and spout gables. The upscale tranquility of the Central Canal Ring gives way in two squares—the **Leidseplein** and **Rembrandtplein**—that are touristed, action-filled centers of nightlife, restaurants, coffeeshops, and bars.

LEIDSEPLEIN

Leidseplein offers some of Amsterdam's most densely concentrated—and best—restaurants and nightlife. Named because it once marked the end of the road from Leiden to Amsterdam, the square punctuates the southern curve of the Canal Ring, just north of Vondelpark and west of Museumplein. It is a gathering point for street performers and their tourist audiences.

see map p. 341

REMBRANDTPLEIN

Rembrandtplein proper is a grass rectangle surrounded by scattered flowerbeds, crisscrossed by pedestrian paths and populated with half-dressed locals lazing about (when weather permits, of course). A bronze likeness of the famed master, **Rembrandt van Rijn,** overlooks the scene, but it's what surrounds the greenery that makes this neighborhood unforgettable. The area

see map p. 340

is littered with bars and cafes—establishments ranging from casual to upscale—and they are all packed most nights of the week with lively night owls but are, unfortunately, also often unnecessarily expensive. By night, Rembrandtplein competes with Leidseplein for Amsterdam's hippest nightlife and nightlife aficionados, with a particularly rich concentration of gay hotspots in the area. South and west of the square lies **Reguliersdwarsstraat,** fittingly dubbed "the gayest street in Amsterdam;" it's always raining a shower of good-looking men here. The city's large gay community usually patronizes the clubs that sit just west of the intersection of Reguliersdwarsstraat and **Vijzelsstraat,** as this area tends to house some of Amsterdam's hottest and least inhibited venues. **Utrechtsestraat,** the street that extends southward from Rembrandtplein, bears a concentration of great, untouristed restaurants.

JORDAAN

Head to the Jordaan when you need to relax in style. Amsterdam's most fashionable neighborhood is low-key and cozy, with some of the best-preserved historical homes leaning over the canals, adorned by overflowing flower boxes. The area began in the 1600s as a working class neighborhood and has only

see maps p. 342

recently become the preferred perch of Amsterdam's yuppie population. To reach this infinitely charming and unmissable side of Amsterdam, take tram #13 or 17 to **Marnixstraat** or **Westermarkt**, or tram 10 to Rozengracht or Bloemgracht. On foot, you can walk from **Prinsengracht** along a succession of languid cafe-bars with canal boat seating. Go farther west to explore quiet, narrow streets and secluded canals such as beautiful **Bloemgracht.** The Jordaan features a host of upscale eateries, craft studios, galleries, and cafes.

WESTERPARK & OUD-WEST

see map p. 346

Not as traveled as more central parts of the city, the area north of Vondelpark and west of the outer Singelgracht spans several neighborhoods. Closest to the center, the **Oud-West** (Old West, bounded by Kostverlorenvaart, Hugo de Groot Kade, Vondelpark, and Nassaukade) is a far cry from the scenic and stately neighboring Jordaan, with a gritty, urban energy not found in the center. With fewer bars and clubs than the Jordaan, it isn't the safest place at night, but during the day, the Oud-West comes vibrantly to life. A walk down **Kinkerstraat, Jan Pieter Heijestraat,** and the neighborhood's other major streets reveal the area's dazzling regional diversity, particularly in cuisine: Moroccan-run call centers, Turkish delis, Ethiopian restaurants, and Surinamese supermarkets all abound in the area in and around the Oud-West.

Westerpark is the opposite of its southern neighbor. Where the Oud-West has crowded, tightly-packed streets, Westerpark is full to the brim with winding canals and picturesque greens; where the Oud-West bristles like a small urban city, Westerpark breathes easy with the relaxed attitude of sedate suburbia. The highlight is its eponymous park, which is a popular retreat for families on sunny summer days. To get there, take tram #3 to Haarlemmerplein or 10 to Van Hallstraat for anything from a brisk walk to a leisurely one-hour stroll. Even further west of the Westerpark lie **Bos en Lommer** and **De Baarsjes,** sleepy residential neighborhoods with little to attract even the most curious traveler. **Rembrandtpark,** on the far edge of De Baarsjes, is relatively popular for local joggers and dogwalkers.

MUSEUMPLEIN & VONDELPARK

see map p. 347

Outside of the Singelgracht, which encircles the wild, spirited city core, Museumplein and Vondelpark occupy a quieter, more gentrified area of the city. The 19th century home to wealthy Amsterdammers, the streets around Museumplein are home to some of the most beautiful and stately mansions in the city. The real draw is the museums that line up along Museumplein, an expanse of park that occupies roughly six square blocks. Towering over the park is the ornate late 19th century **Rijksmuseum,** with its world-class collection of such works as Dutch Golden Age paintings, applied arts, and Asian objects. Along Van Baerlestraat you'll find both the **Stedelijk Museum,** the city's main center for Modern and contemporary 20th-century art, and the immensely popular **Van Gogh Museum.** In this peaceful neighborhood you'll also find some of Amsterdam's most expensive shopping (especially along P.C. Hoofstraat) as well as the city's world-famous concert hall, the **Concertgebouw.**

With meandering walkways and a paved path for both bikers and skaters, the **Vondelpark,** just southwest of Leidseplein, draws large crowds any sunny day of the week. Located inside the Vondelpark is the **Openluchttheater,** or open-air theater, where music and dance shows as well as all manner of film screenings are held throughout the summer months. The excellent **Filmmuseum,** adjacent to the park, is home to the world's premier archive of Dutch cinema and features daily screenings from its holdings.

DE PIJP

Just outside the southern stretch of the canal ring, De Pijp (pronounced "pipe") is gentrification-in-process. Once known for its immigrant authenticity, De Pijp is ballooning in hype as new high-design restaurants and bars pop up next to ethnic eateries. The neighborhood's main drag, **Ferdinand Bolstraat,** and the streets around it have pretty much gone over to the trendsters, see map p. 348 while **Albert Cuypstraat** maintains some of its former grittiness. It's home to the **Albert Cuypmarkt,** the largest outdoor market in Europe, where shopkeepers hawk household wares and other sundries to huge crowds every day. **Sarphatipark,** a grassy and befountained plot of parkland, lies in the heart of De Pijp.

JODENBUURT & PLANTAGE

Amsterdam has always been a place of mixed blessings for the Jews, who arrived in The Netherlands in the early 17th century. In time, the area roughly bounded by the streets **Jodenbreestraat, St. Antoniebreestraat,** and **Waterlooplein** gained definition as a **Jewish quarter (Jodenbuurt),** full of synagogues, theaters, shops, businesses, and schools, and some 55,000 Jews. The quarter grew see map p. 349 ever outward to include wealthier areas like **Plantage Middenlaan** and **Nieuwe Keizersgracht.** When the Germans invaded Amsterdam in 1940, that all changed. The Nazis forced the residents of the Jodenbuurt into isolation, deportation, and mass extermination. Only 5200 Dutch Jews survived the war and the Jodenbuurt, though still existing in name, would never be the same. Today this is home to various excellent museums and monuments for the Jews and the Dutch Resistance, as well as other sights like **Hollandsche Schouwberg, Stadhuis-Muziektheater, Holland Experience 3D,** and the **Museum Het Rembrandt.**

To the southeast of the Jodenbuurt lies the verdant **Plantage.** This district is a leafy, shaded escape full of many historical and ethnographic museums (namely the **Nationaal Vakbondsmuseum** and **Tropenmuseum**) as well as various centers for exploring the outdoors and nature; try outdoors spots like the **Hortus Botanicus, Artis Zoo,** or the sprawling **Wertheim Park.**

BIKING & WALKING TOURS

The moment you step out of Centraal Station into the crush of tourists, locals, street performers, pan-handlers, and miscellaneous characters, you'll immediately realize that this is not a city for drivers. One of the best ways to see the city, to understand Amsterdam's layout, and to appreciate all of its architectural beauty is to traverse the myriad canals and back alleys by foot. Amsterdam proper is littered with pedestrian walks, parks and squares, all within close proximity to each other—despite the city's daunting map layout, the city is smaller than you think. The walking tours on the following pages offer suggested self-guided walks all over the city according to various themes. **A Stoner's Tour** (p. 18) gives you the city's best coffeeshops and other sights to titillate and/or soothe your addled mind. If you'd rather get high-brow than high, try **The Sophisticated City** (p. 20), a sampling of Amsterdam's most urbane museums, landmarks, and restaurants. **A History Lesson** (p. 22) is precisely that: this daylong tour puts you in touch with Amsterdam's past, from Jewish immigration in the 17th century and Golden Age affluence to the sometimes sordid, liberated present. Walkers beware: you'll have to jostle for space with bikers—and more than the occasional tram—for supremacy over labyrnthine pathways. The best way to cope with the sound of bike bells ringing in your ears is to succumb and become cyclist yourself; **A Biking Tour of Amsterdam** (p. 16) starts off at the city's best bike rental shop and takes you on a whirlwind tour of the city.

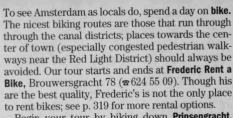

To see Amsterdam as locals do, spend a day on **bike**. The nicest biking routes are those that run through through the canal districts; places towards the center of town (especially congested pedestrian walkways near the Red Light District) should always be avoided. Our tour starts and ends at **Frederic Rent a Bike**, Brouwersgracht 78 (☎624 55 09). Though his are the best quality, Frederic's is not the only place to rent bikes; see p. 319 for more rental options.

Begin your tour by biking down **Prinsengracht**. Turn left onto **Reestraat**, which becomes **Hartenstraat** and **Gasthuismolensteeg**. Continue over the **Singel** to **Dam Square**.

1. DAM SQUARE. Amsterdam's central square is surrounded by the Nieuwe Kerk, Nationaal Monument, and Koninklijk Paleis, home to the Dutch royal family. Stop and check out the street performers in good weather.

2. SPUI. Go back towards Singel, turn left on Nieuwezijds Voorburgwal and go south for a few minutes. Pronounced "spow," the square is home to a Sundays art market, a Friday book market, and is surrounded by bookstores (see p. 179). If you're up early, head into the **Begijnhof** (see p. 60), the peaceful courtyard for observant lay-women. Ride back to the Western Canal Ring via Heistraat. Turn left onto Herengracht and right onto Leidsegracht; pause at the beautiful intersection of canals Leidsegracht and Keizersgracht canals.

3. DE APPEL. Continue down Leidsegracht, turn left at Keizersgracht, and left on Nieuwe Spiegelstraat. Stop at Nieuwe Spiegelstr. 10 to tour Amsterdam's premier space for contemporary art. (see p. 88).

4. GOLDEN BEND. After some art-gazing, head to this stretch of Herengracht, between Leidsestraat and Vijzelstraat, known as the "Golden Bend" because of its opulent houses. Officials bent the strict house-width rules for wealthy citizens who were willing to invest in the construction of the Herengracht, or gentleman's canal.

5. MAGERE BRUG. Turn right at Utrechtsestraat and then left at Prinsengracht. Continue until you hit the Amstel. Turn left; the Magere Brug (skinny bridge) is on your right. This is the oldest of the city's pedestrian bridges, and the only one operated by hand (see p. 65).

6. NIEUWMARKT. Cross the bridge, turn left and head north along the Amstel; cross at Herengracht. Veer left, go right around the far side of the Stadhuis, and cross the bridge at Staalstraat. When you hit Groenburgwal turn right, right again at Raamgracht, and then left at the first bridge. Cross over, turn left and double back along the far side of Raamgr. Turn right at Kloveniersburgwal and follow it to Nieuwmarkt, an open-air market. Head back to Frederic's via Zeedijk, which becomes Prins Hendrikkade and passes Centraal Station.

BIKE TOUR

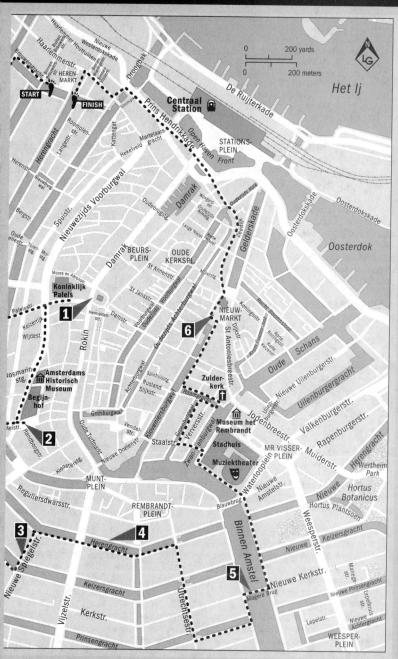

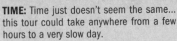

TIME: Time just doesn't seem the same... this tour could take anywhere from a few hours to a very slow day.

SEASON: 4/20, or any other day of the year. Coffeeshops will chill you out on those hazy, humid summer days; any of their wares will also take the edge off the most brutal cold snap of a rainy winter.

Sometimes traveling can be a little confusing when you're stoned, so this tour offers a pre-rolled sampling of the city's best coffeeshops, excellent grub, and psychedelic sights. While it's tempting for some just to find the coffeeshop nearest Centraal Station and stay there for their whole vacation, the city's best cannabis is sold outside the city center—this day-long *trip* will help you explore.

1. BARNEY'S. Haarlemmerstraat 102. Wake and bake, sunshine! Start your day with Barney at noon–there's a long trek ahead of you. Tuck into a hearty breakfast of bacon, eggs, sausages and toast while toking on a big fat joint. Barney's has received the Cannabis Cup (best weed strain) three years running and was named "Best Coffeeshop" in 2002 (see p. 135).

2. ELECTRIC LADYLAND. 2e Leliedwarsstraat 5. This lesser-known museum will befuddle your already-boggled mind. Hippie soulmate/owner Nick Padalino will guide you through this collection of fluorescent sculptures and everyday objects (see p. 90).

3. ABRAXAS. Jonge Roelensteeg 12-14. Top off your breakfast with a refreshing hash smoothie. Mellow mood lighting, mosaics, and a tree sculpture make this Amsterdam's most beautiful coffeeshop. The drink will fortify you for the long, befuddling walk ahead (see p. 131).

4. VONDELPARK. Take a break and relish the park's soft greenery with other locals who come here to relax. Marvel at the hilariously entertaining street performers (see p. 68).

5. VAN GOGH MUSEUM. Paulus Potterstraat 7. Catch some Van Gogh paintings and chill out in this breezy, bright space. The sunflowers may look a little strange and you might think the birds in *Wheatfield with Crows* are raring to eat you after the morning you've had (see p. 91).

6. BOAT TOUR. Tour Boats will take you on a relaxing, immobile journey through the Jordaan's winding canals and will eventually deposit you exactly at the departure point on Singelgracht outside the Rijksmuseum (see p. 94).

7. DAMPKRING. Handboogstraat 29. The high has worn off by now, so here's another coffeeshop—one of the city's classiest. Choose from 18 pre-rolled joints and relax in this deep-blue subterranean space. Brain addled by your day? Ask the expert staff for help (see p. 132).

8. CANNABIS COLLEGE. Oudezijds Achterburgwal 124. Learn everything you've ever wanted to know about the stuff you're smoking—including effects, medicinal uses, and political dimensions—in the company of some hard core cannabis lovers. Best of all, it's free (see p. 80).

9. TASTE OF CULTURE. Zeedijk 109. The munchies have finally kicked and you're ready for this restaurant's hearty challenge: all you can eat in 1hr. for only €7.50. Greasy Chinese food in all its glory will level you out for the stumble to the last coffeeshop stop. (see p. 105).

10. GREY AREA. Oude Leliestraat 2. Your last smoke of the day! Go light with the "Double Bubble Gum" weed or knock yourself out with the "Grey Mist Crystal" hash. Grey Area has sold great stuff for years—they have received 18 awards at the Cannabis Cup since 1996 (see p. 132). You're probably going to pass out right now, so trip on home to your comfy bed; if not, don't worry —you're near some of the city's best nightlife. Only minutes away, **NL Lounge,** Nieuwezijds Voorburgwal 169 (see p. 148) plays trance music that matches your heightened state. Alternatively, **Café 't Smalle,** Egelantiersgracht 12, is ideal for a mellow night of drinks (see pp. 158).

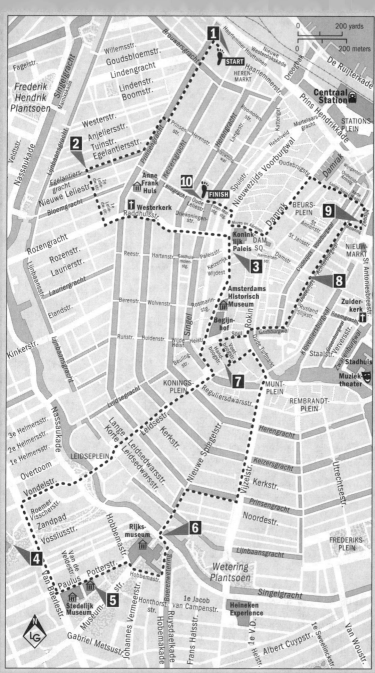

0 | 200 yards
0 | 200 meters

1 START
HEREN-
MARKT

Centraal
Station

STATIONS-
PLEIN

Haarlemmer Houttuinen
Nieuwe
Westerdokskade
Droogbak
De Ruijterkade
Haarlemmerstr.
Prins Hendrikkade

Fagelstr.
Willemsstr.
Goudsbloemstr.
Lindengracht
Lindenstr.
Boomstr.
Brouwersgracht

Frederik
Hendrik
Plantsoen

Roomolen-
str.
Langestr.
Kattengat
Martelaars-
gracht

Westerstr.
Anjeliersstr.
Tuinstr.
Egelantiersstr.

2

Egelantiers-
gracht
Nieuwe Leliestr.
Bloemgracht

Anne
Frank
Huis

10 FINISH

Westerkerk
Raddhuisstr.

Prinsengracht
Keizersgracht
Herenstr.
Prinsenstr.
Leliegracht

Squistr.
Oude
leliest.
Torensl.
Driekoningen-
str.

Nieuwezijds Voorburgwal
Damrak

Hekelveld
Oudebrugste.

BEURS-
PLEIN

9

Rozengracht
Rozenstr.
Laurierstr.
Lauriergracht
Elandstr.

Reestr.
Hartenstr.
Gasthuis-
molen-
stg.
Paleisstr.

Koninklijk
Paleis

3

DAM
SQ.
Damstr.
Hermensteeg
St Jansstr.
St Annenstr.

Oudezijds Voorburgwal

NIEUW-
MARKT

St Antoniesbreestr.

Keizerrijk
Wijdest.

8

Berenstr.
Wolvenstr.

Amsterdams
Historisch
Museum

Rosmarin-
stg.

Zuider-
kerk

Begijn-
hof

Rusland
Slijkstr.

Reaamgracht

Runstr.
Huidenstr.
Wilde
Heist.
Heist.

Spui

Oude Turfmarkt
Grimburgwal

Koningsbergwal
Zwaanburgwal
Verversstr.

Staalstr.
Stadhuis

Kinkerstr.
Lijnbaansgracht

Beulingstr.
Singel

Rokin

Vendel-
boogs-
hand-
boogstr.

Muziek-
theater

7

MUNT-
PLEIN

REMBRANDT-
PLEIN

KONINGS-
PLEIN

Reguliersdwarsstr.

Leidsegracht

3e Helmersstr.
2e Helmersstr.
1e Helmersstr.

Lange
Korte
Leidsedwarsstr.
Leidsedwarsstr.

Leidsestr.
Kerkstr.
Nieuwe Spiegelstr.

Herengracht

Keizersgracht

Utrechtsestr.

LEIDSEPLEIN

Vijzelstr.
Kerkstr.
Prinsengracht
Noordestr.

FREDERIKS-
PLEIN

Overtoom
Vondelstr.
Roemer
Visscherstr.
Zandpad
Vossiusstr.

4

Rijks-
museum

6

Lijnbaansgracht

Wetering
Plantsoen

Van de
Veldestr.
Potterstr.
Hobbemastr.

Boerenwetering

Singelgracht

Paulus
Potterstr.
str.

5

Stedelijk
Museum

Museumstr.
Johannes Vermeerstr.
Honthorst-
str.
Ruysdaelkade
Hobbemakade
Frans Halsstr.

1e Jacob
van Campenstr.

Heineken
Experience

1e V.D.
1e Helstr.

Gabriel Metsustr.
Albert Cuypstr.
1e Sweelinckstr.
Van Woustr.

Van Baerlestr.

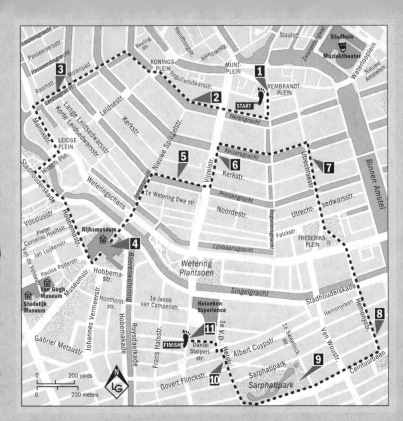

Amsterdam is not a pretentious city; its sophistication is simple, unaffected, and relaxed—perfect for a leisurely walk. This walking tour takes you through Golden Age art, the history of the Central Canal Ring, and the hotspots of De Pijp, the city's most up and coming neighborhood.

TIME: One day.

SEASON: Year-round. The canals are particularly pleasant in spring and autumn, with picturesque foliage and temperate weather.

1. REMBRANDTPLEIN. The Rembrandtplein's gaudy nightclubs are the very antithesis of sophistication, the exact opposite of what you'll find on this walking tour. The square is also a crush of locals of every stripe, particularly locals who loll about half-dressed when the weather is warm enough. The only vestige of anything remotely refined here is a statue of its namesake—master painter Rembrandt van Rijn—who surveys the square's revelry (see p. 13) .

2. GOLDEN BEND. A stretch of houses on the Herengracht between Leidsestraat and Vijzelstraat is known as the Golden because of the affluence of its 17th-century inhabitants and the opulence of the homes they built. Though very few of the structures here are open to the public, you survey the elegant, doubly-wide houses on this picturesque stretch of the "Gentleman's Canal," particularly #495 for its rare balcony, 507 for its fine columns and doubly-wide plot, and 527, the former home of Tsar Peter (see p. 65).

3. NOA. Leidsegracht 84. NOA distinguishes itself from the rather mundane restaurants in nearby Leidseplein for its elegant design and pan-Asian dishes. This is one of the hottest spots for urbane gourmands, who sink into plush sofa seats while sipping some of the city's best and classiest cocktails flavored with international flair (see p. 113).

4. RIJKSMUSEUM AMSTERDAM. Stadhouderskade 42. Marvel at Rembrandt's shadowy, dynamic *Night Watch,* and Johannes Vermeer's luminous, shimmering *Milkmaid* in the National Museum. Both exemplify different facets of Golden Age portrait painting—artwork that was subsidized by the aristocracy. The building itself is also a sight. The huge neo-Gothic structure designed by Pierre Cuypers was once deemed to be the height of aesthetic sophistication and is one of the most readily identifiable landmarks in Amsterdam (see p. 94).

5. PRINSENGRACHT. Compare the skinnier residential houses on the "Prince's Canal" with their more opulent Herengracht counterparts. Note the different gables along the row: a spout gable at #1075, an ornamented neck gable at 1081, and a bell gable at 1099. Along the Prinsengracht, a number of houseboats—lodgings long used to alleviate crowding in the city center—still house occupants throughout the year (see p. 65).

6. MUSEUM VAN LOON. Keizersgracht 672. Revel in the lavishly appointed splendor of a canal house just as it appeared in the Golden Age. This museum preserves the residence of the van Loon family, whose ancestors founded the Dutch East India Company and had a particularly cultivated, expensive interior designer. The unusually ornate gilt banister along the central staircase has words subtly worked into its curves (see p. 89).

7. COFFEE & JAZZ. Utrechtsestraat 113. Smooth jazz and surprisingly chic bamboo furniture complement the city's best coffee at this classy cafe. Finish off a lunch of Dutch-Indonesian fusion dishes with sweet, fruity *pannekoeken.* If you're here later in the evening, great, strictly Indonesian cuisine will surely satisfy. Show off your insider knowledge by calling ahead and booking the loveseat table outside—and watch other sophisticates sidle by (see p. 112).

8. YO YO. 2e van der Heijdenstraat 79. While smoking cigarettes may seem refined, lighting up a joint hardly seems like the soignée thing to do—at least at other coffeeshops. Thanks to a motherly proprietor, this airy, homey establishment is so warm and friendly it's almost wholesome. (Normal) brownies, praiseworthy coffee, quiche, or deservedly famous apple pie completes a particularly sophisticated smoke (see p. 141).

9. SARPHATIPARK. Wait out the high by the sinuous pond in this small but beautifully manicured park named for the cultured philanthropist Dr. Samuel Sarphati. Careening wildly through gentrified De Pijp while under the influence is simply not the suave thing to do, even if you will meet the riff-raff of tourists spilling out from the Heineken Experience (see p. 69).

10. MME. JEANETTE. Settle in for a pre-dinner *aperitif* at this cosmopolitan, velvet-smooth lounge—some of the best, most exotic (but priciest) cocktails in the city. The renowned staff behind the bar make a brilliant Basil Grande Martini with fresh strawberries, but they're too cosmopolitan to be known by any plebian name: they're "shakers," not "bartenders." Famous cocktail workshops will put you on par with these sublimely talented drink mixers (see p. 160).

11. CAFE DE PIJP. More low-key than other pretentious style-restaurants, this surprisingly affordable eatery positively breathes cultivated charm. Soups and innovative appetizers give way to sumptuous mains; melting desserts are a perfect way to polish of a particularly refined day (see p. 119). If you have the need for more sophistication, De Pijp boasts some of the city's most cultured and bars and lounges, perfect for an evening among equally classy urbanites.

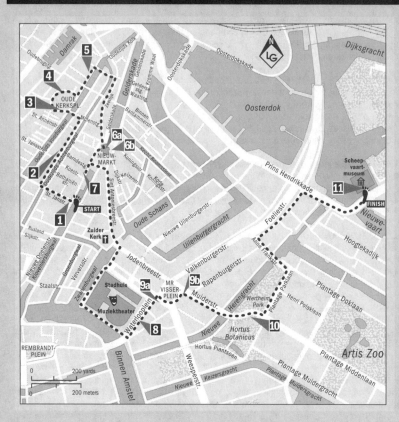

This tour will take you on a whirlwind trip around the Centrum and beyond to relive some of its storied past and witness many facets of contemporary life.

TIME: All morning, most of an afternoon.

SEASON: Year-round.

1. OOST INDISCH HUIS. This monument to Dutch colonial history was once the headquarters of the Dutch East India Company (VOC). The conglomerate established a global trading empire that at its height surpassed wealth and excesses of the British Empire. A vast trade network extended as far as Bengal and Indonesia and dealt mainly in silks, spices, and cotton. Though the facade remains roughly as it did when the VOC prospered, today the building's interior is used for conference rooms and lecture halls for the University of Amsterdam (see p. 58).

2 OUDEZIJDS ACHTERBURGWAL. Vicariously experience the liberated spectacle of the Red Light District by ambling along this street which is at the heart of Amsterdam's commercial sex trade. Wall-to-wall window prostitutes window pose alluringly for passing patrons, while brothels are the more discreet cousins to the overt sexuality of sex workers behind windows. The **Casa Rosso**, at numbers 106-108 features Amsterdam's most famous live sex show and the district's most famous landmark—a giant marble penis complete with rotating testicles—across from the entrance. However, not all of the Oudezijds Achterburgwal's thrills are from sex trade—coffeeshops abound in this seedy street (see p. 58).

3 OUDE KERK. Oudekerksplein 23. Find salvation beyond the red haze in Amsterdam's earliest parish church, constructed in the 14th century. The structure features some beautiful stained glass windows and its organ—which dates back to 1724—is still played regularly for concerts. The church that once was stripped of its artwork and religious artifcats now houses traveling exhibitions—artistic and otherwise (see p. 59).

4. PROSTITUTION INFORMATION CENTRE. Enge Kerksteeg 3. Find out everything there is to know about the "oldest profession" at this decidedly un-seedy center. Founder and operator Mariska Majoor is more than willing to answer any question that you might have, no matter how outlandish. Take a picture of the replica sex worker booth—something you can't do near the real red lights. The center is unfunded, so be sure to leave a donation (see p. 124).

5. MUSEUM AMSTELKRING. Oudezijds Voorburgwal 40. Religious resolve is preserved in this "Attic Church." During the Alteration, when Protestantism swept The Netherlands, Catholics were officially disbarred from practising their faith; instead, they covertly attended so-called "secret churches" like Amstelkring, a beautiful little chapel that spans the attics of three adjacent buildings. The rather plain exterior once masqueraded as a shop front (see p. 81).

6A. WAAG. See the ancient "Weigh House," Amsterdam's oldest surviving medieval building in **Nieuwmarkt**. The building was intially constructed as a gate through the city's fortified walls and its topmost floor was the setting for Rembrandt's painting *The Anatomy Lesson of Dr. Tulp*. Today the glorious imposing building is home to the ritzy restaurant, **In de Waag** (see p. 107).

6B. WAAG MARKETS. The Waag presides over an organic food market Sa 10am-3pm and an antiques market Su 9am-4pm (see p. 58).

7. DE BEIAARD. Kloveniersburgwal 6. The Netherlands is a beer drinker's paradise, and at this beautiful wooden brew house, the Dutch dedication to heady yet smooth beer is alive and kicking. Five brews are made on premises, one of which has an alcohol content of a whopping 7%. Arrange beforehand to take a tour of the brewing facilities (see p. 160).

8. WATERLOOPLEIN. After passing the "Stopera" City Hall and Theatre complex, scramble for bargains at the flea market (M-Sa 9am-5pm) at Waterlooplein (you may recognize it from the photo on p. 172). This area was the de facto home of Amsterdam's vibrant Jewish community prior to World War II, when Nazi forces deported over 70,000 Jews (see p. 179).

9A. JOODS HISTORISCH MUSEUM. Celebrate Jewish culture at the museum dedicated to preserving the religion's cultural legacy. The Museum links together four different 17th- and 18th-century Ashkenazi synagogues for a comprehensive history of Judacia. Features include an ark holding Torah silver shields and an excellent childrens' wing (see p. 96).

9B. PORTUGUESE SYNAGOGUE. This temple miraculously escaped being razed by the Nazis during World War II. The synagogue still holds services and features a plain but beautiful *chuppah* (a Jewish wedding canopy) crafted from Brazilian jacaranda wood (see p. 98).

10. HORTUS BOTANICUS. One of the world's oldest medicinal gardens (established in 1675) has over 6000 rare plants mostly smuggled into the country by members of the Dutch East India Company during the Golden Age. Treasures include a minute Ethiopian coffee plant that spawned many plantations throughout Brazil (see p. 71).

11. SCHEEPVAART MUSEUM. Kattenburgerplein 1. The Maritime Museum documents The Netherlands' once-glorious naval history and boasts the Dutch East Indiaman Den Ary, a ship infused with mythological character. Near the museum, the Naval Monument on Prins Henrikkade commemorates WWII sailors with gallant horses and serene angels (see p. 99).

WALKING TOUR

Once in Amsterdam

WHEN TO GO

Amsterdam's weather is mild and temperate, but unpredictable. Since the area around the city is flat, blustery winds can enter from all directions, sweeping away morning clouds, or bringing in late-afternoon showers. Winters in Amsterdam are rainy, and in recent years drops below freezing with less and less frequency, so be sure to bring an umbrella or a raincoat. The fog that hangs over the canals on spring and fall mornings is a bit disorienting but rather comforting with its gauzy haze; fog usually burns off by mid-morning. These same canals can become less charming in the summer months when they become a sometime breeding ground for mosquitoes.

AVERAGE TEMP.	JANUARY		APRIL		JULY		OCTOBER	
	°C	°F	°C	°F	°C	°F	°C	°F
LOW/HIGH	-9/10	16/50	-2/20	28/68	6/29	43/85	0/21	32/69
MEAN	2	36	8	46	17	62	11	51

TRANSPORTATION

BY PLANE

Amsterdam's sleek, glassy **Schiphol Airport** (☎0900-SCHIPHOL, €0.10 per min.; ☎0800 SCHIPHOL from outside of The Netherlands; www.schiphol.nl) serves as The Netherlands' major hub for transatlantic flights.

Signs (in English and Dutch) direct incoming travelers through the arrivals halls and into the vaulted, airy expanse of Schiphol Plaza, where tourist services abound. There's a branch of the **VVV,** the Dutch tourist office organization (open daily 7am-10pm) near the entrance to Arrivals Terminal 2, though lines can be long.

You can **exchange cash** at ABN AMRO branches in the arrivals halls or in the lounge areas (hours vary depending on location, but all are at least open daily 8am-11pm), or at the 24hr. GWK branch in Schiphol Plaza. For **luggage storage** head to the lockers throughout the plaza. (Storage €3-8 per 24hr., depending on size; max storage time 7 days). If you've misplaced your belongings, there are **lost and found** counters located in the lounges in the arrivals and departures levels. (☎0900-SCHIPHOL. Open M-F 7:30am-5:30pm, Sa-Su 9am-5pm.) Schiphol Plaza also contains six **rental car** companies: Avis, ☎655 6050; Budget ☎604 1349; Europcar ☎316 4190; Hertz ☎601 5416; National/Alamo ☎316 4081; Sixt ☎405 9090. (All open daily 6:30am-11pm). Price gouging abounds in the plaza's array of shops and restaurants.

The most efficient way to traverse the 18 kilometers between Schiphol and central Amsterdam is via **sneltrein,** a fast, smooth, light rail connection. Purchase tickets (one-way fare to Centraal Station €2.90; 15-20min.) at any of the kiosks that dot both Schiphol Plaza and the arrivals halls. Board the trains by descending to underground platforms directly below the airport via elevator or escalators located directly in the middle of Schiphol Plaza. **Taxis** (☎653 1000; www.schipholtaxi.nl) make the trek to Amsterdam. They congregate in front of the plaza. Fare to Centraal Station runs €30-35; base charge €2.50. The per kilometer rate is €1.54, but prices click upwards unpredictably—taxis are prohibitively expensive and should be avoided if possible.

BY TRAIN

The hub of rail transport—as well as for trams, buses, and subways—is **Centraal Station,** Stationsplein 1, a magnificent structure adorned with baroque carvings and ornate gables at the end of Damrak (rail schedules: www.ns.nl). The area immediately around Centraal Station buzzes with activity; congested with locals, backpack-toting tourists, and assorted beggars, hustlers, buskers, and preachers, it's a marvelous spot for people-watching. There's a branch of the **VVV** tourist office at platform #2 (open daily 9am-5pm) as well as coin-op **lockers** (€2-4, depending on size; max storage time 24hr.), and a GWK bank with **currency exchange.**

The Netherlands' national rail company is the efficient **Nederlandse Spoorwegen** (NS; ☎0900 92 96; €0.35 per min.; www.ns.nl). Train service tends to be faster than bus service. *Sneltreins* are the fastest; *stoptreins* make the most stops. One-way tickets are called *enkele reis;* normal round-trip tickets, *retour;* and day return tickets (valid only on day of purchase but cheaper than normal round-trip tickets) are called *dagretour.* Tickets to all Dutch trains can generally be bought with a credit card from vending machines or at box offices, though the latter usually means longer lines. The NS sells train passes solely for travel within The Netherlands. The **Summer trip (Zomertoer)** allows unlimited three-day train travel for two people July 1-September 9 (€59). The **Day Travel Card (Dagkaart)** is a less attractive savings—it costs only slightly more than the most expensive one-way fare across the country (€37.10). For another great rail deal, see **The Kindness of Strangers on a Train,** p. 27.

Eurail and **InterRail** passes are valid in The Netherlands. For Netherlands-only travel, the **Holland Railpass** (US$52-98), offered by many travel agencies, is good for three or five travel days in any one-month period. All railpasses for travel in The

Netherlands are only available from overseas. If you "lose" (i.e. do not buy) your train ticket and are caught by authorities, it is possible to buy tickets on board; however, doing so will cost you **twice the original fare.**

BY TRAM, BUS, & SUBWAY

All public transportation—trams, buses, and the subway—runs daily 6am-12:30am, but the most convenient way to navigate Amsterdam's maze of canals and crooked streets is to use its highly efficient and comprehensive **tram system.** With over 13 lines, these streetcars traverse most of the main streets of the city, with tram stops located every few blocks. The currency of trams is the **strippenkart,** a card with anywhere from two (€1.40) to 45 (€17.40) strips. The city is divided into several zones: Centrum, West, Oost (East), Noord (North), and Zuid (South); most of touristed Amsterdam falls within the Centrum zone. You can buy a two-strip one-time *strippenkart* when boarding any tram (€1.40, good for unlimited trips for one hour), but if you're planning on navigating the city it's advisable to buy one of several passes. *Strippenkarts* are much cheaper when bought in bulk (8-*strippenkart* €5.60; 15-*strippenkart* €5.90, seniors and kids €3.70; 45-*strippenkart* €17.40); day passes *(dagkaarten)* for unlimited use in all zones (€5.20, seniors and kids €3.60); and unlimited-use passes *(sterabonnement)* for one week, month, or year in the same zone (one-week pass €8.90, seniors and children €5.65). Passes require a passport-size photo that can be taken in any of the photo booths found in Centraal Station, but holders also require proper ID to use them. You can purchase bulk passes at **GVB (public transportation) offices,** post offices, train stations, and many city convenience stores. *Strippenkart* can be used for all public transportation throughout The Netherlands.

The same basic system governs **buses,** which cover many of the same routes as trams as well as traveling to more distant locations of greater Amsterdam. While other public transport options shut down at 12:30am, night buses rumble through the sleeping city until 6am when the trams start up again (single trip €2.50). The zone transit system that governs Amsterdam applies to **long-distance buses** as well. *Strippenkarts* can be used to travel throughout the country via bus; the number of strips required depends on the number of zones traversed.

on the cheap

kindness of strangers on a train

Dutch students ages 18-27 in possession of an O.V. (Openbaar Vervoer, or "public transport") card are allowed free train travel within The Netherlands during the work week and a 40% discount on weekends. Best of all, they're entitled to take up to three guests with them at any time—for the same 40% reduction. If you're lucky enough to know someone with an O.V. card, you've been graced with an excellent way to save some cash in your travels across Holland. If you haven't already found your way in to the Dutch student circle, though, making friends on the railway platform isn't hard. Next time you're waiting for your next train to Rotterdam or Maastricht, take a moment to chat with the person next to you: if you end up becoming friendly, he or she may offer to let you sit with her. In this case, you need a discount ticket from the electronic ticketing machine (press *korting* for discount) and make sure that your new friend is with you through your final destination. On longer train trips, ticket-checkers will pass up to three times per ride, and if you're caught using a discount rate without appropriate identification, you'll be forced to pay the on-train fare—which is often more than double the price you pay at the station.

The **subway,** known as the Metro, is only useful for a few locations in the downtown core. After departing south from Centraal Station, trains stop at Nieuwmarkt, Waterlooplein, and Weesperplein, and then continue to Amsterdam's surrounding suburbs. If you find yourself in need of this service, simply look for the blue "M" sign.

Confused and overwhelmed? For information and tram passes, head to the **GVB** (public transport authority) on the Stationsplein across from Centraal Station in the same building as the VVV. Be sure to ask for the special multi-colored tram map. (Open M-F 7am-9pm, Sa-Su 8am-9pm. Information ☎09 00 92 92; €0.30 per min. Local info line ☎460 59 59 operated M-F 9am-6pm.) While the tram and bus operators tend to be lax about checking your tickets, the uniformed inspectors are not. If you're caught without a valid pass, you'll be fined €30 plus the cost of the ticket.

BY CAR

The Netherlands has well-maintained roadways and the Dutch drive on the right side of the road. North Americans and Australians need an International Driver's License; if your insurance doesn't cover you abroad, you'll also need a green insurance card. On maps, a green "E" indicates international highways; a red "A," national highways; and "N," other main roads. Speed limits are 50km per hr. in towns, 80km outside, and 120km on highways. Fuel comes in three types; some cars use benzene (about €1.12 per liter), while others use gasoline (€0.40 per liter) or Diesel fuel (€0.80 per liter). The **Royal Dutch Touring Association** (ANWB; ☎0800 08 88) offers roadside assistance to members. For more info contact the branch at Museumplein 5 (☎0800 05 03) or at Wassenaarseweg 220, 2596 EC The Hague, (☎070 314 71 47).

BY BIKE

The long, flat spaces that connect The Netherlands' cities and towns, as well as the bicycle-friendly streets that snake through the cities themselves, make cycling a cheap, convenient, and ecological mode of transport. Amsterdam's streets teem with bikes and bike paths, which can be easily navigated if you follow the basic rules:

First, observe and follow all street signs and stop lights. Amsterdammers violate these with impunity, thanks to instincts born of years of experience. Because you do not have this experience under your belt, a failure to observe traffic rules on Amsterdam's complicated roads may find you in an unexpected tête-a-tête with a tram or car. Second, remember that you must **yield to all traffic coming from the right,** whether car or cycle. Second, always stay on the right side of the road. Third, be careful of tram tracks—they're just wide enough for bike wheels to become wedged in between. If you do find your bike stuck, don't linger while a tram bears down on you, just get away—better to lose your bike than your life. Five, be sure to signal all turns and stops, ensuring that you don't get rear-ended by an unassuming truckdriver.

Finally, **always lock your bike**—bike theft is rampant in Amsterdam. All rental bikes come with locks and keys; use them even when you stop for a few moments. The majority of thefts take place when riders briefly leave their cycles unlocked to snap a photo. Also keep in mind that most bike insurance does not cover bikes that are stolen with the key left on the bike; you have to produce the key to get back your deposit. Especially if you're locking your bike for an extended period, ensure that it is left in a quiet and safe spot, as locks don't always deter bike theft. If you have any questions regarding liability, ask the bike-rental salesperson for advice.

Bike rental shops abound, but not all are created equal. Your best bet is ▉**Frederic Rent a Bike,** Brouwersgracht 78, in the Shipping Quarter which has the best-quality wheels in the city. Although Frederic is slightly pricier than his competitors, it's well worth the ten-minute walk from Centraal Station. Head west along Prins Henrikkade and cross Singelgracht. Turn left down the canal and then right onto the northern side of Brouwersgracht. Frederic rents for €10 per day or €40 per week; a credit card is required. (☎624 55 09; www.frederic.nl.) Another good option is **Mac Bike,** with three locations around the city: Marnixstraat 220, Weteringschans 2, and Mr.

Visserplein 2. This popular chain offers many options, from same-day rentals (€6.50) to six-day stints (€27.25). Be sure not to rent one of the bikes that has a garish "Mac Bike" logo on the front, lest you brand yourself a tourist. (☎ 626 69 64; www.macbike.nl.) For more bike rental options, see the **Service Directory**, p. 319.

KEEPING IN TOUCH

BY MAIL

Post offices are generally open Monday Friday 9am-5 or 6pm, and some are also open Saturday 10am-1:30pm. To find out exact times for specific branches, the best resource is the phone book, as there is no central number or English-language website for the Amsterdam postal service. Mailing a postcard or letter to anywhere within The Netherlands costs €0.39; to anywhere in the, EU €0.59; to destinations outside Europe, postcards cost €0.54, letters (up to 20g) €0.75. Mail takes 2-3 days to the UK, 4-6 to North America, 6-8 to Australia and New Zealand, and 8-10 to South Africa. Mark envelopes "air mail," or "par avion," or your letter or postcard will probably never arrive (surface mail and mail by sea take one to four months at best). To send an international letter, there's no need to go to a post office; just drop it into the *overige* slot of a mailbox.

RECEIVING MAIL IN AMSTERDAM

There are several ways to arrange pick-up of letters sent to you by while you are abroad. Mail can be sent via **Poste Restante** (General Delivery) to almost any city or town in The Netherlands with a post office, Address *Poste Restante* letters accordingly:

Rem KOOLHAAS
Poste Restante
Amsterdam, The Netherlands

The mail will go to a special desk in the central post office, (Singel 250; see p. 323) unless you specify a post office by street or postal. It's best to use the central office; mail may be sent there regardless. Bring a photo ID for pick-up. If the clerks insist that there is nothing for you, have them check under your first name as well.

American Express's travel offices throughout the world offer a free **Client Letter Service** (mail held up to 30 days and forwarded upon request)

Canals & Sint Nicolaaskerk

Pickpocket Reminders

Dam Pigeons

the hidden deal

sim city

Cell phones in The Netherlands are expensive: the cheapest are usually €90-100. But if you're planning on staying in Amsterdam for a longer period of time and are looking for a more reliable means of wireless communication, you may want to consider getting your existing mobile phone un-SIM-locked. For a fee of €20, the centrally-located phone shop **TeleTools**, Nieuwezijds Voorburgwal 91 (☎ 620 00 02), can program just about any American or European cell phone to be compatible with all Dutch SIM cards. This means that once your phone is unlocked, you'll be able to buy a pre-paid SIM card at any phone shop in town; the best and cheapest providers can be picked up at the **Bel-Company,** which has several locations around Amsterdam (Leidsestraat 69, ☎ 620 41 88; Nieuwendijk 205, ☎ 330 88 14). A normal pre-paid SIM card will set you back €16-25, depending on the provider and on how much credit you want; you can buy recharge cards at newsstands, tobacco shops, and phone stores around town. Best of all, incoming calls on all European cell phones are free of charge, and you can usually use your phone anywhere else in Europe (although roaming charges are normally exorbitant). TeleTools is available to unlock phones W only, 5-6pm.

for cardholders who contact them in advance. Address the letter in the same way shown above. For locations, see the **Service Directory,** p. 319.

BY TELEPHONE

Almost every pay phone in The Netherlands requires a "Chipknip" card. You can buy them almost anywhere (hostels, train stations, tobacconists) for as little as €5 and receive between 10 and 30 minutes of call-time, depending on which country you call. It is possible to use a calling card, you just need to gain access to the phone system via a chipknip card; you always need to insert the card, even for toll-free numbers. If you have a calling card that gives you good rates, just buy one Chipknip card and you'll never need another. With Chipknip, international calls are cheapest 8pm-8am. For directory assistance dial ☎ 0900 80 08; for collect calls dial 06 04 10. International direct dial numbers include: **AT&T,** ☎ 0800 022 91 11; **Sprint,** ☎ 0800 022 91 19; **Australia Direct,** ☎ 0800 022 20 61; **BT Direct,** ☎ 0800 022 00 44; **Canada Direct,** ☎ 0800 022 91 16; **Ireland Direct,** ☎ 0800 02 20 353; **MCI WorldPhone Direct,** ☎ 0800 022 91 22; **NZ Direct,** ☎ 0800 022 44 64; **Telekom South Africa Direct,** ☎ 0800 022 02 27. All 0800 numbers in Amsterdam are toll-free; 0900 numbers charge a per-minute fee.

TIME DIFFERENCES

Amsterdam is one hour ahead of Greenwich Mean Time (GMT), six hours ahead of New York and Toronto, nine hours ahead of Vancouver and San Francisco, at the same time as Johannesburg, Rome, and Paris, two hours behind Moscow, and eight or nine hours behind Sydney, depending on the season. The Netherlands observes daylight savings time.

BY INTERNET

Internet is fairly easy to find in Amsterdam (for listings, see the **Service Directory,** p. 322), though it may be more difficult to find places with floppy disk drives. The best place for internet can be found in Amsterdam's wonderful libraries (see **Bibliotheek-nophilia,** p. 31).

TOURIST, FINANCIAL, & LOCAL SERVICES

Every town in The Netherlands has a VVV, or Dutch tourist office. While the resources at these offices—brochures, maps, and tickets—can be helpful, the employees may be weary of the crowds, and show it. The main VVV offices in Amsterdam are located across from Centraal Station, and Leidsestraat, near Leidseplein. For more specific information on the VVV and other tourist services, see the **Service Directory**, p. 324.

BANKING. The major banks in Amsterdam are **ABN-AMRO** and **Rabobank.** Standard banking hours are between 9am-5pm on weekdays and often include extended hours (9am-7pm) on Thursdays. See **Service Directory: Banks,** p. 319.

SAFETY & SECURITY

PERSONAL SAFETY

EXPLORING. To avoid unwanted attention, avoid the tourist profile; don't speak English loudly and avoid wearing a camera around your neck. Familiarize yourself with your surroundings before setting out, and walk confidently; if you must check a map, duck into a shop. If you are traveling alone, be sure someone at home knows your itinerary, and **never admit that you're traveling by yourself.** When walking at night, stick to busy, well-lit streets. If you feel uncomfortable, leave as quickly and directly as you can.

DRIVING. If you are using a car, learn local driving signals and wear a seatbelt. Children under 40lbs. should ride only in a special car seat, available from most car rental agencies. If your car breaks down, wait for the police to assist you. Be sure to park your vehicle in a well traveled area. **Sleeping in your car** is one of the most dangerous—and illegal—ways to get your rest.

CON ARTISTS & PICKPOCKETS. Don't ever let your passport and your bags out of your sight. Beware of **pickpockets** in crowds, especially in the Red Light District, Dam Square, near Centraal Station, and on public transport.

ETIQUETTE

While Amsterdam is known for tolerance, it is important to respect the city's customs.

SMOKING (TOBACCO). Typically, restaurants will allow their patrons to smoke cigarettes while dining; thus, do not expect a smoke-free environment when eating out, or any other place for that matter—Amsterdam is a tobacco smoker's paradise. Legislation that bans smoking in public places is set to take effect in January 2005 (p. 44).

on the cheap

bibliotheek-nophilia

Forget about Amsterdam's slick internet cafes and their Javanese espressos, frosted brownies, and retro aluminum decor; the best budget place to check your email is the local library. Web-browsing and emailing is always free at Amsterdam's *bibliotheeks,* and there are usually plenty of computers free: however, you'll usually have to limit your session to 30 minutes, and you may have to schedule a slot in advance during busy times. Most locations are strict in enforcing a one-session-per-day rule. The two most centrally located branches are the **Centraal Bibliotheek,** Prinsengracht 587 (☎523 09 00; open M 1-9pm, Tu-Th 10am-9pm, F-Sa 10am-5pm, Su 1pm-5pm), and **Pintohuis,** St. Antoniesbreestraat 69 (☎624 31 84; open M, W 2-8pm, F 2-5pm, Sa 11am-4pm). Other locations include **Cinetoi,** Tolstraat 160 in **De Pijp** (☎662 31 84; open M, W 2-8pm, Tu 2-5pm, F 10am-5pm, Sa 11am-5pm), and **Saatsliedenberg,** Van Limburg Stirumstraat 133 in **Westerpark** (☎682 39 86; open M, W 2-8pm, F 10am-5pm, Sa 11am-4pm). You can pick up a leaflet with library hours for all locations in any branch, or check www.oba.nl for more details.

Playing Around at Artis

A View from Metz & Co.

Small-Time Crooks

SMOKING (DRUGS). Marijuana and other soft drugs are tolerated in Amsterdam, but along with experimentation comes the need for responsibility and respect. Be sure to regulate your drug intake out of a basic respect for the city you're visiting. Refrain from smoking up outside, unless it's on the terrace of a coffeeshop; not only is this an easy way for pickpockets and con artists to pick out a tourist, but locals also consider it offensive. Be sure to **ask if it's okay to smoke** before lighting a joint. Coffeeshops are legally not allowed to cause a disturbance; if you are being rowdy, you may be asked to leave. For more information, see **Only in Amsterdam,** p. 126

LOVE FOR HIRE. As visitors to the Red Light District know, prostitution is legal in Amsterdam. Most of the prostitutes that you see belong to a union called "The Red Thread" and are tested for HIV and STDs, although testing is on a voluntary basis. While it's okay to look, **do not take photos** unless you want to explain yourself to the angriest—and largest—man you'll ever see. If you're in a group of tourists, don't crowd in front of a window for a long time; this tends to discourage customers and is thus frustrating to the prostitute. Here are the basic do's and don'ts:

First, be sure to show the women basic respect. Looking is fine, even necessary, but leering and catcalling are absolutely uncalled for. Keep in mind that prostitution is an entirely legal enterprise, and windows are places of business. Second, show up clean and sober. Prostitutes always reserve the right to refuse service. Third, be sure to be extremely clear and straightforward in your negotiation. Specifically state what you get for the money you're paying—that means which sex acts, in what positions, and especially how much time you have in which to do it. Window prostitutes are self-employed and can set their own prices. Moreover, they aren't required by any means to do anything you want; they must consent to it beforehand. Fourth, don't make trouble. If anyone becomes violent or threatening with a window prostitute, they have access to an emergency button that sets off a loud alarm. It not only makes an ear-splitting noise, it also summons the police, who invariably side with prostitutes in disputes. If you feel you have a legitimate complaint or have any kind of question about commercial sex, head to the extremely helpful ⛟**Prostitution Information Center** (see p. 124) and discuss it with them. Fifth, don't ask for a refund if you're not satisfied; all sales are final. Sixth, always practice safe sex. A prostitute should not be expected to—and indeed will not—touch an uncondomed penis.

GENERAL BUSINESS HOURS. Most shops are open M-F 9am-5pm and generally are not open late at night. During holidays and the tourist season, hours are extended into the night and shops open their doors on Sundays, but only in the more touristed districts. Most outer neighborhoods are silent and locked on Sundays. Lunch is typically served from 11am to 3pm; dinner might be served from 5:30pm to 11pm, but in many neighborhoods it's difficult to find a kitchen open later than 9pm.

TIPPING. Service charges are included in all hotel, restaurant, and shopping bills as well as taxi fares, so tips are not necessary—but certainly accepted and appreciated. Taxi drivers and waiters are customarily tipped 10%, and bathroom attendants usually receive €0.10-0.20 per visitor.

LANGUAGE

Dutch is the official language of The Netherlands, but in Amsterdam most natives speak English—and speak it well. Thanks to mandatory education in schools and English-language media exports, most locals have impeccable grammar, vast vocabularies, and a soft Continental accent that makes conversing very pleasant. Knowing a few key Dutch words and phrases can't hurt, particularly in smaller towns where English is not spoken as widely. Dutch spellings frequently resemble German, but pronunciation is very different. For example, Dutch uses a gutteral "g" sound for both "g" and "ch," meaning that legendary painter Van Gogh's name is pronounced "Van Goch." For pronunciation help, see below. To initiate an English conversation, politely ask *Spreekt ü Engels?* ("SPRAYKT oo angles?"). Even if your conversational counterpart speaks little English, he or she will usually try to communicate, an effort you can acknowledge by thanking them: *Dank u wel* ("DAHNK oo vell").

PHONETIC UNIT	PRONUNCIATION	PHONETIC UNIT	PRONUNCIATION
au	ow, as in "now"	g, ch	ch as in "loch"
ai	sounds like "eye"	ie	ee as in "see"
aa	sounds like "laa"	ij	ay, as in "may"
ei	ay as in "may"	oe	oe as in "shoe"
eu	u as in "hurt"	uu	oo as in "too," but longer
ee	ay as in "may"	ui	oe as in "foe"

PHRASEBOOK

ENGLISH	DUTCH	ENGLISH	DUTCH
NUMBERS			
0	nul	15	vijftien
1	een	16	zestien
2	twee	17	zeventien
3	drie	18	achttien
4	vier	19	negentien
5	vijf	20	twintig
6	zes	21	eenentwintig
7	zeven	30	dertig
8	acht	40	veertg
9	negen	50	vijftig
10	tien	60	zestig
11	elf	70	zeventig
12	twaalf	80	tachtig
13	dertien	90	negentig
14	veertien	100	honderd

ENGLISH	DUTCH		ENGLISH	DUTCH
DAYS, TIME				
Monday	*maandag*		**June**	*juni*
Tuesday	*dinsdag*		**July**	*juli*
Wednesday	*woensdag*		**August**	*augustus*
Thursday	*donderdag*		**September**	*september*
Friday	*vrijdag*		**October**	*oktober*
Saturday	*zaterdag*		**November**	*november*
Sunday	*zondag*		**December**	*december*
January	*januari*		**Winter**	*de wnter*
February	*februari*		**Spring**	*de lente*
March	*maart*		**Summer**	*de zomer*
April	*april*		**Fall**	*de herfst*
May	*mei*		**day**	*dag*

ENGLISH	DUTCH	PRONOUNCIATION
GENERAL		
Hello/Hi	*Dag/Hallo*	Dach/Hallo
My name is...	*Mijn naam is...*	Mayn nahm iss
Do you speak English?	*Spreekt ü Engels?*	Spraykt oo angles
I don't speak Dutch	*Ik spreek geen Nederlands*	Ik sprayk chayn Nay-der-lans
I don't understand	*Ik begrijp het niet*	Ik bech-rayp 'et neet
Good morning	*Goedemorgen*	Choo-de-mor-chuh
Good afternoon	*Goedemiddag*	Choo-der-mid-ach
Goodevening	*Goedenavond*	Choo-de-na-vondt
Goodbye	*Tot ziens/Dag* (Informal)	Tot Seens/Dach
Yes/No/Maybe	*Ja/Nee/Misschien*	Yah/Nay/Miss-cheen
Please	*Alstublieft*	Als-too-bleeft
Thank you	*Dank u wel*	Dahnk oo Vell
You're welcome	*Alstublieft* (like "Please")	Als-too-bleeft
Excuse me (getting attention)	*Pardon*	Par-don
Excuse me (to apologize)	*Neemt u mij niet*	Naymt oo mey neet
Go away!	*Ga weg!*	Cha vech!
Help!	*Help!*	Help!
Stop!	*Stop!*	Stop!
I'm lost	*Ik ben verdwand*	Ik ben ferd-vahnd
Sorry!	*Sorry!*	Sorry!
QUESTIONS		
Who?	*Wie?*	Vee?
What?	*Wat?*	Vaat?
When?	*Wanneer?*	Va-neer?
Why?	*Waarom?*	War-ohm?
Where is...?	*Waar is...?*	Vahr iss?
...the museum	*...het museum*	het mu-say-um
...the church	*...de kerk*	de kairk
...the bank	*...de bank*	de bahnk
...the hotel	*...het hotel*	het hotel
...the shop	*...de winkel*	de vin-kul
...the market	*...de markt*	de marrkt
...the consulate	*...het consulaat*	het con-sul-aat

...the train station	...het station	het staht-see-ohn
...the bus stop	...de bushalte	de buus-hahlt
...tourist office	...de VVV	de fay fay fay
What time is it?	Hoe laat is het?	Hoo laht iss 'et?
When does the (house) open?	Waneer gaat het (huis) open?	Van-eer chaht 'et (hows) oh-pen?
ACCOMMODATIONS		
I have a reservation	Ik heb een reservering	Ik hep ayn res-er-vay-ring
Single room	eenpersoonkammer	ayn-per-sohn-kah-mer
Double room	tweepersoonkammer	tvay-per-sohn-kah-mer
How much per night?	Hoeveel kost het per nacht	Hoo-fayl cost 'et payr nacht?
Yesterday	gisteren	chis-te-ruh
Today	vandaag	fan-dach
Tomorrow	morgen	mor-chuh
Bath	bad	badt
Shower	douche	douch

HEALTH

Should you require a house call for a condition not requiring hospitalization, contact the appropriate number from the list of emergency numbers listed in the **Service Directory,** see p. 320. Any hospital should be able to refer you to a dentist, optometrist, or ophthalmologist. Request documentation (including diagnoses) and receipts to submit to your home insurance company for reimbursement. EU citizens can get reciprocal health benefits, entitling them to a practitioner registered with the state system, by filling out a E111 or E112 form before departure; this is available at most major post offices. Other travelers should ensure they have adequate medical insurance before leaving; if your regular insurance policy does not cover travel abroad, you may wish to purchase additional coverage. With the exception of Medicare, most health insurance plans cover members' medical emergencies during trips abroad; check with your insurance carrier to be sure. The Dutch medical system will generally treat you whether or not you can pay in advance.

Pharmacies, *apotheek* in Dutch, can be found all of Amsterdam's neighborhoods. For more information on pharmacies, see the **Service Directory,** p. 323.

If you need a **doctor** *(dokter)* for more serious health matters, call the local hospital for a list of local practitioners. If you are receiving reciprocal health care, make sure you call a doctor who will be linked to the state health care system. Contact your health provider for information regarding charges that may be incurred. Note that the same medicines may have different names in The Netherlands than in your home country; check with your doctor before you leave. If you do not have insurance, go to the **Kruispost Medisch Helpcentrum,** Oudezijds Voorburgwal 129, a first aid walk-in clinic for those without insurance. (☎624 90 31 Open daily 7-9:30pm.)

Life & Times

Though the popular conception of The Netherlands is preoccupied with sex, drugs, and a breezy, liberal culture, the keystones of Dutch history are much more staid and subdued: colonialism and civil engineering. While foreign history glorifies the Dutch trading empire that once rivaled—and was at war with—Great Britain, the domestic story is one of continual battle to fend off the encroaching seas. Locals say that though God created the rest of the world, the Dutch created The Netherlands. The country is a masterful feat of engineering; since most of it is below sea level, many dikes and windmill-driven pumping were used to create dry land, making civilization possible.

HISTORY OF THE NETHERLANDS

EARLY HISTORY: TRIBES & TERPEN

The early history of the so-called **"Low Countries"** is as murky and difficult to navigate as its boggy marshlands. The region includes Belgium, Luxembourg, and The Netherlands, but also encompasses regions of modern Germany and France. Nomads first roamed the area in 150,000 BC, camping out on hills near Utrecht, with the first farmers settling the low countries around 9000 BC. Writtten history of the Low Countries began in 57 BC when Julius Caesar conquered a number of tribes, including the **Eburons,** the **Menapians,** and the Celtic **Belgae.** Two other tribes, the Germanic **Frisians** and **Batavi,** escaped Roman domination, but not out of benevolent intentions: because the lands they inhabited were subject to frequent flooding, the Romans deemed it worthless. The Frisians and Batavi

in the know

xxx—not as racy as you think

While some travelers speculate that the triple cross pattern on Amsterdam's civic shield is somehow related to the city's liberal attitude toward sex, the truth of the matter is far less sensational. Found on every *amsterdammertje*—the capped metal poles separating streets from sidewalks—this 400-year-old pattern represents the crucifixion of the apostle Andrew, patron saint of fishermen and fishmongers. Given the significance of the sea in developing Amsterdam's prosperity and success, the pattern is a fitting choice for the adornment of the city's shield. But each cross represents one of Andrew's moral values: *vastberaden* (courage), *heldhaftig* (determination), and *barmhartig* (altruism). And although the locals are not always fully aware of the symbol's significance, they will be sure to react if it's ever mistaken for sexual innuendo.

were eventually granted the status of trading allies, and these bellicose tribes maintained a tenuous relationship with Rome for over three centuries. This era witnessed the region's first engineering innovations—tribes succeeded by living on **terpen**, (stone mounds to keep lodgings above flood levels), while Roman attempts to dam the land and build canals from 12 BC to AD 50 proved futile, as the area remained abysmally marshy. The historian Pliny even went so far as to call their home "wretched" in AD 50.

CHRISTIANITY & CHARLEMAGNE

Roman influence began to decline in AD 300 and vanished after an invasion by Germanic tribes—who by this time had unified to become collectively known as the **Franks** and the **Saxons**—in AD 406. Most of the Roman advances were reversed with the invasion, and a less complex agrarian society based on small clans replaced the technocracy from Rome. **Clovis I,** king of the Frankish Merovingians, ascended the throne in AD 481 and inaugurated the **Pactus Legis Salicae** (Law of the Salian Franks), a unique system of Roman and Christian law that paved the way for Christianity to permeate northern Europe. **Saint Willibrod** became the first **Bishop of Utrecht** in the beginning of the 8th century—Utrecht was one of the most important Dutch towns in the spread of Christianity (see p. 256). Upon Willibrod's death, **Saint Boniface** strove to complete his predecessor's work. The Frisians killed St. Boniface in 754 in a last (but ultimately futile) attempt to resist conversion.

In 800 **Charlemagne's** forces took control of the Low Countries. He saw himself as retaining the legacy of the Roman emperors who had ruled hundreds of years earlier. The empire had no specific capital—Charlemagne alternately held court in The Netherlands, at his palace in Nijmengen, and in France. Though Charlemagne ruled in name, his Dutch legacy is contested—historians maintain that the that country remained more or less under Frankish control until 1519 and local officials in the Low Countries were quite influential. Nevertheless Charlemagne, crowned as Holy Roman Emperor **Charles I** in 800, presided over an unprecedented cultural renaissance. Romanesque churches still remain in Nijmengen, cultural remnants of this window of light in the Dark Ages.

The rule of Louis I after Charlemagne's death saw the decline of the Carolingian empire. The area's new-found independence left it open for the Danish **Vikings** to attack and plunder. Viking threats abated after the 900s; the peace allowed towns in the Low Countries to flourish economically as trade blossomed. The principalities composing the modern-day Netherlands began to coalesce in the 11th century. The **County of Holland**—in which Amsterdam is located—was one of the first to form, along with **Flanders, Hainaut, Brabant, Liège, Utrecht,** and **Groningen,** all of which began to assert autonomy under various Counts, early proponents of feudalism.

AMSTERDAM'S EMERGENCE

In spite of Holland's emergence as a political body, the area that is now Amsterdam was not truly populated until the mid 1200s. In 1270, the inhabitants of the mouth of the **Amstel River** built the first dam between the dikes—constructed on either side of the river—to keep the sea waters at bay. The town grew as maritime trade flourished between northern Europe and Flanders, but went officially unnamed until 1275 when Count **Floris V** wrote of a town inhabited by people living near the *Amstelledamme,* the "Dam on the River Amstel," in a tariff document; the name later evolved into its current form. The city gained its **charter** in 1306, and by the end of the 15th century, Amsterdam had become the largest and most important town and port in Holland. Emperor **Maximillian I** was so indebted to Amsterdam's support that he allowed the city to adorn itself with the imperial crown of the Burgundian-Austrian empire.

PROTESTANT REFORMATION & EIGHTY YEARS' WAR

The French **Burgundian Dynasty** controlled the region following the decline of the Holy Roman Empire's influence in the Low Countries. Under French rule, Dutch provinces had evolved into clearly delineated, interdependent territories by the mid- to late-14th century. The Burgundian territories were again absorbed into the Holy Roman Empire when **Charles the Bold** died, ceding his lands to the Hapsburgs. In the early 15th century, many continental Europeans were disillusioned by the excesses of the Catholic church. The genesis of that discontent was partly attributed to a Dutch intellectual. Martin Luther, who openly questioned the Catholic Church's indulgence system, was heavily influenced by **Erasmus of Rotterdam,** the humanist scholar. When Luther posted his *95 Theses* to the door of a church in Wittenberg, Germany, Erasmus was attacked on both sides: by the Catholics for having incited Luther's radicalism, and by the Lutherans for not aligning himself with their new faith. His particu-

Begijnhof

Oldest Wooden Building in Amsterdam

Canal House

the indonesian side of the story

Though the history of Dutch colonial efforts in the so-called "East Indies"—modern-day Indonesia—was instrumental in building The Netherlands' wealth and prosperity, the effects on Indonesia's population were not as beneficial.

At the end of the 16th century, Portuguese forces, who had ruled the country since 1511, withdrew from Indonesia, leaving ruined infrastructure and a vestige of Catholicism—only the beginning of colonial turmoil. In place of the Portuguese, Calvinist Dutch entrepreneurs seized upon the opportunity to exploit the island and it's neighbors for spices and produce under the auspices of the Dutch East India Company (VOC). Military force and exploitative diplomacy gave the Dutch a trade monopoly and funneled all profits away from locals—a "divide and subjugate" strategy created segregated pockets of Indonesians and power imbalances among increasingly Dutch-dependent local rulers.

The VOC went bankrupt in 1799, but the Dutch, accustomed to colony-fueled wealth, pressed the government to step in and continue trade within the region in Southeast Asia then known as the Dutch East Indies. The early 20th century saw the creation of the Ethical Policy, aimed at improving education and public health and bringing Indonesians closer to European ideals. Indonesians began formulating religious or ethnic identity and political ideology independent of their colonizers.

Continued on next page

lar dilemma foreshadows the years of religious turmoil that would follow during the radical and sweeping Protestant Reformation.

While the Reformation swept the Low Countries, the Spanish took over Amsterdam in 1519. In 1543 Spanish king **Charles V** created the **Political Union of The Netherlands** (present-day Belgium, Luxembourg, and The Netherlands) as part of his mission to conquer the world. Only a few decades after its creation, the union collapsed due to religious differences. **Philip II,** the new king of Catholic Spain, tried to squelch the Protestant Reformation. Outraged, dissidents commenced the **Breaking of the Images,** desecrating churches and destroying religious icons. Stern military reprisals from Philip's forces ignited a Dutch resistance against the Spanish government in 1568, the beginning of a period of intermittent armed rebellion: the **Eighty Years' War,** led by **William I,** Prince of Orange.

William I led and personally funded a number of revolts in the country, but the city of Amsterdam remained loyal to Philip and hesitated to join the Dutch. Though he was unsuccessful in effecting the freedom of The Netherlands himself, when the provinces claimed their independence in the 1579 **Union of Utrecht,** William was named the first leader of the **United Provinces of The Netherlands.** The proclamation that unified the provinces also returned Amsterdam to the The Netherlands, by then deeply rooted in Protestantism—specifically the strict, ascetic Calvinism. (One year before the union, Spanish citizens and many members of the Roman Catholic Church were deported from the city). This period was known as the **Alteration.** Any remaining Catholics in Amsterdam were forced to practice in hiding, as their public worship areas were confiscated by the Protestants (see p. 81); simultaneously, the town of Antwerp fell to Spain during the war. The resulting Dutch exodus from that town to Amsterdam resulted in a surge in the city's intellectual and cultural energies.

William's assassination was sponsored by Philip in 1584, and by 1588, the southern provinces again fell into Spanish hands. The short-lived Twelve Years' Truce established the current Dutch boundaries in 1609; after 1621 skirmishing resumed. The arrival of France as an emerging power so preoccupied Spain that Dutch independence was recognized in 1648.

GOLDEN AGE (1609-1713)

The seeds of The Netherlands' future commercial dominance were laid in the 1590s, when two ships set sail from Amsterdam on separate voyages bound for **Indonesia.** They were but a harbinger of The Netherlands' imperial might. During the first half of the 17th century, while Rembrandt van Rijn was building an artistic legacy, two newly established commercial trading companies were securing an economic imperial legacy on the international stage. Because of its fortuitously situated northern ports, The Netherlands were prime candidates to assume the reins of a quickly expanding global trading enterprise. Both the Verenigde Oostindisch Compagnie (VOC) or **Dutch East India Company,** and the West-Indische Compagnie (WIC) or **West India Company,** founded in 1602 and 1621, respectively, began creating a vast network of Dutch trading posts throughout Southeast Asia, West Africa, and South America.

The VOC was the larger of the two companies and established major trading posts in India, Indonesia, Thailand, China, Sri Lanka, and Bengal, importing spices, silks and cotton. The Dutch also colonized Indonesia (see p. 40). The WIC traded slaves, gold, and ivory off the western coast of Africa, and established busy ports in Brazil and Suriname—these territories won independence in 1975. The WIC even had a brief stint beginning in 1626 as the colonizers of **New York** (previously **New Amsterdam**), which Peter Minuit purchased from the Native Americans for 60 guilders. Dutch governor Peter Stuyvesant tried to whip the city's residents into obedient Calvinism until the British took over in 1664.

At the height of the Dutch trading empire, the navy numbered over 15,000 vessels (five times more than Britain), which guaranteed it a monopoly over trade routes. One of the primary engines behind the expanding success of the Dutch global enterprise was the arms industry. Because of the standardization of the Dutch army during the Eighty Years' War, the need for regular weaponry increased, and, following independence, the rest of Europe sought to obtain these vaunted Dutch arms for themselves. It was these weapons, both in their use and their sale, that made possible The Netherlands' rise to world power.

As a result of this new-found glory, Amsterdam became both the commercial and social capital of Europe. Religious freedom and abundant employment opportunities attracted emigrants from all over Europe. Portuguese, German, and Eastern European Jews seeking refuge from religious persecution, flocked to the city, as did others seeking work in commercial enterprise. In this age of economic prosperity, aristocrats, merchants, and financiers built homes along Amsterdam canals and revitalized

Continued from previous page

Trade cooperatives and Communist parties became vehicles for political action but internal conflicts prevented the formation of a united nationalist movement.

Growing domestic dissent led to the rise of the Partai Nasional Indonesia (PNI), a nationalist party founded in 1927 and led by charismatic President Sukarno. The PNI practiced civil disobedience to resist Dutch interference and succeeded in pushing to adopt Bahasa Indonesia as the national language in 1928 to foster a sense of national unity.

During WWII, Japan defeated the Dutch and invaded Indonesia for its oil. Indonesians welcomed the Japanese for liberating them from European control, but soon discovered that incorporation into the "Greater East Asia Co-Prosperity Sphere" was a fate worse than Dutch. Power again changed hands as Japan's brutal, $3\frac{1}{2}$-year regime ended with their surrender to the Allies in 1945. The island fell under Dutch control, at least nominally.

Eager to take charge before the Dutch physically returned to the island, Sukarno declared independence several days later. The Netherlands had hoped to restore their former colonial empire, but, to their dismay, they found a mobilized military and chaotically defiant population willing to fight for the newly declared Republik Indonesia. The Indonesian Revolution (1945-50) further unified the nation against the Dutch, who quietly bowed out of the region. By 1950, the Dutch, embarrassed by international criticism, officially transferred sovereignty to Indonesia.

the city. Its population swelled from 50,000 in 1600 to 200,000 in 1650, accelerating an already booming economy. Artists also found The Netherlands to be a haven. In addition to Rembrandt, notable artists Johannes Vermeer, Jan Steen, and Pieter de Hoogh among others painted, chiseled, and carved out The Netherlands' reputation as a creative hotbed. Writers like Constantijn Huygens and poet Joost van den Vondel also flourished during this era. The Dutch preeminence in global trade would last until the beginning of the 18th century, when both England and France wrested control by waging war with The Netherlands.

END OF EMPIRE

Years of war with Britain were not helpful in keeping the Dutch Golden Age afloat, but perhaps even more detrimental to The Netherlands was peace with the naval power to the north. When the 1688 Glorious Revolution in England dethroned James II, **William III of Orange** (*Stadholder* of the United Provinces) was asked to take the British throne with his wife, Mary. In England the Dutch now had an ally against the French, against whom they had waged intermittent war since 1672. In this new alliance, England was to focus its naval strengths in the war against France, while The Netherlands levied its land powers. Because Britain was the stronger member of the Anglo-Dutch alliance, William focused most of his energies on the former. Neglect of The Netherlands increased discontent with his rule; tired of costly wars, Amsterdam was rife with popular uprisings. William's focus on land armies eventually led to the downfall of the Dutch navy—and with the navy went the Golden Age.

After The Netherlands attempted to trade with newly independent American rebels in 1776, the **Fourth Anglo-Dutch War** broke out in 1780. Years of neglect had decimated the Dutch navy and Britain easily emerged victorious, ending Dutch international trade. Th war's economic fallout only served to entrench the deepening divide between upper and lower classes. The influence of the French Enlightenment, which touted the potential and reason of the individual and trumpeted the ideal of democratic rule, fueled the 1780s **Patriot movement.** The movement denounced the conservatism of the ruling Orthodox Protestant monarchy and those aristocrats loyal to **William V.** Internal tensions drew the attention of other nations; France supported the Patriots, while England and Prussia backed the land-owning *stadholders*.

DUTCH REPUBLIC

Fueled by the momentum of the French Revolution, French forces swept through The Netherlands and brought it under their control by 1795. The territory, then the **Batavian Republic,** began the process of political modernization moving towards the democratization for which the Patriots had so long fought. In 1813 after Napoleon's seemingly unending string of military victories finally come to an abrupt and spectacular end, The Netherlands returned to autonomous rule. Ruled by **King William I,** the Kingdom of The Netherlands was declared in 1815. William sought to maintain control over all of the Low Countries, but Belgium declared its independence in 1830; its status was confirmed when William signed a treaty recognizing Belgium in 1839. So great was William's disappointment that he abdicated the throne in 1840.

Constitutional reform followed William's abdication; The Netherlands adopted a liberal charter based on the British system, making the monarch a servant to—rather than a master of—the **States-General,** a body composed of elected officials. Today the Dutch government remains a constitutional monarchy, with Queen Beatrix on the throne. The final major political reforms came in with the **Pacification of 1917,** when universal male suffrage and equal funding to religious and secular schools were established.

WORLD WAR I & II

Despite pressures from both Britain and Germany, The Netherlands maintained its neutrality for the duration of **World War I.** The country thankfully escaped the disastrous fate suffered by its Low Country neighbor Belgium—another neutral nation—

which was invaded in August of 1914. Following what was known as the "Great War," The Netherlands joined the **League of Nations,** but nonetheless continued to maintain its neutrality.

During World War II, The Netherlands was not able to remain as aloof as they had been during the First World War. On May 10, 1940, the army of Nazi Germany crossed the borders of The Netherlands. Military resistance allowed the government and **Queen Wilhelmina** to flee en masse to England (where they formed a parliament in exile), but the Germans overran Dutch forces within a week by bombing much of the country. The Germans occupied The Netherlands for most of the war, flooding its delicate lands to make it more difficult for the Allies to invade neighboring Germany. In response, the Dutch created a clandestine—and largely unsuccessful—Resistance movement that spanned various ideological groups in the country, from conservatives to communists.

The Nazis dissolved political parties and began to persecute Jews, deporting them to concentration and extermination camps. Staying true to their history of tolerance, in one instance, Amsterdam dockworkers, went on strike upon hearing of the deportation of Dutch Jews. This active resistance, which was met with military violence, was one of the few overt and organized acts of resistance that took place during the war. **Anne Frank,** famous for the diary that she kept during her time in hiding, lived with her family in the "secret annex" of her father's warehouse in Amsterdam. Her diary traces a young girl's experience of Jewish persecution. After two years in the annex, the Frank family was found and Anne was taken to the Bergen-Belsen concentration camp, where she died. Her covert existence in a cramped annex illustrates the tragic atrocities of World War II. Now open to the public, the Anne Frank House highlights the inhumanity of World War II and the generosity and courage of some individuals in the Dutch Resistance movement (see p. 85 and p. 84).

Yet Anne Frank and her family's experience was not typical—for the most part the Dutch did not hide their Jews. Fewer Jews from Amsterdam survived (less than 10%) than in any other Western European city; 70,000 were taken to their deaths. Over 75% of the country's Jewish population did not survive the war. Though many buildings in the Jodenbuurt (Jewish Quarter) survived, the area was left empty as its residents were isolated and shipped off to Westerbork (p. 269), a holding camp near Groningen, and then to Death Camps farther east.

lgb history: a timeline

The oldest group for gays and lesbians in Europe, the COC (the full name of which means Dutch Association for the Integration of Homosexuality; p. 308) has been working for over 50 years to expand the rights of gays and lesbians in The Netherlands. Here's a short history of gay rights in Holland:

1950s—The COC begins to organize small meetings where gays and lesbians are allowed to dance together for the first time without persecution.

January 27, 1971—The courts repeal the distinction between homosexual and heterosexual legal age of consent.

October 22, 1973—The courts no longer recognize homosexuality as reasonable grounds for rejection from the military. The move is followed by the creation of a subsidy for social inquiry into the causes of discrimination against homosexuals.

1981—Dutch Parliament legislates that those discriminated against on the basis of homosexuality can be granted political asylum in The Netherlands.

1992—Discrimination against homosexuals on the basis of their sexuality is made illegal.

November 14, 1998—Homosexual parents are granted the right to adopt children.

December 19, 2000—The Netherlands becomes the first country in the world to grant full and legal marriage rights for same-sex couples. The provision went into effect on April 1, 2001.

43

smoke-free?

Attempting to create healthy workplaces for service industry employees, in May 2003, the Dutch government enacted legislation to prohibit smoking in public places—including bars, restaurants, and clubs. The bill, originally set to take effect on January 1, 2004, has been met with resistance from the general population, as smoking tobacco is a common practice among Dutch citizens. But businesses are most outraged because of projection that the ban could cause the loss of 50,000 jobs and €1.5 billion in revenue due to reduced patronage. Although this bill is targeted toward the reduction of tobacco smoke, coffeeshops will be hit the hardest. Technically, the bill bans all smoking in all public places; it would therefore be illegal to light up in a coffeeshop—relaxing with a joint being the primary (or indeed only) reason why these establishments are so highly patronized.

Bas Kuik, the spokesman for Amsterdam's health ministry has stated formally that the proposed bill is not geared toward coffeeshops, but most owners, workers, and customers dismiss that statement given the government's politics. The incumbent right-wing Christian Democrat coalition has reduced the number of the city's coffeeshops by allowing existing shops to go out of business and refusing to

continued on next page

POSTWAR RECONSTRUCTION

Recovery from the war was gradual but marked by significant rebirth in The Netherlands. Wilhelmina returned from England, and with her, legislation to guarantee female suffrage. The country, rebounding from 10-15 billion guilders worth of damage, was forced to rebuild many of its cities. In the postwar period, The Netherlands abandoned its carefully preserved neutrality and joined **NATO.** Wilhelmina abdicated in favor of daughter Juliana in 1948. By the 1950s the country, if not all of its citizens, had recovered, but was again plunged into turmoil when a catastrophic engineering failure troubled the nation. In 1953 high spring tides and hurricane-force gales assaulted the coastlines, breaching dikes that protect the southwestern Netherlands and inundating the countryside; in the torrents of water, over 1800 people died and the economy was devastated. The Netherlands completed its economic recovery and joined the European Economic Community, a precursor to the European Union, in 1957.

PROTEST IN THE 1960s

Amsterdam was at the forefront of the radical movements that sent the entire world reeling in the 1960s. Public demonstrations kept the streets alive, although the causes—environmental and social—were often not as free-lovin' or free-for-all as in North America. **Robert Jasper Grootveld,** founder of a movement called Provos (an abbreviation of *provocatie,* meaning "provocation"), began an anti-smoking campaign in which he spray-painted over cigarette ads with the letter K, for the Dutch word *kanker,* or cancer. His style of protest influenced the anti-war demonstrations in the United States—his followers always remained playful and peaceful. Some remnants of the Provos movement remain in the Spui (see p. 62). The Provos also disrupted the royal wedding of Princess Beatrix to ex-German soldier Claus van Amsberg in 1966 (see p. 50). The influence of the Provos is widely credited with prompting Amsterdam's move to more liberal drug laws.

In another frenzy of edgy Dutch radicalism, people fought for the **White Bicycle Plan,** a proposal to install some 20,000 bicycles throughout the city for shared use. While the plan ended up being less than successful (people just took the white bikes and painted them some other color), they did leave a legacy of environmental conscientiousness behind, and Amsterdam remains a city of cyclists.

1970S & 1980S: HOME SWEET HOME

Housing problems in Amsterdam began after the World War II and continued through the 1970s. The city council's plans to build metro lines involved kicking out residents in the Nieuwmarkt area and moving them to the suburbs. The occupants refused to budge, and police had to resort to tear-gas and brutality finally to remove them. While the metro line was finally constructed in 1980, housing continued to be a problem for the following decade.

The **squatters' movement** (see p. 152) in Amsterdam became a significant political force in the 1980s; during its strongest moments, over 20,000 people occupied buildings without authorization. On April 30, 1980, the day of **Queen Beatrix's** coronation—her mother Juliana abdicated earlier that year—squatters organized huge demonstrations against the excessive spending on royal residences. Once again, violence broke out in the streets of Amsterdam.

Soon the squatters realized that change was better effected through politics. When the 100 squatters living in the old Wyers building learned that their home was to be converted into a hotel, they prepared counter-proposals to present to the city council. Though their proposal was unsuccessful, they succeeded in creating a voice against gentrification, and their eventual eviction occurred without violence.

THE NETHERLANDS TODAY

The Dutch have always been at the forefront of progressive politics, and that position is still evident today in legalized prostitution and drug policy. The Dutch government tolerates soft drug usage—they are highly regulated, (but not legalized; see **Drug Laws,** p. 127) in an attempt to create the safest environment possible for those who partake. As a result, Amsterdam has now become a mecca for drug use and experimentation; such a reputation has led to something of a local backlash against so-called "drug tourism."

Amsterdam and The Netherlands continue to play a disproportionately large role in international politics relative to their geographic size. The Netherlands was an original member of the **European Union (EU),** formed by the Maastricht Treaty signed in 1991. The Netherlands is also the home to the **United Nations' International Court of Justice,** which is in The Hague (see p. 231).

In recent years, The Netherlands has taken on a role of an entirely different stripe: that of international arbiter. The International Court of Justice, housed in the Vredespaleis (Peace Palace)

continued from previous page

issue licenses for new establishments. This subtle policy has weed supporters believing that conservative powers are purposefully trying to eliminate coffeeshops entirely.

For its part, the government believes that the wild and dangerous aspect of weed has driven away gentrified tourists who would otherwise visit Amsterdam for more cultural reasons: history, art, and architecture. But Amsterdam's tourism industry is also partially grounded upon its liberal policies toward drugs and sex, so it seems quite unlikely that the city would improve its tourist numbers and revenues by removing coffeeshops.

All of these musings may be moot, for most citizens believe the bill will never come into effect. In fact, due to the intensity of public outcry, the government has already decided to grant the law a one-year reprieve until January 2005. Opponents reason that other European nations such as France and Spain are still planning on continuing to allow tobacco smoke in public areas, so it seems quite unlikely that the Dutch, who have a history of combatting restrictive conservative policies, would allow Amsterdam to become a smoke-free environment in tobacco-philic Europe.

But even if the bill has no chance of succeeding, that it was merely proposed in the first place reminds visitors that Amsterdam's policy on drugs is a contentious issue and could change the city they know forever. Many travelers come to Amsterdam expecting impossible, rarefied freedom; clearly, even the stoner's haven can be bound by certain limitations.

in recent
news

shifting right

From 1994 to 2002, Holland's center-left Labor Party has ruled over the country's coalition government. But in that final year, only nine days after the May assassination of firebrand right-wing politico Pim Fortuyn, conservatives swept the elections. The Christian Democratic Party—a right-leaning group that led the government from 1977 to 1994 but had until recently fallen out of favor—stormed in and formed a minority government, snaring 43 of Parliament's 150 seats. The "Pim Fortuyn List," a party formerly helmed by its leader and founder, took second; and the smaller, conservative, VVD garnered third. The three parties form the most conservative government in ages—The Netherlands had previously seen almost a decade under Prime Minister Jan Peter Balkenende, but not the same ultra-conservative composition of the coalition government.

The hottest issue of debate now and during the election is unquestionably that of immigration, which some Dutch link to rising crime rates. Voters are frustrated with center-left governments that do little to stem the tide of crime; these voters largely blame immigrants

continued on next page

in The Hague, has overseen disputes between sovereign nations since 1946. Its 15 judges are elected to nine-year terms by a special assembly of the United Nations. Its highest profile defendant has undoubtedly been Slobodan Milosovich, the former leader of the former Yugoslavia who as of press time was still on trial for his "ethnic cleansing" of Albanians.

One of the most unique aspects of the country—but one of the least remarked on in the popular press—is its coalition government, in which no one party gains absolute control of the electorate. The parliament house is divided into two chambers: the second chamber is popularly elected by **proportional representation,** which in turn elects the members of the first chamber. The makeup of the coalition is determined by which parties fare best in the second chamber elections; from the most popular party emerges the Prime Minister. In the 1960s the coalition was led by the Roman Catholic People's Party, which has since faded into obscurity. From 1977-1994 the Christian Democratic Party (CDP) remained in power until it was upset in 1994 by the left-leaning Labor Party. Recent times have seen a move back to the right, and the CDP returned to the top spot following the 2002 elections (see p. 46). This shift to the right was best characterized by that political hand grenade Pim Fortuyn, who died by an assassin's bullet in May 2002. In March 2003, Volkert van der Graaf, a vegan animal rights crusader, claimed sole responsibility for the assassination. In May later that year, Graft was convicted and sentenced to 18 years in prison. The CDP coalition still runs the country, helmed by Fortuyn's replacement Jan Peter Balkenende. The party is also responsible for enacting country's controversial anti-smoking legislation (see p. 44).

In religious affairs, the government of The Netherlands continues its history of tolerance and upholds the doctrine that freedom of religion is a fundamental right. Church and state are separate, and individuals have the right to practice as they wish provided their actions do not harm others. No single religion dominates: 31% of the Dutch are Roman Catholic, 21% are Protestant, and 4.4% are Muslim.

Amsterdam has long been one of the world's "gay capitals"; there are so many gay and lesbian clubs, hotels, and other establishments that a specific scene is difficult to distinguish from the normal tolerance that pervades everyday Dutch life. In addition to the annual **Pride Festival**— which explodes into a flurry of unabashed canalside revelry in early August—Amsterdam is also notable for having legalized the world's first gay marriages—on April 1, 2001. For more background information on the queer history of the city, see **LGB History: A Timeline**, p. 43.

VISUAL ART

The Dutch have a long and varied history in art. Dutch painters are responsible for the departure from the International Gothic Style, the development of the Northern Renaissance, and the perfection of oil painting. In general, Dutch artwork reflects the country's Calvinist tradition: they are characterized by attention to the everyday over religious iconography. Golden Age Dutch paintings are surprisingly small—save for Rembrandt's mammoth *Night Watch*—because they were made for private homes instead of being commissioned by the church.

VAN EYCK

One of the most famous Dutch painters was Johannes van Eyck (1390-1441). Though he didn't invent **oil painting** as once thought, he did perfect the technique. Painting with oil allows the artist more control over his images—van Eyck used the medium to great effect, creating strikingly realistic, minute details in his work. He was particularly adept at portraying the minutiae of architecture and nature, but in doing so, van Eyck often neglected perspective. Van Eyck was also renowned for being a passionate, accurate portrait artist: he even brought out burnished, glittering qualities in metals and jewelry. Critics have suggested that he likely used live models; consequently, his figures appear less graceful but even more realistic than the accuracy-minded Gothic tradition. To see van Eyck paintings, visit the **Rijksmuseum** (see p. 94).

The Betrothal of the Arnolfini, van Eyck's most famous painting, from 1434, shows an everyday scene of two people being promised to each other. He was likely present at the actual event and may have served as a sort of notary—the words "Johannes de eyck fuit hic" (Johannes van Eyck was here) appear on the back wall of the painting. This painting is also a precursor to Velazquez's *Las Meninas*, as the mirror in the back of the room shows a reflection of the scene along with the painter, hence beginning the tradition of the "painting of a painting."

HIËRONYMUS BOSCH

Though only seven of the 40 paintings attributed to Hiëronymus Bosch (1450-1516) bear his name (none are dated), he was legendary for his departure from the prevailing Flemish style embodied by van Eyck. His symbolic triptychs presented

continued from previous page
from the Middle East and from North Africa.

However, the government's agenda ranges far beyond simply cracking down on immigration policies; many of The Netherlands highly-touted liberal traditions are expected to come under stern review. There was a review of the law that legalizes euthanasia, and there are also plans to severely cut social welfare spending. Most significant for visitors, however, the party has always wanted to take a hard look at so-called "drug tourism" and explore ways to curb it. The CDP's latest actions have been to ban smoking in the workplace, which may hurt coffeeshops—see **Smoke Free?**, p. 44.

The Netherlands, of course, is not alone in its fast and major shift to the right. Across Europe, especially in France, Italy, and Spain, rising crime and general voter discontent have led to resounding and often surprising victories for conservative —often extremely conservative—parties and candidates. All this is happening in the context of the further consolidation of the European Union. While the 17 member nations are attempting to systematize their laws and practices, a minor but nevertheless contentious issue is that of marijuana legalization. As the EU seeks to create a collective law on this issue, its many countries will have to come to an agreement on the status of the popular drug, which could have ramifications on Amsterdam's deeply entrenched cannabis culture.

The Changing, Controversial History of Tolerance

Holland is legendary for tolerance of drugs, prostitution, and alternative lifestyles. Prostitution and gay marriage are legal, and although marijuana is not, it is till tolerated in limited quantities (see page p. 127). Some attribute the lax attitude as a historical way of avoiding chaos among the hundreds of territories of which Holland was originally composed. But it was not until 1976, when the Dutch parliament revised the Opium Act and distinguished between hard and soft drugs, that The Netherlands' best-known form of permissiveness came about.

Since The Netherlands began liberalizing drug policy in the mid 1970s, it has become the sweetheart of NORML (the National Organization for the Reform of Marijuana Laws) and legalization movements everywhere. Meanwhile, it has incurred the wrath of drug warriors, most recently former Bill Clinton drug czar Barry McCaffrey, whose tirade against Dutch drug policy included the false claim that the Dutch murder rate is twice as high as in the United States (it is one-fourth as high).

French President Jacques Chirac joined McCaffrey in blaming French narcotics problems on Dutch drug laws, even though only two percent of marijuana in France originated in The Netherlands. Ironically, Chirac's criticisms came at a time when Dutch authorities were tightening regulations. The attacks shocked many Dutch, who view alcohol as a worse vice. According to a 1999 report from the Dutch Ministry of Health, Welfare, and Sport, "the social and health damage that results from alcohol abuse and alcoholism…is many times greater than the damage resulting from drug abuse."

The Dutch are hardly lax when it comes to hard drugs. Recent surveys show that 7 percent of Amsterdam residents over age 12 have used Ecstasy. Dutch authorities are cracking down on production and use of Ecstasy and of other synthetic drugs, just as the US and other countries do. More than 300 seizures were reported in 1998, over 30 production sites were closed, and traffickers were stripped of their financial assets.

Like the US, the Dutch are strict on hard drug use, but they wage a different kind of "war on drugs." When it comes to individual users, the Dutch view hard drug use not as criminal behavior, but as a public health problem. To fight and regulate hard drug use, police have cornered the market by regulating coffeeshop sale of marijuana, and municipal authorities embrace "harm reduction" and "demand reduction."

Despite criticism from the US, France, and others, many European countries are slowly beginning to move toward the Dutch model of decriminalization. Britain recently announced that it will no longer arrest individual soft-drug users, citing thousands of wasted on-duty hours. While the 1961 Convention on Narcotic Drugs, which classifies pot as a drug "with high abuse potential and no medical value," still prevents nations from formally legalizing marijuana without violating international law, countries like Switzerland who are not signatories are considering moving in that direction. The Swiss States Council (the upper house of parliament) voted to decriminalize pot in 2001. Although the lower house has yet to follow, several Swiss cantons have already decriminalized the drug for anyone over 18. "Coffeeshop" style establishments and the sale of cannabis have begun to proliferate.

Despite these trends, US officials still cling stubbornly to the "gateway theory," maintaining that marijuana is a dangerous stepping-stone to harder drugs. But statistics from the Dutch Ministry of Health, Welfare, and Sport tell a different story. According to a recent report, 15.6 percent of Dutch citizens 12 and over have tried marijuana, compared to 32.9 percent of Americans; likewise, only 2.1 percent have used hard drugs compared to 10 percent of Americans. It seems that the combination of regulated tolerance, hard drug prohibition, and a public health approach to drug abuse is showing some results. More of The Netherlands' neighbors may soon be taking note.

Sasha Polakow-Suransky writes for The American Prospect *magazine.*

terrifying scenes that mused pessimistically on human morality. Bosch's worlds were vividly gruesome and wildly fantastical, but he imbued his visions of demonic creatures with striking realism. As such, Bosch's work often evokes the Surrealism movement, which came some 400 years later.

The vivid, demon-filled *Temptation of St. Anthony* presents man as tormented and tempted by sinful pleasures, while St. Anthony himself resists and perseveres through these temptations. His most famous work, *The Garden of Earthly Delights*, a three-part altarpiece, tells the history of the world, from creation through Adam and Eve to mounting human sins and progression into hell. The work laments man's predisposition to pleasure in a dream-like haze; nudes and other-worldly beasts cavort across the paradisiacal middle panel and are confronted with a nightmarish hell on the right.

GOLDEN AGE

The **Golden Age** of the 17th century was one of the most glorious periods in Dutch painting. During the Reformation, religious authorities in northern Holland began to question whether painting should continue at all, as Protestants objected to pictures of religious figures or artwork in religious places. Parishes ceased to fund northern painters while southern artists (still commissioned by the Catholic Church) continued using religious themes. Thus, Dutch artists turned to painting daily life and portraiture. As the demand for religious paintings diminished and artists found that a normally lucrative income source running dry, painters started creating pieces for wealthy private patrons rather than at the discretion of the Church.

REMBRANDT

Rembrandt van Rijn, one of the most famous and talented artists in history, is looked upon by the Dutch with a pride that Italians reserve for da Vinci. Born in 1606 in Leiden, he was part of a new generation of artists that established the **Realist Movement,** whereby artists tried to show the world around them as they actually saw it. He enrolled in the University of Leiden but soon discovered his true passion: painting. He left the university for Amsterdam and married the wealthy Saskia Uylenburgh who supported him for much of his life. He became a portrait painter and upon leaving Leiden became the most sought after in Amsterdam. In 1642, the same year he completed the monumental *Night Watch*, Saskia died, and with her much of his elevated social status. Rembrandt's popularity soon declined as his work became more experimental, alienating his clientele; but though he did declare bankruptcy in 1656 and lived in poverty, he was never completely rejected by the Amsterdam aristocracy and still maintained a relatively high social status until his death in 1669.

In strictly technical terms, few artists have ever rivaled Rembrandt's talent. His paintings are of great renown, but his etchings and drafting skills were also beyond compare. Rembrandt's technique evolved greatly over his lifetime, but he is most famous for his lifelong mastery of *chiaroscuro*, or elements of light and dark. These contrasting lighting techniques allowed Rembrandt to reveal extraordinary emotional details in his subjects' faces, including his own. While other artists kept extensive records of their work and research, Rembrandt instead painted a series of self-portraits ranging from the time of his youth until right before he died. These serve as an autobiographical account and track his artistic development. Rembrandt tended to use coarse strokes and a darker palette (though laced with flashes of brilliant color), lending them an air of brooding mystery.

One of his most famous works, *The Night Watch* (1642), currently resides in the Rijksmuseum (p. 94). For more on Rembrandt, visit the **Museum het Rembrandt**, p. 97.

VERMEER

One of Rembrandt's contemporaries, Johannes Vermeer (1632-1675) is known for painting everyday scenes with a magnificent attention to detail. A slow worker, he studied every angle and curve of his subjects so as to better mirror nature on the

dutchland?

Ever since World War II, the Dutch have displayed a certain unease when it comes to Germany. You'll never meet a Dutchman happy to hear how much the Dutch language sounds like—or spells with the same rules as—German. No one wants to have the number one, *een* (ane), pronounced like the German *ein* (eye-n), mainly because the Germans occupied the country throughout World War II, shipping off over 70,000 of the nation's Jews to concentration camps and destroying dikes to flood the land and slow Allied progress. Though relations are friendly now, it took years for war wounds to heal.

Following WWII the Dutch government demanded German territory as a safety precaution and acquired almost 70 sq. km of German land containing 10,000 inhabitants before normalizing the borders in 1963. It was not until 1969 that a German head of state paid an official visit to The Netherlands, laying a wreath at the National Monument on Dam Square and at the Hollandsche Schouwberg, in memory of the victims of the Holocaust. Given the long-standing tensions between these two countries, it is perhaps not surprising that Princess Beatrix's decision to marry Claus von Amsberg—a German who had served in the Nazi army during the war—caused a Dutch uproar. But Prince Claus has been an adept diplomat, winning the respect of the Dutch along the way. The Netherlands also tasted sweet revenge when they beat West Germany in the semi-finals of the European Championship after losing the World Cup to them in 1974.

canvas. One of his most famous paintings, *The Milkmaid*, shows a woman in a Dutch household performing the simple and ordinary task of pouring milk. What the painting, lacks in dynamicism of subject is more than made up with its honesty. Vermeer produced very few paintings—only 35 have survived. Vermeers in Amsterdam can be found in the Rijksmuseum (see p. 94). For more on Vermeer's work and the location of his works throughout The Netherlands, see **On the Trail of Vermeer,** p. 95.

HALS

Frans Hals (1580-1666) was one of the artists most greatly influenced by the religious turmoil in The Netherlands. To escape religious persecution, he fled the southern Netherlands to Haarlem—it was there that Hals carved out a niche by conveying the upheaval of the time.

Hals favored group portraits and used a painting technique characterized by coarser, "unrefined" brush strokes. In his *Pieter van den Broecke*, we see how he captured his subject in what appears to be an instantaneous moment, lending a sense of familiarity and spontaneity that uniquely brings his subjects to life. His *The Merry Drinker* (1630) appears in the Rijksmuseum and serves as a prime example of his expressive painting. Hals's work was also co-opted by politicians: the robust subjects in *The Banquet of the Officers of the St. George Militia Company* (at the **Hals Museum** in Haarlem, see p. 214) were hailed as model citizens for the new Dutch Republic founded before his birth.

POST-IMPRESSIONISM & VAN GOGH

Working a few centuries later, **Vincent Van Gogh** (1853-1890), born in Zundert, is widely considered the finest Dutch painter after Rembrandt. His early work, as exemplified by *The Potato Eaters* (1885), was darker and more concerned with social commentary; upon moving to Paris in 1886, van Gogh's style changed markedly. There, his **post-Impressionist** work was characterized by his expressive use of bright, often harshly contrasting colors painted with rapid, thick brush strokes, as witnessed in his *Self-Portrait* and *Starry Night* (both from 1889).

Van Gogh settled in Arles, France in the last years of his life; he captured the dry, sunny landscape and the bright colored interiors of Provençal homes in works such as *The Harvest* (1888) and *The Bedroom at Arles* (1888). The mental illness that led him to cut off part of his own left ear is perhaps one of the most famous

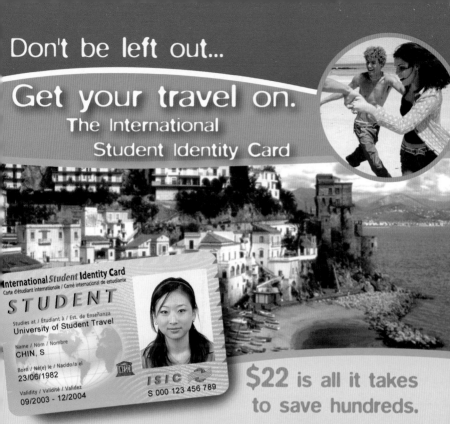

enough already...
Get a room.

Book your next hotel with the people who know what you want.

examples of his psychosis; his derangement ultimately resulted in his suicide in 1890. Van Gogh only sold one painting during his lifetime, but his works became highly prized soon thereafter. His *Sunflowers* sold for US$39.5 million in 1987. For the most extensive collection of his works, visit the **Van Gogh Museum** (see p. 91).

PRIMARY COLORS: MONDRIAN'S WORLD

Twentieth-century Dutch painting was dominated by the primary colors and rigid geometry of **Piet Mondrian's** works. Though early paintings involved largely abstract nature scenes, by the end of his career, Mondrian's style had evolved into one in which forms were reduced to horizontal and vertical elements, exemplified, for example, in *Composition in Red, Black, Blue, Yellow and Grey* (1920). Though his works seem simplistic, x-rays have recently revealed that Mondrian labored over the texture of his whites and the shades of his colors. Mondrian's work and his search for purity of artistic essence was representative of the *De Stijl* ("the style") movement, which not only encompassed painting but also the worlds of sculpture, architecture, and design.

Antique Painted Shutters

MODERN ART

What Mondrian contributed in terms of simplicity was countered by **M.C. Escher's** zany and illusory drawings. Escher drew circular staircases and waterfalls without end and created tessellations that gradually morphed from polygons into living creatures. Art in the post-World War II era was marked by the group of writers and artists who called themselves **CoBrA,** after their native towns of Copenhagen, Brussels, and Amsterdam. CoBrA member **Karel Appel** painted in a bright, simplistic style similar to that of Joan Miró or Paul Klee. For the CoBrA Museum in Amsterdam, see p. 100

de Gooyer Windmill

ARCHITECTURE

Amsterdam is an architectural marvel. The complexities of building a city on top of marshland have resulted in a testament to innovative architectural planning and execution. For example, canal houses were built with many large windows to help reduce the weight of the building on top of unstable topsoil. Tall, narrow houses were constructed on an angle to allow large pieces of furniture to be hoisted through windows without hitting the buildings. The **hooks**

Grotekerk Organ

the local story

gay amsterdam

*Australian-born **Richard Keldoulis** moved to Amsterdam 10 years ago and currently helps to run Pink Point (see p. 67).*

Q: How do you like the city?
A: It's a great city, very small, very international, it's very liberal of course; being gay is really easy here. It's got all the advantages of a small city and none of the disadvantages; it's not provincial.

Q: Do you think, in general, that the people of Amsterdam are as accepting as the laws? Are people's beliefs a reflection of the legislation?
A: It's probably the best city in the world as far as tolerance is concerned, but it's not perfect. The center of the city is pretty good, but as you go a bit out in the suburbs, and outside of Amsterdam and the big cities, it's less good. Homosexuality is pretty much accepted in a lot of areas. In Australia, you have no idea who's gay or not; here, it's standard that everyone is out.

Q: What are your thoughts on Pim Fortuyn [a gay, extremely conservative politician]?
A: Personally, I hated his politics, and everything he stood for. *[Laughs.]* But he did some good things, and he was gay. He was loved by people who would normally

continued next page

that served as pulleys still stick out from just about every canal house; some are still used. By the middle of the 16th century, a law was passed to limit the angle which a house could be built to prevent buildings from falling into the streets.

The canal houses that remain today feature architectural elements dating from many different eras. Medieval houses were constructed with timber and clay, but as locals realized their structures' flammability, brick construction became more prevalent. The only remaining elements of medieval construction are the timber facades of **Begijnhof 34** and **Zeedijk 1.** The Herengracht has wider houses in the area called the **Golden Curve**—city officials bent the rules and let wealthy merchants build wider houses to support the construction of the canal.

Like other European artists of the period, Dutch architects drew their inspiration from the Italians during the **Renaissance. Henrick de Keyser** (1565-1621) left the greatest Renaissance mark on the city, designing the **Zuiderkerk,** the **Westerkerk** (see p. 63), the **Noorderkerk,** and the **Bartolotti House,** (now the **Theater Instituut Nederland;** see p. 86). His work was characterized by rich ornamentation of building facades. In reaction to the decadence of the Renaissance came **neo-Classicism** in the **Golden Age.** Neo-Classical Dutch houses resemble Greek and Roman temples, with columns and decorative scrolls. The movement's austerity was exemplified by the designs of **Adriaan Dortsman** (1625-82), who constructed the **Museum van Loon** on Keizersgracht (see p. 89). During the 18th century an interest in French design and architecture brought Rococo decorations to houses in the cities.

Every visitor to Amsterdam has seen at least one work by 19th-century architect **Pierre Cuypers** (1827-1921). His **Centraal Station** and **Rijksmuseum** fuse of Gothic and Renaissance styles. **Hendrik Petrus Berlage** (1856-1934) was known as the father of modern Dutch architecture—his vision of spartan and utilitarian design frowned upon frivolous ornamentation. For Berlage and his **Amsterdam School,** decoration functioned to support a building and not merely cover up its supports, as was the function of Rococo ornaments. In something of a creative dissent, followers of Berlage's legacy still preferred some excesses in their individual works. One of the most spectacular works created by **Amsterdam School** members **Piet Kramer** (1881-1961), **Johan van der May** (1878-1949), and **Michel de Klerk** (1884-1923) is the **Scheepvaarthuis** (Shipping House), in which shipping companies could conduct their business. The building's design incorporates the street to resemble a ship's bow.

FILM

The film industry in The Netherlands unfortunately suffers from both underfunding and an international Dutch-speaking audience. Despite these constraints, a number of gifted directors have left their marks on the world of cinematography. Prominent Dutch directors include lesbian filmmaker **Marleen Gorris** (1948-), whose *Antonia's Line* (1995) won an Oscar for Best Foreign Film. **Johan van der Keuken** (1938-2001), known as JVDK to his fans, studied as a photographer and filmmaker in Paris before beginning a long career producing short films devoted to the perception of reality. **Joris Ivens** (1898-1989) was both a masterful documentary director and an innovative cinematographer. One of Ivens's most notable works, *Rain*, a 15-min. film capturing rainfall in Amsterdam, took four months to produce.

The city of Rotterdam (see p. 244) is the center of the Dutch film industry, edging out the capital city due to its greater accessibility and rivaling aesthetics. International directors also flock to film in Rotterdam; of most recent interest is *Who Am I* (1998), starring action film star **Jackie Chan.** The Netherlands is home to several prominent film festivals, including the International Film Festival Rotterdam (every January), The Netherlands Film Festival (Utrecht, every September), the Holland Animation Film Festival (Utrecht, November 2004), the International Documentary Film Festival Amsterdam (every November), and CINEKID—the International Children Film, and TV Festival Amsterdam (every October).

THEATER

Since the Dutch film industry has been at times threadbare, Dutch actors have turned their efforts toward theater. Dutch theater has consequently seen rich talent throughout the years; a history of outdoor performances greatly benefitted the genre's popularity. Since the 1960s, avant-garde and experimental theater has flourished in Amsterdam. Today, with over 14,000 theater performances annually in Amsterdam, live drama continues to boom. The scene is characterized by the prominence of many small companies. The **Theater Instituut Nederlands** (p. 86) chronicles the history of Dutch actors and the stage. The **Hollandsche Schouwberg,** on the edge of the Jewish quarter in Amsterdam, was a popular venue for Dutch plays and operettas before World War II (see p. 70).

continued from previous page

be beating gays up. On the other hand, he also brought out a lot of intolerance [against immigrants].

Q: Do you feel that tourists here are accepting and tolerant of homosexuality?
A: Well, I notice from the kiosk, we get a lot of people walking by and laughing. [But] I always think that tourists are quite open-minded; they're on holiday, they're relaxing, they expect something like this in Amsterdam, so it kind of fits into their picture of how the city is. Even people that you'd imagine would be quite anti-gay, they're usually fine; you know, stumbling into a gay kiosk...it's very funny sometimes, people that don't realize it's gay, and suddenly they realize it's gay, grab the kids and run. *[Laughs.]*

Q: Do you think it's unfair that marijuana, prostitution, and gay marriage are all lumped together when foreigners discuss Amsterdam, even though gay marriage is really a civil rights issue?
A: Yeah, maybe, but it is funny that Holland is so bleeding on all those issues, but we've got a new government coming in, so it's going to be very conservative here. Whether things will change and turn back, gay marriage won't be, but things like marijuana laws might be. It's been really liberal; Amsterdam has got its own mentality, it's sort of different from the rest of Holland, it's always been very separate and had its own thing.

LITERATURE

In terms of international recognition, Dutch literature faced the same problem as Dutch film or theater: the language barrier. The most important Dutch moralist was **Erasmus**, whose humanist philosophy influenced Luther. In theater, *Gijsbrecht van Aemstel* (1637) and *Lucifer* (1654), by Amsterdam native **Joost van den Vondel,** figure among the most prominent of the Dutch Renaissance. Perhaps the most brilliant representative of Golden Age literature was **Pieter Corneliszoon Hooft** (1581-1647), whose name now graces Amsterdam's highest-rent shopping street, near the Museumplein. Hooft, a poet and playwright, went to Italy and was strongly influenced by the Renaissance there, bringing the style back to his hometown of Amsterdam.

The **Multatuli Museum** in Amsterdam (see p. 87) celebrates the life and works of **Eduard Douwes Dekker** (1820-1887), who took **Multatuli** (Latin for "I have suffered greatly") for a pen-name. Multatuli used his experience in the Dutch East Indies as fodder for all of his novels. *Max Havelaar*, his most famous work, is the story of an official's attempts to expose the exploitation of natives in the Indonesian Dutch colonies. The book was a criticism of Dutch imperialism and of the static, self-satisfied Dutch attitudes in The Netherlands. Needless to say, Multatuli's attempts to defend the victims of the Dutch East Indies was not appreciated by colonial authorities.

Twentieth-century Dutch literature is extraordinarily diverse. The atrocity of World War II prompted a surge of literary works, both reflective and accusatory. Of these the most famous is the diary kept by **Anne Frank** as she and her family hid in Amsterdam (see p. 85). Her diary is in select company as one of the few Dutch works to be widely translated into other languages.

In a completely different vein, one of the best-selling works of Dutch 20th-century writing is *The Happy Hooker* (1971) by **Xaviera Hollander** (1942-). The book chronicles her experiences as a call girl in the United States. Hollander has continued to popularize Dutch writing by penning articles for *Penthouse* magazine. Mainstream modern authors include **Harry Mulisch** (1927-), who wrote *The Assault* (*De Aanslag;* 1982), a story about life in The Netherlands during and shortly after World War II. The story's movie adaptation won an Academy Award for Best Foreign Film in 1987, the crowning achievement in Mulisch's already spectacular international reputation. One of Mulisch's more recent works is *Discovery of Heaven* (1992), a reflective theological and philosophical narrative.

MUSIC

The Netherlands has not produced composers rivaling the stature of its neighbors but instead has made great contributions in classical music performance. The world-class **Concertgebouw Orchestra,** housed in the Concertgebouw performance hall in Amsterdam (see p. 164) is known for a daring program of classical and contemporary works, led by the illustrious chief conductor Riccardo Chailly. The Netherlands Opera performs at the **Stadhuis-Het Muziektheater,** called the "Stopera," (see p. 73); star performers include Charlotte Margiono, Jard van Nes, and Jan-Ate Stobbe.

Amsterdam's popular music scene is vibrant and cosmopolitan. Dutch colonial past lives on in a genre called **paramaribop,** which fuses Surinamese rhythms and jazz—paramaribop and Latin music appear at venues all over the city. Amsterdam also throbs all night every night thanks to the myriad of dance clubs and rave parties. Perhaps the biggest contribution to club music from the Dutch is the genre **gabber,** like synth-techno, but the number of beats per minute is unbelievably high. Dutch pop, or **Neder Pop,** has always been less popular than British and American exports.

DANCE

Classical ballet and contemporary dance is spearheaded in The Netherlands by the **Dutch National Ballet** and the **Nederlands Dans Theater.** The Dutch National Ballet performs in the Stadhuis-Het Muziektheater (see p. 73), and the Nederlands Dans Theater uses venues throughout Amsterdam. Even the streets sometime become stages for dance performances, especially in June during the International Theatre School Festival, when performances are held on Amsterdam's oldest street, the Nes.

SPORTS

FOOTBALL

Football (soccer) is the Dutch national sport, and on the world stage, The Netherlands has enjoyed a long and (almost) glorious history. The Dutch national team is known as the **Oranje**, arguably one of the better squads never to have won a World Cup. In the 1970s, the Dutch invention of "total football"—a relentlessly attacking style where all players are involved in the offensive and players endlessly change positions—enabled the team to cruise to two World Cup championships but lose both times. The past decade has witnessed mixed fortune for the team: The Netherlands, ousted in the quarter-finals at USA 1994, was knocked out in the semi-finals at France 1998. To the dismay of Dutch football fans, the Oranje failed to qualify for the 2002 World Cup in Korea and Japan, garnering the ignominious moniker the "thirty-third team" (the best nation not to qualify).

Amsterdam's team—and the nation's best—is **Ajax** (the Amsterdamse Football Club Ajax), which plays at the **Amsterdam ArenA** (see p. 75). Top scorers of Ajax include **Piet van Reenen** and **Johan Cruijff**, but top-notch players like the surgical strikers **Edgar Davids** and **Patrick Kluivert**, as well as explosive mid-field general **Clarence Seedorf**, play in foreign leagues. These players, managed by the new Head Coach **Dick Avocaat,** give the nation a good shot at redeeming the team's fortune's at Euro 2004. The Euro 2004 tournament is second in prestige only to the World Cup. If the Oranje qualify—expect cities throughout The Netherlands to shut down on days when football matches are played. Not all the country's residents will be pulling for The Netherlands, as its large Turkish population will be fervently following their own squad, so expect television sets in all Dutch bars to blare non-stop football news. After all, Brazil's championship over Germany in the final was cheered by day-long celebrations in Leidseplein and Dam Square by the city's Brazilian community.

OTHER SPORTS

When the canals freeze, Amsterdam becomes a **skating** rink; but since most residents own their own skates, rentals may be hard to find. Canal boats chug through the ice, though, and often only the Keizersgracht is left untouched for skaters. Those in good shape can skate to nearby towns. Every January, when the weather is cold enough, the Elfstedentocht race covers 11 towns and 200km of frozen canals and rivers. The Netherlands also has a semi-professional **cricket** team that played in World Cup 2003 in South Africa.

A Dutch creation, **korfball** is a bizarre amalgam of basketball (without backboards) and netball. Invented in 1901 by Amsterdam schoolteacher **Nico Broekhuysen,** korfball was played on an international level in the 1970s. The **Federation Internationale de Korfball** has members from over 30 countries, from Armenia to the US. For an underwhelming virtual version of the game, visit www.korfballsa.asn.au/virtual.html.

Sights

OUDE ZIJD

see map p. 344

The name **Oude Zijd** (Old Side) is deceiving because the neighborhood is actually newer than the **Nieuwe Zijd** (New Side; see p. 60). If you can see past the neon lights and through the thick haze of smoke that hang over the northern end, you'll be able to dig up a bit of the past—most of the compelling and historically significant buildings in the south have remained in tact, though many have been claimed by the University of Amsterdam. While closed to the public, the canal houses in particular boast pleasantly picturesque facades. The **Oudemanhuispoort** (Old Man's Gateway) refers to a covered pedestrian walkway that runs between Kloveniersburgwal and Oudezijds Achterburgwal as well as the gate that guards it. The building was once an almshouse for elderly men and women and now houses a used book market (open M-Sa 11am-5pm). There you can find reams of paperbacks—ranging from esoteric philosophy to banal love stories—in a variety of languages (€1-30; most €1). Walled in on three sides by the Voorburgwal, Achterburgwal, and Grimburgwal canals, **Huis aan de Drie Grachten,** the "House on the Three Canals," at Oudezijds Voorburgwal 249, was erected in 1609. The Huis is a geometrical oddity; three of the four sides feature step-gables, arranged so that one gable looks out onto each canal. A dusty, antique bookshop now occupies the premises. (open M, W, F 1-5pm). With a pretty, secluded courtyard protected by an elaborate, ornamental gate, **Sint Agnietenkapel,** Oudezijds Voorburgwal 231 promises seclusion from the whirlwind of the Oude Zijd. Erected in 1470, the building features a disproportionately angled facade. Now owned by the University of Amsterdam, the great hall of this, formerly-Catholic chapel is the only interior room open—albeit unpredictably—to the public. In 1660 the brothers Louis and Hendrick Trip commissioned the architectural quirk now known as the **Trippenhuis,** Kloveniersburgwal 29. The coal-black facade appears to belong to a single building but really covers two—one for each brother. For comparison, glance over at other side of the canal, where the 2.44m wide **Kleine Trippenhuis,** Kloveniersburgwal 26, still stands. This impossibly narrow building was once home to the brothers' coachman. Further north along the canal, the former headquarters of the Dutch East India company reside at the **Oost Indisch Huis,** Kloveniersburgwal 48, though the building is now only used for University of Amsterdam classes.

If for no other reason, **Nieuwmarkt,** on the border between the Oude Zijd and the Jodenbuurt, is worth a visit simply to take a look at the **Waag,** Amsterdam's largest surviving medieval building. Dating from the 15th century, the Waag came into existence as one of Amsterdam's fortified city gates (at the time it was known as Sint Antoniespoort). As Amsterdam expanded, the gate became obsolete and it was converted into a house for public weights and measures. At the end of the 17th century, the Surgeon's Guild built an amphiteater at the top of the central tower to house public dissections and private anatomy lessons—as famously depicted by **Rembrandt's** *The Anatomy Lesson of Dr. Tulp,* which the Guild commissioned. The Waag has also housed a number of other sites, including the Jewish Historical Museum and the Amsterdam Historical Museum. Today it is home to ⬛ **In de Waag,** an outstanding restaurant and cafe (see p. 105).

FO GUANG SHAN HE HUA TEMPLE

🚩 *Zeedijk 106-118, just north of the Nieuwmarkt.* ☎ *420 23 57. Open M-Sa noon-5pm, Su 10am-5pm. Free services Su 10:30am open to the public. 30min. tours by appointment only.*

While Amsterdam's Chinatown might be small, the city is home to approximately 20,000 Chinese people, most of whom hail from Hong Kong. On February 2, 2000, Amsterdam's first house of Buddhist worship opened to little fanfare. It is the largest traditional Chinese temple on the European continent, the product of the International Buddhist Progress Society's efforts to introduce more Europeans to Buddhist traditions and values. Its gold and red facade is a marvelous sight.

MUSEUM IN THIS AREA
Amsterdams Centrum voor Fotografie (Amsterdam Center for Photography), see Museums, p. 80.

see map p. 344

RED LIGHT DISTRICT

If you have come to witness the spectacle, there's no better time to appreciate the Red Light District than at night. Though prostitutes work all through the day, it's at after dark the area actually takes on a red radiance, sex theaters throw open their doors, and the main streets are so thick with people that you may have to slip out to Damrak for some air. It is a heavily touristed area, though the promise of seediness remains largely unfulfilled because of the unabashed openness of the window prostitutes. If you're looking to dip your toes into the carnality of the Red Light District, there are always **sex shows,** in which actors perform strictly choreographed fantasies on stage for 1hr; the most famous live sex show takes place at **Casa Rosso,** Oudezijds Achterburgwal 106-108 (other Casa owned are down the street at #37 and 54), where €25 will buy you admission to 8 or 9 consecutive acts and complimentary drinks. Beware that shows—here and elsewhere—are often more depressing than titillating, as jaded, weary "artists" go at it. (☎ 627 89 54; www.janot.com. Open daily M-Th 8pm-2am, F-Sa 8pm-3am.) Although few tourists will pass through the area without snapping a smiling photo in front of the Casa's **marble penis fountain** (complete with rotating testicles), the Red Light District offers quite a bit at its fringes as well, where the red glow fades and some of the most historic buildings still stand.

During the day, the Red Light District is comparatively flaccid, though you can get an eyeful any time of day. Tourist families parade down **Oudezijds Achterburgwal,** under the impression that if it must be seen, it's better to take the kids in the daylight hours, before things *really* get bad. Police patrol the area 24 hours a day; they are usually in control of any disturbance within a few minutes. No trip to Amsterdam is complete without a visit to its most notorious district.

Oudemanhuispoort

OUDE KERK

🏛 *Oudekerksplein 23. From Centraal Station, walk down Damrak, take a left at the corner of Oudebrugstg. (just before the Beurs van Berlage), and turn right on Warmoesstr.; at the next left is the church.* ☎ *625 82 84, www.oudekerk.nl. Open M-Sa 11am-5pm, Su 1-5pm. €4, students €3. Additional admission for exhibitions.*

Reopened to the public in 1999, Oude Kerk may come as a welcome shock, located smack in the middle of the otherwise lurid Red Light District. History breathes in this stunning structure with an enormous, yawning interior and magnificent stained glass windows. The earliest parish church built in Amsterdam, it is now a center for cultural activities, hosting photography and modern art exhibitions. At the head of the church is the massive Vater-Müller organ, which was built in 1724 and is still played for public concerts. Saskia, Rembrandt's first wife, and Kiliaen van Rensselaer, a founder of the city of New York, were both buried in tombs here. The 14th-century Gothic church has seen hard times, having been stripped of its artwork and religious artifacts between 1566 and 1578 during the Alteration. Between then and now, the Catholic church has served a number of functions: a home for vagrants, a theater, a market, and a space for fishermen to mend broken sails. Today, though there is still an empty, spare feeling inside the building (ideal for the changing art exhibitions that currently grace the hall), the church is nevertheless one of the most impressive and prominent structures in the city.

Touring the City by Boat

SINT NICOLAASKERK

🏛 *Prins Henrikkade 73. A 2min. walk from Centraal Station; turn left when you exit the Stationplein.* ☎ *624 87 49. Open M 1-4pm, Tu-F 11am-4pm, Sa noon-3pm. Su mass at 10:30am. Free.*

A burst of color emanates from the stained glass windows over the impressive columned altar of the otherwise forbidding and gray Sint Nico-

Smallest House in Amsterdam

laaskerk. Designed by A.C. Bleys and completed in 1887 to honor the patron saint of sailors, it replaced a number of Amsterdam's secret Catholic churches from the era of the Alteration (see p. 57). Designed in the neo-Baroque style, the structure houses stern black marble columns, a domed ceiling, and wooden vaults that create a heavy but grand interior. (Organ festival July-Sept. Sa 8:15pm; contemporary and classical organ concerts occasional Sa 3pm—call ahead.)

MUSEUMS IN THIS AREA

Museum Amstelkring "Ons' Lieve Heer Op Solder" ("Our Lord in the Attic"), see Museums, p. 81.

Cannabis College, see Museums, p. 80.

Hash Marijuana Hemp Museum, see Museums, p. 80.

Amsterdam Sex Museum, see Museums, p. 80.

NIEUWE ZIJD

see map p. 344

Despite being home to several of Amsterdam's important historical landmarks, the Nieuwe Zijd (the New Side) is one of the city's most heinously overpopulated, commercial neighborhoods. Hordes of panting tourists fresh off the train from Centraal Station descend upon the **Damrak** and **Nieuwendijk,** two major pedestrian arteries, in search of the neighborhood's innumerable coffee shops (see p. 131). If you manage to stick to the quieter side streets—as well as the slightly less congested **Spuistraat** and **Nieuwezijds Voorburgwal**—an afternoon in the Nieuwe Zijd can be entertaining. Just keep your hand to your purse and avert your gaze from the sea of H&M shopping bags. The neighborhood's heart and soul is the bustling **Dam Square** flanked on either side by two of the city's more significant monuments, the **Koninklijk Paleis (Royal Palace)** and the **Nieuwe Kerk,** as well as the **Nationaal Monument.** On any given summer day, this expanse of white cobblestone is full of jugglers, pickpockets, babies, shoppers, dogs, acrobats, musicians, and street vendors. In the past, the square has seen executions, protests, markets, and celebrations, as well as the erection and destruction of both the first town hall (now the royal palace) and the public weights and measures house. (Louis Bonaparte, King of The Netherlands until his abdication in 1810, razed the latter on the grounds that it spoiled his view from the palace.) Visiting the area can consume the better part of a day, especially if you take the time to try out perfumes at the **Magna Plaza Shopping Center** (open Su-M 11am-7pm, Tu-Sa 9:30am-9pm), originally constructed in 1899 as a post office, or nurse a *mojito* in the back room of one of the area's swank bars (see p. 148).

BEGIJNHOF

From Dam, take Nieuwezijds Voorburgwal south 5min. to Spui, then turn left and then left again on Gedempte Begijnensloot; the gardens are on the left. Or follow signs to Begijnhof from Spui. No groups, guided tours, bikes, or pets. Begijnhof open daily during summer 8-11am; Sept.-May 9am-5pm. Free. Het Houten Huys, ☎ 623 55 54. Open M-F 8-10am. Engelsekerk, Begijnhof 48. ☎ 624 96 65; www.ercadam.nl. Open for prayer Su 10:30am. Begijnhofkapel, Begijnhof 30 (☎ 622 19 18), open M-F 9am-5pm, Sa 9am-7pm; services Su 10am in Dutch and 11:30am in French. Free.

You don't have to take vows to enter this secluded courtyard, the 14th-century home to the Beguines—a sect of free-thinking and religiously devoted laywomen—but you will have to get up early in the morning: last year the residents elected to cease afternoon access during the summer months. Early risers will be rewarded with access to one of the area's more attractive sights. Begijnhof's peaceful, rose-lined gardens, beautifully manicured lawns, gabled houses and tree-lined walkways afford a much-needed respite from the bustling excesses of the Nieuwe Zijd. The women who currently live in Begijnhof are not required to be Catholic, but when the site was founded in 1346, the women were considerably more sequestered: while they didn't take vows, they devoted themselves to a life of religious contemplation, charity, and manual labor. The oldest house in Amsterdam, **Het Houten Huys (The Wooden House),** is located on the premises, while most of the other homes were rebuilt in the 17th and 18th centuries following major fires in the 1400s. While there, be sure to visit the court's two churches. **Engelsekerk,** the English Presbyterian Church, which holds one of the city's few all-English services. The building is believed to date from 1392, when it served as Begijnhof's Catholic chapel. In 1607, as a result of the Reformation, the Beguines were forced to turn it over to Amsterdam's English-speaking Presbyterians. It was enlarged in 1665 and restored thirty years ago. Across from Engelsekerk is **Begijnhofkapel,** constructed in 1680, once one of Amsterdam's *schuilkerken* (**hidden churches;** see p. 81).

DAM SQUARE & KONINKLIJK PALEIS

🏠 *From Centraal, take tram #5, 13, 17, or 20 to Dam. Koninklijk Palace.* ☎ *620 40 60; www.kon-paleisamsterdam.nl. Square open 24hr. Palace open June-Aug. daily 12:30-5pm; hours variable in winter. €4.50, children and seniors €3.60, children under 6 free.*

Right beside the **Nieuwe Kerk** (see **Museums,** p. 82) on Dam Square is one of Amsterdam's more impressive architectural feats, **Koninklijk Palace,** built as the town hall in 1655. Young Philip Vingboons aimed to replace the entrenched Amsterdam Renaissance style with a more profane Classicist one. (Compare this palace to the Westerkerk, up Raadhuisstraat from the back of Koninklijk, at Prinsengracht.) Koninklijk did not become a palace until the arrival of finicky Louis Napoleon in 1808, who had it renovated and remodeled to better serve as a royal residence. Today Queen Beatrix still uses the building for official receptions, though she makes her home in The Hague. The palace's indisputable highlight is the airy, white-marble Citizen's Hall, intended—by virtue of its celestial floor maps and allegorical sculptures—to be the universe contained in a single room. Across Dam Square is the Dutch **Nationaal Monument,** unveiled on May 4, 1956, to honor Dutch victims of WWII. Inside the 21-meter white stone obelisk is soil from all twelve of Holland's provinces and the Dutch East Indies. Along the back of the monument, you'll find the provinces' crests bordered by the years 1940 and 1945. Today, in addition to this reminder of Dutch suffering during the war, the monument is one of Amsterdam's central meeting and people-watching spots.

from the road

queen of hearts?

Any visitor to Buckingham Palace in London knows that the Queen of England's public appearances, no matter how brief, are always accompanied by media and throngs of people. Imagine my surprise when, traipsing through Dam Square, I witnessed a very subdued royal spectacle. In Dam Square, the crowds are constant, centering around whatever attraction pops up. But one afternoon in June, I came across a gathering of a different sort. A barely noticeable group had formed around the back door of the Koninklijk Paleis, where a few informed citizens were hoping to catch a glimpse of the Queen.

Two guards flanked the exit of the building, while three policemen talked on their handsets. An hour later, once most observers had already dispersed, Queen Beatrix emerged from the building, gave a simple, unadorned wave to her devotees, and was whisked off in souped-up Ford Taurus. The event was over almost before it began. Within a minute of her exit, all that remained behind were a few pigeons and policemen. The Netherlands' Queen had come and gone, little noticed by the milling throng. It would appear that one of Europe's last remaining monarchs attracts less of a crowd than do the jugglers on the other side of the square.

–Stefan Atkinson

Dam Square

Nieuwe Kerk

Begijnhof Gardens

SPUI

🚊 *Tram #4, 9, 14, 16, 20, 24, or 25 to Spui.*

Pronounced "spow," this tree-lined, cobble-stoned square, perfect for quiet lounging on summer afternoons, is home to an art market on Sundays, a book market on Fridays, and is surrounded by bookstores—notably the slick, international **Athenaeum Boekhandel** (see **Bookstores**, p. 175). The Begijnhof (see above) is sometimes accessible through a small door off the northern side of the square. Look out for **Het Lievertje** (The Little Urchin), a small bronze statue by Carel Kneulman that became a symbol for the Provos and was the site of many meetings and riots in the 1960s (see **Life and Times**, p. 44).

MUSEUMS IN THIS AREA

🖼 **Nieuwe Kerk**, see Museums, p. 82.

🖼 **Amsterdams Historisch Museum (Amsterdam Historical Museum)**, see Museums, p. 82.

Beurs van Berlage, see Museums, p. 82.

Allard Pierson Museum, see Museums, p. 84.

Madame Tussaud's Wax Museum, see Museums, p. 84.

SCHEEPVAART BUURT

see map p. 342

Just north of the Jordaan and west of the center, Amsterdam's **Shipping Quarter** functioned as the conduit for the city's thriving maritime commerce during the 18th and 19th centuries. When Amsterdam's shipping industry shifted away from the banks of the Ij in the late 1800s, the area was abandoned. The Shipping Quarter underwent various gritty transformations, and until about ten years ago, the quarter housed little more than an assortment of criminals and junkies. But thanks to urban renewal (and an outpouring of investment from the city's coffers), the Scheepvaartbuurt now boasts some of the city's best restaurants, coffeehouses, and shopping venues: all without the crowds, lines, and tourism that pervades neighborhoods closer to the center.

The Shipping Quarter begins where Niewendijk intersects with the Singel and the district's main drag—the **Haarlemmerstraat**—begins. In the east, the quarter doesn't feel that much different than the city center; it's slightly more residential but packed with restaurants and coffeeshops—this is where entrepreneurs and architects have worked their greatest magic. The district's western half, where Haarlemmerstraat becomes **Haarlemmerdijk** across the Korte Prinsengracht (a crucial and confusing fact for navigating local addresses), is significantly more residential. The area's maritime past has largely been forgotten; the only reminders are bronze ship-related monuments—propellers, anchors, and nautical steering wheels—that dot the street corners. Amid the bustle of Haarlemmerstraat and Haarlemmerdijk, it's easy to forget that the Shipping Quarter is bordered on the south by one of Amsterdam's most beautiful canals, the **Brouwersgracht.** It's an ideal place to relax, only two blocks and yet a world away from the Scheepvaartbuurt's frenetic urban pace.

Few sights appear along the Haarlemmerstraat—though the street, with its unparalleled collection of eateries and coffeeshops, is almost a sight in itself. It's worth stopping at the **West Indisch Huis (West Indies House),** Haarlemmerstraat 75, at Herenmarkt. The white, ornately gabled structure dates back to 1617 and originally functioned as the headquarters of the Dutch West Indies Company back when the Dutch ranked among the world's most enterprising imperialists.

Royal Palace

CANAL RING WEST

see map p. 342

There are some 2200 buildings in the canal ring, 1550 of which have been named national monuments, making the neighborhood a sight in itself. Any visit to the Western Canal Ring must begin at the Westermarkt (Tram #6, 13, or 17, from Centraal), the jumping-off point for all touristic sites. The Anne Frank Huis and the Westerkerk are both mere steps away, while the Bijbels Museum and the Theater Instituut Nederlands can be found in their respective magnificent canal houses after a brief stroll through the neighborhood.

Canals

WESTERKERK

🅰 *Prinsengracht 281. On the corner of Prinsengracht and Westermarkt. ☎ 624 77 66. Trams #13, 17, or 20 to Westermarkt. Open Apr.-Sept. M-F 11am-3pm; July-Aug. M-Sa 11am-3pm. Tours of the tower every hr. €3.*

This stunning Protestant church was designed by Roman Catholic architect Hendrick de Keyser and completed in 1631. It stands as one of the last structures built in the Dutch Renaissance style, which can be distinguished by its use of both brick and stone. The blue and yellow imperial crown of Maximilian of Austria—the Hapsburg ruler of the Holy Roman Empire in the late 15th century—rests atop the 85m tower; the

Magna Plaza

in recent
news

religious tolerance

When Rotterdam-based Islamic leader Khalil El-Moumni called homosexuality a "contagious disease" in May 2002, the Dutch government responded by instituting a mandatory seminar on Dutch culture and values, designed specifically for newly-immigrated religious leaders, according to a BBC world report (November 28, 2002, "Imams on Dutch culture course"). In the words of one respondent, "knowing the basics of the Dutch language isn't enough" for these Islamic leaders, or *imams*, who often serve as influential social and political guides for immigrant communities. Designed for *imams* from countries like Morocco and Turkey, this integration course purports to inform leaders about Dutch regulations regarding soft drug use, prostitution, euthanasia, freedom of speech, and non-discrimination. "We wanted *imams* to be informed as much as possible without confronting their religious beliefs," said Halim El-Madkouri of Utrecht's Multicultural Institute, one of the course organizers. While El-Moumni was cleared of discrimination charges that year, the potential and perceived tensions between "Dutch" and Muslim values are a source of continued legal conflict.

tower has become a patriotic symbol for the citizens of Amsterdam. Rembrandt is believed to be buried here, though the exact spot of his resting place has not yet been located. In contrast to the decorative exterior, the Protestant church remains properly sober and plain inside—it is still used by a Presbyterian congregation. Climb the **Westerkerkstoren** tower in a 45min.-1hr. tour for a great view of the city.

FELIX MERITIS

🚩 *Keizersgracht 324.* ☎ *626 23 21; www.felix.meritis.nl. Open M-F 9am-7pm.*

This imposing structure is more than just a cafe with outdoor seating, though you wouldn't know it just by walking past. The monument housed the Felix Meritis Society of arts and sciences when it was first built in the late 18th century to celebrate Enlightenment ideals—the building once served as a cultural center for the city's intellectual elite. After a stint as the headquarters for the Dutch Communist Party during post-World War II reconstruction, Felix Meritis returned to its original function as an institution for arts and sciences. The center now hosts cultural events, debates, classical and world music concerts, and art exhibits. Meritis even houses a summer university which offers 2-3 day courses taught in English (including intensive Dutch for non-native speakers; see www.amsu.edu), and the arts television channel, Kunstkanaal. The canal-side cafe serves as a forum for impromptu political and intellectual discussions. Usually only the cafe and information center are open to the public, unless events are scheduled.

INSTITUTE FOR WAR DOCUMENTATION

🚩 *Herengracht 380.* ☎ *523 38 00; www.oorlogs-doc.knaw.nl. Open M 1-5pm; Tu-W, F 9am-5pm; Th 9am-9pm. Free.*

The degree of intricacy in its carvings and other ornamental decoration set this stone mansion apart from the other banal canal houses. Nazis occupied the opulent space during World War II, and the building now houses the Nederlands Instituut voor Oorlogsdocumentatie (Dutch Library of War Documentation). In addition to a comprehensive collection of Dutch war resources and photographs, the library has English-, French-, and German-language books concerning World War II and other major international conflicts. The study and library are both open to the public.

MUSEUMS IN THIS AREA

⬛ **Anne Frank Huis,** see Museums, p. 85.

⬛ **Bijbels Museum,** see Museums, p. 86.

Huis Marseille, see Museums, p. 86.

Theater Instituut Nederland, see Museums, p. 86.

Multatuli Museum, see Museums, p. 87.

Netherlands Media Art Institute, Montevideo/ Time-based arts, see Museums, p. 88.

CENTRAL CANAL RING

see map p. 340

Two of Amsterdam's most famous bridges span the Amstel near City Hall in the Central Canal Ring. At Amstelstraat the **Blauwbrug** (Blue Bridge), adorned with very detailed nautical carvings, stretches across the river. Capped with ornate blue-and-gold crowns, it offers one of the city's more spectacular river views. To the right of this bridge is the **Magere Brug** (Skinny Bridge), which sways precariously above the water. The Magere is the oldest of the city's many pedestrian drawbridges and the only one still operated by hand. Its original construction in 1670 replaced an even older, skinnier bridge that was built—according to city lore—for two sisters who lived on opposite sides of the canal from one another and sought a convenient way to pay each other a visit.

The canals that make up the Central Ring weave through underrated troves of tranquil, historic homes and quirky neighborhood hangouts that teem with locals on those rare sunny days. This area of the Central Canal Ring is also home to a small stretch of Herengracht called the **Golden Bend,** so named because of the sparkling affluence of the merchants who built the especially lavish canal houses found in this area. In the 17th century, residents of the city were taxed according to the width of their homes, and houses could not be more than one plot wide. To encourage investment in the Herengracht's construction, the city government allowed its elite to build doubly wide homes in the area. From June 21st to 23rd in 2004, the popular **Amsterdam Canal Garden Foundation** (www.amsterdamsegrachtentuin.nl) opens up about twenty of the private back gardens to the public, and people throughout The Netherlands come to see theses tiny hidden treasures of landscape (€10 for a 3-day pass); the rest of the year you can get a taste of Golden Age canal life at **Museum van Loon.**

Seahorse Bridge

Homomonument

Hofje van Staats

check, checkmate

Of all the peculiar Dutch national icons, perhaps none is more peculiar than **Max Euwe** (1901-1981), the only Dutchman to win the world championship chess title, which he did in 1935. A professor of mathematics, he wrote volumes on chess theory and served as president of the World Chess Federation later in life.

For all his trouble, Euwe can now boast (albeit posthumously) a square that not only bears his name, but pays homage to him and his chosen pastime with an enormous chessboard and two-foot-tall pieces. Visit Max Euweplein, off Weteringschans between Leidseplein and the Paradiso, for the biggest chess game of your life.

If outside play is not your style, try the **Schaak Cafe**, Bloemgracht 20 (☎ 622 1801), a basement chess cafe in the Jordaan with boards on every table and a small but loyal cadre of regulars. There's little in the way of food—beer and coffee are both less than €2—but you'll find any number of would-be Max Euwes up for a game.

CAT'S CABINET

🏠 *Herengracht 497.* ☎ *626 53 78; www.kattenkabinet.nl. Open M-F 10am-2pm, Sa-Su 1-5pm. €4.50, under 12 €2.25.*

Housed in the only public building on the Canal Ring's scenic Golden Bend, the Cat's Cabinet is a temple to all things feline—including statuary, portraiture, pop art, and assorted knick-knacks. The Cat's Cabinet collection was started by a businessman with an unusually strong attachment to his cat, who he named J. P. Morgan (after the famous multimillionaire American industrialist); check out his feline face gracing the doctored dollar bill in the museum. After 18 years of eating, sleeping, and showering with his cat, the businessman opened the bottom two floors of his beautiful canal-side mansion when J. P. died in 1990. Feline lovers will purr in appreciation at the collection, but it might cause others to take a catnap.

MUSEUMS IN THIS AREA
🖼 **De Appel**, see Museums, p. 88.
🖼 **Foam Photography Museum**, see Museums, p. 88.
Museum Willet-Holthuysen, see Museums, p. 88.
Museum van Loon, see Museums, p. 89.
Nationaal Brilmuseum [National Spectacles Museum], see Museums, p. 89.
Torture Museum, see Museums, p. 89.

LEIDSEPLEIN

see map p. 341

Leidseplein proper is a crush of street musicians, blaring neon lights, and fragrant open-air urinals. Daytime finds the square packed with countless shoppers, smokers, and drinkers lining the busy sidewalks around the square. When night falls, tourists—and those who want to meet them—emerge in packs of skin-tight jeans and greased-down hair. A slight respite from the hordes is available just east of Leidseplein along Weteringschans, at **Max Euweplein.** Named for the famous Dutch chess master, the square sports an enormous chess board with people-sized pieces (see **Check, Checkmate**, at left). One of Amsterdam's more bizarre public spaces, it is notable both for the tiny park across the street (where tons of **bronze iguanas** provide amusement) and the motto inscribed above its pillars: *Homo sapiens non urinat in ventum* ("A wise man does not piss into the wind").

JORDAAN

The Jordaan's restored gabled homes and flower-filled terraces, its mellow canals and tiny galleries—these are among the most memorable sights in this upscale neighborhood once reserved for the city's impoverished citizens. The whole area is suffused with gentrified calm, but *hofjes* in the Jordaan are particularly ideal for finding a moment of silence. Before the Alteration

see maps p. 342

(see p. 40), these almshouses were subsidized by the Catholic church to serve as housing for the poor and the elderly. For some tranquil time, step behind the nondescript green door that separates **Sint-Andrieshof**, Egelantiersgracht 107-145, (open 9am-6pm; free) from the street and take a slow stroll around the gentle garden, beneath austere sloping roofs. Be quiet, though—the courtyard has the hushed solemnity of a church, which probably has less to do with its holy history and than the private residences that now enclose it.

HOMOMONUMENT & PINK POINT

🔃 *In front of Westerkerk. Take tram #13 or 17 to Westermarkt. Homomonument is the 3 pink granite triangles. Pink Point: ☎ 428 10 70; www.pinkpoint.org. Open Apr.-Sept. daily noon-6pm. Starting in 2004, Pink Point may start winter hours; check website for updates.*

Since 1987 the Homomonument has stood in the center of Amsterdam as a testament to the strength and resilience of the homosexual community. Conceived by Karin Daan, its pink granite triangles allude to the signs homosexuals were required to wear in Nazi concentration camps. Her design was chosen out of numerous competitors partly for its underlying theory that the structure would become a part of its surroundings. The three triangles integrate with the bend in the canal's quay wall, and in the space between them, daily activity continues.

The raised triangle points to the **COC** (Dutch Association for the Integration of Homosexuality; see p. 43), one of the oldest gay rights organizations in the world. The ground level triangle points to the **Anne Frank Huis** (see p. 85) and reads *Naar Vriendschap Zulk Een Mateloos Verlangen*, a line from a poem by Jacob Israel de Haan that translates, "such an endless desire for friendship." The triangle with steps into the canal points to the National War Memorial on the Dam, as a reminder that homosexuals were among those sent to concentration camps. In sum, Homomonument serves as a tripartite memorial to men and women persecuted for their homosexuality in the past, a confrontation with continuing discrimination in the present, and an inspiration for the future. On Liberation Day (May 5) and Queen's Day (April 30), massive celebrations surround the monument.

If the Homomonument serves as a valuable testimony to the ongoing civil rights struggle of homosexuals worldwide, then its neighbor, Pink Point, stands as a reminder of everything vibrant and fun about gay life in Amsterdam. Since 1998 the Pink Point kiosk has served as a clearinghouse for information on homosexual happenings in the city and beyond. Pick up free listings of BGL bars, clubs, restaurants, and cultural life. The kiosk also sells a great selection of souvenirs, postcards, and knick-knacks. From June to September, Fantasy City's walking tour on the history of the city's gay life departs here every Saturday at 1pm. (☎ 672 3993; www.fantasycity.org. €18.) Start here if you're attending the **Gay Pride** festival in the first weekend of August. The party lasts all weekend, culminating in a Sunday celebration at the Stadhuis-Muziektheater.

MUSEUMS IN THIS AREA

Electric Ladyland: The First Museum of Fluorescent Art, see Museums, p. 90.

Woonboot (Houseboat) Museum, see Museums, p. 90.

Stedelijk Museum Bureau Amsterdam, see Museums, p. 90.

Pianola Museum, see Museums, p. 90.

WESTERPARK

see map p. 346

🚹 *Take tram #3 to Haarlemmerplein.*

The Westerpark neighborhood is mostly residential, but its park is worth a visit. The gates—tall wavy blue monstrosities—open onto a wide expanse of green like no other in the city. Banks of thick grass slope into the Haarlemmervaart, which looks more like a river than a canal, and any number of winding dirt paths invite visitors to wander down them. In the center of it all is a large pond, filled with ducks and fish, and the park's sole curiosity: a white, revolving, headless statue. Benches line the pond, and a large playground attracts parents with their children. It's an excellent place to while away an afternoon.

MUSEUMPLEIN & VONDELPARK

VONDELPARK

see map p. 347

🚹 *In the southwestern corner of the city, outside the Singelgracht. Take tram #1, 2, 3, 5, 6, 12, or 20; just a short walk across the canal and to the left from the Leidseplein. www.vondelpark.org.*

With meandering walkways, green meadows, several ponds, and a 1.5km paved path for bikers and skaters, this English-style park, the largest within the city center, is a lovely meeting place for children, skaters, seniors, stoners, soccer players and side-walk acrobats. Named after Holland's Shakespeare, Joost van den Vondel (1587-1679), Vondelpark has, in addition to a few good outdoor cafes (see p. 68), an open-air theater: the **Openluchttheater** (☎673 14 99; www.openluchttheater.nl) where visitors can enjoy free music and dance concerts Wednesday through Sunday during the summer. Every Friday you can meet up with about 350-600 roller- and in-line skaters at 8pm by the **Filmmuseum,** Vondelpark 3 (see p. 96) for a group skate through Amsterdam. If you can't wait until the weekend, head to the east entrance—you'll find rows of skaters zigzagging through lines of cones. For the more pacific at heart, try wandering around the hexagonally-shaped, beautifully maintained rose gardens. There's also a special children's play area toward the center of the grounds.

MUSEUMS IN THIS AREA

▧ **Van Gogh Museum,** see Museums, p. 91.

▧ **Stedelijk Museum for Modern and Contemporary Art,** see Museums, p. 93.

▧ **Rijksmuseum Amsterdam,** see Museums, p. 94.

Filmmuseum, see Museums, p. 96.

DE PIJP

see map p. 348

De Pijp (pronounced "pipe") is a work in progress, a gentrification project occurring in a neighborhood once known for its immigrant authenticity. This is no Jordaan bourgeoisie quite yet—some streets in De Pijp remain humble with rows of discount shops and low-priced ethnic food joints. But De Pijp is ballooning in hype, as new high-design restaurants and chic bars get written up in socialite magazines and attract slim fashionistas with the promise of the next big thing.

The neighborhood was named after its narrow hallways of crowded row houses that supposedly create the appearance of being in a pipe. Right next to the Museumplein but far from its tourist hordes, the district retains a multicultural grittiness. Originally planned in the late 19th century as a bourgeois suburb, De Pijp later attracted a mix of immigrants from Surinam, Indonesia, Turkey, Kurdistan, and Morocco. Today's residents still hail from around the globe but have been joined by an influx of youthful, would-be bohemians.

Most of De Pijp is best experienced by wandering around its skinny streets and popping into its cheap, low-end restaurants and shops. The best place to start is amid the crowded, bustling din of the **Albert Cuypmarkt,** a vibrant market and home to some of the best budget-eatery deals in the city (see **Markets,** p. 179)—the market is along Albert Cuypstraat between **Ferdinand Bolstraat** (the district's largest thoroughfare) and Van Woustraat. A short stroll will take you to the lovely, diminutive **Sarphatipark,** named for the Doctor Samuel Sarphati, a philanthropist who instituted a series of public works programs in the 19th century. Smack in the center of De Pijp, the Sarphatipark is a pleasant stretch of green criss-crossed by a series of paths and a sinuous pond. Along the Amstel River lies the strikingly elaborate building of the **Gemeentearchief,** Amsteldijk 67, which houses the city's municipal records and shows exhibitions. (☎572 02 02; Free.) The park and areas to the south are safe enough by day but should be approached with caution after dark.

Heineken Brewing Tanks

HEINEKEN EXPERIENCE

🛈 *Take tram #16, 24, or 25 to Heinekenplein.* ☎523 96 66; www.heinekenexperince.com. Open Su, Tu-Sa 10am-6pm; last entry at 5pm. Under 18 must be accompanied by a parent. €7.50, includes 3 free beers or soft drinks and a souvenir Heineken glass.

Busloads of tourists pour in daily to discover that beer is not made in the Heineken Brewery. Plenty is served, however. The factory stopped producing here in 1988 and has turned the place into a corporate altar, an amusement park devoted to their green-bottled beer. In the "Experience," visitors guide themselves past holograms, virtual reality machines, and other multimedia treats that inform you more than you ever needed to know about the Heineken corporation and beer production. There's even a kiosk where you can email a picture of yourself on a Heineken bottle cap to envious friends. Some of the attractions can get wonderfully absurd (e.g., the "Bottle Ride," designed to replicate the experience of becoming a Heineken beer), but after a few drinks you'll go with it and have fun. A visit includes three beers and a souvenir glass, all of which is in itself well worth the price of admission. To avoid the crowds, come before noon.

Schreierstoren

Scheepvaarthuis Doorway

JODENBUURT & PLANTAGE

see map p. 349

The Jodenbuurt and Plantage neighborhoods, with their extensive green spaces and varied, excellent assortments of museums, differ greatly from the city center. The Jodenbuurt, or Jewish Quarter, was home to nearly all of the city's Jews until World War II when Nazi forces deported 70,000 Jews to concentration camps. Until that time, the area known as **Mr Visserplein,** home to the **Portugees-Israelietische Synagoge** (Portuguese Synagogue), and **Waterlooplein** were the de facto centers of the vibrant Judaic community's cultural life, though the quarter was not only home to Jewish inhabitants. Rembrandt lived at Jodenbreestraat 4, and his Ashkenazi neighbors were frequent subjects for his paintings. The Quarter's lively and subsequently solemn past is commemorated by a host of monuments and remembrances. Postwar developers unfortunately all but neglected the Jodenbuurt. The streets in this area are a tangled jumble of graffiti and abandoned traffic lights—its bleak gray surfaces a drab contrast to the greenery of Plantage further west.

The Plantage, by contrast is positively lush with verdant spaces. The land originally provided wealthy 17th-century canal ring residents with plots for gardens and parks so they could escape from the city—hence the name "Plantation." One of the most prominent horticultural spaces, **Hortus Botanicus,** was founded here in 1638 as a medicinal garden. As metropolitan limits pushed outwards in the 1850s, the region became one of the city's first suburban developments. Members of the burgeoning merchant class lived in elegant villas that lined wide, tree-lined streets. Today the Plantage is home to **Artis Zoo** and its own fine assemblage of museums.

PORTUGEES-ISRAELIETISCHE SYNAGOGE (PORTUGUESE SYNAGOGUE)

Mr. Visserplein 1-3. Take tram #9 or 14, to Waterlooplein. ☎ *624 53 51; www.esnoga.com. Open Apr.-Oct. Su-F 10am-4pm; Nov.-Mar. Su-Th 10am-4pm., F 10am-3pm. €5, under 15 €4.*

This centuries-old, beautifully maintained Portuguese synagogue still holds services. The building dates to 1675, and has remained largely unchanged despite the destructive force of the Nazi occupation during World War II. Descendants of Jews expelled during the Spanish Inquisition in 1492 began seeking refuge in relatively tolerant Amsterdam in the 17th century; since the Dutch Republic was then at war with Spain, the refugees opted to call themselves "Portuguese Jews." One of the few tangible remnants of Amsterdam's once-thriving Jewish community, the synagogue features a plain but beautiful *chuppah* (a Jewish wedding canopy) crafted from Brazilian jacaranda wood. Foundation vaults and wooden piles that support the synagogue can be viewed by boat from the water beneath the synagogue. A video presentation called *Esnoga*, the Portuguese name for the synagogue, gives background on Amsterdam's Jewish community as an introduction to your visit.

Just after you leave, take a look at **The Dockworker.** Unveiled in 1952, this bronze statue just behind the Synagogue memorializes the strike held by the Amsterdam dockworkers in February 1941. The men were among the first groups in Amsterdam to respond to the German occupation, specifically to the arrest of over 400 Jewish men at the order of the German chief of police.

HOLLANDSCHE SCHOUWBURG

Plantage Middenlaan 24. Take tram #9 or 14 to Waterlooplein. Walk through Mr. Visserplein and southeast on Muiderstraat, which becomes Plantage Middenlaan. ☎ *626 99 45; www.jhm.nl. Open daily 11am-4pm; closed on Yom Kippur. Free.*

This monument, museum, and historic building stands today as one of the region's most enduring symbols of freedom, a moving testament to Dutch life before, during, and after Hitler. Now housing a memorial "In Memory of Those Who Were Taken

Away, 1940-1945," Hollandsche Schouwburg began its life at the end of the 19th century as a Dutch theater on the edge of the old Jewish quarter. The Schouwburg underwent a terrible metamorphosis in 1941, when the Nazi occupiers converted it into the Joodsche Schouwburg, the city's sole establishment to which Jewish performers and Jewish patrons were granted access. Not long after, the building was changed into an assembly point for Dutch Jews who were to be deported to **Westerbork**, the transit camp to the north (see p. 269). The majority of those passing through met their end in Auschwitz, Bergen-Belsen, or Sobibor. Its modern incarnation is a monument to the 104,000 Dutch Jews who were deported and exterminated during World War II. When you walk into the memorial room, 6700 surnames are engraved and illuminated behind an eternally-lit flame. A stone monument occupies the space where the theater's stage used to be, and poplar trees grow in the one-time courtyard. Upstairs is an exhibition that details the gradual isolation and ultimate death of the majority of Dutch Jews who first entered the theater as prisoners.

Portugees-Israelietische Synagoge

ARTIS ZOO

🚏 *Plantage Kerklaan 38-40. Take tram #9 or 14 to Waterlooplein. Walk southeast through Mr. Visserplein and down Muiderstraat, which becomes Plantage Middenlaan at Nieuwe Herengracht. Turn left on Plantage Kerklaan. ☎ 523 34 00; www.artis.nl. Open daily 9am-5pm; 9am-6pm during daylight savings time. €14, ages 4-11 €10.50, seniors €12.50.*

Reverent Angel

Artis is the oldest zoo in Europe, as well a zoological museum, a museum of geology, an aquarium, and a planetarium. A day of good weather is enough to make the Artis complex worth a visit, especially for children sick of historical landmarks and their weary parents, as well as for nature-buffs looking for an escape from the urban rush. During World War II, up to 300 Jews were hidden in the zoo's empty cages.

HORTUS BOTANICUS

🚏 *Plantage Middenlaan 2A. Take tram #7, 9, or 14 to Waterlooplein/Plantage Parklaan and follow the "Hortus Botanicus" signs. ☎ 638 16 70; www.dehortus.nl. Open Apr.-Oct. M-F 9am-5pm, Sa-Su 11am-5pm; Dec.-Mar. M-F 9am-4pm, Sa-Su 11am-4pm. Guided tours Su 2pm €1. €6, children and seniors €3.*

With over 6000 species of plants, Hortus, founded in 1638, is one of the oldest gardens of its kind in the world and a modern refuge for a number of plants headed toward extinction. It was originally established as "Hortus Medicus,"

Hortus Botanicus

life's green

bean there, done that

While The Netherlands are universally celebrated for their ability to cultivate the world's finest tulips, the country's horticultural flair extends beyond these highly attractive flowers. When Amsterdam's **Hortus Botanicus** was founded in 1638, it nursed primarily medicinal plants used regularly by Dutch apothecaries to concoct natural cures for taxing diseases. With the emergence of the Dutch East India Company in the 16th and 17th centuries, however, botanical gardens throughout The Netherlands came to serve wholly new purposes. Merchants with the shipping company would often smuggle goods to their homeland, bringing back exotic plants and seeds among the many souvenirs. Many of these were brought to the Hortus Botanicus for cultivation and still thrive as healthy specimens. Perhaps the most interesting of these foreign returns is the garden's still-thriving coffee plant.

Transported to Hortus Botanicus in 1706 by an East India Company merchant who had returned from Ethiopia, it can proudly claim to be the first coffee plant grown in European soil. Impressively, it was also the forebear of many of the now ubiquitous coffee plantation in Brazil. No small feat for a rather tiny plant.

a medicinal garden for the town's physicians. Many of its more exceptional specimens, including a coffee plant smuggled out of Ethiopia, whose clippings spawned the Brazilian coffee empire (see **Bean There, Done That,** at left), were gathered during the 17th and 18th centuries by members of the Dutch East India Company. Visitors can wander through a number of simulated ecosystems, a rock garden, a rosarium, an herb garden, three multi-climate greenhouses, and a butterfly room. Don't miss Hortus's *Welwitschia mirabilis*, a rare desert plant from Namibia with a maximum 2000 year life span but sprouts a grand total of two leaves during that time. In late summer, check out the giant water lily, *Victoria amazonica*, planted anew every year. Rest among the branches at the greenhouse cafe, with outdoor seating when weather permits. (Sandwiches and snacks €1-6. Open M-F 10am-5pm, Sa-Su 11am-5pm.)

ZUIDERKERK

🚹 *Zuiderkerkhof. From Nieuwmarkt, head southwest on Kloveniersburgwal and turn left at Zandstraat; the church will be on your left. zuiderkerk@dro.amsterdam.nl. Guided tower tours June-Sept. W-Sa 2, 3, and 4pm. Children under 9 need adult supervision. €3.*

South of the Nieuwmarkt, Zuiderkerk—especially its elegant spire—is the Jodenbuurt's most visible landmark. Constructed between 1603 and 1614 under the supervision of architect Hendrick de Keyser, it was the first Calvinist church to be built after the Reformation. During and after Holland's Hard Winter of 1944-45, in which temperatures and foodstuffs reached record lows, the building was a makeshift morgue. Its tower is open in summer and boasts some of the best views of the city. Zuiderkerk houses the **Municipal Information Center for Physical Planning and Housing** and features exhibits on the history and planning of Amsterdam's neighborhoods. (☎552 79 87. Open M 11am-4pm, Tu-W, F 9am-4pm, Th 9am-10pm. Free.)

ARCAM (ARCHITECTURE CENTER AMSTERDAM)

🚹 *Oosterdok 14. Take tram #9, 14, to Waterlooplein. ☎620 48 78; www.arcam.nl. Open Tu-Sa 1-5pm; closed on bank holidays. Wheelchair-accessible. Free.*

Staffed by professionals with training in design, ARCAM is a fantastic resource for finding out all you could possibly want to know about Amsterdam's vibrant architecture scene. While the center is not really a museum, it hosts a number of changing exhibitions that provide guests and residents of the city with some insight into what's behind (and inside) Amsterdam's newest and oldest structures. ARCAM also sells a detailed architectural map of the city (€5).

BROUWERIJ 'T IJ

🚋 *Funenkade 7. Take bus #22 out to the Zeeburgerstraat stop. Walk behind the windmill.* ☎ *622 83 25 or 320 17 86. Open W-Su 3-7:45pm. Tours F 4pm. Free.*

This former bathhouse and current daytime bar is a no-frills, die-hard brewery for the serious enthusiast. Situated on the body of water known as 't Ij, the building bears the sign of the Brouwerij 't Ij: an ostrich and its egg. The origin of the logo derives from the similarity between the sound of " 't Ij" and the Dutch *de ei*, which means "the egg." There's plenty of cigarette smoke and lively conversation from the locals that pack the bar and large canal terrace. Bring your camera, because after sampling the Brouwerij's nine home brews (six regulars and three seasonal beers for €1.70 each), you're sure to have a foggy memory of this unique brewery.

Wooden Bridge

HOLLAND EXPERIENCE 3D

🚋 *Waterlooplein 17.* ☎ *422 22 33; www.holland-experi-ence.nl. Open daily 10am-6pm; showings hourly every hr. 10:30am-5:30pm. €8; under 16 and seniors €6.85, children under 4 free, family pass (2 adults and 2 children) €25. Combination ticket with Museum het Rembrandt €12.50. MC/V.*

For a unique and unforgettable Dutch experience, check into this movie/bizarro festival of the senses, which takes viewers on a thirty-minute, language-free tour of Holland. The "experience" includes some rather puzzling shots of aquatic ballet, little girls playing with umbrellas, dikes bursting under the pressure of the sea, and women posing for photographs next to a giant Buddha made of sand. The moving theater, wind and sound effects, images of modern and traditional Dutch culture, and real water rushing through the theater make the experience an assault on the senses. Be sure to view the breathtaking aerial photography also on display.

Artis Planetarium

STADHUIS (HET MUZIEKTHEATER)

🚋 *Waterlooplein. Take tram #9 or 14 to Waterlooplein, or take any Metro line to Waterlooplein. Box office* ☎ *625 54 55; online bookings at www.hetmuziektheater.nl. Box office open M-Sa 10am-curtain, Su and holidays 11:30am-curtain; if there is no evening performance, the box office closes at 6pm. Tours Su 3pm €4.50, under 12 free. AmEx/DC/MC/V.*

Paddleboats

Nicknamed the "Stopera" by protestors who objected to the demolition of historic buildings in the old Jewish quarter in favor of new buildings, the Amstel-bound Muziektheater is home to The Netherlands Opera and the National Ballet. Enthusiasts can tour the performance and backstage spaces of both companies, which include wigs, props and costumes from past performances. Productions in 2004 will include Mozart's *Idomeneo*, Britten's *Peter Grimes*, and Verdi's *Don Carlo*. The rotund red-brick, marble, and glass complex also houses Amsterdam's city hall, or Stadhuis.

MOZES EN AÄRONKERK (MOSES & AARON CHURCH)

🚈 *Waterlooplein 207. Take all sneltrams or to Waterlooplein.* ☎ *622 13 05; www.mozeshuis.nl.*

This daunting piece of Neoclassical architecture was built as a Roman Catholic church in 1841, and is the only Christian edifice in the Jodenbuurt. The site now hosts exhibitions, symposia, social service groups and an adult education center. Moses and Aaron was once graced with concerts by Franz Liszt and Camille Saint-Saëns—it has carried this lively musical past into the present with frequent performances. Call for information on upcoming events.

WERTHEIM PARK

🚈 *Plantage Middenlaan, across from Hortus Botanicus. Open daily 8am-sundown.*

Home to the **Auschwitz Nooit Meer** (Auschwitz Never Again) monument, this small park on the Nieuwe Herengracht is a great place to stretch out on a sunny day. One of several wonderful green spaces in Plantage, Wertheim Park provides many a contemplative spot for its visitors.

MUSEUMS IN THE AREA

🖼 **Joods Historisch Museum (Jewish Historical Museum),** see Museums, p. 97.

🖼 **Museum het Rembrandt,** see Museums, p. 97.

🖼 **Tropenmuseum (Museum of the Tropics),** see Museums, p. 97.

Verzetsmuseum (Dutch Resistance Museum), see Museums, p. 98.

NEMO (New Metropolis), see Museums, p. 98.

Scheepvaartmuseum (Maritime Museum), see Museums, p. 99.

Nationaal Vakbondsmuseum "de Burcht" (National Trade Union Museum "The Fortress"), see Museums, p. 99.

GREATER AMSTERDAM

It doesn't hurt to leave the chaotic Canal Ring sometimes. Here are some major sights that just don't fit on our maps.

AMSTERDAMSE BOS (AMSTERDAM FOREST)

🚈 *Main entrance at Nieuwe Kalfjeslaan 4. Take bus #170 or 172 from Centraal, Dam, Westermarkt, Leidseplein, Museumplein, or Stadionplein to Van Nijenrodeweg, or just ask for Amsterdamse Bos.* ☎ *643 14 14; www.amsterdamsebos.amsterdam.nl.*

Sculpted in 1934, the forest impressively spans a 10 square km southwest of the city center. With 19km of bike trails, excellent picnic spots, weaving waterways, a small petting zoo, and a picturesque pancake house, these woods may well be the city's best-kept secret. The expansive green space feels more like a park than like a forest at times, with several football pitches and roads covering the land; however, many quiet acres do provide some a well-needed repose from the city of red lights. With six pedestrian routes and 13 bike paths, the forest provides a natural environment for daily exercise. **Rental bikes** are available at the main entrance at Van Hijenrodeweg (☎ 644 54 73) for €3.50 per hr., €5 per 2hr., and €7 per day. Better yet, dip your feet in the Bosbaan River with three-hour **canoe, waterbike,** or **electric boat** rides. (☎645 78 31. 2 people per canoe €8; 2 people per water-bike €8; 5 people in an electric boat €22.) The forest's most popular attraction is its Geinten-boerderij, or **petting zoo.** Located about 3km southwest of the entrance, it allows children to buy a €0.60 milk bottle to feed a thankful goat or sheep. (☎645 50 34. Open daily 9am-6pm.) Another fun spot for kids is the **Bosmuseum** at the northwestern corner of the woods, with interactive nature exhibits, including an underground tunnel that allows visitors to explore life beneath the earth's surface. (☎676 21 52. Open daily 9am-5pm.) Open Mar.-Oct. daily 10am-7pm; Nov.-Feb. F-Su 10am-6pm.) Recline to a film in the **Openluchttheater,** or **open-air theater,** through the summer (located just north of the A9 freeway) or ice-skate upon the frozen Bosbaan during the winter season. The forest offers plenty of green for field hockey, cricket, tennis, and has numerous fishing ponds besides. If you're walking, be prepared for a long hike by the river before reaching the first sites.

ARENA STADIUM

🚩 *ArenA Boulevard 1. Metro #50 or 54 or bus #29, 158, 174, 177, 178 to Strandvliet/ArenA or Bijlmer. Dir: Gein; 2 zones; 15min. €2.10 for metro. Enter on the far side of the stadium, near ingang (gate) F. ☎311 13 33, 311 13 36, or 311 14 44 for tickets; www.amsterdamarena.nl; team website www.ajax.nl. Open daily 10am-5pm, tours every 90min. Guided 1hr. tour of stadium €8; under 12 and over 65 €7. Ajax Museum (including short tour of stadium) €3.50.*

The Dutchman's undying passion for football (soccer) is magnificently demonstrated by the state-of-the-art, 52,000-seat stadium built in Amsterdam's outskirts in 1996. ArenA, a massively modern creation, even boasts a mobile domed roof that slides open or closed due to weather conditions. For a small nation, The Netherlands enjoys a distinguished football history (see p. 55). Amsterdam's love for the "the beautiful game" is devoted to the Amsterdamsche Football Club (AFC) Ajax, The Netherlands most successful football club. The team, founded in 1900, is almost unanimously supported by Amsterdammers. AFC rewards its fans with consistently high-level play, having won both the Dutch Cup and Dutch Championship in 2002. With 40,000 season ticket holders, the stadium's 12,000 remaining tickets (from €15) sell quickly but are usually still available in the weeks before matches. However, games against hated metropolitan rivals like Feyenoord Rotterdam, PSU Eindhoven, and FC Utrecht usually

Brouwerij 't IJ

Sint Nikolaaskerk

Graffiti Near U of A

sell out instantly and are often reserved for locals so as to ensure that die-hard fans pack the seats. If you're lucky enough to score a ticket, beware that local hooligans occupy the western of the ArenA (F-Side), where they'll be madly cheering Ajax to victory. A tour of the facility will take you onto the actual field, home to large concerts, an ice skate rink in the winter and club football matches. The museum attached to the stadium gives visitors an impassioned look at the town's pride team, delving into the "World of Ajax" through videos, famed uniforms, photographs, and team documents. (ArenA Boulevard 3. ☎311 16 85.)

MUSEUMS IN THE AREA
CoBrA Museum, see Museums, p. 100.

TOURS

Boat tours of the city are a great way to start off any trip to Amsterdam—the layout makes much more sense when you view it from the waterways. Bike tours can get you out of the downtown to see parts of The Netherlands you might never discover by train. And diamond tours are just about the only way visitors can get into a diamond workshop without becoming an apprentice.

BOAT TOURS

Amsterdam Canal Cruises, Nicholas Witsenskade 1A (☎626 56 36), boards opposite th Heineken brewery. From Centraal, take tram #16, 24, or 25 and exit at "Ferdinand Bolstraat," and backtrack 80m to Singelgracht. 1¼hr. tour. €8, children €3.50. Open 9:30am-5pm.

Canal Bike (☎626 55 74, www.canal.nl), at 4 moorings: Rijksmuseum, Leidseplein, Keizersgr. at Leidsestraat, and Anne Frank Huis. These paddleboats offer a more exercise-intensive experience. For 1-2 people €8 per hr., for 4 people €7 per hr. €50 deposit. Printed route guides €2. Also offers boat tours of the city (day pass €15, for 10+ people €10.50). Open 10am-9pm, low season 10am-7 or 8pm.

Canal Bus (☎626 55 74; www.canal.nl), travels 3 routes with 11 stops; buy tickets at kiosks or on board. Worthwhile only if you plan on doing heavy sightseeing over a 12hr. period. Adults €15, children €10.50. Pass valid until noon the next day and gives discounts at some museums and restaurants. Open daily 10am-6pm, in summer 10am-9:30pm.

Lovers Boat Company, Prins Hendrikkade 25-27 (☎530 10 90; www.lovers.nl), offers several different options in canal travel. For €8, you can hop on a 1hr. canal cruise (every hr. 10am-5pm) that leaves from the main depot across from Centraal Station. **Museumboot** has pickups every 30min. at Centraal, Anne Frank Huis, Rijksmuseum, Bloemenmarkt, Waterlooplein, and the old shipyard. Day ticket €14.25; €12.50 after 1pm. Patrons can board and disembark at all stops. For romance, try a candlelight cruise, which includes a drink (2hr., 9pm daily, €24) or a dinner cruise (2½hr., 7:30pm daily, €68.50), each of which leaves from outside Centraal. A simple 1hr. night cruise costs €8.50.

Wetlands Safari (☎686 34 45; www.wetlandssafari.nl) takes visitors on a different kind of boat tour, allowing tourists to escape urban Amsterdam and explore the beautiful landscape of its surroundings. The 5hr. bus and canoe tour (€30) includes light lunch and loads of lush scenery. May 1-Sept. 15 M-F 9:30am from the VVV outside Centraal Station.

BIKE & BUS TOURS

To rent your own bike, see the **Service Directory,** p. 319.

Lowlands Travel, Korvelplein 176, Tilburg (☎62 334 20 46; www.lowlandstravel.nl). Now every week Lowlands Travel takes small groups on personalized 3- to 4-day tours of The Netherlands in the hope of revealing the places still untouched by souvenir shops and camera-wielding tourists. Several tours are available, expeditions through northern or southern Holland. All tours include transportation, meals, and accommodations, and start at €199.

Mike's Bike Tours, Kerkstraat 134 (☎622 79 70; www.mikesbiketours.com), runs very popular tours of the city and surrounding areas led by hilarious, well-informed guides. 3-4hr. tours meet daily at the Rijksmuseum's west entrance, Stadhouderskade 42. Mar.-Apr. and Sept.-Nov. 12:30pm; May-Aug. 11:30am and 4pm. Rain gear provided. Tours €22, including bikes. No reservations necessary. Traveler's checks accepted, no credit cards.

Yellow Bike, Nieuwezijds Kolk 29 (☎620 69 40; www.yellowbike.nl). Tour Amsterdam by bike with an English-speaking guide or rent a bike and ride off into the sunset, or even into wine and cheese country (tours Apr.-Oct.). Bike rental a bit pricey (€8 per day; credit card swipe or €100 deposit per bike), but guided tours are a great way to get to know Amsterdam. 3hr. city tour departs Su-F at 9:30am and 1pm, Sa 2pm (€17), 6hr. country tour departs daily at 11am and stops at a pancake bakery (€22.50). Rental shop open 8:30am-5:30pm.

DIAMOND TOURS

In the late 19th- and early 20th-centuries, Amsterdam was a major world diamond center, with massive quantities of this precious gem brought in from colonial efforts in Africa—the rocks were cut and sold in the Jodenbuurt, particularly around Waterlooplein. Today many of the original manufacturers offer free tours highlighting their process and final result. For those so inclined, the factories are also a great place to purchase the gem, with wholesale prices and eliminating the significant tax for tourists. Make sure to ask for a VAT receipt for a later refund.

Gassan Diamonds, Nieuwe Uilenburgerstraat 173-175 (☎622 53 33; www.gassandiamonds.com), behind the flea market at Waterlooplein. Take any Metro line to Jodenbreestraat and take Nieuwe Uilenburgerstraat east. An impressive showroom and particularly friendly tour guides. Free tours every few minutes. Open daily 9am-5pm.

Stoeltie Diamonds, Wagenstraat 13-17 (☎623 76 01; www.stoeltiediamonds.com), from Rembrandtplein, take Amstelstraat east and turn left on Wagenstraat. Offers comprehensive free tours of their beautiful diamond factory. Open daily 9am-5:30pm.

Amstel Diamonds, Amstel 206-208 (☎623 14 79). Take any Metro line to Waterlooplein, take the Stadhuis/Muziektheater exit; the factory is on the other side of the Amstel. A small diamond manufacturer that has worked on the river since 1876, Amstel is one of the oldest workshops still in operation. Free guided tours M-Sa 9:30am-4:30pm, Su 10am-5pm.

Museums & Galleries

Amsterdam's museums contain enough art and history to arouse even the most indifferent of curiosities. Whether you want to admire Rembrandts and van Goghs, observe cutting-edge photography, pay tribute to Anne Frank's memory, or marvel at sexual oddities, Amsterdam has a museum geared toward every purpose. Above all, however, Amsterdam is an art-lover's paradise. The most popular art museums—including the Stedelijk, the Rijksmuseum, and the Van Gogh museum—are crowded into the Museumplein, but other neighborhoods hide smaller collections. If you're itching to have your finger on the contemporary pulse of the city's cultural life—or if you want to take a piece of it home—you should consider spending a morning gallery-hopping in Amsterdam (p. 101).

Amsterdam has also witnessed thriving museum counter-culture, best exemplified by a swelling of so-called "alternative art spaces". These extraordinarily compelling spaces, usually housed in former squatted buildings, explore a range of artistic expression that includes, but goes beyond painting and installation art to performance pieces and innovative mixed media. They are a sometimes elusive part of Amsterdam's artistic life, but should not be missed. For more information and listings, see p. 101. In an entirely different—and frequently non-artistic—vein, the city enjoys a smattering of specific collected artifacts and objects that cater to come truly obscure niche interests; for more information on these curious curators, see **Bizarre Amsterdam,** p. 83.

the hidden deal

museums for less

Those planning to hit even just a handful of museums while in the city may want to invest in a **Museum Jaarkaart** (MJK). An especially good deal for younger travelers, the pass (€29.95, under 25 €17.55, including the one-time "handling fee") entitles the holder to admission at most of the major museums in Amsterdam, including the Van Gogh Museum, Rijksmuseum, and the Anne Frank Huis.

The card is also valid at many first-rate museums all over The Netherlands: the Mauritshuis in The Hague, the Nederlands Architectuurinstituut in Rotterdam, the Frans Hals Museum in Haarlem, and the Bonnefanten Museum in Maastricht. The cards are good for one year, but can be worth it even for those staying a week (combined admission to the Van Gogh Museum and Rijksmuseum is about the price of an under-25 card). Bring a passport photo and buy the MJK card at most of the participating museums.

It will save you money, but it may not save you any time; card-holders still have to wait in line. For more information, check www.museumjaarkaart.nl. Cards may be purchased at this website—but these may only be sent to an address in The Netherlands.

OUDE ZIJD

see map p. 344

AMSTERDAMS CENTRUM VOOR FOTOGRAFIE (AMSTERDAM CENTER FOR PHOTOGRAPHY)

⑦ *Bethanienstraat 9, between Kloveniersburgwal and Oudezijds Achterburgwal.* ☎ *622 48 99. Open W-Sa 1-6pm. Closed July to mid-Aug.*

A brimming forum emphasizing the talents of young photographers, the Centrum voor Fotografie holds five- to six-week-long exhibitions by up-and-coming, mainly Dutch artists. The level of talent and breadth of subject matter displayed is highly variable, but there are always some remarkable and vibrant pieces throughout the three floors of open, sunny display rooms. One exhibition per year focuses on the work of an international artist. Darkrooms are available when not being used for teaching students, (€3.20 for 2hr, €9.10 per day), though a membership is required (€10 for 2 months, €25 for 1 year). **Gallerie 39,** right down the street at Bethanienstraat 39, is a newly opened branch of this museum and displays additional photographs by the same artists.

RED LIGHT DISTRICT

see map p. 344

THE VICES

If weed piques your interest, your best bet is the staggeringly informative 🏫**Cannabis College,** Oudezijds Achterburgwal 124. For unadulterated knowledge on the uses of medicinal marijuana, the War on Drugs, the sensationally healthy high of the Vaporizer, or the creative applications of industrial hemp, it's ounce-for-ounce the equal of the Hash Museum (see below), just more potent—and free. The staff is unbelievably friendly and knowledgeable; they are so eager to answer any questions you could possibly have that you'll leave a cannabis connoisseur. See an artfully designed and adoringly cared-for growroom for a donation of €2.50. (☎ 423 44 20; www.cannabiscollege.com. Open daily 11am-7pm. Free.) You're better off blowing your €5.70 on a bag of grass at one of the many coffeeshops right down the street than dropping it on admission to the **Hash Marijuana Hemp Museum,** Oudezijds Achterburgwal 148. Mostly pro-pot leaflets, exploring hash history, uses, and creations, are tacked to partitions designed to make a small room seem much larger than it is. The museum's only real attraction is its growroom, which does little more than prove that watching grass grow is indeed as exciting as it sounds. (☎ 623 59 61; www.sensiseeds.com. Open daily 11am-10pm. €5.70.)

For a taste of Amsterdam's underbelly in a museum, your best bet is to get your jollies right off the train at the **Amsterdam Sex Museum**, Damrak 18, less than a 5min. walk from Centraal Station. The low admission fee won't leave you feeling burned if you find that walls plastered with pictures of bestiality and S&M are not your thing. The first of four floors features some amusing life-size mannequins of pimps, prostitutes, and even one immodest fellow who literally flashes you from behind his trench-coat. With the many moans, whispers, and cackles emitting from these dolls, at times the experience feels more like a horror show than a sexual adventure. The museum features such ancient artifacts as a stone phallus from the Roman age, but the exhibits are hardly informative and not particularly sensational. Watch out for the gallery of fetishes, though: the montage of horses, whips, and nipple clamps is not for the weak of stomach. *Let's Go* recommends this museum over all other similarly themed collections. (☎ 622 83 76. Open daily 10am-11:30pm. €2.50.)

MUSEUM AMSTELKRING "ONS' LIEVE HEER OP SOLDER" ("OUR LORD IN THE ATTIC")

🖪 *Oudezijds Voorburgwal 40, at Heintje Hoeksteeg.* ☎ 624 66 04; www.museumamstelkring.nl. Open M-Sa 10am-5pm, Su and holidays 1-5pm. €6, students €4.50, under 18 €1.

Hidden in a canal house that's actually worth visiting, this once-secret church on the edge of the Red Light District is now open to all of the marveling public. Amstelkring, which once masqueraded as a shop front, provides a number of remarkable surprises without the mile-long lines at better-known attractions. The only 17th-century attic church preserved in its original state, the museum recalls the time when Amsterdam was officially Protestant and Catholics could not freely practice their religion (see **Shhh...It's a Secret (Church),** p. 81). The stunning little chapel—which spans the attics of three adjacent buildings—makes clever use of its clandestine space with an ornate pulpit stored under the altar and galleries suspended from the roof by cast iron rods. There is also an organ

in the know

shhh...it's a secret (church)

Amsterdam is currently one of the world's most liberal and tolerant cities these days, but the road to acceptance was not always so easy, especially along the axis of Protestant-Catholic conflict. Until the late 16th century, The Netherlands was ruled by the Holy Roman Empire. At that time, Dutch forces fought to free themselves from the then-regnant family, the Spanish, Catholic Hapsburgs. The family's forces struggled to stem the tide of the local Protestant Reformation—but to no avail. In 1579, The Netherlands proclaimed independence from Spain and installed Protestantism as the official religion. During this tumultuous time—known as the Alteration (see p. 40)—Protestants demolished Catholic churches, looting and destroying artwork and artifacts from many structures, including Oude Kerk. Catholics were not allowed to practice their religion openly during the Alteration, so they constructed "secret churches" located in private residences, indistinguishable from neighboring canal houses. These hidden churches were painfully small but in otherwise similar to normal Catholic churches. One such secret church **Ons' Lieve Heer Op Solder ("Our Lord in the Attic"),** is now open to the public as a not-so-hidden museum (see p. 81).

81

"Our Lord in the Attic"

Armor, Historisch Museum

Main Gallery, Historisch Museum

tucked into the ceiling, abundant artwork on each floor, and a grand collection of silver reserved for services. The rooms on the lower levels of the museum are equally interesting as examples of the rigid Dutch Classical style, an aesthetic that valued** symmetry above all else. One of these rooms, the family's reception or "Sael," includes a false door just to preserve that symmetry. Today, Amstelkring still hosts occasional services, including Christmas Eve mass.

NIEUWE ZIJD

NIEUWE KERK

see map p. 344

🔲 Adjacent to Dam Sq., beside Koninklijk Palace. ☎ 638 69 09; www.nieuwekerk.nl. Open Su-W, F 10am-6pm; Th 10am-10pm. Organ recitals Th 12:30pm, Su 8pm, June-Sept. Call ahead for exact times. €8, ages 6-15 and seniors €6.

Nieuwe Kerk ("New Church"), the extravagant 15th-century brick-red church at the heart of the Nieuwe Zijd, now serves a triple role as religious edifice, historical monument, and art museum. Through 2004, the originally Catholic church will open its doors to rotating exhibits from the Stedelijk collection's depository while that museum is being renovated. Take a moment to stray from the main exhibit to discover the ornate hexagonal pulpit, with its intricate bas-reliefs where tiny angels slide down carved mahogany ropes. The pulpit was carved over 15 years by Albert Jansz Vinckenbrinck. Jacob van Campen, architect of the Koninklijk Palace, designed the undulating organ case. Also be sure to tilt your head upwards to catch a glimpse of winged cherubs who appear to be bearing the weight of the vaulted ceiling. The church, which has been rebuilt several times after fires, is still used for coronations and royal weddings. Queen Wilhelmina was crowned here in 1898, followed by her daughter Juliana in 1948, and granddaughter Queen Beatrix in 1980. In February, 2002, Prince Wilhelm Alexander, the future king of Holland, was married to an Argentine belle in Nieuwe Kerk's hallowed sanctuary.

AMSTERDAMS HISTORISCH MUSEUM (HISTORICAL MUSEUM)

🔲 Kalverstraat 92, Sint Luciensteeg 27, and Nieuwezijds Voorburgwal 357. Tram #4, 9, 14, 16, 24, or 25 to Spui, or #1, 2, or 5 to Nieuwezijds Voorburgwal. ☎ 523 18 22; www.ahm.nl. Open M-F 10am-5pm, Sa-Su 11am-5pm; closed Apr. 30. €6, ages 6-16 €3, seniors €4.50.

The building itself oozes history: the house, constructed in the 17th century, used to be Amsterdam's city orphanage. And even though nothing beats a walk around the city itself, this archival museum offers an eclectic introduction to Amsterdam's historical development by way of medieval manuscripts, Baroque paintings, and multimedia displays. While the layout is often needlessly labyrinthine and the spare wall texts don't provide a coherent enough narrative, the collection of artifacts alone provides a useful introduction to the city's rise and fall—and rise.

The story is organized into a "Grand Tour" of Amsterdam's history, beginning on the ground floor with "The Young City, 1350-1550" and continuing through the Reformation, Industrial Revolution, and finishing in "The Modern City, 1850-2000." The section of the museum that features artistic accounts of gory Golden Age anatomy lessons (Rembrandt's among them) is particularly interesting. The illustrations of Amsterdam's maritime history narrate the curious struggles of the Dutch East India Company. Be sure to catch one of the Historical Museum's hidden surprises: in the covered passageway between the museum and Begijnhof there is an extensive collection of large 17th-century paintings of Amsterdam's civic guards. During Amsterdam's Golden Age, these pictures were a genre to themselves: they were commissioned by the governing boards of municipal bodies seeking painterly immortality. Beyond the passage, the remainder of the museum illustrates Amsterdam's more contemporary history with photographs, films, and creative displays.

BEURS VAN BERLAGE

🗺 *Damrak 277, near Dam Square.* ☎ *530 41 41; www.beursvanberlage.nl. Open Tu-Su 11am-5pm. €5, students €3, under 12 free.*

Architecture buffs will salivate over this old stock and commodities exchange, designed by Hendrik van Berlage in 1903. The edifice was influential because of its neo-Romanesque style and the techniques developed to sustain its massive weight in the porous Amsterdam soil. If you look closely in this newly renovated museum, you'll notice double portices, designed by Berlage to support the mass of the building on sinking ground. In 2000 a wide tunnel was built under the structure, continuing the everlasting Dutch battle with land. While the restored interior chambers—part of an ongoing project to restore spaces to their original states—provide a fascinating look at the workings of the Dutch economy at the turn of the century, the highlight

bizarre amsterdam

The Van Gogh Museum, the Anne Frank Huis, and the Rijksmuseum are obvious must-sees for the museum-goer. But Amsterdam is also host to a very eclectic collection of collections. Convince your friends and family that your trip to Amsterdam has been truly educational by sending them a postcard from one of the following (very different) museums:

Amsterdam Sex Museum, in the Oude Zijd (p. 80).

Bijbels Museum, in the Canal Ring West (p. 86).

Cannabis College, in the Red Light District (p. 80).

Electric Ladyland: The First Museum of Fluorescent Art, in the Jordaan (p. 90).

Nationaal Brilmuseum (National Spectacles Museum), in Rembrandtplein (p. 89).

Pianola Museum, in the Jordaan (p. 90).

Woonboot (Houseboat) Museum, in the Jordaan (p. 90).

Torture Museum, in Nieuwmarkt (p. 89).

83

in recent news

betrayal revisited

The Frank family's betrayal is a six-decade-old mystery that remains solved. It is an enigma that continues to infuriate readers of Anne Frank's diary so frequently that The Netherlands Institute for War Documentation (NIOD) has thrice reopened the case in the past 60 years. The most recent investigation began in July 2002 in response to recent books that proposed probable suspects. The two main speculations for the betrayal had always been Willem van Maaren, an employee of Otto Frank and Lena Hartog, the family's cleaning woman, but they were vindicated after the first two NIOD investigations. In 2002, Carol Ann Lee published The *Hidden Life of Otto Frank*, presenting new facts and reasoning resolute enough that she convinced the NIOD to start its third report on the Frank mystery. The book incriminated a first-time suspect Anton Ahlers, a Dutch Nazi and Otto Frank's business associate. On April 25, 2003, at the end of their investigation, historians authored a report entitled "Who Betrayed Anne Frank?" and rejected all suspect theories, stating that the Frank family mystery may be impossible to solve due to the utter lack of conclusive evidence. The report also proclaimed Lee's theory to be unreliable as she had reached her conclusions based on mere speculation.

of the museum may well be the vertiginous ascent up a rickety staircase to the top of the clock tower. Those gutsy enough to brave the climb will be rewarded with a sweeping 360-degree view of the city. The interior space has since been changed from a trading floor into a gallery space featuring rotating modern art exhibits that focus on the study and exhibition of architectural models, paintings, and photographs. The recently renovated halls also provide space for events such as craft fairs and conferences; check the website for details.

ALLARD PIERSON MUSEUM

🔝 *Oude Turfmarkt 127. Located across the Amstel from Rokin, less than 5min. from Dam Square.* ☎ *525 25 56; www.uba.uva.nl/apm. Open Tu-F 10am-5pm, Sa-Su 1-5pm. €4.30, students €3.20, seniors €2.30, ages 12-15 €1.40, 4-11 €0.45, under 4 free.*

Experience a Classical blast from the past at the University of Amsterdam's Archaeological Museum. While the well-balanced and handsome collection of artifacts from ancient Egypt, Greece, Mesopotamia, Etruria, and Rome is not exactly world class, it does have a surprising collection of Roman figurines, Egyptian reliefs, and Greek pottery—as well as some of the city's classiest, albeit 20-millennia-old, full-frontal nudes. The museum inhabits the former headquarters (1869-1967) of the Dutch central bank, and the building's history is evident: the bright, institutional feel of the space can at times interfere with the antiquarian quiet of the exhibitions, and artifact captions are sparse and sometimes only in Dutch. Nonetheless, the holdings—30,000 excavated objects, 10,000 year old skulls, and a carefully restored mummy—are worthy attractions for fans of classical antiquity.

MADAME TUSSAUD'S WAX MUSEUM

🔝 *Dam 20. Take any tram to Dam Sq.; Madame Tussaud's is on the corner.* ☎ *522 10 10; www.madame-tussauds.com. Open July 15-Aug. daily 10am-5:30pm; Sept.-July 14 daily 9:30am-7pm. Closed Apr. 30. €17.50, ages 5-15 €10, seniors 60+ €15. Groups over 10 €14.50 per head. Brochure €7.50. AmEx/DC/MC/V.*

While the idea of going to see wax sculptures of famous people at an international, Brit-owned chain may seem nauseating, Madame Tussaud's could actually be fun—if you're in the right mood, and if it weren't for those long lines and prohibitive prices (regular entrance has been upped to €17.50). This temple of kitsch, which just spent €4 million on renovations in 2002, tries to justify its existence in the historic center of Amsterdam by starting its "exhibit" with a condescending and cartoonish precis of Dutch history. The tour begins with the fight for Dutch independence and ends with a soppy tribute to assassinated right-wing politico Pim Fortuyn (see **Shifting Right,** p. 46). Just about the only worthwhile part of the exhibit is the chance to walk through a life-size model of Vermeer's famous painting, "The Allegory of the Artist."

Whoever makes it past this ochre-colored history lesson will reach the air-conditioned hall of fame located upstairs: this floor contains room after room of Dutch politicians, American pop idols, and international sports celebrities. If seeing George W. Bush or Kylie Minogue "in the wax" turns you on, forget about the Red Light District; for the rest, this museum remains an absurd anomaly in midst of Amsterdam's fleshy historic neighborhood.

Nationaal Brilmuseum

CANAL RING WEST

◪ ANNE FRANK HUIS

see map p. 342

◪ Prinsengracht 267. Tram #6, 13, 14, or 17 to Westermarkt. ☎556 71 00; www.anne-frank.nl. Open Apr.-Aug. daily 9am-9pm; Sept.-Mar. daily 9am-7pm; closed on Yom Kippur. Last admission 30min. before closing. €6.50, ages 10-17 €3, under 10 free.

Anne Frank was just ten years old when World War II commenced in 1939, but her literary legacy has inspired many across the globe. In 1942 the Nazis began deporting all Jews to ghettos and concentration camps, forcing Anne's family and four other Dutch Jews to hide in the *achterhuis*, or annex, of Otto Frank's warehouse on the Prinsengracht. All eight refugees lived in this "Secret Annex" for two years, during which time Anne penned her diary, a moving chronicle of her life as a Jew in Nazi-occupied Holland. Her journal continues to be one of the most widely read books in the world, revealing in its innocent sincerity the destructive consequences of prejudice and hate.

Interactive Exhibit, Anne Frank Huis

Displays of various household objects, text panels mounted with pages from the diary's first and second copies, and video footage of the rooms as they looked during Anne's time give some sense of life in that tumultuous time. However, save Anne's original magazine clippings and photos left plastered to the walls, the rooms are unfurnished; the cramped, exposed conditions and lack of privacy described in her writing are left to the visitor's imagination. Footage of

Westerkerk Belltower

interviews with Otto Frank (Anne's father), Miep Gies (an office worker who supplied the family with food and other necessities), and Anne's best childhood friend provide further insights.

After walking through the house, be sure to check out the CD-ROM exhibit, which gives the visitor a chance to learn more about World War II, and navigate through a virtual tour of the furnished house. Adjacent, an interactive display that strives contextualize the Holocaust in relation to current human rights issues, asks visitors to vote on whether they believe in the freedom of expression or in non-discrimination—assuming of course that the two are mutually exclusive. In the exhibit visitors watch a film documenting recent civil rights issues, including the 2002 Gay Pride eruption in Rome. While the effort at linking the past and present is appreciated, the gratuitous use of modern technology diminishes the exhibit's solemnity.

The endless line stretching around the corner attests to the popularity of Anne Frank Huis. With extended hours in the summer, there is no reason to queue up for an hour in order to get inside—the admissions line diminishes considerably after 7pm and before 10am.

BIJBELS MUSEUM

Herengracht 366-368. Tram #1, 2, or 5 to Spui. ☎ 624 24 36; www.bijbelsmuseum.nl. Open M-Sa 10am-5pm, Su 11am- 5pm. €5, children €2.50.

This museum bridges the gap between the Bible and Dutch culture. Housed in two canal houses built by 17th-century architect Philip Vingboons, the museum presents information both on the contents and history of the Bible and on the cultural context in which the Bible was written. Opened in 1851 with Reverend Leendert Schouten's public displaying of his ancient Israeli Tabernacle, it includes the first Bible ever printed in The Netherlands. The exhibits benefit from their surroundings; the house is a monument in itself, containing artistic designs that call forth biblical themes and demonstrate the Bible's influence on culture and society. The bottom floor is devoted to the study of canal house architecture, with emphasis on the ceiling paintings by Jacob de Wit and the elliptical English grand staircase. Make sure to examine the 17th-century kitchen and don't miss the two Aroma Cabinets that offer samplings of "exalted" fragrances—lotus and myrrh—and "everyday" scents from biblical times—fig and pomegranate. The large garden located at the back of the museum is an oasis of calm with its lily pond and arrangement of biblical sculptures.

HUIS MARSEILLE

Keizersgracht 401 ☎ 531 89 89; www.huismarseille.nl. Open Su, Tu-Sa 11am-5pm; in summer Tu-W 11am-5pm, Th-F 11am-8pm. €2.80, students €1.40, under 12 free.

The first locale in the city to curate photography exhibits on a permanent basis, the Marseille is a must for shutterbugs. Every three months, a handful of new displays grace this 1665 canal house—only a few prints are selected from each artist, but their works are invariably expressive, informative, and thoughtfully arranged. Exhibits through 2004 include Victorian photographs by Benjamin Brecknell Turner and contemporary displays by Dutch artists Ispeth Diederix and Marnix Goossens. The museum also has its own permanent collection of contemporary works by international photographers whose pieces also branch out into other forms of visual art. The collection includes transcendent pieces by Andreas Gursky and Sam Samore.

THEATER INSTITUUT NEDERLAND

Herengracht 168-174. Take any tram to Dam, walk up Raadhuisstraat away from the back of the palace. Turn left at Herengracht. ☎ 551 33 00; www.tin.nl. Open Tu-F 11am-5pm, Sa-Su 1-5pm. €3.85; students, children, and seniors €1.95.

Located in five majestic Herengracht canal houses, the Theater Instituut Nederland is a celebration of artistic and theatrical expression. The main building of the Instituut is Herengracht 168, which in 1638 was transformed by architect Philip Vingboons from a bakery into a resplendent house with the city's first neck-gable (an ornamentation that capped off thin canal houses). The museum also extends into the notable Bartolotti house, built in 1617 by Guillelmo Bartolloti. The buildings now hold a provocative collection of theater costumes, stages, and props, described thoroughly by side panels printed in both Dutch and English. Be sure to check out the walls and ceilings of the front reception area; the landscapes depicted here, painted by artist Issac de Moucheron, tell the legend of Jefta, the commander of the Israelite army, and the figures, by renowned painter Jacob de Wit, glorify Flora, Roman goddess of the spring. The building also houses a comprehensive library specializing in Dutch theater. In the back, a bare but well-lit cafe stocks snacks and drinks.

Bijbels Museum

MULTATULI MUSEUM

🖪 Korsjespoortsteeg 20. Take tram #1, 2, 5, 13, or 17 to Nieuwezijda Kolk, get off at the Herengracht stop, and walk toward the Shipping Quarter. ☎ 638 19 38; www.multatuli-museum.nl/en. Open Tu 10am-5pm, Sa-Su noon-5pm. Free.

"I am a coffee broker, and I live at No. 37 Lauriergracht, Amsterdam." So begins *Max Havelaar, or the Coffee Auctions of the Dutch Trading Company*, one of the few 19th-century Dutch novels still popular with contemporary literati. Its author, Eduard Douwes Dekker, was lauded by most Dutchmen for his visionary political leadership. Douwes was also recently named The Netherlands' most significant author. He penned the work after a 20-year sojourn in Indonesia, during which time he became disillusioned by the Dutch government's exploitation of the Javanese. Because Holland profited greatly from colonial spoils, Dekker wavered on whether to publicize his controversial beliefs; eventually he wrote his tome under the pseudonym *Multatuli*, Latin for "I have endured much," in 1860. The novel's critique of colonialism and its passionate witticisms instantly made it a vivid classic, for it breathed life into the conventional world of pedantic mid-19th century Dutch literature.

Museumplein

Today you can visit a museum dedicated to Dekker's legacy—not on Lauriergracht in the Jordaan, but at the author's birthplace on **Korsjespoortsteeg.** The Museum serves mainly for scholarly research, but the upstairs room displays Multatuli's personal book collection, desk, and the sofa on which he died. A fantastically knowledgeable staff of volunteers will eagerly recount Dekker's life.

Filmmuseum

NETHERLANDS MEDIA ART INSTITUTE, MONTEVIDEO/TIME-BASED ARTS

🏛 *Keizersgracht 264. Tram #13, 14, or 17 to Westermarkt.* ☎ *623 7101; www.montevideo.nl. Front desk open M-F 9am-5pm; gallery and exhibition space Tu-Sa 1-6pm; Mediathèque open M-F 1-5pm. Entrance to exhibition €2.50, students and seniors €1.50; Mediathèque free.*

Founded in 1978, this former canal house functions as an exhibition space, video library, and educational institution devoted to the promotion of time-based media. The Nederlands Instituut voor Mediakunst, which also manages De Appel's video holdings (see below), currently has a collection of over 14,000 books and videos available for study in the Mediathèque downstairs. Upstairs, Institute curates five to seven exhibitions per year on various issues in time-based arts, such as a retrospective of the work of Marina Abramovic. Montevideo also organizes lectures, symposia, workshops, and educational programs; check the website or call for details.

see map p. 340

CENTRAL CANAL RING

🖼 DE APPEL

🏛 *Nieuwe Spiegelstraat 10.* ☎ *625 56 51; www.deappel.nl. Open Tu-Su 11am-6pm. €2.*

De Appel can be depended upon to provide the unexpected—this art museum does not house a permanent collection, but a well-chosen roster of contemporary exhibitions makes even the Stedelijk look old-fashioned. Curators assemble provocative contemporary collections—a single artist on the first floor and exhibits of "cinema, sounds, and synergy" on the second floor. The first museum to show video art in The Netherlands, De Appel is now a testing ground for the newest, most daring multimedia installations. Check their website for occasional Tuesday programs (8pm, €2).

🖼 FOAM PHOTOGRAPHY MUSEUM

🏛 *Keizersgracht 609. Tram #16, 24, or 25 to Keizersgracht, between Vijzelstraat and Reguliersgracht.* ☎ *551 65 00; www.foam.nl. Open daily 10am-5pm. €5, students with ID €4. Cafe open W-Su 10am-5pm.*

Housed in a traditional canal house, the Foam Photography Museum stages a fearless exploration of modern photography. Every genre of the photographed image is fair game—the purely aesthetic, the overtly political, fashion photography, and historical exhibits. The keyword here is dauntless: a recent exhibition of the work of Dutch documentary photographer Ad van Denderen tested the boundaries, so to speak, of the issue of refugees in Europe. Sixteen years of work yielded wrenching images and artifacts of African migrants swimming the strait of Gibraltar and portraits taken in asylum centers.

MUSEUM WILLET-HOLTHUYSEN

🏛 *Herengracht 605, between Amstel and Utrechtsestraat. Tram #4, 9, 14, or 20 to Rembrandtplein or Metro to Waterlooplein.* ☎ *523 18 70; www.ahm.nl. Open M-F 10am-5pm, Sa-Su 11am-5pm. €4, ages 6-16 €2, over 65 €3, under 6 free.*

Walk into life in the Golden Age. Run by the Amsterdam Historisch Museum, this 17th-century canal house has been preserved as a fascinating museum with 18th-century furnishings, so you can see how the wealthy in Amsterdam lived over 300 years ago. In 1895, Sandrina Holthuysen donated the family home she shared with her collector husband Abraham Willet. Now the marble and gilt mansion has been redone in a Baroque, early 18th-century style, with gilt-edged walls, glittering chandeliers, family portraits, Rococo furnishings, and other signs of conspicuous consumption, including Abraham's collection of fine porcelain, glassware, and silver. Read the accompanying book—available in the museum book shop—to find out the details of daily life here, such as 19th-century water filtration methods. The French Neoclassical garden located behind the house remains as finely manicured as it was in the Dutch Golden Age.

MUSEUM VAN LOON

🔽 *Keizersgracht 672, between Vijzelstraat and Reguliersgracht. Tram #16, 24, or 25 to Keizersgracht. ☎ 624 52 55; www.museumvanloon.nl. Open M and F-Su 11am-5pm. €4.50, students €3, children under 12 free.*

The tenant history of this preserved canal house mirrors that of The Netherlands' prosperous centuries. It was built in 1672 for a Flemish merchant attracted by the international trading boom; his first tenant was Ferdinand Bol, Rembrandt's most famous pupil. It eventually fell into the hands of the Van Loon family, descendants of Dutch East India Company co-founder Willem Van Loon. Check out his portrait in the entrance hall, as well as the "Moor" that adorns the family crest, thought to commemorate the family's colonial past. The unusually ornate gilt banister along the central staircase has words subtly worked into its curves.

NATIONAAL BRILMUSEUM (NATIONAL SPECTACLES MUSEUM)

🔽 *Gasthuismolensteeg 7. Take any tram to Dam Sq., walk around to the left of the Palace, turn left, walk half a block and turn right onto Paleisstraat, which becomes Gasthuismolensteeg. Cross the Singel; the museum is on the left in the middle of the next block. ☎ 421 24 14; www.brilmuseumamsterdam.nl. Open W-F 11:30am-5:30pm, Sa 11:30am-5pm. €4.50, under 12 €2.50.*

By virtue of its location on one of Amsterdam's quieter side streets, it is easy to breeze right by the Nationaal Brilmuseum (National Glasses Museum), located in the home of a family that has been collecting specs here for over four generations. The four-story building, which dates all the way back to 1620, is stuffed to the gills with all styles of eyewear—the result of a fourth-generation optician's 35-year mission to gather and present the world's most fascinating spectacle specimens to the curious public. While the museum itself doesn't offer much in the way of twists and turns (the exhibits take you through the history of optical science, craftsmanship, and fashion), its novelty alone might make it worth a visit. Inside you'll find famous frames from the past century—such as Schubert's, Buddy Holly's, Dame Edna's—that have not been worn since their owners bequeathed them to the museum. And even if the hefty admission fee is too steep, the shop that occupies the ground floor of the building that houses the museum is definitely worth a peek (sunglasses from €9, most eyewear around €100).

TORTURE MUSEUM

🔽 *Singel 449. Tram #1, 2, or 5 to Koningsplein; cross the canal and turn right onto Singel. ☎ 320 66 42. Open daily 10am-11pm. €5, children €3.50.*

Just about every means of medieval torture imaginable is displayed at the appropriately dark and claustrophobic Torture Museum. Though the array of centuries-old racks, guillotines, and thumbscrews lack much context beyond a glib explanation of their use, the light they shed on the sheer intricacy of the darker side of European feudal history—when civil and religious authorities sought to subdue the plebes by any means possible—is worth a look. Be warned: as the rather campy advertisements plastered all over town might indicate, this museum is something of a tourist trap. However, if the rest of Amsterdam—with its mind-boggling collection of brothels, head shops, coffeeshops, and live sex shows—is simply too cheerful for you, this subdued celebration of torture may be just what the executioner ordered.

JORDAAN

▣ ELECTRIC LADYLAND: THE FIRST MUSEUM OF FLUORESCENT ART

see maps p. 342

🗹 *2e Leliedwarsstraat 5, below the art gallery, off of Prinsengracht between Bloemgracht and Egelantiersgracht. Tram #13, 14, or 17 to Westermarkt; tram #10 to Bloemgracht; or bus #21, 170, or 171 to Westermarkt. ☎ 420 37 76; www.electric-lady-land.com. Check website for how to get there; people often get lost despite written directions. Open Tu-Sa 1-6pm. €5, under 12 free.*

From the mines of New Jersey to the heights of the Himalayas, owner Nick Padalino has been inspired by the title of Jimi Hendrix's 1968 album and collected a singularly impressive assortment of fluorescent objects. These include gorgeous rocks that glow green in black light and an array of everyday objects that reveal hidden shades. Even better is Padalino's mind-bending fluorescent sculpture, which he deems "participatory art." Visitors are encouraged to dive into the interactive space and play with the many switches and buttons that turn various lights on and off; try to find the miniature statues and concealed periscopes all around the sculpture. It took him seven years to make, and Padalino—to whom the adjective "knowledgeable" does not do justice—won't hesitate to spend anywhere from one hour to three explaining the science behind the art. Indeed, a visit to the museum is essentially a private tour with the endearingly eccentric owner. The other side of the small museum displays the scientific and cultural artifacts in Padalino's collection, and upstairs his fluorescent art—prints, sculptures, cards, etc.—is sold.

WOONBOOT (HOUSEBOAT) MUSEUM

🗹 *In Prinsengracht canal opposite #296, facing Elandsgracht. ☎ 427 07 50; www.houseboatmuseum.nl. Open Mar.-Oct. W-Su 11am-5pm; Nov.-Feb. F-Su 11am-5pm. Closed Jan. 5-30. €3, children shorter than 152cm €2.50.*

Houseboats in Amsterdam began as a way to relieve overcrowding and the severe housing shortage following World War II. Since then, living on the water has become quite popular, with 2500 houseboats now lining the canals. This houseboat lets you see what the floating life might be like, complete with a tiny bathroom, a play area, and a book-lined living room. A slide show of boats around Amsterdam uses Enya's *Sail Away* as a soundtrack.

STEDELIJK MUSEUM BUREAU AMSTERDAM

🗹 *Rozenstraat 59. ☎ 422 04 71; www.smba.nl. Open Tu-Su 11am-5pm. Free.*

This adjunct of the Stedelijk devotes itself to exhibiting the newest in Amsterdam art. A pure white space made light and breezy by a vaulted glass ceiling, the museum bureau is something of a testing ground for avant-garde artists and material designers. The 10-12 shows per year range from the rather traditional forms of painting and sculpture to more outrageous attempts at installation art, performance pieces, as well displays of furniture and fashion design. Shows in the bureau can run anywhere from a weekend to a few months.

PIANOLA MUSEUM

🗹 *Westerstraat 106. ☎ 627 96 24; www.pianola.nl. Open Su 11:30am-5:30pm and by appointment during weekdays. €4, children €2.50.*

You wouldn't expect to find a pianola museum, well, anywhere, but least of all tucked into an unassuming corner of bustling Westerstraat. For the uninitiated, the pianola (frequently referred to as a player piano) is an upright piano whose internal mechanism has been partially replaced with machinery so as to play automatically; different songs are recorded on paper pianola rolls and inserted into the instrument.

This offbeat curiosity of a museum lets the visitor explore not only the history of the pianola, but the entire scope of the 1920s, when the popularity of this dodo of musical instruments was at its peak. The collection began as a private obsession but now provides a unique glimpse into this otherwise marginalized niche culture. It also houses a collection of 15,000 vintage player piano rolls and hosts regular weekend concerts (check website for details). The kind curator may even demonstrate some of the selections on the piano himself.

MUSEUMPLEIN & VONDELPARK

▨ VAN GOGH MUSEUM

see map p. 347

Grassy Knoll, Museumplein

🄵 *Paulus Potterstraat 7. Tram #2 or 5 to Paulus Potterstraat. Tram #3, 12, and 16 also stop nearby at the Museumplein. ☎570 52 52; www.vangoghmuseum.nl. Open daily 10am-6pm; ticket office and restaurant close 5:30pm; museum shop closes 5:45pm. A desk on the ground floor rents audio guides for €4. €9, ages 13-17 €2.50, under 12 free. AmEx/MC/V accepted with min. €25 purchase. Ticket price includes admission to the exhibition wing.*

Contemplating Van Gogh

With a futuristic new wing completed in 1999, the Van Gogh Museum seems to be set on propelling this modern Dutch master into 21st-century stardom. The original 1973 building by de Stijl designer Gerrit Rietveld has large, white exhibition spaces that reverberate with aloof Modernist cool. Here you'll find the permanent collection, including the largest collection of paintings and sketches by Van Gogh in the world, arranged chronologically. The second floor is home to a study area with web consoles and a small library, while the third floor houses a substantial collection of important 19th-century art by Impressionist, post-Impressionist, Realist, and Symbolist painters and sculptors.

PRACTICAL INFORMATION

For better or for worse the Van Gogh Museum is one of Amsterdam's biggest cultural tourist attractions, and as such suffers from some of the longest lines in town. If you think you'll beat the crowd by showing up a few minutes before the museum opens, you're wrong—on weekends, the queue even weaves down the stairs and onto the sidewalk before the cash register warms up. You'll encounter the shortest wait if you show up around 10:30am, when the initial line has dissipated, or after 4pm, when the crowds are head-

Downstairs at the Van Gogh Museum

Entrance, Museum Het Rembrandt

Living Room, Museum Het Rembrandt

Ante Room, Museum Het Rembrandt

ing home. To avoid hassle, you can also reserve your tickets online at www.vangoghmuseum.nl or, for a small service charge, through the Uitburo (www.uitlijn.nl).

You can pick up a copy of the incredibly earnest (and sometimes melodramatic) audio tour near the front desk—although the museum has enough wall texts to make this unnecessary.

ORIENTATION

The museum is relatively small; count on seeing it all in one morning or afternoon. The meat of the museum, the Van Gogh **masterpieces,** occupies the **first floor** (upstairs from the ticket desk and book shop); this is where you should concentrate your time. The collection unfolds in chronological order, beginning with the painter's dark and ponderous Dutch period. The famous **Potato Eaters (1885),** a sober depiction of a struggling peasant family at the dinner table, is the crowning achievement of the painter's early experimentation. In 1886 Van Gogh moved to Paris, where he was confronted with modern art for the first time. As a result, his paintings became brighter and more experimental. Vincent's love for *japonaiserie* emerged with **The Bridge in the Rain (after Hiroshige)** and **The Courtesan** in which he incorporated the flatness and stylization of Japanese woodblock prints into his nascent mature style. The last phases of his artistic development coincide with his travels—to Arles, Saint-Remy, and Auvers-sur-Oise—and these galleries contain some of his most recognizable works. One of the museum's decided gems is the equivocally cheerful **Bedroom at Arles,** where the thick violence of *impasto* paint collides with an insipidly pale range of pastel colors. Despite the fame their sibling garnered from fetching a then-record US$39 million at a 1987 auction, his studies of **Sunflowers,** made for close friend and rival Gauguin, are not the most spectacular works of Vincent's career; other masterpieces like **Branches of an Almond Tree in Blossom** and **Wheatfield with Crows**—the latter of which was completed just before Van Gogh's suicide in 1890—steal the show.

The **second-floor study area** is disappointingly uninformative and antiseptic. An excellent collection of smaller works by Van Gogh and his contemporaries—including some unbeatable self-portraits—are hung like specimens behind glass, while the souped-up computers only allow you to surf the museum's website. A demonstration of how Van Gogh chose and mixed the colors of his palate provides rare pedantic insight into the minutiae of his craft.

The **third floor's** collection of European painting and sculpture from 1840-1920 does far more than simply contextualize Van Gogh's painterly development; several of the pieces are masterly in their own right. Don't miss Gauguin's stunning **Self-portrait with Portrait of Bernard,** the collection of paintings by friend Emile Bernard, Symbolist Odillon Redon, or Pointillist Georges Seurat.

The partially subterranean **exhibition wing,** designed by Kisho Kurokawa and completed in 1999, is so curvaceous that it's known as "the mussel." This hyper-modern space, swooping around an outdoor patio, is the venue for the museum's top-notch traveling exhibitions. For a list of upcoming exhibitions for 2004, see below.

SPECIAL EXHIBITIONS

FROM KIRCHNER TO BECKMANN (NOV. 7, 2003-FEB. 8. 2004). Expressionist drawings and prints on loan from the Hamburger Kunsthalle. This show will feature 80 prints and drawings by Max Beckmann, Emil Nolde, Otto Dix, Ernst Ludwig Kirchner, and the artists associated with Die Brucke.

DANTE GABRIEL ROSSETTI (FEB. 27-JUNE 6, 2004). This first retrospective of the British Pre-Raphaelite painter Rosetti (1828-1882) will focus on the artist's famously erotic portrayal of *femme fatales.*

FORGET ME NOT! (MAR. 26-JUNE 6, 2004). "Photography and Remembrance" will expose a ritual side of the photographic image: how early family photographs were enhanced to become decorative, three-dimensional, immemorial objects. The collection includes photographs from India, Mexico, and Europe.

EDOUARD MANET: IMPRESSIONS OF THE SEA (JUNE 18-SEPT. 26, 2004). In collaboration with The Art Institute of Chicago and the Philadelphia Museum of Art, this is the first exhibition to focus on Manet's (1832-1883) marine paintings. Manet's works are shown alongside Whistler, Courbet, and the French Impressionists.

L'ART NOUVEAU (NOV. 26, 2004-MARCH 6, 2005). An exposé of Siegfried Bing's (1838-1905) Paris gallery, L'Art Nouveau, which became synonymous with the 19th-century movement. The exhibition displays a large assembly of Japanese woodblock prints (which influenced many European artists), a collection of decorative arts, and paintings by Toulouse-Lautrec, Munch, and Bonnard.

▧ STEDELIJK MUSEUM FOR MODERN & CONTEMPORARY ART

◪ Paulus Potterstraat 13. Tram #2, 5, or 20 to Paulus Potterstraat. Tram #3, 12, and 16 stop at nearby Museumplein. ☎ 573 27 45, recorded info 573 29 11; www.stedelijk.nl. Open daily 11am-5pm. €7, ages 7-16, over 65 and groups over 15 €3.50, under 7 free, families €17.50.

With the largest holding of Malevich paintings and drawings in Western Europe, a good selection of American art from the 60s and 70s, and extensive work by top-notch contemporary artists like Anselm Kiefer and Jan Dibbets, the Stedelijk (pronounced "STAID-ah-lick") has succeeded in amassing a world-class collection on a par with the Tate Modern or the MoMA. Unfortunately fraught with protracted restoration problems, this bastion for avant-garde and contemporary art, constructed in 1895, is slated to close in January 2004 for up to three years (though the museum was also scheduled to shut down in 2002, so its future is still uncertain). If it does undergo renovations, the museum will exhibit selections from its collection in different venues around Amsterdam; check the website for more up-to-date information. If you're lucky enough to catch a glimpse of the museum's holdings, don't miss its collection of works by Joseph Beuys, Robert Rauschenberg, Sigmar Polke, Damien Hirst, R.B. Kitaj, Gilbert and George, and Sol LeWitt as well as its first-rate photography collection.

Contemplating Rembrandt

Main Wing, Rijksmuseum

Rijksmuseum From Across the Singel

RIJKSMUSEUM AMSTERDAM

Stadhouderskade 42. Tram #2 or 5 to Paulus Potter-straat or tram #6, 7, or 10 to Spiegelgracht. Cross the canal; it's the huge neo-Gothic castle. ☎674 70 00; www.rijksmuseum.nl. Open daily 10am-5pm. Audio guides €3.50, €2.50 for students and under 18. Maps available at the ticket counters. €8.50, under 18 free.

Even though the main building of the museum will close for renovations in December 2003, the Rijksmuseum is still a mandatory Amsterdam excursion. During restoration, the smaller Philips Wing will remain open to show masterpieces of 17th-century painting, including works by Rembrandt van Rijn, Johannes Vermeer, Frans Hals, and Jan Steen. Originally opened in 1800, the Rijks, or "state" museum settled into its current monumental quarters, designed by Pierre Cuypers (also the architect of Centraal Station), in 1884. As the national museum of The Netherlands, it houses an encyclopedic collection of top-notch Dutch art and artifacts from the Middle Ages through the 19th century, a comprehensive exhibit on Dutch history, a collection of Asiatic art, and an enormous selection of furniture, porcelain, and decorative objects. Unfortunately, while the museum undergoes renovation, much of this collection will not be on display, but you may be able to catch a glimpse of some of the museum's holdings on loan at venues around the city. For details on the locations that will temporarily hold the Rijksmuseum's voluminous collection, check the website.

PRACTICAL INFORMATION

The two main entrances off the main building of the Rijksmuseum will be closed for the duration of the museum's renovation; visitors must enter instead through the Philips Wing, adjacent to the main building.

ORIENTATION

You will find few crucifixion scenes at the Rijksmuseum; traditional Dutch art is distinguished from its traditional European counterparts by its focus on the secular and the everyday. Nearly all 17th-century Golden Age painting in Holland was the product of free-market mercantilism: most of the domestic interiors, civic portraits, landscapes, and "vanitas" pictures on display were commissioned by wealthy Dutch merchants for display in their private homes.

Of this tour-de-force collection, Rembrandt's gargantuan militia portrait **The Night Watch** is a crowning, and deservedly famous, achievement. Equally breathtaking is the museum's collection of paintings by **Johannes Vermeer.** Only 31 paint-

L istening to "Visions of Johanna," I swore I heard Bob Dylan sing, "She's delicate and seems like a Vermeer." I wasn't surprised, because no other painter so pervades the contemporary Western imagination as the 17th-century Dutchman Johannes Vermeer. His renderings of the intimate, domestic circumstances of women evoke by turn interaction and introspection that suggest delicate and complex interior lives. "Like a Vermeer" has become shorthand for wistful and sensitive femininity with a hint of emotional vulnerability. Every time Vermeer's works, painted in Delft between 1653 and his death in 1675, are exhibited, lines stretch around the block. Scholars unanimously accept only 31 of his works, a small total by 17th-century Dutch standards. Painted at a rate of two a year, each was a considered statement, the result of intellectual contemplation as meticulous as their physical execution.

Visitors to Amsterdam and The Hague can see only seven Vermeers in just two museums. Any one of them is worth the trip—this is as good as art gets. The truly smitten can visit Vermeer's home town Delft, though there are no Vermeers there. Although you won't find the house he painted in *The Little Street* (Rijksmuseum, Amsterdam), you'll find plenty like it. Neither will you get precisely the same vantage point of the *View of Delft* (Mauritshuis, The Hague), but the harbor in front of the city walls remains. Narrow streets open onto large squares dominated by huge medieval churches, and light from canals reflected into limpidly lit rooms, vividly evoke Vermeer's physical world. The *View of Delft*, an imposing cityscape that set the standard for the genre ever after, was the first Vermeer to enter a Dutch museum. King Willem I made funds available when it was auctioned in 1822 and decided that it should be placed in the royal gallery, the Mauritshuis, rather than in the Rijksmuseum. This was the work that first brought Vermeer to the attention of curators, dealers, and critics beyond The Netherlands. New railroads opened the country to tourism, and soon one French critic, Theophile Thoré, was urging visitors to see the *View of Delft*, and two other paintings in the possession of the aristocratic Six family in Amsterdam. The Sixes' policy of opening their collection to the public ensured that thousands of visitors could see *The Milkmaid* and *The Little Street* prior to their entry into the Rijksmuseum in 1908 and 1921 respectively.

We are also indebted to banker Adriaan van der Hoop. Among the paintings in his collection was the *Woman in Blue Reading a Letter*, bequeathed to the city of Amsterdam in 1854. Thoré knew only six

paintings by Vermeer at this time, so he accepted Hoop's unsigned canvas after careful comparison with the others. The *Woman in Blue* is still owned by the city of Amsterdam, but it has been on loan to the Rijksmuseum since 1885. This brings to the fore a fact that easily eludes us: we take the identity of Vermeer's paintings for granted, but they are varied, so recognizing them as his work was no easy task. Nine years earlier the Mauritshuis had acquired a painting that exemplifies the difficulty of identification: *Diana and her Companions*, bought in 1876 as a Nicolaes Maes. The discovery of Vermeer's badly worn signature led to the correct attribution, but the dissimilarity between this scene and the *View of Delft*, hanging in the same room, led many to wonder if they were by the same artist. Not until the discovery of other, similar, early works were scholarly doubts allayed.

In 1892 the Rijksmuseum acquired another Vermeer: the *Love Letter*. Uniquely in his body of work, Vermeer used the device of a view through a doorway to establish a private interior domain. A seated woman has just received a sealed letter from a maid standing behind her. Though the painting on the wall behind them, a sailing vessel on a calm sea, suggests that the course of love may well be running smooth, the recipient's expression is anxious, and revelatory of an unguarded emotional moment. In the *Love Letter* the exchange of glances is internal to the picture; in a Vermeer acquired by the Mauritshuis in 1903, the gaze of its one figure meets our own as enigmatically and as devastatingly as any in art. *The Girl with a Pearl Earring* had been lost to sight since the late seventeenth century until it was offered, unattributed, at an auction in The Hague in 1881. A local collector bought it for all of two guilders. He bequeathed it to the Mauritshuis where it has since become the "Dutch Mona Lisa," emblematic, above all other works, of Vermeer's meltingly sympathetic pictorial account of the physical manifestation of young women's psyches. Although seemingly crushingly familiar from countless reproductions, this little painting—just 17½ by 15½ inches—flusters the heart. No more beautiful human achievement exists.

"She's delicate and seems like a Vermeer" brings visions of the *Pearl Earring* to mind. But Dylan's diction is notoriously indistinct at times. I misheard—"...and seems like the mirror" is the true lyric. Yet inasmuch as Vermeer's paintings mirror our desires, my version is true to their contemporary reflections. Go to see the seven Vermeers. They will shimmer prismatically—unforgettably—in the minds of anyone who stands before them.

Dr. Ivan Gaskell is the Margaret S. Winthrop curator at Harvard University's Fogg Art Museum.

GET smart

violence on
the night watch

Patrons flock to Rembrandt's storied *The Night Watch* (actually titled *The Militia Company of Frans Banning Cocq*), to see the master's impressive use of light and lively portraiture. Most visitors don't realize that they're seeing a reduced version of the original. The painting was moved in the 1670s, 30 years after it was completed (in 1642). When the work didn't fit in the new space, someone trimmed a considerable chunk off the left side and most of the bottom foreground. A reduced copy of the uncut original hangs beside the painting to give you a point of comparison.

In 1975, another knife cut into the canvas; this time it belonged to a crazed visitor who viciously slashed the painting's two foremost figures. The painting was restored without removing it from the gallery, but the scars can still be seen from just the right angle. Another disturbed person tried to throw acid on the work in 1990, but guards prevented major damage and only the varnish had to be repaired. To get a better sense of the damage, ask at the museum's information desk for a picture of the painting before it was repaired.

ings by the master of Delft survive; the Rijks possesses four. **The Kitchenmaid,** from 1668, has become something of an icon of Dutch genre painting: it shows a woman in front of an open window pouring a pitcher of milk into a bowl. Despite this motion, the picture retains the tranquility of a still life. Light glitters on the bread, and the plain back wall is scarred with nail marks, creating a sense of space out of a flat plane. The other paintings by Vermeer in the museum's collection share a similar luminous intensity and voyeuristic intimacy. For more on Vermeer's work, including **The Love Letter,** see the article **On the Trail of Vermeer,** p. 95.

Hans Bollonger's vanitas painting is a reminder of human ephemerality; this painting of a vase of vibrant tulips was painted two years after the collapse of the tulip market, while the insects on the table serve as a reminder of death. The subversive morality of **Jan Steen's** painting is evident in **The Merry Family,** which depicts a family boisterously singing and drinking—even the young children have glasses of wine in hand. Meanwhile, a hidden message in the rightmost corner of the canvas reads "as the old song is, so will the young pipe play," a warning to parents that their children will inevitably follow in their footsteps. Be sure not to miss **Pieter de Hooch's** interior scenes, the fine miniature panels of **Gerard Dou, Pieter Saenredam's** paintings of luminous church interiors, or **Frans Hals's** magnificently gestural brushwork.

FILMMUSEUM

📍 *Vondelpark 3, in the park between the Roemer Visscherstraat and Vondelstraat entrances.* ☎ *589 14 00; www.filmmuseum.nl. Free.*

Although the Filmmuseum is dedicated to the celebration and preservation of film, don't come here expecting to find mundane museum exhibits: most visitors come to see movies. As the national center for cinema in The Netherlands, the museum's collection holds 35,000 titles stretching back to 1898. In addition to screening several films a day (see p. 169), they maintain an information center at 69 Vondelstraat (across the path when exiting the Filmmuseum), which houses the largest collection of books and periodicals on film in The Netherlands, many of them in English. You can do film research in the non-circulating archives or on the computerized databases; the friendly staff will help you with any request. At the information center, videos from the museum's collection screen in the library's booths (€12.50, students €4.50), but you'll probably need to reserve ahead of time.

JODENBUURT & PLANTAGE

■ JOODS HISTORISCH MUSEUM (JEWISH HISTORICAL MUSEUM)

⚑ *Jonas Daniel Meijerplein 2-4 at Waterlooplein. Tram #9 to Waterloop-* **see map p. 349**
lein; museum is near the northwestern corner. ☎ *626 99 45; www.jhm.nl.*
Audio Tour €1. Open daily 11am-5pm; closed Yom Kippur. €6.50, seniors and ISIC holders €4,
ages 13-18 €3, ages 6-12 €2.

In the heart of Amsterdam's traditional Jewish neighborhood, the Joods Historisch Museum aims to celebrate Jewish culture and document the religion's cultural legacy. The complex links together four different 17th- and 18th-century Ashkenazi synagogues with glass and steel connections, symbolically—and literally—bridging past and present. Through exhibits by Jewish artists and galleries of historically significant Judaica, the museum presents The Netherlands' most comprehensive picture of Jewish life—photographs, religious artifacts, texts, artwork, and traditional clothing remain in the permanent collection, while an excellent children's wing is geared towards educating younger visitors. Some of the more notable artifacts include an ornately embroidered 18th-century Torah mantle and a Holy Ark holding silver Torah shields. Temporary exhibits change every four months—*Where Mokum is Home*, a children's educational display, and *Jewish Emigrants to the New World* will run through 2004. The staff also organizes trips to the Portuguese Synagogue (€12.50 per person; discounts for groups over 10).

■ MUSEUM HET REMBRANDT

⚑ *Jodenbreestraat 4, at the corner of Oudeschans Canal. Tram #9 or 14 to Waterlooplein, head*
northeast across Mr. Visserplein to Jodenbreestraat. ☎ *520 04 00; www.rembrandthuis.nl. Open*
M-Sa 10am-5pm, Su 1-5pm. €7, with ISIC €5, children ages 6-15 €1.50, children under 6 free.

Dutch master Rembrandt van Rijn's house at Waterlooplein, from which he was evicted by tax-hounds in 1658, is now the happy home of the artist's impressive collection of 250 etchings. Travel through all four levels of the beautifully restored house and see the inhumanly claustrophobic box-bed in which Rembrandt slept, tour the studio in which he mentored promising painters, and explore the kitchen in which his mistress is said to have "lashed out" at him. In the upstairs studio, Rembrandt produced some of his most important works. On display are some of his tools and plates, and a new wing houses temporary exhibitions—check the website for 2004 exhibits. Enthusiasts should also stop at Rozengracht 184, in the Jordaan, where Rembrandt lived out the remainder of his life. On Wednesdays and weekends year-round, artisans re-enact the paint-making and printing techniques of his time.

■ TROPENMUSEUM (MUSEUM OF THE TROPICS)

⚑ *Tropenmuseum: Linnaeusstraat 2. Tram #9 and bus #22 stop right outside the museum.*
☎ *568 82 15; www.tropenmuseum.nl. Open daily 10am-5pm. €6.80, students and seniors €4.50,*
ages 6-17 €3.40, under 6 free; family ticket, 1-2 adults and max. 4 children, €18.25. Kindermu-
seum, in the museum's basement. ☎ *568 82 33; www.kindermuseum.nl. Ages 6-12 €4.50. Spe-*
cial programs in the Kindermuseum in Dutch only; reservations must be made 2 weeks in advance.

The Tropenmuseum takes guests on an anthropological tour of Southeast Asia, Oceania, South Asia, West Asia, North Africa, Africa, Latin America, and the Caribbean. Sponsored by the KIT (Koninklij Instituut voor de Tropen), or Dutch Royal Institute of the Tropics, the museum is situated in one of Amsterdam's most awe-inspiring modern buildings, a massive, arched dome slotted with skylights. Take the elevator up to the second floor and wend your way down through the enormous world tour of ancient artifacts, contemporary objects, and religious pieces. Most of the works on display were obtained through Dutch colonial expansion; others are contemporary ethnographic studies.

NEMO

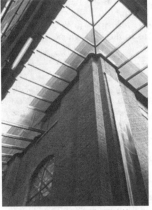

Joods Historisch Museum

Bizarro Wig Collection

The museum is also home to the celebrated **Kindermuseum (Children's Museum).** Only for children between six and 12 and those accompanying them, the Kindermuseum tries to provide something for all ages to enjoy. Permanent exhibitions combine video footage, music, computer technology, and models to create simulations of real environments—including narrow Indian streets, South American traditional medicine shops, and a Middle Eastern bazaar.

VERZETSMUSEUM (DUTCH RESISTANCE MUSEUM)

🚩 *Plantage Kerklaan 61. Tram #9 to Plantage Kerklaan; #6 or 14 to Plantage Middenlaan/Kerklaan.* ☎ *620 25 35; www.verzetsmuseum.org. Open Tu-F 10am-5pm, Sa-M noon-5pm, public holidays noon-5pm. €4.50, ages 7-15 €2.50. Tour of neighborhood available by phone or email appointment (€7.50 per person, groups smaller than 10 €75).*

Though the Nazi-German military quickly overran Dutch armed forces in May, 1940 The Netherlands maintained an extraordinarily active resistance throughout World War II. The Resistance Museum focuses on the members of this secret army, providing visitors with the details of their lives and struggles. Displays allow visitors to track the occupation and Resistance chronologically, from German invasion through liberation, ending with an enlightening exhibit on postwar Dutch regeneration. Model streets, buildings, and tape-recorded radio reports recreate the rebels' experiences—from smuggling food to issuing anti-propaganda on a printing press. On display are photos and letters from those who hid, escaped, or perished before the war's end in 1945. Temporary exhibits examine current forms of resistance in order to acknowledge ongoing struggles to fight oppression. The museum is housed in the historic Plancius Building, originally built in 1876 as the social club for a Jewish choir.

NEMO (NEW METROPOLIS)

🚩 *Oosterdok 2. East of Centraal Station in/on the Oosterdok.* ☎ *0900 919 11 00 (€0.35 per min.); www.e-NEMO.nl. Open Tu-Su 10am-5pm. €10, students €6, under 4 free.*

The green hull-like structure rising out of the water is NEMO, a science and creative exploration center geared towards children ages 6-16 and their accompanying adults. The structure, Renzo Piano's modern homage to The Netherlands' seafaring past, spans four stories and is littered with science exhibits just begging to be poked at, jumped on, and experimented with.

The provocative and thoughtfully designed displays at NEMO include permanent fixtures like "Why the World Works," "Machine Park," and "Bamboo House." For the more mature crowd, "Super Banker," a simulation/interactive exhibit where participants invest and gamble money to make it big, is addictive enough to consume an entire afternoon. Other temporary displays change regularly to keep up with evolving technology. Don't miss the spectacular view of the shipyard and the historic city offered by the museum; on the eastern side of the building, a staircase traverses the structure's slanted roof.

SCHEEPVAARTMUSEUM (MARITIME MUSEUM)

🚩 *Kattenburgerplein 1. From Centraal Station, follow signs past NEMO for about 10min. Or take bus #22 or 32 to Scheepvaartmuseum. ☎ 523 22 22; www.scheepvaartmuseum.nl. Open Tu-Su 10am-5pm; mid-June to mid-Sept. daily 10am-5pm; closed Jan. 1, Apr. 30, and Dec. 25. €7, seniors €6, students €5.25, children 6-18 €4.*

For lovers of the sea, the vast three-tiered Scheepvaartmuseum or Maritime Museum—one of the largest museums of its kind in the world—leaves no shell unturned in its exploration of The Netherlands' long and storied sea-faring history. The museum is run by the Verenigde Oost-Indische Compagnie (Dutch East India Company), the trade and shipping organization that in the Golden Age added what is now Indonesia to the Dutch empire. In addition to the 70 real vessels on display, multiple model ships are spread throughout the museum—including the spectacular Dutch East Indiaman Den Ary, a ship that seems to have sailed straight out of the mythical age of pirates and mermaids.

Plenty of attractions also sit outside the museum on the Oosterdok. Don't miss the full-size replica of the Dutch East Indian ship *Amsterdam*, parked right in front of the museum—it's not as if you could. On weekends at 11am, noon, 2, and 3pm, actors stage historic re-enactments of life on board this ship. The **Vereniging Museumhaven Amsterdam,** a collection of 18 antique boats, is tucked quietly between NEMO and the Scheepvaartmuseum. While visitors cannot board these late-19th- and early-20th-century vessels, placards explaining the history of each one are posted on the docks. (Open daily. Free.) For those in a more somber mood, the **Second World War Naval Monument** is right beside the Maritime Museum. This magnificent fountain, populated with statues of gallant horses and serene angels, was built to commemorate the hundreds of Dutch navy-men who died as a result of German U-boats between May 1940 and May 1945.

NATIONAAL VAKBONDSMUSEUM "DE BURCHT" (NATL. TRADE UNION MUSEUM "THE FORTRESS")

🚩 *Henri Polaklaan 9. Tram #9 to Artis Zoo. ☎ 624 11 66; www.deburcht-vakbondsmuseum.nl. Open Tu-F 11am-5pm, Su 1-5pm. €2.30, ages 13-18 and trade unionists €1.15.*

"The Fortress" documents the trade-union crusade of Jewish diamond worker Henri Polak (1868-1943), and now hosts rotating and permanent labor rights exhibits. The building, designed by the famous socialist "community style" artist Hendrik Petrus Berlage, was the original headquarters for the ANDB, the socialist diamond-workers' union. Polak wanted the building to be a monument for the workers' struggle, and so the design was meant to fit into the populist and socialist underpinnings of trade unionism. Countless paintings depicting aspects of Dutch social history are on display as part of the museum's permanent collection. When the eight-hour workday was introduced in 1912, socialist painter **Richard Holst** created a triptych for the building's board room showing that the day must be divided into three equal parts: work, relaxation, and sleep. On the way out, you'll see the gardens in front of many houses on Henri Polaklaan; at the turn of the century, many of the wealthier Jews running the union moved here and built homes behind what continue to be Amsterdam's only front yards.

GREATER AMSTERDAM

COBRA MUSEUM

🏛 *Sandbergplein 1-3, south of Amsterdam in Amstelveen. Take bus #170, 171, or 172 for 15min.; the museum is across the street from the station. Or, tram #5; the stop is a 10min. walk from the museum. ☎547 50 50, to pre-arrange a tour 547 50 45; www.cobra-museum.nl. Open Tu-Su 11am-5pm. Adults €6, students and seniors €4, ages 5-16 €2.50. AmEx/MC/V.*

The CoBrA Museum pays tribute to The Netherlands' second great 20th-century art movement (after de Stijl, see p. 51): the name is an abbreviation of the capital cities of the groups's founding members (Copenhagen, Brussels, and Amsterdam). CoBrA was founded after WWII by artists who desired to rebel against artistic conventions, venting their fury at postwar disjunction through abstract expressionism. The collective the included artists like Asger Jorn, Corneille, Constant, and famed Dutchman Karel Appel, all of whom were committed to progressive political activism and the "search for a vital image of reality." After CoBrA disbanded in 1951, the Stedelijk maintained many of their works, but the CoBrA Museum contains a more comprehensive display. The modern museum, overlooking a pond and centering around a small "Zen garden," effectively presents a range of the movement's work from the soft, Klee-like geometry of Corneille to the colorful, painterly frenzy of Appel. The highlight of the collection is Appel's large *Femmes, Enfants, Animaux* (1951), recently sold to the museum by Metallica drummer Lars Ulrich.

GALLERIES

The **Jordaan** has the highest density of top-quality contemporary art: the area bounded by Prinsengracht, Lijnbaansgracht, Elandsgracht, and Bloemgracht has a numerous galleries that specialize in cutting-edge pieces and installation. A stretch of Lijnbaansgracht just east of Vijzelstraat is home to nine excellent, welcoming galleries and is known as the **Galerie Complex Lijnbaansgracht** (see below). Best of all, the galleries along this convivial canal all throw their openings the same night: be sure to find out the date and get there early. The best way to plan a gallery-hop of Amsterdam's better spaces is to pick up a free copy of **AKKA's** gallery guide and map (online at www.akka.nl/agenda). The free monthly *Uitkrant* (www.uitkrant.nl), available at the Uitbureau and other locations, also has gallery listings and reviews.

CENTRAL CANAL RING

Van Zoetendaal, Keizersgracht 488 (☎624 98 02; www.vanzoetendaal.nl). Top-notch contemporary photography in a gorgeous space overlooking Keizersgracht. Open W-Sa 1-6pm.

Paul Andrisse, Prinsengracht 116 (☎623 62 37; andriesse@euronet.nl). Well-known gallery represents internationally renowned artist Marlene Dumas. Also displays work by others like Giuseppe Penone. Open Su-F 11am-6pm, Sa 2-6pm, 1st Su of the month 2-6pm.

Galerie Binnen, Keizersgracht 82 (☎625 96 03; interno@xs4all.nl). Über-cool designers mix up high and low: futuristic Eames-like chairs, molded porcelain tableware, and fluid metal lamps. Open W-Sa noon-6pm.

Clement, Prinsengracht 845 (☎625 16 56; www.galerie_clement.nl). The original 1958 print shop that worked with Hockney and Jim Dine closed this year, but the shop and exhibition space remain. Contemporary abstract work is not always on the cusp, but space has beautiful canal views. Shop sells excellent modern prints. Open Tu-Sa 11am-5:30pm.

Galerie Louise Smit, Prinsengracht 615 (☎625 98 98; www.louisesmit.nl). Beautiful contemporary art-jewelry crosses the line between fashion and gallery art. Open W-Sa 2-6pm.

Frozen Fountain, Prinsengracht 629 (☎622 93 75), in the Central Canal Ring. Not quite as cool as Binnen, Frozen Fountain nonetheless displays colorful, cutting-edge furniture and interior design by young Dutch creators. Open M 1-6pm, Tu-F 10am-6pm, Sa 10am-5pm.

JORDAAN

Galerie Fons Welters, Bloemstraat 140 (☎423 30 46; fax 620 84 33; www.fonswelters.nl). The most interesting section of this excellent, sky-lit gallery is the front-hall, known as "Play-station": a space where young Dutch and European artists are invited to install cutting-edge work. Open Tu-Sa 1-6pm, 1st Su of the month 2-5pm.

Galerie Diana Stigter, Hazenstraat 17 (☎624 23 61; www.dianastigter.nl). Sculpture, painting, installation, and photography from artists like Pierre Bismuth and Steve McQueen. Two of their artists, Saskia Olde Wolbers and Monika Sosnowska, won the Baloise "artist statement" prize at 2003 International Art Fair in Basel. Open Tu-Sa 1-6pm, 1st Su of the month 2-5pm.

Torch, Lauriergracht 94 (☎626 0284; www.torchgallery.com). Heats up with fiery exhibitions (shows like "Icons, Idols, & Fetishes") and super-slick selections of European and American artists (including Jake and Dinos Chapman, Takashi Murakami, Tracey Moffat, and occasionally Cindy Sherman). Open Tu-Sa 2-6pm.

Annet Gelink Gallery, Laurierstraat 187-189 (☎330 20 66; annet.gelink@wxs.nl). Large, airy exhibition space shows contemporary Dutch artists with a few strong international names. Open Tu-F, Sa 1-6pm.

De Expeditie, Leliegracht 47 (☎620 47 58; www.de-expeditie.com). Expect some hyper-real, pop-inspired contemporary art by young Dutch painters. Open W-F 11am-6pm, Sa 2-6pm.

GALERIE COMPLEX LIJNBAANSGRACHT

Galerie Akinci, Lijnbaansgracht 317 (☎638 04 80; www.akinci.nl). The most international of the Lijnbaansgracht spaces, representing world-class artists like Stephan Balkenhol, Axel Hutte, and Ilya Rabinovich. Tu-Sa 1-6pm, 1st Su of the month 2-5pm.

Canvas International Art, Lijnbaansgracht 319 (☎428 60 40; www.canvas-art.nl). An independent private art center in the Lijnbaansgracht complex that promotes artists from Latin America, Asia, and Australia. Open W-Sa 1-6pm.

Galerie Lumen Travo, Lijnbaansgracht 314 (☎627 0883; www.lumentravo.nl). International artists from Shirin Nesat to Jimmie Durham. Open W-Sa 1-6pm, 1st Su of the month 2-5pm.

Van Wijngaarden/Haakens, Lijnbaansgracht 318 (☎626 49 70; www.galerievanwijngaarden.nl). Surprisingly fresh painting, video, photography, and installation work by small group of Dutch artists. Open W-Sa 1-6pm, 1st Su of the month 2-7pm.

Vous Êtes Ici, Lijnbaansgracht 314 (☎612 79 79; www.vousetesici.nl). Slick, bright young painters from The Netherlands, Germany, and the US exhibit in this friendly space. Open W-Sa 1-6pm, 1st Su of the month 2-5pm.

ALTERNATIVE ART SPACES

Art-lovers know Amsterdam for its museums and galleries. However, there are a cluster of institutions (mostly former squats) that host rotating exhibitions by contemporary artists. In these "alternative art spaces," artwork is never for sale and entrance is always free.

W 139, Warmoesstraat 139 (☎622 94 34; www.W139.nl), in the Oude Zijd. The best of city's alternative art spaces, this former squat is an Amsterdam institution, hosting elaborate, edgy, punky, raucous, awe-inspiring, and politically-charged installations that use every inch of this amazing, sprawling space. Six shows per year. Open W-Su 1-5pm. Free.

SMART Project Space, 1e Constantin Huygensstraat 20 (☎427 59 51; www.smartprojectspace.net), near Vondelpark. Anti-squat known for its art-house cinema. Exhibitions sometimes less polished than W 139. Gallery open Tu-Sa noon-10pm, Su 1-10pm. Free.

Food & Drink

When it comes time to sit down for a meal, you'll thank your lucky stars that colonial history and a medley of immigrants have diversified your choices. In fact, in most areas the sheer number of options—from shawarma snack-bars to Argentinian barbecue to pan-Asian noodle joints—can be dizzying. Though Dutch food is common in the city, it's not nearly as exciting, or often as well prepared, as some of the selections from the former Dutch empire. Indonesian cuisine, omnipresent in the city, is one of the safest and tastiest bets for vegetarians and vegans, as traditional Dutch cuisine is hearty, heavy, meaty, and wholesome. During regular meals expect a lot of bread and cheese at breakfast and lunch, and generous portions of meats and fishes for dinner. Popular seafood choices include all sorts of grilled fishes and shellfish, wholesome seafood stews, and raw herring. For a unique, truly authentic Dutch meal, ask (especially in May and June) for white asparagus, which can be a main dish on its own, served with potatoes, ham, and eggs. But if you do decide to go Dutch, the best of it can be found in the bakeries; the *stroopwafels* and *pannekoeken* are sweet, thick and utterly perfect rounding out a meal. Between daily sittings, the Dutch conception of a light snack, often served in *eetcafes* (cafe-restaurants) includes *tostis*, piping hot grilled cheese or ham and cheese sandwiches, *broodjes* (familiar sandwiches), *bitterballen* (spiced meatballs with mustard dipping sauce), *oliebollen* (doughnuts), or *poffertjes* (small pancakes). However, the best food in Amsterdam underscores the city's pluralist, international character. An adventurous palate will serve you best as you navigate the jumble of Surinamese, Italian, Tibetan, and Ethiopian restaurants—among others. Die-hard meat-eaters will also find themselves in paradise, as South American steak houses abound.

BY TYPE

FOOD & DRINK BY TYPE

AFRICAN
Abyssinia Afrikaans Eet-cafe (117) WO ❷
Axum (113) CCR ❷
Rendez-Vous en Afrique (109) SQ ❶❷

AMERICAN
🍴 Eat at Jo's (113) LP ❶
Mister Coco's (107) NZ ❸
🍴 Harlem: Drinks and Soul Food (108) SQ ❸
Old Highlander (108) NZ ❷

BAKERY
Bakkerij Paul Année (111) CRW ❶

CAFES & SANDWICHES
Aguada (121) JP ❸
Broodje Mokum (116) J ❶
🍴 Cafe-Restaurant Amsterdam (116) WO ❸
🍴 Cafe de Pijp (119) WO ❸
🍴 Cafe Vertigo (118) MV ❷
Coffee and Jazz (112) CCR ❷
Dimitri's (111) CRW ❷
Foodism (106) NZ ❷
Het Blauwe Theehuis (118) MV ❶
La Place (108) NZ ❷
Plancius (121) JP ❸
Ruhe Delicatessen (111) CRW ❶
Soup En Zo (121) JP ❶
Theehuis Himalaya (105) OZ ❶
Vennington (112) CRW ❶

CHINESE
Hoi Tin (105) OZ ❸
Sea Palace (106) OZ ❺
Taste of Culture (105) OZ ❶
New Season (105) OZ ❷
Nam Tin (121) JP ❸
Wolvenstraat 23 (110) CRW ❷

DESSERT
Jordino (110) SQ ❶
🍴 Lanskroon (112) CCR ❶
Peppino Gelateria (119) DP ❶

DUTCH
Cafe De Pels (112) CRW ❶
Café Koosje (121) JP ❷
🍴 Cafe Latei (121) JP ❶
Cafe Westers (118) WO ❷
Carousel Pancake House (113) CCR ❶
De Belhamel (109) SQ ❺
De Smoeshaan (114) LP ❶
De Soepwinkel (119) DP ❶
Granny (120) DP ❶
Hein (111) CRW ❶
Het Molenpad (112) CRW ❷

DUTCH (CONT'D.)
🍴 Lunchcafe Neilson (110) CRW ❶
🍴 Pannenkoekenhuis Upstairs (106) NZ ❶
Spanjer en Van Twist (111) CRW ❸

FUSION/"GLOBAL"
18 Twintig (119) DP ❹
De Ondeugd (119) DP ❹
🍴 Kitsch (112) CCR ❹
Restaurant Wanka (117) WO ❸
🍴 In de Waag (107) MV ❹
Zouk (117) WO ❹

INDIAN & PAKISTANI
Balraj (109) SQ ❷
Bombay Inn (114) LP ❷
Dosa (117) WO ❸
Koh-i-noor (112) CRW ❸

INDONESIAN
Aneka Rasa (105) OZ ❹
Bojo (113) LP ❸
Esoterica (117) WO ❷
Padi (109) SQ ❷
Sie Joe (107) NZ ❶

IRISH
Tig Barra (118) WO ❷

ITALIAN
🍴 Abe Veneto (121) JP ❷
🍴 Cinema Paradiso (116) J ❷
Prego (111) CRW ❺
🍴 Ristorante Caprese (106) NZ ❸
Santa Lucia (114) LP ❶

JAPANESE
Go Sushi (118) MV, J ❷
Tomo Sushi (115) RP ❺
Wagamama (114) LP ❸
Shinto (120) DP ❷

JUICE BARS
Jay's Juice (109) SQ ❶
La Fruteria (107) NZ ❶
Tasty and Healthy (107) NZ ❶

MARKET
De Avondmarkt (117) WO ❶

MEXICAN
Rose's Cantina (115) RP ❸
La Margarita (115) RP ❹

MIDDLE EASTERN & KOSHER
Ben Cohen Shawarma (116) J ❶
King Solomon Restaurant (121) JP ❷
Snackbar Aggie (116) J ❶

104

SPANISH & PORTUGUESE	
Manzano (116)	J ❹
Mas Tapas (120)	DP ❸
Rest. La Sala Comidas Caseras (121)	JP ❹
Tapa Feliz (118)	MV ❹
Tapas de Kelderhof (114)	LP ❷
Toussaint Cafe (117)	WO ❸

SURINAMESE & AFGHANI	
Moksie (120)	DP ❷
Usama (108)	NZ ❷

THAI & SOUTHEAST ASIAN	
Cambodja City (120)	DP ❷
NOA (113)	CCR ❹
Rakang (116)	J ❹
Top Thai (111)	CRW ❷

TIBETAN	
Tashi Deleg (113)	CCR ❹

TURKISH & KURDISH	
Eufraat (120)	DP ❷
Kismet (117)	WO ❶
Saray (119)	DP ❸
⚑ Zagros (119)	DP ❷

VEGETARIAN & VEGAN	
⚑ Bolhoed (116)	J ❸
⚑ Restaurant de Bolhoed (110)	CRW ❸
De Vliegende Schotel (116)	J ❷
Golden Temple (113)	CCR ❸
Green Planet (106)	NZ ❶
Tis-Fris (121)	JP ❶

CCR central canal ring **CRW** canal ring west **DP** de pijp **J** jordaan **JP** jodenbuurt & plantage **LP** leidseplein **MV** museumplein & vondelpark **NZ** nieuwe zijd **OW** oud-west **OZ** oude zijd **RLD** red light district **RP** rembrandtplein **SQ** shipping quarter (scheepvaartbuurt) **WO** westerpark & oud-west

BY NEIGHBORHOOD

OUDE ZIJD

There's plenty of food in the Oude Zijd, but most options are less than tempting. Run-of-the-mill shawarma huts clutter the Red Light District's Warmoesstraat, but they don't exactly provide fine—or even decent—budget dining. Head over to Nieuwmarkt's Chinatown has excellent Asian fare in all price ranges. see map p. 344

⚑ **In de Waag,** Nieuwmarkt. See p. 107.

Aneka Rasa, Warmoesstraat 25-29 (☎626 15 60). A beacon of elegance amidst the seediness of the Red Light District, this Indonesian restaurant will let you and a friend chow down on a huge helping of *rijsttafel* for €16.50-26.80 per person. Other main dishes, like the popular beef in spicy coconut sauce, satisfy the palette (€11-13); plenty of tasteful vegetarian plates as well (€8). Open daily 5-10:30pm. AmEx/MC/V. ❹

Theehuis Himalaya, Warmoesstraat 56 (☎626 08 99; www.himalaya.nl). Though it appears to be just a New Age book shop, the back room houses a Buddhist-themed *theehuis,* serving light vegetarian and vegan lunches. With 40 varieties of tea, the shop provides peaceful respite from the lurid grit of Warmoesstraat. Tasty *tostis* (€3-3.50), and pies (€3-3.25). Open M 1-6pm, Tu-W and F-Sa 10am-6pm, Th 10am-8:30pm, Su 12:30-5pm. AmEx/MC/V. ❶

New Season, Warmoesstraat 39 (☎625 61 25). There is no shortage of choices at this pan-Asian, family-style, sit-down eatery. Menu includes Cantonese, Szechuan, Thai, and Malaysian dishes. Main courses on the extensive menu around €7-10. Vegetarian plates €5-6. Try the sizzling Teppan meals for €16-18.60. Open Tu-Su 3-11pm. AmEx/MC/V. ❷

Hoi Tin, Zeedijk 122-124 (☎625 64 51). Remarkably authentic dim sum (11am-5pm) and dinner meals await at this slightly upscale local favorite in Chinatown. Most meat dishes €9.50-11. Egg and vegetable dishes €8-14.50. Dim sum €2.25-3.75. Vegetarian options (€8-14.50), but you have to scour the menu for them. Open daily 11am-11pm. Cash only. ❸

Taste of Culture, Zeedijk 109 (☎638 14 66). It's easy to imagine that many an eating contest has been inspired by Taste of Culture's tempting offer: all you can eat for 1hr., €7.50. Start with the dim sum (dumplings, eggrolls) and then move on to heartier dishes (chicken drumsticks, egg-fried rice). Plenty of vegetarian options. Open M-W noon-11pm, Th-Su until midnight. Another location at Rokin 152 (☎638 12 49). Cash only. ❶

tasty treats

Here is a guide to the delectable sweet delights that you can sample during your trip:

Drop: Dark licorice has never been so popular. This is the candy to suck on in Amsterdam, created from a type of licorice found only in the city.

Haagse hopjes: These coffee-flavored caramels come in a quaint tin container; you won't be able to eat just one.

Stroopwafels: There's no resisting this cookie comprised of honey and sugar syrup stuffed sinfully between two thin layers of battered waffles.

Poffertjes: Take a bite of pure heaven with these mini-pancakes drizzled with melted butter and doused with a layer of powdered confectioner's sugar.

Limburgase Vlaai (Flan): A tempting alternative to just another pastry, these cakes are made from yeast dough and filled with fruit or creamy rice.

Boterkoek: A buttery biscuit that melts on your tongue while you're drinking your morning coffee.

Suikerbrood: A plump breakfast bread speckled with granular sugar and sweet spices.

Speculaas: A spiced biscuit that the Dutch lay out for Sinterklaas (St. Nicholas) on Christmas Eve—a more luxurious ginger bread.

Sea Palace, Oosterdokskade 8 (☎626 47 77). Though the restaurant itself—a gargantuan floating palace in gaudy pagoda style—may be the initial attraction, the edibles will certainly not disappoint. The Odyssey-length menu offers Chinese, Cantonese, and Indonesian 2-4 person meals (€27-40). The 3-course Peking duck meal (€57) is a treat. Open daily noon-4pm, 6pm-midnight. Kitchen closes 11pm. AmEx/MC/V. ❺

NIEUWE ZIJD

see map p. 344

🏠 **Pannenkoekenhuis Upstairs,** Grimburgwal 2 (☎626 56 03). A 2min. walk from the Rokin tram stop. This tiny nook caters to the creative traveler: with vintage photos of Dutch royalty, only 6 tables, and antique teapots hanging from the ceiling, Upstairs is an experience—and that's what you're paying for. The traditional pancakes are said to be among the better in Amsterdam, but running up to €9 apiece, they don't accommodate slimmer budgets; if you bring an old teapot as an offering, you'll get a free powdered-sugar pancake. Take the ultimate lunchtime plunge with the Miranda (pear, egg nog, chocolate sauce, and whipped cream; €7.90). Open M-F noon-7pm, Sa noon-6pm, Su noon-5pm. ❶

🏠 **Ristorante Caprese,** Spuistraat 259-261 (☎620 00 59). From Dam, follow Spuistraat south a few blocks. Authentic Italian food, relaxed jazz, peach-colored walls, and comforting candlelight. The chef's handmade pastas, homemade tomato sauce, and the restaurant's inexpensive wine (glass of montepulciano €2.50) make Ristorante Caprese an excellent dinner spot. Try the sumptuous penne arrabbiata (€8.50). Open daily 5-10:45pm. No reservations. ❸

Foodism, Oude Leliestraat 8 (☎427 51 03). From Dam, walk up Raadhuisstraat, turn right at Singel, and the restaurant is between Singel and Herengracht on your left. With swanky green- and-violet decor, this small restaurant serves sandwiches like chicken mango (from €4), soups and salads (from €3.50), and pasta dishes (from €8; try "pinky"—tagliatelle, salmon, and creamy pesto sauce) on a lovely canal-side street. Vegetarian options (sun-dried tomato, avocado, red onion, and alfalfa sandwich €4.50). Open Su-Th 11am-10pm, F-Sa 11:30am-11pm. ❷

Green Planet, Spuistraat 122 (☎625 82 80; www.greenplanet.nl). This hot new die-hard vegetarian restaurant may advertise itself as "more than a restaurant, a lifestyle"—but after one sip of the Thai-style pumpkin cream soup with coconut milk, lemongrass, and ginger (€5.50) or the sweet-potato dumpling with spinach, ricotta, and cashews (€13), you won't think that this lifestyle is quite so corny. Organic wines and beers from €2.50. The only restaurant in The Netherlands to use bio-degradable packaging for takeout. Open M-Sa 11am-11pm. ❷

Sie Joe, Gravenstraat 24 (☎624 18 30). Between Nieuwendijk and Nieuwenzijds Voorburgwal, behind Nieuwe Kerk. Pronounced "see you": a phonetic transcription into Dutch of the owners' hopes that you'll be back again for more; at this warm, family-run hole-in-the-wall, you probably will. Sie Joe serves up great Indonesian lunch and dinner at good prices, especially compared with nearby Indonesian stops. In this cozy *lunchcafe*, vegetarians should sample the delectable *gado gado* (mixed vegetables in peanut sauce; €6). *Tjendol* is a delicate drink made of soft green noodles, palm sugar, coconut milk, and crushed ice (€3). Lamb and chicken *satay* €6. Open M-W, F-Sa 11am-7pm; Th 11am-8pm. ❶

La Fruteria, Nieuwezijds Voorburgwal 141 (☎623 29 17), north of Dam against Nieuwe Kerk. A colorful little store selling fruit shakes and juices made with the freshest produce. Mix and match your own combo of three juiceables. Small €2.40; medium €2.90; large €3.50. Yogurt with granola €2.40-3.50. Host of sandwiches (€3-3.60) on fresh-baked bread: dig into the artichoke salad sandwich or the vegetarian sandwich with tomato, grilled zucchini, and cucumber (both €3.60). Open M-Sa 10am-6pm, Su 11am-6pm. ❶

Mister Coco's, Nieuwendijk 11 (☎623 62 60; www.mrcocos.com). From Centraal, turn right at the main street, left at Martelaarsgracht, and right onto Nieuwendijk. Mr. Coco is the guy on the sign outside— a bald, drunk, ugly clown promising "lousy food and warm beer" to a carnivorous crowd, thankful for his sense of irony. Although a big English hangout and in the middle of the Nieuwe Zijd's most hideously touristed shopping street, Mr. Coco's serves up some of Amsterdam's tastiest ribs (all-you-can-eat €13). 2 floors get crazy on weekend nights, especially when there's a football game on the big-screen TV. Massive burgers advertised as the "world's biggest" and slathered with toppings €6.30-11.25. All-day English breakfast €6.95. Open Su-Th 11am-1am, F-Sa 11am-3am. AmEx/MC/V. ❸

Tasty and Healthy, Korte Lijnbaansteeg 4-6 (☎320 19 34). Between Nieuwezijds Voorburgwal and Spuistraat, north of Dam. Snug spot off a small side street vends fresh fruit juices (€2.50-3.50) and light snacks. Sandwiches €1.60-2.85. Try the more exotic fruit shakes: the energizing "atomic" is an explosive cloud of dates, organic yogurt, muesli, banana, kiwi, ginseng, mango, bee pollen, and vitamins (€3.40-4.55). The owner, a nutrition whiz, may recommend some wheatgrass juice for €3, a little cheaper and less compromising than the city's other "grass" beverages. Open daily 7:30am-7pm. ❶

the BIG $plurge

in de waag

Dine in medieval elegance when you step into the magnificent castle that stands formidably at the center of Nieuwmarkt. ▨ **In de Waag,** is a pleasurable culinary experience in the stately antiquity of Amsterdam's oldest secular structure. In 1488, the building served as the eastern gate into the city and later served as a public weighing house, history museum, and medical amphitheater—Rembrandt's *The Anatomy Lesson of Dr. Tulp* was painted here during one such medical session.

Today you'll find nothing but richly-flavored cuisine. The basic lunch menu has sandwiches and salads (€4-8.50) while dinners at In de Waag are Italian, French, or Norwegian specialties served under the 250 candles hanging from the ceiling. The casually hip patrons pack between the stone walls and delight in a satisfying menu that changes every three months; the filet mignon (€23.50) is one exceptional item that stays true to customers throughout the entire year. If you're so inclined, bring your laptop to surf the wireless Internet while you dine, but doing so just seems so uncouth amid such perfect, antiquated elegance.

(Nieuwmarkt 4. ☎452 77 72; www.indewaag.nl. Open Su-Th 10am-midnight, F-Sa 10am-1am; often open until 3am on busy evening. ❹)

the hidden deal

the wonderful mensch of maoz

During Hanukkah, the Jewish festival of lights, a day's worth of oil lasted eight full days; at ◼ **Maoz Falafel,** hungry travellers can make their sandwiches last nearly as long. Owned by two Israeli brothers, Maoz is an Amsterdam-based chain known for its endlessly replenishing salad bar, fresh handmade falafel, and incomparably low prices. A small falafel costs €2.50, and with the right technique, you can make it your daily meal. Ordering any falafel gives you access to the all-you-can-stack salad bar. Pile up a Middle Eeaster Dagwood of couscous, carrots, tomatoes, spicy onions, beets, peppers, and tahini—and don't be shy about going back for seconds. Expert stackers say the secret is leaving the pita intact: that way there's room for the second trip.

The original, 13-year-old shop is a hole-in-the-wall at Regulierbreestr. 45 (☎624 92 90), but the other Amsterdam spots are just as good: outside Centraal Station (☎623 07 93); Muntplein 1 (☎420 74 35); Leidsestr. 85 (☎427 97 20); Ferdinand Bolstr. 67; and 1e v/d Helststr. 43 (☎676 76 12); www.maozfalafel.nl. Open daily at least 11am-11pm; hours vary by location. ❶

La Place, Kalverstraat 201 (☎622 01 71). From the Muntplein tram stop, take Kalverstraat northwest; the restaurant is on your right. In the Vroom and Dreesmann department store, with another entrance on Kalverstraat. Don't expect culinary advice from the security guards at the door: at this upscale cafeteria, they're there to protect the merchandise, not to serve you. Sumptuous market-style buffet boasting fresh fruit bowls (€2.80-3.49), soup (€3.79), panini sandwiches (from €2.29), and rotating main dishes (€6-10). Menu and prices change with the season. Open M-W, F-Su 9am-8pm; Th 9am-9pm. MC/V. ❷

Old Highlander, St. Jacobstraat 8 (☎420 83 21). From Dam, take Nieuwezijds Voorburgwal northeast about 300m; St. Jacobstraat is on your right. Old Highlander is a compelling contradiction: waiters wear kilts at this Scottish-owned, American-style restaurant where the kitsch cool of an indoor waterfall and wooden bridge crossing a faux river compete for visual attention with compelling abstract paintings. No blood pudding, but indulge in high tea with scones, clotted cream, and sandwiches (€14). If that highland style is too steep, try a healthy breakfast (€8), homemade soups (€4), sandwiches (from €6.50), and salads (€5-8). Children's portions and takeout available. Open daily 9am-10pm; kitchen closes at 9pm. ❷

Usama, Spuistraat 50 (☎422 64 94), a few blocks from Centraal on Spuistraat. This tiny takeout spot serves up big portions of Surinamese, Pakistani, Indian, and Afghan chow for cheap, even if the "dining room" is actually a mom-and-pop convenience store. Curry, *roti, nasi,* and more, almost entirely under €9; most dishes around €7. Tasty *tandoori* chicken €8.25. Open daily noon-1am. ❷

see map p. 342

SCHEEPVAART BUURT

To get to the Scheepvaartbuurt's plentiful restaurants and bars from Centraal Station, turn right on Prins Hendrikkade, then left and then an immediate right onto Nieuwendijk, which turns into Haarlemmerstraat as it crosses the Singel. Haarlemmerstr. turns into Haarlemmerdijk at Korte Prinsengracht. Alternatively, head north on Prinsengracht, which intersects the street two blocks past the Brouwersgracht.

◼ **Harlem: Drinks and Soulfood,** Haarlemmerstraat 77 (☎330 14 98), at the Herenmarkt. Spelled with a single "a," Harlem's high-class fusion cuisine blends American-style soul food, like catfish and macaroni, with Cajun and Caribbean flavors. Rotating dinner menu boasts about 10 creatively prepared and generously proportioned dishes, each with a large helping of delicious vegetables and rice (€12-17). Lighter lunch includes creamy peanut soup (€4.75), sandwiches (€4-5) like Franky's Goat to Hollywood (goat cheese, peach, and pine nuts; €4.30), as well as unique salad selections such as Marvin's Gay (€8.35). Inside at the bar, relax to cool jazz and chat with the lively folk who pour drinks; alternatively, head outside to the patio for a prime view of Haarlemmerstraat. Especially packed Th night. Open M-Th 10am-1am, F-Sa 10am-3am, Su 11am-1am. Kitchen closes 10pm. MC/V. ❸

🏷 **De Belhamel,** Brouwersgracht 60, See right.

Padi, Haarlemmerdijk 50 (☎625 12 80). Locals rave about this Indonesian *eethuis*, lined with Indonesian fans and rustic wood decor. Appetizers are cheap (*loempia*, spring rolls, only €2), but the best is *pangsit goreg* (fresh shrimp in a paper-thin edible wrapper; €4). Entrees like *rendang* (€8) or *ikan rica* (€7.25) will fire up your palette, while *lontong opor* (coconut-simmered chicken; €7.50) will cool it down. Vegetarian options include the variation on *gado gado*, a dinner salad with spicy dressing and hard-boiled egg (€5.25). Open daily 5-10pm. Cash only. ❷

Balraj, Haarlemmerdijk 28 (☎625 14 28). First-rate North Indian and Punjabi cuisine in a narrow space that's usually jammed with locals. The prices are not always budget, but if you're in the mood for something hot enough to fry your taste buds, try the chicken *madras* (€10.75). The lamb *jai puri* is considerably mellower, but still tasty (€11.75). *Biryani* dishes—both lamb and chicken—are aromatic, simmered with cardamom and coconut and served with sides of curd and lentils (€9.75-10.75). Vegetarian dishes are less expensive: *saag paneer* and *alu mattar* each €9.75. Open daily 4-10pm. Cash only. ❷

Jay's Juice, Haarlemmerstraat 14 (☎623 12 67). Jay, the self-proclaimed "King of Juice," presides over this den of good vibes where everything, as Jay says, "comes from the heart." The small interior feels large thanks to colorful island-themed murals, and the juice is made from only of the freshest fruits and vegetables. "Jay's Booster" features tomato, ginger, carrot, and celery; you can add ginseng, guarana, or even "hornygoat grass" (10mg of herbal Viagra) if you're in the mood—or would like to be (each €0.50). Homemade vegetarian soups available in winter (€4.75). Buy 10 juices and get 1 free. Juices available in 0.3L (€2.30-3.55), 0.5L (€3.10-4.60), or 1L (€5.50-8.20) bottles. In summer noon-1pm buy-2- get-3 special. Open daily 8am-7pm. Cash only. ❶

Rendez-Vous en Afrique, Haarlemmerdijk 108 (☎620 33 25). Follow the zebra-print doorway into this small Cameroonian restaurant that serves up mild Central-Western African cuisine like *heri-heri*,

the BIG $plurge

de belhamel

This century-old Art-Nouveau cafe in the Shipping Quarter may just have the most lovely and intimate canal-side view of any restaurant in Amsterdam. At the intersection of Brouwersgracht and Herengracht, 🏷 **De Belhamel's** interior matches the outdoor scenery, with burnished walls that glow with velvety light as dusk descends. The menu, portions of which change every three months, serves up creative Franco-Dutch and Italian-Dutch cuisine. For a splurge, try one dish that has long been the restaurant's staple: the classic "beef Belhamel" (€20; min. of 2 persons) with Chinese spinach, oysters, mushrooms, and tarragon sauce. The service is excellent—no wonder Amsterdam epicures frequently patronize De Belhamel—so come in attire to match the beautifully-appointed surroundings. An intimate bar downstairs makes an ideal spot for a truly elegant *aperitif* before dinner or a dessert wine after the meal. Appetizers run €8-11, mains around €20, and decadent desserts €8.50. Reservations obligatory: call after 4pm.

(*Brouwersgracht 60*. ☎*622 10 95; www.belhamel.nl. Open M-Th 6-10pm, F-Sa 6-10:30pm. AmEx/MC/V.* ❺*)*

salted codfish with boiled cassava, plantains, and yams (€11.10), in addition to more far-out options like crocodile tail (€17.45) or ostrich with banana chips (€16.55). Sandwiches are cheaper (spicy lamb sausage €2.30). Delicious banana-flavored Mongozo beer (€3.50) alone makes the restaurant worth a visit. Service is friendly, but slow, so be prepared to come early. Open 5:30-11pm. Cash only. ❶-❷

Jordino, Harlemmerdijk 25 (☎420 32 25). This choc-olateria serves decadent, delectable confections. Ice cream and *gelato* (1 scoop €1; each additional scoop €0.50) made with seasonal ingredients. The real draw is the finely wrought handmade chocolate (100g bag €3.50). Open Su-M 1-7pm, Tu-Sa 10am-7pm. ❶

Carousel Pancake House

Noordermarkt Sausage

Sea Palace

CANAL RING WEST

see map p. 342

⬚ **Lunchcafe Nielson,** Beren-straat 19 (☎330 60 06). An extra bright ray of light in an already shining neighborhood. Breakfast and lunch served all day. Dig into french toast or eggs (€4). For a slightly heavier dish, try the Belgian waffles (€5.25) or hefty omelets (€6). Salads from €8. Open Tu-F 8am-5pm (4pm in warm weather), Sa 8am-6pm, Su 9am-5pm; kitchen closes 30min. before restaurant. ❶

⬚ **Restaurant de Bolhoed,** Prinsengracht 60-62 (☎626 18 03). A popular vegetarian and vegan spot adorned with stained glass lamps and wild plant life. 90% of the dishes are made with purely natural ingredients but include the flavor and cre-ativity that many organic meals lack. A different vegan meal, complete with grains, proteins, and beans, offered each day (€13). Juices squeezed on the spot and fresh homemade pasta. Fancy vegan cakes (€3.05 per slice) complete a refreshingly healthy meal. Dinner menu starts at 5pm. Open M-F, Su noon-10pm; Sa 11am-10pm. Cash only. ❸

Wolvenstraat 23, Wolvenstraat 23 (☎320 08 43). Unmarked except by its address, this trendy stop is no ordinary restaurant. A cushioned, lime green lounge welcomes visitors, giving way to an orange and green interior decorated with velvet pillows, candles, and fur-covered stairs. Lunch here means sandwiches (€2-5.20), salads (€6), and omelets (€3-4). Can-tonese chefs take the helm for the dinner's strictly Chinese cuisine. Popular with young professionals Sa-Su and daily after 10pm. Lunch menu 8am-3:30pm, dinner 6-10:30pm. Open M-Th 8am-1am, F 8am-2am, Sa 9am-2am, Su 10am-1am. Cash only. ❷

Top Thai, Herenstraat 22 (☎623 46 33; www.topthai.nl), serves traditional Thai cuisine under Asian sunshades that cover the ceiling. Sample pad thai variations (€10) and entrees like the Flying Chicken or Thai Hot Beef (€14.50), or try the eclectic Top Thai Pearls, a sampler of the restaurant's appetizers (€7). Open daily 4:30-10:30pm. MC/V. ❷

Ruhe Delicatessen, Prinsenstraat 13 (☎ 626 74 38). A thrilling stop for the busy budget traveler. Quality, but reasonably priced meats, breads, cheese, wine, fruit, pies, bon-bons, vegetables, and snacks pack the shelves at very reasonable prices. No tables here, just browse this smallish supermarket or ask the friendly staff to cut off pieces of salami or brie. Make yourself a full meal for under €5, or buy a packaged dish for €6-9. Open daily noon-10pm. Cash only. ❶

Currant Boats

Dimitri's, Prinsenstraat 3 (☎ 627 93 93). It's rare to find a place in Amsterdam that serves all 3 meals, especially as good as Dimitri's. Breakfast (8am-noon) sticks to the basics. Lunch (noon-5pm) branches out to substantial sandwiches (€4-6) and *crostinis* (€3.50-4.50) that are just as tasty. Dinner (5-10pm) blooms with huge salads, burgers, fajitas (€10), and pasta dishes (most under €11). Customers swear by his egg sandwich (€5.25). No reservations. Open M-Sa 8am-10pm, Su 9am-10pm. Cash only. ❷

Hein, Berenstraat 20 (☎ 623 10 48). It's a one-woman show at this relaxed neighborhood lunchery with an open kitchen. Everything is homemade by Hein herself with the freshest ingredients. Lunch menu includes soups, crepes, and *croques monsieurs*. Snacks and sandwiches €2-18. Open daily 9am-6pm. Kitchen closes 3pm. Cash only. ❶

Slicing Edam Cheese

Bakkerij Paul Année, Runstraat 25 (☎ 623 53 22). Super-cheap baked goods just begging to be taken home. Savory cookies, bread, and tarts are most fresh early in the day. Don't miss the *appeltas*, baked apples with nuts wrapped up in a pastry puff of goodness, the best in the city (€1.30). Open M-F 9am-6pm, Sat 9am-5pm. Cash only. ❶

Prego, Herenstraat 25 (☎ 638 01 48). If you want great Italian food served in understated elegance, save up to visit Prego, between Herengracht and Keizersgracht. Known for its fresh meats and fish, this classy local offers a special brochette of sole and prawn (€21.50); other mains around €10. Ask genial waiters for a wine recommendation from their huge selection. A well-deserved break from the shawarma huts and sandwich shops. Open daily 6-10pm. ❺

Spanjer en Van Twist, Leliegracht 60 (☎ 639 01 09). This cafe-restaurant is ideal for a leisurely meal or mid-day drink, with summertime canal seating. For lunch, sandwiches, salads, and pasta run €4-7. At dinner, satisfying entrees like the Thai Chicken Salad around €12. No reservations, so the wait can be up to 1½hr., especially 7-9pm. Open daily 10am-1am. Lunch served M-F until 4pm, dinner 6-11pm. Sa-Su lunch until 5pm, dinner 5-11pm. MC/V. ❸

Afternoon Coffeebreak

the BIG
$plurge

retro refreshment

Amsterdam is full of campy chic, as any number of 70s-style hostels and hippie holdovers will attest. But no one does retro irony quite as elegantly as ★**Kitsch,** which will simultaneously satisfy your cravings for TV's *Charlie's Angels* and inventive fusion cuisine. With padded blue walls, plush red booths, chandeliers, and a cute hipster crowd, the 70s and 80s never looked this good. Customers refill their own water at personal silver faucets at every table. While you wait for your meal (entrees €16-25), crane your neck toward the gold-framed TV, which has a nonstop feed of movies rife with shag carpeting and tacky teased haircuts.

Stand-out cuisine includes Thai and French selections; "Pussy & Potatoes," an inexplicably named kitsch "special," features 16 oysters with fries and salad (€15). The house special dessert drink, *sgropino* (lemon ice cream, vodka, and champagne, with mint and fresh raspberry; €5.75) will cleanse your palate in time for dessert. Tell them it's your birthday and they'll bring you ice cream with a pink layer-cake that jiggles and dances. Go straight for the sorbet and skip the cake--it's plastic.

(Utrechtsestraat 42. ☎625 92 51; www.restaurant-kitsch.nl. Open M-Th 6pm-1am, F-Sa 6pm-3am. ❹)

Het Molenpad, Prinsengracht 653 (☎625 96 80). The Dutch word *Gezelligheid* (coziness) was created to describe eateries like this. Escape from the bustle take your meal to the wooden benches out back. In mid-summer, locals fill up the canal-side seats in front, and in winter, they gather at the inviting bar of this traditional *bruin cafe.* Usual *eetcafe* offerings (soup €4.75; entrees €13-16; dessert €6) go well with a *vaasje* of beer (€1.90). Lunch served until 4pm (sandwiches €4-5; salad €8-14). Dutch snacks like *bitterballen* (€3.40) available 3-10:30pm. Open Su-Th noon-1am, F-Sa noon-2am. Cash only. ❷

Cafe de Pels, Huidenstraat 25 (☎622 90 37). A no-frills neighborhood hangout popular with the after-work crowd, especially for drinks, coffee, and sandwiches. This is the lone place that makes good use of the *amsterdammertjes* (3-foot poles that separate the sidewalks from the roads) by putting table tops on them for outdoor seating. Bar snacks and *broodjes* (sandwiches) €2-2.60. Same menu for lunch and dinner 6 days a week, excluding Su brunch served 11am-2pm (€3.75-8.50). Open M-Th 10am-1am, F-Sa 10am-3am, Su 11am-1am. ❶

Vennington, Prinsenstraat 2 (☎625 93 98). If you venture into this popular sandwich shop during the lunch hours, you won't be able to find a table. But the club sandwich creations (under €6) are filling, and the fruit shakes (under €4) are perfect for warm days. Breakfast (€3.65-9) served until 11am. Open M-Sa 7:30am-5pm, Su 8am-5pm. AmEx/MC/V. ❶

Koh-i-noor, Westermarkt 29 (☎623 31 33). Offering a taste of traditional culture with authentic music and vibrant paintings and tapestries, it serves an endless variety of Indian delicacies. Try the chicken *tikka tandoori* or the fish *dhansak* (€13.50) while digesting cultural facts from the informative placemat. Open daily 5-11:30pm. ❸

see map p. 340

CENTRAL CANAL RING

★ **Kitsch,** Utrechtsestraat 42. See **The Big Splurge: Retro Refreshment,** at left.

★ **Lanskroon,** Singel 385 (☎623 77 43), at the Spui. Locals have been getting their fix of traditional Dutch pastries at this famed *banketbakkerij,* reputed to be the best in Amsterdam, since 1908. *Koningsstroopwafels* (honey-filled cookies; €1.35) and other delights are still made on site, as is the impressive range of sorbets. Open Tu-F 8am-5:30pm, Sa 8am-5pm, Su 10am-5pm. Cash only. ❶

Coffee and Jazz, Utrechtsestraat 113 (☎624 58 51). Local regulars swear that this is the best coffee in town. Here among the bamboo furniture and smooth jazz, the Dutch-Indonesian fusion seems only natural. Sweet, fruity *pannenkoeken* (€4.50-7) share the menu with tender lamb and chicken *satay* (€7-9). At dinner time only Indonesian food is served: chicken, lamb and beef dishes around €15. Delectable fruit shakes (€4.50 combine mango, banana, and orange—big enough for 2. If the sun is shining, call ahead and reserve the loveseat table out front—it's a prime people-watching spot. Open Tu-F 9:30am-8pm, Sa 10am-4pm. ❷

NOA, Leidsegracht 84 (☎626 08 02; www.withnoa.com), just outside the Leidseplein hype. In a sea of middling eateries, NOA distinguishes itself as much for its elegant design as for its pan-Asian dishes. Urbane gourmands sink into plush sofa seats, with their pad thai (€12) and salads (€13). Get your cocktail fix here—they make great *caipirinhas*, apple martinis, and *mojitos* (€7-9). AmEx/MC/V. ❹

Golden Temple, Utrechtsestraat 126 (☎626 85 60), between Frederiksplein and Prinsengracht. Even committed carnivores can find something to love at the Temple, which features food from around the globe in entirely vegetarian and mostly organic renditions. Try the filling but not overly rich Indian *thali* which allows you to mix and match a meal from various regional delicacies (€12.50). Pizza €6.50-9.50. Vegan ice cream €2.25. Open daily 5-9:30pm. AmEx/MC/V. ❸

Axum, Utrechtsedwarsstraat 85-87 (☎622 83 89). Tram #4 to Frederiksplein, go north on Utrechtsestraat for a block, then turn right on Utrechtsedwarsstraat. Homey, family-run eatery serves great Ethiopian fare. No silverware here; use your hands to scoop up your food with tart *injera*. Entrees (€12) come steaming in pots and include sides of lentils, salad, and veggies. Highlights are *yebeg wot* (zesty lamb; €11) and *doro wot* (tangy chicken; €9.75). Plenty of veggie options, including the excellent *shiro wot* (fried chickpeas in Ethiopian herbs; €8.75). Open M-F 5:30-11pm, Sa-Su 5:30-11:30pm. ❷

Tashi Deleg, Utrechtsestraat 65 (☎620 66 24). Savor traditional Tibetan cooking at this mellow *eetcafe* under Tibetan tapestries and a shrine to the Dalai Lama. *Momos* make for a rich appetizer (steamed dumplings with beef; €5.50). Main courses range from the spicy Himalaya *sha latsa* (beef €11) to *Tse Nezom*, mixed vegetables lightly sauteed with herbs and bamboo (€9.50). Menus for 2 will satiate with 3-course meals (€18, vegetarian €17, €20.50 for more extensive choice) and pack in the most Deleg delight for your buck. Balance the meal with piquant *Tib Chang*, Tibetan rice beer (€1.75), or their speciality, buttered tea. Open Tu-Su 3-11:30pm. V. ❹

Carousel Pancake House, Weteringcircuit 1 (☎625 80 02). Tram #6, 7, 16, 24, or 25 to Weteringcircuit. It all comes full circle at this donut-shaped *eethuis* surrounding a small, old-fashioned immobile merry-go-round, where delectable pancakes are the main feature. Somewhat touristy with non-existent atmosphere, but the location in the greenery of Weteringcircuit is ideal when weather permits eating at the abundant outdoor seating. The *pannenkoeken*—buttery, warm, flaky—come in full-plate size or in little silver dollars *(poffertjes)* with countless varieties of toppings from fruit to bacon to cheese (€3-7.50). Divine apple *pannekoek* is liberally dusted with powdered sugar (€4.75). Open daily 10am-8:30pm. Cash only. ❶

LEIDSEPLEIN

🖼 **Eat at Jo's,** Marnixstraat 409 (☎624 17 77; www.melkweg.nl), inside Melkweg. Tram #1, 2, 5, 6, 7 or 10 to Leidseplein and then turn down the smaller side street to the left of the grand Stadsschouwberg theater. Chicago-born chef Mary Jo first came to the Melkweg when her musician husband played there; today she feeds musicians, hipsters and tired old ladies alike with a multi-ethnic, freshly-prepared menu

see map p. 341

that changes daily. You can't do better in this enclave of cool just outside of Leidseplein. Soups (€3.40) and numerous vegetarian options (entrees €10) earn raves. Open W-Su noon-9pm. Cash only. ❶

Bojo, Lange Leidsedwarsstraat 51 (☎622 74 34). On a street beset with touristy food dives of every stripe, Bojo is a culinary stalwart. At this popular Indonesian eatery, Javanese chow is the real star. You can't go wrong with the tender savory lamb or chicken *satay* smothered in

the local story

christmas twins

Just over 70 years old and sporting a white Mohawk haircut, **Gary Christmas** is one of Amsterdam's most beloved expats. With his now-deceased twin brother Greg, the American-born Gary once graced stages around the world for decades as the Christmas Twins. Today having adopted Amsterdam as his home, Gary maintains a circle of friends of every age and proclivity, and claims to have the keys to the apartment of just about everybody in his neighborhood near Rembrandtplein. He can be found in his store on Utrechtsestraat—sometimes called Twins, sometimes called Backstage—selling his collection of hats and dresses, which he crochets himself, despite having only nine fingers. You can grab some food here, named with characteristic Christmas twin flair—the vegetarian Dirty Gertie sandwich, or the Gang Bang sandwich ("meat, meat and more meat."). But don't miss talking to Gary himself, the true attraction here.

On his showbiz past: Christmas is our real name. And I was born on New Year's Eve, right before 12. And my mother kept her pace, and at five after 12, my brother came. So I was born in the old year and my brother was born in the New Year. And Mary Christmas, my mother, had twins on New Year's...

continued on next page

peanut sauce (€5.75-7.50). House fave *Ayam Banjar* features chicken in a sweet and spicy sauce (€10.75). If the choices simply overwhelm, just grab the mini *rijsttafel* with a sampling of Indonesian specialities piled onto one plate (€10.50). Lychees make for a great dessert (€2). Open M-Th 4pm-2am, F 4pm-4am, Sa noon-4am, Su noon-2am. MC/V. ❸

Santa Lucia, Leidsekruisstraat 20-22 (☎623 46 39). Great pizza in a city where decent slices are hard to come by. Corner location puts you just off Leidseplein. Hot pies bubbling with cheese (€5) and toppings (mushroom €6.75; pepperoni €7.75). Gooey lasagna €8.50. Open daily noon-11pm. MC/V. ❶

Wagamama, Max Euweplein 10 (☎528 77 78; www.wagamama.com). This London import is somewhat of a cultural phenomenon: sleek, minimalist decor, masses of scrubbed, mostly youthful hipsters crowd long, cafeteria-style tables to slurp Japanese noodles. It's pristine, quick, and a great deal for these heaping entrees. Among the best are the *Yaki udon* (shiitake mushrooms, prawns, chicken, and Japanese fish sauce); and *Zasai gohen* (stir-fried chicken, shiitake, and veggies in a spicy sauce). Open M-Sa noon-11pm, Su noon-10pm. AmEx/DC/MC/V. ❸

De Smoeshaan, Leidsekade 90 (☎625 03 68; www.desmoeshaan.nl). De Smoeshaan is a cozy *eet-cafe* with real Dutch flavor just off the main drag. Sample a drink (beer €2; wine €2.60-3) or light snack (*tostis* €1.30; *bitterballen* €3) on the patio and watch canal life drift by or in the cozy wooden room under the theater, plastered with posters from past shows. The kitchen closes at 9pm; the late night bar is mellow enough to have a chat with friends or even an intimate *tête-à-tête*. Open Su-Th 11am-1am, F-Sa 11am-3am. AmEx/MC/V. ❶

Bombay Inn, Lange Leidsedwarsstraat 46 (☎624 17 84). Among the constellation of Indian restaurants that dot this part of the Leidseplein, Bombay Inn stands out for delicately spiced dishes at excellent value. The choice for budget travelers is clear: just ask for the generous "tourist menu" and gorge on 3 courses: *papadum* and soup; chicken or lamb curry, mixed rice, and salad; and coffee or dessert (€8.50 for chicken; €9.50 for lamb; also available for 2). Meatless eats such as *alu palaak* and *saag paneer* come cheap as well (€5). Don't expect any extras, like rice unless you're willing to pay (€2.25). Open daily 3-11pm. AmEx/MC/V. ❷

Tapas de Kelderhof, Lange Leidsedwarsstraat 53-59 (☎622 0682; www.kelderhof.nl). Classier than the dozens of restaurants lining this street, Kelderhof has an extensive *tapas* menu served on the terrace or in the glowing interior. Try their homemade sangria (€11.35 per 0.50L). Tourist menu with samples of 10 different *tapas* €12.50. Open daily 5:30-11pm. ❷

REMBRANDT PLEIN

The Rembrandtplein area overflows with countless restaurants and pubs, but only a few of these offerings

see map p. 340

are worth a try, even with the promise of the area's prime people-watching. **Utrechtsestraat,** running south of Rembrandtplein from its southeasternmost corner, is where you will find the best restaurants here.

Maoz Falafel, Regulierbreestraat 45. See the box **The Hidden Deal: The Wonderful Mensch of Maoz,** on p. 108.

Rose's Cantina, Reguliersdwarsstraat 40 (☎625 97 97; www.rosescantina.com). Take a tram to Koningsplein or Muntplein. Rose's offers endless fun and fiesta amidst luscious greenery and elegant statues. The enormous restaurant, decorated with the tiles of a Mexican hacienda and strewn with pink roses, is always bustling. There's a quieter garden terrace in back for warmer nights, and the mood is always lively, accentuated by sultry salsa music. €13.60 gets you a choice of 2: quesadilla, enchilada, burrito, or taco, served with sides of rice, beans, and guacamole; 1 choice €11.20. Fajitas €16. Margaritas are small (€4.60) but quality and presentation take precedence: all cocktails €4.20-5; pitchers €27.90. Open M-F 5pm-midnight, Sa-Su 5pm-2am; kitchen open M-F 5:30pm-11pm, Sa-Su 5:30-11:30pm. AmEx/MC/V. ❸

La Margarita, Reguliersdwarsstraat 49 (☎623 07 07). La Margarita is a lighthearted Caribbean restaurant that serves creative meals native to the Islands. Peach walls, straw umbrellas, and vibrant greenery add an authentic touch to a dining experience accentuated by fun, rollicking music. Try unique tropical dishes such as marinated red snapper (€17.50); all mains (€15-20) include rice, beans, sweet potato, and tropical vegetables. Abundant vegetarian dishes (€15). Extensive cocktail menu (€5.30-5.90). Open Su-Th 5pm-1am, F-Sat 5pm-3am; kitchen open 5pm-11pm. AmEx/MC/V. ❹

Tomo Sushi, Reguliersdwarsstraat 131 (☎528 52 08; www.tomosushi.nl). Hip sushi joint with Jetsons-like furnishings. Style, when accompanying ultra-fresh fish, comes with a price: sushi and/or *sashimi* combos €15.50-27, most about €22. *Nigiri* (including scallop and yellowtail) €1.40-3.70; *maki* cucumber or pickle €3.70; salmon €5. Tempura €15.50. Cleanse your palette with green tea ice cream (€4). Reserve for dinner. Domestic beer €2.80; imported Japanese beer €3.50; warm sake €4.40. Open daily 5:30pm-11:30pm. AmEx/MC/V. ❺

continued from previous page

I don't want to sit here and say, 'Oh, we knew this one when we knew that one.' We knew Johnny Mathis, Ray Charles, Stevie Wonder—all those people we've known in our show business, you know? But I don't want to sit here and list people, because that sounds so egotripper. We've met friends in show business, okay? And we worked all around the world. But our biggest dream was to have a shop somewhere. So we came to Holland one day.

On Amsterdam: You're free here. There's no segregation. They're tolerant. You can be yourself. You can be whoever you want to. If you're a little clever, you can have a nice life here. And we have a nice life here, living over the shop, designing dresses and making clothes. Doing interviews and being in different magazines. Doing shows ourselves. We're doing a small film on the life of my brother and I [with Dutch filmmaker Hugo Metsers].

On his appearance in Dutch Playboy, surrounded by nude models: It was because I'm talented. No, really, I'm funny. And I like screwing around. How can I say it without sounding...people love me. I dress crazy. They always want to invite me to the party because I'm a good dancer...I'm a character who does a lot of things. I dress very weird. And when my brother was here, there where so many interviews with us where they said, "Well, finally we have some glamour in Holland." Because we wore gold. My brother wore headpieces. We gave Holland glamour. I don't mean to say there's no glamour here—but we gave it to them.

JORDAAN

It's worth heading out west to the Jordaan to for classy eats on an outdoor terrace. Cuisine here tends to be more discriminating than in the center, though not necessarily more expensive.

see maps p. 342

■ **Bolhoed,** Prinsengracht 60-62 (☎626 18 03). The best in vegetarian and vegan fare—fresh, flavorful, and lovingly prepared. The canal-side setting is sweet, but so is the chill pale-green interior. Besides a variety of pastas, casseroles, and Mexican dishes (€12.50-15), the key attractions here are the fresh-squeezed juices and the organic and vegan desserts made here daily, particularly the banana cream pie (€3.05). Imperative to make a reservation for dinner. Open Su-F 11am-10pm, last reservation 9pm. Cash only. ❸

■ **Cinema Paradiso,** Westerstraat 186 (☎623 73 44). Word of mouth has filled this cavernous former cinema with fans of its purist Italian food and candle-lit charm. *Antipasti* €4-10. *Bruchette* €5-7. *Pasta* €9-15. No reservations, so be prepared for a wait unless you arrive early. Open Tu-Su 6-11pm; kitchen closes 11pm. AmEx/MC/V. ❷

Manzano, Rozengracht 106 (☎624 57 52; www.manzano.nl). Glowing with golden light, this *tapas* retreat also oozes a homey, familial atmosphere. Inside, bottles from the wine bar's extensive cellar grace the walls while the terrace is a blithe venue for open-air eating. Dips and *tapas* €2.50-10; special *tapas* menus €18-27. Main dishes €10-20. Reservations for dinner advised, but not mandatory. Desserts €5-7.50. Open Tu-Su 5:30pm-midnight. Margaritas and sangria €5.50-6.50. AmEx/MC/V. ❹

Snackbar Aggie, 2e Goudsbloemdwarsstraat (☎774 79 61). Odds are you'll get the munchies once or twice while in Amsterdam, and if you're starving at 2am, there's no better place to go than here. Grab falafel, fries, or an ice-cream cone at this ideal late-night snack joint; nothing's more than around €3. Open Su-Th 11am-1am, F-Sa 11am-3am. ❶

Rakang, Elandsgracht 29 (☎627 50 12 or 620 95 51). For those who favor high design in their decor and tradition on their plate, Rakang offers upscale Thai dining. All meals are served family-style, in the center of the table. Appetizers €6-12. Main dishes €15-19; many fixed-price menu choices. Wine and *aperitifs* served in unique hand-blown glass goblets. Open daily 6-10:30pm. ❹

Ben Cohen Shawarma, Rozengracht 239 (☎627 97 21). Tram #10 to Rozengracht or 3, 14, or 17 to Marnixstraat. Nothing but bare-bones eating here. Open late and won't break the bank. Shawarma €3.50. Open daily 5pm-3am. ❶

De Vliegende Schotel, Nieuwe Leliestraat 162-168 (☎625 20 41; www.vliegendeschotel.com). From tempura to goulash, this casual vegetarian restaurant's diverse menu is ideal for a quick bite. Wide variety of organic salads, as well as some fish dishes (€7.50-€9.50). Open daily 4pm-11:30pm; kitchen closes 10:45pm. AmEx/MC/V. ❷

Broodje Mokum, Rozengracht 26 (☎623 19 66). No-frills, deli-style restaurant great for grabbing a fast sandwich with any number of meats and cheeses. Sandwiches around €2. Open M-F 6:30am-6pm, Sa 8am-5pm. Cash only. ❶

WESTERPARK & OUD-WEST

see map p. 346

■ **Cafe-Restaurant Amsterdam,** Watertorenplein 6 (☎682 26 67; www.cradam.nl). Worth the trek out to Van Hallstraat in Westerpark, the terminus of tram #10, this converted water pumping station has inherited wonderfully high ceilings and a minimalist charm from its industrial roots. Surprisingly casual and child-friendly, it's also got a crowd-pleasing menu of meat and fish choices (€9-15), as well as a few veggie dishes. The terrace is particularly enjoyable. Open M-Th 11am-midnight; F-Sa 11am-1am; kitchen closes M-Th 10:30pm. AmEx/MC/V. ❸

■ **De Avondmarkt,** De Wittenkade 94-96. See the box **The Hidden Deal: Midnight Munchies Madness,** at right.

Restaurant Wanka, Bosboom Toussaintstraat 70 (☎412 61 69). Tram #3 or 12 to Overtoom. This beautifully appointed restaurant serves "global" cuisine, justifying that label with a menu containing sashimi and falafel. Appetizers €5-7. *Tapas* menu €2-7.50. Main courses €11-16. Always 2 vegetarian items on menu. After dark, Wanka becomes a chic lounge serving cocktails; a DJ spins F 11pm-3am. Open Su-Th 6pm-1am, F-Sa 6pm-3am; kitchen closes M-Th 10pm, F-Sa 11pm. AmEx/MC/V. ❸

Zouk, 1e Constantijn Huygensstraat 45 (☎689 11 33). Tram #1 or 6 to 1e Constantijn Huygensstr. Like its sister Cafe de Pijp, Zouk doesn't take its own trendiness too seriously. Dinner of Thai, Mexican, or ribeye steak at this casual, stylish spot done up in red will run you €12-15. Beer €1.90; *caipirinha* €5. Open Su-Th noon-1am, F-Sa noon-3am. Cash only. ❹

Abyssinia Afrikaans Eet-cafe, Jan Pieter Heijestraat 190 (☎683 07 92). Tram #1 to Jan Pieter Heijestr. Ethiopian eatery (and Let's Go) encourages eating the *injera* (fermented pancake) with your hands but will provide forks on request. Most meals €8-10, including a wide selection of vegetarian options. Reservations suggested. Open daily 5pm-midnight. AmEx/DC/MC/V. ❷

Esoterica, Overtoom 409 (☎689 72 26). Tram #1 to Overtoomsesluis. Walk 3 blocks on Overtoom away from the canal (worth the walk). An eccentric, placid spot specializing in vegetarian and Indonesian cuisine. Chess tournaments every Su afternoon; if you're not a player, peruse one of the many English-language volumes on the bookshelves. Starters €2.40-5; main dishes €7.50-8.50. Indonesian rice table €12.50. Open W-Su 2-10pm. Cash only. ❷

Toussaint Cafe, Bosboom Toussaintstr. 26 (☎685 07 37). Tram #1 or 6 to 1e Constantijn Huygensstr., or tram #3 or 12 to Overtoom. Walk away from Overtoom 4 blocks on 1e Constantijn Huygensstr. and take a right on Bosboom Toussaintstr. Locals flock to this small restaurant and bar with sidewalk seating where they can sample *tapas* all day (combo plate €10.50). Ask about daily specials and quiche. Always vegetarian choices on the menu. Dinner entrees €10-13. Reservations for 3 or more strongly recommended. Open daily 10am-midnight. Cash only. ❸

Kismet, 350 Kinkerstraat (☎683 99 75). Tram #7 or 17 to 10 Katestr. Walk 2 blocks on Kinkerstr. toward Jan Pieter Huygensstraat. Small takeout place with tasty Turkish treats like grape leaves and baklava. Combo menus €5.50. Open daily 9am-9pm. ❶

Dosa, Overtoom 146 (☎616 48 38; www.dosa-southindian.nl). Tram #1 or 6 to 1e Constantijn Huygensstraat. As its name implies, Dosa serves straightforward South Indian cuisine in a pleasant setting. Plenty of vegetarian choices and a surprisingly

the hidden deal

midnight munchies madness

De Avondmarkt, de Wittenkade 94-96 in Westerpark is an Amsterdam institution.

Though shopping here means a bit of a trek away from the Centrum, if coffeeshop Paradox has just closed and you've still got the munchies, or if you're holed up in a hotel out in the Jordaan, De Avondmarkt is extremely convenient. This "Evening Market" never opens any earlier than 4pm during the week and stays open daily until midnight.

Here you'll find a wide selection of reasonably-priced wines (from €5 per bottle, but pricier vintages also line the shelves) as well as a huge array of fresh fruits and vegetables, meats, breads, and every other product you can imagine to satisfy your late-night munchies. All manner of Dutch sweets (see **Tasty Treats,** p. 106) are available here for those after-hours sugar cravings.

Best of all, there's no mark-up, and unlike other evening markets, it carries much more than just luxury goods—it still stocks the necessary, no-frills staples to get you through the night.

(☎686 4919 Open M-F 4pm-midnight, Sa 3pm-midnight, Su 2pm-midnight ❶)

large variety of *naan* (€1.80-3.65). For dessert, try *kheer,* the traditional Indian rice pudding (€3.20). Sides hover around €6; main dishes about €13. Open daily 4pm-midnight; kitchen closes 11pm. AmEx/MC/V. ❸

Tig Barra, Overtoom 31 (☎412 22 10; www.tigbarra.nl). Tram #1 or 6 to 1e Constatijn Huygensstr. Walk towards the Singlegr., and Tig Barra is on the right side of the street. From the orange, green, and white flags flying over the door to the constant stream of football matches on the TV, this is a full-on Irish pub. Abide by the "homage to the gargle" painted above the bar and have a pint of Guiness (€4.30) alongside Irish pub grub (€8-11.50). Open M-Th noon-1am, F-Sa 10:30am-1am, Su 10:30am-1am. ❷

Cafe Westers, 1e Constantijn Huygensstraat 35-37 (☎612 16 91). Tram #1, or 3 to Overtoom. Cafe Westers has the cozy feeling of a *bruin cafe* in a sizeable space, plus a typical Dutch menu and a pleasant outdoor terrace. Appetizers and salads run €6-8; mains are around €9-15. Several vegetarian options available as well. Beers start at €1.80. Dinner served daily 5:30-10:30pm. Bar open M-Th 3pm-1am, F 3pm-2am, Sa 11am-2am, Su 11am-1am. Cash only. ❷

MUSEUMPLEIN & VONDELPARK

see map p. 347

If you're looking for a quick bite while gallery-hopping in the area, Museumplein's major museums all have cafes with unexceptional food. Lining the surrounding park and boulevards, food stands offer equally unexceptional, somewhat greasier, slightly cheaper food (sandwiches and hot dogs €2-3). You might want to stock up on snacks at the **Albert Heijn** supermarket on Van Baerlestraat, near the Concertgebouw. For more quality sit-down fare, try one of the following area eateries.

◪ **Cafe Vertigo,** Vondelpark 3 (☎612 30 21; www.vertigo.nl). Adjacent to the Filmmuseum (see p. 96) and overlooking a placid duck pond towards the *North (by Northwest)* corner of the park, *Vertigo's* expansive, tree-lined terrace is the perfect place to kick back and watch *The Birds*—or order a beer. The cafe offers a free drink with admission to the outdoor films shown by the Filmmuseum (films F €2.50; starting about 10-10:30pm). Skip the cafe's pricier dinner menu in favor of the filling lunch sandwiches (turkey with pesto and tomato €3.40) and tasty fresh-baked pastries (€2). Basket lunches for a picnic in the park are available for just €7.95. Sept.-Mar. Sa disco nights. M-Sa lunch until 4pm, Su until 5pm; dinner daily 6-10pm. Open daily 10am-1am. MC/V. ❶

Het Blauwe Theehuis, Vondelpark 5 (☎662 0254; www.blauwetheehuis.nl). In the middle of the park, just north of the Open-Air Theater. Through the trees in the park, you may glimpse a linoleum-colored flying saucer full of people having a good time. This is in fact Het Blauwe Theehuis, a cafe with circular terraces. Lunch sandwiches (€4) and evening *tapas* (€3-4) are pretty standard; stop by Het Blauwe instead for a drink and chill on the outdoor patio in the warmer months, or nestle into the comfortable mothership when the weather turns colder. Sa-Su summer, BBQ €6-7. DJ F-Sa nights. Open Su-Th 9am-midnight, F-Sa 9am-2am; kitchen closes 10pm. Cash only. ❶

Go Sushi, Johannes Verhulststraat 35 (☎471 00 35). Tram #16 to Jacob Olbrechtstraat. No relation to the famous London conveyor-belt sushi chain Yo! Sushi, Go Sushi is a tiny "Japanse Eetwinkel" tucked into a quiet street. 3 pieces of *maki* €1.90-2.60; *nigiri* €1.20-2.95; 10-piece sushi "lunchbox" €8.95. Open M-F noon-7pm. Recently-opened annex location in the **Jordaan** at 1e Goudsbloemdwarsstraat 5 (☎320 82 31) is bigger and open later for dinner (T-Sa 4-9pm), but this is the quality original. Cash only. ❷

▸a **Feliz,** Valeruisstraat 85hs (☎364 12 83). Tram #16 to Emmastraat. Advertising itself ▸ *tapas* bar and international restaurant, Feliz serves multicultural dishes in a multi-col-▸iled 2-floor restaurant. Sip sangria (0.5L €8) and nibble on *tapas* (most €5) with the ▸n Feliz's pleasant terrace. Warm sandwiches at lunchtime (€4-6.25) are kinder to the ▸an the expensive dinner entrees, though the large *paella* (€16) is nicely spiced. ▸v 11:30am-3pm, dinner M-F 5:30-11pm, Sa-Su 4-11pm. AmEx/MC/V. ❹

DE PIJP

The food scene at De Pijp is bustling, and it reflects neighborhood's current transition. Simple, no-frills eateries run by immigrant families now share streets with high-priced, elegantly appointed bar-restaurants, where "international cuisine" means something altogether different. Making a value comparison

see map p. 348

between these restaurants is therefore difficult. If you're looking for a tasty, affordable meal and decor is not a priority, head to **Albert Cuypstraat** and environs for Surinamese/Chinese/Indonesian combos, as well as scores of Middle Eastern and Turkish choices. If you like cocktails and plush with your dinner, head to the dozen or so upscale restaurants that are proliferating in the neighborhood. Restaurants of both types are listed here.

Cafe De Pijp, Ferdinand Bolstraat 17-19 (☎670 41 61). Brand-new Cafe De Pijp has all the style of the young crop of restaurants to which it belongs, but it's a trifle more low-key than its sisters, and affordability is a stated goal. Soup of the day €3.90. Appetizers like shrimp with tomato sauce and fried feta €7.90. Main courses €13-15. Cocktails €5. Open Su-Th noon-1am, F-Sa noon-3am. Cash only. ❸

Zagros, Albert Cuypstraat 50 (☎670 04 61). Tram #16, 24 or 25 to Albert Cuyp. Here's your chance to experience little-recognized Kurdish cuisine. The food is influenced by the 5 countries spanned by Kurdistan—Turkey, Iran, Iraq, Syria, and Armenia—in a plain but appealing candlelit atmosphere. Lamb dominates the menu: grilled lamb chops come with couscous and salad (€11.50); *beste berxe* includes cubed, marinated lamb, rice, and a salad (€10.50). Plenty of Veggie options available. Try the sticky, sugary baklava if you're not already full (€3.50). Takeout available. If you come with a group, you can order a belly dancer (€150-200; call at least 1 day ahead). Open daily 3pm-midnight. AmEx/MC/V. ❷

Peppino Gelateria, 1e Sweelinckstraat 16 (☎676 49 10). Tram #4 to Albert Cuyp. Silvano Tofani makes the best homemade gelato, using only fresh cream and fruit (right before your eyes), in the city (from €0.75 per scoop). Flavors range from coconut to banana to pineapple. Excellent cappuccino (€1.80). Open M-F 10am-11pm. Cash only. ❶

De Soepwinkel, 1e Sweelinckstraat 19F (☎673 22 93), just off Albert Cuypmarkt. A hip kitchen that elevates soup-making to a fine art form. The bright, cheery, streamlined decor focuses your attention on their masterpiece soups: 6 specialities that change every month but always include a vegetarian option and soup for kids, all served with fresh breads. Small €3.50; medium €5.75; large €9. Fixed-price lunch menus (€6.65-€9.65). Non-soup menu features include quiche (€2.10) and homemade pie (€2.30). Open M-F 11am-8pm, Sa 11am-6pm. Cash only. ❶

De Ondeugd, Ferdinand Bolstraat 13-15 (☎672 06 51; www.ondeugd.nl). "We want to do something a little naughty with food," explains a manager as to why the place is called "The Naughty One." These days, it's a wonder what is particularly sinful about a French-Asian kitchen, but then, this was one of the first gentrified restaurants in De Pijp. Entrees like the rich Madeira-infused "Beefy de lomo" or delicate duck confit €9-14. DJs occasionally F-Sa in the stunning back dance rooms. Open Su-Th 6pm-1am, F-Sa 6pm-3am; kitchen open 6-11pm. AmEx/DC/MC/V. ❹

Saray, Gerard Doustraat 33 (☎671 92 16). Tram #16, 24, or 25 to Albert Cuyp. Turkish delicacies under beautiful colored-glass lamps in an establishment that's been around for 25 years. *Kofta* (lentils, onion, and ground beef; €3.40) is a great starter, or sample the fi courgette with yogurt and garlic (€3.40). Grilled mains are well within budget rang dishes (€9-13.30), fish dishes (€11-15). Wash it down with *Efes*, the Turkish na (€2) or Turkish liqueurs (€2.70). Takeout available. Open daily 5-11pm. AmE

18 Twintig, Ferdinand Bolstraat 18-20 (☎470 05 51). Undulating w tulip-backlit nooks help, but nothing signals 18 Twintig's entrance into hype-happy crowd. Pan-Asian fish dishes and nouveau Italian app 19. It's worth coming back after 9:30pm Th and Sa for DJs noon-1am, F-Sa 11am-2am. Kitchen closes at an unparalle

Clog Cafe

Heart Attack on a Plate

Moksie, Ferdinand Bolstraat 21 (☎676 82 64). The name of this mellow Surinamese spot refers to its signature dish, a mixture of chicken, sausage, beef, and pork in soy sauce (€7.50; large €8.80). Plenty of *roti* and rice dishes, including vegetarian options (€5-10). Open Tu-Sa noon-10pm, Su 4-10pm. Cash only. ❷

Eufraat, 1e van der Heltstraat 72 (☎672 05 79; www.eufraat.com). On a block where yuppie joints flourish, Eufraat is rather unassuming, specializing in cuisine in from the regions around the Euphrates River (Syria, Turkey, and Iraq). Start your geographically-themed feast with lentil soup (€3.30) or Assyrian *rissoles* (pancakes stuffed with cheese, lamb, or chicken; €3.90), and move on to *koutleh* (pastries stuffed with minced lamb and fried in egg; €10.80) or the *doboh* (leg of lamb in a herbed garlic tomato sauce; €12.60). Hearty vegetarian stew, "The Mesopotamia," combines eggplant, mushrooms, tomato, and peppers (€8.30). Turkish wine by the glass from €2.10. Open Tu-Su noon-10:30pm. AmEx/MC/V. ❷

Mas Tapas, Saenredamstraat 37 (☎664 00 66; www.siempre-tapas.com). Tram #16, 24 or 25 to Albert Cuyp. This spot aims for quaint, with lavender white-washed walls and shabby-chic peeling furniture. Apparently the formula works; the place is usually jam-packed. Selection of 12 *tapas* (€2.75 each, 5 for €13) include garlicky mushrooms and *ceviche* (marinated fish). Meals include *pinchos morenos* (€8.75). Spanish San Miguel beer €2; Brandy de Jerez €3.25. Open daily 4:30pm-midnight. Cash only. ❸

Shinto, Govert Flinckstraat 153 (☎670 46 90). Sushi bars are surprisingly rare finds in a city packed with ethnic eateries. This straightforward, immaculate spot fills miso and eel cravings. The combo meals (€6.90-20.90) are made with fresh ingredients before your eyes. Sake €4.50. Takeout and delivery available. Open daily noon-11pm. AmEx/MC/V. ❷

Granny, 1e van der Heltstraat 45 (☎679 44 65). Tram #16, 24, or 25 to Albert Cuyp. This "petit grand cafe" is a throwback to the early 1900s, with tintype photos of guys on big-wheeled bikes and flappers advertising Coca-Cola. Great for families. For a non-Dutch treat, try a big, basic cheeseburger (€3). Great *appelgebak* comes loaded with whipped cream (€2.20). *Pannenkoeken* €3.65-6.10. *Broodjes* €1.60-3. Open M-Sa 9am-6pm. Cash only. ❶

Cambodja City, Albert Cuypstraat 58-60 (☎671 49 30). Tram #16, 24, or 25 to Albert Cuyp. Specialties from Thailand, Vietnam, and, yes, Cambodia. Lacking ·n atmosphere, Cambodja City compensates with ·eat value: the food is good, cheap, and generously ·rtioned—perfect for takeout to Sarphatipark. Viet- ·nese noodle soup is loaded with chicken-beef ·ls and makes for a full meal alone (€6). Thai ·ken or lamb curry €7.75; mains under €13.50. ·ial dinners for 2-4 people: 10 choices for €20- ·pen Tu-Su 5-10pm. Cash only. ❷

119

·ed
·lamb
·onal beer MC/V. ❸
·benches and
·vinyl
·the trend cycle like the €16-
·tizers €5-12; mains Open Su-Th
·d €5 cocktails. AmEx/MC/V. ❹
·ed 11pm.

JODENBUURT & PLANTAGE

see map p. 349

Cafe Latei, Zeedijk 143 (☎625 74 85). At this unique cafe-*cum*-curiosities-shop, nearly everything is for sale—even your plate. The brainchild of 2 vintage knick-knack enthusiasts, Cafe Latei is ideal for a quick bite or leisurely conversation. Hanging lamps, old-fashioned crockery, and wall hangings may come and go, but the affable atmosphere remains. Large sandwiches about €3. All-day continental breakfast €6.40. Fresh juices €2-4. Th couscous nights; call for other special events. Open M-F 8am-5pm, Sa 9am-6pm, Su 11am-6pm. ❶

Abe Veneto, Plantage Kerklaan 2 (☎639 23 64). This homey Italian eatery has food and prices to make any traveler happy. A dizzying selection of freshly made pizzas (€4.50-9.50), pastas (€6.50-9.50), and salads (most under €5). Wine by the bottle or the carafe (half carafe €6.50). Takeout available. Open daily noon-midnight. Cash only. ❷

King Solomon Restaurant, Waterlooplein 239 (☎625 58 60). Run by a hospitable Orthodox family, this is the only kosher restaurant in sight of the old Jewish quarter. Serves falafel (€7.25), veggie platters (€13.50), and the specialty of any Jewish grandmother, gefilte fish (€6.75). Try *the malaouakh,* the delicious, hard-to-find Yemenite pancake (€6.25). Open Su-Th noon-10pm, F noon-5pm; winter Sa 45min. after sundown-10pm. AmEx/MC/V. ❷

Soup En Zo, Jodenbreestraat 94a (☎422 22 43). Let your nose guide you to the amazing broth at this tiny soupery. Homemade soup and fresh bread make a great lunch combo, especially for vegetarians. Several soups and sizes (€2.20-5.50) with free bread and fresh toppings (coriander, dill, cheese, nuts). Check out their new location at Nieuwe Spiegelstraat 54. Open M-F 11am-8pm, Sa 11am-7pm, Su 1-7pm. ❶

Plancius, Plantage Kerklaan 61a (☎330 94 69). Terrifically chic with its minimalist industrial design, yet still accessible, Plancius serves stylish, international breakfasts (on weekends), lunches, and dinners. Sandwiches €2-5; pasta €8. Menu changes every few months; past favorites include risotto with gorgonzola and shallots. Open daily 10am-2am; kitchen open 10am-4:30pm and 6-10pm. ❸

Nam Tin, Jodenbreestraat 11-13 (☎428 85 08). This enormous, elegant Chinese banquet hall is replete with pink tablecloths, tuxedoed waiters, and Buddhist statues. Cantonese food is Nam Tin's specialty, with dim sum served all day (most dishes under €4) and a large array of noodle soups (around €8-12). Open M-Sa noon-midnight, Su noon-11:30pm; kitchen open daily noon-10pm. Cash only. ❸

Restaurante La Sala Comidas Caseras, Plantage Kerklaan 41 (☎624 48 46). Spanish and Portuguese food is served at this cafe-restaurant across from the Artis Zoo. Tasty *tapas* (from €3.40) and authentic Spanish entrees (from €16.60). Sip wine on the outdoor terrace. Open Tu-Su 4pm-midnight. Cash only. ❹

Cafe Koosje, Plantage Middenlaan 37 (☎320 08 17). A pleasant place to grab a bite, complemented with a classic Dutch wooden interior. For lunch, you'll find *ciabattas* (€3-5) and the soup of the day (€4). For dinner, Koosje floats out a more serious menu (mains €10-15). At night, drinkers hit the full bar, with people as varied as students from nearby University of Amsterdam to nursing home residents from down the street. Cash only. ❷

TisFris, St. Antoniesbreestraat 142 (☎622 04 72). Watch the world go by on this chic cafe's terrace or through the enormous windows facing Sint Antoniesbreestraat. There's plenty for vegetarians and even a few dishes for the hard-core vegan (avocado, pine nuts, and red onions on a roll €3.80). Signature oven-grilled sandwiches €4-5. Warm goat cheese salad with croutons, honey, and walnuts €9. Open M-Sa 9am-7pm, Su 10am-7pm. Cash only. ❶

Aguada, Roetersstraat 10 (☎620 37 82). Cheese fondue (€11), salads (from €4), and tasty grills (steak €11) all delight at this comfy, antique-filled cafe across the street from the University of Amsterdam. *Tapas* €2-4. Open M-F noon-11pm, Sa-Su 4-11pm. Cash only. ❸

CASA ROSSO
AMSTERDAM

Only in Amsterdam

The Netherlands is unique for its liberal attitude in regards to soft drugs and prostitution—though other countries are beginning to follow suit (see **Soft Drugs and Rock 'N Roll,** p. 48). This chapter outlines the laws and etiquette of the unique Dutch culture and lists the best coffeeshops and smartshops around.

COMMERCIAL SEX

The "world's oldest profession" has flourished in Amsterdam since the city's inception around the 13th century. The main locus for prostitution has always centered around what today is the Red Light District, though it is practiced elsewhere in the city as well. The Red Light District originally grew up in the 13th century around what up around what is now known as Zeedijk as prostitutes congregated to service sailors who came into port. Window prostitution, which grew out of the practice of prostitutes showing off their goods from the front windows of private houses, was officially legalized in 1911, and in 2000, the law outlawing brothels was taken off the books, making informal streetwalking the only prohibited form of prostitution.

Legal prostitution in Amsterdam comes in three main forms. By far the most visible is **window prostitution,** where scantily-clad women tempt passers-by from small chambers fronted by a plate-glass window. These sex workers are self-employed and rent the windows themselves, and accordingly, each sets her own price. This form of commercial sex gave the Red Light District its name, as lamps both outside and in the windows emit a red

the local story

mother madam

*We interviewed Mariska Majoor, a former prostitute who founded the **Prostitution Information Centre** (PIC; p. 124).*

Q: Why did you start the PIC?

A: I started PIC in August 1994 because I think it is extremely important to have a place where everybody can come with questions about prostitution. I started the Centre for prostitutes, clients, tourists, students, people who want to start a brothel, people who are in trouble, people who want to go to a certain place to have commercial sex. I used to work as a prostitute myself. I started when I was 16 years old because I needed money for a dog–it was a stupid reason. I'm from a Catholic family, I grew up good, healthy, normal: normal family, nothing special–no incest past, no rape, nothing sensational.

Q: How are prostitutes treated in Dutch society?

A: If you were a prostitute, it doesn't matter because you'll always be an ex-prostitute. Most girls want to stay anonymous, so they lead a double life. It's only a very small group that are open about what they're doing. That's difficult, because at the moment you stop your career and you want to do something else, people always ask

continued on next page

glow that bathes the whole area by night. The most popular spot for window prostitution in the **Red Light District** is between **Zeedijk** and **Warmoesstraat.** There are two more areas, in the **Nieuwe Zijd,** between Spuistraat and Singel, and in **De Pijp** along Ruysdaelkade—in both regions, sex workers are self-employed. Those in the Nieuwe Zijd and De Pijp tend to be more discreet and more frequented by Dutch men than by tourists. Don't take pictures of prostitutes—it is **disrespectful.** Doing so will likely prompt an encounter with large, angry men.

If you're interested in having sex with a window prostitute, go up to the door and wait for someone inside to open it. Any act is permitted long as you clearly agree on it beforehand; negotiation occurs and money changes hands before any sexual acts take place. Be aware that once your time is up, the prostitute will ask you to leave, and there are no refunds (for more etiquette, see **Love for Hire,** p. 32).

Increasingly popular are the recently legalized **brothels,** which come in two main varieties. The term brothel usually refers to an establishment where you enter a bar in which women will make your acquaintance and are available for hour-long sessions. Brothels, also called **sex clubs,** can be pricey. In addition to costly drinks in the bar—women are encouraged by the management to entice patrons into buying bottles of champagne—they charge a cover just to enter the building. A less expensive and more confidential alternative to the sex club is the variation known as the **private house.** In contrast to brothels, in which you enter a bar with prostitutes and other patrons, in a private house you enter a room and the currently available women walk by for your inspection. Select the one you like (or don't—there's no problem with walking out if none of the prostitutes are to your taste), and rent a room (the cost of which includes the women's services). Most of these establishments are located in Amsterdam's southern districts. **Escort services** are legal in Amsterdam as well. Offering even more discretion than private houses, these services arrange for a call girl to visit you at your home or hotel room.

The best place to go for information about prostitution in Amsterdam is the **Prostitution Information Centre,** Enge Kerksteeg 3, in the Red Light District behind the Oude Kerk. Friendly, helpful staff can answer any question you might have, no matter how much you blush when you ask it. For an interview with Mariska Majoor, an Information Centre employee, see **Mother Madam,** p. 124. You can also pick up copies of several informative publications: *The Most Fre-*

quently Asked Questions about Amsterdam's Red Light District, a basic guide to the ins and outs of the window prostitution scene (€1.50); *Best Places to Go in Amsterdam*, a single sheet with the PIC's top picks of establishments (€2.50); and the *Pleasure Guide*, a magazine with ads and articles about commercial sex in the city (€2.50). The Centre offers handmade souvenirs and a mock-up of a window brothel interior, where you can take pictures—something you can't do at real window-prostitution booths. If you come to poke around, leave a donation; the PIC is not yet state-supported and depends on the generosity of visitors to continue its work. (☎420 73 28; www.pic-amsterdam.com. Open Tu-W and F-Sa 11:30am-6:30pm.)

Sex shops and **live sex shows** are related elements of the industry. The former litter the Red Light District, vending pornos (mags and videos), dildos, lubricants, stimulants, lewd souvenirs, and the like. **Porn theaters** abound here as well, where an hour of lurid on-screen sex costs less than €10. Sex shops and porn theaters cluster along **Reguliersbreestraat**, just off Rembrandtplein, as well. Live sex shows are venues where the "performers" on stage will strip and engage in intercourse before your very eyes. There are quite a few live sex show establishments in the Red Light District, but the most famous (and by some accounts, "classiest") is **Casa Rosso**, right behind the penis fountain, where you can get an eyeful for €25. These are a few Amsterdam's most infamous and/or reputable sex shops.

Absolute Danny, Oudezijds Achterburgwal 78 (☎421 09 15; www.absolutedanny.com). Slick leather suits in all colors accompanied by stiletto boots and late-night toys. Vibrators, collars, erotic videos round off this sexually pleasing collection under one singularly saucy sign. Open M-W, Sa noon-8pm; Th noon-9pm; F noon-10pm; Su noon-7pm. AmEx/MC/V.

Chickita's Sex Paradijs, Warmoesstraat 65 (☎623 78 18). An all-purpose sex shop with an endless supply of vibrators and dildos, porn magazines, and videos explores the most outlandish fantasies. Booths of 64 channels sit outside for quick pleasure while inside, low priced (but not cheaply made) whips, lingerie, and fetish-like get-ups abound. Small gifts include nude playing cards and chocolate genitals. Open daily 10am-1am. V.

Christine Le Duc, Spui 6 (☎624 82 65; www.christineleduc.com), vends naughty lingerie, videos, and toys. Open M-F 9am-6pm. AmEx/MC/V.

Condomerie het Gulden Vlies, Warmoesstraat 141 (☎627 41 74; www.condomerie.com). With its selection of condoms in every shape, size, and flavor possible, you'll be sure to find your own special brand.

continued from previous page

what you did before. If there's a couple years' hole, they try to find out what you did. They find out, and you're in trouble.

Q: What's the biggest problem facing Dutch prostitution?
A: Work circumstances are unclear at the moment, and the stigma of course, but that has to do with working conditions. As a prostitute, we can choose to work for ourselves, as independent business-women, or as a brothel or club employee. The rules [like health insurance] for a normal job, they don't apply. The government doesn't know how to deal with it.

Q: Have things changed since brothels were legalized?
A: Everyone who makes money has to pay taxes. Officially, the prostitutes have had to pay taxes for a long time, but if they didn't pay, the tax people didn't do anything. Since the law, it's been easier for the tax people to find prostitutes and make them pay taxes.

Q: Does being part of tax-paying society make life better?
A: Yes and no. We talk with prostitutes and try to tell them that if they pay taxes, you can put money in the bank account, you can get interest, and after a while you can buy a house or use the money to start your own business. But, if she wants to want to borrow money, banks say "No. You've made your money through prostitution," so they will not give you a loan...Even if a prostitute is aware of the benefits, it's like society is punishing her for her honesty.

125

life's* green

cream of the shop

Here are our picks for the **best coffeeshops** based on ambiance, staff knowledge, and selection combined:

Abraxas: By far the city's most beautiful coffeeshop, Abraxas has a refreshingly pressure-free atmosphere to boot (p. 131).

Barney's: Huge, gloriously greasy breakfasts served all day almost overshadow the high quality smokeables. Almost— Barney's weed has been voted best in the city for three years running (p. 135).

Bluebird: A relaxing space infused with the deepest azure, Bluebird doesn't just let you read what's on the menu, but attaches actual cannabis samples for your perusal (p. 141).

The Dolphins: An unassumingly small, kitsch facade belies an elaborate, tranquil interior for soothing, albeit fishy tripping under the sea (p. 137).

La Tertulia: The van Gogh mural outside and shimmering crystals inside go surprisingly well with the leafy botanicals within: plants and smokes (p. 140).

Paradox: When the munchies hit, get the world's best veggie burger at this relaxing, neighborly coffeeshop (p. 140).

Yo Yo: Toking up hardly seems like the best thing to with family, but Yo Yo is so homey it makes getting high feel wholesome. Tremendous apple pie (p. 141).

Express your Dutch pride and invest in a "football package" (1 condom adorned with a soccer ball and 11 others the bright orange team color) to support the national team even when you're back at home. Open M-Sa 11am-6pm. AmEx/MC/V.

Stout, Berenstraat 9 (☎ 620 16 76). Woman-friendly shop selling gorgeous lingerie sure to entice any partner. Aims to provide a touch of intimacy rather than kinkiness. Pricey Italian lingerie, vibrators, steamy videos, chains, and clamps sold here are displayed for the experimenting, loving woman. No leather or rubber. Open M-F noon-7pm, Sa 11am-6pm, Su 1-5pm. AmEx/MC/V.

COFFEESHOPS

A far cry from your friendly neighborhood Starbucks, the coffee at coffeeshops in Amsterdam isn't the focal point (in fact, at many you'll find that the coffeemaker is out of order, and few patrons seem to care). Places calling themselves coffeeshops sell pot or hash or will let you buy a drink and smoke your own stuff. Look for the green and white "Coffeeshop BCD" sticker that certifies a shop's credibility. Although Amsterdam is known as the hash capital of the world, **marijuana** is increasingly popular. You can legally purchase up to 5g of marijuana or hash, although you are permitted to possess up to **1 oz.** (about 28g) at a time. For info on the legal ins and outs, call the **Jellinek clinic** (☎ 570 23 55). If your questions pertain only to cannabis or hemp matters, try the **Cannabis College** (see **Museums,** p. 80).

As with any kind of recreation and experimentation, safety precautions must be taken. **Never buy drugs from street dealers.** Street dealers are mostly strung-out addicts and are often out to mug tourists. Don't get too caught up in Amsterdam's narcotic quirk; use common sense, and remember that any experimentation with drugs can be dangerous. **If a friend is tripping, it is important to never leave their side.** Take them to a relaxed place and give them sugar, food, or anything with Vitamin C in it. If they don't get better in a few hours, then **call ☎ 112 for an ambulance.** Beware that an ambulance may not arrive as soon as you'd like—authorities are generally fed up with drug-tourists who have smoked or eaten too many drugs. However, if you choose to indulge, you will find that coffeeshops carry a range of products which are described below. It is a courtesy to tip coffeeshop attendants, even by simply saying, "Keep the change." When you move from one coffeeshop to another, it is obligatory to buy a drink in the next coffeeshop even if you already have weed. As long as you're buying drinks, you can stay as long as you want.

While it's all right to smoke on the outdoor patio of a coffeeshop, don't go walking down the street smoking a joint like you're James Dean with a cigarette: it's simply not done, especially outside of the **Red Light District.**

While there are hot spots in Amsterdam that seem to feature as many coffeeshops as restaurants (i.e. Nieuwendijk, Warmoesstraat, and much of the Red Light District), you'll find that the best offerings aren't necessarily concentrated in any particular location. As a general rule, the farther you travel from the touristed spots, the better and cheaper the establishments. When a shop is frequented mainly by Dutch customers, it means they've established a loyal clientele, which in turn means they sell good stuff. Pick up a free copy of the *BCD Official Coffeeshop Guide* for the pot-smoker's map of Amsterdam, or try the *Smoker's Guide* (€3), sold at most coffeeshops. There's nothing wrong with walking in and checking a place out before you settle on smoking there. Peruse the listings below before coffee-shopping and be sure to take your time making your selections. When you enter a shop, ask for the menu—establishments are not allowed to advertise their products or leave menus on the tables. The quantity of soft drugs in Amsterdam might be unlimited, but your cash flow isn't; taking that extra minute to pick the best spot for what you're after will help to guarantee you get the most bang for your buck.

HASH. Hashish comes in three varieties: black (Indian), blonde (Moroccan), and Dutch (also called ice-o-lator hash), all of which can cost from €4 to €30 per gram, though it's the increasingly popular **ice-o-lator hash** that tops out at around €20-30 per g. Typically, the cost of the hash is proportional to its quality and strength. Black hash hits harder than blonde, and ice-o-lator can send even a seasoned smoker off his head. What separates hash from weed is that, while weed is the flower, hash is the extracted resin crystals, which give a different kind of high.

DRUG LAWS

The Netherlands' policy towards **soft drugs** is one of tolerance **(not legalization or decriminalization, as many believe),** meaning that smoking cannabis or hash is an offense, but one that is rarely prosecuted. The definition of soft versus hard drugs according to the 1976 revision of The Netherlands' Opium Act depends on the abuse potential and safety of use. Laws against processed **hard drugs** such as cocaine and heroin are strictly enforced, and being caught with them can lead to prison sentences of up to 10 years. With marijuana and hash, possession of up to 5g is considered a "minor offense;" drugs may be confiscated but usually no legal action will be taken. Any more, and you'll be suspected of **dealing,** a crime; the sale of weed is generally only tolerated in licensed coffeeshops.

Those under 18 may not buy weed or be on coffeeshop premises. Taking drugs outside the country (including via mail) is illegal. Drug-sniffing dogs often greet trains or planes arriving from The Netherlands.

MARIJUANA. Marijuana is a dried, cured flower also referred to as weed, mary jane, and pot. Different weeds come in and out of favor much like different beers. Any weed with white in its name is guaranteed to be strong, such as White Widow, White Butterfly, and White Ice. Pot in The Netherlands is incredibly strong; today's strains have 10-25% THC content, as opposed to weed two or three decades ago, which might have only 6-7%. The "heads" of the plant also contain more THC than the remainder. Take it easy so you don't pass out. The Dutch tend to mix tobacco with their pot as well, so joints are harsher on your lungs and throat if you're not a cigarette smoker. Pre-rolled joints are always rolled with tobacco; most coffeeshops also offer pure joints at up to twice the cost. Dutch marijuana is the most common and costs anywhere from €3-12 per g; most coffeeshops sell bags in set amounts (€6, €12, etc.). Staff at coffeeshops are accustomed to explaining the different

the local story

hemp ph.d.

Lorna Clay volunteers at ▨ *Cannabis College (p. 80), the city's foremost authority on all things related to marijuana, hashish, and hemp. She said the following about cannabis in the city:*

On coffeeshop history: In the 60s, originally the coffeeshops were known as teahouses. You couldn't buy cannabis, but you could go and buy tea and smoke it there. Then, when the licenses came out, it was just to provide a bit more choice for people and take it away from the criminals. Right off, there only used to be about four or five coffeeshops here, and that was fine for the people that lived here. Then, since the late 70s, Amsterdam's become a bit of a mecca for smokers.

On quality establishments: Unfortunately, Amsterdam has seen a big amount of drug tourism and that's been exploited by a lot of horrible owners. They think "I can sell [tourists] bad cannabis and they'll never come back, and that's fine because I've made my money." There's 281 coffeeshops in Amsterdam and I can recommend you 15, honestly... a lot of the owners don't even smoke. A good thing to look out for are the members of the BCD—basically a union of coffeeshops. We can give you a BCD map. There are about 30 members and these guys care about their customers.

continued on next page

kinds of pot on the menu to tourists. It is recommended that you buy a gram at a time. Most places will supply rolling papers and filter tips—Europeans only smoke joints. When pipes or bongs are provided they are usually for and used by tourists. Another increasingly popular way of getting high in Amsterdam is to use a **vaporizer.** These devices heat up cannabis products, until the hallucinogenic substances like THC to become gaseous, extracting more THC out of the product than regular burning via cigarettes; beware that vaporizers with copper piping may release nasty (and potentially carcinogenic) copper particles into your lungs.

SPACECAKES, SHAKES, & SWEETS. Spacecakes, shakes, and sweets are made with hash or weed and the butter used is usually hash or weed-based. Because the THC only takes affect when it gets into your blood, and is digested, the drugs take longer to affect a person. That means they also take longer to filter out, producing a body stone that can take up to two hours or longer to start. Don't go for a second sweet because you don't feel anything immediately—start off with half a serving and see how you feel after an hour or two. It's always easier to eat more than to wait out a higher dose than you can handle. The amount of pot or hash in baked or frozen goods cannot be regulated—and it is impossible to know what grade of drugs is in them. This makes ingesting this form of cannabis much more dangerous than smoking, where you can control your intake.

SMART SHOPS

Smart shops are also legal, and peddle a variety of "herbal enhancers" (see p. 134) as well as **hallucinogens** that walk the fine line between soft and hard drugs. Some shops are alcohol-free and all have a strict no-hard-drugs policy, as **hard drugs**—including heroin, ecstasy, or cocaine—are **illegal and not tolerated** and possession is treated as a serious crime in Amsterdam. Always remember that experimentation with drugs is dangerous and can cause either short or long-term damage. If you're interested in experimenting with **magic mushrooms ('shrooms),** it is crucial, as with all soft drugs, to do your research beforehand. Here's a brief run-down of the different types of mushrooms and a few guidelines:

TYPES OF MUSHROOMS. All 'shrooms have the same psychedelic chemical, psilocybin, but different types of mushrooms offer very different trips. **Mexican** and **Thai** mushrooms are generally used by beginners: they are the least potent and give a laughing, colorful, and speedy high with some visual hallucination. **Philosophers' stones** (which have an Xtasy-like effect) and **Hawaiians** (which give an intensely visual trip similar to LSD) are significantly more intense, and should be taken **only by experienced users.**

DOSES. It is currently illegal to "prepare" mushrooms—that includes drying, baking, or any other kind of handling because the process concentrates the hallucinogenic chemicals tenfold. A mild high is a dose of about 10-15g of fresh 'shrooms; a weak trip 15-30g; and a strong trip 30-50g. Be sure to ask the salesperson exactly how many grams there are in your purchase so that you know the amount you eat.

EFFECTS. 'Shrooms will start to work at around 30-60 minutes following ingestion, and the effects will last, depending on the amount of the dose, anywhere from three to eight hours. The effects you feel will depend on your mood and environment. Your emotions will be heightened such that you could feel absolute bliss, unadulterated fear, or stark, seemingly endless depression. Overall, you will experience a distorted reality: lengths of time will randomly expand or contract, colors, forms, shapes, and experiences will be unpredictably intensified or subdued. Blips will appear on your sensory radar, blinding you to all other realities; conversely, certain sounds and smells may captivate you such that you become obsessed with their existence. To cut the effect at any time, take a lot of vitamin C (i.e. several glasses of orange juice) and eat a lot of sugar; the trip will neutralize within 45 minutes.

WARNINGS. Do not take more than once dose at a time—many first time users take too much because they don't feel anything immediately. Shrooms take at least 30 minutes to kick in. As with pot and hash, never look for mushrooms outside of a smart shop, and **do not buy from a street dealer;** it is extremely difficult to tell the difference between those that are poisonous or hallucinogenic. A bad trip will occur if you mix hallucinogens or other controlled substances. If you smoke marijuana when shrooming, you can have flashbacks up to several days later. Try to avoid eating before taking 'shrooms, as this will likely dull their effect or could intensify nausea. Be sure that you take them in a safe surrounding with people you know, preferably outside and during daytime hours—in any strange environment, your neurological worries are bound to affect your high. Do not take 'shrooms after a night of little sleep and avoid balconies, bridges,

continued from previous page

On types of weed: Know the difference between Sativa and Indica. Sativa will get you high and giggly and energized and that is something that "Haze" or "Kali Mist" will do. When you smoke the Indica, that gets you really stoned and relaxed, and that's like "Afghani Shiva" or "Buddha." The choice is: do you want to get high or stoned?

On what to ask: Don't ask: what's the strongest? It's difficult for someone to answer, because what's strongest for one is not strongest for someone else. Ask them for their most flavorsome, not their strongest. Ask them what they recommend. Never go in and ask for a name because it depends on who grows the particular plant, not the strain. For example, White Widow—it's just been made famous by the name. You will find they will bump up the price. Never ever be afraid to ask the guy or the girl about their weed. Just like if you walk into a wine bar, you want to ask advice about wine. If they give you [a hard time], honestly, turn around and walk straight out... Don't give them your business.

On growing: If a company doesn't even distinguish on their menu between bio or hydro, it's not worth buying. Bio is when weed's grown in soil and hydro is when it's grown in water. Usually when you're growing hydro, you're filling it with artificial chemical nutrients. Good quality coffeeshops will sell good quality hydro but in these bad quality coffeeshops, they don't flush the chemicals out of their plants so you're getting high off the harmful chemicals... I only grow bio using natural food. I personally believe the plant gets a lot of its flavors from the earth.

Rolling One at Abraxas

Penis Fountain, Casa Rosso

Breaking Off a Chunk of Sweet Tooth

and rooftops. If you are depressed, pregnant, or on medication, you should not take mushrooms. If you are having a bad trip, don't be ashamed to tell someone, because you won't be arrested in Amsterdam for using—it's not a crime here, and locals have seen it all before.

SHOPS BY NEIGHBORHOOD

OUDE ZIJD & RED LIGHT DISTRICT

see map p. 344

Despite the proliferation of coffeeshops in the area, you're better off looking outside the Red Light District for a quality joint. Because of the heavy tourist traffic, shops don't have to rely on repeat business so customer satisfaction is a low priority. Shops can sell you lousy weed and get away with it, as the knowledgeable Dutch smokers (who don't visit the Red Light District) will readily affirm. However, some reasonable places do exist if you're craving a hit in the area.

Hill Street Blues, Warmoesstraat 52. Don't let the loud rock music wafting into the street drive you away; it's all about leisurely comfort inside at this busy but mellow coffeeshop and bar. Add to the liveliness by bringing your own CDs to play at the bar and decorate the graffiti-laden walls with personal messages or postcards. If you don't want to smoke (weed and hash €4.50-11.50 per g), you won't be able to resist the incredibly cheap beer (pint €2.80; €2.10 during Happy Hour 6-9pm). Cocktails available for an equally measly €3.20 during Cocktail Happy Hour Tu-Th 9pm-10pm. Space shakes €4.60; space tea €4. The bar hosts a pool competition every other Su. (€5 entrance fee). Open Su-Th 9am-1am, F-Sa 9am-3am.

Rusland, Ruslandstraat 16 (☎627 94 68). Known as Amsterdam's oldest coffeeshop, Rusland is an intimate nook with huge selections of non-spaced tea, milkshakes (€2), and fruity vitamin shakes (€2.80). If you like the handblown lamps on the walls, go downstairs and admire the selection of handblown pipes while relaxing on the pillowed benches for an afternoon smoke. Pre-rolled joints €2.30; 1.3-4.3g of hash and grass available in €12 quantities. Open Su-Th 10am-midnight, F-Sa 10am-1am.

Route 99, Haringpakkerssteeg 8 (☎320 75 62). Take a roadtrip through the American Midwest with Elvis, Marilyn, and a White Widow joint. A vibrant mural of highways, cowboys, and sand decorates the walls of this coffeeshop whose cinematic paradise stars the King and his blonde bombshell. Trip in style: 1.7-3.5g weed and 1.2-2.5g hash both €12. Joints €3.5, pure weed €5.5. Entice your taste buds with all things space: cakes, hot chocolate, and tea €3.50. Pool table €5 per hr. Open Su-Th 9am-midnight, F-Sa 9am-1am. Big sister to **Route 66,** Warmoesstraat 77.

The Greenhouse Effect, Warmoesstraat 53 (☎623 74 62; www.the-greenhouse-effect.com). Also a hotel and bar, this all-purpose establishment provides almost all of the Red Light District's (non-sexual) thrills. One of the area's most pleasant and welcoming spots with extremely friendly staff. Smoke on the couches in the back or just buy your goodies and head to the Greenhouse bar next door for Happy Hour (8-10pm; pints €2.30). Discounts at coffeeshop and bar for hotel patrons. €3.60-7 per g of weed; €3.50-16 per g of hash (including ice-o-lator). Pre-rolled joints €3. Open Su-Th 9am-1am, F-Sa 9am-3am.

Funny People Coffeeshop, Nieuwebrugsteeg 24 (☎623 86 63; www.funnypeople.nl). Snug coffeeshop offers perfect wake 'n' bake with its early opening time, sun-soaked windows, and hilarious staff. Grass €3-6.50 per g; hash €3.50-7 per g. Rolled joints €3; pure joints €6. Also sells pipes and grinders. Open M-F 8am-midnight, Sa-Su 7am-midnight.

Cafe del Mondo, Nieuwmarkt 28 (☎624 13 73; www.cafedelmondo.nl). Booming stereo system, 3 big-screen televisions, outdoor terrace, and convenient location make this bar and coffeeshop one of the prime stops along Nieuwmarkt. Serves beer and cocktails including the "Screaming Orgasm" (€5.25). Breakfast menu €8, pastries €2. *Tostis* (€2.50-3.90). 1.4-4.5 g weed €12. Pre-rolled joints €3.50. Open Su-Th 9am-1am, F-Sa 9am-3am.

SMART SHOP

▓ **Conscious Dreams Kokopelli,** Warmoesstraat 12 (☎421 70 00). This smart shop is perhaps the best place in Amsterdam to begin with psychedelic experimentation. Books, gifts, pipes, and lava lamps available with an overwhelming selection of magic 'shrooms, oxygen drinks, fertility elixirs, vitamins, and herbs. A staff with background in neurobiology and botany is on hand to advise the unknowing consumer. DJs spinning tunes F-Su 5-10pm give you even more reasons to smoke up or begin a trip in this animated shop overlooking a canal. Internet access (€1 for 15 min.). Herbal XTC €11.50-14. Mushrooms €12.50 for happy/funny effect, €18 for a real "Hawaiian" trip. For the most powerful trip of all, ask about Salvia (0.5g €14-23, 1g €23-41, depending on strength), but discuss its intensity and safety with the staff first. Open daily 11am-10pm.

NIEUWE ZIJD

The **Nieuwe Zijd** has one of the highest coffeeshop-per-square-kilometer ratios in all of Amsterdam. While most of these hash and weed purveyors are barely preferable to smoking alone in your hotel room, those listed below are some of Amsterdam's honest-to-goodness gems.

see map p. 344

▓ **Abraxas,** J. Roelensteeg 12-14 (☎625 57 63; www.abraxas.tv). Between Nieuwezijds Voorburgwal and Kalverstraat, just south of Dam. With colorful, sprawling mosaics, an undulating tree sculpture growing over bar, and mood lighting on each of its 3 floors, Abraxas is one of Amsterdam's most beautiful coffeeshops. Serves the full palette of hash and weed products plus juice and sodas in a casual, sophisticated, and no-pressure atmosphere. On weekends (Th-Sa nights), get high to the beat of a DJ playing mellow lounge tunes and jazz for the 18- to 35-year-old clientele. Serves space cakes and shakes as well as tropical space tea (all €3.70), but use caution: Abraxas's space drinks and baked goods are strong. 12min. free Internet access with a drink or any purchase, €4 per hr. after that. Open daily 10am-1am.

▓ **Grey Area,** Oude Leliestraat 2 (☎420 43 01; www.greyarea.nl). From Dam Square, follow Raadhuisstraat to Singel, turn right and then left on Oude Leliestraat. Where coffeeshop owners themselves go for the best. One of the only owner-operated spots left in the city, the petite shop plastered with bumper stickers and images of American pop culture has received 18 awards at the Cannabis Cup since 1996. No wonder Amsterdammers flock here, whether look-

life's
green

and the winner is...

Every year, on the American Thanksgiving (the fourth Thursday of November), Amsterdam plays host to the **Cannabis Cup,** the largest marijuana-tasting festival in the world, held at Melkweg (p. 168). Cannabis Cup (best marijuana strain) winners from 2002 listed in *Let's Go: Amsterdam* are below. For more information on next year's Cannabis Cup, visit www.420tours.com.

1ST PLACE: Morning Glory from Barneys, p. 135.

2ND PLACE: NYC Diesel from De Tweede Kamer, p. 133.

3RD PLACE: Super Kali Mist from Green House, p. 141

4TH PLACE: Super Sage from Katsu, p. 141.

5TH PLACE: Stella Blue from Coffeeshop Anyday, p. 134.

ing for the light "Double Bubble Gum" weed or the more ponderous "Grey Mist Crystal" hash (€7.50 per g). The yankee expat who works behind the counter will be happy to let you borrow one of the coffeeshop's classy glass bongs. Amsterdam's cheapest pure marijuana joints (€3.50) and juice (€1.50) are also available. Open Tu-Su noon-8pm.

Kadinsky, Rosmarijnsteeg 9 (☎624 70 23), a few blocks north of the intersection of Spui and Nieuwezijds Voorburgwal, between the 2 streets. Stylish 3-story joint hidden away off an alley near Spui and one of the city's most comfortable, friendly, and hip stoneries. Grandiose fresh flower bouquet greets you upon entrance and window-side bar opens onto the street for indoor/outdoor chillage on sunny days. Great weekly deals on house weed and hashish (from €5 per g) plus 20% off all drugs every 8th day (call ahead if it excites you that much), or 20% off a 5g purchase any day. Mixed joints €3.20-3.70; pure €3.90. 20min. free Internet with purchase. Trippy pinball machine €0.50 per play. Since 2002, Kadinsky has added two small, modish annexes—one at Langebrugsteeg 7A and the other at Zoritsteeg 14, though nothing beats the original. Open daily 10am-1am.

Dampkring, Handboogstraat 29 (☎638 07 05; www.dampkring.nl). From Muntplein, take Singel to Heiligweg, turn right and it is near the corner of Heiligweg and Handboogstraat. The dark underground to Abraxas's sweet and colorful decor: in this deep blue subterranean space, psychedelic trees reach for the ceiling, and ambient flourescent lighting guides your way to the bar. Even though many patrons are experienced smokers and growers, the place is not pretentious: Dampkring is inviting enough for even the stinkiest backpacker to feel at ease. Extremely detailed cannabis menu with 18 choices of pre-rolled joints from €2.80-5.70. Same owner as De Tweede Kamer (see below), with the same excellent value and strong cannabis, like "Salad Bowl" (€4 per g) or the special NYC Diesel (€8 per g). Some of the strongest ice-o-lator hash in the city. Open M-Th 10am-1am, F-Sa 10am-2am, Su 11am-1am.

Dutch Flowers, Singel 387 (☎624 76 24; info@dutch-flowers.nl). From Muntplein, follow the Singel past 2 bridges; Dutch Flowers will be up on your right. With a huge menu, Dutch Flowers is widely regarded as offering some of the best weed in the city, evidenced by the nearly continuous line at the cannabis bar at the front. More than cannabis has gone to their heads, though: as past winners of the coveted "High Life" prize for best hash in Amsterdam's annual Cannabis Cup, the staff can sometimes have a stand-offish attitude. But with crooked paintings on the walls, outside terrace seating along the beautiful Singel canal, and one of Amsterdam's best bakeries around the corner for when you get the munchies (**Lanskroon,** Singel 385, see p. 112), Dutch Flowers remains a steadfast purveyor of the high life. Beer €1.60. Loose weed from €8.50. Open Su-Th 10am-1am, F-Sa 10am-2am.

De Tweede Kamer (The Second Room), Heisteeg 6 (☎422 22 36; www.channels.nl/amsterdam/twka-mer.html). Head north along Nieuwezijds Voorburgwal from Spui for a block, then turn left onto the dinky alleyway that is Heisteeg. You might mistake this *gezellig* (cozy) smokery's deep burgundy curtains and calligraphic window signs for the facade of a Parisian restaurant. The sister store of **Dampkring** (see p. 132) with a slightly larger—and equally high-quality—selection will tickle the fancy of any marauding puffer. Strongest hash, the cannabis ice-o-lated in Afghani-stan and grown in Morocco, "only for experienced smokers," sells at €20-23 per g. For bud, sample "Kalimist" (€9 per g). Even the cheapest choices (€7.50 per g of hash and €5 per g of pot) kick well. Open M-Sa 10am-1am, Su 11am-1am.

Cannabis College Grow Room

Wolke Wietje, Kolksteeg 1a (☎462 93 25), from Dam take Nieuwezijds Voorburgwal north to Nieuwez-ijds Kolk, turn left, and the coffeeshop is on your right near Nieuwendijk. Rock-crystal in the chandelier, a "stoned" Buddha figurine, and mosaic-covered tables—this small, open-air cafe is best known for its hash and black hash (from €6 per g), pure joints (€3.50), weed (from €5-9.50 per g), cookies, *tostis*, and other munchies. Relax to Frank Zappa tunes by the blue glow of the exotic fish tank while you sample your purchases. Open daily 8am-1am.

La Canna, Nieuwendijk 121-125 (☎428 44 82; www.lacanna.nl). Follow Damrak straight out from the station, turn right on Karnemelksteeg and then left on Nieuwendijk. With a bar, coffeeshop, smart shop, res-taurant, hostel (see p. 191), and tattoo parlor, this jungle-themed party complex, on one of Amsterdam's most touristed streets, is one-stop shopping: all that's missing is a floor of gartered prostitutes. The 1st floor houses a bar with restaurant (beer €2.25; snacks €3-5, space tea €3.75); 2nd floor has pool tables (€1 per game) and a coffeeshop with an irritating mini-mum buy requirement of 5g or €20. On the 3rd, there's more pool, another bar, and a tattooist just in case you think getting Jerry Garcia's mug tattooed to your nether regions seems like a good idea. If the scene starts to run you down, pep up with the house-brew energy drink (€3). Smart shop on the ground floor vends magic mushrooms (€14-20) and smart drugs like ephedra (€3-25) or recovery pills (€3.50). Open Su-Th 9am-1am, F-Sa 9am-3am.

Fetish Gear

420 Cafe (de Kuil), Oudebrugsteeg 27 (☎623 48 48; www.420cafe.com). From Centraal, take Damrak straight out and turn right at Oudebrugsteeg. Though it's only a few blocks from Centraal Station, this cof-feehouse provides a mellow escape from the intensity

Trippin' the Light Fantastic, Abraxas

GET smart

herbal enhancers

Smart shops have begun competing with coffeeshops and sell the following types of "natural" products. Most aren't coffeeshops—more like pharmacies than bars; don't plan on whiling away an afternoon at one. Many of these substances have potentially dangerous adverse side effects; if combined with other substances, they could cause serious problems.

Cola Nut: Brazilians chewed this nut to stay awake. Can be an appetite suppressant. Don't combine with ephedra.

Ephedra: Highly controversial supplement often consumed in a tea-like substance, said to speed up heartbeat and increase alertness. Has been linked to heart attacks, seizures, permanent nerve damage, and death.

Guaraná: Supposedly enhances endurance and concentration. Similar effect as caffeine. Often added to coffee or cola to give a powerful kick. Been known to cause potentially fatal irregular heartbeats.

Skullcap: Reputedly gives a marijuana-like high, although they have also been linked to an irregular heartbeat.

Valerian: Supposedly produces an effect like Valium; a powerful muscle relaxant. Helpful for insomnia. Do not take in conjunction with other tranquilizing drugs. In excess, may cause paralysis or a weak heartbeat.

of the city center. Classic rock vibe draws an older crowd that appreciates Hendrix, the Beatles, and house fave Frank Zappa. Beer €1.70-3.20; martini just €2. And, as the sign outside demonstrates, it's always 4:20, with hash and pot, sold in increments of 1-5 g, ranging from €5-9 for 1g and €25-40 for 5g. Examine your purchase with the house microscope, through which you can look at the important THC content of the goods. Or, smoke up using one of the bar's 2 state-of-the art German vaporizers. Standard joints €3.20; pot-only joint €4.60. Pool €1 per game. Open Su-Th noon-1am, F-Sa noon-3am.

Softland, Spuistraat 222 (☎420 97 99). From Dam, walk a few blocks south on Spuistraat. Enter the otherworldly Softland intergalactic space-ship, complete with android eye tables, exposed silver piping, and green Martian lighting, for some of their space cakes (€5), hemp tea (€3.50), milkshakes, coffee, munchies, and, of course, joints (€3-4). Hash, and weed that will "beam you up" to whatever planet you came from. The winner of 3 Cannabis Cup prizes (People's Cup 3rd prize, Best Weed 2nd prize, Best Hash 3rd prize), is light years away from the other classy cafes and coffeeshops along Spuistraat. Internet €2 per 45min. Open daily 11am-1am.

Coffeeshop Any Day, Korte Kolksteeg 5 (☎420 86 98). Take Spuistraat a few blocks north from Dam and you'll find the store on your right at Korte Kolksteeg. It might be tiny (15 seats), but a sizable selection, low prices (hash €2.30-23 per g, marijuana €2.10-8 per g), and friendly staff are ready to help you any day. Coffee and fruit drinks (€1.50-3). Known around town for both its pure pot joints (skunk €4.10; haze €6.80). Don't miss out on one of their *verdampers*, or vaporizers, that look like middle school science projects with a somewhat less virtuous purpose. Avoid vaporizers with copper coils, however, as they are known to release copper particles into the vapor (see **Marijuana**, p. 127). Open daily 10am-1am.

SMART SHOPS

The Magic Mushroom, Spuistraat 249 (☎427 57 65; www.magicmushroom.com), 5min. south of Dam. At this astroturfed museum of a smartshop, get all the mushrooms, herbal XTC, energy and smart drinks, smart drugs, and stoner art you've been dreaming of. Halogen-lit display cases present merchandise and offer great insight into the world of hallucinogens and smart drugs. Chill-out corner with pillows and candles where you can try newly bought merchandise, check your email (€2 per 16min.), and sip free tea or lemonade. Also at Singel 524 (☎422 78 45). Open Su-Th 11am-10pm, F-Sa 10am-10pm. D/MC/V.

The Essential Seeds Company Art and Smart Shop, Hekelveld 2 (☎622 10 33; www.seedsexpress.nl). From Centraal, turn right, and then left at Martelaarsgracht; it's on your right just after the street becomes Nieuwezijds Voorburgwal. Hole-in-the-wall smartshop run by knowledgeable Amsterdam natives. Though they don't have weed or hash, Essential Seeds boasts 40 different kinds of seeds, 7 varieties of shrooms, and some original concoctions (mushroom chocolate bars with 3g of shrooms, €17.50; mushroom joints, €5) along with a more traditional selection of smart products. The "art" in the title is a trippy collection of colored glass pipes and bongs. Open Su-W 9am-7pm, Th-Sa 9am-9pm. MC/V.

Magic Valley, Spuistraat 60 (☎320 30 01). Just a few blocks north of Dam Sq. Magic Valley offers magic mushrooms, hemp seeds, herbal XTC, energizers, and sex stimulants in a small colorful shop that looks like it was molded from psychedelic plaster. Only expert trippers should try their Hawaiian Copeladia shrooms (€18), while novices can begin with Mexican (€13) or Thai (€14). Show this book and the owner will hook you up with a free Energizer energy drink or 10% off all magical fungi. Open daily 10am-10pm. AmEx/MC/V.

SCHEEPVAART BUURT

see map p. 342

The two-block stretch of Haarlemmerstraat just over the Haarlemmersluis and the section of Singel on either side of the bridge is home to the majority of the coffeeshops in this area. Though some are just smaller branches of larger chains—such as the **Rokerij,** at Singel 10, and **Bulldog,** at Singel 12—some have a more distinctive flavor.

Barney's, Haarlemmerstraat 102 (☎625 97 61; www.barneys-amsterdam.com). Deserved champion of the coffeeshop world: winner of the prestigious Cannabis Cup 3 (best marijuana strain) years in a row, it captured 2002 title of "Best Coffeeshop"; victorious entries Sweet Tooth (2000/2001) and Morning Glory (2002) can be bought for only €9 per g. With extraordinarily friendly staff and a full kitchen serving everything from the city's best breakfasts (omelettes €7, pancakes €4.50), delicious lemonmint shakes (€2.70), and vegetarian burritos (€8.30), Barney's is a popular spot in the heart of the Shipping Quarter. **Brasserie ❷** next door serves creative fruit shakes, cocktails (apple julep €5.20), as well as full Irish breakfasts (bacon, sausage, egg, beans, mushrooms, tomatoes, and toast; €9.50) and rib-eye (bacon, egg, beans, toast, and big-ass steak; €13.50). At the coffeeshop, both pot and hash are sold in increments of 1-5g; pot €5-11 for 1g; hash €4.50-11.50, with the popular but incredibly potent

Breakfast & a Bong at Barney's

Wolke Wietje, Nieuwe Zijd

Saucy Stuff at Absolute Danny

GET sm**art**

hash screening

If you're going to devote some time in Amsterdam to smoking, you might as well save some money and impress your friends with your knowledge of good- and bad-quality hash. To conduct your test, place a small quantity of the hash on a flat, non-flammable surface. Take a lighter and move the flame lightly over the hash for a few seconds; if the hash catches on fire after the first few attempts, you're looking at a quality smoke. If, after much time and effort, you still haven't been able to light the lump, you're probably wasting your money on hash that contains way too little THC. If you don't want to burn the THC from your hash, hold your lighter very close to the ball; if the hash starts to bubble quickly, it's a good piece. If you're smoking a joint, it should catch on fire immediately and stay lighted with a rising flame. The smoke emitted from your hash should be white or bluish-grey, and its smell should be thick and sweet, earthy instead of heavily chemical. Unpleasant odors signal the presence of nasty, unwanted contaminants in your stash.

If you don't have access to a lighter, check the general consistency of the hash by crumbling it between your fingers. Soft, malleable hash indicates large THC crystals; rock-hard hash means you're getting the dregs of some bad-quality THC.

"Helter Skelter" variety going for €25 per g. Rolled joints also available (€3-5). Two vaporizers free of charge. Coffeeshop open daily 7am-7pm. Brasserie open M-Th 10am-midnight, F-Su 8am-midnight.

Blue Velvet, Haarlemmerstraat 64 (☎627 73 29). White and ice-blue environs feel as cool as they look. The snow white cat on the premises attests to the quality of the goods available—she spends most of her time passed out on the bar. Beer €1.80; mixed drinks €3-5. Pre-rolled joints €3-4; hash and weed sold in €12 bags—visitors rate the ice as especially good. Internet kiosks in the back €1 per 15min. Open daily 11am-midnight.

Pablow Picasso, Haarlemmerstraat 6 (☎638 8079). Despite its name, this neighborhood coffeeshop isn't exactly high art—it's often crowded and not as personal as some of the other establishments just down the street. But Pablow Picasso—whose reverence for the painter apparently stops short of spelling his name correctly—does offer a blunt of a deal: buy €12.50 worth of weed or hash between 8am-noon any day of the week and you get a free breakfast. It's not quite the greasy breakfast feast that Barney's serves up, but hey—it's free. Pre-rolled joints €3-3.50. Open daily 8am-8pm.

see map p. 342

CANAL RING WEST

🌿 **Amnesia,** Herengracht 133 (☎638 30 03), at the corner of Herengracht and Bergstraat. Quiet, welcoming spot with pleasant canal views, a funky red interior, painted tables, and plush pillows. The staff here is fun and eccentric; take advantage of their free stories and advice on all topics. 1g starts at €5, 5g at €22.50. Weed joints €3. Space cake €3.50. Open Su-F 9am-11pm, Sa 9am-midnight.

🌿 **Siberie,** Brouwersgracht 11 (☎623 59 09; www.siberie.nl), just past the intersection at Singel. Unassumingly tucked into the top corner of the Canal Ring, this coffeeshop exudes a warm, serene atmosphere. However, if you get high enough, you just might start to think the *Little Shop of Horrors*-esque light fixtures are gunning to eat you. Offers a wide selection of weed and hash from all over the world, including, for 1 month each year, special ice-o-lator hash (about €13.50 per g). *Tostis* €1.60; coffee €0.70. Internet €1.15 per 30min. Open Su-Th 11am-11pm, F-Sa 11am-midnight.

Extreme Amsterdam, Huidenstraat 13 (☎773 56 98; www.coffeeshopXtreme.com). Between Herengracht and Keizersgracht and below street level, this gem of a coffeeshop offers free Internet access to its patrons

(30min. a very flexible maximum). Good quality weed and hash evidenced by the large number of regular Dutch customers. Wide variety of sizes and prices (rolled joints €2.50-5; pure weed €4-5) as well as a very friendly, helpful staff, able to answer questions and join in your indulgence. Selection of florescent bongs to use or to buy complements the colorful decor. Comfortable couch for the lounging of long-term patrons. Open M-Th 10am-midnight, F-Sa 10am-1am, Su noon-midnight.

CENTRAL CANAL RING

see map p. 340

🎴 **The Dolphins,** Kerkstraat 39 (☎ 625 91 62; www.thedolphinscoffeeshop.com), around the corner from Leidsestraat. Enter the underwater world of coral reefer madness: this ocean-themed coffeeshop, which won third place in last year's Cannabis Cup for its Royal Dolphin hash (€12.50 per gram), has a dazzlingly elaborate decor, complete with fishtanks hanging from the ceiling, wavy blue lights, and intricate coralwork on the walls. Bar serves up drinks (beer €2.75, mixed drinks €5.25) and space tea and cakes (€5). Pre-rolled joints €3.50, White Dolphin weed €8 per g. Open Su-Th 10am-1am, F-Sa 10am-3pm.

Dutch Flowers, Nieuwe Zijd

🎴 **The Noon,** Zieseniskade 22 (www.thenoon.net). From Leidseplein, head east on Kl. Gartmanpints, then cross to the south side of Lijnbaansgracht and continue for about a block. Great atmosphere near the buzz of Leidseplein but immune to the tourist hordes. Buddha mural, embroidered velvet pillows, and wooden statues of writhing dragons on the bar aim for the ambience of an Asian temple—just don't ask how the ivy hung on the ceiling fits in. Weed and hash range from standard to extremely powerful; try the Blue Berry bud (1g €7, 5g €23). White Melon (1g €6, 2.5g €11) and the Noon Blueberry Ice hash (1g €27) also come highly recommended. Intense pot-only blueberry joints €7. The staff highly recommends the Honey hash (1g €10.). Open daily 9am-1am.

Anything Goes

Stix, Utrechtsestraat 21 (www.stix.nl), near Herengracht. A mostly local crowd chills to cool jazz in this tiny, sophisticated coffeeshop with clean wooden tables and park bench-like seating. Large picture windows and high ceilings make for a light, airy feel. The staff at Stix is always happy to let you inspect samples of their high-quality, all-organic smokeables. Glass bongs €7.50-28. Royal Stix, Shiva, and their homemade Gunpowder—which is pure THC—pack the strongest kick. Sold in 1g increments for €5.50-8; buy 5g and get a 10% discount. Pre-rolled joints €4. Open daily 11am-1am.

Magic Valley, Nieuwe Zijd

137

the local story

pot quiz, hotshot

Mark has owned The Rookies coffeeshop (p. 139) in Leidseplein for over 10 years. He's a "second-generation cannabis retailer" and on the board of two cannabis unions.

Q: What do you like about working in a coffeeshop?

A: It's not aggressive, it's a very tolerant atmosphere and people from all over the world come in.

Q: What is it about Dutch culture that makes cannabis permissible here and nowhere else?

A: It started because they needed to separate the soft and hard drug markets. If a young person wants to get high, he goes to a coffeeshop and doesn't get involved with other stuff. In other countries, the same person who sells cannabis will sell ecstasy, pills, cocaine, etc. Coffeeshops are very clean; there are no hard drugs here. They're still here because it's working. Neighboring countries are beginning to follow our system. The Christian Democrats Party wants to get rid of everything, but it's unrealistic to think you can get rid of drugs; there's always going to be people who use them. It's better to leave it in the open, not shove it under the carpet; if it's still in the open you have more social control on it.

continued on next page

Coffeeshop Little, Vijzelstraat 47 (☎420 13 86; www.coffeshoplittle.com). Tram #16, 24, or 25 to Weteringcircuit and backtrack ½ of a block; it's on the right. Descend the yellow-tiled stairs to this mellow coffeeshop that feels like a homey living room. True to its name, this coffeeshop is as *gezellig* (cozy) as they come, with a chess table and cushy couches. Good deals on hash and weed (€6-7 per g; joints €3). Open Su-Th 8am-midnight, F-Sa 8am-1am.

Tops, Prinsengracht 480 (☎638 41 08). Homages to Jimi Hendrix and Led Zeppelin characterize this canal side coffeehouse, which has an impressive 8 Internet terminals available for customers (€1.60 per 20min.). Weed sold in €6, €12 or €23 bags, which gets you up to 4.3g of bud. Beer €1.60; in a bottle, €2.80. Mixed drinks from €3. Open Su-Th 10pm-1am, F-Sa 10pm-3am.

Global Chillage, Kerkstraat 51 (☎777 99 77; www.globalchillage.org), between Leidsestraat and Nieuwe Spiegelstraat. Take tram #1, 2, or 5 to Prinsengracht, then walk back along the tram line for 1 block. From there, take a right onto the small Kerkstraat. A mural of mythical creatures, bright purple-and-red booths, and an artificial tree whose butterfly-adorned leaves overhang the ceiling give visitors to Global Chillage a feeling that you've entered the world of *The Hobbit*. Fantasy furnishings and mellow ambient trance music provide a good environment to get high or to trip. Chillage has a standard array of pot and hash available in €6 and €12 bags, which buys 0.8-1.1g and 1.7-2.2g of goods, respectively. Joints with 0.5g of hash €4; the organic, pot-only Surprise spliff packs all different weed varieties in one bag (€12 for 3g). Open daily 10am-midnight.

SMART SHOPS

Dreamlounge Smartshop, Kerkstraat 93 (☎626 69 07; www.consciousdreams.nl). Five kinds of mushrooms, from Mexican to truffles to Hawaiian. Mushrooms €12.50 or €17.50; herbal ecstasy €3.85-13.95. Staff is willing to guide your experience. Affiliated with Conscious Dreams Kokopelli (see p. 131). Internet access €1.20 per 15min. Open M-W 11am-7pm, Th-Sa 11am-8pm, Su noon-5pm. AmEx/MC/V for purchases over €25.

Seeds of Passion, Utrechtsestraat 26 (☎625 11 00; www.seedsofpassion.nl). Seeds of Passion's giant plastic pot fronds and little stools hewn from tree stumps complete the sense that you've walked into some kind of drug-happy fairytale at this upscale store that sells cannabis seeds from all over the world (€12.50-125 for 10 seeds). A huge, impressive specialty selection of seeds makes this the place to go if you're in the market; just keep it in the country. Open M-Sa 11am-6pm.

LEIDSEPLEIN

⬛ The Rookies, Korte Leidsedwarsstraat 145-146 (☎ 639 09 78). One of the few remaining places outside of the Red Light District that serves both liquor and marijuana, The Rookies

see map p. 341

feels more like a bustling neighborhood bar than a trippy coffeeshop. Entertainments include a pool table, chess game, and TV. Outdoor seating in summer. All bags, such as the potent house-specialty Rookie Skunk, sold in €12 increments. Pre-rolled joint €3; pot-only joint €5, or you can borrow a bong. Shoot a rack of pool for €1. Beer €1.60. Open Su-Th 10am-1am, F-Sa 10am-3am.

SMART SHOP

Tatanka, Korte Leidsedwarsstraat 151A (☎ 771 69 16). Gorgeous two-story feels as much like a museum as smart shop. Range of goods includes shrooms (Mexican and Thai €12, "The Philosopher" €15), smart drugs, grow-your-own kits, and sterling silver and turquoise jewelry. Homemade herbal ecstasy with Tatanka label. Mural-covered chill room upstairs, where, as the owner says, you can "enter the feeling of mushrooms." Open July 1-Oct. 1. Buy 4 packs of mushrooms, get 1 free. Open 11am-10pm.

REMBRANDT PLEIN

The Other Side, Reguliersdwarsstraat 6 (☎ 421 10 14; www.theotherside.nl). Tram #1, 2, or 5 to Koningsplein.

see map p. 340

Friendly, bustling coffeeshop popular with the gay scene but open to everyone. There's very little decor here, but the staff is so personable it almost feels homey. Bags are sold in increments of €11.50, €23, and €46 for everything from 1.5g to 13.59g; €1-2 discount for buying in bulk. Pure joints €4.75; space cake €3.60. Open daily 11am-1am.

Free I, Reguliersdwarsstraat 70 (☎ 622 77 27). Tram #1, 2, or 5 to Koningsplein. A beach mural atop bamboo walls adds nicely to this casual, lazy atmosphere. The knowledgeable staff can help with recommendations for any smoker. Try the potent "Power Haze" grass (€9.50 per g, €42.75 per 5g) or knock yourself out with the "Spice Ice" hash (€30 per g), which has a mind-blowing 65% THC content; The Afghan hash (€13 per g) is much milder. Buy 2g grass and get 0.5g "Yellow" weed free during daily Happy Hour (noon-2pm and 6-8pm). Joints €3.40; space cakes/ candy €5. Open daily 9am-1am.

continued from previous page

Q: When the laws on marijuana were first relaxed in the early 70s, did anyone protest?
A: Of course; only 10% of the Dutch population smokes. Even now if you want to open a coffeeshop, some are against it. It's still somehow a conservative country.

Q: 10%?
A: More youngsters smoke [cannabis] in England than in The Netherlands. Maybe 1.5% of users have a problem... but with alcohol it's as high as 20%. A lot of people are pointing at the 1.5%—I think it's ridiculous.

Q: Since cannabis isn't legal, just tolerated, how socially accepted is it? Would employers hesitate to hire someone who'd worked in a coffeeshop?
A: Not really, it depends on the person. I had a manager who worked here four years and is now a policeman.

Q: How do you think membership in the EU will affect the status of coffeeshops?
A: It's a minor thing. They recently made a law that allows French policemen to arrest someone here if he committed a felony. But there are two exceptions: one is for coffeeshops selling soft drugs and the other is euthanasia. Only France and Sweden are giving us problems about it, France especially. But their alcoholism rate is so high; it's really ridiculous that they're complaining about drugs. They complain that drugs come from Holland, but so many drugs come from Morocco. And if it comes from Morocco, then it has to come through France.

The Saint, Regulierssteeg 1, on an alley off Reguliersbreestraat. Dank, dim nest pulses to constant reggae. Middle Eastern wall decorations and Bob Marley posters overlook a handful of tables. Not the most inviting, but has a bar serving fresh fruit juice and hash fruit shakes (€5; without hash €3.50). Hash coffee, tea, and hot chocolate €4-4.50. Cannabis sold in €13 bags (1.4-3.2g). Open daily 9am-1am.

JORDAAN

see maps p. 342

☘ **Paradox,** 1e Bloemdwarsstraat 2 (☎623 56 39; www.paradoxam-sterdam.demon.nl). To match its neighborhood location, the emphasis at Paradox is on color, freshness, and relaxation. Weed and hash €5-24; bongs for the borrowing. More than just munchies: grab positively the best veggie burger you've ever had in your life for just €4.10, or a big yogurt shake for €3.50. Freshly-squeezed juices €2.30-€3.40. Open daily 10am-8pm; kitchen closes 3pm.

La Tertulia, Prinsengracht 312. Most coffeeshop "themes" offer more camp than charm, but La Tertulia's casual botanical decor isn't too heavy-handed, with rickety garden furniture and leafy plants everywhere. Pot brownies €4; rolled joints €3. Special Hawaiian haze, extolled by *Smoker's Guide*, runs €12 per g. Bubble ice-o-lator hash €20 per g. Also sells seeds. Open Tu-Sa 11am-7pm.

Black Star Coffeeshop, Rozengracht 1a (☎626 9469; www.coffeeshopafricanblackstar.nl). This coffeeshop prefers weed Jamaican-style, with a reggae soundtrack, Bob Marley posters, and red, yellow and green motif. Predominately African-Dutch clientele. Bags of grass for €10 (1.5-3g, depending on the type). Internet access available (€1 per 20min.). Open Su-Th 11am-midnight, F-Sa 11am-1am.

Spirit Coffeeshop, Westerstraat 121 (☎625 46 50; www.coffeeshop-spirit.com). Open later than most coffeeshops, Spirit will keep the discriminating stoner busy with pool, arcade games, and foosball (€0.50). All beverages €1.50-2.95; grass will run you €6 or €12 a bag, amounts vary based on quality. Pre-rolled joints €2.25-4.55. Open daily 1pm-1am.

OUD-WEST

see map p. 346

☘ **Kashmir Lounge,** Jan Pieter Heijstr. 85-87 (☎683 22 68). Tram #17 to J.P. Heijestr., or tram #1 or 6 to Jan Pieter Heijestr.; walk away from Overtoom up J.P. Heijestr. and cross Lennepkanal. From the dark interior, mysteriously lit by candlelight, to the intricate ornamentation on every wall to the large pillow corner, it's the perfect place to sit back and toke up. Reflecting its location in the diverse and lively Oud-West, Kashmir attracts customers of every stripe. Hash €3.10-8 per g. Marijuana €4.55-9 per g. DJs every M-F from 9pm, Sa-Su from 10pm. Pre-rolled joints €2.30-4.55. Open M-Th 10am-1am, F-Sa 10am-3am, Su 11am-1am.

The Top, Gilles van Ledenberchstr. 135. Tram #3 to Hugo de Grootpl., then walk away from the Nassaukade for 2 blocks; The Top is on the corner. This living room-style coffeeshop will bring back memories of smoking up at home—if home involved a giant turquoise mural and a seemingly limitless supply of grass (€3-7 per g). Hash €3-10. Pre-rolled joints €3-4. Open M-F 10am-midnight, Sa noon-midnight, Su 1pm-midnight.

MUSEUMPLEIN & VONDELPARK

see map p. 347

tWEEDy, Vondelstraat 104 (☎618 03 44), at 2e Constantijn Huygen-straat. Low-key coffeeshop with a pool table. Known for its friendly, knowledgeable staff. Park-side location makes it a great place for grab-bing a joint before a nature walk. Excellent, oily hashish Malana Cream is a specialty. €7.50-15 buys 1.2-2.26g of several varieties, from White Widow to stronger Power Plant weed. Open daily 11am-midnight.

DE PIJP

Yo Yo, 2e van der Heijdenstraat 79 (☎664 71 73). Tram #3, 4, or 20 to Van Wou/Ceintuurbaan. So warm it's nearly wholesome, Yo Yo is unlike any other coffeeshop. The mother who runs this place keeps it stocked with famous apple pie (€1.50 per slice). One of the few coffeeshops where non-smokers will come just to have a cup of coffee. *Tostis,* soup, and (normal) brownies also served. Homemade quiche €1.15. All weed is organic and sold in bags for €5 or €10, with a monthly €3.50 special. Open daily noon-7pm.

see map p. 348

Katsu, 1e van der Helststraat 70 (www.katsu.nl). Probably the most popular coffeeshop in De Pijp, a centrally located neighborhood spot with a pleasantly beat-up feel that's loud, lively, and packed every day with locals of all ages. Its "Crystal Clear" water hash comes highly recommended (€12 per 0.5g); the Sage weed is also famed. All marijuana and hash sold in €12 increments, which gets you 1-3.8g of weed or 0.5-3.4g of hash. A vaporizer is available for use. Open M-Th 5-11pm, F-Sa 11am-midnight, Su noon-11pm.

Bom Shankar Chaishop, Albert Cuypstraat 17 (☎673 08 95). Great local spot with a friendly, open vibe. South Asian motif prevails with cool mural of Goa Beach and delicious house specialty spicy chai (€1.50). Smokeable selection includes many varieties of Moroccan hash and weed (€4.50-€20 per g), including the storied "incredible Dutch hash cream," topping the price list at €20 per g. 20% discount on purchases of €50 or more. Good customers can use the music studio with bongo drums and computers in the back. Also, check out the pretty "Rio Grande" bathrooms. Chess tournaments too; check with store for times. Open M-W 9am-10pm, Th-Sa 10am-midnight, Su 10am-10pm.

Club Media, Gerard Doustraat 83-85 (☎664 58 89). Pick a poison: football, media, or marijuana or pick them all. The coffeeshop earns its name with 2 TVs and a daily selection of newspapers and magazines. It's also popular with supporters of the Ajax Football Club; thus it's populated by a tougher, but still very friendly, crowd. And the 3rd obsession: pot in increments of €5.75 gets 0.7-1g or 1.6-2.2g of pot, and 0.7-1.5g or 1.8-3.3g of hash. Pre-rolled joints €2.80-3.40. Free fruit plate with purchase. Free pool and darts. Open daily 10am-1am.

JODENBUURT & PLANTAGE

Bluebird, Sint Antoniesbreestraat 71 (☎622 52 32). 2 stories of azure chill space include a big overstuffed leather couch for a communal vibe as well as quieter alcoves for a thoughtful smoke. At this companionable spot, the vast menu is presented in 2 thick scrapbooks that include real samples of each variety of hash and marijuana for inspection. Sample the high-quality house blend (1.4g for €12) or try the ice-o-lator hash (0.5g for €12). Tasty, fresh juices come in a rainbow of fruit flavors (€2-2.30). Open daily 9:30am-1am.

see map p. 349

Green House, Waterlooplein 345. Travelers pour into Green House for its reliable selection and cozy setting. The shop features ethnic paraphernalia, tasteful murals, and seating on leather or plush velvet couches. Indica Big Bang €8 per g. Prerolled joints: weed €2.80; hash and tobacco €5.50; pure weed mix €5.50. Open Su-Th 10am-midnight, F-Sa 10am-1am.

Het Ballonnetje, Roetersstraat 12 (☎622 80 27). Across the street from the University of Amsterdam. With 35 kinds of tea (€1.20), soup, cookies, and plenty of other homemade goodies, this coffeeshop is a pleasant stop not only for smokers, but also for those just looking for a bite to eat and a place to rest. Terrariums, houseplants, and a healthy mix of students and locals make the shop a welcome respite from the more commercial coffeeshops in the city. Popular Super Skunk €6 per g. Hash €3-9 per g. Open daily 10am-midnight.

Hortus De Overkant, Nieuwe Herengracht 71 (☎620 65 77). Order from an informative menu, and take it to go–there's no seating here. Weekly deals on wide array Dutch-grown skunk and a microscope for scrutiny. €4.40 per 0.8g for all varieties. "StudentSmoke" deal gets 20% more weed. Complimentary soft drink with purchase. Open daily 10am-midnight.

141

Nightlife

Amsterdam's reputation as a capital of libertinism is most famously embodied by its coffeeshops, but its nightlife provides ample opportunity to do (or be) anything (or anyone) you want. Clubs cater to gay and straight, observers and dancers alike, while bars alternate between classic, old-Amsterdam *bruin cafes* (brown cafes—whose ceilings are weathered and brown from years of tobacco smoke) and their modern counterpart, the fancily named **grand cafe.** Step out into Amsterdam after dark and you'll acquire first-hand knowledge as to why it's said that the best visit to this city is one that you can't remember.

Though Amsterdam boasts a world-class nightclub scene, it is one that is refreshingly focused on dancing and having a good time rather than posing and outglamming the other clubsters. That said, you'll find a few long lines and discerning bouncers at the most popular establishments, which cluster near **Rembrandtplein** and lie along **Reguliersdwarsstraat.** The clubs closer to the center of town, particularly in the Nieuwe Zijd, are generally bombarded with boisterous tourists. To increase your chances of admission, try one or all of the following: be neatly dressed; be sober in mind and behavior (bouncers revel in throwing out swaying drunks); and be female (or in the presence of same-sex clubs, seek to achieve gender balance). If you want to return to a club, it's wise to **tip the bouncer** as you leave to assure his grace on your next visit. Lines are short before midnight, so showing up early can help you get in. Keep in mind, though, that this works well only because people don't show up at clubs until about midnight or 1am. Before then, locals pack into bars to pre-party. While coffeeshops may seem attractive, for an evening of revelry, they are not popular haunts for local nightlife. Smoking up in clubs is also frowned upon.

LGB ▼
AMSTERDAM

gay nightlife

The rainbow flag flies proudly in Amsterdam—the city enjoys one of the most open and accessible gay scenes in the Western world. The country legalized gay marriage in 2001—the first country to do so—and entertains a very active **gay nightlife** scene with dozens of clubs and bars geared towards LGB customers. However, labeling nightlife in Amsterdam as "gay" or "straight" is very misleading—Amsterdam's after-hours scene usually admits all; men- or women-only scenes are specified as such in our listings. The area near **Rembrandtplein** (especially **Reguliersdwarsstraat**) is lined with bars, clubs, and cafes and serves as Amsterdam's gay center, though there's still plenty open to the straight set. The city's **leather scene** is particularly prominent, and there are a variety of **sex shows** and **safe-sex parties.** Though there's plenty for men to rave about, lesbians may find the scene a little disappointing. The number of places and activities catering only to lesbians (well-represented by the lively **Saarein II** and **Vive La Vie**), are unfortunately few—a better bet is to look for gay or straight establishments with lesbian-themed nights. For more information on all of LGB Amsterdam, particularly nightlife, visit **Pink Point** in the Canal Ring West (see p. 67).

GAY & LESBIAN NIGHTLIFE

Amsterdam's gay nightlife may very well claim the prize as Europe's best, capturing intensity and fun through its many outlets. **Reguliersdwarsstraat** reigns as the undisputed king of the gay party scene with large clubs that tend to be upbeat, cruisey, and unabashedly flamboyant. For a taste of kinkiness, try the smaller, darker clubs at **Warmoesstraat,** which feature quite a bit of rubber and leather, housing an occasional anything goes (so long as it's safe) darkroom for the truly intrepid adventurer. There are fewer bars and clubs that cater specifically to lesbians, but those that do are popular. They are not always heavily populated but have decidedly less attitude than their male counterparts. Many gay clubs host lesbian-themed nights as well, so party-loving ladies can always explore a fair share of options. The distinctive gay and lesbian nightlife scene does not suggest a separation of sorts however, as most clubs welcome any type of sexual orientation, with predominantly straight venues drawing a fair number of gay patrons on any given night. For gay and lesbian events, the best publication is the monthly *Gay and Night* (written in Dutch with some English articles) which provides information on gay life in the city with updates on upcoming parties, and ads for singles and escorts.

BEER & SPIRITS

Amsterdam is a blissful paradise for the frugal beer drinker. In addition to its native brews—the familiar Amstel, Grolsch, and Heineken, and the more exotic De Koninck and Wieckse Witte—you'll also find bars vending a panoply of Belgian Trappist ales and hearty German lagers. A small glass (*fluitje*, about 220 cL) of native brew runs about €1.60-2.80; larger *vaasjes*, (about 250 cL), generally run €1.90-3.50. Pints, generally consumed by over-zealous American or British expats and tourists, are €3-5. The Belgian ales—Vos, Duvel, and Palm—tend to be pricier (€2.70-4.50 for a *vaasje*-sized glass), but they pack a headier kick due to their high alcohol content.

A glass of Dutch spirits, including the beloved local gin, *jenever*, will usually run about €1.80-2.20, while other sorts of hard liquor go for €2.20-3.50. When the Dutch want it hard, they'll take it straight, but you can order a mixed drink by adding the price of a tonic, juice, or soda (usually €1.60-2.50) to a straight shot of liquor. If you're completely undecided, ask the bartender for a *kopstoot* (kop-stout; meaning "head-butt"), a balanced combination of a *fluitje* of local beer and a shot of *jenever*. Cocktails are not very popular in Amsterdam, but you'll be sure to find a menu for frilly drinks at most posh, upscale bars (around €6).

TYPES OF BARS

Amsterdam offers two varieties of bars. *Bruin cafes* (brown cafes), deriving their names from the dark tone of their interiors, are the traditional wooden pubs that cater largely to locals. With brown, smoke-stained walls and hard benches, these bars epitomize *gezellig* (coziness), the small space jammed with old-style beer ads, ancient paintings, and other random detritus. Grand cafes, on the other hand, are a modern riposte to their brown counterparts. As sleek and airy as the *bruin cafes* are cozy and dim, grand cafes cater to a younger, hipper, international crowd with fashionable outdoor terraces and elegantly modern furniture.

Whether brown or grand, Dutch bar life has a distinctly mellow tenor. Locals tend to chat at a table for hours while nursing a single glass, leading many a foreigner to remark on the minimalism of Dutch drinking. There is, of course, a fair share of lively, drunken haunts, but in those establishments, you'll most likely be getting sloshed with a group of fellow tourists. The line between bar and cafe blur as well, as most bars offer food and just about all cafes serve alcohol. Bar-cafes are thus quite popular, serving nourishment serenely by day, then morphing into a crowded bar by 9-10pm at night. Drink prices at bars and even at more upscale clubs tend to be fairly constant within the range prescribed above. A gratuity of about 10% is expected in bars and clubs, and the easiest and most common way to tip is by rounding up to the nearest Euro.

If **live music** is your game of choice, head straight to **Leidseplein,** home to the city's most famous and popular venues. Be warned, however, that due to byzantine regulations, the Melkweg and Paradiso, among others, charge a membership fee to patrons. The fee lasts for the duration of the month in which you purchase it and will tack on an additional €2.50 to the first ticket you buy. See **Live Music,** p. 165.

BY NEIGHBORHOOD

OUDE ZIJD

Café de Jaren, Nieuwe Doelenstraat 20-22 (☎ 625 57 71). From Muntplein, cross the Amstel and proceed ahead for half a block. Sweet relief on a hot day, this fabulous 2-floor cafe's air of sophistication doesn't quite mesh with its budget-friendly prices. Gaze at sweeping views of the Amstel through vaulted plate-glass windows or dine in style atop the Café de Jaren's waterfront deck. This is as authentic a slice of

see map p. 344

Amsterdam cafe society as you're likely to find, and a bona fide student haunt as well, thanks to the University of Amsterdam's location right across the street. Bottom floor serves same light menu all day with soups and salads (€3.40-6), sandwiches (€2.50-4.50), and full hot meals (€11). Upstairs changes to dinner menu after 5:30pm (main courses around €14).

inside

SECRETS TO...

nachtcafes

Even in Amsterdam, all good things must end. In fact, the city heavily regulates bar closing times, limiting hours of operation for bars to 1am Sunday through Thursday and 3am Friday and Saturday. But if you're not ready to call it an evening, fear not; just head to one of Amsterdam's **nachtcafes (night bars).** These establishments that have a special license to stay open an hour or two later than their standard counterparts. Nachtcafes are all about drinking, so you won't find anything elaborate in the way of atmosphere or decor. In fact, most have to adhere to a subdued aesthetic motif per local regulations. Getting a license requires having an unobtrusive exterior and interior (both are usually black and dim), and the music stays low so as not to disturb sleeping neighbors.

Drink prices tend to be on the steep side—a *fluitje* runs about €2.40 and pints cost €4.50. The whole affair has a vaguely illicit, speakeasy feel, especially because you must ring a bell to gain admittance.

One of the most famous nachtcafe is **San Francisco,** Zeedijk 40-42, where an edgy crowd of hard drinkers piles in when most of the Red Light District has gone to bed (open Su-Th midnight-4am, F-Sa midnight-5am). There is also a moderate concentration of night bars in **De Pijp.**

Two impressive bars serve cocktails and beer (€1.80-3.10). Open Su-Th 10am-1am, F-Sa 10am-2am; kitchen open Su-Th until 10:30pm, F-Sa until midnight; dinner menu 5:30-10:30pm.

Cafe Heffer, Oudebrugsteeg 7 (☎428 44 90), at Beursstraat. Situated in the former house of the city tax collector, the Heffer blends the traditional Dutch *bruin cafe* motif with modern touches. High ceilings, ample light, and a sprawling patio decked with sun umbrellas provide an oasis from the ebb and flow of the pushers, pimps, and prostitutes in the Red Light District. The Venloosh Ale is a bit pricey (glass €2.10; pint €4.60), but the cafe's pleasant atmosphere makes it a stylish refuge to relax and people-watch. Open Su-Th 10am-1am, F-Sa 9:30am-3am; kitchen closes 5pm. Cash only.

Casablanca, Zeedijk 24-26 (☎625 56 85; www.casablanca-amsterdam.nl), between Oudezijds Kolk and Vredenburgersteeg. Casablanca has been around since 1946 and, though its heyday as *the* jazz bar in Amsterdam has faded, it's still one of the best for live jazz. Dim and smoky, the Casablanca retains a moody feel and is still quite popular with locals. At Zeedijk 26, live jazz Su-W nights; Th-Sa DJ-hosted house dance parties, occasional karaoke. Right next door at 24, Casablanca serves dinner 4pm-1am accompanied by variety shows that dabble in magic, cabaret, drama, and even clown acts. Check the website for up-coming performances. €5 cover (Zeedijk 24 only). Open Su-Th 8pm-3am, F-Sa 8pm-4am. MC/V.

Café de Engelbewaarder, Kloveniersburgwal 59 (☎625 37 72). An enjoyable bar atmosphere any time of the week but truly comes alive on Su for a set of superb live jazz. Belgian Maes beer on tap €1.70. Large, welcoming room and exceptionally friendly bartenders round out the experience. Jan.-June and Sept.-Dec. Su live jazz 4:30pm-7pm. Open M-Th noon-1am, F-Sa noon-3am, Su 2pm-1am. Kitchen open noon-3pm and 5:30-10pm. Cash only.

Getto, Warmoesstraat. 51 (☎421 51 51; www.getto.nl). In the heart of the Red-Light District, this joint-friendly bar and cafe is beloved for its kicky cocktails (try "Getto Blaster" or "Thirsty Vampire"; €6) and its hip, loungey decor. Primarily a gay and lesbian establishment, but everyone feels welcome here. Serves appetizers for €4-6 and main dishes like the favorite veggie burger (€10-15). Tarot card readings Su 8pm-11pm (about €10). Tu-Sa 2-for-1 cocktail Happy Hour 5-7pm; Su Cocktail Bash (all cocktails €4) 5-7pm. Open Tu-Th 4pm-1am, F-Sa 4pm-2am, Su 4pm-midnight. Cafe open daily 6-11pm.

Lokaal 't Loosje, Nieuwmarkt 32-34 (☎627 26 35). This classic *bruin cafe* is beloved by Oude Zijd locals for its mellow come-as-you-are vibe and its well-preserved classic art deco wall tile decor. Frequented mainly by a 20-something-and-older crowd, Lokaal 't

Loosje is a popular spot to sit outside and watch the buzz of the Nieuwmarkt ebb and flow around you. A glass of Heineken beer runs an average of €1.70. Open Su-Th 9:30am-1am, F-Sa 9:30am-3am. Cash only.

Durty Nelly's Pub, Warmoesstraat 115-117 (☎638 01 25). From Centraal Station, go south on Damrak, turn right on Brugsteeg, and then right on Warmoesstraat; Nelly's is 2 blocks down on the left. Down and durty Irish pub on the edge of the Red Light District where Celtic barkeeps draw a mean pint of Guinness (€4.60; other beer €2-4.60). Superpowered A/C and big-screen TV featuring the latest sporting events make Nelly's a great place to beat the heat on sweltering summer days. Good quality pub grub; grab a lighter meal (baked potato loaded with your choice of toppings €4-5) or heartier fare (hamburger with fries) for €10-14. Vegetarian lasagna €8.50. Open Su-Th 9am-1am (until 4am for hostel guests, see p. 147); F-Sa 9am-3am (until 5am for hostel guests). Kitchen open noon-10pm. Cash only.

Lime, Zeedijk 104 (☎639 30 20), just north of Nieuwmarkt. The ultimate lounge with all the accoutrements of the space-age bachelor pad—a disco ball casts slivers of light on pleather couches and a projection of floating globs covers the wall behind the bar. Popular with the pre-club crowd and refreshingly low on attitude. Soul, house, and jazzy tunes make for easy listening. For a quick sugar fix, chomp on some chocolate bars from the Twix dispenser in the back corner of the room. Beer €1.80; Bacardi Breezers and imported brew €3.85. Cigarettes sold at bar. Open Su-Th 5pm-1am, F-Sa 5pm-3am. AmEx/MC/V.

Wijnand Fockink, 31 Pijlsteeg (☎639 26 95), on an alleyway just off Dam Sq. Perhaps the most unique bar you'll visit in Amsterdam, the place is over 300-years old and looks it: dusty and creaky floors, dark, antique decor, and no chairs. The hook: unequivocally the best *fockink* liquor (Dutch gin) in the city. available in over 60 flavors: appletart, peppermint, and the famous half and half. Try a glass of the potent brand (20% alcohol) for only €2.50. Room is cramped so stop by the *slijterij* where you can bring bottles home to show your friends what *fockink* in Amsterdam is all about (bottles €20). Open daily 3-9pm. Cash only.

Cock & Feathers, Zeedijk 23-25, (☎624 31 41; www.cockandfeathers.nl). Mood lighting and a low-key environment make this gay bar the perfect pre-club spot to hit for a drink or a lively chat. Music plays and the disco ball revolves with a DJ Fr-Sat, but the atmosphere is much more "sit and talk" than "get up and shake your groove thang." Bottles of beer €2.60, pints €4.50. Primarily gay clientele but everyone is and feels welcome. Open Su and Tu-Th 5pm-1am, F-Sa 4pm-3am. Kitchen open 6pm-10pm. Cash only.

Stablemaster, Warmoesstraat 23 (☎625 01 48). This cowboy-and-western-themed bar is strewn with gay erotica and famed for its "JO parties," for which patrons strip down to the buck and let it all hang out (from 9pm every night of business). Any form of sex goes here, as long as it's safe; condoms are provided free of charge, there are lube dispensers by the bar, and there's even a saddle on a stool located upstairs. Men only. Cover €6; 1-drink min. Beer €3; hard alcohol €4.50. Open Su-M, Th 9pm-1am; F-Sa 7pm-3am. AmEx/MC/V only for payments of €25 and higher.

Cafe de Stevens, Geldersekade 123 (☎620 69 70), just off Nieuwmarkt. If you're put off by the unmitigated pretension of its neighbors, head to the welcomingly understated Stevens, a great spot to read in the afternoon or enjoy an after-dinner *apertif* while listening to the low-key mix on the stereo. Down a cheap pint of Heineken (€3.50) or dig into the freshly made apple tarts (€3). Warm snacks and *broodjes* served daily noon-4pm with light treats available afterward. Open Su-Th 11:30am-1am, F-Sa 11:30am-3am.

CLUBS

Cockring, Warmoesstraat 96 (☎623 96 04, www.clubcockring.com). Just look for the giant cockring on the sign. Living up to its self-awarded title as "Amsterdam's Premier Gay Disco," Cockring straddles the line between a sex club and a disco; you can come to dance or get lucky. DJs play for studly men who readily doff clothing as things heat up. Live sex shows and strippers Sa 11pm-4am (Sa €5; Th and Su free). Special "SafeSex" parties May-Jul. and 3rd Su of every month—dress code "shoes only" or "naked" (€6.50; free condoms and sandwiches). Dark room in the back where anything goes. Disco M-Tu, techno/trance Th-Su. Men only. No cover, except for special parties. Open Su-Th 11pm-4am, F-Sa 11pm-5am.

out & about

jenever– proost!

Though The Netherlands is a beer drinker's paradise there's more to Dutch drinking than the typical lineup of Heineken, Amstel, and any number of imported Belgian beers. Not for the faint of heart or weak of stomach, **jenever** is Dutch gin, or grain spirits infused with juniper berries. Jenever is something of a national drink, as many controversially claim that Dr. Sylvius de Bouve of Leiden invented gin when he first performed the process in the mid-17th century. The drink was originally valued for supposed medicinal properties, and the older Dutch generation now down the oily beverage without regard to any sort of health benefits (or dangers). There are two types of jenever, jonge (young) and oude (old). The names are misleading, however, because they have nothing to do with the age of the actual drink. Oude jenever is light yellow and has a stronger taste than the jonge, which is clear and more similar to the gin familiar to the rest of the world. The Dutch sip shots of gin, or drink it with black currant flavoring, though the younger set, especially students, avoid it like the plague.

see map p. 342

NIEUWE ZIJD

BARS

▨ **NL Lounge,** Nieuwezijds Voorburgwal 169 (☎622 75 10), just south of Dam, on the same side of the street. Far too cool for an outside sign, the trendy NL is the unmarked destination where some of Amsterdam's slickest, best-dressed, and most sophisticated insiders of all persuasions come to get lost in the stiff drinks (€6) and intense red theme. Early in the evening, music varies, but at 1am, the beat invariably switches over to trippy techno. Get there early (before midnight) on weekend nights, and dress to the nines—the bouncers are picky, and obnoxious tourists will be turned away. No cover; mandatory €1 coat-check. Open Su-Th 10pm-3am, F-Sa 10pm-4am.

▨ **Absinthe,** Nieuwezijds Voorburgwal 171 (☎320 67 80), just south of Dam. Recently remodeled with variegated layers of magenta leather couches and intimate, candle-lit corners, Absinthe looks poised to attract a sleek crowd of young sophisticates—although during the week there may be more British tourists than you might want. Lively bar that fills with the purple light of several disco balls. Don't leave without some of the fluorescent-green house drink: a variant called "Smart Absinthe" with 10% wormwood (€10). Buzzing bar with a few quiet corners for intimate chats. Trancy music sets a good tone, and it's soft enough to speak without shouting. Open Su-Th 8pm-3am, F-Sa 8pm-4am.

The Tara, Rokin 85-89 (☎421 26 54; www.thetara.com), a few blocks south of Dam. Vast Irish-themed watering hole with an enormous, maze-like interior. Velveteen wallpaper, red leather couches, and huge stone fireplaces give Tara the feel of a 19th-century drawing room or hunting lodge. Cozy, candlelit corners are ideal for blustery winter evenings, but don't get caught in a romantic tête-à-tête here on soccer days—the slightly older crowd of British expats can get raucous. Three bars where they know how to pull a real pint of Guinness (€4.50; regular draft beer €1.90-3.90). DJs or bands (traditional Irish, Flamenco, and jazz) usually turn up Th-Sa—call ahead or check the website for details. Open Su-Th 11am-1am, F-Sa 11am-3am. AmEx/D/MC/V.

Vrankvijk, Spuistraat 216 (www.vrankvijk.org). 3 blocks north of the Spui; look for the building whose facade is covered by a Lichtenstein-inspired mural. Booming punk music and incredibly cheap drinks (fluitje €0.90; bottle of Gulpener €1.10; glass of Chouffe €1.30) in a long-standing, well-known squat with no visible tourists (see **Squat Culture,** p. 152). Leave your bourgeois accoutrements at home when you come here: the crowd consists largely of mohawked, leather-jacketed folks who still seem pissed about the death of Sid Vicious. Sprawl out beneath the political-poster-plastered walls and drink up; all the beer is from small European breweries and proceeds go to support progressive causes. Ring the bell to be let in. M gay and lesbian night; Tu proceeds go to refugees; Th 8-9:30pm squatter information hour; Sa disco night. Open M-W 9pm-1am, Th 9:30pm-1am, F 9pm-3am, Sa 10pm-3am, Su "when they feel like it"-1am.

Rockstar Lights, Melkweg

Bep, Nieuwezijds Voorburgwal 260 (☎626 56 49). Created in the image of the space-age bachelor pad with fake stone walls, wrap-around bar, olive-green decor, and a glittery disco ball. Small, swank, and popular with the pre-clubbers, Bep is crowded on weekend nights when sharply done-up hipsters spill out onto the front patio with their fancy cocktails. Both lunch (*broodjes* and soup €4) and dinner are on the pricier side (Thai curries €11-15.50). Beer €1.80; spirits €3.40-4.80; *mojito* €5.80. Open M-Th 5pm-1am, F 5pm-3am, Sa 1pm-3am, Su 1pm-1am; kitchen closes 10pm.

Gollem, Raamsteg 4 (☎330 28 90), between Spuistraat and Singel, a few blocks south of Dam Square. Young, fun, and convivial, Gollem is truly a mecca for beer aficionados in Amsterdam. The bar has a menu of brews spanning 2 walls and covering over 200 varieties on tap: most varieties are Belgian but there are also Dutch, Czech, and German staples (€2.20-7.70). The house brew is Holland's delicious Leeuw (*fluitjes* €1.80, pints €3.60). If you're really thirsty, spring for the Belgian special McChouffe (€10.50), which arrives in a huge (0.75L) tankard. Patient bartenders can help you navigate the massive menu. Open Su-Th 4pm-1am, F-Sa 4pm-2am.

Rembrandtplein at Night

Why Not & Blue Boy, Nieuwezijds Voorburgwal 28 (☎627 43 74). From Centraal, turn right at the main street then left at Martelaarsgracht; it becomes Nieuwezijds Voorburgwal. Downstairs, the **Why Not** trumpets itself as "Amsterdam's oldest and largest Boy's Club," a mostly gay bar populated with men (and a few women) of all ages. Studly bartenders serve cheap drinks (€1.80) to men on the prowl. Weekends feature go-go dancing shows (9pm-10am; no cover, 1 drink minimum). Upstairs, the **Blue Boy** is a steamy sex club and bar, with live sex shows F-Sa nights starting at 11pm (€25; reserve early). Drinks €3. Escorts available. Why Not open Su-Th 4pm-1am, F-Sa 4pm-2am; Blue Boy open daily noon-2am.

Harry's Bar, Spuistraat 285 (☎624 43 84), south of Dam. Harry's Bar's subscription to *Cigar Aficionado* says it all. Conspicuously consume cocktails and cigars with well-dressed, slightly older patrons at this decadent den. Comfy leather chairs, hardwood floors, delicate wine vessels, and 3 stories to enjoy a smoke (Cubans €3.90-28.40) and a dry martini (€8.25) in

Night Owls, Lellebel

consummate style. The popular Bellini (peach schnapps and champagne; €6,75) packs quite a kick, but isn't overly sweet. Beer €2-5.50. Open Su-M 5pm-1am, F-Sa 5pm-3am. AmEx/DC/MC/V.

Belgique, Gravenstraat 2 (☎625 19 74), behind Nieuwe Kerk and between Niewendijk and Nieuwezijds Voorburgwal. If you're ready to graduate from keg swill to the real stuff, step up to this bar with over 40 varieties of high-quality (and high-alcohol) Belgian brew. House specialties are 8 beers on tap, including la Trappe and la Chouffe, fresh from the asceticism of a Trappist monastery and ready to fuel Amsterdam debauchery (€1.80-5). The rest come in bottles; after perusing the detailed beer menu, you'll be able to rattle off the names of the monks that packed your brew. Open M-Th 2pm-1am, F-Su noon-3am.

Blarney Stone, Nieuwendijk 29 (☎623 38 30; www.theblarneystone.freeservers.com). From Centraal Station, turn right on the main street, left on Martelaarsgracht, and right on Nieuwendijk. Honest-to-goodness Irish pub where local staples abound: drafts of Guinness, Kilkenny, and Strongbow. Big-screen TV features major soccer and rugby matches. Tasty English breakfast 10am-2pm (eggs, bacon, and toast; €4.90). Beer €2; pint €4. Open Su-Th 10pm-1am, F-Sa 10pm-3am, opens earlier for major Irish and British sporting events.

The Getaway, Nieuwezijds Voorburgwal 250 (☎627 14 27). Five min. south of Dam. Popular spot to go out before clubs and after other places close down. Trendy decor mixes and matches flowery wallpaper, bizarre elf statues, and a big aquarium. Music played quietly enough that you can talk without yelling. The party usually starts kicking at 11pm. Beer €2; mixed drinks €5. Open Su-Th 10pm-3am, F-Sa 10pm-4am.

CLUBS

Meander, Voetboogstraat 3b (☎625 84 30; www.cafemeander.com). From Muntplein, take the Singel to Heiligweg, turn right, and then left at Voetboogstraat. Live bands jam at this bar-cafe populated by crowds of youthful hipsters. Dim, smoky atmosphere, constant din, and dense crowds make for a raucous, high-energy good time. Shows nightly in a number of different genres: top 40, jazz, funk, soul, blues, R&B, salsa, and DJ-hosted dance sessions (monthly schedule posted on website). M student night, Th band, F-Sa disco, Su "Chill Out" party. Beer €1.80. Cover from €2.50-5. Open Su-Th 9pm-3am, F-Sa 9pm-4am.

Dansen Bij Jansen, Handboogstraat 11-13 (☎620 17 79; www.dansenbijjansen.nl). Near Konigsplein. *The* student dance club in Amsterdam, as popular with locals from the nearby University of Amsterdam as with the backpacking set. Each night features a different DJ with a distinctive style—a fun, if slightly hokey, blend of R&B, hip hop, disco, and top 40. Dionysian dance frenzy dominates downstairs; a more relaxed bar is upstairs. Emphasis is on drinking and dancing; there's not a shred of snooty clubster attitude. You must show a student ID to enter or be accompanied by a student. A great way to meet local university kids. Beer €1.70-3.30; mixed drinks from €3.30. Open Su-Th 11pm-4am, F-Sa 11pm-5am.

020, Nieuwezijds Voorburgwal 163-165 (☎428 44 18; www.020ams.nl), just south of Dam. Trendy, gritty, industrial-themed night club features drum and bass, jazz, techno, and house music. May feel a bit like a souped-up warehouse, but when the music gets going, there's plenty of space to dance or chill out. Beer €2.20; mixed drinks €6.50. Open M midnight-4am, W-Th 11pm-4am, F 11pm-5am, Sa midnight-5am, Su 10pm-4am.

SCHEEPVAARTBUURT

see map p. 342

🍷 **Cafe de Wilde Zee,** Haarlemmerstraat 32 (☎624 64 06). Elegant, black-clad literati congregate in this small, maroon wine bar to sip real Italian espressos (€1.70), explore a range of great wines (€2.60-3 per glass), and converse to cool jazz. Classical music in the mornings. Reasonably priced sandwiches (€2.60-4); 6 Belgian and Dutch beers on tap (€2.50-3). Open M-Tu 11am-8pm, W-Su 11am-1am.

Dulac, Haarlemmerstraat 118 (☎624 42 65). With a miniature station-wagon hanging over a bright blue pool-table, gothic spires radiating from the bar, and über-hip knick-knacks plastering the walls, Dulac looks like the fantasy treasure trove of Amsterdam's hippest gnome. The garden-terrace out back is a lovely, intimate spot to enjoy a pint of beer (€3.50) or *tapas* (€2.95-5.50). Cocktails and mixed drinks are a little pricey at €7. DJ spins every F-Sa 10pm-3am. Gothic party first Sa of the month 10pm-3am. No cover. Open Su-Th 4pm-1am, F-Sa 4pm-3am. Kitchen open daily until 10:30pm. AmEx/MC/V.

De Blauwe Druife (The Blue Grape), Haarlemmerstraat 91 (☎626 98 97), at Binnen Bowers Straat. Old-school neighborhood *bruin cafe*, popular with locals since 1733. Its interior bears marks of its age; it's dark and packed with trinkets (including a slot machine) that clutter the walls and hang from the ceiling. The terrace outside is popular on pleasant days. Snacks are within budget: *broodjes* €2.50-3.50, *bitterballen* €4.20. Beer on tap €1.80. Open Su-Th noon-1am, F-Sa noon-3am.

CANAL RING WEST

see map p. 342

⚔ **Cafe Kalkhoven,** Prinsengracht 283 (☎624 86 49). Kalkhoven represents "Old Amsterdam" in all its brown, wooden glory; tacky and commercialized ambiance is sure to be found elsewhere—the old wooden barrels on the wall behind the bar, chandeliers extending from darkly painted ceilings, and food choices all have a markedly traditional Dutch flavor. *Tostis* (ham and cheese sandwich) and *appeltas* (apple strudel) both €1.80. Settle down for a drink (Heineken €4) in the back, where candles populate every table. Despite the otherwise authentic atmosphere, the owner is heard to say over the sounds of U2, "we *don't* play Dutch music because people don't like it" Open daily 11am-1am.

CENTRAL CANAL RING

see map p. 340

Mankind, Weteringstraat 60 (☎638 47 55; www.mankind.nl). Tram #6, 7, or 10 to Spiegelgracht or tram #16, 24, or 25 to Westeringcircuit. From Leidseplein, facing the Marriott Hotel, turn left down Kl. Gartmanplants for 2 blocks. This is a mellow neighborhood bar with a loyal local following. Two outdoor porches: one with views of the Rijksmuseum and the other situated along the sparkling Lijnbaansgracht. Mixed crowd, but gay-owned and very gay-friendly. Standard array of snacks (*tostis* €2; *bitterballen* €3.40; cheap, tasty *dagschotel* €8.10). Open daily noon-midnight. Kitchen closes at 8pm. Cash only.

LGB ▼

boys' night out

Amsterdam sports a wall-to-wall range of gay nightlife to rival any city in the world. Here's an agenda that will keep you busy every night of the week. **Monday:** Hang out at the "Jackoff" parties at Stablemaster (p. 147) where the mandated dress code is "shoes only." **Tuesday:** Belt out a ballad at the drag-queen-hosted karaoke night at Lellebel (p. 156). **Wednesday:** Dress up sexy for Heat, a gay party at the Back Door that pumps out some hard-hitting house music (p. 156). **Thursday:** Drop into Cockring for dancing and live sex/strip shows (p. 147). **Friday:** After 11pm, go to Montmartre, voted best gay club in Amsterdam by *GayKrant* magazine, for Euro and American pop hits (p. 154). **Saturday:** live sex shows at Why Not starting at 11pm—€25; reserve early. (p. 149). **Sunday:** Unwind at the Tea Dance at the Back Door, with free food, cigarettes, and joints.

The above listings are enough for a week's hard partying, but some clubs have more infrequent events: **Cockring;** "SafeSex" parties first and third Sunday of every month. **The iT;** third Saturday of each month reserved for gay men (see p. 156). **Escape;** first Friday of every month gay party "Salvation" (see p. 156).

in recent news

squat culture

What began as a radical movement against the housing shortage exacerbated by speculative landowners has now settled into a quieter counterculture throughout The Netherlands. Any building sitting unoccupied for a year and a day can be legally squatted in by anyone who offers to furnish the space with a mattress, chair, and table, announcing his or her intent to inhabit. Squats have become communes of sorts, housing those who live at the very fringe of society. The practice has been surprisingly permitted by law in order to deter real estate investors from buying buildings without ever using them, ultimately selling them at a huge profit a few years later.

Although the last mayor of Amsterdam, Schelto Patyn, devoted his career to a thorough cleansing of the city, thereby eradicating many of the squats, a handful of the large ones still do exist in Amsterdam and its environs (see **Vrankvijk**, p. 148). However, the communities, a wonderfully eclectic mix of artists, punks, and expats, lead a precarious existence, never quite certain of when their next boot will come.

One of the most vibrant squats is **De Peper** (☎779 49 12; www.ot301@squat.net), in the former **Film Academie**, located at Overtoom 301

continued on next page

152

LEIDSEPLEIN

see map p. 341

The dense concentration of nightlife in and around Leidseplein comes in all stripes: steps away from Sex-O-Rama and Mama's Restaurant (which, for a Freudian field day, are next door to each other) are the smoke machine-filled clubs frequented by teenage tourists. Nearby, an older crowd sheds its inhibitions at jazz-oriented bars. For a reprieve just around the corner that might as well be a million miles from Leidseplein, Marnixstraat's string of chic, well-designed bars attract expats and a reasonably large local contingent. Don't come expecting any fancy liquor—a surprisingly large number of these upscale spots don't serve cocktails.

BARS

▓ **Lux,** Marnixstraat 403 (☎422 14 12). The pseudo-tacky mobster motif belies how classy this place actually is. The red plush walls and leopard-print curtains are distinctly ironic when peopled with languid expats and a significant Dutch crowd. There's not much dancing, but the candles, wave lamps, and DJ spinning Th-Su will all get you pumped to go hit the clubs later on. Beer €2; hard liquor €4. Open Su-Th 8pm-3am, F-Sa 8pm-4am. Cash only.

▓ **Paradiso,** Weteringschans 6-8 (☎626 45 21; www.paradiso.nl). When big-name rock, punk, new-wave, hip-hop, and reggae bands come to Amsterdam, they almost invariably play here in this former church converted into a temple to rock 'n' roll. Grace the place where Lenny Kravitz got his big break and the Tones taped their 1995 live album. Upstairs is a smaller stage where up-and-coming talents are showcased. Tickets €5-25; additional mandatory monthly membership fee €2.50. The cool kids come here for the nightclub "Paradisco" M, Th-Su. Nightclub €6 weeknights, €12.50 weekends. Open until 2am.

▓ **Melkweg,** Lijnbaansgracht 234a (☎531 8181; www.melweg.nl), off Leidseplein. Take tram #1, 2, 5, 6, 7, 10 to Leidseplein, then turn down the smaller side street to the left of the Stadsschouwberg theater. At this legendary nightspot in an old milk factory (whose name means "Milky Way"), it's one-stop shopping for forward-looking live music, food (see **Eat At Jo's,** p. 113) film, and dance parties. There's even a photography gallery (free W-Su 1-9pm). Concert tickets from €9.50-22 plus €2.50 monthly membership. Prices below factor in fee. Th Latin music €7.50. Sa danceable pop midnight-5am; cover €9.50. Box office open M-F 1-5pm, Sa-Su 4-6pm; show days from 7:30pm to end of show on show days.

Bourbon Street Jazz & Blues Club, Leidsekruisstraat. 6-8 (☎623 34 40; www.bourbonstreet.nl). From Leidsestraat, take first right onto Lange Leidsestraat, and then turn left onto Leidsekruisstraat. A slightly older traveler crowd dances with abandon to blues, soul, funk, and rock bands. Mostly smaller bands play this intimate venue, although in the past they have drawn the Stones and Sting. Musicians can join in the M and Tu jam sessions for free (€3 for the rest of us). Call or check the web or the sheet posted in the window to find out what's on. Beer €2,50, pints €5. Cover Su and Th €3; F-Sa €5, free if you enter 10-10:30pm. Open Su-Th 10pm-4am, F-Sa 10pm-5am.

Kamer 401, Marnixstraat 401(☎320 45 80), between Leidsegracht and Leidseplein. Gorgeous bar-restaurant right around the corner from the Leidseplein scene. Done up stylishly in chrome and glass with a shiny zinc bar, the Kamer has an international menu that changes monthly but always has around 6 excellent options (main courses about €13, soups €4.50). Before 10pm it's more of a restaurant; after, a bar with a local crowd that lounges rather than dances. *Vaasje* of Dommelsch €2; Corona and Hoegaarden €3-3.50; spirits €3.80. Open Su-Th 5pm-1am, F-Sa 5pm-3am; kitchen closes at 10:30pm.

Cafe de Koe, Marnixstraat 381 (☎625 44 82). A relaxed crowd, rock music, and slightly haphazard decor make this restaurant and bar a happening spot. Live music 1st Su of every month, Sept.-June, and a music trivia "pop quiz" the last Su of the month. Nicer for a sit-down dinner than most bars, try the daily special (€8.50), or choose from the meat, fish, veggie, and pasta dishes (€8-12). Cafe open daily 4pm-1am, Sa 4pm-3am; kitchen open 6-10:30pm. AmEx/MC/V.

Alto, Korte Leidsedwarsstraat 115, in Leidseplein. Take a right in front of Haagen Dazs; it will be 1 block down on your left. Hepcats left over from the 50s—literally—mingle with young aficionados at this busy nightspot where the vibe is cool but the jazz is hot. Show up early to get a table up front, though you can hear (if not see too clearly) the act from the bar. Free nightly jazz: Su-Th 10pm-2am, F-Sa until 3am. Open Su-Th 9pm-3am, F-Sa until 4am. Cash only.

Weber, Marnixstraat 397 (☎622 99 10), between Leidseplein and Leidsegracht. All the style and sophistication of Amsterdam's edgiest bars with none of the attitude. Friendly, come-as-you-are bar hosts crowds of pre-club drinkers and grizzled locals alike. Though velvet curtains, felt-patterned wallpaper, and the occasional Buddha may seem incongruous, it all comes together nicely. Downstairs grotto provides a *gezellig* spot for chilling and conversations. Open Su-Th 8pm-3am, F-Sa 8pm-4am. Cash only.

Aroma, Leidsestraat 96 (☎624 29 41; www.cafe-aroma.nl). Smack in the center of Leidsestraat's flurry of activity, Aroma is a bit of space-age couture:

continued from previous page

Take tram #1 or 6 to Jan Pieter Heijestraat, cross the street, and look for a large door with a bulletin board pinned to its left. De Peper has negotiated with the local government so that it can now legally rent to tenants while still maintaining the independent spirit of a squat. It holds social and political workshops, providing a stage for drama, dance, and musical performances. Tuesday, Friday, and Sunday usually see indie movie screenings; a vegan cafe opens at 7pm. Call ahead so they can cook enough food; same-night reservations are accepted from 4pm. Artists and performers are welcome Th from 10pm (free). Open Tu, F, Su 6pm; dinner (€5) 7-8:30pm.

A very recent development has been the blossoming of the "anti-squat," an abandoned house whose owners allow tenants to rent for free except for the cost of utilities. The government has encouraged the use of anti-squats in an attempt to discourage the further squat spreading, and as of now, both tenants and owners seem to be pleased with the current landlord/tenant relationship. However, those participating in anti-squat culture seem very much to be young professionals who simply cannot find another source of housing in Amsterdam's extreme shortage of options; they may not exactly desire the alternative community of a squat.

For more on squats in The Netherlands and beyond, check out www.squat.net. The bi-weekly *Shark* also has Amsterdam squat events listings; find it at many bars, restaurants, and coffeeshops.

153

out & about

fiesta in the sand

Skip Rembrandtplein for just one night and head out to the beach for some unforgettable clubbing in the sand. Amsterdam's hottest party occurs just once a month, taking over the tiny town of **Bloemendaal-aan-Zee** (see p. 220) with its uninhibited exhilaration. **Beach Bop,** held on the last Sundays of June through October, sounds pathetically teen-fabulous but captures all ages and personalities with its offer of insatiable fun. The beach clubs lining the shores of Bloemendaal are already chic by day, serving up drinks, music, and soporific lounges amidst stretches of sandy shores, but for Beach Bop, the clubs go into overdrive—the party starts at a ridiculously premature 1pm and rages until it is forced to shut down at midnight. Creatures crawl in from all over The Netherlands for these endless raucous nights (and afternoons), crowding the clubs to such capacity that they're bound to spill out onto the beach for dancing under the stars. Each beach pavilion blasts their own tunes, with **Woodstock 69** spinning soulful house and **Solaris** mixing disco and hip hop, but the music all just blends together at the end of the night when no one's sane or sober enough to care. To get there, take a train from Centraal station (25min., 3 per hr., €3.50).

scoop-style plastic chairs, everything in white and lit by warm orange light. International entrees €7-16. DJs spin classic rock, house, funk, world music, or garage (depending on the night) to a superhip crowd. Beer €2-€3. Breakfast served until 5pm. Open Su-Th 9am-1am, F-Sa 9am-3am.

Bamboo Bar, Lange Leidsedwarsstraat 64 (☎624 39 93; www.bamboobar.com). *Noir* decorations, disco ball, and slick hardwood bar share space with tribal masks and tiki torches in a jungle motif that manages to feel simultaneously classy and hokey. Beer (€2) or vast menu of cocktails (€4-7.50, most €6.30) includes the down-home Alabama Slamma' (€4.50) and killer Long Island Iced Tea (€7.20). Shooters like the "Slippery Nipple" €3.20. Open Su-Th 8pm-3am, F-Sa 8pm-4am. Cash only.

CLUBS

De Beetles, Lange Leidsedwarsstraat 81 (☎625 95 88; www.beetles.nl). A drink house with a sometimes-hopping dance floor and a motley crowd. Look for bartender Bart, who can flip a bottle and do bar tricks like no other. Eclectic house tunes nightly; Su reggae, Th rock night, Sa oldies and dance classics. No cover F before midnight; after midnight, €5 includes €2 drink. Beer and soda €2, hard liquor €3.50-5. Open Su-Th 9pm-4am, F-Sa 9pm-5am. Cash only.

REMBRANDT PLEIN

see map p. 340

BARS

🖼 **Arc Bar,** Reguliersdwarsstraat 44 (☎689 70 70). Done up with leather lounge chairs and silver walls, Arc is a hip, cutting-edge choice for a night out with friends. Cocktails are delightfully frilly (martinis €6.50; *caipirinha*, margarita, *mojito*, or Long Island iced tea €7.50), a perfect match for the young, trendy crowd that overtakes the bar weekend nights. Dine in beige elegance (dinner 6pm-10:30pm) then move into a dark haze of lights for socializing. The black tabletops in front are mechanically lowered for dancing on the weekends and used for serving "special" drinks (made only by particular guest bartenders) on W Cocktail Night (5pm-1am; cocktails only €5). Open daily noon-1am, F-Sa noon-3am. AmEx/MC/V

🖼 **Montmartre,** Halvemaarsteg 17 (☎620 76 22). Rococo interior with flowers and rich draperies houses some of the wildest parties in Amsterdam for men who love men. Disarmingly cute bartenders serve 2-for-1 beers during daily Happy Hour 6-8pm (beer €2; liquor €3.90-5.70). Voted best gay bar by local gay mag *Gay Krant* 6 years running, though it's definitely straight-friendly. Don't expect pretense or pressure—just everyone having a good time. The party rages hardest Th-Su after 11pm, when the boys get down and dirty to European or American pop. Open Su-Th 5pm-1am, F-Sa 5pm-3am. Cash only.

Cafe April, Regulierdwarsstraat 37 (☎625 95 72; www.april-exit.com). Tram #1, 2, or 5 to Koningsplein. Popular gay bar that's laid-back by day, increasingly active and cruisey as the night wears on. It's the brother establishment of popular gay nightspot **Exit** (p. 157), but not quite as image-conscious. Clusters of marble tables spill onto the sidewalk up front, while in back a circular rotating bar is also a huge tourist attraction. Siren lights embedded in the ceiling blast the jingle from *The Price is Right* at odd intervals F-Sa nights, signaling 2-for-1 drinks and a mad rush of manhood to the bar. Happy Hour 2-for-1 drinks Su 6-8pm, M-Sa 6-7pm. Open Su-Th 2pm-1am, F-Sa 2pm-3am. Cash only.

Traditional *Bruin Cafe*

Coco's Outback, Thorbeckeplein 8-12 (☎627 24 23, www.cocosoutback.com), just east of Rembrandtplein. There's no better place to grab some "lousy food and warm beer" than the Australian Outback at Coco's, complete with plastic crocs, wooden ladders, and an abundance of handsome Aussie waiters. During the day, the Outback serves fried favorites such as the Blooming Onion (€4.60). After 11pm, the creatures crawl out to play, with DJs spinning Th-Su, pop hits blasting, and British expats strutting their stuff on the tabletops—wildly popular with tourists on the prowl. Frozen pint €3.50-4.20; 20mL shots €2-3.50. Open Su-Th noon-1am, F-Sa noon-3am, kitchen closes 10pm. AmEx/MC/V.

Boys Only

Cafe Menschen, Amstel 202 (☎627 87 27), at Amstelstraat. Cornerside bar has great views of the picturesque Blauwbrug and, best of all, pours (small but satisfying) glasses of Dommelsch beer for a mere €1. Locals and tourists take advantage of the cheap booze and relaxed environment, but only true regulars like Eddy, Hans, and Olaf get their names plaqued on bar by their favorite stool. Snap a photo and tack it to the wall while you're there; this bar is all about retaining memories. *Tostis* €1.50. *Broodjes* €1.30. Open M-Th 2pm-1am, F-Sa 1pm-2am. Cash only.

Soho, Reguliersdwarsstraat 36 (☎616 12 13). Tram #1, 2, or 5 to Koningsplein. Looks like an old boys' club, but all kinds of characters crowd into this bustling mixed bar. Leather wallpaper, aged armchairs, and dusty bookshelves line the walls, elegant staircases snake between the 2 floors, and an impressive 2-story mirror exposes all the drama of the night. Traditional accoutrements don't quite match the crowd that's young, cruisey, and a little preppy. Well-situated in the thick of Reguliersdwarsstraat, making it ideal for pre-club drinking and lounging. DJ Th-Su. Open Su-Th 8pm-3am, F-Sa 8pm-4am. Cash only.

Breakdancing at Melkweg

M Bar, Reguliersdwarsstraat 13-15, just off Leidsestraat. Tram #1, 2, or 5 to Koningsplein. Sleek, minimalist bar, located on a famously gay street but drawing a mainly straight crowd. Small, dim space with sparse decorations and even fewer seats. Forego your comfort and perch on the tiny stools at the bar, or pose in the red light that glows against the back wall. DJs spin house, club, and techno Th-Sa. Beer €2, bottles €3; wine €3; mixed drinks €5.90. Open W-Th 9pm-3am, F-Sa 9pm-4am. Cash only.

Vive La Vie, Amstelstraat 7 (☎ 624 01 14; www.vivelavie.net), just east of Rembrandtplein. Fun, friendly lesbian bar where the emphasis is on good times, good company, and good drinking, all without a shred of attitude. Small but lively and comfortably packed on weekends. No dance floor, but that doesn't stop the ladies—and a few lucky men—from busting out to jazz, Latin, and feel-good pop anthems. Pretty cocktails €8; beer €2. Busiest nights are Th-Sa; Su is mellower. Open Su-Th 4pm-1am, F-Sa 4pm-3am. Cash only.

Lellebel, Utrechtsestraat 4 (☎ 427 51 39; www.lellebel.nl), just off the southeastern corner of Rembrandtplein. Welcoming local crowd comes to this campy, vampy mixed bar run by a cadre of outrageous drag queens. Your saucy hostesses Desiree and Susilari tend bar almost every night for their fun-loving crowd of admirers. Women always welcome. Fabulous theme nights include: karaoke on Tu; open podium contest on F; popular drag show featuring queens from all over Amsterdam on Sa; and DJ-hosted "world music" evening on Su. Open M-Th, Su 9pm-3am, F-Sa 8pm-4am.

CLUBS

The iT, Amstelstraat 24 (☎ 489 72 85; www.it.nl), Break out your best leather ensemble for this famed discotheque specializing in house and trance—The iT is why other clubs in Rembrandtplein are sometimes empty. Amsterdam's brazen beauties come here to dance the night away; be prepared to lose yourself in a packed room radiating with heated sensuality. Dry ice adds smoky intrigue and an elevated platform shrouds swaying silhouettes in purple haze. Bar with couches near the dance floor for those too tired to stand anymore (beer €4, mixed drinks €7.50). Most nights are mixed but the 2nd Sa of each month reserved for gay men. Cover €15. Casual wear is acceptable but you'll want to look your best to match the liberated extravagance inside. Open Th, Su 11pm-4am, F-Sa, 11pm-6am. Cash only.

Escape, Rembrandtplein 11 (☎ 622 11 11; www.escape.nl). Party animals pour into this massive venue for their moment of glory at one of Amsterdam's hottest clubs. It features 2 floors with 6 bars, a breezy upstairs lounge, and an enormous, sensually charged dance floor downstairs, where impeccably dressed scenesters groove to house, trance, disco, and dance classics. Sa is Chemistry, a hugely popular and fashionable party with famed DJ Marcella spinning trance and house; the same renowned model-turned-DJ hosts a smaller party, Rush, on Th, for a styling student crowd. F continually changes theme nights to keep the usual crowd entertained, but the first F of every month is always the gay party Salvation. Lines grow long through 2am, and hulky bouncers scan the crowd for miscreants; be well-dressed and relatively sober to increase your chances of entry. Metal detector, full pat-down, and thorough bag check required before entry. Beer €2.30. Mixed drinks €7.50. Cover €10-15. Open Th-Su 11pm-4am, F-Sa 11pm-5am. Cash only.

The Ministry, Reguliersdwarsstraat 12 (☎ 623 39 81; www.ministry.nl). The popular Ministry is upscale enough to be classy and hip, but lacks the unnecessary attitude or exclusivity of other clubs. Crowd of all ages and races come for music you can actually dance to, and though some clubbers are content to lounge in the corners, others move unabashedly to the beat. Theme nights change constantly with live music, dance classics, R&B, UK garage, 2-step, hip-hop, and old-school disco (check website for latest schedule). M open live jam session fills up quickly, so come before midnight. Cover M and F €7, Sa €10. Free-admission tickets for weekday nights often handed out on commercial streets. Open Su-Th 11pm-4am, F-Sa 11pm-5am. Cash only.

The Back Door, Amstelstraat 32 (☎ 620 23 33; www.backdoor.nl). The Door provides 2 different dens—a red-walled, smoky dance area and a chatty, upbeat bar—and several different theme club nights. W is Heat, a gay party with harder house music (€5), Th is Latin and Salsa; F-Sa DJs spin house and R&B classics for a mixed crowd (about €10), and Su is Tea

Dance, a packed and popular gay party that features free food, joints, and cigarettes, in a sleek red and black setting (€10). Downstairs cocktail cafe (open W-Th and Su 6pm-1am, F-Sa 6pm-3am); show your receipt at the club, you may get half-priced cover. Open F-Sa 11pm-5am, Su 9pm-4am. Cash only.

Exit, Reguliersdwarsstraat 42 (☎625 87 88; www.april-exit.com). Enter Exit to find one of the most popular gay discos in The Netherlands. Downstairs bar plays dance classics for the laid-back boys; upstairs is a DJ-driven high-energy techno party where a young, handsome crowd sheds its inhibitions. Balcony overlooks dance floor to better facilitate cruising. In the back, there's a darkroom reserved just for men where the most secret of fantasies await fulfillment. Mostly male clubbers, though female friends often appear. Cover F-Sa €9, Th €4. No cover Su. Open Su-Th 11pm-4am, F-Sa 11pm-5am. Cash only.

Lux

You II, Amstel 178 (☎421 09 00; www.youll.nl). From Rembrandtplein, head east down Amstelstr., turn left at Bakkerstraat and then right when you come to the river; it's 1½ blocks up on the left. Amsterdam's most popular lesbian nightclub. The middle-aged clientele tend to sidestep the tiny dance floor, opting to chat at the bar or in intimate nooks instead. A circular bar in front serves beer (€2.50) and liquor (€4), leading to a room that's elegantly modeled but sparsely inhabited. F-Sa are more lesbian-oriented; Th, Su geared toward gay men. Cover only Sa €7. Open Th, Su 11pm-4am; F-Sa 11pm-5am. Cash only.

K2 Apres-Ski Lounge, Paardenstraat 13-15 (☎627 27 10; www.apres-skilounge.nl). From Rembrandtplein, walk east down Amstelstraat and take a left onto Paardenstraat; K2 is on your right. Done up like a ski chalet, the K2 packs in young Dutch folks intent on dancing and drinking. The rooms are adorned like the interior of a log cabin, complete with skies, sleds, antlers, and wooden furniture. The nonstop music—hosted by "Ski-Jays"—is loud and upbeat, and though the crowd is a bit snobby, clubbers are uninhibited and always up for a rockin' good time. Bring a friend and compete to see who can hammer a nail into a wooden stump the fastest; winner lucks out with a free tequila shot. On occasion, the Ski-Jay will turn on the snow machine, providing you all the amenities of a vacation to Vail. No cover, but pay the wardrobe folks €1 per item you check. Draft beer €2.20; bottles €4.50-5; Red Bull and vodka €8. Th, Su 10pm-3am; F-Sa 10pm-4am. Cash only.

Canal Bridge at Night

De Duivel, Reguliersdwarsstraat 87 (☎626 61 84, www.deduivel.nl). The only club in Amsterdam devoted to hip-hop, De Duivel, "The Devil," has been visited by Cypress Hill, the Roots, and loads of other musical greats. Small, smoke-filled room hosts lively guests who dabble a bit in dancing but mostly just

Korsakof

chat to the music. Nightly DJs mix hip-hop beats with rap and ska, catering to loyal regulars. A stained-glass devil looks on forbiddingly but can't stop the extremely laid-back crowd from enjoying their night. Beer €1.80; liquor €3.60. Open Su-Th 8pm-3am, F-Sa 8pm-4am.

JORDAAN

BARS

see maps p. 342

■ **Café 't Smalle,** Egelantiersgracht 12 (☎623 96 17), at the corner of Prinsengracht and Egelantiersgracht. A bar rich with its own history, 't Smalle was founded in 1780 as the tasting room of a neighboring distillery. A good place in the afternoon as well as the evening, and rightfully one of the most popular cafes in the city's west, 't Smalle has summertime canal-side seats and a warm, old-fashioned interior for colder nights. Famous pea soup (€4.35) served in winter. Draft Wieckse Witte €2.45. Open Su-Th 10am-1am, F-Sa 10am-2am.

■ **Sound Garden,** Marnixstraat 164-166 (☎620 28 53). Tram #10 13, or 17 to Marnixstraat or Rozengracht. Amsterdam's true rock 'n' roll dive. Diverse in age and style, patrons share one thing in common: a love of beer. Try the house brew—Flater's Kater (€3), a Dutch expression meaning "hangover," with a kicking 9.5% alcohol content. Inside are listings of the latest music happenings in and around town; if the music's not your thing, head out to the gorgeous canal-front terrace. "Fuck Disco" DJ series W and F nights. Live acoustic guitar Su 9pm-midnight. Open M-Th 1pm-1am, F 1pm-3am, Sa 3pm-3am, Su 3pm-1am. Cash only.

Proust, Noordermarkt 4 (☎623 91 45; cafe_proust@hotmail.com). Proust has endured as a place where the beautiful people go to relax; its next-door neighbor **Finch** is the same idea. The setting, if not the crowd, is trendier than your average Jordaan *bruin cafe,* done all orange and gold, and the terrace is always packed. Lunch served until 5pm, dinner 6-10pm. Open daily 11am-1am, F-Sa 11am-3am. Cash only.

Duende, Lindengracht 62 (☎420 66 92; www.cafeduende.nl). Live free Flamenco music every Sa at 11pm might be what attracts the well-dressed crowd, or perhaps it's the €4 *tapas.* It's also a base for Flamenco lessons, so the bar is often full of women sipping sangria (€3) after a workout. Open M-Th 4pm-1am, F 4pm-3am, Sa 2pm-3am, Su 2pm-1am.

Wil's Cafe, Prinsengracht 126 (☎ 320 27 53). On a nice day, try the outside tables or come inside for the funky candles, beat-up sofa, and homey interior that set Wil's apart from its Prinsengracht neighbors. Get a baguette sandwich (€3-4) with a glass of Grolsch (€1.80), or come for the live blues M 10pm. In the evening, Wil's becomes a hip place for all ages. Open Su-Th 10am-1am, F-Sa 10am-3am. Kitchen open 6-10pm. Cash only.

Cafe Thijssen, Brouwersgracht 107 (☎623 89 94; www.cafe-thijssen.nl). After a dinner in one of Lindengracht's many burnished bistros, come here for a glass of beer (€1.70-3) or a cocktail in a casual outdoor setting. Open Su-Th 8am-1am, F-Sa 8am-3am. Cash only.

Saarein II, Elandstraat 119 (☎623 49 01), at Hazenstraat. Tram #7, 10, or 17 to Elandsgracht. Upscale lesbian bar with velvet curtains and a piano attracts mostly women on weekends, though on weeknights it's filled with all orientations and dispositions. Full bar (beers €1.75) and pool table. Open Su-Th 5pm-1am, F-Sa 5pm-2am. Cash only.

Cafe P96, Prinsengracht 96 (☎622 18 64). When you're not ready for the night to end just yet, go to P96 for the full bar and the pub snacks. This is the one of the few "late night" bars in a neighborhood that notoriously shuts down early, so you never know what kind of people you'll see. The terrace boat, open every evening and weekend days, is roomy enough for you not to care. Beer €1.90. Open Su-Th 8pm-3am, F-Sa 8pm-4am. Cash only.

Café de Tuin, 2e Tuindwarsstraat 13 (☎624 45 59). Another favorite Jordaan spot, this one is tucked away on a side street, away from the hordes. Beer starts at €1.80 in this cool yet traditional *bruin cafe.* Open M-Th 10am-1am, F-Sa 10am-2am, Su 11am-1am. Cash only.

CLUBS

On warm summer nights in the Jordaan, clubs don't really start swinging 'til midnight or 1am.

Mazzo, Rozengracht 114 (☎626 75 00; www.mazzo.nl). One of the less pretentious dance floors in the city, Mazzo's avowed goal is hospitable clubbing. There's usually no rope burn at the door, no dancing skill hierarchy, and the cover remains stable. Beer €1.85; mixed drinks €5. Th Techno, F Drum 'n' Bass, Sa Techouse; check website for changing events on W and Su. Cover W-Th, Su €5-10; F €8-10; Sa €10. Open W-Th, Su 11pm-4am; F-Sa 11pm-5am.

Club More, Rozengracht 133 (☎528 74 59; www.expectmore.nl). An uninhibited half-local, half-tourist crowd lines up to see what all the hype is about. Revolving cast of DJs spin techno, club house, and funk groove Th-Sa nights. Cover €10-12. Open Th-F 11pm-4am, Sa 11pm-5am, Su 4pm-midnight.

Korsakoff, Lijnbaansgracht 161 (☎625 78 54). Keeping the flame of 80s goth-industrial alive through its mid-90s revival by Trent Reznor and followers, this smoky club is the place to flail to hard core industrial music and compare dreadlocks and facial piercings. Open Su-Th 10pm-3am, F-Sa 10pm-4am.

Shirtless at Exit

WESTERPARK

Blender, Van de Palmkade 16 (☎486 98 60). Tram #10 to Van Hallstraat. Its remote location somehow manages to distinguish Blender from the pack of chic designer bars. Skyy

see map p. 346

Vodka cocktails (€7) and orange airport-lounge decor aren't *that* hard to find, but the canal side privacy is enviable—the international fashion *cognoscenti* make the trip. DJs spin Th-Sa. Open M-Th 6pm-1am, F-Sa 6pm-2am. AmEx/MC/V.

DE PIJP

Dancing Queen, Club More

BARS

▩ **De Engel (The Angel),** Albert Cuypstraat 182 (☎675 0544; www.de-engel.net). Look for the angel on the roof. The

see map p. 348

heavenly decor is no accident: this used to be a church. Nowadays, only the god of hedonism is worshiped under these sumptuous gold chandeliers. Beer from Heinekein (€1.90) to premiere Belgian La Chouffe (€7). Check the website for live music events: jazz most F, Su 11am brunch with live classical music (€12.50). Dinners served on the balcony (€20). Open M-F 10am-1am, Sa-Su 10am-2am.

▩ **Chocolate Bar,** 1e van der Helststraat 62a (☎675 76 72). This hyper-chic yet low-key spot is completely unmarked; you'll know the Chocolate Bar only by its distinctive, brightly zebra-striped exterior—and in sum-

Narcoleptic Cat, Soundgarden

mer, by the crowds of local hipsters lounging outdoors. Winning DJs spin nearly every night here. 12-15 kinds of cocktails run €6.50 each. Fresh shakes €2.80. Open Su-Th 10am-1am, F-Sa 10am-3am. AmEx/MC/V.

De Vrolijke Drinker, Frans Halstraat 66a (☎771 43 16). Elegant neighborhood bar on a quiet street with mellow jazz and excellent, friendly service. Chess and Monopoly available. Beer €1.70; Johnnie Walker €3.40-11. Open M-F 4pm-1am, F-Sa 4pm-3am. Cash only.

Mme. Jeanette, 1e van de Helststraat 42 (☎673 33 32; www.id-t.com/jeanette). Cosmopolitan within an inch of its life, this velvet-smooth lounge serves some of the best, if priciest, cocktails in Amsterdam, such as the Basil Grande Martini (with vodka, basil, and fresh strawberries; €8.50). DJs nearly nightly. Open Su-Th 6pm-1am, F-Sa 6pm-3am. AmEx/MC/V.

Kingfisher, Ferdinand Bolstraat 24 (☎671 23 95). Hipsters and yuppies alike congregate in this bar. Low-priced, global beer selections include Australian James Boag (€3.30), Indian Cobra and, of course, Kingfisher (on tap €1.90, bottle €3.30). Great food, too. Club sandwiches €4.50. *Dagschotel* €11 (vegetarian option always available). *Jenever* €1.50, cocktails €4.20. Frozen fruit smoothies €3. Open M-Th 11am-1pm, F-Sa 11am-3pm. Cash only.

O'Donnell's, Ferdinand Bolstraat 5 (☎676 77 86). Though the prices are on the high end of the budget range, this Irish pub has a friendly buzz and authentic atmosphere, with wood paneling and Guinness ads (pints €4.50). British and Irish sports matches screened on 1 big-screen and 2 small-screen TVs. Breakfast M-F 11am-3pm, Sa 11am-5pm (€9); traditional Irish roast Su 11am-3pm (€12.50). Lunch €4.50; dinner €10-14. Open M-F 11am-2am, Sa-Su 11am-3am. Kitchen open M-Sa 11am-3pm and 5-10pm, Su until 9pm. AmEx/MC/V.

Cafe Berkhout, Stadhouderskade 77 (☎320 98 01), opposite Heineken Experience (p. 69). Casual, breezy *eetcafe* jammed with locals. Cheap drinks: *vaasje* €2; pint €4.50; martini €2.50. Good Dutch snacks (*bitterballen* €3.90; chicken *satay* €8.99) and *dagmenu* (full, filling meal €7.49). Open M-Th 7am-1am, F 7am-2am, Sa 9am-2am, Su 10am-1am. MC/V.

De Badcuyp, 1e Sweelinckstraat 10 (☎675 96 69 www.badcuyp.demon.nl), on Albert Cuypstraat. Vibrant cobalt-and-yellow venue for world music in an immigrant neighborhood. Tu 9pm-midnight blues and world (free), W salsa dance (€3), Su jazz (free). African dance party last Su of every month (€2.50); didgeridoo 2nd Th of every month (free). Check the website for more events. Open Su-Th 10am-1am, F-Sa 10am-3am. Closed M. MC/V.

JODENBUURT & PLANTAGE

see map p. 349

BARS

De Beiaard, Kloveniersburgwal 6-8 (☎423 01 12; www.beiaardgroep.nl). A beautiful wooden brewhouse just south of Nieuwmarkt. Though part of a Dutch chain, it's worth stopping in for the fabulous brews, 5 of which are made on the premises. Alcohol content can get to a heady 7%. And if you want to see the suds develop from start to finish, make an appointment to take a spin through the on-site brewing facilities (min. 10 people, €8 per person). Open M-Th 10am-1am, F-Sa 10am-2am, Su 11am-midnight. Cash only.

Cafe Elfendig, Roetersstraat 4 (☎422 96 49), opposite the University of Amsterdam. Prime location means this snug, unpretentious cafe-bar is hottest Th nights, starting at the Happy Hour (4:30-6pm). DJs spin most nights. Open M-F 10am-1am, F-Sa 5pm-3am. Cash only.

CLUB

Arena, Gravesandestraat 51-53 (☎850 24 00; www.hotelarena.nl), in the Oost. Take night bus #76 or 77, or tram #9 to Tropenmuseum; turn right on Mauritskade and then left on Gravesandestr. Former chapel throws great parties, but there's no predicting what you'll get on a given party night, so do your homework. Every F and Sa at 11pm (cover €10-25), dance to an eclectic mix in large party spaces. The crowd is young, down-to-earth, and keeps it rockin' until the early hours. Perhaps a bit touristy, with the pricey Hotel Arena next door, but the colorful wall lights and fluorescent wall-hanging help maintain a very chill atmosphere. Open F-Sa 11pm-4am, Su 6pm-3am.

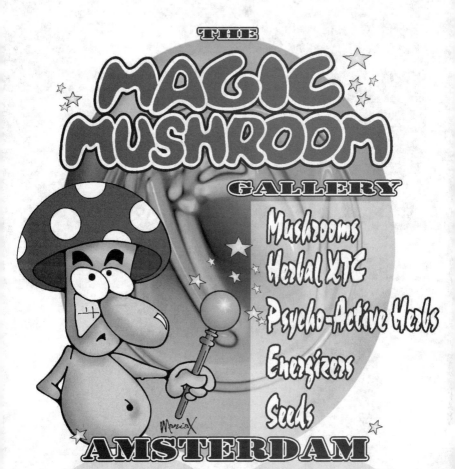

Arts & Entertainment

Throughout the year, Amsterdam is a whirlwind of artistic activity, providing venues for hundreds of plays, concerts, festivals, and fairs. With so many opportunities, even long-term residents are liable to feel overwhelmed, so travelers shooting through the city are bound to find themselves inundated. To thwart such confusion, the **Amsterdams Uit Buro (AUB),** Leidseplein 26, right on Leidseplein square, is stuffed with free monthly magazines, pamphlets, and tips to help you sift through the seasonal offerings. The most comprehensive publication is the free monthly *Uitkrant,* and for visitors staying longer, the *Uitgids,* which often advertises reduced fares for advance purchases. For a slightly edgier guide to Amsterdam entertainment, consider picking up a *Shark*—also available at assorted restaurants, bars, and shops throughout the city—which provides comprehensive listings for clubs, squats, music, film, and gay events. The AUB also sells tickets and makes reservations for just about any cultural event in the city for a commission—around €2 per person per ticket. (☎0900 01 91; www.uitlijn.nl. AUB office open M-W, F-Sa 10am-6pm, Th 10am-9pm, Su noon-6pm.) The **VV's** theater desk, Stationsplein 10, can also make reservations for cultural events (☎0900 400 40 40, €0.55 per min. Open M-Sa 10am-5pm). The monthly *Day by Day,* available from the tourist office, also provides comprehensive cultural listings. If you're still thirsty for more, the mini-magazine *Boom!,* free at restaurants and cafes around the city, is chock full of tourist info.

CLASSICAL MUSIC, OPERA, & DANCE

Amsterdam is world-renowned for its innovative classical performing arts, especially for its avant-garde, contemporary chamber ensembles. In 1986, the city invested in the construction of the prestigious and controversial **Stadhuis-Muziektheater** complex, which now houses both the **National Ballet** and **The Netherlands Opera** in addition to regularly featuring **The Netherlands Philharmonic Orchestra** (see below). At Museumplein, the **Concertgebouw** attracts top-notch performers and is home to one of the world's finest classical orchestras. Tickets for all of these events are available through the AUB (see above).

Churches throughout the city also host regular organ, choral, and chamber music concerts (tickets usually from about €2.50). While almost all of Amsterdam's churches host concert programs, the **Oude Kerk** (see p. 59), **Engelsekerk** (see p. 60), **Westerkerk** (www.westerkerk.nl, p. 63) all have regular summertime programs that feature some wonderful chamber, choral, organ, and early music. An international center for **contemporary music,** the famous, ground-breaking **IJsbreker** theater, features dozens of superior contemporary avant-garde ensembles who breathe life into the works of folks like Schönberg, Steve Reich, and Arvo Pärt every year. Amsterdam's rock, pop, world music, and jazz music scene is similarly vital, with hundreds of bubbling hot venues scattered throughout the city.

VENUES & COMPANIES

Concertgebouw, Concertgebouwplein 2-6 (☎671 83 45; www.concertegebouw.nl), across Paulus Potterstraat from the open expanse of the **Museumplein.** Take tram #2, 3, 5, 12, or 16 to Museumplein. This gorgeous concert hall, constructed in 1888, is home to one of the world's finest classical ensembles, the Royal Concertgebouw Orchestra. Programs are star-studded, with occasional jazz, world, and folk performances mixed with the Mendelssohn and Mozart. Stop by the hall to get a program of concerts, some of which cost as little as €7. Su morning concerts with guided tours before the performance are a cheaper option, running usually around €12 (tours, €3.50, start at 9:30am). Sept.-June, under 26 rush tickets from €7. Additional free lunchtime concerts during Fall, Winter and Spring; W 12:30pm, no tickets necessary. Ticket office open daily 10am-7pm; until 8:15pm for same-day ticketing. Telephone reservations until 5pm. AmEx/MC/V.

Stadhuis-het Muziektheater, Waterlooplein (☎625 54 55; www.hetmuziektheater.nl) in the **Plantage.** Take tram #9 or 14 or metro #21, 53, or 54 to Waterlooplein. Also known as the "Stopera" after a recent protest against its construction, the Muziektheater's gargantuan complex is home to the Dutch National Ballet, the Holland Symfonia, and The Netherlands Opera. Tickets can be bought through either the Muziektheater box office or through the AUB (see above). Box office open M-Sa 10am-curtain up, Su and holidays 11:30am-curtain up (usually 8pm). Opera tickets start at €22; ballet tickets from €11. For ballet only, student rush tickets available 30min. before the show (€6). Closed July-Aug. For more information, contact the individual companies: National Ballet, ☎551 82 25, www.het-nationale-ballet.nl; The Netherlands Opera, ☎551 89 22, www.dno.nl; Holland Symfonia, ☎551 88 23, www.hollandsymfonia.nl. AmEx/DC/V.

Bimhuis, Oudeschaans 73-77 (☎623 13 61; www.bimhuis.nl), in the **Jodenbuurt.** Take a tram to Waterlooplein. Amsterdam's premier venue for jazz and improv. music for over 20 years, Bimhuis features the famous, the obscure, and the local legend. Performers from Europe, the Americas, Asia, and Africa, are united in their devotion to unscripted melody. Beyond the bar, the stage is surrounded by benches and a ring of cafe tables. Tickets run €12-14 students and seniors €10-12. Free Tu jam session 10pm. MC/V.

Conservatorium van Amsterdam, Van Baerlestraat 27 (☎571 25 00; www.cva.ahk.nl) in the **Museumplein.** Tram #2, 3, 5, 12, or 16, or buses #145, 170, 197. The Conservatory of Amsterdam's students study here all year round—the jazz, classical, and the occasional opera performances are free.

Beurs van Berlage Theater, Damrak 277 (☎627 04 66; www.beursvanberlage.nl), in the **Nieuwe Zijd.** This monumental building, the former stock exchange, and now architectural museum (see p. 83), is home to 3 grand concert halls that host The Netherlands Philharmonic Orchestra and The Netherlands Chamber Orchestra. Concerts €8-20, student and senior discounts, depending on the show. MC/V.

Koninklijk Carré Theater, Amstel 115-125 (☎0900 25 25 255, www.theatercarre.nl), in the **Jodenbuurt.** Tram #4 to Frederiksplein or 6, 7, 10 to Oosteinde or Metro: 51, 53, or 54 to Weesperplein. Grand, old-fashioned theater with red velvet opened in 1888 showing old-time amusements such as cabaret, the circus, and musical theater. Other offerings from touring companies such as Irish dance, lesser-known pop groups, Chinese acrobatic troupes, and Israeli percussion ensembles. Tickets €10-50, €5 student tickets on the day of performance. Tickets sold at box office (open M-Sa 10am-7pm, Su 1-7pm) or through the AUB (see above). MC/V. Slated to close temporarily starting Jan. 2004—check website or call for details.

IJsbreker, Weesperzijde 23 (☎668 18 05; www.ysbreker.nl). Tram #6, 7, 10 to Weesperplein or #3 to Ruyschstraat; it's just south of the Jodenbuurt. Avant-garde music center, known for being one step ahead, nourishes Amsterdam's contemporary music scene. Both local and international talent, experimental programs, and a chamber music series. €6-16, students and seniors about €2 less. MC/V.

Marionette Theater, Nieuwe Jonkerstraat 8 (☎620 80 27; www.marionettentheater.nl). In an intimate, charming space on a quiet street in the **Oude Zijd,** the Marionette Theater performs a full program of Mozart and Offenbach operas entirely with—you guessed it—marionettes. Performances twice monthly, tickets available through phone, web, or AUB (see above). €10, students and seniors €7, kids €3.50.

Kit Tropentheater Kleine Zaal, Linnaeusstraat 2 and Grote Zaal, Mauritskade 63 (☎568 85 00; www.tropentheater.nl), in the **Plantage.** Take tram #6, 9, or 10. Features non-Western performing arts, from Ghanan dance to Inuit music to Surinamese theater. Box office open M-Sa noon-4pm and 1hr. before performance. Tickets reasonably priced (€5-20), but no reduced rates. Ticket office open M-Sa noon-6pm, or reserve online or by phone. MC/V.

LIVE MUSIC

In addition to the venues (€5-20), you can also catch occasional live jazz at **Elsa's Jazz Cafe,** Middenweg 73 (☎668 50 10), and **Toomler's** on Friday nights (see p. 167). World music can sometimes be found at the **Melkweg** (see p. 168), **Carre Theater** (see p. 165), or the **Tropeninstitut** (see p. 165).

Skate Park

I'm Really Pierced Off Right Now

The Next Generation's Rising Star

Bourbon Street Jazz & Blues Club, Leidsekruisstr. 6-8 (☎ 623 34 40; www.bourbon-street.nl). Take the tram to **Leidseplein,** head north on Leidsestraat, go east on Lange Leidsedwarsstraat, and then turn north on Leidsekruisstraat. Blues, soul, funk, and rock bands keep the crowds heavy every night. Mostly smaller bands play this intimate venue, although in the past they have drawn the Rolling Stones and Sting. M and Tu free jam sessions while the weekends are typically more about rock. You won't find schedules in local papers; instead, call or check the web or the sheet posted in the front window to find out what's on. Beer €2.50, pints €5. Cover Su and Th €3, F-Sa free if you enter 10-10:30pm. Open Su-Th 10pm-4am, F-Sa 10pm-5am.

Maloe Melo, Lijnbaansgracht 163 (☎ 420 45 92; www.maloemelo.com), in the Jordaan. Maloe Melo is the best deal in the **Jordaan** for a night out: the beer is cheap and the bands are free. Both local and visiting amateur groups play on W, F, and Sa; mostly blues, rock, and alternative country. Stop in and you might catch an act before its big break. Regular jam sessions other nights of the week. Check website for line-up details. No cover. Music in the back room from 10:30pm. Open Su-Th 9pm-3am, F-Sa 9pm-4am. Su Tu Th jam sessions; Tu, Th electric jam sessions, music starts 11pm. Cash only.

Melkweg, see p. 152.

Paradiso, Weteringschans 6-8 (☎ 626 45 21; www.paradiso.nl). Tram #1, 2, 5, 6, 7, or 10 to **Leidseplein.** When big-name rock, punk, new-wave, hip-hop, and reggae bands come to Amsterdam, they almost invariably play here in this former church that has converted into a temple to rock 'n' roll. Grace the place where Lenny Kravitz got his big break, and the Stones taped their 1995 live album. Upstairs there's also a smaller stage where up-and-coming talents are showcased. Tickets range from €5-25; additional *de rigueur* monthly membership fee €2.50. The cool kids come here for the nightclub "Paradiso" Th-M (€6 weeknights, €12.50 weekends).

JAZZ, CONTEMPORARY, & WORLD MUSIC

Alto, Korte Leidsedwarsstraat 115, in Leidseplein. Take a right in front of Häagen Dazs; it's 1 block down on your left. Hepcats left over from the 50s—literally—mingle with young aficionados at this busy nightspot where the vibe is cool but the jazz is hot. Show up early to get a table up front, though you can hear (if not see too clearly) the act from the bar away from the stage. Free nightly jazz Su-Th 10pm-2am, F-Sa until 3am. Open Su-Th 9pm-3am, F-Sa until 4am. Cash only.

Casablanca, Zeedijk 24-26 (☎ 625 56 85; www.casablanca-amsterdam.nl), between Oudezijds Kolk and Vredenburgersteeg. Casablanca has been around since 1946 and, though its heyday as *the* jazz bar in Amsterdam has faded, it's still one of the best for live jazz. Dim and smoky, the Casablanca retains a moody feel and is still quite popular with locals. Live jazz Su-W night. €5 cover (at Zeedijk 24 only). Open Su-Th 8pm-3am, F-Sa 8pm-4am. MC/V.

Cristofori, Prisengracht 581-3 (☎ 626 84 85; www.cristofori.nl). Tram #1, 2, or 5 to Prisengracht. Su night jazz and other contemporary and chamber music in an old canal house. Two concerts per month, from Sept.-Apr. Chamber music at 3pm, jazz at 8:30pm. €12.50, seniors €10. Cash only.

De Badcuyp, 1e Sweelinckstraat 10 (☎ 675 96 69; www.badcuyp.demon.nl), on Albert Cuypstraat. A vibrant cobalt-and-yellow venue for world music in an immigrant neighborhood. Tu 9pm-midnight blues and world (free), W salsa dance (€3), Su jazz (free). African dance party last Su of every month (€2.50); didgeridoo 2nd Th of every month (free). Pick up a schedule or check the website for more events. Also houses a cafe with €10.50 dinners. Open Su-Th 10am-1am, F-Sa 10am-3am. MC/V.

Meander, Voetboogstraat 3b (☎ 625 84 30; www.cafemeander.com). From Muntplein, take the Singel to Heiligweg, turn right, and then left at Voetboogstraat. Live bands jam at this barcafe populated by crowds of youthful hipsters. There are shows nightly, ranging from jazz to funk to soul to blues to R&B to salsa to DJ-hosted dance sessions (monthly schedule posted on website). Dim, smokey atmosphere, constant din, and dense crowds make for a raucous, high-energy good time. Cover from €5. Open Su-Th 9pm-3am, F-Sa 9pm-4am. Cash only.

Panama, Oostelijke Handelskade 4 (☎311 86 86; www.panama.nl), in the Eastern docklands. From Centraal Station, take bus #32 or 39. The abandoned warehouse location means they lure you to their opulent playland for the whole night: this theater and nightclub usually attracts a crowd in their 30s and 40s. The live music is mostly Latin, with some jazz and Caribbean; usually accompanied by dance, impromptu or otherwise (€5-20). "Twilight Zone" Sa 10:30-11pm. The last Su of every month is a gay night, "Club BPM," with a special performance at 10pm (€15 before 9:30pm, €20 after). Cover Th €6, F-Sa €12. Cash only.

THEATER

If it's live theater you're after, the Amsterdam Uitburo (AUB) is your best resource, hands down. Year-round (but especially in the summer), the city is bursting with opportunities to see live theater, both Dutch and international. There are many different varieties of theater in the city, including **cabarets, musicals, stand-up comedy** (often in English) **spoken dramas,** and **dance.** Ticket prices vary widely; cheaper tickets are usually €11-23 and more expensive ones €23-46.

COMEDY

Boom! Chicago, Leidseplein 12 (☎423 01 01; www.boomchicago.nl). Tram #1, 2, 5, 6, 7, or 10 to Leidseplein. You don't have to travel to Amsterdam to find funny Americans, but you can. This 11-year-old troupe performs sketch and improvisational comedy at the theater on Leidseplein. These expats promise a wry look at life on the continent that makes fun of people on both sides of the Atlantic. Shows Su-F 8:15pm, Sa 7:30 and 10:45pm. Heineken Late Nite (€10.50) is an all-improv show F 11:30pm. Restaurant and theater open at 6:30pm (6pm on Sa); arrive early. Bring a copy of *Boom!,* (their witty guide to Amsterdam that's distributed free around the city) for a €3 discount on tickets 6pm Su-Th. Tickets Su-Th €17, F-Sa €19. Boom! Chicago also organizes **boat trips** in small, open boats through the non-profit organization Sint Nicolaas Boat Stichting (€10). Tours arranged at irregular times, so call ahead or drop by Boom! Chicago. AmEx/MC/V.

Comedy Cafe, Max Euweplein 43-45 (☎638 39 71; www.comedycafe.nl). Tram #1, 2, 5, 6, 7 or 10 to Leidseplein. A rotating line-up of comics from around the world, some in English and some in Dutch; call or check the web (Th-Sa 9pm; €12). W open-mic night, with a typically unpredictable bag of performances (9pm; €5 cover includes 1 drink). New show "Without Ties" delivers wacky improv comedy in English (Tu and Su 9pm; €11). Three-course dinner (Th-Sa €34, Su €31) includes a ticket to the show; reservation usually necessary. Box office open M-F 9am-5pm, after that and on weekends, buy your tickets at the cafe.

Toomler, Breitnerstraat 2 (☎670 7400; www.toomler.nl), next to the Hilton Amsterdam. Tram #16 to Cornelius Schutstraat, or #5 or 24 to Apollolaan and walk left across the canal for 3 blocks. Or, take bus #15, 145, 170, or 197. Hosts Comedy Train International, a laugh-riot in English (Sa 7pm and midnight). Features on other nights include live music and more comedy, although it's frequently in Dutch (€2-5).

LIVE THEATER VENUES

Stadsschouwburg, Leidseplein 26 (☎624 23 11; www.stadsschouwburgamsterdam.nl). The main theater for Dutch-language plays in Amsterdam and the base for the Holland Festival in June. Also features some modern dance and opera. July Dance Festival (www.julidans.com). Theater tickets €10-20, more for opera. Box office open M-Sa 10am-6pm. Sprintpass (under age 24), allows purchase of €10 tickets 30min. before the show.

Bellevue Theater/Nieuwe de la Mar, Leidsekade 90 (☎530 53 01; www.theaterbellevue.nl or www.nieuwedelamartheater.nl). Tram #1, 2, 5, 6, 7, or 10 to Leidseplein. Three stages for popular theater, musicals, modern dance, and cabaret. The Bellevue, which merged with Nieuwe de la Mar 15 years ago, runs more experimental theater out of the same and complex. Most shows in Dutch, but check the current offerings. Bellevue tickets usually €15-75, Nieuwe de la Mar up to €20. Box office open daily 11am-6pm.

truth is stranger than *fiction*

In that touchstone of contemporary American pop culture, Quentin Tarantino's film *Pulp Fiction*, Amsterdam is hailed as a bastion of hedonism as compared to the more stodgy US. In one of the movie's first scenes, mobster Vincent Vega regales another hitman, Jules Winfield, about the "little differences" that make Amsterdam special. Among them are:

Bars in movies theaters. As Vincent reports, in Amsterdam you can go into a movie theater and get a beer—"I mean, a glass of beer." True enough—most movie theaters, even the commercial chain Pathé, will have at least Heineken and Amstel on tap and many more besides. To drink up and see a flick, see Film, p. 168.

Smoking in the city. "It's legal but it ain't a hundred percent legal, I mean, you just can't walk into a restaurant, roll a joint and start puffin' away," Vincent reports. It's a bad idea to walk into any bar or restaurant with a lit joint. It is considered impolite and not done—you will likely be asked to leave; ask if you want to smoke shomewhere other than a coffeeshop.

On the legality of cannabis. It's legal to buy it, it's legal to own it, and if you're the proprietor of a hash bar, it's legal to sell it," says Mr. Vega. Partially right: unless you have a license, you will be prosecuted for buying, selling, or carrying over 5g of hash or marijuana. Actually cannabis is only *tolerated* in

continued on next page

De Kleine Komedie, Amstel 56-58 (☎624 05 34; www.dekleinekomedie.nl). Tram #4, 5, or 9, to Rembrandtplein. One of Amsterdam's oldest theaters and The Netherlands' premiere cabaret spot. Full program of drama and musical theater, most in Dutch.

Badhuis-Theater de Bochel, Andreas Bonnstraat 28 (☎065 355 3982; www.badhuistheater.nl), near Oosterpark. Tram #3. An irregular schedule of various off-beat productions (experimental theater, children's workshops, dance parties) in this bathouse-turned-theater. Jazz Th night, weekends often open parties. Most shows €5-7.50. Buy your ticket at the door.

Melkweg, Lijnbaansgracht 234a (☎531 8181; www.melkweg.nl). Along with the cinema, club, and art gallery, the Melkweg is a popular venue for touring theater groups. See p. 166.

De Balie, Kleine-Gartmanplansoen 10 (☎553 51 00; www.balie.nl), just off Leidseplein. Housed in a former court of justice, De Balie is a center for film, photography, theater, and new media. Interesting contemporary theater is almost a guarantee. Check with box office for info on whether a film is subtitled in English.

Vondelpark Openluchttheater (☎673 14 99; www.openluchttheater.nl), in the center of the park. Free summer (May-Aug.) outdoor theater as well as music, dance, and kids shows.

Marionette Theater, see p. 165.

Casablanca, Zeedijk 24-26, (☎625 56 85). A small variety theater and circus with an old-time feel (€5). Children's magician Su afternoon. Old-World dinner around €17.

FILM

The Dutch love affair with the movies is expansive, encompassing a cinematic range from the tackiest American blockbuster to the most obscure indie art-house flick. The city distinguishes itself by the **Filmmuseum,** a national cinematic library. Fortunately for tourists and non-locals, films are only rarely dubbed into Dutch, which means that you won't need to have expert lip-reading skills. Bearing this in mind, you must remember that if you're planning to view a non-English film, it will be shown in its original language with Dutch subtitles. Some theaters may offer English subtitles for foreign films, but you should check with the box office first or look for an "EO" or "Engels Ondertiteld" sign. Most movies are released in The Netherlands a few months after their debut, although big box office hits will occasionally get to the Dutch screen right away. Check out www.movieguide.nl for listings or stop by any movie theater and pick up a copy of *Film Agenda*, a free guide to what's playing during a given week throughout the city. At the AUB, the *Film Krant* provides comprehensive listings and is an especially good resource for retrospectives and art house films. Alternatively, you can pick up an edition of the weekly *K-Pasa* or check the web at www.k-pasa.nl. The best site for Dutch film news is www.filmfocus.nl, which has showtimes as well as critical reviews and festival information.

The French company **Pathé** owns four of the bigger cinema houses in the city—The City, The Arena, Pathé de Munt, and the historic Tuschinski; information for all these is at www.pathe.nl. Pathé tends to show mainstream films although there are independent flicks in the lot as well. Prices for Pathé de Munt range €5-9.50, depending on how long the movie has been playing. At the other houses, prices are as follows: M-Th €7.90, students and seniors €6.80 (M only student tickets €4.50), matinees €6.50; F-Su morning and evening shows €8.75, seniors €7.65. Pick up the program at any theaters for listings to all of Pathé's cinemas.

Even if you're going to see *Dumb and Dumber III*, you should still be aware of cultural differences in Dutch cinema-going. For example, in Amsterdam, people do not eat while watching films, and many theaters do not serve popcorn; instead the Dutch like to bring a drink in with them. In *Pulp Fiction*, Vincent says one of the coolest things about Amsterdam is that you can go into a movie theater and order a beer. Well, here you are, so go to the movies and get your glass of beer. (See **Truth is Stranger Than *Fiction,*** at left, for more Vincent Vega wisdom.)

Filmmuseum, Vondelpark 3, between Roemer Visscherstraat and Vondelstraat entrances. (☎589 14 00; www.filmmuseum.nl). Walk across Singelgracht from Leidseplein to **Vondelpark,** or take tram #1 to 1er Constatijn Huygensstraat or #3, 12 to Overtoom. A stately house with at least 4 daily screenings, many of them older classics or organized around a special theme like the works of Fellini, American Westerns, or Jacques Tati. Every summer, the Filmmuseum shows a retrospective of a film diva, like Sophia Loren or Elizabeth Taylor. €6.25-7, students and seniors €5. F night witnesses an outdoor screening for €3, which also gets you a free drink at the next door Cafe Vertigo (see p. 118). A new exhibition space will open in late 2003 to complement the screenings. The newly-opened annex, **Filmmuseum Cinerama,** Marnixstraat 400 (tram #1, 2, 5, 6, 7, 10) has a smaller pick of classic and contemporary films. Pick up a copy of *Zine* magazine at either theater for the month's listings or call the main Vondelpark box office. Box office open 9am-10:15pm.

continued from previous page

The Netherlands. It is technically an offense to possess any amount—the Dutch merely allow its use. The toleration policy means that you will not get arrested for smoking, carrying, or buying under 5g in any 24hr. period. Vincent goes on to say, "It's legal to carry it, which doesn't really matter 'cause— get a load of this—if the cops stop you, it's illegal for them to search you. Searching you is a right that the cops in Amsterdam don't have." Again, only partially true: the police do have the right to stop you, but in order for them to search you, they must take you to the police station.

Dutch fetish for mayo on fries. As Vincent says, "they drown 'em in that shit." If you get french fries here, they will probably come slathered in—or with an ample side of—mayo. Though North Americans may cringe, the taste is not unpleasant. Aside from the standard white goop, there are a number of exotic variations—like flavored with curry spices or spicy Japanese "samurai" tincture. Once your taste adjusts, you may even find it delicious, and maybe even forget that you're eating mayonnaise. If you're anywhere near Wetplein in the south of the Central Canal Ring, grab some fries at **Snackbar Eucalyptus ❶,** Nieuwe Vijzelstraat 3, just across from the Weteringcircuit stop on either tram #16 or 24.

Vincent Vega's take on Amsterdam is mostly right, so don't knock foreign-seeming local customs. As Vincent admonished Jules, "You'd dig it the most!"

The Movies, Harlemmerstraat 159 (☎624 57 90; www.themovies.nl), in the **Shipping Quarter.** Take Bus #18 or 22, or tram #3 to Haarlemmerplein. The Movies, a restored Art Deco building, is Amsterdam's oldest movie theater and shows an engrossing range of independent films from all genres. Sa "Seize the Night" series plays recent favorites and dusty classics. In the adjacent restaurant and bar, the savory *dagschotels* tend to be quite dear (about €17), but budget travelers are sure to be able to afford the appetizers (€6), light snacks, and drinks. There is a 4-course set menu, including the price of a movie ticket, for €27, making for an elegant dinner-and-a-movie package. Movie only €7.50, students and seniors €6.50. MC/V in restaurant only.

Kriterion Theater and Cafe, Roetersstraat 170 (☎623 17 08; www.kriterion.nl), in **Plantage.** Tram #6, 7, or 10 to Weesperplein. Run by a student collective from the nearby University of Amsterdam, Kriterion is a real art-house movie theater with a laid-back cafe, where local students come to discuss everything from Bogart to Bond over cigarettes and jazz. Independent and studio films run daily at the theater, and children's movies are also shown regularly throughout the year. Cafe open Su-Th 11am-1am, F-Sa 12:30pm-3am. €6.20, weekends €6.60; students and seniors €5, weekends €5.40. Cash only.

Smart Project Space, 1e Constantijn Huygensstraat 20 (☎427 5951; www.smartprojectspace.net), in the **Oud-West.** Tram #1 to 1er Constatijn Huygensstraat or #3, 12 to Overtoom. The Smart Project Space is both an exhibition space and a movie theater, run by an anti-squat organization, that has a variety of arts-related events. Experimental and independent films in addition to monthly live performances. Restaurant and bar in front is hip, if prohibitively expensive. Films €5.50, students and seniors €4.50. Cash only.

Tuschinski Cinema, Reguliersbreestraat 26-28 (☎626 26 33), between Rembrandtplein and Muntplein. Step from the gaudy whirlwind of the **Rembrandtplein's** porno shops and fast food stands into the Tuschinski Cinema's oasis of Old World elegance. This ornate movie theater, built back in 1921, was one of Europe's first experiments in the Art Deco style. Although a group of drunk Nazis once got out of hand and started a fire in the theater's cabaret, the theater miraculously survived WWII and has remained in operation for over 75 years. Guided tours July-Aug. Su-M 10:30am. A ticket to a screening of one of their Hollywood features allows you to explore on your own. Theater 1 is the main stage and has private boxes—it tends to show a commercial hits while the other screens are devoted to artsy shows. Tuschinski is a Pathé cinema (see above).

De Balie, Kleine-Gartmanplansoen 10 (Ticket counter ☎553 51 00; reception tel. 553 51 51; www.balie.nl). Just off of **Leidseplein.** Tram #1, 2, 5, 6, 7, 10 to Leidseplein. An intellectual center in a former courthouse, De Balie offers alternative films (€6.25, students and seniors €5), theater (€8.75/€7.50), new media, political debates, and lectures (€7.50/€5). Films are generally non-commercial and on topics such as contemporary life in China. Cafe (food €3-8) with changing art displays and free Internet (you're expected to buy a drink). Pick up a program in the lobby or check the website for more info. Cash only.

Het Ketelhuis, Haarlemmerweg 8-10 (☎684 00 90; www.ketelhuis.nl), west of the **Shipping Quarter.** Tram #10 to Van Limburg Stirumplein. A living room for Dutch cinema in an abandoned warehouse. While the majority of Amsterdam's cinemas show mostly foreign films, Het Ketelhuis, located in the Westergasfabrik complex, is dedicated to the promotion of Dutch works. Films very are rarely in English, so brush up on your Dutch or come during the summer when they often show international art house films. €7.50, students €6.50.

Rialto, Ceintuurbaan 338 (☎675 39 94; www.rialtofilm.nl), in **De Pijp.** Tram #3, 24, or 25 to Ferdinand Bol. The Rialto is a wonderful art house cinema in a newly renovated complex showing a wide variety of international movies on 2 screens. Features an engaging number of retrospectives and series; documentaries Th 8pm. €6.50, €7.50 on weekends; students and seniors €5.50/€6.50

Cinecenter, Lijnbaansgracht 236 (☎623 66 15; www.cinecenter.nl), just off **Leidseplein.** Not catering to the masses, the Cinecenter runs medium-artsy films, many of which are foreign. €6.50 weekdays, €7.50 weekends; students and seniors €5.50/€6.50.

SPORTS & OTHER ENTERTAINMENT

Bungy Jump Holland, Westerdoksdijk 44 (☎419 60 05; www.bungy.nl). Jump from a crane 75m above the Ij canal. You get to choose whether you end up wet or dry. First jump €50, 2nd €40; duo jump €100. Open Apr. Sa-Su noon-6pm; May-June Th-Su noon-7pm; July-Aug. W-Su noon-8pm; Sept.-Oct. Th-Su noon-6pm.

Deco Sauna, Herengracht 115 (☎623 82 15; www.saunadeco.nl). Pamper yourself amidst fabulous 20s art deco surroundings with a massage—Shiatsu or reflexology. €27 for 25min., €44 for 55min. Fiery sauna and turkish bath hidden among damp tiled columns. Towel rental €2. Salon next door at Herengracht 117 offers facials, manicures, and special "beauty days" from €100 (☎330 35 65) Open M-Sa noon-11pm, Su 1-6pm. Cash only.

Holland Casino Amsterdam, Max Euweplein 62 (☎521 11 11; www.hollandcasino.nl). Head through Max Euweplein's columns past a lovely curved fountain for the mammoth temple to Mammon. The largest and ritziest of The Netherlands' national gaming houses, the casino generously presents a variety of pocket-emptying diversions—electronic slots, blackjack, roulette, poker and wily one-armed bandits. 18 to enter, but even seniors without a government-issued ID will be turned away. Flashy restaurant inside, open same hours as casino. Open daily 1pm-3am. €3.50 entry fee. Min. wager at some tables €1.30-2, for slots €0.50.

Klimmuur Centruum, De Ruyterkade 160 (☎427 57 77; www.deklimmuur.nl), east of Centraal Station; it's the enormous corrugated tilting block. An unsurpassed indoor wall climbing facility. €9 per climb; €15 for rental of full equipment. Open M-F 6-10:30pm, Sa 1-7pm, Su 1-10:30pm. Cash only.

Knijn Bowling, Scheldeplein 3 (☎664 22 11; www.knijnbowling.nl) in the South. Tram #4. The Dutch aren't famous for bowling but Knijn makes a noble try. "Twilight Bowling" with luminous balls and pins as well as lighting, smoke and dance music (F 11pm-12:30am, Sa 11:30pm-1am) €10.50 per person. Hourly prices for groups up to 6 people, including shoe rental: M-F 10am-5pm €15; M-Th 5pm-1am €20.50; F-Sa 5pm-1am €23.50; Sa noon-5pm €20.50; Su and public holidays noon-midnight €23.50.

Snooker & Poolclub Oud-West, Overtoom 209 (☎618 80 19). Tram #1 or 6 to Constantijn Huygensstr. and walk down Overtoom. Full-size snooker in a converted church with 2 pool tables on the balcony and 2 dart lanes. Full bar on the side for added merriment. Monthly membership for use of pool tables €5 (€8 for 1 hr. before 2pm, €7.50 after); no membership needed for snooker. Open Su-Th noon-1am, F-Sa noon-2am. Reserve 2 days ahead for F-Sa.

Shopping

Amsterdam is brimming with specialized boutiques offering all sorts of quirky but well-designed goods. The little passageways that cross the three central canals in between Raadhuisstraat and Leidsegracht—famously known as the "Nine Streets"—are strewn with fun designs. Passages in the **Jordaan** posses similarly charming shops. Other roads ripe with goodies include **Utrechtsestraat,** south of Rembrandtplein; **Nieuwe Hoogstraat,** in the Jodenbuurt; and **Haarlemmerstraat,** in the Shipping Quarter. **Kalverstraat** and **Nieuwendijk** are also two popular pedestrian-packed commercial strips near Dam Square. The cheapest goods in the city can be found in shops in **De Pijp,** which brim with bargain finds from all over the world. By contrast, the most prestigious (and expensive) shops are found on **P.C. Hoofstraat** in Museumplein, which teems with international clothing designers. However, in comparison to the rest of Amsterdam, this stretch is actually quite sterile and banal. Art aficionados will find delight in the Jordaan, and the Central Canal Ring, which are home to several fine ventures that feature contemporary art and more antique prints. One of the best one-stop shops for artwork is the **Galerie Complex Lijnbaansgracht,** a center home to nine equally excellent galleries. Despite the number of quality goods found in specialized boutiques and commercial European chains Amsterdam's bustling **market** scene is by far the best option for bargain hunting. Markets hawking everything from organic produce random detritus operate daily in the city, including the tulip and bulb market at **Bloemenmarkt** (see p. 179) and the **Dappermarkt** (see p. 179), which has been claimed by the city's North African and Middle Eastern communities. The true gem of Amsterdam's abundant market is **Albert Cuypmarkt** (p. 179), which merits an exploration for its unparalleled abundance of cheap treasures.

BY NEIGHBORHOOD

OUDE ZIJD

Episode (175)	clothing
Oudemanhuispoort (179)	market
⊠ The Book Exchange (175)	books
Waterlooplein (179)	market

NIEUWE ZIJD

American Book Center (175)	books
Athenaeum Boekhandel (175)	books
Bloemenmarkt (179)	market
Dance Tracks (179)	music
Hema (176)	department store
Japanese Winkeltje (178)	international
Laundry Industry (176)	clothing
Magna Plaza (176)	department store
Roots Music (180)	music
Soul Food (180)	music
Spui (179)	market
The Old Man (180)	smoking
Tibet Winkel (179)	international

CANAL RING WEST

Architectura and Natura (175)	books
Beadies (177)	gifts
Cine Qua Non (177)	gifts
Cortina Paper (177)	gifts
De Witte Tanden Winkel (177)	gifts
In Oprichting (177)	gifts
La Savonnerie (178)	gifts
Laura Dols (180)	vintage clothing
Nic Nic (174)	antiques
ROB (178)	gifts
Ree-member (180)	vintage clothes
⊠ Saga (176)	clothing
Zara (176)	clothing
Zipper (181)	vintage clothing

CENTRAL CANAL RING

A la Carte (175)	books
Concerto (179)	music
Local Service (176)	clothing
⊠ Maranon Hangmatten (178)	home goods
Uptodate (178)	gifts

MUSEUMPLEIN & VONDELPARK

Schot CD Shop (180)	music

JORDAAN

A Space Oddity (178)	gifts
Back Beat Records (179)	music
De Plaatboef (179)	music
⊠ English Bookshop (175)	books
Kitsch Kitchen (177)	gifts
Megazino (176)	clothing
Noordermarkt (179)	market
Petticoat (181)	vintage clothing
⊠ Twee (de) Handjes (180)	vintage clothing
Wenterwereld Records (180)	music
Westermarkt (179)	market

WESTERPARK & OUD-WEST

Hera Kaarsen (177)	gifts

DE PIJP

Abracadabra (177)	gifts
Albert Cuypmarkt (179)	market
⊠ Betsy Palmer Shoes (175)	clothing
De Beestenwinkel (180)	toys
De Emaillekeizer (178)	home goods
De Kinderfeestwinkel (177)	gifts
Gallerie Casbah (178)	home goods
Morning Glory-yocha (178)	international
Santa Jet (175)	antiques
The Head Man (180)	smoking

NIEUWMARKT

Biba (175)	clothing
De Bijenkorf (176)	department store
⊠ De Hoed Van Tijn (175)	clothing
Dun Yong (178)	international
Juggle Store (180)	toys
Nieuwmarkt (179)	market

JODENBUURT & PLANTAGE

Dappermarkt (179)	market
Puck (176)	clothing

SHIPPING QUARTER

The Purple Onion (178)	home goods
Wini (181)	vintage clothing

BY CATEGORY

ANTIQUES

Also see **Markets**, p. 179.

Nic Nic, Gasthuismolensteeg 5 (☎ 622 85 23). Nearly everyone who passes the exceptionally cluttered window of Nic Nic just *has* to go inside and take a peek. The offerings in this antique and curiosities shop are simply too unusual to pass up. Everything from art deco furniture to 50s dishware and dolls are on sale for reasonable prices; take the time to dig through the intimidating piles and you're sure to surface with an incredible find. Open M-F noon-6pm, Sa 10am-5pm. AmEx/MC/V.

Santa Jet, Albert Cuypstraat 69 (☎675 51 35). Folk art and artifacts from Latin America, including bags, clothing, mirrors, love potions, and candles. Large variety of religious shrines and icons as well. Second location at Prinsenstraat 7 (☎427 2070). Open Tu-Sa 10am-10pm, Su noon-10pm. Cash only.

BOOKS, ETC.

▨ **The Book Exchange,** Kloveniersburgwal 58 (☎626 62 66), between the Oude Zijd and the Jodenbuurt, deals in used texts and has a friendly, tasteful, knowledgeable staff. Frightfully good selection of used English-language books, from basic fiction and nonfiction to the more esoteric, all reasonably priced (paperbacks €3-11). Also buys used paperbacks; true to its name, the Exchange offers a more favorable deal if you're willing to trade. Open M-F 10am-6pm, Sa 10am-5:30pm, Su 11:30am-4pm.

▨ **English Bookshop,** Lauriergracht 71 (☎626 42 30), in the Jordaan. Renovated and reopened in July 2002, it now offers coffee and tea to sip while you browse its strong selection of books and American magazines. Open Tu-Su 10am-6pm.

A la Carte, Utrechtsestraat 110-112 (☎625 06 79; www.reisboekhandel). Tram #7 or 10 to Frederiksplein. A cozy travel bookstore specializing in maps from around the world, as well as various editions of Dutch- and English-language travel guides. Open M 1-6pm, Tu-F 10-6pm, Sa 10-5pm. AmEx/MC/V.

American Book Center, Kalverstraat 185 (☎625 55 37; www.abc.nl) in the Nieuwe Zijd, advertises itself as the largest English-language bookstore on the continent. 10% discount for students and teachers. Open M 1pm-6pm, Tu-Sa 11am-6pm.

Architectura and Natura, Leliegracht 22 (☎623 61 86; www.architectura.nl), in the Canal Ring West. Can't read Dutch? Well, it doesn't matter, because it's the pictures that make these coffeetable books extraordinary. Enough of them are in English, anyway. Heavy and beautiful, the tomes here tend to be expensive. Open M noon-6:30pm, Tu-Sa 9am-6pm. AmEx/MC/V.

Athenaeum Boekhandel, Spui 14-16 (☎622 62 48; www.athenaeum.nl), at the bottom of the Nieuwe Zijd in the Spui. Stocks obscure literary treasures, cultural criticism, and philosophy as well as beautiful art coffeetable books; most are in English. Also maintains a newsstand with a very extensive selection of American and British magazines. Open M 11am-6pm, Tu-W and F-Sa 9:30am-6pm, Th 9:30am-9pm, Su noon-5:30pm. AmEx/MC/V.

Waterstone's, Kalverstraat 152 (☎638 38 21), carries a wide selection. Open Su-M 11am-6pm, Tu-W 9am-6pm, Th 9am-9pm, F 9am-7pm, Sa 10am-7pm.

CLOTHING

▨ **Betsy Palmer Shoes,** Van Woustraat 46 (☎470 97 95; www.betsypalmer.com), in De Pijp, or Rokin 9-15 (☎422 10 60), in the Nieuwe Zijd. Heels, sandals, and boots in funky yet elegant styles. Although these chic women's shoes are priced on the high side, the store has frequent sales. Open M noon-6pm, Tu-F 10am-6pm, Sa 10am-5pm.

▨ **De Hoed Van Tijn,** Nieuwe Hoogstraat 15 (☎623 27 59). Fedoras, berets, pork pie hats, and every other style of head ornament are here, ranging in price from €20-200. Steep prices but, when hunting for a stylish chapeau, there's no better place to look. Open M noon-6pm, Tu-F 11am-6pm, Sa 11am-5pm.

Biba, Nieuwe Hoogstraat 26 (☎330 57 21; fax 330 57 22). Many items here cost a pretty penny, but the dazzling collection of classic and ultra-modern jewelry makes it more than worth a stop for the design-conscious trinket lover. Open M 1-6pm, Tu-Sa 11am-6pm, Su 1pm-5pm. AmEx/MC/V.

Episode, Waterlooplein 1 (☎320 30 00). An eclectic selection of inexpensive second-hand clothing awaits your discovery and creative mismatching at this shop. Located alongside the Waterlooplein flea market. Open M-Sa 10am-6pm. MC/V.

life's green

recycled garments

Clothing store ◼**Saga** has taken the art of recycling to an aesthetic level. For two years designer Noel has created clothing and accessories from recycled products—using postage, tires, and even Ukranian army uniforms. The outfits are chic, with off-the-shoulder tees proudly boasting a postal emblem or cargo pants cut from army discards. Tote bags are brightly colored and craftily sculpted so the store's clientele hardly look as if they're sporting used tires on their shoulders.

But the prices at Saga are steep; with t-shirts €39-49 and dress shirts and pants €109-139, many may wonder why they're paying so much for a (former) piece of garbage. Noel has a message for all cotton devotees. Inspired by an environmentally-conscious friend, he's become attuned to the needs of a sustainable earth, combining recycling with fashion so he can use his talent to preserve the planet. Cans and paper are just the start of conservation: if Noel can reuse an ancient couch—upholstery wallets are his specialty—he knows every little trinket can be turned into a fashion work of art.

(Huidenstraat 30, Canal Ring West. ☎ 422 64 07. Open Tu-Su 11am-6pm.)

Laundry Industry, Spui 1 (☎ 420 25 54), in the Nieuwe Zijd. The Dutch are proud to call this respected international brand their own. The debonair and crisp, clean-cut suits, semi-casual wear, and lingerie run middle to high range prices. Open M 11am-6:30pm; Tu, W, F 10am-6:30pm; Th 10am-9pm; Sa 10am-6pm; Su noon-6pm. AmEx/MC/V.

Local Service. Keizersgracht 400-402 (☎ 626 68 40 or 620 86 38). Men's and women's modern designer clothing with a colorful flair. Choose from casual or dressy items. Trendy accessories and shoes complete this fashion statement of a store. Open M 1pm-6pm; Tu, W, F 10am-6pm; Th 10am-7:30pm; Sa 10am-5:30pm; Su 1-5:30pm.

Megazino, Rozengracht 207-213 (☎ 330 10 31; www.megazinobv.com), in the Jordaan. A designer outlet with name brands for ¼ the price. They get their items (sometimes a season or two behind) directly from the factory. Disorderly array of clothes, shoes, and accessories. Open Su-M noon-7pm; Tu-W, F-Sa 10am-7pm; Th 10am-9pm. AmEx/MC/V.

Puck, Nieuwe Hoogstraat 1a (☎ 625 42 01). New and used goods in a bright, airy shop in the Jodenbuurt. Second-hand clothes are classics and in excellent condition. Best of all, items (dresses, suits, hats, accessories, linens, Japanese and Korean kimonos, and children's apparel) come without the musty smell that characterizes many vintage goods. Open M 1-6pm, Tu-F 11am-6pm, Sa 11am-5pm.

Zara, Kalverstraat 67-69 (☎ 530 40 50). This Spanish store delivers the fashion world's hottest outfits straight from the runway to you. Sporty, casual, and dress clothes are accompanied by trendy shoes and chic accessories at pleasantly cheap prices. One floor of the store is reserved for men's styles. Open M, Su noon-6pm; T, W, F, Sa 10am-6pm; Th 10am-9pm. AmEx/MC/V.

DEPARTMENT STORES

De Bijenkorf, Dam 1 (☎ 621 80 80). Situated in the heart of Dam Square, Amsterdam's best-known department store sells books, clothes, home goods—standard (but classy) department store stock. Open M 11am-7pm, Tu-W 9:30am-7pm Th-F 9:30am-9pm; Sa 9:30am-6pm; Su noon-6pm.

Hema, Nieuwendijk 174 (☎ 638 99 63). Compared to De Bijenkorf, Hema is a more affordable department store carrying many of the same items and more household goods. Open M-W, F 9:30am-4:30pm; Th 9:30am-9pm; Sa 9:30am-4pm; Su noon-4pm.

Magna Plaza, Nieuwezijds Voorburgwal 182 (☎ 626 91 99). A popular shopping mall with high-end fashion boutiques. Open M 11am-7pm, Tu-Sa 10am-7pm, Su noon-7pm.

GIFTS

Amsterdam, especially the Canal Ring West, abounds with one-of-a-kind boutiques.

Abracadabra, Sarphati Park 24 (☎676 66 83), in De Pijp. Abracadabra stocks glittery delights at very low prices: jewelry, lanterns, picture frames, pillows, incense, and additional baubles, all imported from India. Remarkable for the great bargains on jewelry, with some necklaces and earrings for only €5. V/MC for purchases €50 and above.

Beadies, Huidenstraat 6 (☎428 51 61; www.beadies.com). This store provides all the ingredients of a colorful trinket but if you don't dare to create your own, plenty of ready-made jewelry is laid out for sale. Bracelets and necklaces from €10 (depending on the cost of beads and clasps). Open M 1-6pm, Tu-Sa 10:30am-6pm, Th 10:30am-9pm. AmEx/MC/V.

Ceramic Clogs

Cine Qua Non, Staalstraat 14 (☎625 55 88). Find posters, books, and related ephemera from movies both classic and camp at this small shop devoted to the by-products of the film industry. Open Tu-Sa 1-6pm. All credit cards accepted.

Cortina Paper, Reestraat 22 (☎623 66 76), in the Canal Ring West. This store is full of elegant stationery, notebooks, and photo albums that make perfect gifts, especially when wrapped in the gorgeous selection of decorative wrapping paper. Open M 1-6pm, Tu-Sa 11am-6pm. AmEx/MC/V.

De Kinderfeestwinkel, 1e van der Helststraat 15 (☎672 22 15), in De Pijp. The store to hit when you're planning a child's birthday party. A fantastical "fairy" shop packed with all sorts of playful, glittery goodies, invitations, toys, party decorations, and children's costumes, all arranged by color. Open M 1-6pm, Tu-Sa 10am-6pm.

Noordermarkt

De Witte Tanden Winkel, Runstraat 5 (☎623 34 43). Hop aboard the ferris wheel of dental hygiene! The White Tooth Shop is a humorous alternative to the local drugstore when you're looking for good ol' American toothpaste. Novelty brushes €2-14. Open M 1-6pm, Tu-F 10am-6pm, Sa 10am-5pm. AmEx/MC/V.

Hera Kaarsen, Overtoom 402 (☎616 28 86). A staggering variety of colorful and curious home-made candles (from €14), shaped into everything from globes to fruits and figurines. Lamps and glass vases round out Hera Kaarsen's luminous experience. Open Tu-F 11am-6pm, Sa 11am-5pm.

In Oprichting, Herenstraat 38 (☎639 28 52). At In Oprichting, peculiar gifts breed with a selection of puzzles, housewares, and toys for the child in everyone. Make sure you leave with the sheep-shaped nightlight for a lucky friend. Open M noon-6pm, Tu-Sa 11am-6pm. AmEx/MC/V.

Buying Books at Oudemanhuispoort

33354

44444333333322

222222222222

Kitsch Kitchen, 1e Bloemdwarsstraat 21-23 (☎428 49 69). A walk into the Jordaan will bring you to an explosion of color in the form of offbeat tupperware, culinary tools, and other home furnishings. Perfect place to stock up on kooky gifts and a cheaply made wardrobe. 2nd store located close by at Rozengracht 183 (☎622 82 61). Open M-W, F 11am-7pm; Th 11am-8pm; Sa 11am-6pm. AmEx/MC/V.

La Savonnerie, Prinsengracht 294 (☎428 11 39; www.savonnerie.nl). Exquisite handmade soaps in 80 colors and scents (€3.90-5). Open Tu-F 10am-6pm, Sa 10am-5pm. V/MC

ROB, Warmoestraat 32 (☎625 46 86). Rubber toys, leather pants, and fetishly outrageous masks and restraints makes this store innocent fun for the whole family. Men's clothing (jeans, chaps, and vests) located in brother establishment at Weterschans 253 (☎428 3000). Open M-F noon-7pm, Sa noon-6pm, Su 1-5pm.

A Space Oddity, Prinsengracht 204 (☎427 40 36; www.spaceoddity,com). Storeowner Jeff Bas has assembled an impressive assortment of sci-fi and comic book paraphernalia, from old action figures to movie promos. The young at heart will find old and rare toy incarnations of their favorite movies and comic books, from *Star Wars* to *Spider-Man*. Prices start at €10 and skyrocket from there. Open M 1-5:30pm, Tu-F 11am-5:30pm, Sa 1-5pm. MC/V.

Uptodate, Herengracht 300 (☎620 59 95). Classy silver items at shockingly low prices, suitable for every age. Unique jewelry, watches, clocks, pocketknives, and keychains elegantly created into spectacular gifts. Open M 1pm-6pm, T-F 11am-6pm, Sa 11am-5pm. Am/MC/V for purchases above €25.

HOME GOODS & FURNITURE

Maranon Hangmatten, Singelgracht 488-90 (☎420 71 21; www.maranon.net), in the Central Canal Ring. Right off the flower market, this is the best place in the city for temporary refuge. Come in for a rest to "test" the colorful, comfortable hammocks hanging from the ceiling. Open M-Sa 9am-6pm, Su 10am-5:30pm. AmEx/MC/V.

De Emaillekeizer, 1e Sweelinckstraat 15 (☎664 18 47; www.emaillekeizer.nl), a block and a half off the Albert Cuypmarket in De Pijp. Sells bright baskets, colorful woven deck chairs, and other knicknacks primarily from Ghana. Incredibly cheap dishware and teapots. If you're in town for a little while and realize you might need a plate, mug, or teapot, this is the place to go. Open M 1-6pm, Tu-Sa 11am-6pm.

Gallerie Casbah, 1e Van Der Helstraat (☎671 04 74), in De Pijp. Beautifully ornate imports from Morocco. Many pieces, especially tiled fountains, vases, and rugs. Also some wonderful plates and book bindings. Open daily 11am-6pm. Cash only.

The Purple Onion, Haarlemmerdijk 139 (☎427 37 50), in the Shipping Quarter. Step into this incense-filled shop to a world of eclectic goods imported from India. The owners, a Dutch anthropologist and an Indian scientist, select items using natural materials, such as wooden sculptures and handmade bedspreads. Open Tu-Sa 11:30am-6pm. MC/V.

INTERNATIONAL STORES

Dun Yong, Stormsteeg 9 (☎622 17 63; www.dunyong.com), on the corner of Gelderskade. A world of Chinese cultural kitsch awaits at this 5-floor shop bursting with foodstuffs, paper fans, decorative lamps, mini ceramic Buddhas, and kitchenware. Second location at Zeedijk 83. Open M-Sa 9am-6pm, Su noon-6pm. MC.

Japanese Winkeltje, NZ Voorburgwal 177 (☎627 95 23; www.japanesewinkeltje.nl), in the Nieuwe Zijd. Sushi plates, fine china, kimonos, art, books, and specialty dry foods from the Eastern island. The affiliated Japanese cultural center next door offers winter-time classes in language and cooking, and will help book trips to Japan as well. Open Su-M 1-6pm, Tu-Sa 9:30am-6pm. AmEx/MC/V for purchases €23 and up.

Morning Glory-yocha, Van Woustraat 48 (☎471 14 00; info@yocha.nl), in De Pijp. Welcome to the world of Hello Kitty, Babu, and Blue Bear. Pretty pastel collection of stationery, bags, and toys with these popular Japanese cartoon characters from Sanrio and Morning Glory. Open M 1-6pm, Tu-Su 10am-6pm. Cash only.

Tibet Winkel, Spuistraat 185a (☎420 54 38; www.tibetwinkel.nl). All proceeds from goods sold in this store (Tibetan music, books, incense, and other cultural knickknacks) help to fund the Tibet Support Group, which aids the Tibetan people in their struggle for self-determination (for more info, see www.xs4all.nl/~tibetsg). Open M 1-6pm, Tu-Su 10am-6pm. MC/V.

MARKETS

Each year on April 30, all of Amsterdam is transformed into a giant flea market in honor of Queen's Day (see p. 8). Fortunately, you can bargain-hunt and shop for treasures in the city's best markets on a daily basis.

Albert Cuypmarkt, in De Pijp. The biggest outdoor market in Europe boasts hoards of food, clothing, hardware, and household goods. Open M-Sa 9am-5pm.

Bloemenmarkt, on the Singelgracht canal by Muntplein. Dig through rows of flower bulbs at this floating market. Open daily 9am-5pm.

Dappermarkt, on Dapperstraat. If you're hoping to get a glimpse of Amsterdam's Middle Eastern and North African communities, stop by the Dappermarkt and sort through piles of useful, useless, and staggeringly cheap artifacts. With everything from pharmaceuticals and underwear to fresh produce, it's worth the trek for the bargain-hunter. Open M-Sa 9am-4pm.

Nieuwmarkt hosts a Boerenmarkt (organic food market) every Sa 10am-3pm, as well as an antiques market May-Sept. Su 9am-5pm.

Noordermarkt in the Jordaan (M 8am-1pm) is known for its collection of antiques, household goods, clothes, and trinkets. Organic produce market Sa 9am-4pm).

Oudemanhuispoort, between Oudezijds Achterburgwal and Kloveniersburgwal, sells cratefuls of both new and antiquated books, from the beloved *Harry Potter* series to steamy bodice-rippers. Open M-F 11am-4pm.

Spui, where on Su, local and international artists present their oils, etchings, sculptures, and jewelry, turning the bustling square into an outdoor modern gallery; open Mar.-Oct 10:30am-6pm. F the area transforms yet again, into a pricey book market that occasionally yields rare editions and 17th-century Dutch romances; open 10am-6pm.

Waterlooplein hosts an open air market M-Sa. Tapestries, used clothing, music and traditional Dutch art are all on sale in this large flea market beside the Stadhuis-Muziektheater. Open M-F 9am-5pm, Sa 8:30am-5:30pm.

Westermarkt, on Westerstraat, offers a small selection of various clothes, fabrics, and watches every M 9am-1pm.

MUSIC

Back Beat Records, Egelantiersstraat 19 (☎627 16 57; backbeat@xs4all.nl), in the Jordaan. Tightly packed collection of jazz, soul, funk, blues, and R&B. Prices are often steep, but some bargains can be found. New CD's as well as new and used vinyl. Open M-Sa 11am-6pm.

Concerto, Utrechtsestraat 52-60 (☎623 52 28; info@concerto.nu), in the Central Canal Ring. Around since 1955 and arguably the best music store in Amsterdam, Concerto sells a broad selection of CDs from 5 adjoining houses: second-hand, dance, pop, jazz/world, and classical. Records downstairs. Listening station where they'll play anything. Open M-W and F-Sa 10am-6pm, Th 10am-9pm, Su noon-6pm. AmEx/MC/V.

Dance Tracks, Nieuwe Nieuwstraat 69 (☎639 08 53). This record/CD shop advertises as "strictly dance music," and that's exactly what it means. Expect to find all sorts of cuts in the dance genre—bootlegs, rare records, and tons of hip-hop, soul, and house music. Open M 1-7pm, Tu-W and F-Sa 11am-7pm, Th 11am-9pm, Su 1-6pm. AmEx/MC/V.

De Plaatboef, Rozengracht 40 (☎422 87 77; www.plaatboef.com), in the Jordaan. Big selection of new and used CDs (around €11). Open M noon-6pm, Tu-Sa 10am-6pm. Credit cards accepted for purchases over €40.

Roots Music, Jonge Roelensteeg 6 (☎620 44 70). For reggae, Latin, or African beats, look no further than this mousehole-sized music shop in Canal Ring West. Roots houses a great selection of vinyl, 7-inches, and CDs at very affordable prices. Open Su-M 12:30-6pm, Tu-W and F-Sa 10:30am-6pm, Th 10:30am-9pm.

Soul Food, Nieuwe Nieuwstraat 27c, in the Red Light District. Specializes in dance music, both CD and vinyl. Wide selection of new and old cuts from Europe, the US, and abroad. Open M 1-9pm, Tu-W and F-Sa 11am-7pm, Th 11am-9pm, Su 1-7pm.

Schot CD Shop, van Baerlestraat 5 (☎662 37 59), between P.C. Hooftstraaat and Vossiusstraat, near Vondelpark. From the Museumplein, walk away from the Rijksmuseum and take your first right on van Baerlestraat. Diverse selection of music, with everything from world music to classical, opera, New Age, jazz, soul, and a larger selection of pop, including corny 70s hits. Prices vary widely, but there are many special deals. Good selection outside (€4.60; 3 for €12). Open daily 10:30am-7pm. AmEx/MC/V.

Wenterwereld Records, 13a 1e Bloemwarsstraat (☎622 23 30). If you've ever wanted to round out the "Nederpop" section of your record collection, this is the place to do it. Wonderful assortment of used and new records (€8.50-17.50); most are Dutch, and many of the American records are quite obscure. Also has an impressive collection of old comics, most in Dutch. In-store turntable lets you listen before you buy. Open M-Sa noon-5:30pm. Cash only.

SMOKING ACCESSORIES

The Head Man, 1e Sweelinckstraat 7 (☎670 78 26). Full-service shop in de Pijp with knowledgeable and helpful staff vending all manner of smoking devices: chillums, pipes, bongs, and more in countless different designs. Ask about the vaporizers—a new, increasingly popular way to take pot or hash (€45-273). Also a huge selection of stonerwear from the world's hemp-producing regions, including t-shirts (€4.50-6.80) and many different styles of rasta hats (€11.30-22.70). Open M-Sa 1-6pm.

The Old Man, Damstraat 16 (☎627 00 43). A massive selection near Dam Square, right in the center of it all. Glass bongs, wooden pipes, scales, hookahs and more. Don't miss the Delftware bong shaped like a clog and printed with a windmill, the combination of nearly every Dutch cliche in existence (€40). Upstairs there's a somewhat unsettling collection of swords and knives for sale. Open daily 9:30am-6pm. AmEx/MC/V.

TOYS & ENTERTAINMENT

De Beestenwinkel, Staalstraat 11 (☎623 18 05), in the Jodenbuurt. Corner shop specializing in cool animal toys of every sort. Be warned: there's an especially cuddly collection of plush animals that you won't be able to resist. Open Tu-Sa 10am-6pm, Su noon-5pm.

Juggle Store, Staalstraat 3 (☎420 19 80; www.juggle-store.com). *The* store for absolutely all of your juggling needs. The expert staff has selected the best juggling products on the market (as well as crafted some great in-shop ones, as well). A free split-second juggling lesson is available on request. Open Tu-Sa noon-5pm

VINTAGE CLOTHING

Twee (de) Handjes, 2e Leliedwarsstraat 23 (☎626 70 87), in the Jordaan. The owner of this little shop truly loves dresses, especially from the 30s and 40s, and a look at her selection of ballgowns, slipdresses, and petticoats will make you love them too. She also does alterations. Open Tu-Su noon-6pm.

Laura Dols, Wolvenstraat 6-7 (☎624 90 66), in the Canal Ring West. Two shops across the street from one another vend fanciful men's and women's clothing, such as tutus and cowboy shirts. Open M-Sa 11am-6pm, Th 11am-9pm, Su 2-6pm. V.

Ree-member, Ree-Straat 26-w (☎622 13 29), in the Canal Ring West. Well-chosen display of beautiful vintage clothes and '60s standards, like Lacoste polo shirts. Also sells shoes and bags. Great selection of coats. Open daily 11am-6pm. AmEx/MC/V.

Wini, Haarlemmerstraat 29 (☎ 427 93 93), in the Shipping Quarter. Young hipsters (men and women) shop here for their cool, stylish clothing. Wini also offers a great selection of bags and shoes. Open M-W and Sa 1am-6pm, Th 10am-8pm, Su noon-5pm. V.

Petticoat, Lindengracht 99 (☎ 623 30 65), in the Jordaan. Quality second-hand clothing for men and women. Open M-F 11am-6pm, Sa 11am-5pm. Cash only.

Zipper, Huidenstraat 7 (☎ 623 73 02), in the Canal Ring West, or Nieuwe Hoogstraat 8 (☎ 627 03 53), in the Jodenbuurt. Most renowned for their vast collection of vintage jeans, Zipper also stocks a sizable collection of young, '70s leaning (Adidas, cutout T-shirts, big belts) clothing for hipsters to fill the gaps in their wardrobes. Open M-Sa 11am-6pm, Th 11am-9pm, Su 1-5pm. AmEx/MC/V.

SIZES & CONVERSIONS

CLOTHING SIZES

WOMEN'S CLOTHING							
US SIZE	4	6	8	10	12	14	16
UK SIZE	6	8	10	12	14	16	18
DUTCH SIZE	32	34	36	38	40	42	44

WOMEN'S SHOES							
US SIZE	5	6	7	8	9	10	11
UK SIZE	3	4	5	6	7	8	10
DUTCH SIZE	36	37	38	39	40	41	42

MEN'S SUITS/JACKETS							
US/UK SIZE	32	34	36	38	40	42	44
DUTCH SIZE	42	44	46	48	50	52	54

MEN'S SHIRTS							
US/UK SIZE	14	14.5	15	15.5	16	16.5	17
DUTCH SIZE	35	36/37	38	39/40	41	42/43	44

MEN'S SHOES							
US SIZE	7	8	9	10	11	12	13
UK SIZE	6	7	8	9	10	11	12
DUTCH SIZE	39	41	42	43	44	46	47

METRIC CONVERSIONS

BRITISH/METRIC	METRIC/BRITISH
1 in. = 2.54cm	1cm = 0.4 in
1 ft. = 0.305m	1m = 3.28 ft.
1 mi. = 1.61km	1km = 0.62 mi.

BRITISH/METRIC	METRIC/BRITISH
1 lb. = 0.454kg	1kg = 2.2 lb.
1 gal. = 4 qt. = 3.79L	1L = 1.06 qt. = 0.264 gal.

Accommodations

Many of the accommodations in these listings are converted canal houses with unbeliev-ably steep staircases. Unless otherwise indicated, these lodgings do not have elevators, which means that you will likely have to lug your baggage up at least two imposing flights of stairs. That mammoth suitcase on wheels won't seem so convenient when you have to drag it while crawling up to the fourth floor—when packing, consider a backpack or two smaller pieces of luggage instead. Some of the shared bathrooms have antechambers so you can get dressed fresh from the shower. Shower shoes to prevent athlete's foot are also a good idea, and those squeamish about nudity may also want to pack a big towel.

Many of the smaller hotels in Amsterdam only accept credit cards with a hefty sur-charge of 4 to 6.5%. These establishments are not trying to cheat their customers, nor are they afraid of last-minute cancellations. Card companies make it difficult for credit cards to be worthwhile for small establishments, so these hotels try to charge patrons the same amount that the company charges them. We attempt to list all surcharges at all hotels, but even ones without extra charges will provide incentives like free breakfast or cheap drinks at their in-house bars as encouragement for customers to pay in cash. Some hotels will require full payment for your entire stay up front. The summer months and the few days before Christmas until New Year's Day are usually considered to be the high season, when hostel and hotel prices are higher.

For each neighborhood, hostels are listed first, followed by hotels and B&Bs. Some hotels are listed as hostels because they provide dorm-style accommodations.

BY PRICE

❶: UNDER €30 PER PERSON

🛏 Anna Youth Hostel (190)	NZ
Bob's Youth Hostel (190)	NZ
Budget Hotel Tamara (191)	NZ
La Canna (191)	NZ
De Witte Tulip Hostel (188)	RLD
Durty Nelly's Hostel (185)	OZ
Euphemia Budget Hotel (195)	CCR
🛏 Flying Pig Downtown (190)	NZ
Flying Pig Palace (201)	MV
Hans Brinker Hotel (196)	LP
Hotel Brian (192)	NZ
Hotel My Home (194)	SQ
International Budget Hostel (197)	LP
Ramenas Hotel (194)	SQ
The Shelter City (185)	RLD
🛏 The Shelter Jordan (198)	J
🛏 StayOkay Amst. Stadsdoelen (184)	OZ
🛏 StayOkay Amst. Vondelpark (HI) (200)	MV
Tourist Inn (190)	NZ
Young Budget Hotel Kabul (188)	RLD

❷: €30-49 PER PERSON

ANCO Hotel and Bar (189)	RLD
Apple Inn Hotel (202)	MV
🛏 Bicycle Hotel (202)	DP
Frisco Inn (185)	OZ
Hotel Royal Taste (189)	RLD
Hotel The Crown (189)	RLD
Hotel ABBA (200)	OW
🛏 Hotel Bema (201)	MV
🛏 Hotel Brouwer (191)	NZ
Hostel Cosmos (191)	NZ
Hotel Crystal (200)	OW
🛏 Hotel Groenendael (192)	NZ
De Oranje Tulp (193)	NZ
Hotel Aspen (195)	CRW
Hotel Asterisk (196)	CCR
Hotel Barbacan (204)	JP
Hotel Belga (195)	CRW
🛏 Hotel Clemens (194)	CRW
Hotel Hegra (195)	CRW
Hotel de Lantaerne (197)	LP
Hotel Museumzicht (202)	MV

❷: €30-49 PER PERSON, CONT'D.

Hotel Pax (195)	CRW
Hotel P.C. Hooft (202)	MV
Hotel Pension Kitty (203)	JP
Hotel Princess (200)	OW
Hotel De Stadhouder (203)	DP
Hotel van Onna (199)	J
Hotel Wynnobel (202)	MV
Old Nickel (189)	RLD
Old Quarter (188)	RLD
🛏 Quentin Hotel (197)	LP
Radion Inn Youth Hostel (196)	CCR

❸: €50-69 PER PERSON

Frederic Rent a Bike (193)	SQ
The Golden Bear (195)	CCR
The Greenhouse Effect Hotel (188)	RLD
🛏 Hemp Hotel (194)	CCR
Hotel Acacia (199)	J
Hotel Adolesce (204)	JP
Hotel La Boheme (198)	LP
Hotel Continental (193)	NZ
Hotel Kap (196)	CCR
Hotel Fantasia (204)	JP
Hotel de la Haye (198)	LP
Hotel Rokin (192)	NZ
Hotel Titus (198)	LP
🛏 Hotel Winston (188)	RLD
Stablemaster Hotel (189)	OZ
Tulip Inn Amsterdam Centre (199)	OW
Westertoren Hotel (195)	CRW
🛏 Wiechmann Hotel (195)	CRW

❹: €70-99 PER PERSON

City Hotel (198)	RP
Hotel Bellington (202)	MV
Hotel Europa 92 (202)	MV
🛏 Hotel de Filosoof (200)	OW
Hotel Hoksbergen (192)	NZ
Hotel International (189)	RLD
Hotel Monopole (198)	RP
Hotel Vijaya (189)	RLD

❺: €100+ PER PERSON

Hotel Nova (192)	NZ

CCR central canal ring **CRW** canal ring west **DP** de pijp **J** jordaan **JP** jodenbuurt & plantage **LP** leidseplein **MV** museumplein & vondelpark **NZ** nieuwe zijd **OW** oud-west **OZ** oude zijd **RLD** red light district **RP** rembrandtplein **SQ** shipping quarter (scheepvaartbuurt)

OUDE ZIJD

HOSTELS

see map p. 344

🛏 **StayOkay Amsterdam Stadsdoelen,** Kloveniersburgwal 97 (☎624 68 32; www.hostelbooking.com). Take tram #4, 9, 16, 24, or 25 to Muntplein. From Muntplein, proceed down Nieuwe Doelenstraat; Kloveniersburgwal will be on your right over the bridge. Located in a quieter corner of central Amsterdam, hostel sleeps 158 and provides clean, drug-free lodgings for reasonable prices. Accommodations are plain, but comfortable and spotless. Breakfast, lockers, and linens included. Reception 7am-1am. Internet (€1 per 12min.). Kitchen and laundry facilities. Pool table, TV room, and bar open 3pm-midnight (Happy Hour 9-10pm; beer €1). Bike rental €5.70 per day. Discounted museum passes and transportation tickets. Book via website or telephone. Locker deposit €20 or passport. Co-ed or single-sex 8-20 bed dorms €21.65; €2.50 discount with HI membership. MC/V. ❶

Durty Nelly's Hostel, Warmoesstraat 115/117 (☎638 01 25; http://xs4all.nl/~nellys). From Centraal Station, go south on Damrak, turn right on Brugsteeg, and then right on Warmoesstraat; Nelly's is 2 blocks down on the left. Cozy hostel above an Irish pub (see p. 184) sleeps 42 in clean, co-ed, dormstyle accommodations. Guests can drink after hours in the bar. Breakfast and linens included. Locker deposit €10. Reception (at bar) 24hr. Internet reservations only. Dorms €25-35. Cash only. ❶

HOTEL

Frisco Inn, Beursstraat 5 (☎620 16 10). From Centraal Station, go south on Damrak, then left at Brugsteeg, and take the next right onto Beursstraat. On one of the quietest streets in the Oude Zijd, this small, central hotel behind the Beurs van Berlage rents 27 beds in solid, but window-less, claustrophobic rooms. Downstairs bar sells beer (€1.90). All rooms renovated at the end of 2002 to add bathroom, safe, and TV. Smoking allowed provided you open windows. Reception (at bar) 24hr. No curfew. Doubles €60-90, quads €120-180, quints €150-225. AmEx/MC/V. ❷

RED LIGHT DISTRICT

HOSTEL

The Shelter City, Barndesteeg 21 (☎625 32 30; www.shelter.nl). Metro: Nieuwmarkt. Finding virtue amid the red lights, travelers will encounter brightly colored, incredibly clean rooms and a friendly all-Christian staff here. Religious slogans abound, but like its smaller Jordaan cohort, everyone is made to feel welcome; the cozy courtyard with lily pond is an oasis from the surrounding debauchery. Breakfast included. No drugs; smoking permitted only in hallways and snack bar. Locker deposit €5. Linens included; towels €1. Curfew Su-Th midnight, F-Sa 1am, signalled by locking of front door. Security guard 11:30pm-7:30am, enforcing drug, alcohol, and curfew rules. Dorms €15.50-18. MC/V with 5% surcharge. ❶

see map p. 344

1001 Nights Room, Greenhouse Effect

Interior, 1001 Nights Room

Fishy Dwellings

STAYOKAY HOSTELS

Stayokay is a chain of 30 hostels located throughout the Netherlands. You will find our hostels at surprisingly lovely places: in the dunes, the woods, along the waterside and in the city. The Stayokay hostels are housed in different unique buildings, ranging from modern facilities to castles or country houses. The same informal, relaxed atmosphere can be found at all Stayokay hostels, where friendly, helpful staff awaits your arrival!

HOSTELLING INTERNATIONAL

Stayokay is part of the Hostelling International network, comprising over 4.000 hostels worldwide. HI members receive € 2,50 discount per night.

RESERVATIONS

You can reserve directly at the hostel or at **www.stayokay.com**. Alternatively you can make a reservation via the Hostelling International IBN network.

OUR HOSTELS IN THE CENTRE OF AMSTERDAM

Stayokay Amsterdam Vondelpark

Zandpad 5
1054 GA Amsterdam
tel +31 (0)20 589 89 96
fax +31 (0)20 589 89 55

Stayokay Amsterdam Stadsdoelen

Kloveniersburgwal 97
1011 KB Amsterdam
tel +31 (0)20 624 68 32
fax +31 (0)20 639 10 35

Diverse, exciting and comfortable Stayokay Amsterdam Vondelpark is one of Europe's largest and most modern hostels. Located in the centre of Amsterdam, in the beautiful Vondelpark.

Downtown Amsterdam, international, exciting Stayokay Amsterdam Stadsdoelen is located in a stately canal house in the city centre.

www.stayokay.com

WE OFFER YOU...

• beds on comfortable 2-, 4-, 6- and 8- bedded rooms and dormitories, most with private sanitary facilities • comfortable double bunks, bedside lights, table and chairs and private cupboards • breakfast included • bedsheets included • restaurant • TV lounge • internet facilities • luggage lockers • laundry facilities (at most hostels) • discounted tickets for local attractions • and more...

OUR HOSTELS NEAR AMSTERDAM

Stayokay Bunnik

Historic hostel surrounded by nature
Stayokay Bunnik
Rhijnauwenselaan 14
3981 HH Bunnik
tel +31 (0)30 656 12 77
fax +31 (0)30 657 10 65

Stayokay Den Haag

City, seashore and dunes
Stayokay Den Haag
Scheepmakersstraat 27
2515 VA Den Haag
tel +31 (0)70 315 78 88
fax +31 (0)70 315 78 77

Stayokay Haarlem

Fabulous Haarlem, Burgundian city of the North
Stayokay Haarlem
Jan Gijzenpad 3
2024 CL Haarlem
tel +31 (0)23 537 37 93
fax +31 (0)23 537 11 76

Stayokay Rotterdam

Culture and architecture in the heart of the harbour city
Stayokay Rotterdam
Rochussenstraat 107-109, 3015 EH Rotterdam
tel +31 (0)10 436 57 63
fax +31 (0)10 436 56 69

Stayokay Heemskerk

Beach and dunes, the genuine castle experience
Stayokay Heemskerk
Tolweg 9
1967 NG Heemskerk
tel +31 (0)251 232 288
fax +31 (0)251 251 024

Stayokay Soest

Comfort, nature and variety
Stayokay Soest
Bosstraat 16
3766 AG Soest
tel +31 (0)35 601 22 96
fax +31 (0)35 602 89 21

GET sm**art**

hotel winston

Most quality hotels in Amsterdam pride themselves on having welcoming, classy decor—but few take design to the extremes of 🔲 **Hotel Winston** in the Red Light District. Half of Winston's rooms are generic, but very comfortable, while the remaining reasonably-priced "art" rooms feel—and indeed are intended to be—more like installation pieces that belong in a contemporary gallery in the Jordaan, and for good reason. Local artists and designers have used the walls and furniture as an outlet for their individual creative musings. From the sleekly elegant minimalism of the "704" room by Gitte Nygaard and Jair to the intense shocking green of the "any minute" room by Moniek Moulon and retro plush in the "Bridal Suite" by Maarten Voskuil, every room is outrageously and wonderfully different from the rest. So that you don't arrive unprepared for your particular suite's theme, Winston's website will let you view every art room, and reserve a specific one online.

(Warmoesstraat 129. From Centraal Station, go down Damrak 2 blocks, then left on Brugsteeg and right when you hit Warmoesstr. ☎ 623 13 80; www.winston.nl. Book well in advance. Breakfast included. Singles €60-72; doubles €74-96; triples €113-128. ❸)

Young Budget Hotel Kabul, Warmoesstraat 38-42 (☎ 623 71 58 or 623 70 59; kabulhotel@hotmail.com), just down Warmoesstraat and about 5min. from Centraal Station. Pleasant hostel experience awaits at Kabul, where 4-16 person dorms have comfortable beds in carpeted, relatively spacious rooms. Surroundings are a bit worn-down but some dorms have a serene view of the canals. Breakfast and sheets included. Internet downstairs (€1 per 17min.). No curfew. Max. stay 1 week. €15 key deposit. Dorms €17-23; private rooms €45-95. AmEx/MC/V ❶

De Witte Tulip Hostel, Warmoesstraat 87 (☎ 625 59 74). You'll find low-key, basic budget digs in this sociable, youthful hostel. Rooms are bright and spotless with large windows; shared facilities are a bit worn-down and not exceptionally clean. Downstairs pub serves drinks (beer €4.50 per pint, liquor €3.50-5.50) and snacks; hotel guests receive a 25% discount on drinks and breakfast. Preferably no smoking in rooms. Sheets included. Dorms Apr.-Sept. €20-35, Oct.-Mar. €15. AmEx/MC/V. ❶

HOTELS

The Red Light District isn't teeming with hotels, but the accommodations here are as expensive as those located in the rest of the city. They're usually booked solid through the summer months, and while it may initially seem convenient to shack up across the street from a brothel, the proximity to the heart of the Red Light District can become a little distracting.

Old Quarter, Warmoesstraat 20-22 (☎ 626 64 29; www.oldquarter.com). Walking away from Centraal Station, make a left onto Prins Hendrikskade, and bear right at Nieuwbrigstg. Warmoesstr. is the 1st right. Smaller rooms are snug but homey; larger ones clean, classy, and bright. All rooms include TV and phone; some have a strikingly good view of the canal. Biggest attraction: elevator that makes hotel wheelchair-accessible. Downstairs *bruin cafe* provides a great place to watch a football match (kitchen open 9am-11pm). M night jazz jam sessions. Breakfast included. Reception 24hr. Singles from €35; doubles from €60. AmEx/MC/V ❷

The Greenhouse Effect Hotel, Warmoesstraat 55 (☎ 624 49 74; www.the-greenhouse-effect.com). Reasonably priced theme rooms (including Arabian Nights, Chinatown, and Tropical Dream) await your discovery. Hotel guests are treated to an all-day Happy Hour at the downstairs bar/reception (pints of beer €2.30). See website for discounts. Rooms located above, across the street, and 5min. walk from bar. Singles €60, with bath €75; doubles with bath €90; triples with bath €120-130; 2-4 person apartments €120-180. AmEx/MC/V. ❸

Hotel Royal Taste, Oudezijds Achterburgwal 47 (☎623 24 78; www.hotelroyaltaste.com). Smack in the middle of the Red Light District, Royal Taste provides clean, comfortable, and almost-fancy accommodations at reasonable prices. The bar downstairs features a big-screen TV for football or rugby games. Rooms with bath, fridge, and TV; some with kitchen area. Breakfast included. Singles €50; doubles €90; triples €135, quads €180. AmEx/MC/V. ❷

Hotel The Crown, Oudezijds Voorburgwal 21 (☎626 96 64; www.hotelthecrown.com). This British-owned hotel provides handsome digs in the picturesque end of the Red Light District. Bar open until 3am, with pool table and dart board (beer €4 per pint; cocktails from €2.50). Cigarette- and joint-friendly. Singles €35-50; doubles €70-100; triples €105-150; quads €140-200; quints €175-250; 6-person room €210-300 (rooms with hall showers €10 less). AmEx/MC/V required for reservation confirmation; only cash is accepted for payment. ❷

Old Nickel, Nieuwebrugsteeg 11 (☎624 19 12). From Centraal, turn left onto Prins Hendrikskade and then bear right onto Nieuwebrugstg. In a quiet corner of the neighborhood, this hotel with a downstairs bar offers a peaceful and inexpensive place to spend the night. Single rooms are disconcertingly tiny but larger rooms are sunnier. Shared facilities (shower and toilet) are very high-end but also a bit cramped. Breakfast included. Singles €35-50; doubles €70-100; triples €105-150; quads €140-200. AmEx/MC/V. ❷

Hotel Vijaya, Oudezijds Voorburgwal 44 (☎626 94 06 or 638 01 02; www.hotelvijaya.com). Clean and basic rooms on the fringe of the bustle. Breakfast is included. All rooms with TV, telephone reception (to place outgoing calls you have to use the phone booth downstairs), and private bathroom. Singles €70, doubles €92; triples €125; quads €150; all about €10 cheaper in low season. AmEx/MC/V. ❹

Hotel Internationaal, Warmoesstraat 1-3 (☎624 55 20; www.hotelinternationaal.com). Smoke-filled bar downstairs (open Su-Th 10:30am-1am, F-Sa until 3am) has old-time charm. Rooms themselves are small but very clean, adding a touch of class with carpets and deep red curtains. Breakfast €5. Doubles €75, with private bathroom €90; triples with shared facilities €100. AmEx/MC/V. ❹

NIEUWE ZIJD

HOSTELS

While some of the Nieuwe Zijd accommodations call themselves "inns" or "hotels," all those listed below offer dorm-style rooms for guests.

see map p. 344

hotels for men

ANCO Hotel and Bar, Oudezijds Voorburgwal 55 (☎624 11 26; www.ancohotel.nl), in the Red Light District. This extremely well-maintained, men-only hotel has crisp apartment-style accommodations, canal views, 24hr. access, free cable TV, and is a 5min. walk from the leather district. The downstairs bar (open 9am-10pm), lined with black plastic and gay posters, is a good springboard to a wild evening of clubbing. No elevators. Breakfast included. 3- to 4-person dorms €40; singles €60; doubles €85, with private bathroom, kitchenette, and minibar €135. AmEx/MC/V. ❷

Stablemaster Hotel, Warmoesstraat 23 (☎625 01 48; www.stablemaster.nl), in the Oude Zijd. Perfect if you want a short walk home after carousing at the downstairs bar's (see p. 147) nightly cowboy-themed gay orgies. This generally men-only hotel sports classy rooms with fridges, radios, TVs, phones, spotless bathrooms, exposed beams, and lots of magazines about the local queer scene. No elevators. Be prepared to shell out a hefty €50 for the key deposit. Singles €65; doubles €95-105; triples €150. Apartments for longer rental €150 per night; women allowed in apartments. AmEX/MC/V. ❸

189

the hidden deal

anna youth hostel

The extraordinary 🏠 **Anna Youth Hostel,** in the Nieuwe Zijd, caters to the quiet, independent traveler. Unlike many of the city's crowded accommodations, there are no drugs permitted, which is a blessing considering the haze of smoke that sometimes hangs over the Centrum. The spacious and airy dorms, supremely tranquil atmosphere, and rustic hippie-chic decor are what make Anna's by far the most traditionally beautiful hostel in the city, replete with red, blue and gold decor; stark plants; purple curtains; and exposed wooden beams.

Owned and operated by a genuinely caring hostelowner—one of the friendliest in Amsterdam—who ensures that everyone's needs are met, this place is a gorgeous and cost-efficient retreat from the bustle of the Nieuwe Zijd. The prices, to top it off, are some of the lowest around for dorms. Walk-ins are welcome, though reservations are recommended.

(☎ 620 11 55. Reception 8am-1pm, 5pm through the night. Towel, linens, soap, and safe all included. 2-night min. stay on weekends. Closed during part of December. Dorms €18-19; doubles with bath M-F €70, Sa-Su €80. Cash only. ❶*)*

🏠 **Anna Youth Hostel,** Spuistraat 6 (at left). ❶

🏠 **Flying Pig Downtown,** Nieuwendijk 100 (☎ 420 68 22; www.flyingpig.nl). From the main entrance of Centraal Station, walk towards Damrak. Pass the Victoria Hotel and take the 1st alley on your right. At the end of that alley, you'll find Nieuwendijk. Helpful and professional staff, knockout location, and colorful decor make the Flying Pig Downtown a perennial favorite among backpackers. The hostel caters to a younger set, mostly 18- to 28-year olds who pack into their spacious dorms. Sprawling, gorgeous gathering space/bar filled with afghan pillows is ideal for reading, smoking, and watching the parade go by on the avenue outside; the bar is open M-F until 4am, Sa-Su until 5am. Breakfast included; there is also a kitchen in which you can make your own meals. Free Internet. Sheets provided. One women-only dorm available. Key deposit, which includes a locker, €10. 4- to 6-bed dorms €27; 8- to 10-bed dorms €24; 16- to 22-bed dorms €21; singles and twins €76. ISIC cardholders receive a free beer at the bar in summer and a 5% discount in winter. AmEx/MC/V. ❶

Bob's Youth Hostel, Nieuwezijds Voorburgwal 92 (☎ 623 00 63). From Centraal Station, head down the right-most artery and veer left at Martelaarsgracht; then, turn right when it becomes Nieuwezijds Voorburgwal. Well-known among European backpackers, Bob's Youth Hostel provides the bare necessities to its guests, no frills attached. The hostel's young, posthippie clientele relax in the Mondrian-style underground reception area, the only place in the hostel where drugs are permitted. With giant dorm rooms, this is a good spot for lone travelers looking to make friends with fellow wanderers. Breakfast included. Lockers and luggage storage included. Linens provided, but bring a towel. Key deposit €10; €10 extra for a locker key. 2-night minimum weekend stay; 7-night max. Reception 8am-3am. No lockout or curfew. No reservations, so arrive before 10am to stand a chance of getting a room. One women-only dorm. Dorms €18; doubles €70; triples €80. If you want a little more privacy, the hostel also has a few spacious, nicely-furnished apartment annexes with shared kitchens around the corner. ❶

Tourist Inn, Spuistraat 52 (☎ 421 58 41; www.tourist-inn.nl). From Centraal Station, turn right at the main street, then left at Martelaarsgracht. A couple blocks ahead, keep right onto Spuistraat. A great value for backpackers and families, the Tourist Inn is clean, friendly, comfortable—even if the cottage-cheese walls smack of early 1950s design. Breakfast included. Lockers €30 deposit plus €1.20 per day. Laundry facilities around the corner; linens and a towel included. Reception 24hr. Walk-ins welcome, but reservations are strongly ad-vised, particularly in summer. Prices vary by season. Dorms €25-35; singles €50-100; doubles €65-120; triples €100-150; quads €100-140; quints €125-160; 6-person room €150-180. AmEx/MC/V. ❶

Budget Hotel Tamara, Nieuwezijds Voorburgwal 144 (☎624 24 84). Friendly Irish staff welcomes backpackers to Amsterdam in true budget style "with a capital B"—with respect to both the cost and the lodgings. The scuffed, rundown walls of Tamara's diminutive rooms may have plenty of stories to tell, but they get the job done. Guests get a free drink at the Blarney Stone Pub (see **Nightlife,** p. 184). Free tea and coffee in the morning. Internet €1.30 for 30min. Reception 24hr. Dorms €15-17.50/€25 on weekends; singles €35/€40; doubles €50/€60; triples €75/€90; quads €80/€120. Cash only. ❶

La Canna, Nieuwendijk 121-125 (☎428 44 82; www.lacanna.nl). From Centraal, take the main street to the right, head left on Martelaarsgracht and then right on Nieuwendijk. If you don't mind sleeping over a roiling mess of an all-night Amsterdam party, La Canna's rooms (see **Only In Amsterdam,** p. 133) are convenient for those looking for a shorter stumble home at the end of the night—a place to crash if you're just looking for a clean bed to sleep in. Check-in at the smartshop. Free lockers (bring your own lock). No curfew. 24hr. security. Co-ed dorms €18; singles with continental breakfast €53-55, with English breakfast add €55-58; singles with bath €63/€68; doubles €71, with shower €86; triples €109/€121; quads €132/€148; larger room €162 and €178 for 4, €5 per additional person. ❶

Hostel Cosmos, Nieuwe Nieuwestraat 17 (☎625 24 38; www.hostelcosmos.com), between Nieuwendijk and Nieuwezijds Voorburgwal, a few blocks north of Dam Sq. A perplexing sign over the desk of this recently renovated, pink, hotel-like hostel claims that "if we don't take care of the customer, somebody will." With 30 beds in 6 clean rooms, it can't be that bad. Some rooms with TV and VCR. Reception 24hr. Online reservation. Prices vary seasonally. 6-person dorms €23-28; 8-person dorms €21-26; doubles €32-38; quads 24-30. Cash only. ❷

HOTELS

A good hotel in the Nieuwe Zijd is hard to find: largely disappointing, options run from grimy to pricey. For a good room, try the apartments at Bob's Hostel or the private rooms in Anna Youth Hostel (see above). Failing those stalwarts, below are a few of the better deals.

🖾 **Hotel Brouwer,** Singelgracht 83 (☎624 63 58; www.hotelbrouwer.nl). From Centraal Station, cross the water, turn right onto Prins Hendrikkade and left onto Singelgracht. Small hotel right off the canal run by the same family for 3 generations and easily the

Conveniently Located

Secluded *Hofje*

Traditional Thatch House

Roof Garden

Ivied Stairs

Room with a View

best hotel in the neighborhood. Eight gorgeously restored rooms, each with private bathroom, canal view, and named for a Dutch painter. Choose from Vermeer, Van Gogh, Mondrian, and Escher, among others. Breakfast in charming dark-wood dining room included. No smoking in the rooms. Tiny elevator. Singles €50; doubles €85; doubles for single use (or vice versa) €70. Cash and traveler's checks only. ❷

Hotel Groenendael, Nieuwendijk 15 (☎624 48 22; www.hotelgroenendael.com). Turn right on the main street out of the station, then go left at Martelaarsgracht and then right on Nieuwendijk. Mellow hotel near Centraal Station and on one of the area's most commercial streets uses shaggy afghan throw-rugs for tablecloths in the dining room. Rooms—some with balconies—are in fairly good shape. Plenty of clean bathrooms, mostly off shared hallways. Breakfast included (8:30-10am); served in a lounge decorated with international knick-knacks. Free towels, soap, and access to safe. Room key deposit €5. Singles €32; doubles €50, with shower €55; triples €75. Cash and traveler's checks only. ❷

Hotel Nova, Nieuwezijds Voorburgwal 276 (☎623 00 66; www.bookings.nl/hotels/nova). Exceptionally large, clean accommodations a stone's throw from the city center. The price is certainly not for a budget, but these slick, modern rooms may provide much-needed respite from other more dingy options. Make sure to get good directions to your room at reception: Nova is a 60-room labyrinth. All rooms come with bathroom, TV, phone, and refrigerator. Breakfast included. Singles €76-107; doubles €95-147; triples €125-180; quads €155-210. AmEx/D/MC/V. ❺

Hotel Brian, Singelgracht 69 (☎624 46 61; www.hotelbrian.com). From Centraal Station, turn right at the Victoria Hotel, then left onto Singelgracht. Extremely basic communal digs in a friendly, low-key (if cramped) hotel with a liberal drug policy. Rooms are clean even if little effort seems to have been made to redecorate. Picturesque canalside location and low price make these tiny crash-pads a little more interesting. Breakfast included. Key deposit €20. Reception 8am-11pm. Dorms €27. Cash only. ❶

Hotel Rokin, Rokin 73 (☎626 74 56; www.rokinhotel.com). Centrally located just a few blocks south from Dam Sq. in a house that leans conspicuously forward over the street. Clean digs include TV and VCR as well as continental breakfast. Despite budget rates, foamy wallpaper, and a faint smell of tobacco, the place is put-together and the staff is eager to please. Prices vary by season. Singles €50-60; doubles €60-75; triples €110-145; quads €140-185; 6-person rooms €195-255. AmEx/MC/V. ❸

Hotel Hoksbergen, Singelgracht 301 (☎626 60 43; www.hotelhoksbergen.nl). Take tram #1, 2, or 5 to Spui. On the east side of the Singelgracht canal,

YOUTH HOSTEL

A unique, chilled-out, quiet and drug-free hostel in the heart of the city. Low priced dorms including free internet, safety deposit box, linen and towels. An artistically inspired interior makes this place one you will want to come back to.

Spuistraat 6, Amsterdam, Netherlands
Tel: +31 620 1155

Show your Hostels of Europe (HOE) membership card for a discount at check-in.

between Rosmarijnsteeg and Paleisstraat. This quaint, 300-year-old canal house offers its patrons a shower, toilet, phone, and television in every room, which is not bad—even if the price is steep for such cramped quarters. Full Dutch breakfast (breads, cheese, ham, and tea) included. Singles €76-90; doubles €90-104; triples €104-130; apartments (4-6 persons) €150-200. AmEx/MC/V with 5% surcharge. ❹

Hotel Continental, Damrak 40-41 (☎622 33 63; www.hotelcontinental.nl). Damrak location puts you right near the action, 2min. from Centraal Station. More upscale than standard budget digs, with small but comfy rooms—which means that you'll get to cozy up with your neighbors. Each room with TV and phone. Continental breakfast served 7:30-9am. Reception 24hr. Singles €50-80; doubles €50-120; triples €90-135. AmEx/MC/V with 5% surcharge. ❸

De Oranje Tulp, Damrak 32 (☎428 16 18; www.oranjetulp.nl) Located 3min. from Centraal, down the main street heading straight out of the station and hidden above a restaurant. With the noise of the Damrak within earshot and the dimly-lit rooms in need of some repair, De Oranje Tulp may not be the 1st choice—but can be an effective, centrally located crash-pad following nights of excess debauchery. Guests receive discounts on dinner in the restaurant downstairs. Breakfast included. Singles €45-70; doubles €75-120; triples €80-150; quads €80-120; quints €80-140. AmEx/DC/MC/V. ❷

SHIPPING QUARTER (SCHEEPVAARTBUURT)

Just northwest of the city center, the Shipping Quarter is less touristy than other centrally-located neighborhoods.

see map p. 342

HOTELS

Frederic Rent a Bike, Brouwersgracht 78 (☎624 55 09; www.frederic.nl). In addition to bikes, Frederic also rents rooms. The best option is to stay in one of 3 lived-in, homey, and cheerful rooms in the back of the rental shop—each named after a different painter (Chagall,

life's* green

hemp hotel

The **Hemp Hotel** has only five rooms, but each is lovingly done up to celebrate one of the world's major hemp-producing regions: India, Tibet, Afghanistan, Morocco, and the Caribbean. Almost everything is made of hemp—the bedclothes, the curtains, and even the soap. An affable mother-daughter management team make staying here a pleasure, as do some eccentric patrons: "We get some real characters here," says employee Kathy Ankers. The hotel has hall bathrooms, and all rooms have TV and sink. Reception (at Hemp Bar) 11am-3am, F-Sa until 4am.

(Frederiksplein 15. ☎625 44 25; www.hemp-hotel.com. Lone single €50; doubles €65-70. ❸)

The **Hemp Bar** downstairs is a quiet, mellow spot popular with English-speaking expats. You can imbibe all manner of booze, but hemp beer is the house speciality (€2; other beers €1.70-2.50). There can be up to five varieties of hemp brew available, depending on current hemp laws abroad; however, hemp brew won't get you high, because it has no THC. If you do want to smoke weed or hash, you're welcome to light up, but the owners don't sell smokeables. Pipes and bongs left over by guests who couldn't take them out of the country are available for use. Open Su-Th 4pm-3am, F-Sa 4pm-4am. V.

Picasso, and Mondrian); 1 with private bath with sauna jets; the others share a bath. Not only will the staff share some of Amsterdam's best-kept secrets, but you'll find an open bar with drinks, rolling papers, smokes, games, soap, towels, and anything else you need. If the rooms are booked, Frederic can also book you a room in various privately listed locations around the city for a 15% commission. Visit Frederic's website for virtual tours of the accommodations, reservations, and tons of information about Amsterdam. Reception 9am-6pm. Singles €50-80; doubles €60-90. Apartments available for short-term stays. Cash only; AmEx/MC/V required for reservation. ❸

Ramenas Hotel, Haarlemmerdijk 61 (☎624 60 30; www.amsterdamhotels.com). Walk from Centraal Station along Nieuwendijk as it turns into Haarlemmerstraat and then Haarlemmerdijk. Above an average cafe of the same name, Ramenas rents ascetic rooms, but they get the job done. Hall bathrooms are clean and the rooms are comfortable. Breakfast included. Reservations via website. Doubles €64-80; triples €96-120; quints €160-200. MC/V ❶

Hotel My Home, Haarlemmerstraat 82 (☎624 23 20; www.amsterdambudgethotel.com). From Centraal Station, head south on Nieuwezijds Voorburgwal, turn right on Nieuwendijk, and continue across the Singelgracht; it is 1 block on your left. Basically clean budget digs in a low-frill environment. Even if the stairwell smells suspect, the hall bathrooms are clean. Breakfast, complete with a bottomless cup of coffee, included. Friendly staff can provide the inside scoop on the city scene. Sheets and towels provided. No curfew. Free Internet and pool. Online reservations available. Reception 8:30am-1pm and 6-11pm. 4- to 5-person dorms €30, in low season €25; doubles €50-60, with shower €63; triples €90; quads €120. Cash only. ❶

see map p. 342

CANAL RING WEST

The atmosphere of the Canal Ring West reflects its geographic placement; accommodations in the area strike a stable balance between residential and legendary Amsterdam, both in terms of surroundings and decorations.

◪ **Hotel Clemens,** Raadhuisstraat 39 (☎624 60 89; www.clemenshotel.nl). Take tram #13 or 17 to Westermarkt. A true gem with elegant deluxe and budget rooms, recently renovated to display different color schemes. Phone, fridge, TV, Internet connection, safe, and hairdryer in all rooms. Deluxe rooms are larger, with private bath. Breakfast €7. Key deposit €20.

Book a month in advance. Min. stay 3 nights including Su during weekends. Rental laptops at reception. Singles €55; budget doubles €70-75, deluxe €110; triples with bath and toilet €125, deluxe €150. Cash only for budget rooms. AmEx/MC/V. ❷

🏨 **Wiechmann Hotel,** Prinsengracht 328-332 (☎ 626 33 21; www.hotelwiechmann.nl). Tram #1, 2, or 5 to Prinsengracht; turn right and walk along the left side of the canal. Three restored canal houses run by an easy-going couple. Spacious hotel with clean, sizeable rooms, many with canal views and patchwork comforters. Breakfast included. Key deposit €20. Min. stay 2 nights on weekends. All rooms with stylish bath. Living room on 1st floor. Singles €70-90; doubles with bathtub €125-135; triples and quads €170-230. MC/V. ❸

Westertoren Hotel, Raadhuisstraat 35b (☎ 624 46 39; www.hotelwestertoren.nl). Tram #13, 17, or 6 to Westermarkt. Clean, plain surroundings and friendly staff. Perfect for groups, Westertoren boasts a handful of "family" rooms that sleep up to 6 people. Various combinations of shared/private shower and toilet; check website for details. Tea and coffee in room. Breakfast included. 3 night min. weekend stay (Su included). Singles €55; doubles €80-90; triples €110-125; family room (4-6 people) €140-205. AmEx/MC/V. ❸

Hotel Belga, Hartenstraat 8 (☎ 624 90 80; www.hotelnet.nl). Tram #1, 2, or 5 to Dam. Walk away from the palace on Raadhuisstraat. Turn left at Herengracht and take the 1st right on Hartenstraat. Rooms are large and sunny if bland, all with TV, phone, and safe. Most rooms with shower and toilet. Breakfast included. Weekend stays include Sa and Su during summer. Singles €41-57; doubles €62-84, with bath €77.50-118; triples €95-140.50; quads €134-188.50. AmEx/MC/V. ❷

Hotel Pax, Raadhuisstraat 37 (☎ 624 97 35). Tram #6, 13, or 17 to Westermarkt. A bit less inviting than its neighbors on Raahuisstraat, with creaky floors and dark, mirrored walls. Minimalist budget hotel with cot beds and shared facilities run by 2 affable brothers. Rooms have sink and TV, but no shower or toilet. Singles Sept.-May €35-70, Apr.-Oct. €25-50; doubles €65-95/€65; triples €69-99; quads €70-109. AmEx/MC/V with 3.5% surcharge. ❷

Hotel Aspen, Raadhuisstraat 31 (☎ 626 67 14; hotelaspen@planet.nl; www.hotelaspen.nl). Tram #6, 13, or, 17 Westermarkt. Friendly staff and clean, comfortable lodgings. All snug rooms with shower and toilet (except singles and 1 small double). Reserve 2 weeks in advance through email to ensure availability. Singles €35; doubles €44-65; triples €75-80; quads €92. Cash only in summer. AmEx/MC/V in winter. ❷

Hotel Hegra, Herengracht 269 (☎ 623 78 77). Take tram #1, 2 or 5 to the Dam. Follow Raadhuisstraat away from the back of the palace. Cross the Singelgracht and turn left. Go right on Romeinsarmsteeg and right at Herengracht. Small family hotel on a lovely canal. 11 basic rooms, most with shower but no toilet. Breakfast included. Hallways and stairs are a bit cramped. Singles €45; doubles €65, with shower €80, with bath €90. AmEx/MC/V. ❷

CENTRAL CANAL RING

HOTELS

🏨 **Hemp Hotel,** See Hemp Hotel and Cafe, p. 194.

Euphemia Budget Hotel, Fokke Simonszstraat 1-9 (☎ 622 90 45; www.euphemiahotel.com), 10min. from Rembrandtplein or Leidseplein. see map p. 340 Take tram #16, 24, or 25 to Weteringcircuit, backtrack on Vijzelstraat for about 200m, and turn right on Fokke Simonszstraat. Welcoming, quiet, budget digs in a former monastery. Rooms are basic but clean, flowery and bright, and recent renovations lend a colorful feel throughout. Gay friendly. Continental breakfast €5. Internet €1 for 15min. Reception 8am-11pm. Doubles, triples, or 4-person mixed dorms €23-55 per person depending on season, availability, and type of room. 10% discount on the 1st night with website reservation. AmEx/MC/V with 5% surcharge. ❶

The Golden Bear, Kerkstraat 37 (☎ 624 47 85; www.goldenbear.nl). Take tram #1, 2 or 5 to Prinsengracht, backtrack 1 block to Kerkstraat and turn left. Opened in 1948, the Golden Bear, may be the oldest openly gay hotel in the world. It's certainly the oldest one in Amster-

Hostel Stairs

Right Side of the Tracks

dam. Mainly male couples frequent the hotel, though lesbians are welcome as well. All rooms include phone, safe, and color cable TV (some with VCRs). Watch out for the winding, narrow stairs—there's no elevator. Breakfast included, served until luxuriously late (8:30am-noon). Basic single from €57, with bath €99; basic double from €78, with bath €112. ❸

Hotel Kap, Den Texstraat 5b (☎624 59 08; www.kaphotel.nl). Tram #16, 24, or 25 to Weteringcircuit. Go left down Weteringschans, then right at 2e Weteringplantsoen, and left at Den Texstraat. Hotel Kap will be on your left. Very personable staff rents clean, comfortable rooms on a quiet, residential street. Breakfast served in lovely lounge, with flower-filled terrace out back (8-10:30am). Television, but no phones in each room. Reception 8am-10:30pm. Check-out 11am. Depending on space and facilities, singles €57; doubles €86-109; triples €109-118; quads €136. AmEx/MC/V with 5% surcharge. ❸

Hotel Asterisk, Den Texstraat 16 (☎626 23 96 or 624 17 68; www.asteriskhotel.nl). Tram #16, 24, or 25 to Weteringcircuit, turn left at the roundabout, and then proceed to Den Texstraat; the hotel is on the right. Orderly, quiet hotel with 40 clean, bright rooms. All rooms include cable TV, phone, and safe. Helpful, personable staff can provide insight on activities in and around Amsterdam. Free breakfast if you pay in cash (€8 with credit cards). High season singles €44, with shower or toilet €48, with both €84; doubles €65, with facilities €115-125; triples €130-136; quads €150. MC/V with 4% surcharge. ❷

Radion Inn Youth Hostel, Utrechtsedwarsstraat 79 (☎625 03 45; www.radioinn.nl). Take tram #4 and exit at Prinsengracht; walk south along Utrechtsestraat for a block and turn left on Utrechtsedwarsstraat; the hotel is on your left. There's no shortage of character at this cheerfully idiosyncratic hostel, somewhere between a 70s garage sale and a budget hotel. Housed in an old radio store, the homey lobby is filled with defunct gadgets and presided over by 2 cats. No 2 of the 8 rooms are the same: televisions lined with fake fur, defunct computers strewn with graffiti, and disassembled mannequins—you get the idea. TV and sink in each room; all rooms share adequately clean hall toilets and showers. Kitchen available 24hr. Free laundry. €25 per person for all rooms. Cash only. ❷

LEIDSEPLEIN

HOSTEL

see map p. 341

Hans Brinker Hotel, Kerkstraat 136 (☎622 06 87; www.hansbrinker.com). Take tram #1, 2, or 5 to Kerkstraat. This "hotel" is really a massive hostel, with cheap bunk-bed rooms

Squatters' Club

and self-service sheets. Spartan, clean rooms, all with shower and toilet. Guest-only bar serves cheap drinks, especially with 2-for-1 beer, wine, and soft-drinks during Happy Hour (5-6pm); bar open 5pm-3am. All-you-can-eat breakfast buffet included (7:30-10am). Free Internet access in basement; disco open 10pm-3am. Key deposit €5; safe €0.50. Reception 24hr. Checkout 10am. No visitors. 4-10 person dorms (single-sex and mixed) €29-35; singles €52; doubles €58-75; triples €90; quads €96; quints €120. AmEx/MC/V. ❶

International Budget Hostel, Leidsegracht 76-1 (☎624 27 84; www.internationalbudgethostel.com). Tram #1, 2, or 5 to Prinsengracht, turn right and walk to Leidsegracht. Pretty second-floor flower-box exterior gives way to cramped rooms with spare white walls and wooden ceiling beams. Sister hostel of Euphemia Hotel (see p. 195) has 12 quads and 2 twins; some rooms have lovely canal views. Dorm-quality shared facilities. Breakfast (€14) served 9am-noon €14. In summer, 3-night min. stay starting F, or 2-night stay starting Sa. Reception with safe and lounge with television, vending machines, telephone, and Internet (€1 per 15min.) open 9am-11pm. Locker key deposit €10; padlock €5. Dorm-style quads €25; July and Aug. €30. AmEx/MC/V accepted with 5% surcharge. ❶

HOTELS

🏨 **Quentin Hotel,** Leidsekade 89 (☎626 21 87). The Quentin proves that you don't have to sacrifice style to get budget accommodations; these digs are jazzy and hip, in a canal-side setting. Hallways are adorned with gilt-framed mirrors, and each room bears a distinctive motif and has cable TV. Recent renovations have given a crisp, modern feeling and added private facilities to most rooms; elevator and full bar in the works. Continental breakfast €7. Reception open 24hr. Singles €40, with facilities €65; smaller "economy" doubles with facilities €80; regular doubles €100; triples €133. AmEx/MC/V with 5% surcharge. ❷

Hotel de Lantaerne, Leidsekade 111 (☎623 22 21; www.hotellantaerne.com). Lovely accommodations in 2 canal houses along the scenic Leidsegracht, near Leidseplein. Stylish rooms include TV, phone, and hairdryer. Breakfast included. Singles with shared facilities in high season

197

€75, low season €55; doubles with shower and toilet €115, €85; triples €150, €115; 4-6-person family rooms €145-185. Special rates offered for longer stays and weekdays. AmEx/MC/V with 5% surcharge. ❷

Hotel de la Haye, Leidsegracht 114 (☎624 40 44; www.hoteldelahaye.com). Tram #1, 2, or 5 to Leidseplein. Walk up Marnixstraat 1 block and turn right. Combines the convenience of Leidseplein and the serenity of a canal view. Breakfast included in a pretty yellow room with a canal view and fresh flowers. Sink and TV in each room. Pay required for whole stay on arrival. Reception 8am-10pm; no curfew. Singles in high season €64, low season €57; basic doubles €95, €87; doubles with bath €105, €95; triples €120, €105; quads €175, €135; quint with balcony and canal view €200, €165. AmEx/MC/V with 5% surcharge. ❸

Hotel La Boheme, Marnixstraat 415 (☎624 28 28; labohemeamsterdam.com). Tram #1, 2, or 5 to Leidseplein and take a right after the theater onto Marnixstraat. Clean, professional hotel with cafe and bar; all rooms have phone and TV. Breakfast included. Reception 8am-11pm. Singles with shared facilities €55; twin doubles with facilities in high season €105, low season €105, depending on day of the week; triples with facilities €140/€100; look for specials on the Internet. MC/V. ❸

Hotel Titus, Leidsekade 74 (☎626 57 58; www.hoteltitus.nl). Tram #1, 2, or 5 to Leidesplein. Walk past the theater on your right, take a right onto Marnixstraat and then left onto Leidsekade. The Titus' somewhat bare rooms come equipped with TV and phones. Breakfast included. Reception 8am-midnight. Singles with shared facilities in high season €55, low season €30; doubles with shared facilities €80, €45; doubles with private facilities €80, €120; triples €120, €160; quads €140-180. AmEx/MC/V with 5% surcharge. ❸

REMBRANDTPLEIN

Accommodations in Rembrandtplein cater to those who want to party all night and then collapse in bed without worrying about a long commute home.

see map p. 340

City Hotel, Utrechtsestraat 2 (☎627 23 23; www.city-hotel.nl). Classy, spacious accommodations above a pub right on the Rembrandtplein. Many rooms have great views of the square, and the ones on higher floors overlook the city skyline. Rooms, hall baths, and showers all immaculately kept. Breakfast included. Rooms without shower/toilet share facilities with 1 other room. Reception 24hr. Doubles in high season €90, in low season €80; doubles with facilities €100/€90; triples €105/€135; quads €180/€140; quints €225/€175; 6-person room €270/€210. AmEx/DC/MC/V. ❹

Hotel Monopole, Amstel 60 (☎624 62 71; www.monopole.demon.nl). Tram #4 or 9 to Rembrandtplein. From Rembrandtplein, go north on Halvemaanstraat, then head right when you hit the river. Lovely setting right by the Amstel offsets simple but charming rooms with flowered bedspreads and pastel walls. Not all rooms have canal views so make sure to ask ahead. Comfortable living room on 1st floor enhanced by fresh flowers. Breakfast included, delivered to door. All rooms with TV, some with bath. Singles €85; doubles €95, with facilities €125; triples €160; quads €200; quints €260. MC/V with a 5% surcharge. ❹

JORDAAN

Lodgings in the Jordaan generally afford peace and quiet a comfortable distance from the frenzied city center.

HOSTELS

see maps p. 342

▨ **The Shelter Jordan,** Bloemstraat 179 (☎624 47 17; www.shelter.nl). Tram #6, 13 or 17 to Marnixstraat; follow Lijnbaansgracht (off Rozengracht) for 50m, then turn right on Bloemstraat. This well-maintained, companionable Christian hostel is a treasure. There are nightly Bible study groups and you'll probably be handed a copy of the Gospel upon check-in, but everyone is made to feel more than welcome. Umbrella rental €0.50; currency exchange with no commission. Cafe with Internet

(€0.50 for 20min.), and even a piano. Breakfast included. Lunch €2-3; dinner €5. Lockers with €5 key deposit and free storage for larger bags and packs. Curfew 2am. Single-sex dorms. No smoking, no alcohol. Age limit 35. Sept.-May dorms €16.50; July-Aug. €18. MC/V. ❶

HOTELS

Hotel van Onna, Bloemgracht 104 (☎626 58 01; www.vanonna.nl). Take Tram #13 or 17 from Centraal Station to Westermarkt, also close to the Bloemgracht stop on tram #10. No televisions and no smoking means visitors get a peaceful night's rest in a restored historic building, situated on arguably the prettiest canal in the Jordaan. The small but very comfortable rooms all have private bathrooms, and the gentle owner will help you with all your needs. Despite the trek upstairs, ask for a top floor room. There, the rooms are sloped by the building's original wooden beams, and the view stretches out over the entire Jordaan. Breakfast included in the superlative dining room. Reception 8am-11pm. Singles €40; doubles €80; triples €120, quads €160. Cash only. ❷

Hotel Acacia, Lindengracht 251 (☎622 14 60). From Centraal Station take bus #18 to Willemstraat. Tram #3 to Bloemgracht is also close. If watching the houseboats peacefully rocking along the canals of the Jordaan isn't enough for you, try living in one. Acacia has 2 lovely houseboats, one new and one older, with rooms for 2-4 people available. All rooms come with private bath and include breakfast. Studios and houseboats include small kitchenette. In hotel: singles, €65; doubles €80; triples €99; quads €120; quints €130. In studios: doubles €90; triples €105. On houseboats: doubles €95-110; triples €115; quads €130. MC/V with 5% surcharge. ❸

Enjoying Boat Life

Steep Staircase Within

OUD-WEST

see map p. 346

The Oud-West district runs west of the canal rings, just north of Vondelpark. Staying in accommodations in this area means a short walk to shopping and nightlife in Leidseplein and the attractions of Museumplein, often at lower prices. Nevertheless, the neighborhood is still fairly rough-edged and commercial.

🏠 **Hotel de Filosoof,** Anna Vondelstraat 6. See **Hotel de Filosoof,** p. 200.

Tulip Inn Amsterdam Centre, Nassaukade 387-390 (☎530 78 88; www.tulipinnamsterdamcentre.com). Take tram #1, 2, 5, 6, 7, or 10 to Leidseplein. Great value for a 3-star, 70-room hotel, the Tulip Inn Amsterdam Centre caters to the quieter traveler, although there is a large lobby with busy bar open until mid-

Exorbitant Canal House

the BIG splurge

hotel de filosoof

This year marks the 15th anniversary of the classiest accommodations in Oud-West—the small, unusually creative **Hotel de Filosoof.** Wittgenstein, Spinoza, Aristotle—whether you've read their works or just like to name-drop, you'll feel the presence of these great philosophers of the world here. The 38 beautiful, meticulously decorated rooms each have a philosophical or cultural theme.

Stay in a room devoted to the Greek classics or try Eastern philosophy in the "Zen" room. All rooms have a bath, phone, and TV, and breakfast included. A bar in the lobby and a placid garden out back allow for heady contemplation. Reception 24hr. Call two or three weeks in advance to reserve for July and August.

(Anna Vondelstraat 6. Tram #1 to Jan Pieter Heijestraat; walk along Overtoom toward Leidseplein, then turn right. If you're coming from Schiphol, get off at Station Lelyland and get on tram #1 from there to cut about 20min. from your trip. ☎683 30 13; reservations@hotelfilosoof.nl; www.hotelfilosoof.nl. Singles €97.50-108, doubles €102-135, triples €160-170. AmEx/MC/V. ❹)

night. All rooms with bath, phone, TV, and safe. Breakfast buffet included. Reception 24hr. Singles €88; doubles €148; triples €166. AmEx/D/MC/V. ❸

Hotel Crystal, 2e Helmersstraat 6 (☎618 05 21; hotelcrystal@planet.nl). Take tram #1, 2, 5, 6, 7, or 10 to Leidseplein, cross the bridge, with the American hotel on your right, and make a right; it's the 3rd street on your left. The 17-room family hotel lies within short walking distance of Leidseplein, Museumplein, and Vondelpark. The rooms aren't palatial, but they're clean and very comfortable, especially those with private bathrooms. The hall bathrooms are well maintained as well; all rooms with sinks. Breakfast included. Credit card reservation required. Singles in high season €50, in low season €30; bunked singles €60/€54; doubles €68/€64; twins with bath €102/€73; triples with bath €125/€95; spacious quads with bath €147/€113. Cash only. ❷

Hotel Abba, Overtoom 122 (☎618 30 58; www.abbabudgethotel.com). Tram #1 to 1e Constantijn Huygensstr, Abba is across the street. Overtoom can get noisy and crowded, but this budget hotel is nevertheless attractive for its proximity to Leidseplein and the museums. Breakfast included. Free safe at reception. Reception until 11pm. Credit card reservation required. Singles €37.50, with bath €55; doubles €60/€80; triples €90/€100; quads €140; quints €175. Cash only. ❷

Hotel Princess, Overtoom 80 (☎612 29 47; hotelprincess@planet.nl). Tram #1 or 6 to Constantijn Huygensstraat. Think of this place as Hotel Crystal's less expensive sister. All rooms share a toilet and shower. Rooms overlooking noisy Overtoom have tiny balconies. Breakfast included (8-10am). Cash payment on arrival. Singles in high season €40, in low season €32; doubles €65/€55; triples €90/€55; quads €110/€100. Cash only. ❷

MUSEUMPLEIN & VONDELPARK

see map p. 347

The beautiful neighborhood around the Museumplein and the Vondelpark, while near to the museums and the central canal ring, is also just across the river from the nightlife hotspot, Leidseplein. There are a handful of pricier hotels along Vondelstraat, most of which rent doubles for upwards of €115 per night.

HOSTELS

 StayOkay Amsterdam Vondelpark, Zandpad 5 (☎589 89 96; www.stayokay.com/vondelpark), bordering Vondelpark. Take tram #1, 2, or 5 to Leidseplein, walk to the Marriott and take a left. Walk a block and turn right onto Zanpad right before the park. A palatial, if slightly corporate, hostel with exceptionally clean rooms. Option of 10 to 20-person single sex dormitory rooms. Smaller, mixed rooms, all with bath, makes for a good family option. With a lobby lounge, bar with terrace on the park, TV/rec room and smoking room (the rest of the hostel is non-smoking), StayOkay takes care of all your needs. Breakfast and sheets included. Lockers in the lobby €2.50; bring a padlock for room lockers. Elevator-access. Bike rental €5.50 per day. Internet access €0.50 per min. Reception 7:30am-midnight. Hostel fills up quickly—make a reservation by paying with credit card at www.hostelbooking.com or reserve a more tentative place by phone or the hostel's website. 12- 14-person dorm in high season €23, low season €20.50; 6- or 8-person dorms €25/€23; quad, €28/ €26; twin room €77/€65. HI members €2.50 discount. MC/V. ❶

Homey Jordaan

Flying Pig Palace, Vossiusstraat 46-47 (☎400 41 87; www.flyingpig.nl). Take tram #1, 2, or 5 from Centraal Station to Leidseplein., walk over the bridge to the Marriott and turn left. Go past the entrance to the park and then take the first right onto Vossuistraat. The Palace is down a long block on your left. Not as clean as the Flying Pig Downtown (see p. 190), but has the same laid-back, friendly attitude in a quieter setting with views of the park. The cozy bar with rugs, books, and pillows at one end is the Pig's unofficial meeting spot. All rooms co-ed. Kitchen. Breakfast included. Sheets free, towels 0.70. Free Internet. Key deposit €10. Reception 8am-9pm. Flying Pig hostels are for travelers ages 18-35. Stop by at 8am or call at 8:30am to reserve for the same night or make reservations via Internet and pay 10% deposit ahead of time. The Flying Pig has queen-sized bunk beds in some of their dorms (sleeps 2 for the price of 1.5). During high season, 10-bed dorms €20, €30 for queen-size bed; 8-bed dorms €23/€34.50; 4- to 6-bed dorms €25/€37.50; twins €63, €66 with shower and bath. If you are staying a while, ask about doing work in exchange for rent. AmEx/MC/V. ❶

Peaceful *Hofje* Doorway

HOTELS

🏨 **Hotel Bema,** Concertgebouw 19b (☎679 13 96; www.bemahotel.com). From Centraal Station, take tram #16 to Museumplein; the hotel is just to the left of the imposing Concertgebouw, across from the main taxi stand. Bema is a charming 7-room hotel with airy accommodations (complete with skylights), movie-theater seats, a very friendly staff, and a funky Indo-Australian neo-hippie style. Free breakfast delivered to the room. Reception 8am-midnight. Singles €50, around New Year's €65; twins/doubles €68/€75, with shower €75/85; triples €85/€105; with shower

You Want to Live Here

€95/120; quads with shower €105/€160. Bema also has several apartments equipped with kitchenette for rent. Two people €95-105; 3 €120-130; 4 €160-173. AmEx/MC/V accepted with 5% surcharge. ❷

Hotel Bellington, P.C Hoftstraat 78-80 (☎671 64 78; www.hotel-bellington.com). From Schiphol Airport, take bus #197 to Hobbemasstraat; from Centraal, take tram #2 or 5. A well-groomed hotel on the city's ritziest street; best rooms have windows with views of the thoroughfare. Phone and TV in each room. Breakfast included. Reception 8am-11pm. Doubles €60, with shower and toilet €80-95; triples €105-115; quads €128. AmEx/MC/V. ❹

Hotel Europa 92, 1e Constantijn Huygenstraat 103-105 (☎618 88 08; www.europa92.nl), between Vondelstraat and Overtoom. Tram #1, 6 to 1e Constantijn Huygenstraat Converted from 2 adjacent houses into 1 labyrinthine hotel. Offers clean, professional, fully modernized rooms and a large garden terrace. Every room with phone, TV, private bath, and hair dryer. Breakfast included. Tiny elevator means you carry your luggage for no more than half a flight of stairs. Singles €65, high season €95; doubles €90/€130; triples €100/€155; quads €125/€180. AmEx/DC/MC/V accepted with 4% surcharge. ❹

Hotel Wynnobel, Vossiusstraat 9 (☎662 22 98 or 673 41 15). Follow directions to the Flying Pig Palace and you will come to this hotel first on Vossuistraat. Managed by a stalwart Frenchman, Hotel Wynnobel possesses both the charms and the set-backs of being old-fashioned. With fireplaces, antiqued wood, high ceilings, beautiful big windows, and a garden in the back, this hotel has the warm feel of a home. But nothing here is mechanized—that means no phones, no TV, no website, and no credit cards. It feels a little cramped and beds are a bit saggy, but huge shared bathrooms have bathtubs. Breakfast included. All 11 rooms share facilities on each floor. Singles €35, doubles €60-70 (the smaller and higher up the room is, the cheaper); triples €90; quads €120; quints €150. Ask about price reductions during the low season. ❷

Hotel Museumzicht, Jan Luijkenstraat 22 (☎671 52 24). Directly from Schiphol Airport, ride bus #197 to Hobbemasstraat. From Centraal Station, take tram #2 or 5. Small charming house with old-fashioned personality. The staff may be brusque, but some rooms have views of the Rijksmuseum and the beautiful window-lined breakfast room is homey. Breakfast included. Reception 8am-11pm. Single €45, with shower and toilet €85; doubles €75, €95; triples €95. AmEx/MC/V accepted with 5% surcharge. ❷

Hotel P.C. Hooft, P.C. Hooftstraat 63 (☎662 71 07). From Centraal Station, take tram #2 or 5 to the Rijksmuseum. You may have to sidestep Ferraris on your way home, but this hotel's slightly worn-in rooms are out of step with the glitzy neighborhood surroundings. The bathrooms are clean, and all 16 rooms have rooms have sink and TV. Some with shower. All toilets shared. Singles €35-50; doubles €60-70, with bathroom €75; triples €85-95; quads €110-115/€115. MC/V. ❷

Apple Inn Hotel, Koninginneweg 93 (☎662 78 94; www.apple-inn.nl). Tram #2 to Emmastraat and walk 200m further in the direction of the tram. More isolated than the other hotels in the area and a little more impersonal, the Apple Inn will nevertheless put you in a peaceful, residential neighborhood. Clean basic rooms with bath, TV, phone, and hair dryer. Breakfast included. Singles €65-85, high season €85-100; doubles €85-100/€100-120; triples €128-140/€140-150; quads €156-175/€175-190. AmEx/MC/V. ❸

DE PIJP

Although it's not quite in the heart of the action, the De Pijp district has a number of affordable accommodations available for travelers; Amsterdam's walkability and easily navigable public transportation system make this area an essential consideration for budget travelers.

see map p. 348

🖾 **Bicycle Hotel,** Van Ostadestraat 123 (☎679 34 52; www.bicyclehotel.com). From Centraal Station, take tram #24 or 16 to Albert Cuyp, the 8th stop on either line. Bicycle's draws include clean digs and spotless bathrooms, plus a large, airy common room and leafy garden. A bicycle-friendly hotel (as its name implies), with a bike garage and maps of recom-

mended bike trips. They also rent bikes (€5 per day), and the cycling motif prevails throughout hotel decor. All rooms have sink and TV and breakfast is included (served 8-10am). Free bike storage. Free Internet and safe. Double €68-70, with bath €99; triples €90/€120; quads with bath €120. Cash only. ❷

Hotel De Stadhouder, Stadhouderskade 76 (☎671 84 28). From Centraal Station, take tram #16, 24, or 25. Located directly across from the Heineken Experience (see p. 69), the Hotel De Stadhouder features 20 well-kept rooms, all with TV and daily linen/towel service; some come equipped with patios or delicious canal views. Breakfast included. Most rooms with private bath; all rooms with sink. Elevator. Reception 8am-10pm. Singles €65, low season €35; doubles €85/€40; triples €100/75; quads €110/95; quints €125/85. AmEx/MC/V with 5% surcharge. ❸

JODENBUURT & PLANTAGE

HOTELS

Hotel Pension Kitty, Plantage Middenlaan 40 (☎622 68 19). Take tram #9 or 14 to Plantage Kerklaan; look out for the small sign. You could stay at the nearby assembly-line chain, or you could try for something different at Kitty's. Under the watchful eye of its gentle 80-year-

see map p. 349

old proprietress, Hotel Pension Kitty provides for those seeking a peaceful respite. Located just a few blocks from Artis Zoo, Hortus Botanicus, and the Jewish Museum, this hotel is 4 floors of grandmotherly warmth and meticulous detail. The environment at Kitty is dignified and tranquil; the staff asks that guests try their best to maintain the quiet atmosphere. Some rooms have private toilets or mini-fridges; all have sinks. No children. Singles €50; doubles €60-70; triples €75. Cash only. ❷

Hotel Fantasia, Nieuwe Keizersgracht 16 (☎623 82 59; www.fantasia-hotel.com). Take tram #9, 14 to Waterlooplein. A clean, friendly, family-owned establishment in an 18th-century house on a quiet canal in the center of Amsterdam. Facilities include radios, telephones, safe, and coffee- and tea-makers. Most rooms with bath. Breakfast included; order a home-made takeout lunch before breakfast for €6. Closed Dec. 14-27 and Jan. 6-Mar. 1. Singles €55-63; doubles €80-90; triples €115; quads €135. AmEx/MC/V with 3% surcharge. ❸

Hotel Adolesce, Nieuwe Keizersgracht 26 (☎626 39 59; adolesce@xs4all.nl). This pristine hotel is located in an old canal house just steps away from Amsterdam's famous Magere Brug ("skinny bridge"). Free coffee/tea served all day. No drugs of any kind allowed. All rooms with sink and TV. Reception open 8:30am-1am; pay on arrival. Singles with private bathroom €60-€65; doubles €80-85; twin room with shared shower and toilet €80; triples €115. MC/V. ❸

Hotel Barbacan, Plantage Muidergracht 89 (☎623 62 41; www.barbacan.nl). Take tram #9 or 14 to Plantage Kerklaan. Shag carpets, soft duvets, and included breakfast show that comfort comes first at this quiet hotel. Internet access €2.50 per 30min. Singles (depending on season) €35-45; doubles €60-75, with bath €85-100; triples with bath €100-130; quads with bath €120-155. AmEx/MC/V with 5% surcharge. ❷

LONG-TERM ACCOMMODATIONS

STUDENT HOUSING

While many **colleges and universities** in Europe open their residence halls to travelers when school is not in session, those in Amsterdam do not. Your best bet is to go through private apartment tenants.

RENTING

Renting an apartment in Amsterdam from abroad is very difficult. If you have connections in Amsterdam, ask them to check a local paper (especially on Wednesdays) or to consult a rental agency. Look in the **Gouden Gids (yellow pages)** under **makelaars (housing agencies),** or try the links below. It is common practice to pay these agencies a fee, usually one or two months' rent. When they quote you a price, be sure to ask if the figure includes commission and utilities. Also beware that renting an apartment in Amsterdam can be very expensive—real estate agents estimate that Amsterdam properties are now more expensive than equivalent housing in Paris, Brussels, or Munich. A decent, furnished, two-room apartment (three-room apartments are as elusive as Loch Ness monster) near the center of town can be around €1500 per month. However, furnished apartments in Amsterdam may be considered equivalent to hotels, which makes it easier for your landlord to evict you.

Such a tight housing market leaves plenty of room for unscrupulous landlords and agencies to take advantage of desperate foreigners. Educate yourself before you sign a contract and you'll be less likely to be cheated. Some tenants in subsidized housing illegally sublet at potentially inflated rates; the dangers of this often outweigh the benefits, as you cannot then register at the town hall, which only allows one tenant or family per address, and you abdicate your right to intercede with the authorities. Amsterdam has standards for a legal maximum rent, based on a points system that takes into account factors like size, location, amenities, and age of the apartment. If you think your landlord is overcharging, you have recourse, as long as you have the time to pursue them. The non-profit Amsterdam **Huurteams** (☎428 38 65, www.steunpuntwonen.nl/english/index.asp) will visit your apartment for free, evaluate the place by the points system, and if necessary help you petition the government's **Huurcommissie** (rental commission) for lower rent. For information on Real Estate and Rental Agencies, see **Service Directory,** p. 323

HOME EXCHANGES

Home exchange offers the traveler various types of homes (houses, apartments, condominiums, villas, even castles in some cases), plus the opportunity to live like a native and to cut down on accommodations fees. For more information, contact **HomeExchange.Com** (☎ 888-877-8723; www.homeexchange.com), **Intervac International Home Exchange** (☎ 800-756-4663; www.intervac.com), or **The Invented City: International Home Exchange** (☎ 800-788-CITY or ☎ 415-252-1141; www.invented-city.com). These organizations charge a fee to view listings and are most useful to those who have homes to exchange.

Daytripping

With all the fantastical tripping and sights at your fingertips in Amsterdam proper, you may wonder why you would ever want to leave the city. The city appears to be the seat of all things urbane and cultural in The Netherlands, but the popular conception that the remainder of the country offers nothing more than quaint provincialism simply isn't true. The decidedly stereotypical—yet wonderfully so—Zaanse Schans will satisfy hankerings for Dutch clogs and cheese, while a 20-minute bus ride out to Lisse will immerse you in fields of lilting tulips. A slightly longer jaunt brings you to Leiden, a bustling university town; to Rotterdam, a modern city with cosmopolitan flavor; or The Hague and Delft for the seat of Dutch government and the birthplace of Johannes Vermeer, respectively. A few hours away, the gloriously desolate Wadden Islands boast the finest beaches in The Netherlands and a nature-minded trip to De Hoge Veluwe National Park will surprisingly reveal the Kröller-Müller museum—the country's best collection not located in Amsterdam. This guide covers most of The Netherlands, all of which is easily accessible by train, or even bike, from Amsterdam. Biking through the low countries is exceptionally easy—the country is largely flat and mostly below sea level. For convenience, you may also take your bike with you on all trains for a €6 fee. Spring, when fields of tulips create a sea of colors along the roads, is an ideal time to see the country.

The towns and cities in this chapter are listed in order of their approximate distance from Amsterdam, by route, so that it's easy to hop from one town to another (e.g. Leiden, The Hague, and Rotterdam are all on the same train line). The closer and smaller ones are an easy two-hour excursion, while larger and more distant areas are better seen over a couple of days. For a run-down of our top five favorite daytrip destinations, see p. 210.

DESTINATION	TRANSPORTATION TIME	COST
Arnhem	1¼hr. from Amsterdam	€12.50
Bloemendaal-aan-Zee	25min. from Amsterdam	€3.50
Delft	1hr. from Amsterdam	€9.50
Gouda	20min. from Rotterdam	€3.70
Groningen	2½hr. from Amsterdam	€24.50
Haarlem	20min. from Amsterdam	€3.10
The Hague	50min. from Amsterdam	€8.50
De Hoge Veluwe National Park	25min. from Arnhem	€4.20 or 6 strips
Leiden	35min. from Amsterdam	€6.60
Lisse	20min. from Leiden	€3.40 or 5 strips
Maastricht	2½hr. from Amsterdam	€24.50
Noordwijk-aan-Zee	10min. from Leiden	€3.40 or 5 strips
Rotterdam	1hr. from Amsterdam	€11.20
Utrecht	30min. from Amsterdam	€5.60
Wadden Islands	2-3hr. from Amsterdam	€14.90-43
Zaanse Schans	20min. from Amsterdam	€2.25
Zandvoort-aan-Zee	10min. from Haarlem	€1.50

TULIP COUNTRY

AALSMEER

BLOEMENVEILING AALSMEER (FLOWER AUCTION)

🏳 *Legmeerdijk 313. Take bus #172, 45min., every 15min., 5 strips. Arrive before 9am for busiest trading; buses leave Amsterdam and Haarlem starting at 6:10am. ☎0297 39 21 85; www.vba-aalsmeer.nl. Open M-F 7:30-11am. €4, ages 6-11 €2, groups over 15 €3 per person.*

Easily accessible by bus from Amsterdam and Haarlem, the quietly quaint town of Aalsmeer is home to the world's largest flower auction. With an impressive trading floor that covers the area of 150 American football stadiums, the Bloemenveiling Aalsmeer acts as a central marketplace where growers sell over 19 million flowers to wholesalers and exporters yearly. Visitors cannot participate in the actual bidding process, through which the world price of flowers is determined in Dutch auction style (prices for items drop rather than rise with time), but audio boxes and leaflets are readily available for in-depth explanations of the action. Observe the trade floor from a surrounding balcony, and prepare to be enthralled by the constant bargaining place below. Europe's largest commercial complex includes a cafe and even a barbershop if your curiosity happens to wane. Avoid visiting on Thursdays, which tend to be slow and quiet, but venture out on Mondays, often the busiest day of the week.

ⓘ ESSENTIAL INFORMATION

HOLLAND VS. THE NETHERLANDS

Many believe that the country has two names—Holland and The Netherlands. And for those who live in America and Great Britain, it's true; the names are easily interchangeable in everyday language. But there is a difference, and mixing up the names might earn a mild correction from your Dutch host. The country's official name is The Netherlands, leaving the elusive question: what is Holland?

Holland is a major province within The Netherlands that includes the city of Amsterdam. The word Holland comes from *houtland*, Dutch for "wooded land," while "The Netherlands" comes from *nederland*, literally "low country." To say that Amsterdam is in Holland is true, though to be more accurate, the city is in North Holland. North Holland and South Holland are the two most populous of the nation's 12 provinces. The two provinces contain such major cities as Rotterdam, Haarlem, Leiden, and The Hague.

HISTORISCHE TUIN

🏳 *Uiterweg 32. From the center of town, turn right along Stationsweg and left on Uiterweg. ☎0297 32 25 62; www.htaalsmeer.org. Open Mar.-Oct. Tu-Th 10am-4:40pm, F-Su 1:30pm-4:30pm. €3, under 12 €1.50.*

These unique historical gardens are worth a visit if you're particularly flower-conscious. They celebrate Holland's botanical history through guided tours, auction sessions, and boat trips. Exhibits on traditional farm life, 55 varieties of the dahlia flower, and an exceptional tree with 13 kinds of pears serve as enticing highlights. Look for special flower sales in the spring.

While in Aalsmeer you may also want to take a ride with **Westeinder Rondvaart** at Zijdstraat 260, which runs a quaint, open-air vessel that traverses the picturesque lakes west of the city center. (☎0297 34 15 82; www.westeinderrondvaart.nl. Operates May-Oct. Tu-W and F-Sa 1:30, 2:45, and 4pm, Su 2:30pm. €6, under 12 €3.) If you're hungry, stop by **Brasserie Westeinder ②**, Kudelstaartseweg 222, a comfortable cafe that serves Dutch and French cuisine for about €10. (☎0297 34 1836. Open M-Sa at 11:30am. AmEx/MC/V.) **Wapen van Aalsmeer ③**, Dorpsstraat 15 is a more upscale restaurant offering typical Dutch meals for around €22. (☎0297 38 55 20. Open M-Su

in the know

top five daytrips

There are so many wonderful destinations outside of Amsterdam—here are our favorites:

5. WADDEN ISLANDS. As desolate as life gets in the gentrified Dutch countryside, the Wadden Islands present a true escape with glorious stretches of sandy-white beaches (p. 274).

4. LEIDEN. One of Europe's most prestigious universities lends Leiden a bipolar personality—a serious intellectual center, with philosophy written (literally) on the walls, and a hopping student's city (p. 225).

3. ROTTERDAM. The biggest port city in the world, a center for contemporary architecture, a multi-cultural city: Rotterdam is as far from Old World as it gets—in Holland, at least (p. 244).

2. THE HAGUE & DELFT. Take on The Netherlands' seat of government in The Hague and be sure to visit the extraordinary ⬛ **Mauritshuis** museum (p. 231). Delft, the birthplace of painter Johannes Vermeer, is a short tram-ride away: it's one of the loveliest and best preserved Dutch towns (p. 239).

1. DE HOGE VELUWE. The Hoge Veluwe's 42km of parklands are home to pine forests, sand dunes, deer, and the ⬛ **Kröller-Müller Museum**—one of The Netherlands' best, period. It boasts a brilliant collection of van Goghs and a world-class sculpture garden (p. 263).

noon-9:15pm. AmEx/MC/V.) For further info on Aalsmeer, visit the town's **VVV,** located at Drie Kolommenplein 1 (☎ 0297 32 53 74).

LISSE

Lisse's main (and indeed sole) attraction is related to horticulture, especially that of the renowned Dutch flower, the tulip.

TRANSPORTATION & PRACTICAL INFORMATION

To reach Lisse, Take **bus** #50 or 51 toward Lisse from the **Leiden** or **Haarlem** train stations (20min.; 5 strips or €3.50); bus #54, the Keukenhof Express, can also be accessed from either the Leiden or Lisse station. The town's **VVV,** at Heereweg 254, gives information on the town's few sights (www.lisse.nl; in Dutch).

FOOD

Lisse has many restaurants, most of which are located on the central street Heereweg. Local favorites are **De Engel ❷** (Heereweg 386; ☎ 025 221 18 80) and **Restaurant De Vier Seizoenen ❷** (Heereweg 224; ☎ 025 241 80 23).

SIGHTS

⬛ **KEUKENHOF GARDENS.** The unquestionable highlight of the comfortable town of **Lisse** are the breathtaking Keukenhof Gardens, which in late spring become a kaleidoscope of color as over seven million bulbs explode into life. Designed in 1949 by the Vondelpark creators, the gardens were a priority of the town's mayor, who wanted a permanent space for annual open-air flower exhibitions. Now the world's largest flower garden, Keukenhof boasts impeccable grounds with fountains, a windmill, and a petting zoo. Visit all three greenhouses, one of which holds the winners from a national tulip contest. From the gardens, where all existing species of tulip are showcased for close examination, take in views of the area's surrounding **tulip fields,** whose long strips of color are the pride of the Dutch, visited each year by tourists from all over Europe. May 2-4 marks the annual summer bulb weekend, featuring the International Flower Exhibition that provides expert lessons and presentations for world-wide gardeners. (Stationsweg 166a. ☎ 0252 46 55 55; www.keukenhof.com/english. Open Mar. 25-May 20 daily 8am-7:30pm; tickets on sale until 6pm. €11.50, children ages 4-11 €5.50. Open also in mid-Oct. for the sale of bulbs; check website for more information.)

ZWARTE TULP MUSEUM (BLACK TULIP). The museum details the historical cultivation and scientific evolution of "bulbiculture," or tulip raising, through videos, photos, drawings, artifacts, tools, and a botanical library. This exhaustingly extensive horticultural centre also concentrates on the quest for the black tulip, explaining that all attempts are most likely futile as the color black is not produced naturally by any flowering organism. (Grachtweg 2a. ☎025 241 79 00; www.museum-dezwartetulp.nl/hollands.html. Open Su, Tu-Sa 1-5pm. €3, children and seniors €2.)

DEVER HOUSE. Older than any standing structure in Amsterdam, the Dever tower-house and dungeon was built in 1375 by Reinier Dever, a knight and vassal of Count van Beieren. The dark, ancient building has been a renowned museum in Lisse since 1978. (Heereweg 349a. ☎0252 41 14 30. Open Su, Tu-Sa 2-5pm. Free.)

HAARLEM   ☎023

Haarlem's narrow cobblestone streets, rippling canals, and fields of tulips make for a great escape from Amsterdam's urban frenzy. Most visitors come to the city for its many artistic and historical sights, littered as it is with Renaissance facades, idyllic *hofjes* (almshouses for the elderly), medieval architecture, and the renowned Frans Hals Museum. Founded earlier than Amsterdam, Haarlem was once the cultural center of 16th- and 17th-century Holland. But there's more than antiquated charm here—Haarlem ebbs with a relaxed energy befitting a mid-sized urban center (pop. 150,000). Coffeeshops, bars, and the most restaurants per capita of any Dutch city ensure that there's fun to be had after the sun goes down. In 2004, Haarlem will host a four-day jazz festival August 20-24 (☎527 33 47; www.haarlemjazz.nl) and a culinary fest July 31-August 3. Grote Markt welcomes a bustling marketplace on Monday afternoons, where vendors hawk everything from clothing to flower seeds.

TRANSPORTATION & PRACTICAL INFORMATION

Travel to Haarlem from Amsterdam either by train from **Centraal Station** (20min.; €3.10 one-way, €5.50 round-trip if returning same day) or by bus #80 from **Marnixstraat** near Leidseplein (20min., 2 per hr., 2 strips). A **Tickets and Service** center provides schedules for trains, and sells tickets and *strippenkarten*. (Open M-Sa 6:15am-midnight, Su 6:15am-11pm). The **VVV tour-**

The Local LEGEND

a darker shade of purple

Flower growers have managed to create every imaginable strain of **tulip,** from smooth-edged to fringed, single-hued to multi-colored. Hybridizers have not succeeded in what seems to be a simple task: the creation of a black tulip. Scientists have come close, growing tulips that are darker and darker shades of purple, but have not achieved an absolute shade of black. The difficulty of this quest has sparked the romantic imaginations of artists and writers: Alexandre Dumas, author of *The Count of Monte Cristo*, wrote a melodramatic novella set in The Netherlands—*The Black Tulip* (1850)—in which an elusive, mysterious specimen of the mythical flower was the center of intrigue.

Despite any literary invention, biology it seems, will have the final word. It is actually impossible for any plant, tulips included—no living organism can produce black pigments for black is the absence of all color. But if you insist on having something in your garden that is as black (or purple) as midnight, try tulip strains "Burgundy," "Black Diamond," or "Black Parrot." For more on the legend, visit the Zwarte Tulp Museum (see p. 211).

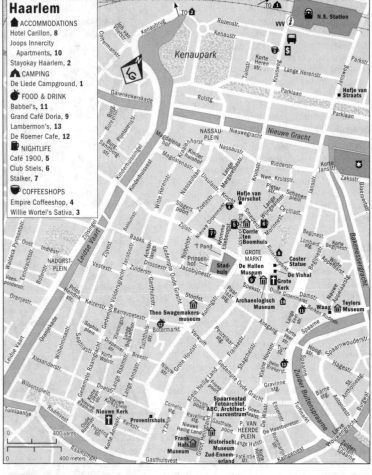

Haarlem

🏠 ACCOMMODATIONS
Hotel Carillon, **8**
Joops Innercity
 Apartments, **10**
Stayokay Haarlem, **2**

🏕 CAMPING
De Liede Campground, **1**

🍴 FOOD & DRINK
Babbel's, **11**
Grand Café Doria, **9**
Lambermon's, **13**
De Roemer Cafe, **12**

🍷 NIGHTLIFE
Café 1900, **5**
Club Stiels, **6**
Stalker, **7**

☕ COFFEESHOPS
Empire Coffeeshop, **4**
Willie Wortel's Sativa, **3**

ist office, Stationsplein 1, just to your right when you walk out of the train station, sells maps (€2) and finds accommodations for a €5 fee. (☎ 0900 616 16 00; www.vvvzk.nl. Open M-F 9am-5:30pm, Sa 10am-3:30pm; in low season M-F 9am-5:30pm, Sa 10am-2pm.)

ACCOMMODATIONS

StayOkay Haarlem, Jan Gijzenpad 3 (☎ 537 37 93; www.stayokay.com/haarlem). Take bus #2 from platform #1 (dir: Haarlem-Noord; every 10min. until 6pm; every 15min. 6pm-12:30am)—the bus stops directly in front of hostel. The best place to stay in Haarlem is 3km from Haarlem's train station, surrounded by a wooded park and situated on the banks of a placid canal. Packed with amenities, the hostel is incomparably suited for young travelers. Rooms are spare but cheery and perfectly clean with private facilities. Staff runs a lively pub, The Shuffle, where, if you're man enough, you can order the 2.5L "boot" of beer (deposit of 1 shoe required). The party spills onto the canal-side patio on summer nights, where an open fire doubles as a barbe-cue. Packages for activities at the nearby Noorder sports park available. Bike rental €6.80 per day (passport or €150 deposit required); canoe and scooter rental also available. Sheets included; sleeping bags not allowed. Breakfast included; box lunches €4.15; 3-course dinner €8.70. Bike rack, bag storage, and laundry room included. Key deposit €10 or passport. Beds in 1- to 8-person dorms in high season €22-24.50, in low season €19-22. €2.50 discount with StayOkay membership. AmEx/MC/V. ●

Joops Innercity Apartments, Oude Groenmarkt 20 (☎532 20 08; joops@easynet.nl). Walk to Grote Markt and take a right; Oude Groenmarkt runs along the right hand side of the giant church. A touch of class for half the price. Centrally located with luxurious, elegant rooms. Rooms and apartments with cream walls and carpeted floors, impeccably clean and very spacious serviced by a Dutch rarity: an elevator. Reception M-Sa 7am-11pm, Su 8am-10pm. Continental breakfast buffet €9.50. Rooms with shower and hall toilet: singles €28-40; doubles €55. Studios with shower, toilet, and kitchenette: small singles or doubles €75; large singles or doubles €85; triples €95; quads €120. Extra large suites with balcony: singles or doubles €110; triples or quads with 2 bedrooms €120. Large apartment with living room, kitchen, and bathroom €107 for 2; €20 extra per person up to 10. AmEx/MC/V. ●

Hotel Carillon, Grote Markt 27 (☎531 05 91; www.hotelcarillon.com). Ideally located right in the town square, to the left of the Grote Kerk and 5min from train station. Bright, basic rooms make up in cleanliness and neatness what they lack in space. Despite their diminutive size, most with TV, shower, and phone. Rooms situated above a classy restaurant/bar with an outdoor patio facing directly into the square (beer from €1.80). Breakfast included. Reception and bar in summer 7:30am-1am; in winter 7:30am-midnight. Singles €30, with facilities €55; doubles €55/€71; triples €92; quads €99. MC/V. ❷

De Liede Campground, Lie Oever 68 (☎535 86 66). Take the *stoptrein* that goes between Haarlem and Amsterdam and get off at the Haarlem-Spaarnwoude stop; the campground is just a few minutes away. Or take bus #2 (dir: Zuiderpolder) and tell the bus driver where you're going; he will give walking directions from the bus stop. Located on a swimmable canal with a restaurant, pool table, tennis, and campsite shop. €2.85 per person, €2.85 per tent, €2.85 per car. Animals allowed. Cash only. ●

FOOD

Haarlem smugly dubs itself the "most delicious city in Holland." The slogan refers to the city's many restaurants, which are definitely satisfying, but unfortunately rather expensive. The unofficial street for culinary excellence is Lange Veerstraat, but for cheaper, casual meals, travelers should try the cafes in the **Grote Markt** or in the **Botermarkt,** which have the added advantage of outdoor patios that soak in the stunning city backdrop.

▨ **Lambermon's,** Spaarne 96 (☎542 78 04; www.lambermons.nl). From Lange Veerstraat, turn down one of the streets on your left, then turn right; it's 2 blocks down, in a formidable brick structure adorned with gold lions. A lavish treat for the culinary enthusiast, Lambermon's is the best in haute cuisine that Haarlem has to offer. The menu changes nightly and consists of 10 small but delectable courses (€8 each)—dishes are served only at 30min. intervals; 4 or 5 per person will usually suffice. Wines (€3.50-4.50 per glass) are selected to complement each dish although full wine and liquor (€4-4.50 per glass) menus are available. The open kitchen functions as a kind of performance art venue, as guests feel inclined to marvel at the creativity of the numerous chefs. Open daily 6pm-1am. 1st course served at 6:30pm; kitchen closes 10:30pm. Reservations mandatory. AmEx/MC/V. ❺

▨ **Grand Café Doria,** Grote Houtstraat 1a (☎531 33 35; www.doria.nl), right in the Grote Markt, to the west of the Grote Kerk. It looks deceptively like a standard Dutch cafe, though it actually specializes in Italian fare, including pizza margherita (€6) and pasta bolognese (€8.50). Main courses €6-19.50, but lighter dishes of *broodjes* (€2.50-7) or ice cream desserts (€2.50-4.50) available as well. Gorgeously designed Italian interior with red walls and green columns, strewn with lush vegetation planted under archways. Its outdoor patio is a fabulous place to relax by day, and turns into a lively bar scene by night. Open Su-Th 9am-midnight, F-Sa 9am-2am. AmEx/MC/V. ❷

The Local LEGEND

coster's last stand

If ever questioned, Haarlem locals will insist that **Laurens Coster** (1370-1440), the city's most celebrated citizen (after master painter Frans Hals, of course), invented the printing press in 1423, 13 meaningful years before Johannes Gutenberg printed the world's first mass-produced bible.

As the story is often told, Coster was carving a letter out of tree bark when he accidentally dropped it into a patch of mud and was thus struck by the inspiration for the basic premise of the printing press. Extremely fragile evidence exists to support this claim, and few historians seriously believe the tale, but Haarlemmers continue to promote the legend as inarguable truth. Of course, myth-mongers are quite aware that Gutenberg has been credited with the inventing the printing press but they are perfectly content to share Laurens Coster's story time and time again.

The statue at the northeastern corner of **Grote Markt** (see above) commemorates Coster. His figure presides heroically over the square, his right hand poised and raised, grasping the letter "A" that, as legend goes, gave rise to the existence of the printed word.

Babbel's, Lange Veerstraat 23 (☎542 35 78). Walk behind the Grote Kerk and take a right onto Lange Veerstraat. Babbel's serves a range of meat and fish dishes in an elegant, candlelit setting. The restaurant has an antique toy shop ambiance with storybook murals and shelves littered with dolls, and trinkets; ask to dine in the closet for a special treat. Prices are slightly lower than the upscale restaurants that surround it, but dishes like the *carpaccio* with fresh Parmesan (€7.50), chicken skewers in peanut sauce (€12), and spare ribs (€12.50) are satisfying. Main dishes served with salad, french fries, and vegetables (€11.50-17.25). Reasonable starters abound (€4.80-9). Open daily 5:30-9:30pm. Cash only. ❷

De Roemer Cafe, Botermarkt 17 (☎532 52 67). A typical Dutch cafe on the Botermarkt, with a young, rambunctious crowd and a large selection of specialty beer (€1.80-8.40 per bottle). The outstanding house specialty is the *gambas piri piri* (€10.20), spicy shrimp tossed in chili, peppers, and garlic. Main dishes €10.20-16.50. Sandwiches €3.10-5.20. *Tostis* (including the mozzarella, tomato, and pesto) €2.20-2.60. Music wafts from inside the restaurant to the lively outdoor patio. Open M-Th 9am-1pm, F-Sa 9am-2pm, Su noon-1am. Cash only. ❷

SIGHTS

The action in Haarlem centers on the 🖼**Grote Markt,** the city's vibrant main square since the town's founding in 1245. To get to the square from the train station, head south along Kruisweg, which becomes Kruisstraat when it crosses the Nieuwe Gracht. Continue south when Kruisstraat becomes Barteljorisstraat, and you'll soon be bombarded by the square's magnificence. Just north of **Grote Kerk,** the 5m high statue of **Laurens Coster** (see **Coster's Last Stand,** p. 214) beckons to the public.

🖼 FRANS HALS MUSEUM

🔢 *Groot Heiligland 62. From Grote Markt in front of the church, take a right on to Warmoestraat and go 3.5 blocks down.* ☎511 57 75; www.franshalsmuseum.com. *Open Tu-Sa 11am-5pm, Su noon-5pm. €5.40, seniors and groups €4, under 19 free. Wheelchair accessible.*

This breathtaking museum leads you through the art of the Dutch Golden Age with an impressive collection of paintings by masters including Jacob van Ruisdael, Pieter Saenredam, and one-time Haarlem resident Frans Hals. Housed in a picturesque 17th-century building that was used as an almshouse and orphanage, the museum offers an unique impression of the 16th and 17th century artwork. Spread through recreated period rooms, the paintings are displayed as they might have been in the Golden Age—above antique oak tables and between cabinets filled with silver, glass, and porcelain. Along with the dramatic Haarlem landscapes painted by Ruisdael and the serene churches depicted by Saenredam, 11 of Haarlem master Frans Hals's works reside here, many of them enormous pieces portraying the ctiy's civic guards. In these works, Hals departed from his contemporaries, as he arranged his militia companies with greater motion and freedom than his colleagues did; most painters of that era preferred to paint portraits with stodgy, rigid poses. In **The Banquet of the Officers of the St George Militia Company,** look for Hals's self-portrait in the upper left row of men. His other portraiture work, commissioned by bourgeois merchants, reveals breezy casual brush strokes that were once considered sloppy but are now understood to have been an initial move toward Impressionism. The museum also houses an intricate doll house, and the courtyard outside provides peaceful repose.

GROTE KERK (ST. BAVO'S)

Grote Markt. ☎553 20 40; www.bavo.nl. Open M-Sa 10am-4pm; Mar.-Oct. closed M. Guided tours by appointment €2. €1.50, children €1. Free organ concerts (www.organfestival.nl) Tu 8:15pm, June-Sept. Th 3pm.

The church's interior glows with light from the enormous stained-glass windows, and houses the splendid, mammoth Müller organ once played by both Handel and Mozart. First built in the early 14th century but reconstructed several times, St. Bavo's holds many an artifact to explore, including Haarlem's oldest safe, model ships celebrating Holland's 1219 first capture of the city from Spanish hands, a cannon ball from the Spanish siege of 1572-3, and a modern statue commemorating Haarlem's resistance during the seven months of besiegement. On the oak pulpit and its handrails, Satan and his serpents flee from the Gospel and the baptismal waters while marble Muses dedicate their work to Piety in front of the richly detailed red and gold organ. To the right of the organ is perhaps the cathedral's strangest sight, the gated "Dog Whipper's Chapel" from which an attendant would emerge to remove troublesome dogs that had entered the church. Pieter Saenredam (who painted the church) Jacob van Ruisdael, and Frans Hals are buried here; the latter's tombstone is marked by a lantern. Weary travelers can rest in the cafe in the Brewer's guild memorial section.

CORRIE TEN BOOMHUIS

Barteljorisstraat 19, 2min. from the Grote Markt. ☎531 08 23; www.corrietenboom.com. Open Tu-Sa 10am-4pm. You must go on a 45min. guided tour that occurs every 30min; call or check the clock outside for times. Free, but donations accepted.

Corrie ten Boom and her family were pillars of strength and generosity in the Dutch Resistance, providing a safe haven for Jews and persecuted Dutch rebels during World War II. This house, despite its public location on a main thoroughfare, served as a network headquarters for the Resistance, and it is estimated that Corrie saved the lives of over 800 people by arranging to have them hidden in houses throughout the city and in the surrounding countryside. She kept the most imperiled refugees in her own house, those who supposedly looked "particularly Jewish" and others whose poor health meant almost certain death in an extermination camp. When the ten Boom family's subterfuge was discovered, they were sent to the Ravensbruck concentration camp, and only Corrie managed to survive the war. Following the war, she won global renown for her message of forgiveness and authored the book *The Hiding Place*, the tale of her wartime ordeal, which was later made into a film. The tour through the ten Boom house is an inspiring glance at her moving life, but the most extraordinary sight is undoubtedly the famed hiding spot, an impossibly narrow space located behind a brick wall. Six fugitives hid here from the Gestapo when the ten Boom family was betrayed, staying in the tiny space for three days without food, water, or facilities.

Haarlem

TEYLERS MUSEUM

🄵 *Spaarne 16. From the Grote Markt, walk behind the church to Damstraat and then take a left at the river.* ☎ *531 90 10; www.teylersmuseum.nl. Open Tu-Su 10am-5pm, Su noon-5pm. €5.50, children ages 5-18 €1, groups of 20 €4 per person. Wheelchair accessible.*

Named after Pieter Teyler van der Hulst, a textile manufacturer who left his fortune for the promotion of arts and sciences, this museum, opened in 1784, is the oldest in The Netherlands. With its antiquated displays of scientific curiosities, the Teylers is a voyage through the ages with a clutter of fossils, dinosaur bones, rocks, old coins, and obsolete scientific instruments; the collection is renowned for its inclusion of the jaws of a Mosasaurus and a Diluvian man. Displays haven't changed much since the museum's opening but a charming selection of 19th-century paintings has been recently added. The Classical facade is a formidable sight along the canal-side and houses, and also houses a small cafe that faces out to a serene landscape of open green.

DE HALLEN MUSEUM (VLEESHAL & VERWEYHAL)

🄵 *Grote Market 16, just to the right of the Grote Kerk.* ☎ *511 57 75; www.franshalsmuseum.com; www.dehallen.com. Open Tu-Sa 11am-5pm, Su noon-5pm. €4, under 19 free.*

Grotemarkt, Haarlem

Now owned by the Frans Hals museum, Haarlem's collection of modern art is housed in the 17th-century Dutch Renaissance *vleeshal*, an indoor meat market built in the early 1600s for sanitation purposes. The building is a magnificent sight in the Grote Markt, with a reminder of its old purpose suitably displayed in the ox and sheep heads adorning the exterior. The museum hosts changing exhibitions of modern and contemporary art, giving special attention to contemporary photography and displaying a large collection of works by 20th century artist Kees Verwey; the adjoining hall is named after this Haarlem painter who died in 1995. A roof terrace provides a sweeping view over Haarlem but is not always open for visitors.

HISTORISCH MUSEUM ZUD-ENNEMERLAND

🄵 *Groot Heiligland 47, oposite the Frans Hals Museum.* ☎ *542 24 27. English cards for captions available. Open Tu-Sa noon-5pm, Su 1-5pm. €1, under 19 free.*

Old Hospital, Haarlem

Haarlem has a fascinating past, and this small museum strives to present the history engagingly. A ten-minute film with an English-language "narration" by Laurens Coster (see **Coster's Last Stand,** p. 214) and an interactive video display in Dutch illustrate memorable moments in Haarlem's past, while a similarly contrived timeline flies through centuries of change with symbolic artifacts, reducing the city's history into material suitable for a high school lecture. The highlight of the museum is an ever-changing exhibit on noteworthy aspects of Haarlem life that features black and white photos and antiquated objects.

OTHER SIGHTS

The city has 19 **hofjes,** or almshouses, which have provided the elderly free housing for over five centuries. Many of the *hofjes*—all of which are still in operation—surround beautiful garden courtyards that visitors can sometimes stroll through. Check out the **Hofje van Oorschot,** where Kruisstraat becomes Barteljorisstraat, whose gorgeous courtyard of lavender and roses contains a statue of Eve before original sin. (Open daily 10am-5pm.) Other ancient *hofjes* worth noting are the **Provenirshuis** at Grote Houtstraat and **Hofje van Staats,** Jansweg 39. (Open M-Sa 10am-5pm.)

At the west end of the Grote Markt looms the glorious medieval **Town Hall,** once the hunting lodge of the Count of Holland. It was built in the 14th-17th centuries, the varying architectural styles reflected in its bricolage of spires and statues. In a small space right by the Grote Kerk is **De Vishal,** a gallery space displaying the contemporary multi-media art. Exhibits of paintings, photography, sculpture and fashion change frequently but do not diminish in their avant-garde experimentation. (www.devishal.nl. Open Tu-Sa 11am-5pm, Su 1-5pm. Free.) Underneath the De Hallen Museum to the right of the Grote Kerk is the **Archeologisch Museum,** displaying centuries of archaeological artifacts through changing exhibits. (☎542 08 88 or 531 31 35. Open W-Su 1-5pm. Free.) The **Theo Swagemakersmuseum,** Stoofsteeg 6, between Koningstraat and Gedempte Oude Gracht, houses 200 of the 20th-century portrait painter Swagemakers's art, including still-lifes and landscape watercolors. The museum also contains a floor with changing exhibitions of contemporary artwork. (☎532 77 61; www.swagemakersmuseum.nl. Open Th-Su 1-5pm. €3.) Upstairs from the **Historisch Museum** (see above) is the **Spaarnestad Fotoarchief,** a free gallery with changing exhibits of contemporary documentary photographs and selections from a permanent collection of 4 million photos. (☎518 51 52; www.spaarnefoto.nl. Open Tu-Sa noon-5pm, Su 1-5pm. Free.) To the left of the Teylers museum is the 1598 **Waag** (weighhouse), which was formerly used for weighing goods during trade on the Spaarne River. Across the Spaarne looms the **Amsterdamse Poort,** built around 1400, the last segment of the city's fortifications still standing from when a defensive wall encircled the whole town. To reach the Poort, cross the bridge to the left of the Teyler's museum, take a left on Spaarne and turn on to Oostvest. The **Nieuwe Kerk,** situated amidst rows of residential houses on Korte Annastraat, is an impressive rectangular structure built in the 1640s by Jacob van Campen, who designed the Royal Palace. It peaks with a graceful tower constructed a generation earlier in 1613 by Lieven de Key in the Dutch Renaissance style. (No entrance allowed.)

COFFEESHOPS

Have no fear, hash and marijuana are as popular here as in the big city. Haarlem's best coffeehouse is **Empire Coffeeshop,** Krocht 8, just off Barteljorisstraat, which delivers a pool table (€1), foosball (€0.50), and speedy Internet (expensive at €1.20 per 15min.) amidst blasting R&B and pop tunes. Weed and hash are €6-12 for 0.8-3g; pre-rolled joints are €3. (☎531 44 53; www.coffeeshop-empire.nl. Open daily 10am-midnight.) Another favorite is **Willie Wortel's Sativa,** Kruisweg 46, conveniently located across from the train station. Weed (1g €5-20), hash chocolate bars (€7), and lollipops (€3.60) are available from the two connoisseur attendants behind the counters. (☎531 77 70. Ridiculously cheap pure joints €2.50-3.60; spacecake €3.60. Bongs available for use for €0.60 or with a drink purchase. Internet €3.50 per hr. Open Su-Th and Su 9am-1am, F-Sa 9am-2am.)

Frans Haals Museum, Haarlem

Frans Haals Museum China Room

Sex Shop, Haarlem

NIGHTLIFE

Haarlem's nightlife doesn't rock as hard as Amsterdam's, but the bars and clubs are more accessible and less crowded. In the summer, you may want to consider taking a bus to nearby Bloemendaal-aan-Zee instead for dinner, drinks, and music on the beach (see p. 220).

Cafe Stiels, Smedestraat 21 (☎ 531 69 40; www.stels.nl), just northwest of the city center, is a stylish, candlelit drinking den that grows hugely active as the night progresses. Extremely popular with locals who appreciate dancing to the quality music that explodes from a powerful stereo system. Su-Th live bands play covers, soul, R&B, and acid jazz, while F-Sa 20-somethings boogie to DJs spinning disco dance classics. Crowded after 11pm with very few seats. Beer €2; cocktails €5. No cover. Open Su-Th 6pm-2am, F-Sa 6pm-4am.

Stalker, Kromme Elleboogsteeg 20 (☎ 531 46 52; www.clubstalker.nl). Located in a former warehouse, the only "real" club in Haarlem, where the locals keep the party bumpin' until dawn. Downstairs features a huge dance floor while upstairs lounge provides seating comfort, and a bar. House, techno, garage, and French disco play for the dancing crowd. Out-of-towners should show up early to ensure admittance. Cover Th €6, F €7, Sa €8-9, Su €3. Open Th-F, Su midnight-5am; Sa 11pm-5am.

Cafe 1900, Barteljorisstraat 10 (☎ 531 82 83), just northwest of the Grote Markt. Dark, bustling cafe that serves a light lunch throughout the day (salads and sandwiches €3-7) then morphs into a chill bar by night. Room for dancing but patrons prefer to socialize over drinks. Free live music Su; Th-Sa DJ hosts a pop music dance party (no cover). Open M-Th 9am-12:30am, F-Sa 9am-1am, Su 11am-1am.

NEAR HAARLEM

ZANDVOORT-AAN-ZEE

From Amsterdam, take a train from Centraal station, 30min., 3 per hr., €4.60. From Haarlem, you can take a train, 10min., round-trip €2.50.

Just seven miles from Haarlem, the seaside town of Zandvoort draws gaggles of sun-starved Germans and Dutch to its expansive stretch of sandy beaches during summer. To find the shore from the train station, follow the signs to the Raadhuis, and from there head west along Kerkstraat until you fall into the warm sand. The ocean water is generally too cold for swimming though brave souls take the plunge year-round, particularly on 20°C August days. You can stake out a spot on the sand for free, but most locals enjoy Zandvoort through the luxurious comfort of "beach clubs," wooden pavilions that run along the shore with enclosed restaurants, outdoor patios, and rows of chaise lounges for sunbathing. These clubs open early each morning, close at midnight, and are only in service during the summer. Each offers its own distinct decor and nourishment, but admission is always free as long as you're buying drinks or food. If you're in a friskier mood, head to one of the several nudist beach clubs on the "Naaktstrand," about 20 minutes south of the main beach.

The VVV **tourist office,** Schoolplein 1, is just east of the town square off Louisdavidstraat and about eight minutes from the beach and the station; signs lead the way from most locations. (☎571 79 47; www.vvvzk.nl. Hours vary according to season, but generally open M-Sa 9am-5:15pm.) There are quite a few hotels in Zandvoort, many of them located on Hogeweg or Haltestraat, including **Hotel Noordzee ❷,** Hogeweg 15, which has rooms with TV and hall shower/toilet. (☎571 31 27. Doubles begin €47-60 depending on season.) **Arosa ❷,** Hogeweg 48 is another viable option. (☎571 31 87; hotel_arosa@hotmail.com. Doubles with shower €45-65 depending on season. AmEx/MC/V). Otherwise you can book inexpensive B&B rooms through the VVV for a €3 reservation fee. In Zandvoort, B&Bs are generally in private residences and discourage smoking; bookings can be done up to three weeks in advance.

Rent bikes at the train station at Stationsplein (☎571 26 00) or at Vondelaan 16 (☎572 00 00). Just north of the town lies the **Kraansvlak Dune Reserve,** a quiet hideaway for a walk or bike ride. (☎0900 796 47 36; www.pwn.nl. Open M-Sa 9am-6pm, Su 10am-6pm.) For a wilder time, try out the **Holland Casino Zandvoort,** Badhuisplein 7, featuring the likes of roulette, black jack, and slot machines. There is also a free **circus,** Gasthuispein 5 (☎23 571 86 86; www.circuszandvoort.nl), with games, miniature rides, and a movie theater. Zandvoort's **restaurants** can bankrupt you in true beach resort style, but some budget deals line the streets radiating from the **Raadhuisplein.** On sunny days, the best choice might be one of the many **food trucks ❶** that park along the beach strip, vending seafood (fried or raw) fresh from the Atlantic (meals €3.50-7). Kerkstraat and Haltestraat in particular are packed with eateries, most of which feature tranquil outdoor patios during the day that transform into lively bars at night. **Grand Cafe 25,** Kerkstraat 25, features a classy bar and comfy, multi-colored linen chairs ideal for lounging with

Tulip Bulbs

Dutch Tiles

Grote Kerk, Haarlem

Teylers Museum, Haarlem

Stads-Koffyhuis

Flea Market

drink. (☎571 35 10. Open daily 11am-3am.) **De Pannekoeken Farm ❶**, Kerkstraat 10A, serves a whirlwind of pancake meals, topped off with friendly, warm service. (☎571 94 98. Open daily noon-10pm.) Off Kerkstraat, to the right when walking toward the beach is **Yanks,** Dorpsplein 2, the rowdy, over-the-top cowboy-themed bar and coffeeshop, decorated with an excess of Native American headdresses and teepees. (☎571 94 55; www.yanks.nl. Open daily in summer 9am-3am; in winter 10am-3am.)

BLOEMENDAAL-AAN-ZEE

🚩 *A 30min. walk to the right of Zandvoort Beach. Take bus #81 from Haarlem or Zandvoort. Or, take a train from Amsterdam Centraal, 25min., 2-3 per hr., €3.50.*

In recent years, Bloemendaal-aan-zee has transformed from a quiet family beach town into the site of Holland's largest and most popular beach party. Local club 🎵**Woodstock 69** (☎573 21 52; www.woodstock69.nl) started throwing **Beach Bop** parties every Sunday—all-out bacchanalia that would stretch into the night with endless hours of drinks, dancing, and music. Unlike Zandvoort, Bloemendaal is mostly visited by the Dutch, so the thousands of clubbers that came in from Amsterdam turned this tiny town into a bastion of cool on the coast. Other clubs sprung up to support the insatiable revelers, but the magnitude of the parties so overwhelmed the small burg of Bloemendaal that authorities have now limited the Beach Bop festivities to the last Sunday of every month (see www.beach-bop.info). Casual gatherings do occur during the other nights of the week, but Bloemendaal should really be visited during the morning or afternoon hours, when the sun shines brightly and travelers can recline peacefully on the sofas or beds placed right in the sand surrounding each club. Unfortunately, the clubs are open only in summer months, generally from April to September and must shut their doors by midnight. Woodstock 69 is a pot of gold at the end of the rainbow, a backpacker's paradise with couches on the beach, hammocks strung lazily from trees, and even a restaurant serving international delights in colorful, casual hippie style.

On the edge of town lies the **Zuid-Kennemerland National Park** (Visitor's Center ☎527 18 71; open Tu, 10am-5pm), where you can ride along lovely bike trails through the dunes—Bloemendaal boasts the Kopje van Bloemendaal, the highest sand dune in The Netherlands. Stay on marked trails because the park doubles as a nature sanctuary. If you can't get enough of the beach, spend a few nights camping at **Bloemendaal ❶**

(Zeeweg 72; ☎ 573 21 78; campingbloe-mendaal@planet.nl; open daily 4pm-2:10am) or **Lakens ❶**. (Zeeweg 60. ☎ 0900 384 62 26; www.kennemerduincampings.nl, €25 per night; includes car, tent, and tax. Open daily 9am-4am.) Hotels are expensive in Bloemendaal, so a few nights of roughing it might be well worth the extra pocket change. The many beach clubs serve satisfying enough meals, but if you're famished for more, head over to cafe-restaurant **Zonnehoek ❸**, which offers dinner for €11.50 and lunch sandwiches for €4, all on a beautiful sunlit terrace right above the beach. (Zeeweg 98. ☎ 573 21 58. Open daily 11:30am-9pm.)

For unstructured club life, just stay near the beach; all clubs close around the same time: whenever the party peters out. **Bloomingdale** (☎ 0900 606 06 66) reclines in chic elegance with tan sofas and plush pillows thrown into a background of pulsing music; with its laid-back grace, Bloomingdale tends to be the favorite of most locals. **De Zomer** (☎ 571 80 08; www.dezomer.nl) and **Solaris** (☎ 573 21 55; www.strandclubsolaris.nl) are two younger clubs that help to support the DJ concert series **Paradiso-aan-Zee** (www.paradisoaanzee.nl).

Zaanse Schans

ZAANSE SCHANS ☎ 075

Unleash your inner tourist for a day at delightful Zaanse Schans, a 17th-century town located only 20 minutes from Amsterdam, on the River Zaan. Feel free to fumble clumsily with an oversized map while fiddling with your fannypack, because Zaanse Schans, with its cheese farm, wooden shoe workshop, and working windmills, embraces and encourages a tourist's curiosity. In the 1950s, the residents of the Zaan region were concerned that industrialization was quietly destroying their historic landmarks, so they transported the wooden landmarks on barges and trucks to this pretty plot of land. While you walk through the town, dodging the numerous group tours, you may feel immersed in a surreal museum village; however, a handful of inhabitants (about 40 in total, occupying 25 historic houses) do in fact work here. The town of Zaanse Schans is the perfect destination for that timeless Golden Age feel that you've been searching for throughout The Netherlands.

Tulip Candies

Most attractions in Zaanse Schans are open daily 10am-5pm in the summer, but only on weekends in the winter. Zaanse Schans is best suited to be a true one-day trip, but if you're just begging to stay, the VVV can direct you to the city's few accommodations.

Bloemendaal-aan-zee

221

Cheese Shop

Dutch Countryside

Say Cheese!

TRANSPORTATION & PRACTICAL INFORMATION

From **Amsterdam Centraal,** take the *stoptrein* heading to Alkmaar and get off at **Koog Zandijk** (20min, €2.25 one-way). From there, follow the signs to Zaanse Schans, a 12-minute walk across a bridge. The **VVV information center** is located at Schansend 1, in the former "Vrede" warehouse. (☎616 82 18; www.zaanseschans.nl. Open daily 8:30am-5pm; in summer 8:30am-5:30pm.)

SIGHTS

The best way to see picturesque Zaanse Schans is just to wander about the town, popping into whichever building that happens to interest you. The highlight of the attractions are inarguably the ◪**working windmills,** some of last remaining ones in the world. You can see the wheels inside grinding with their breeze-fueled power and then head up to the deck for a dramatic view of the town. Zaanse Schans houses eight windmills in all but only two regularly allow visitors. The lovely **De Kat Windmill,** Kalverringdijk 29, has been grinding plants into paint pigments since 1782. (☎621 04 77. Open Apr.-Oct. daily 9am-5pm; Nov.-Mar. Sa-Su 9am-5pm. €2, ages 6-12 €1, groups of 10 €1.50.) The **De Zoeker windmill,** Kalverringdijk 31, is the oldest oil mill in the world, restored to its current condition in 1978; it works by a deafening banging beam that will certainly catch your attention. (☎628 79 42. Open Mar.-Oct. daily 9:30am-4:30pm. €2.)

Other highlights include **Cheesefarm Catharina Hoeve,** Zeilenmakerspad 5, a replica of the original cheese farm which offers free bite-sized samples of its various homemade wares as well as a free tour of its workshop. (☎621 58 20. Open daily 8am-6pm. Free.) Watch craftsmen mold blocks of wood into attractive clogs at **Klompenmakerij de Zaanse Schans,** Kraaienest 4. (☎617 71 21. Open daily 8am-6pm.) Don't miss the charming display that unravels the mystery of the wooden shoe's prominence in Dutch history.

Discover the ubiquitous Albert Heijn supermarket craze right where it all started at the man's original old shop, now a museum aptly named the **Albert Heijn Museumwinkel,** Kalverringdijk 5. A grocery shop that opened in 1820, this quaint museums smells comfortingly of the past, with spices and dried meats that bring you back to the 19th century. (☎659 25 75. Open Mar.-Oct. daily 10am-1pm and 2-5pm; Nov.-Feb. Sa-Su 9am-1pm and 2pm-4pm. Free.) Next door you can stop by the **Museum van het Nederlandse**

Uurwerk (Museum of the Dutch Clock), Kalverringdijk 3, to sneak a peek at the oldest working pendulum clock in the world, as well as a number of other fascinating timepieces. (☎617 97 69. Open Apr.-Oct. 31 daily 10am-5pm. €2.30.) Other attractions include the pint-sized **Museum Het Noorderhuis,** Kalverringdijk 17, a restored home that features original costumes from the Zaan region in two reconstructed rooms. (☎617 32 37. Open Mar.-June and Sept.-Oct. Su, Tu-Sa 10am-5pm; July-Aug. daily 10am-5pm; Nov.-Feb. Sa-Su 10am-5pm. €1, seniors and children ages 4-11 €0.50.) At the **Hut van de Kapitein,** De Kwakels 2, boats are still repaired and built once a week; the rest of the time it's just a store selling nautical clothing and trinkets. (Open Mar.-Dec. daily 10am-5pm.) If travel by water is your thing, consider cruising around Zaanse Schans with **Rederij de Schans.** (☎614 67 62. Hourly departures Apr.-Sept. daily 11am-4pm. €5.)

NOORDWIJK-AAN-ZEE ☎071

Beautiful beaches can be found about an hour from Amsterdam and the Hague in the town of Noordwijk-aan-zee. While this stunning hamlet on the coast of Holland has always been a favorite resort for Dutch and German tourists, tourists from outside of Europe are only beginning to discover its wonders—visit before the town is overrun by traveling hordes. Outdoor activities abound, and visitors can ride horseback through dunes and woods, surf brisk sea-coast water, or toss frisbees on over 13km of sparkling white sand.

TRANSPORTATION

To get to Noordwijk, first take a train from **Centraal Station** to **Leiden** Centraal Station. Outside the station in Leiden is a terminal where you can catch **bus #57** to Noordwijk (last stop) for five strips or €3.40 (10min.). A better (but lesser known) bet is the Flying Pig summertime shuttle bus (€2) that leaves from their downtown hostel in Amsterdam at 7pm and from the Vondelpark hostel at 8pm. (☎071 36 22 533. Reservations required.) The bus will drop you off at the Flying Pig Beach hostel (see below). The return leaves from the hostel for Amsterdam at 7pm.

ORIENTATION & PRACTICAL INFORMATION

At the last stop, get off the bus; there you'll see the **VVV Noordwijk,** De Grent 8, where you can pick up a free map to the town. (☎361 93 21; www.vvvnoordwijk.nl. Open M-F 10am-6pm, Sa 9am-4pm, Su 10am-2pm.) The beach is just a four-minute walk away from the bus stop— Koningen Wilhemina Blvd. is the street that runs parallel to the beach along the center of town, while its adjacent neighbor is conveniently named Parallel Boulevard. Wilhemina turns inward and becomes De Grent at the police station on the beach while Koningin Astrid Boulevard continues along down the coast.

Noordwijk-aan-Zee is easily walkable; however renting a bike is an engaging way to take in the nearby dune trails or leave the sand-bound crowds behind. Bike, scooter, and roller-skate rentals are available at **J. Mooijekind,** Schoolstraat 68, starting at €6 a day. (☎361 28 26. Open daily 8:30am-6pm.)

ACCOMMODATIONS

▨ **Flying Pig Beach Hostel,** Parallel Blvd. 208 (☎362 25 33; fax 362 25 53; www.flyingpig.nl). From Leiden, take bus #40 or 42 for 20min. to "Vuurtorenplein," or Lighthouse Square; face south with the lighthouse to your right. The Pig is 100m on your left side. Located in the center of town, 2min. from the beach, the Beach Hostel is a rare find among budget accommodations, offering excellent service and clean, brightly decorated lodgings. A favorite with backpackers who want to meet other travelers in a fun, laid-back ambiance. Staff members prepare home-cooked meals for guests every Sa night (€6). A full range of activities is offered through the Pig for the more energetic guests. Kite Surfing Experience €20. Surfboard, in-line skates, bike rental available. Breakfast included with full kitchen facilities. Free Internet. Key deposit €10. Reception 9am-2am at bar. Open Mar.-Oct. 14-bed dorms €15, queen size bed in dorm (sleeps 2) €22.50; 7-bed dorm €19; 4-bed dorm €22.50; doubles €56, with bath €66. MC/V. ❶

StayOkay Sportherberg, Langevelderlaan 45 (☎0252 37 29 20; www.stayokay.com/noordwijk). Take bus #57 and walk 30min., following the signs to Sancta Maria. Or call a bus taxi for €1-2 (☎023 515 53 17). This clean, sizeable hostel lying deep in the dunes is especially geared towards groups, though the well-maintained facilities certainly cater toward individual travelers as well. Canoe, scooter, mountain bike, archery, and power kite rentals available only 15min. from the beach. Bring a towel as rentals are not available. Breakfast and linens included. Reception (and bar) 8am-midnight. Check-in before 6pm. Members €21.70; non-members €24.20. MC/V. ❶

Op Hoop van Zegen Camping, Westeinde 76 (☎025 237 54 91; http://members.lycos.nl/ophoopvanzegen). Quiet woodsy campsite with heated facilities 2.5km from the beach. Animals allowed. €4.50 per person, €2.25 per tent, €1.50 per caravan. ❶

FOOD

Hoofdstraat, a two-minute walk from the Flying Pig Beach Hostel, is lined with small shops and restaurants. The cafes and bars on **Koningin Wilhelmina Boulevard** offer terraces that overlook the North Sea.

🦑 **Chicoleo,** Koningin Wilhelmina Blvd. 7b (☎361 21 21; www.chicoleo.nl). This colorful Mexican restaurant and Argentinian steakhouse is a local favorite. Wicker furniture strewn outside and bright lights jazz up the interior. Stop in on the weekend and catch live music acts (F-Su 6pm) to add some spice to your salsa. Full vegetarian menu. Lunch €4-9; dinner €11-€21. Open daily noon-midnight or 1am; kitchen closes 11pm. AmEx/MC/V. ❹

Harbour Lights, Koningin Wilhelmina Blvd. 9 (☎361 77 05; www.harbourlights.nl). Swig a beer while playing a harrowing game of darts at this intimate seaside pub. The bar and grill attracts locals and tourists of all ages, most of whom rely on this locale to serve up a mean pint of Guinness (€4). Domestic beers (10 on tap and several more in bottles) will cost you slightly less. *Dagschotel* (daily special) €8. Dinners €10-14. Open daily noon-1am. ❷

Vivaldis, Koningin Wilhelmina Blvd. 17 (☎361 67 04). Stuff your toppling cone with Vivaldis's superb ice cream, available in 50 homemade flavors including hazelnut and pear. Cones €0.70-2.30. Open in summer daily noon-midnight. Cash only. ❶

Restaurant de Filosoof, de Grent 4 (☎364 90 03; www.defilosoof.nl), next to the VVV. Slightly expensive but satiating food in a cheerful, upscale setting. Inhale a *tostis* (€2.50), dip into the shrimp salad with mango and pineapple (€8.50), or sit down for the hearty Thai beef (€15). Menu changes often but tasty fare, topped off with rich desserts, is always guaranteed. Open daily 11am-2am; kitchen closes 10:30pm. AmEx/MC/V. ❹

OUTDOOR ACTIVITIES

Visitors come to Noordwijk for the beach, but they refuse to merely laze under the beating sun. The waves are perfect for surfing—boards, wetsuits, and all other equipment are always available for rent. One popular activity is **kite-surfing,** which is surfing on a board while attached to a kite that catches the wind high above you; lessons are mandatory for novices. **Beach Break,** Bomstraat 13, will cater to your water sporting needs. To reach this sand-ridden haven, walk from the beach at the police station, head down Hoofdstraat, and turn left onto Bomstraat. Surf lessons run two hours and cost €35; surfboard rental is €10 per hour; wetsuits €5 per hour. A beginning kite surfing class for four hours is €95, and rental of complete equipment is €40. They also sell bathing suits, sarongs, towels, and other beach goodies. (☎407 70 55; www.beachbreak.nl. Open Su-W, F-Sa 9:30am-6pm; Th 7am-9pm. MC/V.)

When you start to tire of the water, set out for the early morning or sunset **horseback rides** on the beach at **Barnhoeve,** Schoolstraat 71. (☎361 21 95. €25 for 2hr. Open 9-11am and 7-9pm.) The **Space Expo,** Keplerlaan 3, a permanent exhibition that attracts thousands of astronomy fanatics each year at the Visitors Center of the ESTEC, the largest branch of the European Space Agency. (☎364 64 89; www.space-expo.nl. Open Su, Tu-Sa 10am-5pm. €6.80, ages 4-12 €4.55.) Across from the VVV is **Mini Golf Huis ter Duin,** de Grent 3, whose competitive game the Dutch tactfully call Midget Golf. (☎361 88 59. Open in summer daily 10am-midnight; in winter Th 10am-midnight. €3, children €1.)

LEIDEN
☎ 071

Panorama

Home to one of the oldest and most prestigious universities in Europe, Leiden (pop. 117,000) brims with bookstores, flowing canals, windmills, gated gardens, antique churches, hidden walkways, and some truly outstanding museums. Approximately 40km southwest of Amsterdam, near the North Sea on the Rhine river, Leiden has historically been The Netherlands' primary textile producer and today stands as one of Europe's intellectual centers. Many of the city's buildings are even painted with famous excerpts from the writings of Shakespeare, Verlaine, and Basho. Home to Rembrandt's birthplace and the site of Europe's first tulips, The Netherlands' third-largest city offers visitors a picturesque gateway to flower country through a rewarding glance at Dutch history.

TRANSPORTATION

Van der Werfpark, Leiden

Trains haul into Leiden's slick, translucent Centraal Station from **Amsterdam** (35min.; every 30min. until 2:45am; €6.60, €11.70 round-trip) and **The Hague** (20min.; every 30min. until 3:15am; €4.20). Be careful as you're exiting the station: there are two exits, one down near platforms 1 and 2 leading toward the city center and the other heading only for the Museum Naturalis (see p. 228).

ORIENTATION & PRACTICAL INFORMATION

The city center lies southeast of Leiden Centraal and the most interesting sights are roughly enclosed within the **Morssingel** canal in the north, the **Witte Singel** in the west and south, and the **Herengracht** in the east. This core can be

Canal Houses, Leiden

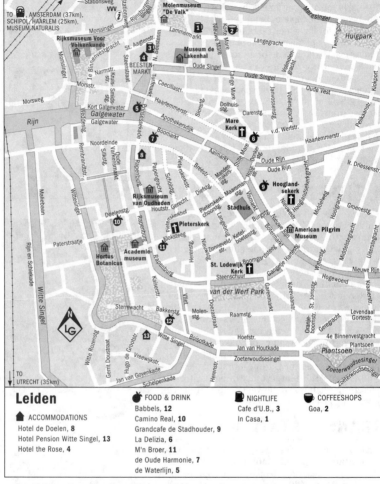

Leiden

🔺 **FOOD & DRINK**
Babbels, **12**
Camino Real, **10**
Grandcafe de Stadhouder, **9**
La Delizia, **6**
M'n Broer, **11**
de Oude Harmonie, **7**
de Waterlijn, **5**

🍺 **NIGHTLIFE**
Cafe d'U.B., **3**
In Casa, **1**

☕ **COFFEESHOPS**
Goa, **2**

🔺 **ACCOMMODATIONS**
Hotel de Doelen, **8**
Hotel Pension Witte Singel, **13**
Hotel the Rose, **4**

enjoyably explored in several hours and has no shortage of picturesque canals, spectacular sights, informative museums, and specialized restaurants. A crowded marketplace overtakes the banks of the Rhine every Wednesday and Saturday 7am-5pm, offering up antique goods and second-hand clothing. To get to the **VV**, Stationsweg 2d, walk (less than 5min.) from the train station's south exit towards the city center on Stationsweg. The center sells maps and walking tour brochures (€2-3) and can help find hotel rooms (€2.25 fee for one person, €1.75 for each additional person), though you can easily locate comfortable accommodations yourself. (☎090 02 22 23 33; www.leiden.nl. Open M 11am-5:20pm, Tu-F 10am-5:20pm, Sa 10am-4:30pm.)

ACCOMMODATIONS

Hotel Pension Witte Singel, Witte Singel 80 (☎512 45 92; wvandriel@pensione-ws.demon.nl). Head south on the street that changes from Turfmarkt to Kaiserstraat until it hits Witte Singel; the Hotel Pension Witte Singel is across the water right on your right. The owner of this hotel is friendly and the lobby area is neatly elegant. A series of well-appointed, immaculate rooms have an excellent view overlooking Leiden's gorgeous gardens and canals. Singles €31; doubles €46.50. ❷

Hotel de Doelen, Rapenburg 2 (☎ 512 05 27; fax 512 84 53; www.dedoelen.com). From the south exit of the station, take Steenstraat until you can turn left onto Morsstraat, then head right onto Prinsessekade. More centrally located and classier than the Hotel Pension Witte Singel, with slightly inflated prices. Stately reception with wall carvings, oriental carpets, and impressive sculptures. Satisfying breakfast €8 served in bright, elegant surroundings. Rooms sparkle with luxury and comfort; all rooms with shower, toilet, TV, and phone. Singles €70-90; doubles €90-120. AmEx/MC/V. ❸

Hotel the Rose, Beestenmarkt 14 (☎ 514 66 30). Take Steenstraat, turn left at Beesten-markt and continue 400m ahead past McDonald's. Located above a crowded, beaten-down cafe. Six surprisingly bright and spacious rooms, often overlooking a canal. Wicker furniture and rose-themed decorations lend an air of tranquility in Leiden's busiest square. Breakfast included. Shower and TV in every room, but hallway toilets are shared. Singles €60; doubles €80; triples €100; quads €120. Cash only. ❸

FOOD & DRINK

Leiden abounds with restaurants of all types, but for a quick bite on the go, stop by the **Super de Boer** supermarket, located opposite the train station at Stationsweg 40. (Open M-F 7am-9pm, Sa 9am-8pm, Su noon-7pm.)

de Oude Harmonie, Breestraat 16 (☎ 512 21 53), just off Rapenburg. Locals and students pack into this popular *eetcafe,* where candlelight and stained glass set the casual mood. Lunch features *broodjes* (under €3) and omelettes (€3.70-4.30). Dinner brings in interna-tional entrees at agreeable prices (€6-12.25); menu changes every 3 months. The place livens up immensely on weekends. Top floor opens Sa nights, with disco balls twirling and lights flashing over to hours of adolescent dancing; theme parties thrown once every 2 months for some added excitement. Lunch in winter 1-3pm; dinner 5-9pm. Open Su 3pm-1am, M-Th noon-1am, F-Sa noon-2am. Cafe opens daily in summer 3pm. Cash only. ❷

La Delizia, Lange Mare 112 (☎ 514 35 79). Follow Apothekersdijk east and keep right at the fork in the canal. A welcoming stopover where you can refuel with an all-day menu, extremely friendly service, and even friendlier prices. Bruschette €2.75-4.50. Soups €3.90-6.20. Sal-ads €5.50-7.50. Good-sized pizza, including the well-loved "Italia" (fresh tomatoes, ham, parmesan, and arugula) and filling pasta dishes €4-9.50. Restaurant doubles as an ice-cream parlor, serving creamy Italian gelato with a mouthwatering selection of sundaes (€5.50). Open M-Sa 1-10pm, Su 3:30-10pm. Cash only. ❶

de Waterlijn, Prinsessekade 5 (☎ 512 12 79). From the station, take Steenstraat south to Morsstraat, turn left, then head right onto Prinsessekade. Floating serenely atop a canal lies this bright, open cafe serving *tostis* (€2.10), sandwiches (€2.60) and the house specialty, the french kiss (baguette with melted brie and tomatoes; a measly €3.60). If weather per-mits, head out to de Waterlijn's wicker-chaired patio for an unobstructed view of the water-front. Cash only. ❶

Babbels, Boisotkade 1 (☎ 514 00 02), along the Witte Singel. University professors and stu-dents mingle here while relishing the exclusive delights of a world-class menu. Lovely patio seating right at the edge of the Witte Singel. Try the escargot appetizer (€6.20) or dip into a tastefully styled main dish (€12.50-26). 4 beers on draft (€1.75-3.30). Lunch served 10am-1pm; dinner 7-10pm. Open daily 10am-midnight. Cash only. ❸

Camino Real, Doelensteeg 8 (☎ 514 90 69), north of the Hortus Botanicus. The restaurant is a vibrant red and sky blue, adorned with mosaic tiles. Lunch dishes such as the *pain fez,* (Turkish bread stuffed with mincemeat), fall well within budget range at €4.75 and are served from a sleek, chrome bar. Dinner appetizers make for a light but delicious meal (sashimi salad €8.65; sushi platter €8). Heavier main courses €12.50-17.50. Many just drop in for a drink. Beer from €1.70 and cocktails €4.75-6.50. Open M-F 11am-2am, Sa noon-1am, Su 12:30-11:30pm. AmEx/MC/V. ❶/❷

Grandcafe de Stadthouder, Nieuwe Rijn 13 (☎514 92 75), is a delightful restaurant high-lighted by its floating patio on the canal out front. On ugly-weather days, the colorful indoor lounge, enhanced with sphere-shaped chandeliers, wooden ceiling beams, and modern wall art, beckons, especially warm and inviting. For lunch (11am-5pm) feast on sandwiches, *tostis,* omelettes, soup, or pancakes, almost all under €5. Dinner is pricier (3-course *tapas* menus from €10; full courses around €15) scrumptiously well-worth the extra pocket change. Open daily 11am-12:30am; kitchen closes 10pm. MC/V. ❹

M'n Broer, Kloksteeg 7 (☎512 50 24), just off Rapenburg, across from the Hortus Botani-cus. French-inspired, this dark dinner spot will delight you with its tantalizing flavors. Grab a vegetarian entree for €9.50, a daily fish specialty for €11, or a decadently rich dessert for under €4.50. Menu changes often but consistent favorites are the delicious rack of lamb (€19.25) and duck breast *à l'orange* (€15.20). Open daily 5pm-midnight. MC/V. ❸

SIGHTS

Leiden is haven for museum-goers, with three collections that are must-sees. Make sure you have a Museumjaarkaart (MJK) to get into them for free (see p. 80).

▓ MUSEUM NATURALIS

◪ *Darwinweg. From the northern exit of Leiden Centraal, near platform 9, follow the yellow webbed feet that will lead you right to the museum. Otherwise, go between the blue and yellow Leiden University Medical Center and the new-age parking complex on the right. Follow the signs to "Naturalis." ☎568 76 00; www.naturalis.nl. Open Sept.-June Su, Tu-Sa 10am-6pm; July-Aug. daily 10am-6pm. €8, ages 4-12, €4.50.*

Museum Naturalis brings natural history to life through spacious, modern, and visu-ally exciting displays that explore the history of the earth and its many various inhabitants. With eye-candy exhibitions of animals, plants, minerals, rocks, and fos-sils—all brilliantly explained with English and Dutch panels—this is an absolute must-see for nature-lovers. Even those who don't normally enjoy museums will appreciate the awe-inspiring wealth of colors and shapes, improved only by the sci-entific and anthropological tales designed to appeal to audiences of all ages. New exhibitions occur every year; 2004 is designated to be a "Journey into the Beating Heart." Free guided tours, children's exhibits, and a domed theater make this museum an exhilarating experience for the whole family.

RIJKSMUSEUM VOOR VOLKENKUNDE (NATIONAL MUSEUM OF ETHNOLOGY)

◪ *Steenstraat 1, just over the canal from the VVV. ☎516 88 00; www.rmv.nl. Open Su, Tu-Sa 10am-5pm. €6.50, ages 4-12 €3.50.*

Displaying ethnic treasures brought back by Dutch explorers and academics since 1837, this anthropological museum displays Inca sculptures, Chinese paintings, Afri-can bronzes and Indonesian artifacts. Totems and togs, swords and statues, and masks and *mukluks* overflow in the regal, grandiose complex. Recent renovations lend technological sophistication to the exhibits; interactive touch screens offer explanations in English as well as Dutch, and guides give illuminating presentations on the international collection. Impromptu play acts and modern interpretations of ethnology on display in the luscious museum gardens provide additional intrigue.

RIJKSMUSEUM VAN OUDHEDEN (NATIONAL MUSEUM OF ANTIQUITIES)

◪ *Rapenburg 28. ☎516 31 63. Open Tu-F 10am-5pm, Sa-Su noon-5pm. €6, ages 6-18 €5.50.*

This branch of the Rijksmuseum proudly harbors the restored Egyptian Temple of Taffeh, a gift to the Dutch that was removed from the reservoir basin of the Aswan Dam when it overflowed. The fascinating collection features mummies and sarcophagi from North Africa and Europe but also includes outstanding Dutch artifacts from the Roman Empire, though the medieval exhibit is a bit less stimulating. The **Nationaal Penningkabinet,** The Netherlands' National Coin Cabinet, is included in admission. The cabinet unveils several old, new, odd, and unreleased Dutch coins. Free English pocket guide available for Dutch-impaired visitors.

OTHER MUSEUMS

Tear yourself away from the three museums listed above to visit Leiden's smaller collections, which certainly merit a peek. Scale steep staircases to inspect the innards of a functioning windmill from 1743 at the ⬛**Molenmuseum "De Valk,"** 2e Binnenvestgracht 1. The living quarters of the mill's ground floor have been preserved

North Sea Jazz Festival, Scheveningen

from their last habitation, with paintings and photographs displayed to depict the life of a 19th-century miller. Video presentations and wall panels explain the technology, history, and craftmanship of a windmill, while broad windows overlook the city's green expanses. (☎516 53 53. Open Tu-Sa 10am-5pm, Su 1-5pm. €2.50.)

The **Museum De Lakenhal,** Oude Singel 28-32, reveals masterpieces by Rembrandt, van Leyden, and Jan Steen in finely styled surroundings. Experience the art and history of Leiden from the Middle Ages to the present, with ancient pieces and ever-changing contemporary exhibits displayed in Dutch and English. Through collections of tiles, tin, glass, and silver, the museum details the city's important 700-year textile industry. (☎516 53 60. Open Tu-F 10am-5pm, Sa-Su noon-5pm. €4, under 18 free.) After the Pil-

Mauritshuis, The Hague

grims departed from England, they found refuge in Leiden and a handful of other Dutch towns before setting off for a tumultuous journey to America. Relive this period (1609-1620) at the small but rich **American Pilgrim Museum,** Beschuitsteeg 9, that is housed in two rooms of Leiden's oldest house, built in 1371. The sign for entrance is rather miniscule, so try not to slip by unknowingly. (☎512 24 13. Open W-Sa 1-5pm. Guided tour €2.)

OTHER SIGHTS

Leiden's appeal extends beyond its museums: the city is awash with lovely canals strewn with covered bridges, stately mansions, 35 almshouses, and stretches of parks. Inarguably the most impressive of Leiden's natural havens, **Hortus Botanicus,** Rapenburg 73, doubles as the University of Leiden's botanic gardens, which offer a showering of greenery with over 400 years of

Knight's Hall, The Hague

229

plant life cultivated on the grounds and in the greenhouses for the enjoyment of visitors. The oldest botanical garden in The Netherlands, it was opened in 1587 as a center for medical research and botanical instruction, allowing Carolus Clusius to plant Western Europe's first tulips in his research with Turkish medicinal plants. An unmissible highlight is the **Clusius Garden** (open M-F), a wonderful reconstruction of his verdant 1594 workshop that showcases tube plants and rare 200-year-old trees. Be sure to stop into the tropical greenhouses as well, which primarily feature first-class plant collections from Asia. Its grassy knolls alongside the delightful **Witte Singel** canal make Hortus Botanicus an ideal picnic spot to round off a perfectly easy afternoon. (☎527 72 49; www.hortusleiden.nl. Guided tours available by appointment. Open Apr.-Oct. daily 10am-6pm; Nov.-Apr. Su-F 10am-4pm. €4, children 4-12 €2.) The Hortus shares a gate with the **Academy Building,** the University of Leiden's main hall whose Vaulted Chamber celebrates local academia through displayed gowns, medals, and inscriptions. (☎527 72 42. Open M-Th 1-5pm, by appointment only except on W. Free.)

While in the area, be sure to take in the newly renovated **Pieterskerk,** Kloksteeg 16, the 500-year-old Gothic church that is now home to the graves of both Dutch painter Jan Steen and renowned pilgrim pastor John Robinson. Founded in 1121 by the Count of Holland, it is dedicated to St. Peter, whose keys to the gate of Heaven appear in Leiden's ubiquitous coat of arms. (☎512 43 19; www.pieterskerk.com. Open daily 1:30-4pm. Free.) When facing the church, look over to your left to see the red-and-white patterned shutters of Leiden's many university buildings. From the church, backtrack toward Hortus and turn left on Rapenburg, following the curve of the canal for a few blocks. The welcoming, lush **van der Werfpark** will be on your right as you walk—this soft, green space, with a small cafe at its northwestern edge, was the site of a gunpowder storage facility that exploded in 1807 and destroyed the surrounding city blocks. Miraculously, **St. Lodewijk Kerk,** located across the canal from the eastern side of the park, survived almost entirely unscathed. Today the park emanates serenity; its weeping willows droop amongst languid afternoon nappers and canal-side readers.

NIGHTLIFE & COFFEESHOPS

The city is undoubtedly a university town, but most students hit up the bars and discos only after they've had their share of private fraternity events. If you're looking to bar- or club-hop, head to the upper stretch of **Nieuwe Beestenmarkt,** just south of the formidable windmill, which is packed with bustling bars, clubs, and coffeeshops.

🔲 **In Casa,** Lammermarkt 100 (☎514 49 79). From Leiden Centraal, take Steenstraat to 2e Binnenvestgracht, turn left and then right on Lammermarkt; the late-night bender is on your left. In Casa is Leiden's self-appointed *studentendiscotheek,* with raucous dance parties lasting long into Th-Su nights. Get your groove on with the student-heavy crowd, and shake to the likes of mainstream hip-hop, salsa, and 70s disco. Open Th 10pm-3:30am, F 11pm-3:30am, Sa 10pm-4am, Su 8pm-midnight. Cover €10-15.

Cafe d'U.B., Nieuwe Beestenmarkt 4 (☎512 04 55). Take Steenstraat south, turn left at 2e Binnenvestgracht, and continue around the corner. A trusty pregame spot with €1.50 beer, €4.50 mixed drinks, and a projection screen for your die-hard football needs. Skip the dancing during the week, but F-Sa nights really move with 20-somethings partying hard to R&B, rock, and house music. Open Su-Th 2pm-1am, F-Sa 2pm-2am (with the party lasting until 4-5am behind closed doors). Cash only.

Goa, Korte Mare 8 (☎522 64 76). Take Steenstraat south and turn left at Beestenmarkt, following Oude Singel a few blocks to Korte Mare. An elegant coffeeshop adorned with reminders of India, from a widespread landscape on the walls to compact sculptures lining the windowsill. With a pool table, and beautiful antique tables and chairs, it's a smoker's refuge of style and cleanliness. Primera (Moroccan hash) €9 per g; Haze weed €7.50 per g; pre-rolled joints €3.50. Open daily 4pm-10pm.

THE HAGUE (DEN HAAG) ☎070

Since The Hague—whose official name is actually "'s-Gravenhage," or "Count's Domain"—wasn't granted municipal rights until 1806, it was perfectly situated to become the neutral seat of political power in The Netherlands. In 1248 Willem II moved his royal residence to Den Haag, and when Prince Maurits transferred his court to the Stadhouder's residence on the Binnenhof (see p. 235) in 1585, the city (current pop. 800,000) became the permanent home of the royal House of Orange. These days all of The Netherlands' important governmental institutions find their homes in The Hague: Queen Beatrix's royal residence off Noordeinde, the Dutch government in the Binnenhof and the International Court of Justice at the Vredespaleis (see p. 234). With all its international lawyers, elected officials, embassies, and imposing government buildings, The Hague might seem a bit stiff in the collar. And while some of the city's monuments will appeal primarily to those with a particular interest in politics and international affairs, The Hague has much more to offer. World-class art museums, a lively (if a bit confused) city center, high-class shopping, more parks per square meter than almost any other Dutch city and one of the world's biggest jazz festivals, make The Netherlands' political capital anything but boring. And if you need a break from sightseeing, The Hague's carefree neighbor on the North Sea, Scheveningen (see p. 237), is a tram ride away.

Bredius Collection, The Hague

TRANSPORTATION

Trains roll in from **Amsterdam Centraal** (50min., 1-6 per hr., €8.50) and **Rotterdam Centraal** (30min., 1-6 per hr., €3.60) to both of The Hague's major stations, **Centraal Station** and **Holland Spoor**. Centraal Station is right on the eastern edge of The Hague's downtown; Holland Spoor is a 10min. walk south of the city center, but is convenient to the StayOkay hostel. Trams #1, 9, 12, and 15 connect the two stations.

Peace Palace, The Hague

PRACTICAL INFORMATION

The Hague's central **VVV tourist office,** Kon. Julianapl. 30, is just outside the northern entrance to Centraal Station, next to the Hotel Sofitel. Staffers book rooms for a €5 fee and sell highly detailed maps of the city center (€2); an interac-

Gemeentemuseum, The Hague

The Hague

ACCOMMODATIONS
Hotel 't Centrum, 2
StayOkay Hostel, 10

FOOD & DRINK
Bamboe, 11
Cafe de Bok, 4
Cafe de Oude Mol/
   Tapaskeuken Sally, 3
Giuliano's, 7
Havana, 6
Make Your Own, 9

NIGHTLIFE
O'Casey's Bar, 1
De Paap, 5
De Pater, 8

(Map of The Hague with streets including Kortenaerkade, Hogewal, Mauritskade, Willemstr., Noordeinde, Paleistuin, Palais Nooreinde, Lange Voorhout, Lange Vijverberg, Hofvijver, Hofvijver, Haags Historisch Museum, Mauritshuis, Grote Kerk, Gevangenpoort, Binnenhof, Ridderzaal, 1E Kamer, 2E Kamer, Lange Poten, Stadhuis, Theater aan het Spui, Malieveld, Centraal Station, VVV. Directions to Scheveningen (2km), Madurodam (4km), Gemeentemuseum (1.5km), GEM/Fotomuseum (1.5km), Vredespaleis (.5km), Holland-Spoor Station (600m). Scale 200 yards / 200 meters.)

tive hotel booking computer (€0.45 per min.) is available 24hr. if you arrive after the VVV closes. (☎0900 340 35 05; www.denhaag.com. Open M, Sa 10am-5pm; Tu-F 9am-5:30pm; June-Sept. Su 11am-3pm.) For comprehensive listings of The Hague's full array of cultural events, pick up a copy of the monthly publication *Den Haag Agenda*, which also has extensive restaurant and shop listings for the city; the magazine is available for free at the VVV office. Also helpful is the **Uitpost Haaglanden** (☎363 38 33; www.uitpost.nl; open M-F 9am-5pm), which offers some information about cultural events in the area and publishes the free and very thorough monthly *Uitpost* magazine. The cheapest option for **Internet access** is **O₂**, Grote Marktstraat 51. (€3 for 1 hr., €5 for 2hr. Open M-W, F-Sa 10am-6pm; Th 10am-9pm; Su noon-6pm.) The **post office**, Kerkplein 6, is right next to Grote Kerk. (Open M 11am-5pm, Tu-Sa 9am-5pm.) While you might be able to rent one of the **bikes** available at HS or Centraal Station (€4), your best bet for two-wheel transport is **Du Nord Rijwielen,** in nearby Scheveningen (see p. 238). For information about cycling in The Hague, check www.citycycleevents.nl.

The Hague has a few special yearly events. The popular **North Sea Jazz Festival** brings some of the biggest names in jazz and blues to the area for three whole days in July (see www.northseajazz.nl for more information). On the third Tuesday in September of every year, The Netherlands' Queen Beatrix makes her annual address from the throne of the regal Knight's Hall, located in the Binnenhof (see p. 235); this marks the **Opening of the Parliamentary Year.** Even if you're not a visiting dignitary in town on business, you'll be able to catch a glimpse of the Royal Family's Golden Coach riding through town.

ACCOMMODATIONS

Let's Go does not recommend staying in one of the budget hotels lining Stationsweg, as they are unfriendly and overpriced. Instead try:

■ **StayOkay City Hostel Den Haag,** Scheepmaker-straat 27 (☎315 78 88; www.stayokay.com/den-haag). Turn right from Holland Spoor, follow the tram tracks, turn right at the big intersection, and Scheep-makerstraat is 3min. ahead, on your right. From Centraal Station, take tram #1 (dir: Delft), 9 (dir: Vrederust), or 12 (dir: Duindorp) to Rijswijkseplein (2 strips); cross to the left in front of the tram, cross the big intersection, and Scheepmakerstraat is straight ahead. One of the best StayOkay hostels in The Netherlands, the City Hostel in The Hague has huge, spacious, sparkling rooms with private baths, a helpful staff, and lots of space to lounge around. Best of all, the downstairs in-house restaurant, **Brasserie Backpackers,** has excellent and healthy dinner meals—like *salade nicoise*—for only €6.60. Buffet breakfast and sheets included. Locker rental €2 for 24hr. Internet €5 per hr. Reception daily 7:30am-10:30pm. 4- to 8-person dorms €24.80; singles €41-43; doubles €61-66; triples €75-83; quads €95-106. €2.50 discount for HI members. Brasserie open daily until 1am. Special night key-card required to stay out later than 1am. MC/V. ❶

Hotel 't Centrum, Veenkade 5-6 (☎346 36 57), right by Paleistuin. Take tram #3. This old but clean hotel is a comfortable place to stay in a quiet corner of The Hague. An easy walk to the city center. Includes breakfast in a pleasant downstairs dining area. Single €40, with bath €65; doubles with bath €75; triples €90; quads €98. AmEx/MC/V. ❷

FOOD & DRINK

The best restaurants in The Hague cluster in the neighborhood of the Grote Kerk; try **Lange** and **Korte Poten,** two streets that run behind the Binnenhof, for takeout joints where you can grab a quick falafel, shawarma, or doner kebab. For more upscale (and expensive) dining, head over to the canals to the north of the city center, along **Hooikade** and **Hooigracht.**

■ **Cafe de Oude Mol,** Oude Molstraat 61 (☎345 16 23). Tram #3 to Grote Halstraat, walk through the pavilion to your right, where you'll hit Oude Molstraat; follow this street for 2 blocks; the restaurant will be on the right. Decorated with colorful Mexican oil-cloth, bric-a-brac paintings, a rococo beer pump, and lavender ceilings, Cafe de Oude Mol is a tiny bar has an excellent upstairs restaurant, **Tapaskeuken Sally,** which is undoubtedly The Hague's best-kept dining

Palestuin Park, The Hague

Grote Kerk, The Hague

Delftware Workshop

secret. Here you'll find delicious *tapas* from €3-5 per dish, accompanied on M by live rock, Cajun, and world music. Restaurant open W-Sa 5:30-10:30pm. Bar open Su-W 5pm-1am, Th until 1:30am, F-Sa until 2am. Cash only. ❷

Giuliano's, Schoolstraat 13a (☎345 52 15), just south of the Grote Kerk. Honest-to-goodness authentic Italian food in an intimate, candlelit dining room. Prices are unbeatable, with almost every pasta dish €9-11. *Tortellone alla verdura* €10. Spaghetti *alla carbonara* €9. Salads like *insalata* salmon are equally well-priced at around €9. Open daily 5-11pm, F-Su also open for lunch noon-3pm. AmEx/MC/V. ❷

Cafe de Bok, Papestraat 36 (☎364 21 62). This charming, country-garden style restaurant prides itself on its extensive international menu—with "a wink to English cuisine." Dishes like vegetarian quiche (€9) and French onion soup (€5) are good non-meat options, while sausage with eggs and chips (€6) and lasagna (€11.50) are heartier options. Join the friendly locals for a half-pint at the bar. British, Irish, Scottish, and Dutch beers around €2.25. Brilliant Su breakfast €9.50. Open Su noon-5pm, Tu-F 12:30pm-2:30pm and 5:30-10pm, Sa 1-10pm. MC/V. ❶/❷

Bamboe, Zuidwal 8a (☎427 86 71). Take tram #16 or 17 to Spui. Cross the street and walk along the canal on Bierkade, which turns into Zuidwal after 2 blocks. Small neighborhood restaurant and bar with a large selection of Indonesian cuisine. Canal-side setting and boat-terrace are charming, but be careful late at night—one street over is The Hague's slightly unsavory red-light district. Starters €2-4. Main courses €6-12. Indonesian *rijstaffel* €16-20 per person. Open daily noon-1am; kitchen open 5-10pm. ❸

Make Your Own, Plein 3 (☎360 44 18; www.myo.nl), is an independently owned salad-bar and do-it-yourself sandwich counter packed with fresh ingredients like spicy chicken salad, pesto, artichokes, feta, roasted pine-nuts, and all kinds of vegetables. Salads €3.75 for a small, €5 for a large. Sandwiches €2.90 small, €3.90 large. Make your own juice €2-3.50. Soups from €2.40. Open M-F 8am-7pm, Sa 9am-5pm. Cash only. ❶

Havana, Buitenhof 19 (☎356 29 00). Take tram #3 or 10 to Buitenhof. Large bar and restaurant specializing in Cuban cuisine is not always budget ("Che's ribs" €13.50)—but the beautiful outside terrace on the Buitenhof is a place to see and be seen. Havana burger €8.50. Seared tuna steak €12.50. Cocktails like tequila sunrise, margaritas, and piña coladas all €4.50. Open daily 10:30am-1am. ❸

SIGHTS

With its 800 years of Dutch political history and its current status as the world's focal point for international law, The Hague teems with countless sightseeing prospects for government buffs.

▣ PEACE PALACE (HET VREDESPALEIS)

🚩 *Carnegieplein 2. Take tram #17, dir. Statenkwartier, for 3min. Or, take tram #8, dir. Scheveningen, to stop: Vredespaleis. ☎302 42 42, for guided tours 302 41 37; www.vredespaleis.nl. Tours M-F 10, 11am, 2, and 3pm. Book in advance. No tours when the court is in session. Admission €3.50, children under 13 €2.30. Cash only.*

The opulent home of the International Court of Justice and the Permanent Court of Arbitration was donated by Andrew Carnegie in 1913. It has served as the site of international arbitrations, peace-treaty negotiations, and war crimes trials since then, the most notorious of which has been the prosecution of Slobodan Milosevic's "ethnic cleansing" of Albanians—at press time, the trial was still ongoing. The tour focuses more on the building's objects (donated from each country participating) and artwork than the workings of the courts, but the items are magnificent, and the tour is the only option for visitors who want to get past the gates. The building is surrounded by impeccably-kept grounds and gardens that are closed to the public, but if you are interested in further acquaintance with the court's work, you can apply to study at the summer Hague Academy of International Law (www.hagueacademy.nl).

MAURITSHUIS

🔲 *Korte Vijverberg 8, just outside the northern entrance of the Binnenhof. Take tram #1, 3, 7, 8, 9, 10, 12, or 16; bus #4 or 22 from Centraal Station. ☎ 302 34 35; www.mauritshuis.nl. Open Tu-Sa 10am-5pm, Su 11am-5pm. Audio tour €2.50. €7, seniors €3.50, under 18 and Museumjaar-kaart free. Entrance to the Picture Gallery of Prince Willem V free with ticket to Mauritshuis.*

One of the most beautiful smaller-sized museums anywhere, the Mauritshuis, originally constructed in 1644 and rebuilt by Jacob van Campen in 1822 in the Dutch Neo-classical style, has a near-perfect collection of Dutch Golden Age art. Museums the world over often have some amount of filler; Mauritshuis only has masterpieces. Nothing but gems line the walls of Prince Johan Maurit's former private residence, and each merits individual attention. Not counting the precious selection of paintings by Rubens, Van Ruisdael, Jan Steen, Hans Holbein, and Judith Leyster, the museum has in its possession several excellent Rembrandts, including one of his last self-portraits and his famous *The Anatomy Lesson of Dr. Tulp*. The showstopping pieces are without hesitation two absolutely gorgeous paintings by Vermeer: the *Girl with a Pearl Earring*, and *View of Delft*, the latter of which is one of the lushest and most stunning depictions of light in landscape ever painted.

BINNENHOF & RIDDERZAAL

🔲 *Binnenhof 8a. The most central point in the city, accessible by trams #1, 2, 3, 6, 7, 8, 9, and 17. ☎ 364 61 44; www.eerstekamer.nl; www.tweedekamer.nl. Open M-Sa 10am-4pm; last tour leaves 3:45pm. Parliament is often in session Tu-Th. Entrance to courtyard free; tours €5; seniors and children €4.30. Cash only.*

Beside the Hofvijver reflecting pool, lies the "home of Dutch democracy," the Binnenhof Parliament building; Binnenhof means "inner courtyard." Built in the 13th century as a hunting lodge for Count Floris IV, it has a long history as home to many of The Netherlands' most prominent historical figures. Show up at **Binnenhof 8a** (tucked behind Ridderzaal, in the center of the courtyard) for a guided tour, which covers both Ridderzaal (Hall of Knights) and the Second Chamber of the States General, The Netherlands' main legislative body. The latter, in a new wing designed in 1992, is in modern shades of blue and green and is somewhat less impressive than the historic Ridderzaal. Because Dutch democracy needs its quiet, tours don't run when Parliament is in session, but if you show up early you can sit in on the proceedings. The tour is in Dutch, though an English translation is provided on paper. If you're not interested in learning about the Dutch political system, skip the tour and just wander around the courtyard, one of The Hague's most photogenic sights.

GEMEENTEMUSEUM

🔲 *Stadhouderslaan 41. From Holland Spoor, take tram #10; from Centraal Station or hop on bus #4; both stop in front of the museum complex. ☎ 338 11 11; www.gemeentemuseum.nl. Open Tu-Su 11am-5pm. €7.50, seniors €5; free with Museumjaarkaart.*

The best reason to visit is for the museum's collection (the world's largest) of paintings by Mondrian. The Gemeentemuseum has a remarkably complete assortment of the De Stijl painter's work, whose development you can trace in his move from symbolic figuration to completely abstract "neo-Plasticity." A highlight of his oeuvre, the eye-popping "Victory Boogie Woogie," finished with paint and colored tape, was recently acquired by the museum. H.P. Berlage's building is a bit awkward as an exhibition space—its red, yellow, and blue tile-work and built-in benches make the museum feel uncomfortably like an Art Deco bath-house. In any case, it would be a shame not to glance at the other highlights of the collection, which include a room of decent paintings by Francis Bacon and a small selection of works by American minimalists like Sol LeWitt and Donald Judd. Much of the museum is devoted to regional art (especially New Hague School), which are sometimes interesting but often derivative. The Schatkamers (treasure room) downstairs is a mishmash of 20th-century work by Redon, Picasso, and lesser-known artists.

GEM/FOTOMUSEUM

🔲 *Stadhouderslaan 43, to the left of the Gemeentemuseum in the far wing of the same building. Gem: ☎ 338 11 33; www.gem-online.nl. Fotomuseum: ☎ 338 11 44; www.fotomuseumdenhaag.nl. Open Tu-Su 2-10pm. €5, students and seniors €3, under 18 and Museumjaarkaart free. For film screenings, events, and parties check the website or call ahead in advance.*

If you've made all the way to the Gemeentemuseum, it would be a mistake not to stop in at the museum's younger next-door neighbors, two of the hottest and most engaging contemporary art spaces in all of The Netherlands. The Fotomuseum is one of the best places to go for creative photography, from images by Edward S. Curtis to in-your-face commercial work. The Gem Museum of Contemporary Art (the name is pronounced "KHEM," a word-play on its older neighbor) holds outstanding rotating exhibitions on contemporary sculpture, video, photography, and painting by artists that you've probably never heard of. Still, you'll be glad you got a chance to see them here first. Gem hosts the annual "Prix de Rome," which goes out to the most innovative young Dutch or European artists exploring issues in sculpture and public space.

MADURODAM

🔲 *George Maduroplein 1. Take tram #1 or 9, dir: Scheveningen, to Madurodam. Or, bus #10, or 20 to Dr. A. Jacobsweg stop. ☎ 416 24 00; www.madurodam.nl. Open Sept.-Feb. daily 9am-6pm; Mar.-June 9am-8pm; July-Aug. 9am-10pm. Ticket office open until 1hr. before closing. €11, seniors €10, children 4-11 €8, under 3 free. Includes free guide booklet.*

Think of it as Holland-in-a-box. It's surprising just how much time you can spend wandering among the detailed miniature recreations (scale 1:25) of almost all of The Netherlands; working trains, boats, drawbridges, windmills, ferries, and even waterskiers are in constant motion throughout Madurodam's insanely miniaturized expanse. You'll lord over picturesque models of Utrecht's Dom Tower, the Binnenhof in The Hague, and Dam Square in Amsterdam—which are most enjoyable if you've already been to the real thing. But for the sake of judiciousness, the park's designers have included a host of decidedly non-scenic monuments including a concrete mixing plant, an insurance company, and a power station in Nijmegen.

OTHER SIGHTS

It's too bad that the 15th-century **Grote Kerk,** on Kerkplein, isn't open more regularly. Nevertheless, it's still one of the Hague's most impressive sights from the outside, even if it now has to tower over the myriad department stores that play at its feet. (☎ 302 86 30. Only open during public events; check entrance or call for information.) Across the street from Mauritshuis, **Haags Historisch Museum,** Korte Vijverberg 7, is less a collection of artifacts than an exploration of history through paintings. Worthwhile exhibits cover one of the country's most famous rulers, William III of Orange, in addition to other topics. (☎ 364 69 40; www.haagshistorischmuseum.nl. Open Tu-F 11am-5pm, Sa-Su noon-5pm. €3.60, seniors €3.20, under 18 free.)

NIGHTLIFE

The Hague's laid-back sophistication means less clubs and more bar-cafes; the best place to find then are around the **Grote Kerk** area, with a few old-style international Brown Cafes along **Oude Molstraat** and a whole group of more boisterous and excellent bars with outdoor terraces on the **Grote Markt,** just south of the church.

🎸 **De Paap,** Papestraat 32 (☎ 365 20 02; www.depaap.nl). The hottest rock cafe in town; stylish 20-somethings come for the almost nightly jazz, punk, funk, and occasional hip-hop acts. Best of all, there's never any cover. Music most nights 10pm-1am, Sept.-June Tu-Th, and Su. Bar open in summer Tu-Th 7pm-3am, F 4pm-5am, Sa 7pm-5am; in winter also open Su 7pm-1am. Beer €2. Cash only.

De Pater (The Priest), Achterom 8 (☎345 08 52), is pious in name only. The beer's pricey at over €2, but it's still one of The Hague's best music bars. De Pater features international sets including salsa, Latin beats, and jazz for a young, lively crowd. Shows start 10:30pm; call ahead for schedules. Open Tu-Sa 10pm-2am, Su 5pm-2am. MC/V.

O'Casey's Bar, Noordeinde 140 (☎363 06 98; www.ocaseys.net). The best pint of Guinness in The Hague (€4). O'Casey's *biergarten* is regally situated just behind the back wall of the Dutch Queen's palace. Pub food like ham and cheese rolls (€3.80) and salads (€6.90). Irish drinking songs on the stereo. Open M-Th noon-1am, F-Sa noon-2am; kitchen closes at 8pm. MC/V.

ENTERTAINMENT

Theater aan het Spui, Spui 187 (ticket office ☎880 03 33, main office 880 03 00; www.theateraan-hetspui.nl). Take tram #16 or 17 to Spui. Experimental theater, opera, jazz and blues, world-class classical ensembles, indie music, and modern dance all find a home at the Spui Theater, with its funky stage design and overall hip approach to entertainment. Though some plays are in Dutch, there are regular concerts featuring the latest cutting-edge sound. Closed late June-Aug.; check website for latest offerings. Pick up a free schedule of events at the box office or the VVV. Ticket office open noon-6pm.

North Sea Jazz Festival (www.northseajazz.nl). Brings the absolute best names in jazz to Scheveningen by the sea for 3 days in mid-July every year, featuring acts as diverse as Herbie Hancock, Wynton Marsalis, Shirley Horn, Tony Bennett, and Van Morrison. Tickets available online. Day passes €50, 3-day passes €135. MC/V.

Parkpop (☎523 90 64; www.parkpop.nl). Hosts what The Netherlands hails as the largest free public pop concert in the world. Held on 3 big stages in the Zuiderpark during late June every year. Past acts include Dandy Warhols, Suzanne Vega, and the Bloodhound Gang.

NEAR THE HAGUE

SCHEVENINGEN

Pronounced "SHKHEvenikher," this beach town directly due north of The Hague is a popular summer vacation spot for the Dutch, and a sort of carefree, libertine antidote to The Hague's cultivated seriousness. Running right along the coast of the North Sea, Scheveningen's main drag, the Strandweg, is a long strip of shoreline packed end to end with hopping bars and night-

NO WORK ALL PLAY

swing by the sea

Northern European countries have long been havens for jazz lovers and musicians, but nothing matches up with the tremendous, three-day ⬛North Sea Jazz Festival (☎015 215 77 56; www.northseajazz.nl), held every July in Scheveningen on the sea, just north of The Hague. This world-class venue for bebop, swing, latin, blues, and fusion attracts the biggest names in music, from Tony Bennet to Chick Corea, Shirley Horn to Kenny Garrett, Cassandra Wilson to Wynton Marsalis. While it might be a once-in-a-lifetime opportunity to hear so much talent in such a short time, it will deal a blow to your pocket book: a day-pass, which allows you to walk in and out of almost every concert across the span of about ten hours, will set you back about €50-60, depending on how far in advance you buy. A three day ticket costs €135, but beware: to get seats to some of the bigger-name acts, you may have to shell out another €15 per concert. Get tickets at the post office, the VVV, or various record shops in The Hague. In Amsterdam, FAME Music, Kalverstraat 2-4 (☎020 638 25 25), has tickets usually up until the week before the festival. You can also order direct from the festival by telephone at ☎010 591 90 00 (M-F 8am-10pm, Sa-Su 10am-8pm; credit card orders only).

clubs. On most sunny summer days, the beaches are packed with all manner of little kids, tourists, locals, beach bums, and sunbathers, while the nightlife, focused around cafes, runs almost year-round.

TRANSPORTATION & PRACTICAL INFORMATION

Trams #1 and 8 make the trek to Scheveningen from The Hague. The Scheveningen branch of the **VVV**, Gevers Deynootweg 1134, has info on rooms. (☎ 09 00 340 35 05, €0.40 per min. Open M 10am-5:30pm, Tu-F 9am-5:30pm, Sa 10am-5pm; Apr.-Sept. also Su 1-5pm; July-Aug. F 9am-7:30pm.) Well-marked paths provide a great hike or **bike ride** (rent from Holland Spoor or Centraal Station, less than €4 per day), which you can then extend into a shoreline cycle trek. For bicycle rental, your best bet is **Du Nord Rijwielen**, Keizerstraat 27-29, in Scheveningen just off the strand, to the West of Gevers Deynootweg. (☎/fax 355 40 60. Rentals from €6 per day, €30 per week. Open Apr.-Oct. M-F 9am-5pm, Sa-Su 10am-5pm; Oct.-Apr. closed M.)

ACCOMMODATIONS

Accommodations in a beach resort like Scheveningen don't come cheap, but there are some noteworthy exceptions. You can also try **Gevers Deynootweg,** where most hotels are located.

Hotel Hage, Seinpostduin 22-23 (☎ 351 46 96; fax 358 58 51). Tram #8 to Gevers Deynootweg, cross the street toward the sea and Seinpostduin is just ahead on your left. Located in a comfortable old wooden house just a hop from the beach. All rooms with toilet and shower. Singles €49; doubles €88; triples €110. AmEx/MC/V. ❸

Hotel Scheveningen, Gevers Deynootweg 2 (☎/fax 354 70 03; www.scheveningen.da.ru). Buzz in at the front door and wait for the owner to come meet you. This worn-in hotel has definitely seen better days, but if you don't mind a little dust and disrepair, this is the cheapest option in Scheveningen. Unlimited breakfast included in the crazy, poster-lined dining room downstairs. All rooms have showers. Reception 8am-10pm. Bathrooms are in the hall. Singles €25; doubles €50. AmEx/DC/MC/V. ❶

Camping Duinhorst, Buurtweg 135 (☎ 324 22 70; www.duinhorst.nl), in the nearby town of Wassenar. Take bus #43 in the direction of Leiden from Centraal Station. Open Apr.-Oct. €13.70 per person, €2.25 per tent. ❶

FOOD & DRINK

Eating in Scheveningen is best done at any of the fresh fish vendors that roll up to the Strandweg and sell *broodjes* (around €4) and meals of cod and calamari, perch, and pike (plates of fish €3-5). At **M'n Schoonmoeder ❶,** Marcelisstraat 255A, all dishes—like *coq au vin* or salad with *chorizo*—in this eatery are €7. Salads and fries on the side are each an extra €2. (☎ 350 75 68). The restaurants along the Strand tend to double as bars and triple as dance clubs, and every one has a particularly garish theme, from the South Seas to giant gorillas to crazy pianos. Dinner at these places isn't cheap, with main dishes running the €10-20 range.

SIGHTS

The **Strandweg** stretches along the beach, scattered with outdoor terraces and a few carnivalesque attractions. The beach itself is dotted with beach clubs that serve food and have space where you can recline with a beer and catch some rays. The prefabricated huts change yearly, but the best ones tend to cluster at the less crowded northern end of the strand (look for the big steel obelisk). The **Beelden-aan-Zee** sculpture museum "on the sea" advertises itself as "a silent sensation:" it houses no big names, and the pieces, culled from the slightly odd-ball collection of a family of Dutch industrialists, is mostly figurative work from the mid- to late 20th century. But it's not the art that you should come here to see—the museum, built under the foundations of a 19th century pavilion and carved literally out of the sand, is a work of art itself. Large skylit galleries curve seamlessly around airy outdoor patios and push up against the sand of hilly beachside dunes. The panoramic views over the ocean offered by this unique space manages to obscure the roiling mess of street-vendors and beach-hoppers on the Strandweg below—giving the impression of stillness and quietude. (Hartevelt-straat 1. To get there, take tram #1 or 9 to Circustheater; from there, follow Badhuisweg to Gevers Deynootweg, then continue to the left until Harteveltstraat. ☎358 58 57; www.beelde-naanzee.nl. Open Tu-Su 11am-5pm. €5, students and ages 5-12 €2.50.) Dead in the center of the strand, **Scheveningen Pier** dates back some 100 years, but recent renovations have erased the ravages of time. The walkway extends several hundred meters out above the ocean, and while it's lined with an endless string of souvenir shops, restaurants, and even a small casino, the pier's undisputed draw is the view of the ocean on nice days—or onto the beach and its summer sunbathers. (☎306 55 00; www.pier.nl. Open 10am-10pm. €1).

Canal Bridge, Delft

DELFT ☎015

The lillied canals and stone footbridges that still line the streets of picturesque Delft are one of the loveliest retreats from the urban buzz of The Hague or Amsterdam. Delft is famously the birthplace and hometown of the 17th-century Dutch painter Johannes Vermeer (1632-1675), whose sumptuous *View of Delft*, now in the Mauritshuis museum in The Hague (see p. 235) is a rare tribute to the town's luminous medieval charm. But other Golden Age artists were also drawn to Delft's placid canals, quiet canal houses, and colorful markets: painters like Jan Steen, Carel Fabritius, Pieter de Hooch, and Willem van Aelst all spent time here. Over the

Delftware Painter

centuries, the city also held court as a royal retreat and is the birthplace of the famous blue and white ceramic pottery known as Delftware. A thriving commercial metropolis in the 1400s, Delft has also seen its fair share of tragedy: two-thirds of Delft was decimated by fire and plague in 1537, and in 1583 the city bore witness to the assassination of national hero William I, Prince of Orange, as he sought refuge during the Eighty Years' War. Today the city is a center for science and technology in The Netherlands: Delft is home to one of the finest engineering schools in the country. Six hundred national monuments, museums, nightlife that caters to nearly includes 13,000 students, and three working Delftware factories make the city a popular destination for tourists. Thursdays and Saturdays, when towns-people flood to the bustling marketplace, are the best days to visit.

William of Orange's Tomb, Delft

Delft

🏠 ACCOMMODATIONS
Herberg de Emauspoort, 5
Hotel Coen, 8

🍴 FOOD & DRINK
Kleyweg's Stads-Koffyhuis, 6
Lunchroom - Tearoom -
   Choclaterie Leonidas, 1
De Nonnerie, 2
Ruif, 3

🌙 NIGHTLIFE
Cafe de Engel, 4
Cafe de Klomp, 7

TRANSPORTATION & PRACTICAL INFORMATION

The easiest way into Delft is the 15-minute ride on **tram** #1 from **The Hague** (2 strips) to Delft station; alternatively you can catch the train from either of the two train stations in The Hague (€1.90), which is a faster option: you'll be in Delft in less than ten minutes. **Trains** also arrive from Amsterdam (1hr., one-way €8.90).

The **Tourist Information Point,** Hippolytusbuurt 4, just by the Stadhuis, has lots of free maps, information on sights and events, and offers walking tours. They also can book you a hotel free of charge. To get there from the train station, head left along the canal, turn right onto Sint Agathaplein, walk straight, cross two bridges, and turn right on Hippolytusbuurt. (☎215 40 15; www.delft.nl. Internet available. Open Su-M 10am-4pm, Tu-F 9am-9pm, Sa 9am-5pm). For info on municipal museums, check www.gemeentemusea.nl. The best way to see Delft is on foot, but **Rondvaart Delft,** Koornmarkt 113, runs water bikes through the canals. (☎212 63 85; www.rondvaart-delft.nl. Open May-Oct. daily 10am-6pm. €4.80, children €3, plus a €15 deposit.)

Thursday is generally **market day** (open 9am-5pm) on the Markt. There is also a flower and plant market held at the same time on Hippolytusbuurt. On Saturday, there is a general market on the Brabantse Turfmarkt (9am-5pm). In the first weeks of August, Delft hosts the **Delft Chamber Music Festival** (☎020 643 20 43; www.delftmu-sicfestival.nl; mailing address Oudezijds Voorburgwal 72, Amsterdam. Single tickets €23, reductions for multiple-event tickets).

ACCOMMODATIONS

There aren't any rock-bottom budget accommodations in Delft; on a shoestring you can always stay in The Hague and take the train (a short 8min ride).

Herberg de Emauspoort, Vrouwenregt 9-11 (☎219 02 19; fax 214 82 51; www.emaus-poort.nl). This friendly old Dutch-style hotel is located above a pastry shop and right on an idyllic canal: best of all, if you plan ahead you can stay in one of two exceptionally clean gypsy-style caravans at no extra cost; check out pictures at www.pipodeclown.nl or www.mammaloe.nl. All rooms with bath, TV, and phone. Pastry shop breakfast included. Free bike rental. Doubles €82.50-92.50; triples €115; quads €140. ❹

Hotel Coen, Coenderstraat 47 (☎214 59 14; www.hotelcoen.nl), right behind the train station. Clean, comfortable, but in a less picturesque neighborhood than other accommodations, this family-run hotel nonetheless has all the comforts, including bathroom, TV, phone, and even a free sauna 6-8pm. Breakfast is disappointingly €11 extra. And if you can't get enough Delftware, the baths are tiled with it. Singles from €70; doubles from €90; quads €125. Tax not included. AmEx/MC/V. ❸

Delftse Hout Recreation Area, Korstlaan 5 (☎213 00 40; www.delftsehout.nl). Camp-gounds about 20min. west of the center of town. Take bus #64 to the end of the line. Cabins are more expensive, but campsites are €22 for 2 people. Reception May-mid-Sept. 8:30am-8pm; mid-Sept.-Apr. 9am-6pm. ❷

FOOD

While a good meal can turn up almost anywhere in Delft, restaurants line **Volderstraat** and **Oude Delft** in particular.

🔲 **Ruif,** Kerkstraat 22-24 (☎214 22 06; www.ruif.nl). With a tiny boat-terrace and verdant canal-side seating, Ruif may just have the most lovely spot in Delft to enjoy a light meal or a glass of beer. Starters €4-6. Main courses like Catalonian fish stew €12-14. Rustic-chic, candlelit dining room with exposed brick walls and ranch equipment hanging from the ceiling is ideal when the weather gets colder. Kitchen serves meals as diverse as dim sum and red-fruit gazpacho. There's always a vegetarian option. Open M 3pm-1am, Tu-Su 11:30am-1am, F-Sa 11:30am-2am; kitchen open until 10pm. ❸

Kleyweg's Stads-Koffyhuis, Oude Delft 133-135 (☎212 46 25; www.stads-koffyhuis.nl). Coffee-house with a boat-terrace is known for interesting coffees (with ginger €2.15) and an enormous selection of pancakes—everything from the currant and raisin (€5.75) to beef stroganoff (€9.85). Sandwiches €5.25. Open M-F 9am-7pm, Sa 9am-8pm. Cash only. ❶

De Nonnerie, Sint Agathaplein (☎212 18 60), across the canal from Oude Kerk and through the gate; beneath Het Prinsenhof (see p. 243). Located just off one of the most beautiful courtyards in Delft, this downstairs lunchroom has brick-vaulted ceilings and a meandering upstairs garden terrace; worth a visit even just for a drink on a warm day. Sandwiches start at €3. Open Tu-F 11am-5pm, Sa-Su noon-5pm. ❶

Lunchroom-Tearoom-Chocolaterie Leonidas, Choorstraat 24 (☎215 78 21), just off Hippolytusbuurt. Sit down for a quiet Dutch meal (sandwiches €4.25-7.75; asparagus soup €3.75) by the fig trees and ferns of the inner garden terrace. Or, treat yourself to high tea. Chocoholics will want to indulge at the adjoining shop where you can buy bon-bons by the boxful (starting at €1.50 per box). Open M-Sa 9am-5pm. ❶

SIGHTS

DELFTWARE

The blue-on-white designs of Delftware pottery was made famous by local artisans in the 16th century to compete with the newly imported Chinese counterpart—and it's been sought after ever since. In the 18th century there were over 35 factories in Delft alone; today only three remain. Of these, two are open to visitors: **De Candelaer,**

Kerkstraat 13a-14, is the most centrally located just off Markt square, to the left of Nieuwe Kerk. Inside, you can see Delftware made from scratch and listen to a free explanation of the process. Each piece comes with a certificate of authenticity. (☎213 18 48; www.candelaer.nl. Open daily 9am-6pm. Demonstrations free. Shop accepts AmEx/MC/V and will ship to the US.) If your thirst for Delftware still isn't slaked, head north to the outskirts of town to see how the bigger factories do it. Try **De Delftse Pauw**, Delftweg 133, which can be reached by taking tram #1, to the Vrijenbanselaan stop. (☎212 47 43; www.delftsepauw.com. Open Apr.-Oct. daily 9am-4:30pm; Nov.-Mar. M-F 9am-4:40pm, Sa-Su 11am-1pm. Demonstrations free.) **Koninklijke Porceleyne Fles**, Rotterdamseweg 196, founded in 1653, is the last remaining 17th-century Delftware factory. The center offers guided tours and information. To get there, take tram #1 away from The Hague, or bus #63, 121, or 129 to the TU Aula stop. (☎251 20 30; www.royaldelft.com. Open M-Sa 9am-5pm.)

These small Delftware factories can teach you to spot genuine Delft ceramic from imitation fakes sold in most souvenir shops around town, most of which are imported from Asia and have silk-screened designs. Since the name "Delft" is reserved for only factories approved by the Chamber of Commerce, imitation manufacturers use names like "Delfts," "Delft Blue," or "Delft-ware." Phrases like "hand-decorated" and "hand-painted" are equally suspect: they may only mean that a few brush strokes were added to printed-on designs. Authentic Delftware should have a model number, the initials of the painter, and usually run around €20-25 for small plates and tiles, €30 for small objects, €50-75 for larger plates and €100-175 for medium-sized vases. If you're interested in antique Delftware, be sure to have your potential purchase checked out by a neutral third party or get a statement of authenticity from the antiques dealer in writing.

NIEUWE KERK

🚩 *On the central Markt.* ☎212 30 25; *www.nieuwekerk-delft.nl. Church open Apr.-Oct. M-Sa 9am-6pm; Nov.-Mar. M-F 11am-4pm, Sa 11am-5pm. Carillon chimes usually Tu, Th, and Sa at noon. Entrance to both Nieuwe Kerk and Oude Kerk €2.50, seniors €2, children 3-12 €1. Tower closes 1hr. earlier, and can be climbed for an additional €2, seniors €1.60, children 3-12 €0.80.*

Built in 1381, Delft's Nieuwe Kerk, recognizable from Vermeer's sumptuous painting *View of Delft* (on view at Mauritshuis in The Hague, see p. 235) has one of the most beautiful brick interiors of any cathedral in The Netherlands. It's also the home to the remains of the members of the House of Orange. The mausoleum of Dutch liberator and Delft-adopted hero William I, Prince of Orange, at the end of the nave, is a sight in itself; the elaborate black and white marble work (which includes a sculpture of the ruler's dog) were magnificently restored in 2001. The church tower, which visitors can normally ascend, will be closed to the public for much of 2004, but no matter: one of the church's best parts is its 36-bell carillon which frequently plays elaborate melodies. The church still hosts regular Sunday services which are open to the public.

NUSANTRA MUSEUM

🚩 *Sint Agathaplein 4-5.* ☎260 23 58; *www.nusantra-delft.nl. Open Tu-Sa 10am-5pm, Su 1-5pm. €3.50, seniors and ages 12-16 €3, under 12 and Museumjaarkaart free. Combination ticket to the Nusantra Museum and Prinsenhof €6, seniors and 12-16 €5. Gamelan concerts held every Sa 11am-1:30pm. AmEx/MC/V.*

Nusantra is post-colonialism at its best, housing a small but gorgeous collection of objects from the former Dutch colonies. Masks, musical instruments, and votive objects from Papua New Guinea, Sumatra, Bali, and Borneo includes a full gamelan orchestra that is played every Saturday. The exhibition begins with a display of V.O.C. (Dutch East Indies Company) artifacts and moves on to displays of indigenous arts. A small gallery by the ticket desk sells objects to interested collectors. All information is in Dutch but the friendly staff can answer your questions.

OUDE KERK

🏛 *Heilige Geestkerkhof 25, across the canal from Sint. Agathaplein. ☎ 212 30 15; www.oudekerk-delft.nl. Open M-Sa 9am-6pm; Nov.-Mar. M-F 11am-4pm, Sa 11am-5pm. Entrance to Nieuwe Kerk and Oude Kerk €2.50, seniors €2, children 3-12 €1.*

The Oude Kerk, built around 1200, is more impressive for its gorgeously imposing brick-red exterior than for its paltry interior decorations; nonetheless, you'll be able to enter the church for free with your entrance ticket from the Nieuwe Kerk. This Dutch Reformed church is home to some elaborate, bas-relief memorial stones for famoush Dutchmen, including those of celebrated naval hero **Piet Heyn** and scientist **Antoni van Leeuwenhoek** (who according to legend may have been the model for Vermeer's famous works *The Geographer* and *The Astronomer*). The church's tower is approximately 75m high and leans a staggering—and slightly unnerving—1.96m out of line.

Dutch Countryside

OTHER SIGHTS

Opposite the Oude Kerk and across the canal is **Sint Agathaplein;** through the gate of this square is the **Waalse Kerk** (Walloon Church), at Oude Delft 179-181, in use as a French church since 1584. Built as a 15th-century nuns' cloister, **Het Prinsenhof,** Sint Agathaplein 1, off Oude Singel, was used by William, Prince I, Prince of Orange, for an abode during the resistance against the Spaniards. The church remained his home until a fanatical French Catholic hired by Spain's Phillip II assassinated him in 1584—you can still see the bullet holes in the wall from the Prince's murder. Today the building houses paintings, tapestries, and pottery, but the real draw is the chance to walk around inside this historic building. (☎ 260 23 58. Open Tu-Sa 10am-5pm, Su 1-5pm. €5, seniors and children 12-16 €4, under 12 and Museumjaarkaart free.) The **Legermuseum (Military Museum),** Korte Geer 1, features an extensive display on the history of the Dutch military and the House of Orange. Original costumes, weapons, armor, and paintings are on display, though with opportunities to dress up and play knight, it's somewhat geared toward kids. (☎ 215 05 00; www.legermuseum.nl. Open M-F 10am-5pm, Sa-Su noon-5pm. €4.40, under 12 €2.20, Museumjaarkaart free.) The **Paul Tetar van Elven Museum,** Koornmarkt 67, was the home of 19th-century Academy painter and collector Paul Tetar van Elven (1823-1896). Magnificent period rooms, curiosities, paintings, drawings, and furniture are on display for visitors. (☎ 212 42 06. Open Apr. 21-Oct. 28 Tu-Su 1-5pm. €2).

World's Largest Port, Rotterdam

Rotterdam

Modern Bridge, Rotterdam

Euromast & Tunnelmarkt Building, Rotterdam

NIGHTLIFE

Cafe de Engel, Markt 66a (☎213 57 08), at the foot of the entrance to the Niewe Kerk on the Markt. The coolest of all the cafe-bars on the Markt, de Engel is also open the latest (usually until 4am). Enjoy a beer (€1.60) on the small terrace in the late afternoon, or head inside when the large projection TV beams the latest soccer or tennis match. Snacks (€2-5). *Tostis* (€2-3.85). Open M-Th 10am-4am, F-Sa 10am-2am, Su 11am-1am. Cash only.

Cafe de Klomp, Binnenwatersloot 5 (☎212 38 10), just off Oude Delft. The oldest pub in The Netherlands (opened in the 17th century), with dusty oil lamps, old velvet seats, Delftware on the walls, and a rotary phone. De Klomp still seems to have its foot in another century—if it weren't for the sounds of trains passing a block away. Still a ch arming local hangout after more than 360 years. Beer from €1.60. Open Su-Th 4pm-1am, F-Sa 4pm-2am. Cash only.

ROTTERDAM   ☎ 010

Bustling metropolis, razor-sharp skyline, steamships and high-speed trains: it's hard to avoid conceiving of Rotterdam (pop. 590,000) without a tinge of post-war terminology. Its urban design—eclectic, eccentric, often terrifically dated—is a veritable architectural manifesto for post-WWII urban renewal. Bombed flat by the Nazis in May 1940, Rotterdam's effort in the interceding years has been to assert itself as a modern European center and a model for reconstruction. An arsenal of experimental architects converted the bombed-out debris into an urban center unlike any other in The Netherlands. You'll find few quaint locales in this thoroughly modern city of steel, concrete, and glass. And it's precisely this high-spirited, innovative creativity that draws visitors to the city today: structures like the new Netherlands Architectural Institute (see p. 248), the Erasmus bridge (see p. 250), or the Schouwburgplein (see p. 250) are some of Europe's most impressive modern architectural achievements. Yet there is more to Rotterdam than its urban design. Designated the "Cultural Capital of Europe" in 2001, it's the hippest and most up-and-coming city in The Netherlands. Events, festivals, art galleries, and interesting nightlife make Rotterdam a lively center of cultural activity. It's also the country's most exciting multi-cultural capital, with the largest traditional immigrant population in The Netherlands. But Rotterdam isn't complete *tabula rasa:* A walk along the old harbor, a trip up the Euromast (see p. 250) or a visit to the Maritiem

Haarlem

Museum (see p. 250) are great ways to learn about Rotterdam's history as the biggest and busiest port city in the world.

ORIENTATION & PRACTICAL INFORMATION

Trains run into Rotterdam Centraal daily from **Amsterdam** (1¼hr., 1-5 per hr., €11.20) and **The Hague** (30min., 1-4 per hr., €3.60). The **VVV**, Coolsingel 67, opposite the *Stadhuis*, books rooms for a €1.60 fee. Free maps of public transportation, as well as maps of the city (€1 for a sightseeing map, but the one for €1.50 is more user-friendly). The VVV also has tourist guidebooks for €2, copies of *R'Uit* with listings of cultural events, and information about tram, bike, and boat tours. (☎0900 403 40 65, €0.35 per min.; from abroad 414 00 00; www.vvvrotterdam.nl. Open M-Th 9:30am-6pm, F 9:30am-9pm, Sa 9:30am-5pm.) For more information on Rotterdam check out www.rotterdam.info or www.rotterdamlinks.nl. You can also stop by the student-oriented ◪**Use-it Rotterdam,** Conradstraat 2 (☎240 91 58; ww.use-it.nl), which also publishes the extremely useful budget guide to Rotterdam, *Simply the Best*, which is stuffed with excellent advice on cheap accommodations, vintage shopping, architecture, restaurants, and up-to-date events. You can pick up a copy of their publication at the VVV or most hostels and hotels. Rotterdam has a network of buses, trams, and two Metro lines (**Calandlijn** and **Erasmuslijn**) that intersect in the center of the city at station Beurs. Metro tickets are equivalent to two strips on the *strippenkart* and are valid for two hours.

Nederlands Architectuurinstituut, Rotterdam

Find your essentials and groceries at **Spar,** Witte de Withstraat 36, next to the Home Hotel. (Open M-F 8:30am-7pm, Sa 8:30am-5pm.) Closer to the center of town, you'll find a large **Albert Heijn** supermarket off Plaatbeurstr. (M: Beurs; open M-F 8am-8pm, Sa 8am-6pm, Su noon-6pm.)

The neighborhood to the west of 's-Gravendijkwal should be avoided at night, as should Chinatown—the area to the north of West Kruiskade and west of Batavierenstraat. The area around Centraal Station (the strip to the north of Weena and east of Batavierenstraat) should also be avoided after hours.

Kijk-Kubus, Rotterdam

ACCOMMODATIONS

Hotel Bazar, Witte de Withstraat 16 (☎206 51 51; fax 206 51 59). Turn onto Schilderstraat from Schiedamse Dijk and follow the street until it turns

Museumpark, Rotterdam

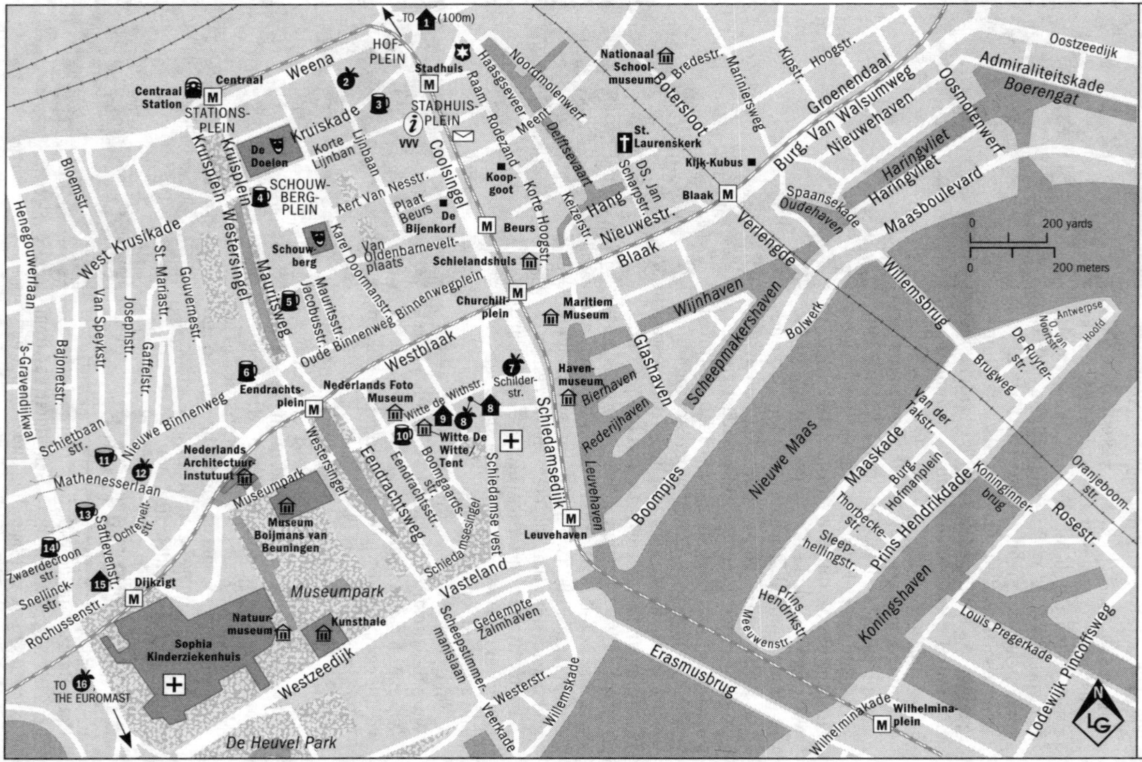

Rotterdam

ACCOMMODATIONS
Home Hotel, 9
Hotel Bazar, 8
Hotel Bienvenue, 1
StayOkay Hostel, 15

FOOD & DRINK
Bagel Bakery, 7
Bazar, 8
De Pannenkoekenboot, 16
Wester Paviljoen, 12
Zin, 2

NIGHTLIFE
Calypso, 4
Dizzy, 14
Off_Corso, 3
Rotown, 6
Strano, 5
De Witte AAP, 10

COFFEESHOPS
Lachende Paus, 11
Sensi Cafe, 13

into Witte de Withstraat. If you're tired of Europe, you can escape to the Middle East, Africa, or South America in one of Bazar's 27 hip, extremely well-decorated rooms—each with its own design. Try to book the room on the South American floor or any of the newly-designed rooms on the African floor. All rooms with bath, and TV. Breakfast included. Elevator access. Check-in 8am-11pm, or until the restaurant closes. Book 2 weeks in advance for weekend reservations. Singles €60-100; doubles €65-120; extra bed €20. AmEx/MC/V. ❸

StayOkay Rotterdam (HI), Rochussenstaat 107-109 (☎436 57 63; www.stayokay.com/rotterdam). Take the Metro to Dijkzigt. Friendly, knowledgeable staff and clean, comfortable rooms compensate for slightly crowded conditions. Kitchen, upstairs TV lounge, downstairs bar, bike rental (€6.45 per day), and laundry (€3.40). Reception 7am-midnight. No curfew. Internet €5 per hr. Dorms €22.50; singles €30.75; doubles €52; triples €74.50. MC/V. ❶

Cube Houses, Rotterdam

Home Hotel, Witte de Withstraat 38 (☎414 21 50; fax 414 16 90). Follow directions to Hotel Bazar. Located right on Rotterdam's coolest street, Home boasts handsome apartments for short- or long-term rent. Rooms are a little old but well-maintained. All with kitchenettes, bathrooms, and telephones. Useful information available in the front office. Reception M-Sa 8:30am-10pm, Su 9:30am-10pm. Singles €60; doubles €70, triples €100, quads €110. Prices do not include 5.5% city tax. Special rates for longer stays. AmEx/MC/V. ❸

Hotel Bienvenue, Spoorsingel 24 (☎466 93 94). Exit through the back of the station, walk straight along the canal for 5min. Close enough to the city center but in a peaceful, canal-lined neighborhood. The hotel is aging—the staircase is almost impossible to climb unless you get down on all fours. One shower for all the rooms—but you'll get all the peace and quiet you need after a night of bar-hopping. Breakfast included. Reception M-F 7:30am-9pm, Sa-Su 8am-9pm. Singles with hall bath €43; doubles with bath €70; triples with bath €90; quads with shower, toilet in hall €115. AmEx/MC/V with 5.5% surcharge. ❷

Vaulted Passageway

FOOD

For food on the cheap, head to **Witte de Withstraat,** where you can easily grab a meal for under €5—generally Chinese takeout or shawarma. Try **Lijbaan** for pubs and bars.

⬛ Bazar, Witte de Withstraat 16 (☎206 51 51; www.hotelbazar.nl), on the 1st fl. of the hotel by the same name (see above). In the middle of Rotterdam's hippest street, Bazar's glittering colored lights, bright blue tables, and gorgeous Middle Eastern fusion cuisine attract crowds nightly. The candlelit basement is

Nederlands Architectuurinstituut, Rotterdam

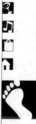

Oude Binnenweg, Rotterdam

Kijk-Kubus Detail, Rotterdam

Shopping in Rotterdam

a little more intimate, but come prepared for a lively, festive atmosphere to the tune of technofied North African music. Sandwiches €3.90. Open M-Th 8am-1am, F 8am-2am, Sa 10am-2am, Su 10am-midnight. AmEx/MC/V. ❷

Wester Paviljoen, Nieuwe Binnenweg 136 (☎436 26 45; www.westerpaviljoen-rotterdam.nl), on the corner of Mathenesserlaan. The expansive, bustling terrace of this large old-style cafe feels like a little bit of Paris in the middle or Rotterdam. This the best place in Rotterdam to enjoy a beer (€1.80) or a sandwich (€3-5), and people-watch under the cool shade of a leafy canopy. Main dishes €10-13. Salads €7.50. Open M-Th 8pm-1am, F 8pm-2am, Sa 9am-2am, Su 9am-1am; kitchen closes 11pm. ❷

Bagel Bakery, Schilderstraat 57a (☎412 1560). Join the rest of Rotterdam's specious gallery-hoppers for a reasonably priced New York-style bagel in this chic lunch cafe. Bagels with cream cheese, banana, cinnamon, and walnuts €3.30; with tapenade, tuna, and capers €3.20. Pastrami with pickles and horseradish €3.85. Bagels with soup €4.10. Open Tu-Sa 9am-5:30pm, Su 10am-5:30pm. Cash only. ❶

De Pannenkoekenboot Rotterdam, Parkhaven t.o. Euromast (☎436 72 95; www.pannenkoeken-boot.nl), right across from the Euromast. Take tram #8 to Euromast. Definitely touristy, Rotterdam's "Pancake-boat" has a series of daily buffet-tours where you can eat as many pancakes as you want while the vessel cruises the harbor. Buffet Sa-Su 1:30, 3, 4:30, and 6pm; W and F 4:30 and 6pm. €12, children €7. Harbor sightseeing Pancake Cruise Sa 8-11pm, Sa 8-11pm. Adults €21, children €15. Cash only. ❸

Zin, Lijbaan 40 (☎281 09 10; www.zin-reizenen-spijzen.nl), just off Weena. A short walk from Centraal station or M: Stadhuis. If you're not afraid to show just how cool you are (and pay for it), then come mingle with Rotterdam's scenemakers over *tapas* (€4-9) and cocktails (€5-6). A world-conscious menu, with culinary curiosities from Japan to Italy, has main courses from €12 and *broodjes* from €4. Open Su-Th noon-midnight, F-Sa noon-2am; June-Aug. opens 11am; kitchen closes 10:30pm. AmEx/MC/V. ❸

SIGHTS

▨ NEDERLANDS ARCHITECTUURINSTITUUT

🗷 *Museumpark 25. Take tram #4 or 5 to Eendracht-splein. Metro: Eendrachtsplein, or bus #32 to Rochus-senstraat. On the northern end of Museumpark.* ☎440 12 00; www.nai.nl. Open Tu-Sa 10am-5pm, Su 11am-5pm. Library and reading room open Tu-Sa 10am-5pm. €7, students and seniors €5, under 15 and Museumjaar-kaart free. Sonnenveld House free with ticket.

Architect Jo Coenen's 1992 design for the new Netherlands Architecture Institute (NAi) beat out that of superstar Rem Koolhaas—and the building is now one of the most extraordinary in all of Rotterdam. The multi-leveled glass and steel construction—which traverses a man-made pool and looks out onto the Museumpark—is home to several exhibition spaces, a world-class archive, a reading room with over 35,000 books, as well as the new **Architecture Biennale** (www.biennalerotterdam.nl). The rotating exhibitions—always innovative if perhaps a bit experimental or theoretical for the uninitiated—explore issues in contemporary architecture, urban design, and landscape planning. A small permanent display explores "200 years of Dutch architecture" through models, photographs, and a short video. Entrance to the museum also grants access to the **Sonnenveld House,** a private residence around the corner, restored to the way it would have looked in 1933.

Canals, Rotterdam

🖼 MUSEUM BOIJMANS VAN BEUNINGEN

🏠 *Museumpark 18-20. Take tram #4 or 5 to Eendrachtsplein. Metro: Eendrachtsplein. Across the street from the Architecture Institute. ☎441 94 75; www.boijmans.nl. Open Tu-Sa 10am-5pm, Su 11am-5pm. €7, seniors €3.50, under 18 and Museumjaarkaart free. Library open M-F 10am-4pm; free with entrance ticket.*

Without a doubt Rotterdam's finest art museum, and in the upper echelon of Dutch collections, van Beuningen reopened in May of 2003 with a modern new wing and an astonishing "Digital Depot." The latter, in the ground floor's main room, includes sophisticated see-through touch-screens that let you access info in the archives, as well as a wall-sized 3D data cloud for navigating through the museum's more than 120,000 objects as though it were a map of the universe. On the ground floor you'll find post-war work by artists like Andy Warhol, Claes Oldenburg, Joseph Beuys, and Bruce Nauman. The second floor is home to a large selection of Surrealist painting by Dali, Max Ernst, and Magritte (check out his famous *Le Modèle Rouge*); expressionist pieces by Kandinsky, Kokoschka, and Munch; and several Monets. Don't miss Jeff Wall's 1992 *Dead Troops Talk* above the main stairwell. This floor also has an impressive collection of Dutch and Flemish art, with two rooms of paintings and drawings by Rubens, Dirk Bouts's moving 15th century *Head of Christ*, Bruegel's *The Tower of Babel*, and various works by the likes of Hans Memling, Van Dyck, Jan Steen, Frans Hals, and Rembrandt.

Anchors Away!

Boat Tour, Rotterdam

KIJK-KUBUS (CUBE HOUSES)

◪ *Overblaak 70. Take tram #1 to Blaak. Metro: Blaak, turn left, and look up. ☎414 22 85; www.cubehouse.nl. Open Mar.-Dec. daily 11am-5pm; Jan.-Feb. F-Su 11am-5pm. €1.75, seniors and children ages 4-12 €1.25.*

For a dramatic example of Rotterdam's eccentric urban design, check out architect Piet Blom's unusual housing complex right on the old harbor. Built in 1982 and nicknamed "Het Blaakse Bos" (the Blaak woods, after its street name), the tilted, yellow, cube-shaped houses are mounted on one corner on tall concrete columns—and look like an upturned de Stijl forest. Though they've been inhabited as private homes for over 20 years, a "show cube" (Kijk-Kubus), fitted with custom-made furniture, is open to the public.

MARITIEM MUSEUM

◪ *Leeuvehaven 1, a 5min. walk from Coolsingel. Take tram #3, 6, 13 or 20. Metro: Beurs. ☎413 26 80; www.maritiemmuseum.nl. Open Tu-Sa 10am-5pm, Su 11am-5pm; July-Aug. also M 10am-5pm. €3.50, seniors and ages 4-15 €2, under 3 and Museumjaarkaart free. Wheelchair-accessible. AmEx/MC/V.*

Water is the lifeblood and the curse of The Netherlands, but there is no city for which it's more important than Rotterdam. Through interactive multimedia displays, exhibits that show what it's like to be inside a ship, and hundreds of model ships constructed with amazing detail, the museum basks in the city's history as the busiest port in the world. The clear highlight is the Wereldhaven (World Port) room, where you can use computer consoles to navigate through 500 years of Rotterdam harbor's history in images, interviews, and amazing 1880 film footage of the docklands at work. On the top floor, Prof. Plons, a children's playground, is a popular stop for those ages 10 and under. A stop aboard the *De Buffel*, a restored 19th-century turret ship, is included with admission. When you're done, swing by the **Verscheurde Stad (Torn City)** monument, behind the museum, designed by sculptor O. Zadkine. The figure with a hole in his heart writing in agony was erected in 1951 to commemorate the WWII bombings 11 years earlier.

EUROMAST

◪ *Parkhaven 20. Take tram #8 to Euromast. ☎436 48 11; www.euromast.nl. Open Jan.-Mar., Oct.-Dec. daily 10am-5pm; Apr.-Sept. 10am-7pm; July-Aug. Tu-Sa 10am-10:30pm. Space Tower: same hours except Jan.-Feb. Sa-Su 10am-5pm only. €7.75, children 4-11 €5.*

The tallest structure in The Netherlands, this popular site is the best way to take in a breathtaking panoramic view of Rotterdam's skyline. Built in only 23 days, one hour, and 59 minutes in 1958, the attraction feels a bit dated: steam and rocket sounds simulate a "space flight" in the high-speed elevator, but a little schmaltz is a small price to pay for the truly astonishing 112m-high views over the old harbor, Delftshaven, and The Hague. From the viewing deck you can take the "Space Adventure," a revolving capsule that ascends to 185m: just below the top of the tower.

ARCHITECTURAL SIGHTS

No trip to Rotterdam would be complete without admiring the futuristic ingenuity and flair of the city's architecture and urban design. In addition to the **NAi, Kunsthale**, and the **Cube Houses** (see above), stop by the centrally located **Schouwburgplein** (M: Centraal, or trams #3, 4, 5, 8) for one of the more impressive sights in Rotterdam. Designed by architect A. Geuze in 1997 and built using wood, rubber, epoxy, steel, concrete, and stone, the huge open space includes the angular and lurching **Pathé cinema building** envisioned by K. van Velzen, as well as four moveable, fire-engine-red lanterns that crane over the open square. Ben van Berkel's **Erasmus Bridge** (M: Leuhaven, trams # 20, 23), which swoops dramatically across the harbor from the city center to Rotterdam Zuid, has been nicknamed "de Zwaan" (the swan) by residents for its graceful, stark white support structure. A less eccentric architectural monument is the **Nationale Nederlanden Building,** whose 151 meters of reflective glass make it by far the tallest building in The Netherlands (Weena 30, next to Centraal Station). For more information about Rotterdam's unique architecture—as well as news of future city developments—stop by the **City Information Center,** Coolsingel 197. (☎489 77 77; www.cic.rotterdam.nl. Open M 1-5:30pm, Tu-F 9am-5:30pm, Sa 11am-5:30pm).

KUNSTHALE ROTTERDAM

🏠 *Westzeedijk 341. On the southern end of Museumpark; entrance from either Westzeedijk or from the park. ☎ 440 03 00, info 440 03 01; www.kunsthal.nl. Open Tu-Sa 10am-5pm, Su 11am-5pm. €7.50, seniors €6.50, students and ages 13-18 €4.50, under 5 €1.*

Designed by famous Dutch architect Rem Koolhaas and built in 1993, the large, modern Kunsthale building is one of Rotterdam's premier venues for contemporary art—with a wide range of exhibitions on artists from photographer Martin Parr to Japanese designer Isamu Noguchi. The museum also has travelling exhibitions on early Modern and 19th century painting and sculpture.

WITTE DE WHITE & TENT

🏠 *Witte de Withestraat 50. Witte de White: ☎411 01 44; www.wdw.nl. Tent: ☎413 54 98; www.tentplaza.nl. Open Su, Tu-Sa 11am-6pm. €2.30, students and seniors €1.10, Museumjaarkaart free. Cash only.*

This address houses two avant-garde art spaces under one roof. The Witte de White and Tent both show work by up-and-coming and international contemporary sculptors, painters, video, and multimedia artists. On the ground floor, the Tent space specializes mostly in works by younger, Rotterdam-based artists: the shows here can be a bit heady if you're not into contemporary art. Upstairs, Witte de White's more international (and digestible) exhibits include an ongoing series exploring "Contemporary Arab Representations," as well as frequent lectures and debates on a wide variety of art-related subjects. The helpful staff (mostly artists) can give advice about art-going in Rotterdam.

MUSEUMPARK

🏠 *Take tram #5 or 8 until you hit the park. Free.*

Of the many parks in The Netherlands, few are as enjoyable as the Museumpark. Conceived by Rem Koolhaas's "Office for Metropolitan Architecture in Rotterdam," the Museumpark seamlessly integrates art and urban landscape architecture. The park features a number of sculptures, mosaics, and monuments—designed by some of the world's foremost artists and architects—interwoven among serene fountains and hedgerows. Nearby **De Heuvel Park,** just across the street toward the Euromast, is also worth a visit.

ST. LAURENSKERK

🏠 *Grote Kerkplein 15. Metro: Blaak. ☎ 413 14 94. Open Tu-Sa 10am-4pm. Services Su 9, 10:30am, and 5pm. Free.*

Though it was bombed and almost completely destroyed on May 14, 1940, the Grote, or St. Laurenskerk, has since been restored to its medieval splendor. While there are no eye-dazzling stained-glass windows or stunning sculptures to be seen here, the church's three organs make it worth the visit. The great red and gold organ at the back of the church is the largest mechanical organ in Europe. In the summer, the church holds organ concerts at 4pm most Saturdays and 8pm on Thursdays (€2.50-5); check with the church for concert listings. There is also a permanent exhibition that commemorates the bombing of Rotterdam with video footage and photographs.

OTHER MUSEUMS

Explore Rotterdam's history and contrast before and after the 1940 bombing at the **Museum Het Schielandshuis (Historical Museum)**, Korte Hoogestraat 31. To get there from Church Plein, turn right on Westblaak, and Korte Hoogestraat is on the left. (☎ 217 67 67; www.hmr.rotterdam.nl. Open Tu-F 10am-5pm, Sa-Su 11am-5pm. €2.70, seniors and ages 4-15 €1.35, Museumjaarkaart free.) Photography enthusiasts should visit The **Netherlands Foto Museum**, Witte de Whitestraat 63, a recently opened exhibition space connected to The Netherlands Foto Archives and a conservation institute. (☎ 213 20 11; www.nederlandsfotomuseum.nl. Open Su, Tu-Sa 11am-5pm. €2.30, under 12 free.) The NFM also hosts the newly inaugurated **Foto Biennale** (www.fbr.nl). If you haven't gotten enough harbor history at the Maritiem museum, you can head a few meters south on Schiedamse Dijk to the free **Havenmuseum (Harbor Museum)**, Leuvehaven 50-72, where you can walk through a small shipyard exhibition. (☎ 404 80 72; www.havenmuseum.nl. Open M-F 10am-4:30pm, Sa-Su 11am-4:30pm). The giant whale skeleton in the front lobby may be the most impressive thing about the **Natuurmuseum**, Westzeedijk 345, which has a diminutive collection of birds, butterflies, and small animals. It's in the southwestern corner of Museumpark, near the Euromast. Take tram #5 or 8 to Museumpark. (☎ 436 42 22; www.nmr.nl. Open Tu-Sa 10am-5pm, Su 11am-5pm. €3; seniors, students, and ages 5-15 €2; Museumjaarkaart free.)

NIGHTLIFE

Bars and clubs line **Mauritsweg, Oude** and **Nieuwe Binnenweg**, and **Witte de Withstraat.** The **Old Harbour,** east of the city center, also has lively, up-and-coming nightlife.

Off_Corso, Kruiskade 22 (☎ 411 38 97; www.off_corso.nl). This abandoned movie theater got a new lease on life in 2001 when 4 young local residents gave birth to what has become Rotterdam's hottest nighttime phenomenon. Good news travels fast: art exhibitions, film screenings, and multimedia festivals share the bill with a continuous flow of hip-hop, house, and techno parties—all in a magisterial, multi-level dance hall. Slated to close at the end of 2005, Off_Corso has benefited from a load of positive press and a certain sense of urgency. Th student dance evening (cover €6, €4 with student ID); F hip hop, soul, R&B, and 80s (€8-15); Sa techno-house (€12.50). Beer €2; mixed drinks €5.60. Open Th-Sa 11pm-5am. Cash only.

Dizzy, 's-Gravendijkwal 127 (☎ 477 30 17; www.dizzy.nl). Take tram #4 to 's-Gravendijkwal. Metro: Dijkzijgt. Rotterdam's premier jazz cafe for 25 years, Dizzy hosts frequent jam sessions and has hosted internationally known performers such as Chet Baker. The back-door patio garden, lined with bamboo and ivy, is the loveliest in Rotterdam. M jam session 10pm-1am (except July-Aug.); Th concert 10pm-12:30am; Sa DJ starting 10pm; Su concert. Beer €1.80; whiskies €5.20. Restaurant serves salads (€4-9) and mains (€8-15) daily until 11pm. Open Su-Th noon-1am, F-Sa noon-2am. AmEx/MC/V.

Strano, Van Oldenbarnevelt Plaats 154 (☎ 412 58 11), on the corner with Mauritsweg. Small, laid-back, and popular gay bar has friendly staff who'll tell you about Rotterdam's BGLT scene. Beer €1.80; cocktails €4.50. Open Su-Th 5pm-2am, F-Sa 5pm-4am.

Rotown, Nieuwe Binnenweg 19b (☎ 436 26 69; tickets 436 26 42; www.rotown.nl). A diverse crowd of hip 20-somethings crowd the terrace of this alt-rock cafe, and heads to the back of the building when there's live reggae, rock, hip-hop, and alternative music playing. During the day the stage leads into an atrium-lit dining room. Sandwiches €3-4. Th indie guitar dance night; F-Sa DJ; Su live music 10:30pm-midnight. Cover usually free, sometimes €4-8. Bar open Su-W 11am-2am, Th-Sa 11am-3a. AmEx/MC/V.

Calypso, Mauritsweg 5 (☎ 201 09 99; www.calypso-rotterdam.com). Unique space right along the canal hosts a range of parties from Latin to Indian to African to gay and lesbian to 70s and 80s, always with a DJ or live band. Once a month the house holds its fabulous "Gaylypso" party; for a full list of events stop by and pick up a flier or check the website for more details. Cocktails €4-5. Cover usually €5-10. Tu 6-10pm salsa night; W 10pm-2am hip-hop night; Sept.-May Th Latin and Flamenco night 7pm-4am. Open Tu-W noon-2am, Th noon-4am, F-Sa noon-6am. Cash only.

De Witte Aap, Witte de Withstraat 78 (☎414 95 65). Of all the small, trendy bars that line Witte de Withstraat, "The White Ape" (whose logo is a monkey with headphones) is the coolest. Huge stuffed apes hang over the bar and wall-sized windows look out onto the street: but the real draw is one of the most diverse and interesting crowds in Rotterdam that spill out onto the street on the weekends. Beer €1.90; mixed drinks €5.60. Open Su-Th 4pm-4am, F-Sa 4pm-5am.

COFFEESHOPS

The coffeeshops in Rotterdam are in general more basic than those in Amsterdam: expect to find few pillow-lined lounges. Nevertheless, for the highest density, check out the **Oude** and **Nieuwe Binnenweg**, especially between 's-Gravendijkwal and Hobokenstraat.

Van Eycks & More Van Eycks

Sensi Cafe, Nieuwe Binnenweg 181 (☎436 46 65; www.sensiseeds.com). With a large yellow wrap-around bar, huge windows overlooking the street corner, cheerful mosaics on the wall, and low drink prices, Sensi cafe is easily the most pleasant place in Rotterdam to have a smoke. Marijuana sold in €5.70 and €11.40 increments. Joints €2 mixed, €3 pure. Cappuccino €1.50; fresh orange juice €1.60. Open daily 10am-1am.

Lachende Paus (The Laughing Pope), Nieuwe Binnenweg 139a (☎436 29 32). A smartshop with everything you might need to get your feet off the ground. Especially friendly staff and a very Zen atmosphere, with little Buddhist and Hindu statues everywhere. Open daily 10am-midnight.

Weighing Cheese

ENTERTAINMENT

A trip to Rotterdam that doesn't take in some of the city's fantastic performance art would be remiss. For up-to-date information on concerts and theater in Rotterdam to pick up a free copy of the monthly magazine **R'Uit** at the VVV or most performance venues.

Rotterdamse Schouwburg, Schouwburgplein 25 (☎411 81 10; www.rotterdamseschowburg.nl). Rotterdam's main theater venue, with over 200 performances of opera, musical theater, modern dance, classical ballet, theater, and family performances. Located in the extravagantly modern Schouwburgplein, which is an architectural sight all to itself.

De Doelen, Schouwburgplein 50 (☎217 17 17; www.dedoelen.nl). De Doelen is the biggest concert hall in The Netherlands. The venue is home to classi-

Boat at Sunset

Outdoor Market, Groningen

Buitenhof, The Hague

Striped Bike, Gouda

cal, jazz, and new and world music concerts, as well as the **Rotterdam Philharmonic Orchestra** (☎217 17 07; www.rpho.nl).

FESTIVALS

Rotterdam, as The Netherlands' most popular up-and-coming city, has an exceptionally strong arsenal of summertime and year-round cultural activities that visitors can take advantage of— and most of them are free. For summer festivals, try www.zomerfestivals.nl, which has information about several festivals listed below. Toward the end of January, the **Rotterdam International Film Festival** (☎890 90 90) provides a venue for hundreds of non-commercial films, special programs, and retrospectives. The **ABN AMRO World Tennis Tournament** (☎0900 235 24 69 or 293 33 00) in Rotterdam Zuid (Metro: Zuidplein) attracts thousands of spectators and top tennis talent in February. In the last week of May, the free **Dunya Festival** (☎233 09 10; www.dunya.nl) features music, poetry, and storytelling from around the world, as well as a special program specifically for younger patrons. **Bang the Drum** (June) turns Rotterdam's Afrikaanderplein into a massive music and dance extravaganza as over a thousand *djembe* players gather together in a celebration of African music. Also in June, the **Poetry International Festival** (☎411 81 10; www.poetryinternational.org) invites dozens of poets from all over the world to read their works in Rotterdam. A book market, interviews, lectures, discussions, and more are included in the gathering. Later in the month, **De Parade** (☎03 34 65 45 77; www.deparade.nl) marches into Museumpark, bringing with it theater, music, film, dance, opera, and variety shows, with a children's parade every afternoon. Admission is free until 5pm, €4 after 5pm; show prices are around €15 each. At end of June and beginning of July, there's the **Festival of Architecture** (☎205 15 36), when remarkably designed buildings all over the city open to the public. In mid-July, both the **Metropolis Pop Festival** (☎433 25 11; www.hetleukstefestivalvannederland.nl) in Zuiderpark, and **Zomerpodium** (☎425 32 92; www.loederevents.nl), in Museumpark, attract a host of Dutch musical acts to the city. If you haven't had enough entertainment by then, the raucous **Zomercarnaval** (☎414 17 72; fax 404 96 30; www.zomercarnaval.com), with its brass bands, DJs, parties, and climactic Battle of the Drums, should do the job. The carnival also features a Caribbean street parade and market. Things begin to quiet down in July with **Kolkkonsert** (☎090 04 03 40 65; www.zomerfestivals.nl)

in nearby Delftshaven, Rotterdam's only historic pre-war neighborhood, which features open-air classical music concerts. The **Chinese Cultural Festival** in July finishes off the month with dragon and lion dances, music, fireworks, and much more. In August, **Ben & Jerry's Pleinbioscoop,** the **open-air cinema,** (☎425 32 92; www.loederevents.nl) projects free cult, classic, action, and international films on a huge open-air screen in the middle of Museumpark. Also in August, the **FFWD Heineken Dance Parade** (www.ffwdheinekendanceparade.nl) rocks the city center with dance music, DJs, 40 trucks, and parades. Things heat up again in November with **DEAF (Dutch Electronic Art Festival),** where artists explore the changing face of art in the computer age. There is also the **Wednesday Night Skate** (www.wednesdaynightskate.nl) in the summertime starting at 6pm in the center of town.

NEAR ROTTERDAM

GOUDA   ☎018

◪ *Trains roll into town from Rotterdam (20min., €3.70) and Amsterdam (1hr., €8). From the station, follow signs to the left towards the VVV: cross the bridge over the canal, walk straight on Kleiweg, which turns into Hoogstraat and leads to the Markt and the VVV tourist office (☎0900 468 32 888; fax 258 32 10; www.vvvgouda.nl). Open M-Sa 9am-5pm; in summer also Su noon-3pm.*

Gouda (HOW-da) is the quintessential Dutch town, with canals, a windmill, and (of course) its well-known cheese. In the 14th century much of the town's infrastructure and fortifications were already developed, and up until the 15th-century it rivalled Amsterdam in size and prestige. Known for crafts like knife-making, syrup-waffles, stained glass, and cheese, Gouda was also the home of **Erasmus:** the medieval humanist scholar was born, educated, and took his religious vows here in town.

In the summer, visitors can witness old-time trading procedures (like the hand-clapping agreements made between salesmen while bartering) during the **cheese market** held in the central Markt (Th 10am-12:30pm). The market features a number of tourist treats, among them cheese-making demonstrations and free samples presented by Gouda's tasty cheese-maidens. If you've ever had a burning desire to see your own weight in cheese, head to **Kaaswaag Gouda (Weigh House Gouda),** Markt 35-36, in the central Markt area. Staffers provide information about Gouda's dairy mainstay. The Kaaswaag features a permanent exhibition about Gouda and the history of its cheese trade. (☎252 99 96. Open Apr.-Oct. Tu-W 1-5pm, Th 10am-5pm, F-Su 1-5pm. €2, seniors €1.50, under 12 €1) If you haven't had enough of those large yellow wheels, every Thursday at 2pm you can join the **Cheese Walk** through town (€3.50; meets at the VVV). While you're in the central market, however, you won't want to miss the spectacular late Gothic **Stadhuis,** right in the center of the square, with its red-and-white clapboard shutters and a mechanical clock whose puppets get set into motion at two minutes past the half and full hour.

Those more interested in delectable Dutch sweets can try **De Vlaam,** Markt 69, tucked in among the many bars and *pannenkoekens,* a bakery famous for its take on *sirupwafels,* the delicious local specialty. (☎251 33 59. €6 for a whole tin. Open M-W and F 8:30am-6pm, Th 8:30am-9pm, Sa 8am-5pm.) The gargantuan, late Gothic **Sint Janskerk** has managed to maintain its collection of 16th-century stained-glass windows, despite attacks by both lightning and Reformation iconoclasts; at nearly 130 meters in length, it is also the longest church in The Netherlands. (☎251 26 84; www.st-janskerkgouda.nl. Open Mar.-Oct. M-Sa 9am-5pm; Nov.-Feb. M-Sa 10am-4pm. €3, seniors and students €1.75, ages 12-18 €1.50, ages 5-12 €1.) The **Goudse Pottenbakkerij "Adrie Moerings,"** Peperstraat 76, produces the same famous Gouda clay smoking pipes since the 17th century, some of which are over a meter long and decorated with elaborate, hand-painted designs. To get there, follow Westhaven along the canal south of the Markt. (☎251 28 42. Open M-F 9am-5pm, Sa 11am-5pm. Free.) Around the corner on Oosthaven, the ⬛**Museum het Catharina Gasthuis,** Achter de Kerk 14, houses a wonderful collection that explores the history of health care in Gouda—using everything from Flemish art and early surgical instruments to period

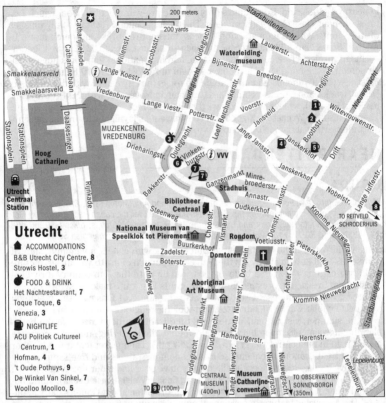

Utrecht

🏠 ACCOMMODATIONS
B&B Utrecht City Centre, **8**
Strowis Hostel, **3**

🍴 FOOD & DRINK
Het Nachtrestaurant, **7**
Toque Toque, **6**
Venezia, **3**

🌙 NIGHTLIFE
ACU Politiek Cultureel
    Centrum, **1**
Hofman, **4**
't Oude Pothuys, **9**
De Winkel Van Sinkel, **7**
Woolloo Moolloo, **5**

furniture, dolls, and weaponry. The Gasthuis is located in a former chapel and adjoining torture chamber. (☎ 258 84 40. Open M-Sa 10am-5pm, Su noon-5pm. €3.60, seniors €2.90, under 18 and Museumjaarkaart free. Cash only.)

UTRECHT   ☎ 0302

The swarms of fraternity boys that fill the city's outdoor cafes are a visible testament to Utrecht's status as The Netherlands' largest university town—with a student population over 60,000. Over 30km southeast of Amsterdam and roughly in the center of The Netherlands, Utrecht (pop. 250,000) is also a wealthy hub: visitors come here for lively festivals, museums, nightlife, and winding, tree-lined canals. Historically the Christian capital of the Low Countries, modern-day Utrecht is alive with religious history; Domtoren, the country's tallest church tower, dominates the provincial landscape, while museum Catharijneconvent displays the region's religious relics. With fewer tourists and more green spaces, Utrecht is an excellent break from the buzz of the nation's capital. Even the canals are more visitor-friendly: lying below street level away from foot traffic, their banks are ideal for afternoon picnicking.

TRANSPORTATION

Take the **train** from Amsterdam (30min., 3-6 per hr., €5.60). When you arrive, you'll be in a building connected to The Netherlands' largest shopping mall, the **Hoog Catharijne.** It's easiest to follow the signs through the mall towards Vredenburg (the

marketplace and music hall), near the center of the city. Turn left out of the mall and walk along the market until Lange Viestraat, then turn right and walk a block to the center. Oudegracht, Utrecht's main canal, will cross beneath you.

ORIENTATION & PRACTICAL INFORMATION

The pulsing center of Utrecht is known as the **Museumkwartier,** and lies a five-minute walk from Utrecht Centraal's Vredenburg exit; to check up on any museum listing, go to www.utrecht-city.com. Generally speaking, the Museum-kwartier is the area bound north and south by Oudegracht and Nieuwegracht. The main east-west thoroughfare is the twice-changing Vreden-burg/Lange Viestraat/Potterstraat. Here you'll find countless churches, museums, fashionable shops, restaurants, art galleries, and a number of theaters and coffeeshops. The center of the city is very commercial, but a stroll farther in any direction will yield more provincial regions. **Beware: the area around Centraal Station should be avoided at night;** in all emergencies, dial ☎112.

Hollyhoekstraat, Haarlem

The city is small enough to be crossed on foot (about 20-40min. across the city center), but if you're itching to put your pedal to the metal, rent a bike at **Bicycle Shop Tusveld,** Van Sijpestein-jkade 40 (☎293 26 79), located in a tunnel that runs under the train tracks, just West of Centraal Station (€5.50 per day). **Shuttevaer,** Bemuurde Weerd O.Z. 17, offers canal tours that leave from the corner of Oudegracht and Lange Viestraat every hour on the hour from 11am to 5pm. (☎272 01 11; www.schuttevaer.com. Open daily 11am-6pm. €6, children under 12 €4.50.) If you need to take a **taxi,** call ☎230 04 00 or pick one up near the station.

Kitty Climbing the Wall

The **VVV** office, Vinkenbrugstraat 19, has an exceptionally helpful and enthusiastic staff. Pick up a map of the city and a complete listing of museums and sights (€2); they can even suggest and book a hotel based on your budget. From the train station, head east on Vredenburg (which turns into Lange Viestraat), cross the canal, and after a block turn right into a small square; the VVV is at the southwestern corner. (☎0900 128 87 32, €0.50 per min; www.utrechts-tad.nl. Open June-Sept. M-W, F 9:30am-6:30pm; Th 9:30am-9pm; Sa 10:30am-5pm; Su 10am-2pm). For cultural information, you may wish to stop by the **RonDom,** Domplein 9, the cultural history visitor's center, also the only place that sells tickets to Dom Tower. (☎233 30 36; www.dom-toren.nl. Open M-Sa 10am-5pm, Su noon-5pm.)

Horse Country, Wadden Islands

The best way to get on the **Internet** is to use the free computers at hostels, but cheap rates (€2 per hr.) can be found at the **Centrale Bibliotheek** (Central Library), Oudegracht 167, north of Dom Tower. (☎286 18 00. Open M 1pm-9pm; Tu-W, F 11am-6pm; Th 11am-9pm; Sa 10am-2pm.)

ACCOMMODATIONS

B&B Utrecht City Centre, Lucasbolwerk 4 (☎0650 43 48 84; www.hostelutrecht.nl). If at Utrecht Centraal station, call and the owner may pick you up. Otherwise, head down Vredenburg, crossing the city center until it turns into Nobelstraat; turn left on Lucasbolwerk. There's nohing on the outside indicating that you're in front of a hostel—you have to ring the bell to be let into this spacious, 3-floor hostel that feels more like a utopian commune. Next to a lovely park, B&B Utrecht operates under a unique set of ideals. For a flat €16 fee, you get a dorm bed, free food 24hr. (the fridge is stocked continually with eggs, bread, and meats), sauna, piano, guitars, didgeridoo, and a home video system (with hundreds of DVDs). Free Internet on 16 top-speed computers, with keyboards from almost every language under the sun. With no max. stay and cheap bike rental (€5 per day), you just might decide to move in. If you do want to stay for a while, you can stay free in exchange for work. Reserve by phone or online. Sheets €2.50. Dorms €16; singles €55; doubles €65; triples €85; quads €100. MC/V. ●

Strowis Hostel, Boothstraat 8 (☎238 02 80 www.strowis.nl). From the station, head east on Vredenburg until it becomes Lange Jansstraat, turn left onto the tree-lined square following Janskerkhof around and turn left again at Boothstraat; the hostel is on your left. Impeccable rooms, shiny dark-wood floors, high ceilings, an outdoor terrace overlooking a garden, and the glimmer of candles on summer nights give this new hostel the feel of an airy country home. Add the laid-back staff, convenient location right around the corner from the ACU Politeek Centrum (see Utrecht: **Nightlife,** p. 260), and unbeatable prices, and it becomes a near-ideal place to spend a night. Breakfast €5. Blankets €1.25. Two-week max. stay. Curfew 2am on weekdays, 3am on weekends. 12- and 14-person dorms €12; 4- and 6-bed dorms €14.50; triples €55; doubles €45. ●

FOOD

Utrecht's affluence is nowhere more apparent than in its lack of extensive budget dining options. For cheap eating, try the pizzerias, pubs, and sandwich shops on **Nobelstraat** (Lange Viestraat becomes Nobelstraat east of the Museumkwartier) or Voorstraat, closer to the center. In fair weather, head to the rows of basement-side canals for picnicking. The less congested stretch of Oudegracht south of Hamburgerstraat is ideal for stretching out and watching the boats row by (there's an Albert Heijn supermarket around the bend on Twijnstraat). Otherwise, you may want to splurge at one of the canal-side restaurants lining **Oudegracht,** near **Domplein.**

Het Nachtrestaurant, Oudegracht 158 (☎230 30 36), on the east side of the canal, just north of the Stadhuis. Co-owned by the popular De Winkel van Sinkel (see Utrecht: **Nightlife,** p. 260), this *tapas* "night restaurant" has a decadent pillow-lined cellar dining room, while the more flashy clientele crowds the canal-side terrace until late. *Tapas* (€2.40-6.80) and *sangria* (€3.20 per glass). Open M-W 6pm-11pm, Th 6pm-midnight, F 6pm-1am, Sa 6pm-10:30pm (on Sa after 11pm the restaurant becomes a night club). MC. ●

Toque Toque, Oudegracht 138 (☎231 87 87), just off Vinkenburgstraat. Deep red walls, an aluminum bar, terrace seats overlooking the canal, and an enormous, multi-colored tissue-paper chandelier make this one of the hipper restaurants along the Oudegracht. Upscale clientele peruses the 9-page wine list, and delicately nibbles large salads (under €12.50) and homemade, fresh pastas (€10.50-15). Open Su-W 10am-midnight, Th-Sa 10am-1am; kitchen open daily 10am-10pm. AmEx/MC/V. ●

Venezia, Oudegracht 105, is Utrecht's most popular ice cream stand. Sundaes from €2, single scoop for €1.10, and heaping 3-scoop cones for €2.70; try the tiramisù, pistachio, or myrtle, and guilt-free fresh fruit sorbets. Open daily noon-10:30pm, although hours vary based on the weather. Cash only. ●

SIGHTS

DOMKERK & DOMTOREN

🔲 *Achter de Dom 1. From Lange Viestraat, turn right on Oudegracht, following it down on the east-ernmost side until Servetstraat; turn left. Domkerk (Dom Church):* ☎ *231 04 03. Open Oct.-Apr. M-F 11am-4pm, Sa 11am-3:30pm, Su 2pm-4pm; May-Sept. M-F 10am-5pm, Sa 10am-3:30pm, Su 2pm-4pm. Free. Free concert every Sa 3:30pm. Domtoren (Dom Tower) accessible only with a guided tour organized by RonDom (see above). Tours Sept.-June daily 10am-4pm every hr. on the hr.; July-Aug. tours every 30min., 10am-4:30pm. Tours in English and Dutch, though tours may be conducted in other languages depending on demand. €6, ages 4-12 €3.60.*

Utrecht's Domtoren is impossible to ignore: the city's most beloved landmark is also the highest church tower in The Netherlands. Lording over the province with flamboyant spires and the music of 60,000kg of bronze bells, it remains a visible (and auditory) reminder of the region's deeply religious past. Begun in 1254 and finished 250 years later in the French Gothic style, the brick-red Domkerk (or Dom Church) was attached to the tower until a wild tornado blew away the nave in 1674. The church was initially Roman Catholic but has held only Protestant services since 1580. Climb the 465 steps to take in panoramic views of Amersfoort and Amsterdam—on clear days, Rotterdam and The Hague are also visible. During the hour-long tour, you'll learn about the history of the church and get a glimpse of the church's 50-plus bells.

MUSEUMS

The Museum Quarter contains the core of Utrecht's extended family of museums. For more general information, check out www.utrecht-city.com or www.utrecht-museumkwartier.nl.

CENTRAAL MUSEUM

🔲 *Nicolaaskerkhof 10. From Domplein, head south on Korte Nieuwstraat (it becomes Lange Nieu-wstraat). Turn right onto at Agnietenstraat; it becomes Nicolaaskerkhof.* ☎ *236 23 62; www.cen-traalmuseum.nl. Open Su, Tu-Sa 11am-5pm. Free audio tour. €8, children under 12 free.*

The five "C"s in the museum's logo stand for the five categories of objects housed in this slick, renovated cloister: Old Masters, Modern Art, Fashion, Design, and Local History. Founded in 1838 and renovated in 1999, the Centraal museum is now the oldest municipal museum in The Netherlands; each of its galleries pays tribute to its the country's national and civic past, with an exquisite collection that ranges from paintings by 17th-century "Utrecht Caravaggists" to 20th-century Dutch masters. The museum oversees the world's largest collection of work by de Stijl designer Gerrit Reitveld (1888-1964), but many of these objects have been transferred to the avantgarde **Rietveld Schroderhuis,** Pritns Hendriklaan 50a (☎ 236 23 10). Designed by Rietveld and constructed in 1924, the house is located towards the east of the city; take bus #4 from Centraal Station to De Hooghstraat. Accessible by guided tour only, so call ahead for reservations. (Open W-Sa 11am-5pm. €8, children ages 4-13 €4.)

MUSEUM CATHARIJNECONVENT

🔲 *Lange Nieuwstraat 38.* ☎ *231 72 96; www.catharijneconvent.nl. Open Tu-F 10am-5pm, Sa-Su 11am-5pm. €6, ages 6-17 €3, seniors €5, family ticket €15, children under 5 free. Some special exhibitions may require extra admission. MC/V.*

Once the Christian capital of the Low Countries, Utrecht overflows with relics from its religious past. In honor of this, the Museum Catharijneconvent, a gorgeously converted convent, has fittingly assembled an historical survey of Dutch Christianity through works of visual art. While the collection contains many traditional Catholic relics, 15th-century manuscripts, and 17th-century paintings, the sections on modern and contemporary religious art are of merely topical significance. Though the museum isn't at afraid to display artwork that is critical of Christianity or the Catholic Church—including a dual portrait of the Devil and the Pope and a painting of a nun and monk caught in the act of coitus—even these attempts at curatorial provocation fall a bit flat.

ABORIGINAL ART MUSEUM

🖪 *Oudegracht 176. South of the Dom on the eastern side of Oudegracht.* ☎ *238 01 00; www.aamu.nl. Open Tu-F 10am-5pm, Sa-Su 11am-5pm. €8, children under 12 and seniors €5, family ticket €15. AmEx/MC/V.*

This collection of acrylic paintings by contemporary Australian Aboriginal artists is the first of its kind in Europe. The paintings from the Central Desert, Arnhem Land, and the Kimberly Region in Australia may look like they're influenced by modern Western abstract art, but they're actually schematic maps of the desert landscape. Most information is in Dutch, but ask for the walk-through pamphlet in English. The museum also has a gallery where you can buy paintings.

OTHER MUSEUMS

Don't miss the **Nationaal Museum van Speelklok tot Pierement** (the National Museum of Musical Clocks and Street Organs), Buurkerkhof 10, and its collection of automats from the 17th-20th centuries. Open T-Sa 10am-5pm, Su noon-5pm. Guided tours where you can see the instruments in motion run every hour. (☎ 231 27 89; www.museumspeelklok.nl. €6, children 4-12 €4) From Steenweg turn onto Buurkerkhof. Farther up Oudegracht you'll find the **Waterleidingmuseum (Waterworks Museum),** Lauwerhof 29, situated in a water tower on the northern side of Lange Viestraat. Here you'll find four floors of Dutch water history delivered by former employees of the Water Company. The colorful 39m water tower from 1895 is worth the five-minute walk from the Museumkwartier. (☎ 232 11 52. Open Tu-F and Su 1:30pm-5pm, Sa 11am-4pm. €2, children ages 6-11 €1.)

For astronomy buffs, the **Observatory Sonnenborgh Museum** Zonnenburg 2, The Netherlands' oldest domed observatory, has telescopes and a large collection of antique scientific instruments. (☎ 230 28 18; www.sonnenborgh.nl. Hours depend on the cosmos and space is limited; call or visit the website to make a viewing reservation. Open M-F 10am-4pm. €3.50, children under 14 €2.50.)

NIGHTLIFE

The Netherlands' largest college town has the nightlife to match. Pick up a copy of *UitLoper* at bars or restaurants to scout the bar and arts scenes—both stay lively seven days a week. As with most student bars and clubs in The Netherlands, big stepping-out nights are Wednesday-Friday; on Saturday many students stay home.

De Winkel van Sinkel, Oude Gracht 158 (☎ 230 30 30; www.dewinkelvansinkel.nl). The city's most popular grandcafe in an old canal side warehouse. The huge, mandarin-colored complex with martinis lining the walls and a hyper-kitsch newsprint menu is open late every night, with discos Sa that spill downstairs into Het Nachtrestaurant (see Utrecht: **Food,** p. 258). Wine from €2.60; beer from €2.30. Open Su-F 11am-2am, Sa 11am-5am.

't Oude Pothuys, Oudegracht 279 (☎ 231 89 70). Musical instruments hang from the ceilings of this candlelit, converted cellar—one of the city's busiest and coolest nightspots. The bar hosts jam sessions M, Tu, Th 11pm-1:30am. Enjoy €1.70 beers in a chill atmosphere with a good mix of young and old. Open daily 10pm-3am.

Woolloo Moolloo, Janskerkhof 14 (☎ 236 08 60; www.woofoto.nl). Run entirely by a local fraternity, this is where Utrecht's student nightlife migrates after everything else closes; show up after 1am for the most fun. Student ID required for entry into the dance hall. DJs every night of the week. Beer €1.10. Cover €3. Open daily 11pm-as late as 7am.

Hofman, Janskerhof 17a, (☎ 230 24 70; www.hofman-cafe.nl). In an beautiful tree-lined square, just next to the Akademietheater, Utrecht's theater school, Hofman's hosts weekly student-friendly events like free Tango night (Tu 9pm), philosophical debates (M 8pm), dance parties (Th, F midnight-4am), and improv competitions (Su 5pm). Food can get expensive, but the *salade nicoise is* €5.50, and samosas are €3.50. Beer €1.60; cocktails like *caipirinha* €5. No cover. Open M-W 11am-2am, Th-Sa 11am-4am, Su 2pm-2am.

ACU Politiek Cultureel Centrum, Voorstraat 71 (☎231 45 90; www.acu.nl). Head east on Lange Viestraat from Oudegracht and turn left onto Voorstraat. A legalized squat with a crowded bar open every night and discos F-Sa until 4am. Also hosts live music on the weekends (mostly hardcore metal, punk, and some folk; cover €4-5), political events, and offers a €5 veggie dinner M-Th 6-7:30pm. Beer €1.60; whisky €2.40. Open Su-W 5pm-1am, Th 5pm-3am, F-Sa 9pm-4am. Cash only.

FESTIVALS

As The Netherlands' central hub, Utrecht is the country's unofficial festival capital. Free events abound throughout the year: check the *UitLoper* magazine—which can be found in pubs and cafes across the city or at www.uitloper.nl. Every Sunday during the summer, Lepelenburg park east of the city, plays host to the free **Lazy Sunday Afternoon** pop concert series at around 2pm. Around the third week of June is **Midzomergracht (Midsummer Canal Party),** Utrecht's famous BGLTQ cultural festival with free movies, concerts and events (www.midzomergracht.nl), as well as the international Utrecht **Blues Festival** (www.blues-festival-utrecht.nl). In late August, the city also hosts the Early Music Festival, **Festival Oude Musiek** (www.oudemuziek.nl), with baroque and classical ensembles playing period instruments. During the second week of November, Utrecht's cafes and pubs open their doors to a less high-brow tradition, the **Smartlappen** festival, which celebrates folk singing—and beer drinking. The city is also home to the **Dutch Film Festival** (www.filmfestival.nl), with red carpets, Dutch film stars, and the "Gouden kalf" award.

ARNHEM ☎026

Arnhem is a good one-night stop on the Lower Rhine, especially on the way to De Hoge Veluwe National Park. A sleepy city (pop. 140,000) that somehow wakes up in the evening, this capital of the province of Gelderland is encircled by a ring of parks and is home several good restaurants and nighteries.

TRANSPORTATION & PRACTICAL INFORMATION

Trains pull in daily from Amsterdam's Centraal Station (80min., every 15min., €12.30). The city center of Arnhem lies south of the main street, Jansbudensingel, which runs east-west from the exit of the train station. The next five blocks are for pedestrians only, and on the southeastern corner (farthest from the trains) of the center is **Eusebiuskerk,** the 15th-century church destroyed in the 1944 Battle of Arnhem and restored thereafter.

To get to the **VVV,** Willemsplein 8, exit the train station, turn left, continue down the street for one block, and you'll see the blue flag on your left. The VVV provides free maps of the town. (☎0900 202 40 75, €0.50 per min.; www.vvvarnhem.nl. Open M 11am-5:30pm, Tu-F 9am-5:30pm, Sa 10am-4pm.)

ACCOMMODATIONS

StayOkay Arnhem, Diepenbrocklaan 27 (☎442 01 14; www.stayokay.com/arnhem). Take bus #3 from the station (10min., €2.10 round-trip) to the Rijnstate Hospital stop. From the bus stop, turn right as you face the hospital (Ziekenhuis Rijnstate), cross the street at the intersection, and turn left on Cattepoelseweg. Then, about 150m ahead, turn right up the brick steps, at the top, turn right. The hostel will be straight ahead. New hostel may feel a bit too polished, but the rooms are exceptionally clean, service is friendly, and rustic setting provides a peaceful entree to the national park. Appeals to a slightly older crowd. Breakfast and linen included. There's a bar and reading room that serves beer (pints €2.50). Laundry available (wash €3.50, dry €2). Key deposit €5. Reception 8am-11pm. No curfew. Free safe box at reception. Lunch €6.75; bag lunch €4.30; dinner €9. Dorms €21.55-22.85; singles €29.55-30.85; doubles €52.30-54.90; triples €71.55-75.45; quads €91-96; quints €113.50-120; 6-bed rooms €128-137. Members of StayOkay network receive €2.50 discount. Children ages 3-10 €4.75, children ages 10-15 €2.50 discount per night. MC/V. ❶

Felix Reijmers, Boaterdijk 23 (☎443 66 06; cell 651 714 274; www.rederijreijmers.nl). From the station, take the main street left, and then hang a right at Nieuweplein. Heading south toward the Rhine, the entrance is by the brown house with green roof on your right along the river. This 5-room "boatel" sits on the Neder Rijn. Rooms are impeccably kept and have bath and brilliant riverside views. A few times a year the boat sets sail for Amsterdam, so make sure to plan your stay in advance. Singles €40; doubles €60. Cash only. ❷

FOOD

Several cheap, greasy sandwich stops and shawarma stands can be found along the bustling **Korenmarkt,** directly southeast of the train station. From the platform, head to your right on Utrechtstraat, turn right after two blocks and then take first left; walk down the street a few meters until you hit the small square.

🍴 **Pizzeria Pinoccio,** Korenmarkt 25b (☎443 22 08), offers good prices, a great location, and even better food in the heart of the city. Sit outside on the square or inside beneath the wine-casks, ivy, and candlelight. Wide selection of generously-sized personal pizzas (€5.60-11; adventurers, try the "surprise pizza" €11), reasonably priced meat entrees (rack of ribs €11.80), and pasta. Open M-W 5-9:30pm, Th-F 5-10pm, Sa-Su 4-10pm. MC/V. ❸

Proef Lokaal de Waag, Markt 38 (☎370 59 60; www.proeflokaaldewaag.nl) at Walburgstraat, just south of Eusebiuskerk, on the southeastern end of the city. Two-floored restaurant in a restored, all-wood mansion from 1761. For lunch, soups €4.10, sandwiches €7-8. For dinner, Proef serves a great veggie lasagna (€13.90) and a well-portioned rack of lamb (€18.90). Open daily 10:30am-1am; kitchen closes 9pm. AmEx/MC/V. ❹

Pasam, Varkensstraat 33 (☎446 07 58). From the train station, turn left on the main street and right at Nieuweplein. Left on Rijnstraat and then a quick left puts Varkensstraat on your right. Not the greatest Middle Eastern food, but portions are reasonable and prices are low. Shawarma combo €6.20, veggie *broodjes* under €3.50. Open daily 1pm-5am. ❶

SIGHTS

In September 1944 the Nazis bombed the town in what has become known as the Battle of Arnhem. Like many Dutch cities, Arnhem had to be completely rebuilt after the war. The town's most conspicuous sight is **Eusebiuskerk,** Kerkplein 1. From the train station, walk out to the main street, turn left and after one block turn right, following Nieuweplein three blocks to Oeverstraat and turn left; the church is up the street about 400m. Here, the grand church, restored in neo-Gothic style soon after its 15th-century tower crashed to the ground during WWII, towers over a frighteningly empty square. Today it is again the base for **Eusebiustoren,** the 93m tower whose 53-bell carillon is the largest in Western Europe. During restoration, a glass elevator was installed to take visitors up to the beautiful views. (☎443 50 68. Open Tu-Sa 10am-5pm, Su noon-5pm. Elevator €2.50, under 14 €2). The hideous gray building behind the church is Arnhem's city hall, **Stadhuis,** which was built in 1964. Between the church and hall and against Walburgstraat, you'll find **Duivelshuis,** Koningstraat 1. This mansion with deformed, distorted faces and animal-like human statues carved into its sides was built in 1545. Untouched by the bombings, it was ironically owned by a successful Dutch warmonger who sculpted the images to protest the town hall's prohibition of gold-coated front steps.

NIGHTLIFE

After witnessing a Saturday night in Arnhem, you'll understand why the city is so quiet during the week: the city's residents are all sleeping off their weekends. It may be the most raucous nightlife in The Netherlands, if not the classiest. Back-to-back pubs and clubs line the Korenmarkt, the nightlife centrum. **Luther Danscafe,** Korenmarkt 26, crowds twenty-somethings into all three floors, with drinking on the 1st, chilling on the second, and grooving to R&B and dance classics on the third. Club dress code is mandatory. Beer €2, most mixed drinks €4. (☎442 81 07. Open in winter Th-Sa 6pm-2am; in summer W 1pm-1am, Th-F 1pm-2am, Su 1pm-1am). The decor at **Le Grand Cafe,** Korenmarkt 16, awkwardly mixes and matches moose heads, palm trees, and fake Greek statuary, but the atmosphere is low-key and the food is tasty. *Tostis* €2.50. Full meals €4.65-6.25; beer €1.80-2. (☎442 62 81. Open M-W 10am-1am, Th-Sa 10am-2am, Su 11am-1am. Cash only).

NEAR ARNHEM

APELDOORN   ☎055

While not a magnificent town in itself, Apeldoorn (pop. 153,000), some 25km north of Arnhem, is another good jumping-off place for **De Hoge Veluwe National Park.** Trains run into Apeldoorn station from both Amsterdam (1hr., every 30min., €11.30) and Arnhem (50min, every 30min, €3.90). The **VVV tourist office,** Stationstraat 72, just a five-minute walk from the station, sells bike maps for €4.20. (☎0900 168 16 36, €0.45 per min.; open M-F 9am-5:30pm, Sa 9am-5pm.) The town is home to the stunning ▓Museum Paleis Het Loo, a 17th-century palace that was home to the many King Willams from Orange. The sizeable grounds are a monument to geometrical excess: the pristine gardens—full of Neoclassical sculptures, fountains, and a colonnade—have been pedantically and symmetrically trimmed for almost 350 years. From the station, walk 40min. or take bus #1, 102, or 104 (20min., 2 strips) to get to the museum; the bus stops outside the entrance. (☎577 24 00; www.paleishetloo.nl. Open Su, Tu-Sa 10am-5pm. Guided tours in English by appointment only. Tours €1.20 per person for up to 20-person group; reserve at least 2 weeks in advance. €9, under 18 €3. MC/V). Also nearby is ▓Apenheul, or (apes' refuge), an interactive zoo in Berg & Bos nature reserve, with 30 different species of apes. Take bus #2 or 3 (10min., 2 strips). Gorillas, orangutans, and bonobos live on islands throughout the park, while smaller apes dwell in the area around the many walking paths. You're more likely to get pickpocketed here than in Amsterdam Centraal—the park provides special monkey-proof money belts. (☎357 57 57; www.apenheul.nl. Open Apr.-May daily 9:30am-6pm; June-Aug. daily 9:30am-5pm; Sept.-Oct daily 9:30am-5pm. €13, seniors €12, under 10 €11.)

DE HOGE VELUWE NATIONAL PARK   ☎0318

De Hoge Veluwe is a far cry from the urban buzz of Amsterdam: at 13,565 acres, the nature reserve is The Netherlands' largest—exploration through the park will reveal wooded areas, moors, grass plains, and, extraordinarily, sand dunes. While the flat landscape may not offer the most dramatic hiking, the Hoge Veluwe is easily traversed by bike. Over 42km of extensively mapped bikepaths cross the reserve, and 1000 white bikes available free of charge at five convenient spots in the park make traversing the landscape a true treat. The handful of lakes and shady glens also make the park ideal for picnicking. Venture to the southern end of the park to watch the wildlife; early morning and late afternoon are the best times to catch a glimpse of the deer, wild boars, and numerous birds that inhabit the park.

TRANSPORTATION & PRACTICAL INFORMATION

Apeldoorn and preferably Arnhem (both 15km from the park) are both good bases for exploring De Hoge Veluwe. From the **Arnhem** train station, take bus #107 to the park's northwestern Otterlo entrance, (25min; every 30min., 6:44-10:14am and 2:44-6:14pm; every hr. 10:14am-2:44pm and 6:14pm-11:14pm.; €4.20 or 6 strips). From **Apeldoorn,** take bus #110 at the train station to the Otterlo entrance (25min.; every hr., last bus leaves the park at 5:45pm; €4.20 or 6 strips). Bus #110 also goes deeper into the park and stops at the main Hoenderloo entrance, the Kröller-Müller Museum, and the Visitor Center. For both routes, if you get off the bus inside the park, you'll have to buy your entrance ticket from the driver: an easier and quicker alternative than standing in the sometimes interminable lines at the ticket booths. The De Hoge grounds are open Apr. 8am-8pm, May and Aug. 8am-9pm, June-July 8am-10pm, Sept. 9am-8pm, Oct. 9am-7pm, Nov.-Mar. 9am-5:30pm. (€5, ages 6-12 €2.50; May-Sept. 50% discount after 5pm. Cars €5. V). Once in the park, begin by picking up a map (€2.50) at any of the park entrances or at the **De Hoge Veluwe Visitor Center,** known as the **Bezoekerscentrum.** (☎59 16 27; www.hogeveluwe.nl. Hours are the same as the park). Note that bike-paths, car roads, and hiking trails are assiduously separated throughout the park. Be sure to read the map legend carefully.

ACCOMMODATIONS & FOOD

Camping is available at a campground near the Hoenderloo entrance. (☎055 378 22 32. Open Apr.-Oct. €3.50 per person, ages 6-12 €1.75. Electricity €2.)

The most economical and enjoyable way to refuel during a day in the park is with a picnic lunch. There are, however, two restaurants within the park. **De Koperen Kop ❸**, a self-service cafeteria-style restaurant at the center of the park and next to the Visitor Center, offers a special (€11.25) for every season in addition to cheap (€3.75-4.75) crepes and salads. (☎59 12 89. Open same hours as Bezoekerscentrum. AmEx/MC/V.). A kiosk next to De Koperen Kop sells ice cream and cold drinks in the warmer months. The more upscale **Rijzenburg ❺**, much farther away from the center (towards the southernmost end of the park) has a three-course menu from €21.30. (☎443 67 33; www.rijzenburg.nl. Open daily noon-8pm). **Monsieur Jacques ❶**, located inside the Kröller-Müller Museum, is a less expensive option. It sells sandwiches and drinks at only slightly inflated prices, and the outdoor terrace makes it worth a stop. (Open same hours as the museum.)

SIGHTS

The park's extensive biking trails are its main attraction—the best route is #2 (2-3 hr. round-trip). Begin at the **Kröller-Müller Museum** and follow the route down past the sand dunes (be sure to pull over and check out the animal tracks, wind-blown streaks, and desert-like flora); make a first left and continue straight ahead, veering to your left: you will pass by the **Deelense Veld's** beautiful lakes on your right. Take the first and second left turns to get back to the Museum or the Otterloo entrance.

◼KRÖLLER-MÜLLER MUSEUM

🚹 *The museum is situated in the center of the park; follow signs from any of the entrances, or ask the bus driver to let you off by the museum. ☎59 12 41; www.kmm.nl. Open Su, Tu-Sa 10am-5pm; sculpture garden closes 4:30pm. €5, ages 6-12 €2.75.*

It's both a blessing and a curse that this world-class gem of a museum should be tucked deep within park's beautiful expanses. The museum's collection, which began with the private holdings of heiress Helene Kröller-Müller, boasts an astounding 91 paintings and 185 drawings by Vincent Van Gogh, including *Four Sunflowers*

Going to Seed, and *Pink Peach Trees*, but the true scene-stealer is his famous *The Cafe Terrace on the Place du Forum*. The sprawling, modern complex is also home to work by other early Modernist masters like Mondrian, Juan Gris, Giacometti, and Seurat. As a museum, the building situates itself firmly in its natural surroundings. Whole galleries look out onto adjacent woodlands, and the gorgeous sculpture garden—with moving large-scale works by Richard Serra, Mario Merz, Carl Andre, and Tony Smith—is an astonishing amalgamation of natural and man-made materials. Be sure not to miss Dubuffet's *Jardin d'email*—a walk-through environment in white and black; just look for the towering, cartoonish tree, or pick up a free map to the garden. The museum and its grounds—both worthy of all hyperbole—should not be missed.

OTHER SIGHTS

A few kilometers north, the central tower of the **St. Hubertus Hunting Lodge** rises up out of the landscape like a large, brick-red ostrich. Designed by Berlage, the castle is open daily for free guided tours. There is also a suggested walk (follow the yellow signs) circling the lodge that rambles past a meditation garden, peat bog, watermill, and sheep meadow. Spots for the lodge tours are limited and fill up especially fast in summer. Reserve early on the day of the tour at the Visitor Center. Also check out the visually inventive **Museonder,** an underground museum in the Visitor Center that teaches travelers about the park's flora, and ecosystems. (Open daily 10am-5pm. Free with park ticket.)

GRONINGEN ☎ 050

Groningen, easily the most happening city in the northern Netherlands, pulses with new life. While the city is far older than Amsterdam—earliest mentions of the city's primitive name *Cruoninga* date from 1040—the mantra here is strictly forward-looking. Heavily bombed in World War II, Groningen rebuilt itself completely. Yet unlike some other Dutch cities, Groningen managed to retain if its Old-World feel alongside its bland 1950s architecture. Some beautiful older buildings remain, including Martinitoren, Stadhuis, the University, and Prinsenhoftuin. The priority now is cutting-edge architecture and design, evidenced, among other things, in the adventurous Groninger Museum and Rem Koolhaas's milk-glass public urinal. The city gates—nine markers that spell out the city's ancient name—were conceived by World Trade Center memorial architect Daniel Libeskind in 1990 to celebrate Groningen's 950th anniversary. More than half of the city's 175,000 inhabitants are under 35, due in no small part to the Rijksuniversiteit Groningen (University of Groningen) and the Hanzehogeschool (Institute for Higher Professional Education). As a result Groningen is known throughout The Netherlands as a party city.

ORIENTATION

The **train** from Amsterdam takes about 2.5 hours (About 2 per hr., €23.80 one way). When you buy your ticket in Amsterdam (or Groningen, on return), ask the attendant if the next train requires a switch in another city; you may have to change trains in Amersfoot. Once you get to the transfer, you will only have to cross the platform and board the opposite train *only* in the section of that train that has a sign listing your final destination. Again, it's best to check with the conductor as even the Dutch seem to get confused in this situation.

PRACTICAL INFORMATION

Groningen's old center is easily walkable and no bigger than a square kilometer. Bordered by public transit in the south and canals in the east, north, and west, the center is a ten-minute walk from the train station. To get there, go out to the main street, **265**

Groningen

⌂ ACCOMMODATIONS
Hotel Friesland, **10**
Martini Hotel, **9**
Simplon Jongerenhotel, **2**

🍴 FOOD & DRINK
Ben'z, **5**
De Kleine Moghul, **1**
Satehuis, **13**

🍷 NIGHTLIFE
Cafe de Vlaamsche Reus, **3**
Tramps, **4**
Vera, **7**

☕ COFFEESHOPS
Dee's Cafe, **6**
Dream Factory, **12**
The Glory, **8**
De Vliegende Hollander, **11**

turn right and cross the second bridge on your left. After crossing, follow Herestraat until its end: Groningen's historic **Grote Markt.** If you need to hit the road for any reason, a bus system reaches all parts of the city (bring your *strippenkaart*). Call for **taxis** at ☎549 49 40. Though Groningen, like many other Dutch cities, boasts a network of canals, here they are referred to as *diep* rather than *gracht*. The **VVV tourist office,** Grote Markt 25, is in the southeastern corner of the Grote Markt next to the Martinitoren. The VVV books accommodations and gives guided walking tours in July and August; reserve in advance. (☎313 97 41; www.vvvgroningen.nl. Open Jan.-June and Sept.-Dec. M-W 9am-6pm, Th 9am-8pm, F 9am-6pm, Sa 10am-5pm; additional hours July-Aug. Su 11am-3pm. Walking tours Su 1-3pm, M 2:30-4:30pm; €3.50, under 12 €2.25.) Get your email fix at **Internet Cafe Groningen,** Turfsingel 94. €0.30 per 5min. (☎311 30 90; www.internetcafe-groningen.net. Open daily noon-1am.)

Groningen heats up on the first weekend in July for its free open-air music festival, **Swingin' Groningen,** which in the past has attracted names like Fishbone and Blackalicious. Book accommodations in advance.

ACCOMMODATIONS

🏠 **Simplon Jongerenhotel,** Boterdiep 73-2 (☎313 52 21; www.xs4all.nl/~simplon). From the train station, take bus #1 (dir. Korrewegwijk) and get off at the Boterdiep stop; the hostel is the white building through the yellow and black striped entranceway. A 10min. walk from the center of Groningen, the Simplon pulls in young and fun residents with its clean, cheap lodgings rock-bottom prices and ultra-friendly, heavy metal-loving staff. Breakfast served

8:30-11am €4; included in price of private rooms. Laundry €4. Reception 24hr. Free lockers with €10 deposit. Linens €2.80 for guests staying in dorms, included in price of private rooms. Lockout noon-3pm. Bed in one of the 5 dorms (4 co-ed, 1 women-only) €11.40; singles €29.50; doubles €43; triples €61.50; quads €79.40. Cash only. ❶

Martini Hotel, Gedempte Zuiderdiep 8 (☎312 99 19; www.martinihotel.nl). From the station, cross the canal at the Groninger Museum and follow that street a few blocks to Gedempte Zuiderdiep. Turn right; Martini is on your right. About halfway between the train station and Grote Markt, this large, new hotel was recently renovated, with a classy new lobby. Private bathrooms TV in every room. Breakfast €7.50. Singles €66; doubles €122; triples €75; quads €96; quints €95. AmEx/MC/V. ❸

Hotel Friesland, Kleine Pelsterstraat 4 (☎312 13 07). It's a 5-10min. walk from the train station: cross the canal at the Groninger Museum (on your right as you exit the station) and walk up Ubbo Emmiusstraat, turn right on Gedempte Zuiderdiep, left on Pelsterstraat, and right onto Kleine Pelsterstraat. Here you'll enjoy friendly service, bright bedrooms with high ceilings, and impeccably clean shared bathrooms. All rooms with sink. Breakfast included. Singles €23.50; doubles €43.50; triples €60; quads €80. AmEx/D/MC/V. ❶

FOOD

🍴 **De Kleine Moghul,** Nieuwe Boteringstraat 62 (☎318 89 05). Entirely organic, lovingly prepared Indian cuisine, in a setting so pretty you won't want to leave. It's a bit of a walk from the center, but convenient to the Noorderplantsoen. Entrees around €9. Takeout available. Open daily 5-10pm. MC/V. ❷

🍴 **Ben'z,** Peperstraat 17 (☎313 79 17; www.restaurantbenz.nl). In the heart of Groningen's party district, this is an unparalleled dining experience. Dinner, a Middle Eastern hodgepodge (starters €2-3.50; multi-course set menus €10-15) is served in a Bedouin tent upon Turkish cushions and lit by lanterns. Finish your meal off with a puff on the *nargila* (water pipe). Perfect for groups; special student menu €7.60-9.10. Cash only. ❷

Satehuis, Herestraat 111 (☎311 28 65). Enjoy the Indonesian-style *satay* in this small world of bamboo and rattan. Meals, 6 sticks of *satay* served with rice and sides, from €6.10-10.40. Special movie deal buys a meal, drink, and ticket to the cinema across the street for €14. Open M 5-10pm, Su, 4:30-10pm. AmEx/MC/V. ❷

SIGHTS

MARTINITOREN

🚩 *On the southeastern corner of Grote Markt. Buy tickets at the VVV, across the street, or at the tower's 1st floor when VVV is not open. Open Apr.-Oct. daily 11am-5pm; Nov.-Mar. noon-4pm. €2.50, children under 12 €1.50.*

The **Martinitoren** offers the best view of the city. Standing at 97 meters, it miraculously survived the war untouched, unlike its neighbors on the northern and eastern sides of Grote Markt, which suffered total destruction. Built as a Catholic church, the middle section dates from the 13th century. When the Protestants took over the church in the late 16th century, they painted over the frescos in white, some of which have been recovered with modern-day restorations. Midway up the tower, you can pull cords and push buttons to simulate bell ringing; let your feet leave the ground and the rope will pull you upward. You can also see the real bells up close, under which people were occasionally tied for torture.

OTHER SIGHTS

While in the area of the Martinitoren, look to the western side of the square and you'll see **Stadhuis,** the Groningen city hall. The Stadhuis prevails over the **Grote Markt,** which becomes a real marketplace every Tuesday and Saturday. For the rare display of open-air urination, head out onto the street that heads out of the square. In a few blocks, it becomes Brugstraat; right before the first canal, turn left onto Kleineder A. There, take in the opaque glass **urinoir** designed by Rem Koolhaas so men can pee publicly in style. Backtrack along the same canal past Brugstraat and take it easy at **Noorderplantsoen,** a rolling, fountained park in the northwestern corner of the city (follow the canal north of Brugstraat and turn left across the last canal before it bends away to the right). The park hosts the annual **Noorderzon (Northern Sun) Festival** of theater in late August. North of Burgstraat along Turftorenstraat sits **Academieplein,** the complex that houses **Rijksuniversiteit Groningen,** the 35,000-student university that provides the city's boisterous nightlife. As you walk up the street, on your left is **Academiegebouw** the administrative center, and on your right, the university's main library. Continue on Academieplein for more sights: one of the oldest stone houses in the city (#24), the house with 13 temples (#23), the former District Court (#36-38), and the one-time residence of the Queen's Commissioner (#44) all lie along the street. Keep walking along Academieplein until you hit the canal. There, escape the city's postwar urbanity in the **Princes' Court Gardens,** which was originally designed in 1625 with a rose garden and covered paths. When in bloom, the fragrant roses make it impossible not to linger, especially when the **Theeschenkerij Tea Hut** inside the garden makes it so tempting to order a cup of tea (€0.80) and lounge in the sun or under one of the charming canopied underpasses. (Tea hut open M-F 10-6pm, Sa-Su noon-6pm.) On your way out, take the advice of the Latin inscription on the sundial above the entrance to heart: "The past is nothing, the future uncertain, the present unstable; ensure that you do not lose this time, which is yours alone."

MUSEUMS

GRONINGER MUSEUM

In the middle of the canal in front and to the right of the train station. Walk across the blue pedestrian bridge. ☎366 65 55; www.groninger-museum.nl. Open Sept.-June Su, Tu-Sa 10am-5pm; July-Aug. M 1-5pm, Su, Tu-Sa 10am-5pm. €7, seniors €6, children €3.50.

The Groninger Museum, housed in a multicolored, almost entropic building, exhibits both modern art, traditional paintings, and ancient artifacts. Built by Italian architects and famed French designer Philippe Starck, with five pavilions and a cafe, its steel-trimmed galleries create a futuristic laboratory atmosphere for its exhibits. It's a museum defined by risk, both architecturally and artistically; there are a few collections from the empire, and some Golden Age paintings, but the point here is revolutionary design and contemporary art.

NOORDELIJK SCHEEPVAART & NEIMEYER TABAKSMUSEUM (SHIPPING & TOBACCO MUSEUM)

Brugstraat 24-26. Head up Ubbo Emmiusstraat and continue, as it becomes Folkingestraat, until Vismarkt. Turn left on the 2nd street leaving Vismarkt from the west; after 2 blocks, that street becomes Brugstraat. ☎312 22 02. Open Tu-Sa 10am-5pm, Su 1-5pm. €2.75, children ages 7-14 and seniors over 65 €1.40, children under 7 free.

With two fascinating museums in one, the Noordelijk is a fun, cheap, hour-long diversion. While the Scheepvaart focuses on the history of Dutch trade from the middle ages, the Tabaksmuseum celebrates the important commercial and political history of the tobacco trade, and displays fabulous ivory and crystal pipes. The museum also charts the current anti-smoking campaign as one of many deterrents to the trade and possession of the luxury good.

NIGHTLIFE

Groningen parties beyond its size; there are 160 pubs and discotheques crammed in this medium-sized city. The best bet for a night on the town lies just off the southeastern corner of Grote Markt on Poelestraat and Peperstraat. The bars and restaurants on these two streets are literally packed shoulder-to-shoulder and offer good prices and a buzzing atmosphere to the mainly student crowd. The students boast that the bars close only when the people stop drinking, usually around 4am on weekends. For outdoor nightlife, try the megabar overlooking the Grote Markt, known familiarly as the **Zuid Zijd** (South Side).

Vera, Oosterstraat 44 (☎313 46 81). Billing itself as the "club for the international pop underground," this center for live music and cinema of all stripes is an unmissable local party nearly every night. Pick up a copy of *VeraKrant,* the newsletter in the box outside, for a schedule of events. Open daily 10pm-3am or 4am; some gigs start at 1am.

Jazzcafe de Spieghel, Peperstraat 11 (☎312 63 00). The intimate, candlelit "cafe" houses 2 floors of live jazz, funk, or blues nightly at 11pm or later. Pick up a free copy of *UILoper* from the VVV to find out what's on. Tokers welcome. Wine €2.20 per glass. Open daily 8pm-4am.

Tramps, Peperstraat 10 (☎318 54 36). Tramps is a hotspot late at night for 30-something locals. Beers €1.70 and a special sweet green shooter called *Boswandeling* (4 for €6.60). Make requests from the bar's 300-CD collection, particularly for 70s and 80s music. Open Su-W 9pm-4am, Th-Sa 9pm-5am.

Cafe de Vlaamsche Reus, Poelestraat 15 (☎314 83 13). A young crowd keeps things lively, with students on both sides of the bar. Beer €1.90. Open daily from 9pm until people start leaving (on Th-Sa as late as 5 or 6am).

COFFEESHOPS

Groningen's streets possess total of 14 coffeeshops, almost all of which offer better prices than those in Amsterdam. Those below have cool, comfortable ambience.

Cafe Dee's, Papengang 3 (www.cafedees.nl). Tucked unassumingly in a small alley between the city's party streets, this is just as much a night spot as a smoke spot, with billiards and foosball (both €0.50). Weed sold in €5 and €12 denominations. Internet €1 per 30min. Space cake €2.50. Some outdoor seating. Open M-W 11am-midnight, Th noon-1am, F 11am-3am, Sa noon-3am.

The Glory, Steentilstraat 3 (☎312 57 42). The Glory is a super-chill spot open late at night with a small projection screen, a vague green, Bob Marley theme, and theater-style seats at small tables. Spacecake or joints €2.50; bud and hash in €5 and €15 increments. Open M-W noon-1am, Th-F noon-2am, Sa 10am-3am.

De Vliegende Hollander, Gedempte Zuiderdiep 63 (☎314 48 07; www.de-vliegende-hollander.nl). The name appropriately means "the flying Hollander" in Dutch. Select your goodies from a touch computer screen in €5 and €15 packets. "Top 44" and "K2" are particularly kind (€6 per 0.8g). Open daily 10am-10pm.

SMARTSHOP

Dream Factory Smart Shop, Zuiderdiep 32 (☎318 87 92; www.the-dreamfactory.com). Energizers, herbals, sexual stimulants, grow kits, CDs, and of course, mushrooms. Truffles €15 per 15g; Mexicans €15 per 30g. Open M 1-6:30pm, T-Sa noon-6:30pm. Cash only.

NEAR GRONINGEN

KAMP WESTERBORK ☎0593

🗹 Oosthalen 8. Take a train from Groningen to Beilin (25min., 2 per hr., €11.20), then a €3.80 trein-taxi to Westerbork's Herinneringscentrum. Call ahead for return pickup. ☎59 26 00; www.kampwesterbork.nl. Open Feb.-June and Sept.-Dec. M-F 10am-5pm, Sa-Su 1-5pm; July-Aug. M-F 10am-5pm, Sa-Su 11am-5pm. Guided tours June-Sept. daily 2pm. €3.85, children ages 8-18 €2.

Built by the Nazis in 1939 as a detainment camp for Jews in The Netherlands, Kamp Westerbork held 100,000 Dutch Jews before sending them east to the concentration camps, from 1942 until liberation. The transport camp was the last stop on Dutch land for virtually all of the country's Jews, including the Frank family in 1944. The **Herinneringscentrum** runs a museum that documents life inside the camp through movies and photos. Ask at reception to borrow the English guidebook.

About 2.6km from Herinneringscentrum is the actual camp, accessible by Wester-bork shuttle from 11am-5pm (every 20min., round-trip €1.75). Not much remains here but open fields, but there are several memorials, including a set of railway tracks rising off the ground, splintered and twisted. They were designed by former Kamp Westerbork inmate and Theresienstadt survivor Ralph Prins. On the drive, look for five stone coffins on your right, one for each of the five concentration camps to which Jews were sent from here. On one side of the coffin is the number sent and on the other is the number exterminated. The exhibits and displays are in Dutch, but a 700-meter walk to the far end of the camp (watchtower and barbed wire), will give you some idea of life inside Westerbork.

After World War II, the site was used as a refugee camp for 12,500 Moluccas. A small population inhabiting the eastern tip of Indonesia, Moluccas joined the drive for Indonesian independence but found the Dutch government unsympathetic to their nationalist causes. They remained an independent community within The Netherlands by living in Westerbork with the hope that they would return home *en masse*. The Moluccans ultimately integrated into the Dutch population.

MAASTRICHT ☎ 043

Maastricht's (pop. 125,000) name marks the city as an important crossing-ground of the Low Countries. Meaning "Maas crossing" in Old Dutch, it was originally settled by the Romans en route to Cologne as a convenient spot to ford the River Maas. Situated in a little pocket of land jutting into territory surrounded by Belgium and Germany, Maastricht's strategic location has made it a hotbed of military conquest throughout history. Although its defensive walls went up in 1229, the town was beseiged 22 times, captured by the Spanish in 1579 and then by the French in 1673. In 1814 it joined the Kingdom of The Netherlands and then resisted siege by the Belgians. After being occupied by the Germans during WWII, Maastricht was one of the first towns to be liberated. This past of international convergence gives Maastricht resonance as the site of the 1991 treaty that established the European Union. As one of the oldest and richest cities in The Netherlands, Maastricht has a pleasingly sedate, Old World feel; neither the rise of modern commercialism nor an active student population manage to take away the city's medieval charm. Old brick fortifications, cobblestone streets, well-preserved churches, and an astounding, vast subterranean defense system, the Caves of Mount St. Pieter, make Maastricht an appealing place to live and to visit.

TRANSPORTATION

Trains to Maastricht (2½hr., every 30min., €24.50) leave from Centraal Station in Amsterdam. To get to the **VVV**, Kleine Straat 1, go straight on Stationstraat, cross the bridge, and walk for another block. When you hit a wall, take a right; the tourist office is one block down on your right. There, be sure pick up a map (€1.25) of the city center or the hefty €1.25 tourist booklet. (☎325 21 21; www.vvvmaastricht.nl. Open Nov.-Apr. M-F 9am-6pm, Sa 9am-5pm; May-Oct. M-Sa 9am-6pm, Su 11am-3pm.)

PRACTICAL INFORMATION

Maastricht is bisected by the River Maas, and the old town (with most of the sights) lies on the western side of the river, across from the train station. The heart of the town is the **Vrijthof**, a large square flanked by two churches, although the Markt and the Onze Lieve Vrouwe Plein are also open to the public. The best way to see Maastricht is to discover its medieval alleyways on foot, and it's small enough that you can **walk** most everywhere in the town—even the Caves of Mount St. Pieter, which lie on the outskirts, are a 30-minute walk. Renting a **bike** might nevertheless be a convenient option if you plan on making more trips across town. Pick one up at cycle shop **Aon de Stasie** on the Stationsplein, to your left just outside the train station. (☎321 11 00. €7 per day, €22.65 deposit and ID required.) If you are going farther, Maastricht has a **bus** system; the information is available at a booth outside the train station or, you can buy a map at the VVV. **Taxi** ranks are located at the Vrijthof, Markt and Central Street; sometimes it is cheaper to pick one up at these stops rather than hailing one on the street. Cafe de Unit offers **Internet** access. (Open M-Th, Sa 11am-7:30pm; F 11am-6pm. €2 per 30min.) To get there from Leliestraat with your back to the Vrijthof, walk onto Paleistraat and take a right onto the first street, a narrow alley. For information on free and special **events,** check the free monthly magazines *Uit in Maastricht* or *Week In, Week Uit:* both are available at the VVV or in hotels and pubs. Most Thursdays at 10pm and Sundays at 4pm, free jazz hits **Bateau Mouche** in the Bassin (to the North of the city up Boschstraat from Markt).

ACCOMMODATIONS

For a small fee (€1.75 per person), the VVV can book rooms in private B&Bs (doubles from €32); many are near the center but rent only one or two rooms total. In general, budget accommodations in Maastricht can be difficult to find.

Botel, Maasboulevard 95 (☎321 90 23). From the train station, walk straight down Stationstraat and cross the bridge. Walk down the river to your left several blocks. This hotel on a moored boat may not offer the most professional service, but these tiny cabins adjoining a cosy deckroom lounge are the best budget digs in town. Try to get one of the rooms abovedeck: they're the same price, but much cheerier. Reception 24hr., but show up early since night hours are especially unreliable. Breakfast €4. Singles €27, with bath €30; doubles €41/€43; triples €60; quads €80; quints €95; 6-person room €114. Cash only. ●

Le Virage, Cortenstraat 2-2b (☎321 66 08; www.levirage.nl). Facing Onze Lieve Vrouwe Basiliek, it's on the square's right hand corner. Four spacious, spotless suites with bedroom, living room, kitchen, and bathroom. Breakfast €9. Reception T-Su 8am-midnight, but hours are spotty, so plan in advance. Doubles €90; triples €112; quads €136. AmEx/MC/V. ●

City-Hostel de Dousberg (HI), Dousbergweg 4 (☎346 67 77; www.dousberg.nl). From Centraal Station, take bus #11 to the Dousberg stop (2 strips) and cross the street. Buses run every 30min., until 6pm. After 6pm, take bus #28 from Centraal or Markt (every 30min., until 11:30pm) to Pottenberg, head towards the right and at the traffic light turn left. On Sa take bus #8 or 18; no bus on Su. Hostel offers somewhat low prices in an inconvenient location. Rooms off cinder-block hallways are nonetheless well-kept and have several amenities: indoor and outdoor pools, and tennis courts (€9 per hr., bring your own racquet). Breakfast included. Lockout 10:30am-3pm. Reception until 10pm. Curfew 1am. All rooms have shower and toilet. Small safe deposit box €1.30. Lunch from €6.75; dinner from €9.05. 10-14 bed single-sex dorm €22-25; triples €74.35; quads €92; quints €110; 6-person room €173; €2.50 discount with HI membership. MC/V. ●

FOOD

Maastricht is known for its *eetcafes:* pubs that serve traditional food along with beer. The best areas to find these establishments are around the **Onze Lieve Vrouwe Plein, St. Amorsplein,** and the **Vrijthof,** but prices in Maastricht are fairly high across the board. For an unglamorous but economical solution, stop by the various Vietnamese and Middle Eastern snack stands that surround the Vrijthof or the fishmarket at **Markt.** Several student-oriented restaurants with slightly lower prices line Brusselsestraat towards the south of the city. The city's various squats often serve cheap vegetarian food: check postings at the **SmartSounds** smartshop (see below) for exact addresses and times, as these are likely to change. Maastricht is also known for its collection of more luxurious (and expensive) French-influenced restaurants. **271**

Chalet Bergrust, Luikerweg 71 (☎325 54 21), just next to the Grotten Noord Caves of Mount St. Pieter to the south of the city (p. 272). A good stop-over after a trip to the caves on perhaps the only hilltop in The Netherlands. Beautiful view over the town and lunch options (sandwiches, pancakes, omelettes) run about €4. Open daily in summer and holiday season 10am-10pm; in winter W and F-M 11am-8pm. ❶

L'Hermitage, St. Bernadusstraat 20 (☎325 17 77), off the southeastern corner of the Onze Lieve Vrouwe Plein. A friendly Mexican cafe that's a favorite with students and locals. Cajun *quesadillas* €9; spareribs €13; vegetarian tacos €8. French dishes round out the cuisine. Open daily 5-10pm. ❸

SIGHTS

🏛 CAVES OF MOUNT SAINT PIETER

🔢 *The best thing to do is go to the VVV in the city center to get exact information about days and times of tours, and hours vary wildly and unpredictably from season to season. There are two entrances to the vast system of caves; the most convenient starting-point is Grotten Noord, Luikerweg 71, accessible by bus, take #4 from Markt. Plan to arrive 15min. before tour departs to buy your ticket from the VVV window by the restaurant. English tours, 1hr. daily Apr.-June and Sept.-Oct. 1:30pm, based upon demand. ☎325 21 21; www.pietersberg.nl. €3.25, children under 12 €2.25; combination with entrance to Fort St. Peter €5.50, children under 12 €3.50. The Zonneberg Caves, Slavante 1, are more difficult to reach; ask at the VVV for walking directions, 50min., or take the boat from the dock at the corner of Maasboulevard and Graanmarkt. English tours June-Aug. 1:45pm—plan to arrive at the docks at 1pm. Prices same as Grotten Noord; combination boat trip and visit, 3hr. €9, children €5.50. V.*

The man-made "caves" of Mount St. Pieter originally began as an old Roman limestone quarry; over centuries, the Dutch expanded it into the world's second-largest underground complex with more than 20,000 passages. Capable of sheltering up to 40,000 people at a time, this enormous underground labyrinth was used repeatedly as a defensive hide-away during the many sieges on Maastricht. They helped Maastricht gain its reputation as the "Iron City" as it rebuffed Belgian forces during several sieges. The caves were used by the French throughout the 18th century, and later by the Nazis. During WWII, the Germans hid several important Dutch paintings, including Rembrandt's *Night Watch*, in Mount St. Pieter's tunnels; similar passages were used to shelter Dutch civilians from Nazi invasion. Nearly 2000 years of history are written, literally, on the walls. Graffiti, carvings, and charcoal drawings dating from as early as Roman times cover the miles and miles of limestone. Visitors can even walk around the bedrooms, feeding troughs, and ovens dug out of the porous stone by local farmers during extended sieges. The Zonneberg tour focuses more on WWII history while the Grotten Noord concentrates on the local farmers' defense efforts. The caves average a temperature of 9°C—wear a coat or sweater.

BONNEFANTENMUSEUM

🔢 *Ave. Ceramique 250. Walk down the river on the side of the train station for 10min.; it's the huge building that looks like a metal rocket ship. ☎329 01 90; www.bonnefanten.nl. Open Su, Tu-Sa 11am-5pm. €7, students and children ages 13-18 €2.50, under 13 free. AmEx/MC/V.*

The 1995 building by Aldo Rossi looks like a cross between a soft-boiled egg and a rocketship; it's a good thing the museum's collection isn't nearly as dated as its outer shell. With a sizeable selection of Southern Dutch and Flemish art on long-term loan from the Rijksmuseum in Amsterdam, the Bonnefanten's collection offers a good range of medieval votive woodcarvings, 17th-century Baroque painting, and 20th-century Minimalist, Conceptual, and post-Conceptual art. Its holdings of mainstream American and European contemporary art are impressive: a good Richard Serra installation fills one of the courtyards; works by Sol LeWitt, Robert Ryman, Joseph Beuys, and Marcel Broodthaers are well represented. The museum also makes a concerted effort to collect pieces by contemporary, up-and-coming Dutch artists. And while some of these artists, Jan Dibbets in particular, have already achieved international success, others less well-known outside Holland at times give the museum a slightly regional feel.

BASILICA OF ST. SERVATIUS

◪ *The huge church on the Vrijthof. The entrance is to the right on Keizer Karelplein. www.sintservaas.nl. Leaflet on the different nooks and statues of the church €3. Open Jan.-June and Sept.-Dec. 10am-5pm; July-Aug. 10am-6pm. €2, seniors €1.80, children €0.60.*

This beautiful church, a central Maastricht landmark, fuses architectural and ecclesiastical history. It is the only church in The Netherlands to be built over the grave of a saint, St. Servatius (d. 384), the first Bishop of The Netherlands. The original church was built over his tomb (c. 570)—the remains have since been excavated. Of the spectacular building that stands today, the inner Romanesque part was built in the 11th century, while the outer Gothic structure was constructed in the 14th and 15th centuries. In a chamber opposite the entrance, there is a tiled labyrinth on the floor; see if you can get from "one of the four corners of the earth" (Rome, Constantinople, Colonge, or Achen) to the "celestial city" of Jerusalem. (Hint: you must go by St. Servatius.) The church surrounds a lovely inner courtyard lined with lavender where sits a huge bell from 1515, affectionately known as the Granmeer (grandmother). On your way into the church, you will pass its treasury, which contains a golden reliquary with part of St. Servatius's skeletal remains, as well as a silver arm containing a bone of the apostle Thomas.

ONZE LIEVE VROUWE BASILIEK (BASILICA OF OUR DEAR LADY)

◪ *Follow signs to the Onze Lieve Vrouwe Plein. ☎ 325 18 51. Open Easter-Oct. M-Sa 11am-5pm, Su 1-5pm. Mass in English Su 5pm in crypt. Free.*

A medieval basilica in honor of the Virgin Mary, with a dark, dank feel punctuated by beautiful colored stained glass. Parts of the cruciform church date to the 11th century. Mary is here affectionately termed "Star of the Sea" because she is said to have saved the lives of sailors at sea during a storm around 1700. See the hundreds of votive candles now placed around her statue in devotion to her miracle-working power. The square outside the church is perhaps the most beautiful in Maastricht.

NATUURHISTORISCH MUSEUM

◪ *De Bosquetplein 6-7. Around the corner from the conservatory; head down Papenstraat from the Vrijthof, veer left on Looiersgracht, and turn left onto Bosquetplein. ☎ 350 54 90; www.nhm-maastricht.nl. Open M-F 10am-5pm, Sa-Su 2-5pm. €3.10, children ages 6-12 €2.30, children under 6 free. Cash only.*

This slick, modern museum features the remains of a newly discovered ancient species, the Montasaurus dinosaur, and giant turtles found fossilized in the sandstone of the Caves of Mount St. Pieter. The rest of the museum follows geological developments from the beginning of time to the contemporary flora and fauna of Southern Limburg (now part of Germany). In the back there are child-friendly exhibits with a fish tank and a lovely botanical garden, including plants from the Late Cretaceous. The museum is curated in Dutch, but there are booklets available in English.

OTHER SIGHTS

St. Jan's Church, a Gothic structure to the left of the St. Servatuis Basilica, has been a Flemish-speaking Protestant church since 1632 and has a beautiful view of the city from its high tower. Its bright red color, restored since the 1980s, was originally painted using ox blood. (Open Mar.-Sept. M-Sa 11am-4pm. Church free; tower €1.15, children €0.45.) On the outskirts of the old centrum lies the **Helpoort,** Sint Bernardusstraat 1, the only city gate from 1229 still standing. Walk along the Onze Lieve

Vrouwe rampart (the cannons point inwards for tourists; they would have been pointing outwards from the walls during a real attack) and learn about the history of the fortified city from the knowledgeable staff. (Open mid-Apr.-Oct. 1:30-4:30pm. Free.) More military sights are at the pentagonal **Fort St. Pieter,** Luikerweg 80, across from the Grotten Noord, which provided protection for the city starting in 1702 (€3). You can also take **boat trips** through the Rederij Stiphout (☎351 53 00; www.stiphout.nl) starting at €5.50 for a basic tour on the River Maas.

COFFEESHOPS & NIGHTLIFE

Marijuana is not accepted here with the same breezy liberalism of Amsterdam. Although coffeeshops exist, they tend to be more discreet. **Tea Room Heaven 69,** Brusselsestraat 146, is located toward the eastern end of town, but once you're there, you might not want to leave: it has a full kitchen serving lunch and dinner (*panini* €3-4) for when the munchies strike. Weed €7-10 per g; mixed joints €2.50. (☎325 34 93; www.heaven69.nl. Open daily 9am-midnight.) For more soft drugs, head to the slick smart shop **SmartSounds,** Oude Tweebergenpoort 7a (from the Vrijthof, take K. Karelplein West until it becomes Oude Tweebergenpoort), which also has a huge collection of vintage records. Also check here for listings of squats serving dinner and beer. (☎351 05 04; www.sirius.nl. Open M-Sa 10am-10pm.)

The nightlife in Maastricht is all about pubbing. Serving over 80 different beers, **Falstaff,** Amorsplein 6, has the best selection in town and is well situated in a beautiful, tree-lined square. Lots of specialty Belgian brews on tap (€2-2.60) and plenty more options in the fridge keep students and beer connoisseurs alike happy. (☎321 72 38; www.cafe-falstaff.com. Open Su-Th 10am-2am, F-Sa 10am-3am.) During the school year, students stay out late to drink at **Metamorfoos,** Kleine Gracht 40-42, a cafe-brasserie. Main dishes €6-8, vegetarian €7; €12 beer card buys 10 beers. (☎321 27 14; www.metamorfoos.com. Open Su, M, F 3-11pm; T-Th, Sa 3pm-5am; kitchen open daily 4-9:30pm; international student night T-Th.) Closer to the river, the über-hip **de Kadans,** Kesselkade 62, serves brasserie food (prix-fixe menu €14.18) and pumps house music F-Sa downstairs at the **K-Club.** (☎326 17 00; www.dekadans.nl. Open M-W 11am-10pm, Th-Sa 11am-5am, Su noon-1am. Kitchen closes 10pm. Cover free-€5.) For more dancing, try **Night Live,** Kesselkade 43, where loud music and a young crowd make this converted church jam. The entrance is to the right of the church down at the end of the alley. (☎362 82 78; www.nightlive.nl. Open F 11am-5am, Sa 11pm-6am; F R&B and hip-hop, Sa global house.) For other entertainment, check out the listings in the free weekly *Uit in Maastricht.*

WADDEN ISLANDS (WADDENEILANDEN)

Tucked away off the northwestern coast of The Netherlands, and inauspiciously named (*wadden* means "mud flat"), the Wadden Islands are an unassuming vacation destination. The Dutch wouldn't have it any other way, happy to keep these idyllic islands to themselves—even when Netherlanders flock in summer, the islands feel sleepy and isolated. Deserted bike paths wind through stretches of grazing land and lead to some of Europe's most pristine nature reserves. The islands offer excellent beaches, where the sun-warmed shallows of the Waddenzee make for temperate swimming. Though transit can tax the wallet of the budget traveler, abundant campsites and good hostels render a trip to these resplendent islands affordable.

The islands arch around the northwestern coast of The Netherlands. Texel, closest to Amsterdam, is the largest and most populous; Vlieland is a sleepy stretch of endless beaches; Terschelling (see p. 278), the middle child of the five, bustles with nightlife and nature preserves. The fourth and fifth islands, remote Ameland and far-flung Schiermonnikoog, fill out the archipelago. Most people travel from the main-

land (from Den Helder for Texel, from Harlingen for the others); island hopping is difficult with the ferry opportunities, so plan in advance with the tourist office. The VVV also sell "Wad-Hop" packages from one island to the next during specific, unpredictable sailing seasons.

TEXEL   ☎ 0222

Texel, because of its proximity to Amsterdam and the less-than-daunting twenty minutes it takes the ferry to cross the Waddenzee, is the most touristed of the Wadden Islands. While its four siblings are certainly quieter by degrees as they arch farther northward away from The Netherlands, Texel is no less charming for its relative popularity. Unlike the other islands in the Wadden archipelago, this one is truly accessible in a single day. For all those travelers who might still want their comforts at hand, the diversity of landscape here is truly dazzling: dunes, woods, heaths, salt marshes, mudflats, all entirely bikeable. There are two major villages among the various clusters of thatched-roof houses lining the landscape of Texel: the quiet Den Burg is located in the center of the island, while the more party-loving De Koog lines Texel's northern shore.

TRANSPORTATION & PRACTICAL INFORMATION

To reach Texel, take the train from Amsterdam to **Den Helder** (90min., €10.90), then grab bus #33 right next to the train station (2 strips); it will drop you off at the docks, from which a **ferry** (☎36 96 00) will take you to 't Hoorntje, the southernmost town on Texel (20min.; every hr. 6:30am-9:30pm; round-trip €4, children under 12 €2, additional €2.70 for bikes). **Buses** depart from the ferry dock to various locales throughout the island, though the best way to travel is to rent a **bike** from **Verhuurbedrijf Heijne,** opposite the ferry dock. (From €4.50 per day. Open Apr.-Oct. daily 9am-8pm; Nov.-Mar. 9am-6pm.) If you prefer public transportation, purchase a **Texel Ticket,** which allows unlimited one-day travel on the island's bus system (runs mid-June to mid-Sept., €3.90). Be warned: the buses arrive at a given stop about once an hour, even in the high season. Pick up a schedule on any bus or at the VVV. The **VV tourist office,** Emmaln 66, is located just outside Den Burg, about 300m south of the main bus stop in Den Burg; look for the blue signs or ask the bus driver to drop you off. (☎31 47 41; www.texel.net. Open M-Th 9am-6pm, F 9am-9pm, Sa 9am-5:30pm; July-Aug. also Su 10am-1:30pm.)

ACCOMMODATIONS

At press time, large budget accommodations on Texel were in a state of flux. The island's hostel, **StayOkay Texel ❶**, Schansweg 7, is 3km outside of Den Burg and accessible via bus #29 from the ferry (4 strips); tell the bus driver your destination. The hostel is snuggled amid lovely but fragrant sheep pastures. (☎31 54 41; www.stayokay.com. Reception 8:30am-10:30pm. Dorms €15.90-22; €2.50 more for HI non-members.) The hostel was slated to close down in May 2004. Plans are in the works for a new hostel to open four months later, with 240 beds in a new location closer to Den Burg. Given the unpredictability of Texel's budget accommodations, your best bet is to let the tourist office book you a spot in any of the dozens of pensions, bed and breakfasts, and bungalows that cover the island. **Campgrounds** provide another cheap accommodations option (€2.50-5 per person; €7 per tent) and allow you to get close to the nature scene; most sites cluster south of De Koog, but there are campgrounds right behind De Koog's main strand, as well as more secluded ones near De Cocksdorp; the tourist office can arrange reservations.

FOOD

In Den Burg, walk anywhere in the center to find a bite. The pub **De 12 Balcken Tavern ❸**, Weverstraat 20, in Den Burg, serves truly heavenly spare ribs, marinated, grilled, and served with salad and a heaping bowl of french fries (€12 serving feeds 2 people). You can also get a shot of *'t Jutterje*, the island's popular liquorice-flavored schnapps, fermented from herbs and wheat, for €2.20. (☎31 26 81. Open M-Sa 1pm-10pm.) **Pizzeria Venezia ❷**, Kogerstraat 7, in Den Burg, offers a pizza in a homey setting with long wooden tables and candlelight; the most savory treat, however, is the calzone, literally as big as your head (€8.75-10.75). Delicious, velvety soups make great starters (€3). Plenty of vegetarian options are available. (☎31 25 70. Pizzas €5-11. Open Apr.-Oct. daily noon-11pm; Nov.-May 4-11pm. MC.) Your best bet for eating in De Koog is to stroll the main drag, Dorpstraat, where vendors hawk *loempia*, fresh fruit, and *appeltaart* (all €2-5). All manner of bars, shawarma huts, *tapas* restaurants and *pannekoekens* are within reach. The Albert Heijn **supermarket,** Waalderstraat 48, in Den Burg, is the best place for self-caterers to grab food and sundries. (Open M-Th and Sa 8am-8pm, F 8am-9pm.) In De Koog, you can also head to **Super de Boer** supermarket on Nikadel. (Open M-Th and Sa 8am-6pm, F 8am-8pm.)

MUSEUMS

A trip around Texel's 54km perimeter will fill an entire day, taking you to the island's best sights. Though the VVV boasts that Texel features five museums, only two are truly worth visiting. **EcoMare Museum and Aquarium,** Ruijslaan 92, 2km south of De Koog, just off the Ruijslaan bike path (take bus #28), features an aquarium and exhibits on Texel's ecology. The museum's real stars, though, are its playful *zeehonden* (seals). EcoMare serves as a home to representatives of each of the several species that thrive in the waters of the North Sea, and the most lively (though crowded) times to visit are during the feeding hours (11am and 3pm). The staff can also arrange tours with outside organizations of the surrounding **nature reserves.** Each reserve focuses on specific ecological niches, such as native birds and tidepool life. For information on tours, call or check the board at the museum. (☎31 77 41; www.ecomare.nl. Open daily 9am-5pm. €7, under 13 €3.50, seniors €5.50.)

On the other side of the island in the quaint burg of **Oudeschild**, a working windmill marks the site of the **Maritime and Beachcomber's Museum** (Maritiem en Jutters Museum), Barentzstraat 21, a monument to the sea and all that's in it. Displays include a relics scavenged from shipwrecks, and a vast assemblage of washed-ashore detritus, astonishing in its volume and variety, and artful in its presentation. The highlight is an exhibit in which you step inside an imagined recreation of a sunken ship, creaky deck and underwater noises included. (☎31 49 56; www.texelsmaritiem.nl. Open Sept.-June Tu-Sa 10am-5pm; July-Aug. M-Sa 10am-5pm. €4.10, children under 14 €2.05)

BEACHES

Texel's greatest treasures lie outdoors. Its bike paths curve along the shoreline and through its pristine nature reserves, past some of the best beaches in The Netherlands. Texel's stretch of sand runs largely uninterrupted up the western coast and is divided into strands, called *paals*, which run in ascending numerical order from south to north. The most popular strands lie near De Koog, especially Paal 20. Just west of town, you'll find all manner of beach clubs and lots of folks sunning and splashing. There are kilometers of shoreline, and it becomes progressively less populated as you travel north and south of paal 20; 12, 13, and 15 are especially worth a visit. All beaches are open to the public, and the water becomes friendly to swimmers when it warms in July and August. At the northern and southern tips of the islands, **nude beaches** beckon the uninhibited; you can bare it all near Paal 9 (2km southwest of Den Hoorn) or Paal 27 (5km west of De Cocksdorp).

NIGHTLIFE

After sun sets on the beaches of Texel, the young and sunburned masses migrate to shoreside De Koog for its sprightly nightlife. By day, **Le Berry,** Dorpstraat 3, has a welcoming, smoky pub atmosphere, but at night the locals let their hair down and dance—a slightly more mature and sophisticated, but no less lively, crowd than at other nearby establishments. (☎31 71 14; www.leberry.nl. Open noon-3am, doors close at 2am. Dancing from 11pm.) **Cafe Sam-Sam,** Dorpstraat 146, always knows how to have a good time. Catering to a crowd that's young but mostly post-pubescent, the Sam hosts nightly dancing to all manner of DJ-driven beats, usually kicking off around 9pm and going until 3am (or whenever the crowd dissipates), including campy 70s and 80s parties every Thursday during summer. (☎31 75 90. Beer €1.80; mixed drinks €4.50.) Den Burg possesses something of a scene, too, though young people tend to stay in De Koog. In Den Burg, nightclubs and bars cluster just off the town square along Kantoorstraat. **De Pilaar,** Kantoorstraat 5, draws a hip crowd with occasional live music, running the gamut from country and blues to rock and soul. Pilaar also features and a wide selection of Belgian and locally-brewed beer, all for €1.60. (☎31 40 75. Open daily 8pm-3am, doors close at 2am.)

VLIELAND   ☎0562

Vlieland is a true escape. The farthest island from the mainland, it is second in the constellation, and is characterized by a serene, untouched feel. In the center, 700 acres of forest shade bike paths, while the long and skinny shape of the island is conducive to beaches along the northern coast. Oost-Vlieland, the closest thing to a village on the island, is a single tree-lined street that is—miraculously—chock full of facilities for travelers, while still retaining its isolated charm.

TRANSPORTATION

Though traveling to Vlieland from adjacent islands can be an unpredictable and maddening experience, it can be reached from the mainland via the ferry from Harlingen (☎051 749 15 00; www.doeksen.nl), either by the standard **Oost Vlieland ferry** (90min., 3 per day, €18.75, ages 4-11 €9.40) or by the **express Koegelwick**. You can also take the tiny **Vriendschap** ferry from **Texel** (☎0222 31 64 51; www.waddenveer.nl; Tu-Th and Su 1 per day; 25min.; €9), which takes you to the eastern side of the island. From the dock, a huge yellow truck will pick you up and take you as far as the village (included in ferry ticket). Unlike Texel, no tourist cars are allowed on the island. Rent a bike at Fiets Verhuur Jan Van Vlieland, with storage across the ferry dock and rental office at Dorpstraat 8 (☎45 15 09. Open M-F 9-12:30am, 1:30-6pm; Su 10-noon, 4-6pm. From €4.50 per day), or at Zeelen Rijwiel Verhuur, Dorpstraat 2. (☎45 10 90. Open M-F 9am-6pm, Su 9am-5pm; July-Aug. open daily 9am-9pm. From €4 per day.) Exorbitantly expensive **taxis** run throughout the island (☎45 12 22), and a bus leaves from the ferry dock once an hour, hitting most major stops.

PRACTICAL INFORMATION

The **VVV tourist office,** 10 Havenweg, is located opposite the ferry dock at the edge of the village of Oost-Vlieland. (☎45 13 45; info@vlieland.net. Open M-F 9am-12:30pm, 1:30-5pm, 6:40pm-8pm; Sa 9:15-11:45am, 3:45-4:45pm, 6:45-8pm; Su 9:15-9:35am, 10:30-11:45am, 3:45-4:45pm.) There is an **ATM** next to the **post office** at Dorpstraat 120 (post office open M-F 9:30am-noon, 1:30-5:30pm; Sa 9:30-noon.) **Internet access** is available at **Informatiecentrum de Noordwester** (€1.60 per 30min.).

ACCOMMODATIONS

Lodging in Vlieland usually falls into one of two categories: village or beach. Staying in one of the many hotels and pensions in Oost-Vlieland means ready access to modern conveniences, while the hotels on the dunes have practically-private beaches as their backyard. **Hotel de Bosrand ❸,** Duinkersoord 113, is a beautiful and well-kept hotel that's one of the best deals on the dunes. Take bus #110 from the ferry to Bosrand, dropping your baggage on the free transport wagon first. (☎45 12 48; www.hoteldebosrand.nl. All rooms with bath. Breakfast and access to tanning studio/sauna included. Singles €51; doubles €82; quads €135; fully equipped apartments for 2-5 people €430-€590 per week. Cash only.) In the village, **Pension de Veerman ❷,** Dorpstraat 173, is clean, comfortable, and homey. (☎45 13 78; www.pensiondeveerman.nl Breakfast included. All rooms with shared bath. Singles €34; doubles €54; apartments €300-600 per week. Cash only.) Reserve ahead for **campgrounds** on Vlieland. **Stortemelk ❶,** Kampweg 1 lies on the outskirts of the village and is Vlieland's largest campground (☎45 12 25; www.stortemelk.nl. €5.25 per person per night, under 10 €2.75; tent fee €4.05-7.30.) **Lange Paal ❶,** 3km west of Oost-Vlieland amid grasslands and sand dunes, is an equally viable, if smaller option. (☎45 15 39; http://members.lycos.nl/langepaal. €4.20 per person per night, ages 3-12 €3.60).

FOOD

Nearly identical restaurants, each serving fish and spare ribs at Amsterdam-style prices line Dorpstraat, Oost-Vlieland's lone street. Pick up sandwiches and shawarma (€2.25-5) at **B.O.L.D. ❶,** Dorpstraat 70. (☎45 15 02, Open M-Sa 10am-10pm, July-Aug. also Su 1:30-5pm). Fill up on provisions at the **SPAR** supermarket, Dorpstraat 38 (☎45 13 47, Open M-F 8:30am-12:30pm, 1:30-6pm; Sa 8:30am-12:30pm, 1:30-5pm.) Nobody comes to Vlieland for the parties, but if you desperately need to hit the town, any town, a couple of *bruin* cafes can be found in Oost-Vlieland. **Discotheek De Stoep,** Dorpstraat 81, even promises dancing. (☎45 14 95. Open daily in high season 10pm- until people start to leave.)

SIGHTS

The entire northern coast of the island offers unspoiled **beaches** that, at their most crowded, boast about 25 people. Book nature excursions of all kinds (usually €5 for 2hr. trips; call ahead to arrange for an tour in English) at **Informatiecentrum de Noordwester,** Dorpstraat 150, (☎45 17 00, www.denoordwester.nl. Open June and Sept. M-F 10am-noon, 2-3:30pm; Sa 2-5pm; Su 1-4pm; July and Aug. M-Sa 10am-5pm, Su 1-4pm.) The best view of the island, if you're willing to trek up the stairs, is at the **Bezichtiging Vuurtoren** (lighthouse), just west of the village. (Open Jan.-June, Sept.-Dec. daily 10:30-noon; Apr. M-W 2-4pm, Sa-Su 10:30-noon; additional hours May-June, Sept.-Oct. M-F 2-4pm. €1.75.)

TERSCHELLING ☎0562

With 80% of the island covered by protected nature reserves, **Terschelling** (pop. 4500) offers secluded beaches that stretch around the western tip and across the northern coast of the long, narrow island. Civilization on this island is traced back to at least the 13th century but now human habitation takes a backseat to an extraordinary variety of plant and bird species. The second-largest of the Wadden Islands, Terschelling can compete with Texel's range of activities, though parts of this large island retain Vlieland's seclusion.

TRANSPORTATION & PRACTICAL INFORMATION

Take a train from Amsterdam directly to **Harlingen Haven,** which drops you right at the ferry landing (3hr., €25.10). **Ferries** (☎051 749 15 00; 24hr. recorded info ☎0900 363 57 36, €0.10 per min.; www.doeksen.nl) depart for **Terschelling** (1-2hr., 3-5 per day, €17.63 one-way). There is a **bus** at every ferry arrival, leaving once an hour and reaching most major spots; bring your *strippenkaart*. To explore the island's striking scenery, **rent a bike** from **Haantjes Fietsverhuur,** W. Barentzskade 23. (☎44 29 29. Bikes start at €4.50 per day, €20 per week.) The **VVV tourist office,** W. Barentszkade 19a, sits opposite the ferry landing. (☎44 30 00. Open M-Sa 9:30am-5:30pm.)

ACCOMMODATIONS

The **Terschelling Hostel (HI) ❶,** Van Heusdenweg 39, is located on the waterfront, just out of town. With your back to the harbor, take a right, walk along the pier, continue 1.5km on the bike path to Midsland. The hostel is on the right, where the paved road curves away from the ocean. The bar (open in summer daily 4:30pm-midnight) and many guest rooms feature sweeping ocean views, and the kitchen serves up a great *dagschotel* for €9.05 (served at 6-6:45pm.). Renovations have made most of the dorms into smaller, 2-to-6-person rooms, but some bunk-style accommodations remain. (☎44 23 38; www.stayokay.com/terschelling. Breakfast included 8-10am. Sheets included; towels €3. Laundry €3.50. Internet €0.13 per min. Reception 9am-10pm. 6-person dorms in high season €23.25, in low season €17.75. €2.50 additional charge for HI non-members) Campgrounds abound on Terschelling, especially along the Midslander Hoofdweg on the southwestern coast. Try **Camping de Kooi,** for its prime location and great amenities, Hee 9 (☎44 27 43; www.campingdekooi.nl), but there are 12 campsites on the island, and all are fairly equal in quality.

FOOD

Terschelling's best food experience is also its most unexpected, at **The Heartbreak Hotel ❶,** Oosterend, where the Elvis-impersonating owner has erected a shrine to The King. There's free live rock n' roll every night July-Aug.; don't miss the huge Elvis Memorial Day party August 16. Diner-style food abounds; the Burning Love Burger is only €4. (☎44 86 34; www.heartbrea-

life's green

transatlantic berries in a bog

Over a century ago, a storm sent a barrel overboard from a ship off the coast **Terschelling** (see p. 278). As the story goes, Pieter Sipkes Cupido found the barrel and rolled it into the dunes, hoping he had found a stash of rum or beer. To his disappointment, he found it filled with bitter-tasting red berries that the sailors kept on board to prevent scurvy; the fruit—cranberries—were rich in Vitamin C and would last longer than citrus. Declaring that the barrel would be worth more than the tart berries, he dumped them on the dunes, where they found a serendipitously favorable environment in which to grow.

This is the story given to explain why Terschelling—and, to a lesser extent, Vlieland—are covered with a bog berry native to North America. Today, Terschelling's cranberry bushes are leased to the company Cranberry Bedrijf Skylge, which picks the berries for wine, jam, tea, and even mustard. The harvest is in September, and after the company's pickers have passed over the main areas, visitors are free to pick from the bushes as well. (Call the Terschelling VVV to find out when certain zones will be available on the island; picking is always free on Vlieland.)

NO WORK ALL PLAY

far-flung theater

You might be walking down a street in the bucolic village of **West Terschelling** and be met by a company of twelve-foot tall live puppets, stopping traffic to engage in simulated coitus with cars and trucks. At the same time, you may witness acrobats dangling nonchalantly from the trees on side streets, or hear the punk-rock circus blaring from the main square. It could only be **Oerol** (www.orel.nl), the 25-year old festival held on Terschelling every year during the third week in June.

It began with Dutch street theater, but now experimental performers of all stripes come from around the world. Selling about 50,000 tickets annually, it's now one of the largest theater festivals in Europe.

Past paid theater performances have included *Ulysses* and Henrik Ibsen's *Peer Gynt,* but you need only set foot on the island to experience the dozens of free performances integrated into daily life. Most of the island's hotel and hostel beds start getting fully booked in May, so make your plans well in advance; however, for hardier travelers, camping may also be a viable option if you procrastinate in booking. Alternatively, it is possible to stay on the mainland or another Wadden Island and ferry into Terchelling every day.

khotel.nl; Open daily 10am-1am. Cash only). **Zeezicht ❸**, W. Barentszkade 20, offers a pleasant, relaxed atmosphere for a great dinner with a sweeping view of the ocean. The main courses pricier (€12-16.50), but come in enormous portions with sides of potatoes and salad, guaranteed to satisfy the heartiest appetite. (☎44 22 68. Next to the VVV, across from the ferry landing. Open daily 10am-midnight; kitchen closes at 9:30pm. AmEx/MC/V.) Follow your nose to the sandwiches and freshly-squeezed juice at **De Dis ❶**, Boomstraat 17. *Broodjes* are €2.30-5.50; pre-made salads run €1.40-1.80 per 100g. (☎443 443. Open M-Sa 9am-9pm, Su 11am-9pm.) Campers can pick up groceries and other supplies at **SPAR Supermarket,** Boomstraat 13. (Open M-F 8am-8pm, Sa 8am-5pm.)

SIGHTS

Hills are rare in The Netherlands, but rolling expanses abound on Terschelling, and make for great mountain biking; the VVV can help in booking organized bike tours. Less strenuous biking is also possible thanks to the island's numerous bike rental shops (see above). Beaches stretch across the northern coast, where, as on the other Wadden Islands, you can go long stretches without encountering another soul. Don't miss the view from the western tip of the island; to get there from the ferry landing, turn left out of the landing dock and walk until you can walk no farther. There you'll behold an unparalleled view of lilting sailboats floating placidly on infinite blue waves. **Oerel,** a huge experimental theater festival, packs the island with revelers every year during the third week of June; book accommodations in advance.

MUSEUMS

Although it's a bit far from town, the **Wrakkenmuseum,** Formerum Zuid 13, is well worth the 8km bike ride from West Terschelling. Indeed, the ride out to the museum is half the fun, with some of the island's most picturesque scenery. To get there, follow the bike path to Formerum; once in Formerum, take a left at the small statue of Rembrandt—the museum is five minutes ahead. (☎44 93 95. Open 10am-8pm, until 11pm in the summer. €2.) Closer to the main drag, the **Zeeaquarium and Natuurmuseum,** Burgemeester Reedekerstraat 11, is a cut above the average taxidermy shop. Though the signs are all in Dutch, most exhibits speak quite well for themselves. (☎44 23 90. Open Apr.-Nov. M-F 7am-5pm, Sa-Su 2-5pm; Nov.-Feb. Sa-Su 2-5pm. €4, ages 4-11 €3.)

NIGHTLIFE

Young people flood Terschelling during the summer, accounting for the island's surprisingly active **nightlife**. The **borrelbus** ("drink bus") runs from about 10pm-2am in the high season, safely transporting drunken revelers home. **Cafe de Zeevaart,** Torenstraat 22, possesses an old-salt, seaside-groghouse feel. (☎44 26 77. Plate of *bitterballen* €4.50. Open daily 10am-2am.) A younger crowd packs the sweaty dance floor at **Braskoer,** Torenstraat 32. (☎464 21 97. *Wieckse Witte* beer €3; Bacardi Breezer €5. Cover €5 after 9pm. Open daily 10am-2am; dancing from 9pm.)

Centraal Statio

Planning Your Trip

DOCUMENTS & FORMALITIES

EMBASSIES & CONSULATES

For foreign consular services in Amsterdam, check the **Service Directory** (see p. 320).

DUTCH EMBASSIES

Australia, 120 Empire Circuit, Yarralumla Canberra, ACT 2600 (☎02 6220 9440; can@min-buza.nl; www.netherlandsembassy.org.au). Open M-F 9:30am-12:30pm and 2-4pm.

Canada, 350 Albert St., Ste. 2020, Ottawa, ON K1R 1A4 (☎613-237-5030; www.netherlandsembassy.ca). Open M-F 9am-5pm, passports and visas 9am-1pm.

Ireland, 160 Merrion Rd., Dublin 4 (☎01 269 3444; www.netherlandsembassy.ie). Open M-F 8:30am-4:15pm, passports and visas 9am-12:30pm.

New Zealand, P.O. Box 840, at Ballance and Featherston St., Wellington (☎04 471 6390; http://netherlandsembassy.co.nz). Open M-Th 8:30am-4pm, F 8:30am-2pm.

South Africa, 825 Arcadia St., Box 117, Pretoria (☎012 344 3910; www.dutchembassy.co.za). Open M-Th 9am-noon, F 9am-11pm.

United Kingdom, 38 Hyde Park Gate, London SW7 5DP (☎020 75 90 32 00; www.netherlandsembassy.org.uk). Open M-F 9am-5pm, passports M-F 9am-noon.

United States, 4200 Linnean Ave., NW, Washington, D.C. 20008 (☎202-244-5300; www.netherlands-embassy.org). Passport office open 9:30am-12:30pm, other offices by appointment only.

one europe

The idea of European unity has come a long way since 1958, when the European Economic Community (EEC) was created to promote solidarity and cooperation. Since then, the EEC has become the European Union (EU), with political, legal, and economic institutions spanning 15 member states: Austria, Belgium, Denmark, Finland, France, Germany, Greece, Ireland, Italy, Luxembourg, The Netherlands, Portugal, Spain, Sweden, and the UK.

What does this have to do with the average non-EU tourist? In 1999, the EU established freedom of movement across 14 European countries—the entire EU minus Ireland and the UK, but plus Iceland and Norway. This means that border controls between participating countries have been abolished, and visa policies harmonized. While you're still required to carry a passport (or government-issued ID card for EU citizens) when crossing an internal border, once you've been admitted into one country, you're free to travel to all participating states. Britain and Ireland have also formed a common travel area, abolishing passport controls between the UK and the Republic of Ireland. This means that the only times you'll see a border guard within the EU are traveling between the British Isles and the Continent.

For more important consequences of the EU for travelers, see The Euro (p. 285) and Customs in the EU (p. 286).

DUTCH CONSULATES

Australia, Level 23, Plaza Tower II, 500 Oxford St., Bondi Junction, NSW 2022 (☎02 9387 6644; fax 9387 3962; syd@minbuza.nl; www.netherlandsconsulate.org.au). Open M-F 9am-4pm.

Canada, Ste. 821-475 Howe St., Vancouver, BC, V6C 2B3 (☎604-684-6448; fax 684-3549; www.netherlands-consulate.org). Open M-Tu, Th-F 9am-12:15pm.

New Zealand, P.O. Box 3816, L. J. Hooker Building, 1st fl., 57 Symonds St., Auckland (☎09 3795 399; fax 3795 807). Open M-F 9:30am-1pm.

South Africa, 100 Strand St., Cape Town 8000; P.O. Box 346, Cape Town 8001 (☎021 421 5660; fax 418 2690; www.dutch-consulate.co.za).

United Kingdom, Thistle Court 1-2, Edinburgh, EH2 1DD (☎0131 220 3226); 18 Carden Pl., Aberdeen AB10 1UQ (☎1224 561616); All-Route Shipping Ltd., 14-16 West Bank Rd., Belfast BT3 9JL, Northern Ireland (☎28 9037 0223).

United States, One Rockefeller Plaza, 11th fl., New York, NY 10020 (☎212-246-1429; fax 333-3603; www.cgny.org); 11766 Wilshire Blvd., Ste. 1150, Los Angeles, CA 90025 (☎310-268-1598; fax 312-0989; www.ncla.org); 2200 Post Oak Blvd., Ste. 610, Houston, TX 77056 (☎713-622-8000; fax 622-3581; www.cghouston.org); 303 E. Wacker Dr., Ste. 2600, Chicago, IL 60601 (☎312-856-0110; fax 856-9218; www.cgchicago.org).

TOURIST OFFICES

For tour info, see the **Service Directory,** p. 324.

The Netherlands Board of Tourism, Vlietweg 50, 2266 KA, Leidschendam (☎070 370 57 05; www2.holland.com; Mailing address: Toerisme Recreatie Nederland, PO Box 458, 2260 MG Leidschendam, The Netherlands). Though travelers cannot visit the head office in person, the Board of Tourism dispenses free info over the phone and maintains a very helpful and comprehensive website with a variety of services including news updates, hotel reservations, and information on Dutch art and culture. From the US and Canada call ☎212-557-3500 for information.

VVV, Stationsplein 10. When exiting Centraal Station, the office is across the tram tracks to the right. Once there, you can get help with hostel/hotel reservations (€3 per person). You can also buy tickets for museums and canal boat tours. Open daily 9am-5pm. Expect a long wait here and at the other offices at platform #2 inside **Centraal** (☎020 201 88 00. Open M-Sa 8am-8pm, Su 9am-5pm). **Leidseplein 1,** around the corner on Leidsestraat. (Open Su-W 9am-5pm, Th-Sa 9am-9pm); **VVV,** De Ruyterkade 5,. west of Centraal. (Open M-F 9am-5pm, Sa 10am-4pm.) For tourist information at all VVV branches, call ☎020 201 88 00

PASSPORTS

REQUIREMENTS. Citizens of Australia, Canada, New Zealand, South Africa, the UK, and the US need valid passports to enter The Netherlands for stays shorter than three months. The Netherlands does not allow entrance if the holder's passport expires in under six months; returning home with an expired passport is illegal, and may result in a fine.

NEW PASSPORTS. Citizens of Australia, Canada, Ireland, New Zealand, the UK, and the US can apply for a passport at any post office, passport office, or court of law. Citizens of South Africa can apply for a passport at any Office of Foreign Affairs. Any new passport or renewal applications must be filed well in advance of the departure date, although most passport offices offer rush services for a very steep fee.

PASSPORT MAINTENANCE. Be sure to photocopy the page of your passport with your photo, as well as photocopying any and all visas, all traveler's check serial numbers, and any other important documents you may have with you during your trip. Carry one set of copies in a safe place, apart from the originals, and leave another set at home. Consulates also recommend that you carry an expired passport or an official copy of your birth certificate in a part of your baggage separate from other documents. If you lose your passport, immediately notify the local police and the nearest embassy or consulate of your home government. To expedite its

---

ⓘ ESSENTIAL INFORMATION

THE EURO

The official currency of the 12 member nations of the European Union—Austria, Belgium, Finland, France, Germany, Greece, Ireland, Italy, Luxembourg, The Netherlands, Portugal, and Spain—is now the euro.

The currency has important (and positive) consequences for travelers hitting more than one Euro-zone country. For one thing, money-changers across the Euro-zone must exchange money at the official, fixed rate, and at no commission (though they may still charge a small service fee). Second, euro-denominated traveler's checks allow you to pay for goods and services in the EU, again at the official set rate, and again commission-free.

At the time of printing, the exchange rate for the euro was €1=US$1.12=1.58CAD=£0.70. For more info, check a currency converter (such as www.xe.com) or www.europa.eu.int.

---

replacement, you will need to know all information previously recorded and show ID and proof of citizenship. In some cases a replacement may take weeks to process, and it may be valid only for a limited time. Any visas stamped in your old passport will be irretrievably lost. In an emergency ask for immediate temporary traveling papers that will permit you to re-enter your home country.

VISAS & WORK PERMITS

VISAS. As of August 2003, citizens of Australia, Canada, Ireland, New Zealand, the UK, and the US need only a passport to stay in The Netherlands for up to 90 days. Those seeking an extended stay, employment, or student status should obtain a visa and a residence permit, though visas are only extended under exceptional circumstances. Citizens of **South Africa** need a visa to enter The Netherlands; contact the nearest Consulate (see **Consulates,** above). Be sure to double-check on entrance requirements at the nearest embassy or consulate (listed under **Embassies & Consulates Abroad,** above) for up-to-date info before departure. The Netherlands Department of Justice also operates a comprehensive website that details visa requirements for every country at http://www.immigratiedienst.nl.

WORK PERMITS. Admission as a visitor does not include the right to work, which is authorized only by a work permit from The Netherlands CWI (www.cwinet.nl). Entering The Netherlands to study requires a special visa. For more info, see **Alternatives to Tourism: Studying,** p. 309.

IDENTIFICATION

Always carry two or more forms of identification on your person, including at least one photo ID; a passport combined with a driver's license or birth certificate is usually adequate. Never carry all your forms of ID together—split them up in case of theft or loss, and keep photocopies of them in your luggage and at home.

TEACHER, STUDENT, & YOUTH IDENTIFICATION. The **International Student Identity Card (ISIC),** the most widely accepted form of student ID, provides discounts on some sights, accommodations, food, and transport; access to a 24hr. emergency helpline (North America ☎877-370-ISIC; elsewhere US collect +1 715-345-0505); and insurance benefits for US cardholders. For example, the Flying Pig hostels offer one free drink at their bar, and many museums discount admission prices. Applicants must be degree-seeking students of a secondary or post-secondary school and be of at least 12 years of age. Because of the proliferation of fake ISICs, some services (particularly airlines) require additional proof of student identity.

The **International Teacher Identity Card (ITIC)** offers teachers the same insurance coverage as well as similar but limited discounts. For travelers who are 25 or under but are not students, the **International Youth Travel Card (IYTC)** also offers many of the same benefits as the ISIC. Similarly, the **International Student Exchange ID Card (ISE)** gives discounts, medical benefits, and allows you to buy student airfares.

Each of these identity cards costs US$22 or the foreign currency equivalent. ISIC and ITIC cards are valid for roughly one and a half academic years; IYTC cards are valid for one year from the date of issue. Many travel agencies issue the cards; for a list of issuing agencies, or for more information, contact the **International Student Travel Confederation (ISTC),** Herengracht 479, 1017 BS Amsterdam, The Netherlands (☎421 28 00; fax 421 28 10; www.istc.org).

CUSTOMS

Upon entering The Netherlands, you must declare certain items from abroad and pay a duty on the value of those articles if they exceed the allowance established by The Netherlands customs service. Note that goods and gifts purchased at **duty-free** shops abroad are not exempt from duty or sales tax; "duty-free" merely means that you need not pay a tax in the country of purchase. For more information on EU customs, see p. 286. Upon returning home, you must similarly declare all articles acquired abroad and pay a duty on the value of articles in excess of your home country's allowance. In order to expedite your return, make a list of any valuables brought from home and register them with customs before traveling abroad, and be sure to keep receipts for all goods acquired abroad. While taking soft drugs home from Amsterdam may seem like a good idea, remember that you're not the only one who knows about drug laws in Amsterdam—sniffer dogs frequently meet all planes, trains, and boats arriving from The Netherlands.

The quoted price of all goods and services in The Netherlands includes the **Value Added Tax (BTW** in The Netherlands), which is set at 6% or 19% depending on the type of goods or services purchased. The tax rate for most services (hotels, taxi fares, and restaurants) as well as smaller goods (groceries) is set at 6%. The going rate for larger purchases like clothing, electronics, and jewelry is 19%. Larger purchases taken back to your home country are eligible for BTW refund; keep your receipts and check at VVV branches for details.

EU CUSTOMS. In addition to freedom of movement of people (see p. 284), travelers in EU member countries can take advantage of the freedom of movement of goods. There are no customs controls at internal EU borders, and travelers are free to transport whatever legal substances they like as long as it is for personal use—up to 800 cigarettes, 10L of spirits, 90L of wine (60L of sparkling wine), and 110L of beer. Duty-free allowances were abolished for travel between EU member states; however, travelers between the EU and the rest of the world still get a duty-free allowance when passing through customs.

MONEY

CURRENCY & EXCHANGE

For current exchange rates, see **The euro**, p. 285, or check the currency converter on financial websites such as www.xe.com, or a major newspaper for the latest exchange rates. As a general rule, it's cheaper to convert money in The Netherlands than at home. However, you should always bring enough foreign currency (in this case, euros) to last for the first 24 to 72 hours of a trip to avoid being penniless should you arrive after bank hours, on weekends, or on a holiday. Travelers from the US can get foreign currency from the comfort of home: **International Currency Express** (☎888-278-6628) delivers foreign currency or traveler's checks second-day (US$12) at competitive exchange rates.

When changing money, go to banks that have at most a 5% margin between buy and sell prices. Since you lose money with every transaction, **convert large sums** (unless the euro is depreciating rapidly), **but no more than you'll need.** If you use traveler's checks or bills, carry some in small denominations (the equivalent of US$50 or less) for times when you are forced to exchange money at disadvantageous rates, but bring a range of denominations since charges may be levied per check cashed. Store your money in a variety of forms; ideally, at any given time you will be carrying some cash, some traveler's checks, and an ATM and/or credit card.

> **ⓘ ESSENTIAL**
> INFORMATION
>
> ### PINS & ATMS
>
> To use a cash or credit card to withdraw money from a cash machine (ATM) in Europe, you must have a four-digit **Personal Identification Number (PIN).** If your PIN is longer than four digits, ask your bank whether you can just use the first four, or whether you'll need a new one. **Credit cards** don't usually come with PINs, so if you intend to hit up ATMs in Europe with a credit card to get cash advances, call your credit card company before leaving to request one.
>
> Those with alphabetic, rather than numerical, PINs may also be thrown off by the lack of letters on European ATMs. The following are the corresponding numbers to use: 1=QZ; 2=ABC; 3=DEF; 4=GHI; 5=JKL; 6=MNO; 7=PRS; 8=TUV; and 9=WXY. Note that if you mistakenly punch the wrong code into the machine three times, it will swallow your card for good.

TRAVELER'S CHECKS

Traveler's checks are one of the safest and least troublesome means of carrying funds while traveling. American Express and Visa are the most widely recognized brands. Many banks and agencies sell them for a small commission. Check-issuers provide refunds if the checks are lost or stolen, and many provide additional services, such as toll-free refund hotlines abroad, emergency message services, and stolen credit card assistance. They are readily accepted in Amsterdam, but less welcome than cash. Ask about toll-free refund hotlines and the location of refund centers when purchasing checks, and always carry emergency cash.

American Express: Checks available with commission at select banks and all AmEx offices. US residents can also purchase checks by phone (☎888-269-6669) or online (www.aexp.com). Checks available in US, Australian, British, Canadian, Japanese, and euro currencies. *Cheques for Two* can be signed by either of 2 people traveling together. For purchase locations or more information contact AmEx's service centers: US and Canada ☎800-221-7282; UK 0800 521 313; Australia 800 25 19 02; New Zealand ☎0800 441 068. In The Netherlands, call ☎0800 023 3405 to report lost or stolen travelers checks.

Visa: Checks available (generally with commission) at banks worldwide. For the location of the nearest office, call Visa's service centers: US ☎800-227-6811; UK ☎0800 89 50 78; elsewhere UK collect ☎+44 020 7937 8091. Checks available in US, British, Canadian, Japanese, and euro currencies.

Travelex/Thomas Cook: US and Canada call ☎800-287-7362; UK ☎0800 62 21 01; elsewhere call UK collect ☎+44 1733 31 89 50.

CREDIT, DEBIT, & ATM CARDS

Where they are accepted, credit cards often offer superior exchange rates—up to 5% better than the retail rate used by banks and other currency exchange establishments. Credit cards may also offer services such as insurance or emergency help and are sometimes required to reserve hotel rooms or rental cars. Although they are widely accepted in Amsterdam, many budget hotels require a stay of several nights or charge a surcharge if you want to use your credit card to pay your bill. It is advisable to make your reservation with a credit card but then to pay in cash. **MasterCard** (sometimes called EuroCard or Access in Europe) and **Visa** are the most welcomed; **American Express** cards work at some ATMs and at AmEx offices and major airports.

ATM machines are widespread in Amsterdam and The Netherlands. Depending on the system that your home bank uses, you can most likely access your personal bank account from abroad. For more information on PINs, see p. 287. ATMs get the same wholesale exchange rate as credit cards, but there is often a limit on the amount of money you can withdraw per day (around US$500), and unfortunately computer networks sometimes fail. There is typically also a surcharge of US$1-5 per withdrawal from your home bank. The two major international money networks are **Cirrus** (to locate ATMs US ☎800-424-7787 or www.mastercard.com) and **Visa/PLUS** (to locate ATMs ☎800-843-7587 or www.visa.com).

GETTING MONEY FROM HOME

If you run out of money while traveling, the easiest and cheapest solution is to have someone back home make a deposit to your credit card or cash (ATM) card. Failing that, consider one of the following options.

WIRING MONEY. It is possible to arrange a **bank money transfer,** which means asking a bank back home to wire money to a bank in Amsterdam. This is the cheapest way to transfer cash, but it's also the slowest, usually taking several days or more. Note that some banks may only release your funds in local currency, potentially sticking you with a poor exchange rate; inquire about this in advance. Money transfer services like Western Union are faster and more convenient than bank transfers—but also much pricier. **Western Union** has many locations worldwide. To find one, visit www.westernunion.com, or call US ☎800-325-6000; Canada 800-235-0000; UK 0800 83 38 33; Australia 800 501 500; New Zealand 800 27 0000; South Africa 0860 100031; Amsterdam 504 8770. Money transfer services are also available at **AmEx** and **Thomas Cook** offices.

US STATE DEPARTMENT (US CITIZENS ONLY). In dire emergencies only, the US State Department will forward money within hours to American citizens care of the nearest US consular office, which will then disburse it according to instructions, all for a US$15 fee. If you wish to use this service, you must contact the Overseas Citizens Service division of the US State Department (☎202-647-5225; nights, Sundays, and holidays 202-647-4000).

COSTS

The single biggest cost of your trip will probably be your round-trip (return) airfare to and from Amsterdam (see **Getting to Amsterdam: By Plane,** p. 293). If you plan to travel throughout Europe, a railpass (or bus pass) may be another important pre-departure expense: you can buy Selectpasses or Youth Selectpasses from Rail Europe for three to five countries to save money (see **Getting to Amsterdam: By Train,** p. 293). Before you go, spend some time calculating a reasonable daily budget that will meet your needs.

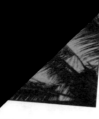

...UDGET. A bare-bones day in Amsterdam (camping or sleeping in ...ses, buying food at supermarkets) should cost about US$30-40; a ...nfortable day (sleeping in hostels/guesthouses and the occasional ...ing one meal a day at a restaurant, going out at night) would run ...r a luxurious day, the sky's the limit. We recommend that you keep ...sh on your person to about $35 because pickpocketing in Amster- ... Also, don't forget to factor in emergency reserve funds (at least ...lanning how much money you'll need.

TIPS FOR ...NG MONEY. Saving just a few dollars a day over the course of your trip might pay for days or weeks of additional travel. Learn to take advantage of freebies. A few times a year, museums will be free and open to the public, although these dates are flexible; check museum websites (see **Museums,** p. 79) for more details. In the summertime or on Queen's Day, April 30, there are tons of free concerts and events; check the **Uitlijn** info-line or website for up-to-date, year-round information about free events (☎0900 01 91; www.uitlijn.nl), or check out **Shark,** Amsterdam's "alternative" English-language guide (☎420 67 75; www.underwateramsterdam.com). In Dutch, "Korting means "discount," while "graitis" means "free."

HEALTH

Common sense is the simplest prescription for good health. For a basic **first-aid kit,** pack: bandages, pain reliever, antibiotic cream, a thermometer, tweezers, moleskin, decongestant, motion-sickness remedy, diarrhea or upset-stomach medication (Pepto Bismol or Imodium), an antihistamine, sunscreen, insect repellent, burn ointment, and a syringe for emergencies (get an explanatory letter from your doctor). In your **passport,** write the names of any people you wish to be contacted in case of a medical emergency, and list any allergies or medical conditions of which you want doctors to be aware. Matching a prescription to a foreign equivalent is not always easy, safe, or possible. Carry up-to-date, legible prescriptions or a statement from your doctor stating the medication's trade name, manufacturer, chemical name, and dosage. While traveling, be sure to keep all medication in your carry-on luggage.

IMMUNIZATIONS

Travelers should make sure that the following vaccines are up to date: MMR (for measles, mumps, and rubella); DTaP or Td (for diptheria, tetanus, and pertussis); OPV (for polio); HbCV (for haemophilus influenza B); and HBV. For recommendations on immunizations and prophylaxis, consult the CDC (see below) in the US or the equivalent in your home country, and check with a doctor for guidance.

AIDS, HIV, & STDS

For detailed information on **Acquired Immune Deficiency Syndrome (AIDS)** in The Netherlands, call the **US Centers for Disease Control's** 24hr. hotline at ☎800-342-2437, or contact the **Joint United Nations Programme on HIV/AIDS (UNAIDS),** 20, Ave. Appia, CH-1211 Geneva 27, Switzerland (☎+41 22 791 3666; fax 22 791 4187). **Sexually transmitted diseases** (STDs) such as gonorrhea, chlamydia, genital warts, syphilis, and herpes are easier to catch than HIV and can be just as deadly. **Hepatitis** B and C can also be transmitted sexually. Though condoms may protect you from some STDs, oral or even tactile contact can lead to transmission. If you think you may have contracted an STD, see a doctor immediately.

MEDICAL ASSISTANCE ON THE ROAD

There is little medical risk to traveling through The Netherlands, but you may want to take out travel insurance just in case. Citizens of the EU and Australia benefit from reciprocal health arrangements with The Netherlands; check at home to find

out which medical and dental services are covered and how. If you're concerned about obtaining medical assistance abroad, consider employing special support services. The *MedPass* from **GlobalCare, Inc.**, 6875 Shiloh Rd. East, Alpharetta, GA 30005, USA (☎800-860-1111; fax 678-341-1800; www.globalems.com), provides 24hr. international medical assistance and medical evacuation resources. The **International Association for Medical Assistance to Travelers** (**IAMAT**; US ☎716-754-4883, Canada 519-836-0102; www.cybermall.co.nz/NZ/IAMAT) has free membership, lists English-speaking doctors worldwide, and offers info on immunization requirements. If your regular **insurance** policy does not cover travel abroad, you may wish to purchase additional coverage (see **Health**, p. 35).

Those with medical conditions (such as diabetes, allergies to antibiotics, epilepsy, or heart conditions) may want to obtain a **Medic Alert** membership (first year US$35, annually thereafter US$20), which includes a stainless steel ID tag, among other benefits, such as access to a 24hr. collect call number. Contact the Medic Alert Foundation, 2323 Colorado Ave, Turlock, CA 95382, USA (☎888-633-4298, outside US 209-668-3333; www.medicalert.org).

INSURANCE

Travel insurance generally covers four basic areas: medical/health problems, property loss, trip cancellation/interruption, and emergency evacuation. Although your regular insurance policies may well extend to travel-related accidents, you may consider purchasing travel insurance if the cost of potential trip cancellation/interruption is greater than you can absorb. Prices for travel insurance purchased separately generally run about US$50 per week for full coverage, while trip cancellation/interruption may be purchased at a rate of about US$5.50 per US$100 of coverage.

Medical insurance (especially university policies) often covers costs incurred abroad; check with your provider. **US Medicare** does not cover travel to The Netherlands. **Canadians** are protected by their home province's health insurance plan for up to 90 days after leaving the country; check with the provincial Ministry of Health or Health Plan Headquarters for details. **Homeowners' insurance** (or your family's coverage) often covers theft during travel and loss of travel documents (passport, plane ticket, railpass, etc.) up to US$500.

ISIC and **ITIC** (see p. 286) provide basic benefits, including US$100 per day of in-hospital sickness (up to 60 days), US$3000 of accident-related medical reimbursement, and US$25,000 for emergency medical transport. Cardholders have access to a 24hr. toll-free helpline (run by insurance provider **TravelGuard**) for medical, legal, and financial emergencies overseas (US and Canada ☎877-370-4742; elsewhere US collect +1 715-345-0505). **American Express** (US ☎800-528-4800) grants most cardholders automatic car rental insurance (collision and theft, but not liability) and ground travel accident coverage of US$100,000 on flight purchases made with the card.

KEEPING IN TOUCH

For more on communications services, see **Once in Amsterdam,** p. 25.

BY MAIL

Airmail letters under 1oz. from North America to Amsterdam take 4-7 days and cost US$0.80 or CDN$1.25. Letters up to 20g take 2-3 days from the UK and cost UK£0.38. UK Swiftair delivers letters a day faster for UK£3.30 more. Allow at least 5-6 workdays from Australia or New Zealand (postage NZ$1.85/AUS$1.65 for letters up to 50g). Check mail rates online at: Australia (www1.auspost.com.au/pac); Canada (www.canadapost.ca/personal/rates/default-e.asp); Ireland (www.anpost.ie); NZ (www.nzpost.co.nz/nzpost/inrates); UK (www.royalmail.com); US (http://ircalc.usps.gov). Amsterdam encompasses several postal districts; to get exact postal codes, surf over to www.postcode.nl.

BY PHONE

To place a call to Amsterdam: first, dial the **international dialing prefix** (if calling from Australia, dial 0011; Canada or the US, 011; the Republic of Ireland, New Zealand, or the UK, 00; South Africa, 09); second, dial the **country code** for The Netherlands, 31; third, dial the **city code** for Amsterdam, 20; and last, dial the **local number.** For information on calling your home country from anywhere in Amsterdam or The Netherlands, see **Once In Amsterdam,** p. 30.

GETTING THERE

BY PLANE

When it comes to airfare, a little effort can save you a bundle. If your plans are flexible enough to deal with the myriad restrictions, courier fares are usually the cheapest. Tickets bought from consolidators and standby seating are also good deals, but occasional last-minute specials, frequent airfare wars, and the odd charter flight fare can often beat these already low fares. The key is to hunt around, to be flexible, and to ask persistently about discounts. Students, seniors, and those under 26 should never pay full price for a plane ticket.

AIRFARES

Airfares to Amsterdam peak from June to September; holidays are also expensive. Midweek (M-Th morning) round-trip flights run US$40-50 cheaper than weekend flights, but they are generally more crowded and less likely to permit

☝ ESSENTIAL
INFORMATION

INTERNET FLIGHT PLANNING

The Internet is one of the best places to look for travel bargains. Make sure sites are secure before handing over your credit card information. For flights headed to Amsterdam, try the sites of **KLM** (www.klm.nl), **Singapore Air** (www.singaporeair.com), or the budget airline **Quick Airways** (www.quickairways.com).

Other sites do the legwork and compile deals for you. Try the sites www.bestfares.com or www.travelzoo.com.

For student discounts on fares, try either ▨**Student Universe** (www.studentuniverse.com) or **STA Travel** (www.sta-travel.com).

For full travel services, try **Expedia** (msn.expedia.com) or **Travelocity** (www.travelocity.com).

Priceline (www.priceline.com) allows you to specify a price but obligates you to buy any ticket that meets it.

Skyauction (www.skyauction.com) has bidding on both last-minute and advance-purchase tickets.

frequent-flier upgrades. Traveling with an "open return" ticket can be pricier than fixing a return date when buying the ticket. Round-trip flights are by far the cheapest; "open-jaw" (arriving in and departing from different cities, e.g. Amsterdam-Paris and Rome-Amsterdam) tickets tend to be pricier.

Budget fares for round-trip flights to Amsterdam from the US or Canadian east coast cost US$500-700, US$300-500 in the low season (roughly Oct.-June); from the US or Canadian west coast US$850-950/US$550-700; from the UK, UK£50-70; from Australia, AUS$1700-2000. Full-price fares from airlines tend to be more expensive. Major carriers include KLM/Northwest (☎800-447-4747; www.nwa.com), Martinair (☎800-627-8462; www.martinaira.com), Continental (☎800-231-0856; www.continental.com), Delta (☎800-241-4141; www.delta.com), United (☎800-538-2929; www.ual.com), Air Canada (☎888-247-2262; www.aircanada.ca), and Singapore Airlines (☎800-742-3333; www.singaporeair.com). Many airlines offer last-minute deals.

BY TRAIN

Thalys, Place Stéphanie 20, 1050 Brussels (☎08 92 35 35 36 in France, €0.35 per min.; www.thalys.com), runs trains from Paris Nord to Centraal Station in Amsterdam (4¼hr., 6-8 per day, €87). The **Eurostar,** Eurostar House, Waterloo Station, **London**

Always Lock Your Bike

Gouda & Edam Cheeses

Synagogue

SE1 8SE (UK ☎ 08705 186 186, US 800-387-6782, elsewhere UK +44 1233 61 75 75; www.eurostar.com), high-speed service goes frequently from London to Paris's Gare du Nord (3hr., 12-14 per day, €120.80).

BY FERRY

Ferries traverse the North Sea, connecting **England** to The Netherlands. Boats arrive at **Rotterdam** from Hull (13½hr.), near York, and at **Amsterdam** from Newcastle-upon-Tyne (14hr.). The following fares listed are **one-way** for **adult foot passengers** unless otherwise noted. Though standard round-trip fares are in most cases simply twice the one-way fare, **fixed-period returns** (usually within five days) are almost invariably cheaper. Ferries run year-round unless otherwise noted. **Bikes** usually cost a few pounds extra. For a **camper/trailer** supplement, you will have to add anywhere from UK£20-140 to the "with car" fare. If more than one price is quoted, the quote in British pounds is valid for departures from the UK, etc. A directory of ferries in this region excluding The Netherlands can be found at www.seaview.co.uk/ferries.html.

DFDS Seaways: UK ☎ 08705 33 30 00; US 800-533-3755; www.scansea.com. Newcastle to **Amsterdam** (14hr., departs daily 5:30pm). Single economy cabins July-Aug. US$200, Sept.-June US$160; 2-, 3-, and 4-person economy cabins US$80 per person.

P&O North Sea Ferries: UK ☎ 0870 129 6002; Netherlands 181 255 555 www.ponsf.com. **Hull** to **Rotterdam** (11hr., departs daily 9pm). UK£52-62.

BY CAR

INTERNATIONAL DRIVING PERMIT (IDP). If you plan to drive a car while in Amsterdam, you must be over 18 and it is highly recommended that you have an International Driving Permit (IDP). In the event that you're in a situation (e.g. an accident or stranded in a small town) where the police do not know English, information on the IDP is printed in ten languages. Your IDP, valid for one year, must be issued in your own country before you depart. An application for an IDP usually needs to include one or two photos, a current local license, an additional form of identification, and a fee. To apply, contact the local or national branch of your home country's Automobile Association.

CAR INSURANCE. Most credit cards cover standard insurance. If you rent, lease, or borrow a car, you will need a **green card,** or **International**

Insurance Certificate, to certify that you have liability insurance and that it applies abroad. Green cards can be obtained at car rental agencies, car dealers (for those leasing cars), some travel agents, and some border crossings. Rental agencies may require you to purchase theft insurance in countries that they consider to have a high risk of auto theft.

SPECIFIC CONCERNS

WOMEN TRAVELERS

Women traveling on their own inevitably face some additional safety concerns, but it's easy to be adventurous without taking undue risks. If you are concerned, consider staying in hostels that offer single rooms that lock from the inside, or in religiously affiliated organizations with rooms for women only. Stick to centrally located accommodations and avoid solitary late-night treks or metro rides.

Always carry extra money for a phone call, bus, or taxi. **Hitchhiking** is never safe for lone women, or even for two women traveling together. When exploring, always look as if you know where you're going and approach older women or couples for directions if you're lost or uncomfortable. The less you look like a tourist, the better off you'll be. Wearing a conspicuous **wedding band** may prevent unwanted overtures. Your best answer to **verbal harassment** is no answer at all; feigning deafness, sitting motionless, and staring straight ahead at nothing in particular will do a world of good that reactions usually don't achieve. The extremely persistent can sometimes be dissuaded by a firm, loud, and very public "Go away!" in the appropriate language. Don't hesitate to seek out a police officer or a passerby if you are being harassed. Memorize the emergency numbers in places you visit, and consider carrying a whistle on your keychain. A self-defense course will both prepare you for a potential attack and raise your level of awareness of your surroundings. Also be sure you are aware of the health concerns that women face when traveling.

TRAVELING ALONE

There are many benefits to traveling alone, including independence and greater interaction with locals. On the other hand, any solo traveler is a more vulnerable target of harassment and street theft. As a lone traveler, try not to stand out as a tourist, look confident, and be especially careful in deserted or very crowded areas. If questioned, never admit that you are traveling alone. Maintain regular contact with someone at home who knows your itinerary. For more tips, pick up *Traveling Solo* by Eleanor Berman (Globe Pequot Press; US$17) or subscribe to **Connecting: Solo Travel Network,** 689 Park Road, Unit 6, Gibsons, BC V0N 1V7, Canada (☎604-886-9099; www.cstn.org; membership US$35). **Travel Companion Exchange,** P.O. Box 833, Amityville, NY 11701, USA (☎631-454-0880, or in the US ☎800-392-1256; www.whytravelalone.com; US$48), will link solo travelers with companions who have similar travel habits and interests.

𝑖 ESSENTIAL
INFORMATION

TRAVEL ADVISORIES

The following government offices provide travel information and advisories by telephone, by fax, or via the web:

Australian Department of Foreign Affairs & Trade: ☎13 00 555135; faxback service 02 6261 1299; www.dfat.gov.au.

Canadian Dept. of Foreign Affairs & Intl. Trade (DFAIT): Canada/US ☎800-267-8376, elsewhere ☎+1 613-944-4000; www.dfait-maeci.gc.ca.

New Zealand Ministry of Foreign Affairs: ☎04 439 8000; fax 494 8506; www.mft.govt.nz/travel.

UK Foreign & Commonwealth Office: ☎020 7008 0232; fax 7008 0155; www.fco.gov.uk.

US Dept. of State: ☎202-647-5225; http://travel.state.gov.

Teyler's Museum

Lilypads at Hortus Botanicus

Guard-Cat Protecting House-Boat

OLDER TRAVELERS

Senior citizens are eligible for a range of discounts on transportation, museums, movies, theaters, concerts, restaurants, and accommodations. If you don't see a senior price listed, ask, and you may be delightfully surprised. The books *No Problem! Worldwise Tips for Mature Adventurers*, by Janice Kenyon (Orca Book Publishers; US$16) and *Unbelievably Good Deals and Great Adventures That You Absolutely Can't Get Unless You're Over 50*, by Joan Rattner Heilman (NTC/Contemporary Publishing; US$13), are both excellent resources. For more information, contact one of the following organizations:

Elderhostel, 11 Ave. de Lafayette, Boston, MA 02111, USA (☎877-426-8056; www.elderhostel.org). Organizes a series of 2-week biking, hiking or boating "educational adventures" in The Netherlands for those 55+.

The Mature Traveler, P.O. Box 15791, Sacramento, CA 95852, USA (☎800-460-6676; www.thematuretraveler.com). Deals, discounts, and travel packages for the 50+ traveler. Subscription $30.

BISEXUAL, GAY, & LESBIAN TRAVELERS

In Amsterdam, anything goes. The Netherlands has the most tolerant laws for homosexuals in the world—it became the first country to legalize gay marriage in 2001, converting all "registered same-sex partnerships" into full marriages. Below are contact organizations, mail-order bookstores, and publishers with materials addressing specific concerns. **Out and About** (www.planetout.com) offers a bi-weekly newsletter and a comprehensive site addressing gay travel concerns. Sidebars throughout this guide will highlight accommodations, entertainment, and nightlife of particular gay-friendly interest.

GAY/LESBIAN RESOURCES

The monthly *Gay and Night* (€2.25) newspaper has info on gay venues and events. The fortnightly *Gay Krant* (€2.25) and *Shark* (€2.25) also provide excellent and thorough listings of what's going down in queer Amsterdam.

▨ **COC,** Rozenstraat 14 (☎626 30 87; www.cocamsterdam.nl), exists as a social network and information center. Maps designed specifically for the gay traveler available in the lobby. Office open M-Tu and Th-F 10am-5pm, W 10am-8pm. The cafe on the ground floor turns into a multicultural discotheque on F and Sa nights. Cafe open Th 8pm-midnight, F 8pm-10pm; disco F-Sa 10pm-4am (Sa is women-only).

Vrolijk, Paleisstraat 135 (☎623 51 42; www.vrolijk.nu), claims to be the largest gay and lesbian bookstore in Europe. With an excellent selection of literature and periodicals, it's an ideal place to stop in for tips on what's hot and what's not in gay Amsterdam. Various knick-knacks abound; also houses a growing DVD selection. Shop online for books. Open M 11am-6pm; Tu-W, F 10am-6pm; Th 10am-9pm, Sa 10am-5pm.

Gay and Lesbian Switchboard (☎623 65 65) is available to answer questions, suggest events, or listen to personal problems. All switchboard volunteers speak English and some speak other languages. Phone staffed daily 10am-10pm. At press time, the service was understaffed; please call again later if they cannot take your call immediately.

Gay Krant Reisservice, Kloveniersburgwal 40 (☎421 00 00; www.gaykrant.nl/reis). A travel service devoted exclusively to gay and lesbian travelers. Also features an impressive display of magazines and newspapers for gay travelers. Newsletters available. Open M 2-6pm, Tu-F 10am-6pm, Sa 10am-4pm.

SAD/Schorerfoundation, P.C. Hoofstraat 5 (☎662 42 06). A counseling center for gay men and women. Open M-F 10am-4pm.

Xantippe Unlimited, Prinsengracht 290 (☎623 58 54; www.xs4all.nl/~xantippe). General bookstore, but with a specialization in women's and lesbian issues. Open M 1-7pm, Tu-F 10am-7pm, Sa 10am-6pm, Su noon-5pm.

FURTHER READING

Spartacus International Gay Guide 2001-2002. Bruno Gmunder Verlag (US$33).

Damron Amsterdam, Damron Travel Guides (US$10). Other Damron publications include: *Damron Men's Guide, Damron's Accommodations,* and *The Women's Traveller* (US$14-19). For more info, call ☎800-462-6654 or visit www.damron.com.

Ferrari Guides' Gay Travel A to Z, Ferrari Guides' Men's Travel in Your Pocket, and *Ferrari Guides' Inn Places.* Ferrari Publications (US$16-20). Purchase the guides online at www.ferrariguides.com.

Gay Vacation Guide: The Best Trips & How to Plan Them, Mark Chesnut. Citadel (US$15).

PACKING

Pack lightly: set out everything you think you'll need, then pack half of it and twice the money. For a longer stay, trade a backpack for a **suitcase.** Bring a **daypack** for carrying things around. Keep your money, passport, and valuables with you in a neck pouch or money belt. Bring a combination lock for your bag or for hostel lockers.

CURRENT & ADAPTERS

In Amsterdam, electric current is 230V AC, enough to fry any 110V North American appliance. North Americans should buy an adapter (which changes the shape of the plug) and a converter (which changes the voltage; US$20). Don't make the mistake of using only an adapter (unless instructions explicitly state otherwise). New Zealanders and South Africans (who both use 220V at home) as well as Australians (who use 240/250V) won't need a converter but will need an adapter for anything electrical. Check http://kropla.com/electric.htm.

DISABLED TRAVELERS

Amsterdam is a particularly difficult city to navigate from a wheelchair. This otherwise tolerant and accommodating city has not yet made significant efforts for handicapped travelers. The streets are narrow, the trams have steps up and narrow doors, and only the better hotels have street-level entrances or elevators. Places that are wheelchair-accessible have been awarded an **International Accessibility Symbol** (IAS). Call the NIZW (☎+31 0 30 230 65 52) or the Afdeling Gehandicaptenvoorlichting (☎+31 0 70 314 14 20) for more information. Those with disabilities should inform airlines and hotels of their disabilities when making reservations; some time may be needed to prepare special accommodations. Call ahead to restaurants, museums, and other facilities to find out about the existence of ramps, the widths of doors, the dimensions of elevators, etc. Unless it is indicated otherwise, readers should assume that all listings in this book are not wheelchair-accessible. **Guide dog owners** should inquire as to the quarantine policies of each destination country. At the very least, they will need to provide a certificate of immunization against rabies.

Rail is probably the most convenient form of travel for disabled travelers in Europe: many stations have ramps, and some trains have wheelchair lifts, special seating areas, and specially equipped toilets. All Eurostar, some InterCity (IC), and some EuroCity (EC) trains are wheelchair-accessible, and CityNightLine trains, French TGV (high speed), and Conrail trains feature special compartments. Most trains in The Netherlands are wheelchair-accessible.

For those who wish to rent cars, some major **car rental** agencies (Hertz, Avis, and National) offer hand-controlled vehicles.

AccessWise, Jachthoornlaan 1a, Arnhem (☎ 26 370 61 61; fax 26 377 67 53; info@access-wise.org; www.accesswise.org). Information for travelers with disabilities on traveling in The Netherlands and from The Netherlands through Europe. Currently the website is only in Dutch, but call—they speak English.

Mobility International Nederland, Heidestein 7 (☎ +31 034 352 17 95). Gives advice on suitable accommodations for the disabled worldwide.

Nederlands Asthma Fonds (☎ 31 033 434 12 36), has information on hotels and other accommodations that are suitable for those with asthma, bronchitis, or emphysema.

USEFUL ORGANIZATIONS & TOUR AGENCIES

Mobility International USA (MIUSA), P.O. Box 10767, Eugene, OR 97440, USA (☎ 541-343-1284, voice and TTY; www.miusa.org), sells *A World of Options: A Guide to International Educational Exchange, Community Service, and Travel for Persons with Disabilities* (US$35).

Society for Accessible Travel and Hospitality (SATH), 347 Fifth Ave., #610, New York, NY 10016, USA (☎ 212-447-7284; www.sath.org). An advocacy group that publishes free online travel information and the travel magazine *OPEN WORLD* (US$18, free for members). Annual membership US$45, students and seniors US$30.

Directions Unlimited, 123 Green Ln., Bedford Hills, NY 10507, USA (☎ 800-533-5343). Books individual and group vacations for the physically disabled; not an info service.

MINORITY TRAVELERS

Amsterdam is an integrated, multicultural city. Surinamese, Indonesian, Moroccan, Turkish, African, and Antillean immigrants—among others—have made their homes in Amsterdam, serving as a lasting reminder of Amsterdam's colonial history. But while Amsterdam has a reputation for tolerance, it also has a surprising reputation for racism. The Netherlands, like many European countries today, is in the process of making tougher penalties for illegal immigrants—most of whom are minorities. This should not discourage non-caucasian travelers from visiting the city—most Amsterdammers are very tolerant and welcoming. But minority travelers should be aware that their presence might possibly elicit a different reaction than those of their non-minority friends.

TRAVELERS WITH CHILDREN

Family vacations often require that you slow your pace and always require that you plan ahead. When deciding where to stay, remember the special needs of young children; if you pick a small hotel, call ahead and make sure it's child-friendly. If you rent a car, make sure the rental company provides a car seat for younger children.

Amsterdam is a great city to visit with children. With lively streets and winding canals, there is always something to see or do. In nice weather, families head to the city's numerous parks, such as the Vondelpark, Sarphartipark, or the Plantage, home also to the Artis Zoo. Museums, tourist attractions, accommodations, and restaurants often offer discounts for children. Children under two generally fly for 10% of the adult airfare on international flights (this does not necessarily include a seat). International fares are usually discounted 25% for children from two to 11.

Look for **Kids in the City** sidebars in this book for kid-oriented sights and activities. For more information, consult one of the following books:

Adventuring with Children: An Inspirational Guide to World Travel and the Outdoors, Nan Jeffrey. Avalon House Publishing (US$15).

Backpacking with Babies and Small Children, Goldie Silverman. Wilderness Press (US$10).

Gutsy Mamas: Travel Tips and Wisdom for Mothers on the Road, Marybeth Bond. Travelers' Tales (US$8).

Have Kid, Will Travel: 101 Survival Strategies for Vacationing With Babies and Young Children, Claire and Lucille Tristram. Andrews McMeel (US$9).

How to take Great Trips with Your Kids, Sanford and Jane Portnoy. Harvard Common Press (US $10).

Trouble Free Travel with Children, Vicki Lansky. Book Peddlers (US$9).

DIETARY CONCERNS

VEGETARIANS & VEGANS

While traditional Dutch food is hearty, heavy, and fish- and meat-based, the proliferation of international cuisine means vegetarians in The Netherlands should have no problems, as there will be suitable selections in most restaurants. Amsterdam boasts the best Indonesian cuisine outside Indonesia, a legacy from colonial days. Indonesian food includes numerous vegetarian possibilities; Indian cuisine is also reliable. And despite the Dutch reputation for eating beef and raw fish, they also early on adopted the Swiss tradition of fondue—a less healthy vegetarian option. The travel section of the **Vegetarian Resource Group's** website (www.vrg.org/travel) has a comprehensive list of organizations and websites geared toward helping vegetarians and vegans traveling abroad. The website www.vegdining.com has an excellent database of vegetarian and vegan restaurants worldwide. For more information, visit your local bookstore or health food store, and consult the guide *The Vegetarian Traveler: Where to Stay if You're Vegetarian*, by Jed and Susan Civic (Larson Publications; US$16).

Planning Your Hat

Under the Bridge

Clog Boat

KEEPING KOSHER

Eating kosher in Amsterdam is easily done—kosher delis, bakeries, butchers are dispersed throughout the city. Many restaurants throughout The Netherlands, including larger cities like the Hague, are under the supervision of the Amsterdam Ashkenazi and Sephardic Rabbinates; all meat in the restaurants under Amsterdam rabbinical supervision is *glatt*. If you are strict in your observance, you may have to prepare your own food on the road. Travelers who keep kosher should contact synagogues in Amsterdam and larger cities like Rotterdam for information on kosher restaurants. Your own synagogue or college Hillel should have access to lists of Jewish institutions across The Netherlands. A good resource is the *Jewish Travel Guide*, by Michael Zaidner (Vallentine Mitchell; US$17).

OTHER RESOURCES

Let's Go tries to cover all aspects of budget travel, but we can't put *everything* in our guides. Listed below are books and websites that can serve as jumping-off points for your own research.

USEFUL PUBLICATIONS

Ethnic Amsterdam: A complete guide to the city's faces, places, and cultures. Uitgeverij Vassalucci 2001. ISBN 90 5000 308 7. €13.50.

Smokers Guide to Amsterdam. Available in the city and online at www.smokersguide.com

WORLD WIDE WEB

Almost every aspect of budget travel is accessible via the Internet. Within 10min. at the keyboard, you can make a reservation at a hostel, get advice on travel hotspots from other travelers who have just returned from Amsterdam, or find out exactly how much a train to Gouda costs. Listed here are some budget travel sites to start off your surfing; other sites are listed throughout the book. Because website turnover is high, use search engines (such as www.google.com) to strike out on your own.

OUR PERSONAL FAVORITE

WWW.LETSGO.COM Our website now includes introductory chapters from all our guides and a wealth of information on a monthly featured destination. As always, our website also has info about our books, a travel forum buzzing with stories and tips, and additional links that will help you to make the most of your trip to Amsterdam and the Netherlands.

ART OF BUDGET TRAVEL

How to See the World: www.artoftravel.com. A compendium of great travel tips, from cheap flights to self defense to interacting with local culture.

Rec. Travel Library: www.travel-library.com. A fantastic set of links for general information and personal travelogues.

Lycos: http://cityguide.lycos.com. General introductions to cities and regions throughout The Netherlands, accompanied by links to applicable histories, news, and local tourism sites.

Backpacker's Ultimate Guide: www.bugeurope.com. Tips on packing, transportation, and where to go. Also tons of travel information about The Netherlands.

Backpack Europe: www.backpackeurope.com. Helpful tips, a bulletin board, and links.

INFORMATION ON AMSTERDAM

City of Amsterdam Online: www.amsterdam.nl. Maintained by the city, the site contains news from local government and links to sports and entertainment.

Amsterdam—The Channels: www.channels.nl. Virtual tour of Amsterdam, tourist and transportation information, and some hotel listings and reviews.

Visit Amsterdam: www.holland.com. Maintained by The Netherlands Board of Tourism, this is a comprehensive site with information on planning your trip and attractions in the city.

The Netherlands Rail Planner: www.ns.nl/domestic/index.cgi. Input your destination, date, and time of your desired travel and you will get a detailed train schedule. Prices only available for trips within The Netherlands.

Alternatives to Tourism

When we started in 1961, about 1.7 million people in the world were traveling internationally each year; in 2002 nearly 700 million trips were made, and this number is projected to be up to a billion by 2010. The dramatic rise in tourism has increased the interdependence of the economy, environment, and culture of many destinations—and the tourists they host. A city full of short-term visitors, tourism has a sizeable impact on Amsterdam and its economy. Over 7 million tourists come to Amsterdam annually, with more making the trek each passing year. In the spirit of sustainable tourism, the Let's Go 2004 series aims to offer travelers a chance to give back to the communities they visit. In this chapter we describe the social, political and economic issues facing Amsterdam, along with listings of volunteer organizations dedicated to these concerns. We will address environmentalism, cultural tolerance and anti-discrimination, help for the homeless, health concerns in Amsterdam, and other service opportunities.

For those interested in saving the environment, Amsterdam, known for its liberal history, is a great place to get involved. In 1998 the Amsterdam Treaty established sustainable development as a priority for the European Union. The organizations listed in this chapter focus on projects as diverse as wildlife preservation on the Wadden Islands to increasing ecological awareness among Amsterdam residents. Notably, Amsterdam is also home to the international office for the global environmental advocacy organization Greenpeace (see p. 307). Those interested in formal green study can take a course at the Amsterdam-Maastricht Summer University on the "Challenges and Risks of Genetically-modified Organisms."

A NEW PHILOSOPHY OF TRAVEL

We at *Let's Go* have watched the growth of the 'ignorant tourist' stereotype with dismay, knowing that the majority of travelers care passionately about the state of the communities and environments they explore—but also knowing that even conscientious tourists can inadvertently damage natural wonders, rich cultures, and impoverished communities. We believe the philosophy of **sustainable travel** is among the most important travel tips we could impart to our readers, to help guide fellow backpackers and on-the-road philanthropists. By staying aware of the needs and troubles of local communities, today's travelers can be a powerful force in preserving and restoring this fragile world.

Working against the negative consequences of irresponsible tourism is much simpler than it might seem; it is often self-awareness, rather than self-sacrifice, that makes the biggest difference. Simply by trying to spend responsibly and conserve local resources, all travelers can positively impact the places they visit. Let's Go has partnered with **BEST (Business Enterprises for Sustainable Travel,** an affiliate of the Conference Board; see www.sustainabletravel.org), which recognizes businesses that operate based on the principles of sustainable travel. Below, they provide advice on how ordinary visitors can practice this philosophy in their daily travels, no matter where they are.

TIPS FOR CIVIC TRAVEL: HOW TO MAKE A DIFFERENCE

Travel by train when feasible. Rail travel requires only half the energy per passenger mile that planes do. On average, each of the 40,000 daily domestic air flights releases more than 1700 pounds of greenhouse gas emissions.

Use public mass transportation whenever possible; outside of cities, take advantage of group taxis or vans. Bicycles are an attractive way of seeing a community first-hand. And enjoy walking—purchase good maps of your destination and ask about on-foot touring opportunities.

When renting a car, ask whether fuel-efficient vehicles are available. Honda and Toyota produce cars that use hybrid engines powered by electricity and gasoline, thus reducing emissions of carbon dioxide. Ford Motor Company plans to introduce a hybrid fuel model by the end of 2004.

Reduce, reuse, recycle—use electronic tickets, recycle papers and bottles wherever possible, and avoid using containers made of styrofoam. Refillable water bottles and rechargable batteries both efficiently conserve expendable resources.

Be thoughtful in your purchases. Take care not to buy souvenir objects made from trees in old-growth or endangered forests, such as teak, or items made from endangered species, like ivory or tortoise jewelry. Ask whether products are made from renewable resources.

Buy from local enterprises, such as casual street vendors. In developing countries and low-income neighborhoods, many people depend on the "informal economy" to make a living.

Be on-the-road-philanthropists. If you are inspired by the natural environment of a destination or enriched by its culture, join in preserving their integrity by making a charitable contribution to a local organization.

Spread the word. Upon your return home, tell friends and colleagues about places to visit that will benefit greatly from their tourist dollars, and reward sustainable enterprises by recommending their services. Travelers can not only introduce friends to particular vendors but also to local causes and charities that they might choose to support when they travel.

Our listings classified under **Anti-Discrimination** (see p. 307) take advantage of Amsterdam's unique reputation for tolerance among persons of different ethnicities, religions, and sexual orientations. For example, we encourage interested travelers to support Gay and Lesbian communities at the COC, the oldest institution of its kind in Europe. However, the fact that organizations dedicated to supporting the gay community have long existed in Amsterdam should not imply that discrimination or cultural intolerance in Amsterdam are problems of the past. For example, in May 2003, prominent religious leader Khalil El-Moumni denounced homosexuality as a "contagious disease" on Dutch public television, to the justified outrage of the country's BGLTQ community (see p. 64).

With the continuing upsurge of immigrants to the city, newcomers are finding a colder welcome from Amsterdam natives, particularly under the current Mayor of Amsterdam, M. J. Cohen, who is continuing the conservative trend of the late Pim Fortuyn. As recently as January 2003, refugees from the Ivory Coast have flocked to Amsterdam to flee anti-French attacks by government loyalists. This comes on the heels of decades of immigration from former Dutch colonies of Surinam, Indonesia, and the Dutch Antilles (Aruba, Bonaire, Curaçao). Unfortunately, these refugees often have difficulty finding jobs and integrating into Dutch society. There is even a marked difference between how immigrants who are not from former colonies (such as Southern Europe, Turkey, and Morocco) and those who are from former colonies are treated in terms of preference for employment. Read on to learn more about how different organizations in Amsterdam respond to the needs of immigrants, Jewish communities, and political refugees—ironically often the very same groups that encountered extreme persecution within the city earlier in the century. In light of the recent crackdowns on "squats" in Amsterdam, we have also listed homeless shelter locations and organizations that are generally dedicated to helping the local needy. Later in this section, we recommend ways to find organizations that best suit your interests, whether you're looking to pitch in for a day or a year.

Studying at a college or language program is another way to integrate yourself into the Amsterdam scene. Amsterdam programs often specialize in international development or intercultural cooperation. Many travelers also structure their trips by the work that they can do along the way—either odd jobs as they go, or full-time stints in cities where they plan to stay for some time.

For more on volunteering, studying, and working in Amsterdam and beyond, consult Let's Go's alternatives to tourism website, **www.beyondtourism.com.**

Before handing your money over to any volunteer or study abroad program, make sure you know exactly what you're getting in to. It's a good idea to get the names of **previous participants** and ask them about their experience with the organization, as some programs sound much better on paper than in reality. The questions below are a good place to start:

—Will you be the only person volunteering or studying in the program? If not, what are the other participants like? How old are they? How much will you be expected to interact with them?

—Is room and board included? If so, what is the arrangement? Will you be expected to share a room? A bathroom? What are the meals like? Do they cater to any dietary restrictions?

—Is transportation included? Are there any additional expenses?

—How much free time will you have? Will you be able to travel around?

—What kind of safety network is set up? Will you still be covered by your home insurance? Does the program have an emergency plan?

VOLUNTEERING

Volunteering can be one of the most fulfilling experiences you have in life, especially if combined it with the thrill of traveling in a new place. Though The Netherlands are considered wealthy by international standards, there is no shortage of aid organizations to benefit the very real issues facing the country. While the majority of volunteer opportunities in Amsterdam and The Netherlands require a strong command of the Dutch language, there are still several opportunities for English-speakers. If you're already in Amsterdam, the best way to begin is to register in person with **Vrijwilligers Centrale,** Hartenstraat 15 (☎530 12 20; www.vrijwilligerscentrale.nl/amsterdam), the city's main volunteer agency. Their free listing service will help you find a short- or long-term volunteer position in a range of local organizations such as day-care centers, human rights programs, circuses, and nursing homes. The national Dutch office also has a **hotline** (☎0900 8998 600; €0.20 per min.) that may be able to give you more general information. Another good way to search for volunteer organizations once in Amsterdam is to check the daily paper: every Saturday newspapers like *Het Parool* and *Telegraaf* post ads for service positions.

Most people who volunteer in Amsterdam do so on a short-term basis, at organizations that make use of drop-in or once-a-week volunteers. Most people choose to go through a parent organization that takes care of logistical details and frequently provides a group environment and support system. You can sometimes avoid high application fees by contacting the individual work camps directly. **Euro-Volunteer** (www.euro-volunteer.org) compiles a list of organizations from five EU countries; search for specific locations in The Netherlands to narrow your search. Some of the listings are partially in Dutch. The websites **www.volunteerabroad.com,** and **Action Without Borders** (www.idealist.org) allow you to search for volunteer openings both in The Netherlands and worldwide.

ENVIRO-FRIENDLY OPTIONS

Environmentalism is on the rise in The Netherlands; during the 1990s the number of Dutch citizens belonging to an environmental organization rose to roughly 3.7 million, with numbers still increasing. Not too shabby for a nation with a population less than 16 million. Most larger organizations are members of the **(IUCN), The Netherlands Committee for the World Conservation Union (www.nciucn.nl).** Based in Amsterdam, the IUCN functions as an umbrella source of funding. The following is a listing of Amsterdam-based organizations, though if you are staying elsewhere in Holland be sure to check out local listings.

A SEED Europe, Minahassastraat 1 (☎668 2236; www.aseed.net; mailing address P.O. Box 92066, 1090 Amsterdam). A SEED: Action for Solidarity, Equality, Environment, and Diversity fights against the exploitation of people and the environment. Volunteers of all ages are accepted in this young, idealistic organization. Participate in campaigns ranging from organic food advocacy to the World Bank boycott. Duration of stay flexible.

Both Ends, Nieuwe Keizersgracht 45 (☎623 0833; pw@bothends.org; www.bothends.org). Environmental action group recruits small number of volunteers for fundraising, information exchange, campaigns promotion, research, and lobbying.

Concordia International, Heversham House, 20-22 Boundary Road, Hove, BN3 4ET, England (☎01273 422 218; www.concordia-iye.org.uk). A small not-for-profit charity, Concordia sponsors volunteer projects worldwide, chiefly for residents of the UK. Past projects include restoring nature preserves. Volunteers pay a subscription fee of £6-10 and a project fee of £75-80 for Western Europe.

Friends of the Earth, The Netherlands (☎550 73 00; www.milieudefensie.nl). Maintains a worldwide "Earth watch" on issues like pollution. Student membership €4.54.

Greenpeace Nederland, Keizersgracht 176 (☎523 622 22 or 0800 422 33 44; info@green-peace.nl). From anti-Genetically Modified foods campaigns to saving the whales, Greenpeace is active in a wide range of regional campaigns. Also home to the international Greenpeace headquarters.

IVN Vereniging Voor Natuur en Milieueducatie (Association for Environmental Education), Plantage Middenlaan 2c (☎622 81 15; fax 626 60 91; mailing address Postbus 20123, 1000 HC Amsterdam). Founded in 1960, this society of volunteers and professionals receives funding from the local and national government to promote environmental awareness through grassroots educational activities.

Wereld Natuur Fonds (World Wide Foundation, Netherlands), Kinkerstraat 142 C-3, 1053 EG Amsterdam (☎ 0614 560 591; www.wwf.nl). The largest animal protection organization in The Netherlands, WNF has regional offices throughout the country. Check out their up-to-date website for the latest campaigns and volunteer opportunities in your area.

Vereniging tot Behoud van Natuurmonumenten in Nederland (Dutch Society for the Preservation of Nature Monuments), Wittenbugergracht 29 (☎625 37 53; www.natuurmonumenten.nl). Founded in 1949, this society is organized by region. Email dcamsterdam@natuurmonumenten.nl for volunteer opportunities in the Amsterdam area.

HELPING THOSE IN CRISIS

Despite the dubious morality of actions taken by the imperialist Dutch East India Company during colonialism, today Amsterdam is home to a wide variety of organizations specifically targeted to meet the needs of the oppressed.

Amnesty International, Keizersgracht 620 (☎626 44 36; n.lute@amnesty.nl; www.amnesty.nl). Dedicated to peace and asylum for refugees worldwide, Amnesty runs an office in Amsterdam that employs volunteers in research, fundraising and publications.

Elandsstraat, Elandsstraat 48 (☎623 4757; www.elandsstraat.com; opfangcentrum@het-net.nl). This crisis center runs a day- and night-shelter for battered women, refugees, and other asylum seekers. Employs 60-70 volunteers. (Not a homeless shelter or for addicts).

Jeannette Noel House, Klieverink 125-126-127 (☎699 89 96). Small Catholic cooperative, offers assistance to refugees, emphasizes the importance of meditation and prayer. A few volunteers are needed for the upkeep of the house. Call before visiting.

Nederlandse Rode Kruis (Red Cross), De Valkenburgerstraat 24 (☎622 62 11; www.nrka.nl). Chapter of the international Red Cross volunteers provide free emergency medical treatment, organize blood donations, and participate in service projects such as instructional swimming for the disabled and assistance for asylum seekers.

Refugee Council Amsterdam, Nieuwe Looiers Dwarsstraat 9 (☎627 7745; info@vvamster-dam.nl; www.vluchtelingenwerk.nl). The local branch of the Dutch refugee council often requires volunteers for office and administrative work.

Stichting Gered Gereedschap, Van Bouwdyk Bastiaansestraat 32 (☎683 96 09; gered@xs4all.nl; www.geredgereedschap.nl), near Vondelpark. Workshop welcomes English-speaking volunteers interested in refurbishing tools and work equipment to be sent to economically impoverished African communities. Contact office or check website for details.

ANTI-DISCRIMINATION

Amsterdam's fame for tolerance is not unmerited, especially because of organizations that promote tolerance in the workplace and groups that are involved in community projects. Organizations—both government-sponsored and private—abound, to battle discrimination. Websites that list information on activist organizations, if not necessarily specific volunteer opportunities, are also abundant. **KIEM** (www.integratie.net) is a great portal dedicated to integrating ethnic minorities in Amsterdam and promoting local tolerance for these groups.

COC, Dutch Organization for the Integration of Homosexuality, Rozenstraat 14 (☎626 30 87; www.cocamsterdam.nl). One of Europe's oldest organizations dedicated to the support and solidarity of homosexuals and their families. Contact for involvement in support groups, gay pride activities, and publications. Open M-Tu and Th-F 10am-5pm, W 10am-8pm.

KAFKA, (☎065 168 2822; www.kafka.antifa.net; Postbus 1471, 1001 LE Amsterdam) in affiliation with Anti Fasistiche Aktie (AFA). Rallies against the 4 fascist parties in The Netherlands and organizes both research and documentation of neo-fascist incidents.

Landelijk Platform Slavernijverleden, 51 - 3013 AR Rotterdam (☎010 413 81 46; fax 010 20 10 222; www.platformslavernij.nl), is an institute dedicated to the residual issues surrounding the former slavery of South Africans, Antillians, Arubans and Surinamese.

LBR, Landelijk Bureau ter Bestrijdgin van Rassendiscriminatie, (National Bureau against Discrimination), Building de Weenahof, Schaatsbaan 51, 3013 AR Rotterdam (☎102 010 201; fax 102 010 222; www.lbr.nl). National office in Rotterdam. Provides legal support and advice to all anti-racist organizations and advocates for laws against fascist parties.

UNITED for Intercultural Action, (☎683 4778; fax 683 45 82; www.unitedagainstracism.org; mailing address Postbus 413, NL-1000 AK) enlists the volunteer efforts of 550 European organizations in the struggle against nationalism, racism, and fascism. Organizes publications, campaigns, and conferences in support of migrants, minorities, and refugees, including the International Day Against Anti-semitism.

ORGANIZATIONS FOR WOMEN

Elandsstraat, see p. 307.

Het Vrouwenhuis (The Women's House), Nieuwe Herengracht 95 (☎625 20 66). A center for several organizations and magazines dedicated to supporting women. Also offers classes and workshops in Dutch as well as a few in English.

Stichting Tussenfasehuis voor Ex-Gedetineerde Vrouwen, Sarphatistraat 92 (☎625 97 39; fax 422 18 54; mailing address P.O. Box 15299, NL 1001 MD Amsterdam). Volunteers for this organization work 9hr. or so per week with women recently released from prison; the program aims to encourage re-socialization.

JEWISH COMMUNITY GROUPS

Amsterdam's strong Jewish community plays an active role in the city's culture and social justice movement. **IJAR, Joodse Studenten en Jongerenverteniging** (Jewish Students and Youth Society; www.ijar.nl) sponsors various activities, events, and trips throughout the year. The **Nederlands Auschwitz Comité,** (☎672 33 88; fax 672 33 88; www.auschwitz.nl; mailing address Postbus 74131, 1070 BC Amsterdam) is dedicated to remembrance of the Holocaust through monuments, bulletins, and public awareness.

HELP FOR THE HOMELESS

In some ways, Amsterdam is the liberal exception to the rest of The Netherlands in their treatment of the homeless. The homeless are given a social security allowance provided they can prove they have resided in the city for at least one month. However, especially in the winter months and in low season, the homeless are in need of additional assistance. **Legerdesheils,** Rodekruisstraat 24b (personnel office ☎630 1115; www.legerdesheils.com), is the Dutch Salvation Army. This large organization runs 46 offices throughout Amsterdam, including service centers and shelters, and organizes projects for youth, the elderly, and the socially disadvantaged. The main **service center** is located at Oudezijds Armsteeg 13 (☎520 8409); the crisis center **Gastenburgh,** Oudezijds Voorburgwal 87 (☎520 8425); and over-night shelter **Harven,** to the north of Amsterdam, is at Sixhavenweg 13 (☎626 0481).

HEALTH

AMOC/DV, Stadhouderskade 159 (☎672 1192; fax 671 9694; www.amoc-dhv.org). Take tram #4 from Centraal Station to Albert Cuypmarkt. The AMOC's aim is to help addicts work and live with their addictions. There is a night shelter and a day care center with room for 40-60 patients. English-speaking volunteers usually work at least 3 months.

HIV Vereniging Nederland, 1e Helmersstraat 17 (☎616 01 60; info@hivnet.org; www.hiv-net.org), near Leidseplein. National organization to safeguard the interests of individuals living with HIV/AIDS. Organizes social activities and workshops, in addition to running a cafe where people can meet. Staff of social workers and doctors are always in need of volunteer service, in a range of capacities. All ages, nationalities, and languages accepted.

SAD-Schorerstichting, PC Hooftstraat 5 (☎662 42 06; www.schorer.nl), provides education on prevention and coping with AIDS, and support to victims.

Stichting Boeng Doti, Roggeveerstraat 12 (☎638 44 36). Volunteers work with children from "problem" families.

Stichting Wegloophuis Psychiatrie, Keizersgracht 252 (☎/fax 626 1067). At this foundation for people with psychiatric handicaps, volunteers can work in the house and garden, play games with the patients, and organize activities.

FOR THE UNDECIDED ALTRUIST

If you're flexible, or unsure of exactly what kind of volunteer opportunities you want to pursue, consider one of these organizations that specialize in task force work camps; duties vary according to immediate need.

Service Civil International Voluntary Service (SCI-IVS), 814 NE 40th St., Seattle, WA 98105, USA (☎/fax 206-545-6585; www.sci-ivs.org). The Netherlands chapter is known as VIA or Vrijwillige Internationale Aktie. Arranges placement in work camps in Amsterdam for those 18+. Registration fee US$65-150.

VIA (Vrijwillige Internationale Aktie), Van Bouwdijk Bastiaansestraat 56 (☎689 2760; main Antwerp office ☎0032 32 26 57 27; www.werkkamp.nl). The Dutch affiliate of **Service Civil International** (www.sciint.org), the VIA's teams of young volunteers run progressively-minded work camps in support of victims of social, economic, and political injustice. Each work camp is a short-term 2-3 week project and encourages team-work and cooperation among volunteers. Volunteers must apply through the office in their home country. Check the international website www.sciint.org, or contact one of the following offices: **Australia** ☎61 296 991 129, www.ivp.org.au; **Canada** ☎416-216-0914, ivscanada@yahoo.com; **United Kingdom** ☎441 206 298 215, www.ivs-gb.org.uk; **US** ☎434-823-9003, www.sci-ivs.org, sciinfo@sci-ivs.org.

Volunteers for Peace, 1034 Tiffany Rd., Belmont, VT 05730, USA (☎802-259-2759; www.vfp.org), arranges placement in work camps in The Netherlands and Belgium. Annual *International Workcamp Directory* US$20. Registration fee US$200. Free newsletter.

Vrijwilligers Centrale, Hartenstraat 16 (☎530 12 22; www.vrijwilligerscentrale.nl). The main volunteer agency in Amsterdam. Provides references and contacts according to your interests. More welcoming than most to foreign volunteers.

STUDYING

Amsterdam is a popular study-abroad destination for its proximity to many European destinations and the high quality of the certification, summer, graduate, and professional courses offered in English. Institutes of International Education, which often offer instruction in English, are generally considered to be on a par with Dutch-language universities. The best resource for English-language programs in the humanities, sciences, and social sciences is **NUFFIC,** Kortenaerkade 11, Den Hague (☎070 426 0260; nuffic@nuffic.nl; www.nuffic.nl; mailing address Postbus 29772, 2502 LT Den Hague), which caters to English-speakers interested in studying in The

Netherlands. Their comprehensive online search engine can help you find a course or degree program that matches your interests, time restrictions, location preferences, and budget. Another good general resource for international students is the **Foreign Student Service,** Oranje Nassaulaan 5, Amsterdam (☎671 5915; www.unesco-centrum.nl/fss/fss.html). The office is a good place to find accommodations and health insurance. It also publishes a newsletter with events of interest to international students, including listings for non-university **Dutch-language programs.**

University applicants are frequently required to have obtained the equivalent of the Dutch VWO, or secondary school diploma.Consequently, many students find it easier, if more expensive, to enroll in study-abroad programs through their home universities. Some study abroad programs are affiliated with universities in Amsterdam or The Netherlands and allow students to take classes directly through the university. These programs may be affiliated with an American university but open to other students as well. They usually arrange housing with a family or in a dorm and excursion throughout The Netherlands. Some also offer an internship placement program for part-time work. In programs that have large groups of students who speak the same language, there is a trade-off. For accommodations, dorm life provides a better opportunity to mingle with fellow students, but there is less of a chance to experience the local scene and learn the language. If you live with a family, there is a potential to build lifelong friendships with locals and to experience day-to-day life in more depth, depending on the family with whom you are placed.

STUDENT VISAS

Study of more than three months for non-EU citizens requires a **student visa,** to be procured at least two months in advance; the program in question should provide all the necessary—and abundant—paperwork. A residence permit for study (not for paid employment) is also required, under which you may work no more than 10 hours per week or perform seasonal work in June, July, and August. Study of less than three months does not require a student visa.

UNIVERSITIES

Some American schools still require students to pay them for credits obtained elsewhere. Most university-level study-abroad programs are conducted in Dutch, but many programs do offer classes in English as well as beginner- and lower-level language courses. Another good resource for finding programs is **www.study-abroad.com,** which has links to various semester-abroad programs based on a variety of criteria, including desired location and focus of study. The following books, available at most libraries and many university career/study abroad offices may also assist you in your search: *Academic Year Abroad 2001-2002* (Institute of International Education Books; US$47); *Vacation Study Abroad 2000-2001* (Institute of International Education Books; US$43); and the encyclopedic *Peterson's Study Abroad* and *Summer Study Abroad 2001* (Peterson's; US$30 each). The organizations listed below place students in university programs abroad or have their own branch in Amsterdam or The Netherlands.

AMERICAN PROGRAMS

AFS (American Field Service) Intercultural Programs, Herenweg 115 C, 3645 ZK Vinkeveen (☎029 721 4076; fax 0297 23 3389; www.afs.nl), organizes home stays and study-abroad programs for high school students ages 15-18 and community service for 18+. An affiliated program allows teachers to live in a host family while teaching in a local school.

American Institute for Foreign Study, College Division, River Plaza, 9 West Broad St., Stamford, CT 06902, USA (☎800-727-2437 ext. 5163; www.aifsabroad.com), organizes programs for high school and college study in universities in The Netherlands.

Center for Cultural Interchange, 17 North Second Avenue, St. Charles, IL 60174, USA (☎888-ABROAD1; fax 630-377-2307; www.cci-exchange.com). High school abroad program,

Central College Abroad, Office of International Education, 812 University, Pella, IA 50219, USA (☎800-831-3629; www.central.edu/abroad), offers internships, as well as summer-, semester-, and year-long programs in The Netherlands. US$25 application fee.

Council on International Educational Exchange (CIEE), 633 3rd Ave., 20th floor, New York, NY 10017-6706, USA (☎800-407-8839; www.ciee.org/study), sponsors work, volunteer, academic, and internship programs in Amsterdam.

International Association for the Exchange of Students for Technical Experience (IAESTE), 10400 Little Patuxent Pkwy. Suite 250, Columbia, MD 21044-3519, USA (☎410-997-2200; www.aipt.org). 8- to 12-week programs in The Netherlands for college students who have completed 2 years of technical study. US$25 application fee. The **Delft Office** can be reached at: University Corporate Office (Universiteitsdienst) P.O. Box 52600, AA Delft, The Netherlands (☎15 278 80 12; fax: 15 278 61 51; www.iaeste.nl).

Institute for the International Education of Students (IES), 33 N. LaSalle St., 15th fl., Chicago, IL 60602, USA (☎800-995-2300; www.IESabroad.org). Offers year-long and semester programs in Amsterdam for college students. US $50 application fee. Scholarships available.

School for International Training, College Semester Abroad, Admissions, Kipling Rd., P.O. Box 676, Brattleboro, VT 05302, USA (☎800-336-1616 or 802-257-7751; www.sit.edu). Semester- and year-long programs in Amsterdam and The Netherlands specialize in "Gender, Sexuality, and Identity." US$10,600-13,700.

PROGRAMS IN AMSTERDAM & BEYOND

▨ **University of Amsterdam,** Spui 21 (☎525 80 80 or 525 33 33; fax 525 29 21; www.uva.nl/english). Amsterdam's largest university offers a full range of degree programs in Dutch. Open to college and graduate students. English **MA programs** offered through the International School in European Studies, film and TV studies, Jewish studies, international relations, and social sciences. Students live either in university dormitories or apartments. For more information write to: Service and Information Centre, Binnengasthuisstraat 9, 1012 ZA Amsterdam. Tuition €1445-10,000 per year, depending on the program. Discounts offered for EU citizens. The following details pertain to specific UVA schools:

International School for Humanities and Social Sciences, Oude Turfmarkt 129 (☎525 3777; www.ishss.uva.nl; mailing address P.O. Box 19268, 1000 GG Amsterdam), offers a range of certification programs including politics, ethnicity, art, and culture; media; globalization and international relations; philosophy. Courses run 21-42 weeks and cost €3300 per semester and €6400 per year. Applicants must have completed at least 2 years of university; some programs have a min. GPA requirement.

Summer Institute on Sexuality, Culture and Society (www.ishss.uva.nl/summerinstitute; summerinstitute@ishss.uva.nl). Offered since 1997; applicants must have a focused interest in sexuality studies. Check the website for enrollment requirements.

Amsterdam-Maastricht Summer University, Keizersgracht 324 (☎620 02 25; www.amsu.edu; mailing address P.O. Box 53066, 1007 RB Amsterdam), offers courses in cultural studies; art history; economics and politics; health sciences; medicine; language; law; public policy; media studies and performing arts. All courses taught in English. Tuition €550-€850 per course. Accommodation €450.

Leiden University, Rapenburg 67, Leiden (☎527 7287; www.leiden.edu; mailing address P.O. Box 9500, 2300 RT Leiden), offers English-language instruction in Dutch, European, and international law; gender studies; culture and politics. Semester- and year-long programs. 2 years university education required. €4150 per semester, €7300 per year.

Universiteit Maastricht, Center for European Studies (CES), Witmakersstraat 10 Maastricht (☎043 321 26 27; www.ces.unimaas.nl; mailing address P.O. Box 616, 6200 MD Maastricht), offers a 6 week certification program with courses on socio-political and economic, aspects of the EU; law and politics; European art and history; intercultural communication. Applicants must have completed at least 2 years of university education.

Utrecht University, (☎030 253 3550; www.uu.nl; mailing address P.O. Box 80125, 3508 TC Utrecht), offers international bachelor's programs, master's, and Ph.D programs in English and Dutch. Range of research programs including biomedical sciences, social sciences, and the humanities. Tuition €1445 for EU and non-EU citizens in 2003. Room and board €3126.

University College Utrecht, Campusplein 1, Utrecht (☎030 253 9900; fax 030 253 9905; www.ucu.uu.nl; mailing address P.O. Box 90145, 3508 TC Utrecht), a subset of the University of Utrecht, offers 3-year English-language BA and BSC programs in the liberal arts and sciences. Classes limited to 25 people. Courses €7050 per year. Requirements: IB, A-levels.

Utrecht University Summer School (☎253 26 96; www.uu.nl/summerschool; mailing address P.O. Box 80125, 3508 TC Utrecht), offers courses in science, health, languages, and behavioral sciences, among other. Popular options include Women's Studies, as well as Dutch Society and Culture. Courses 2-4 weeks; tuition €450-850. Check website for more details. Application deadline: April 15.

LANGUAGE SCHOOLS

Unlike American universities, language schools are frequently independently-run international or local organizations or divisions of foreign universities that rarely offer college credit. Language schools are a good alternative to university study if you desire a deeper focus on the language or a slightly less-rigorous courseload. These programs are also good for younger high school students that might not feel comfortable with older students in a university program.

Goethe Institut, Herengracht 470 (☎623 04 21). A German cultural center offering German language courses, lectures, drama and film (with English subtitles).

Italian Cultural Institute, Keizersgracht 564 (☎626 53 14), offers Italian language courses.

Maison Descartes, Vijzelgracht 2A (☎531 95 00; www.maisondescartesnl). Music, expositions, symposia, and cinema à la française. Language courses €300-550 per 45hr.

The National Registration Center for Study Abroad, P.O. Box 1393, Milwaukee, WI 53201, USA (☎414-278-0631; fax 414-271-8884; www.nrcsa.com). Students live in their language tutor's home and take up to 25 Dutch lessons per week (starting at US$1310).

Nuffic Language Laboratory, Kortenaerkade 12, (☎070 42 60 141; www.nuffic.nl; mailing address Postbus 29777, 2502 LT Den Haag). Individual lessons, including conversational Dutch, English, and French. 12 2-hr. lessons €298 plus materials. €12 registration fee.

ALTERNATIVE STUDY ABROAD

For a chance to learn in a style less ordinary, check out these opportunities in agriculture, art, archaeology, and culinary technique. Also check out www.nuffic.nl for information on The Netherlands' 55 "professional universities," known as **hogescholen,** which specialize in everything from finance to the arts.

Agriventure (International Agricultural Exchange Association), 1000 1st Ave. S, Great Falls, MT 59401, USA (☎406-727-1999; www.agriventure.com), runs an agricultural and horticultural exchange program. Participants are placed with a host family, receive room, board, and stipend, learn Dutch farming techniques. Exchanges last 4-15 months.

Amsterdam Hogeschool voor de Kunsten, (☎527 77 00; fax 527 77 12; www.ahk.nl; mailing address P.O. Box 15079, NL-1001 MB Amsterdam). The School of the Arts is an umbrella organization including the schools listed below. Note, however, that several Academy classes and websites are presented in Dutch only. Tuition varies.

> **Theater School,** Jodenbreestraat 3 (www.the.ahk.nl), offers degree programs in dance, theater, and technical media. Dance ☎527 76 67, info.dans@the.ahk.nl; theater ☎527 7837, info.theater@the.ahk.nl; technical media ☎527 76 20.

> **Conservatorium van Amsterdam (Amsterdam School of Music),** Van Baerlestraat 27 (☎527 75 50; fax 676 15 06; www.cva.ahk.nl) accepts speakers of either Dutch or English. Foreign student contact person: Heleen de Kam (☎527 75 84; h.dekam@cva.ahk.nl). Entrance by audition and examination.

The Academy of Fine Arts, Hortusplantsoen 2 (☎527 72 20; fax 527 72 22; www.bvo.ahk.nl; info@bvo.ahk.nl), offers instruction in drawing and painting.

Maurits Binger Film Institute, Nieuwezijds Voorburghwal 4-10 (☎530 96 30; www.binger.nl), offers experimental short- and long-term courses taught in English on film theory and production for students with extensive experience in the film industry. Prices for most Hogeschool programs €1839 per year for non-EU students, €1445 for EU citizens.

Keizer Culinair, Keizersgracht 376 (☎427 92 76; www.keizerculinair.nl). Choose a sumptuous Dutch or Italian 5-course feast—then learn to cook it in a lovely canal house (€53.50).

NJBG (Nederlandse Jeugdbond voor Gescheidenis) or the **Dutch Youth Association for History,** Prins Willem Alexanderhof 5, 2595 BE Den Haag (☎070 347 6598; fax 070 335 2536; www.njbg.nl). Based in the Hague, NJBG sponsors archaeological excursions and building restoration projects. Prices of excursions vary, ranging roughly €100-500.

WORKING

Some travelers want long-term jobs that allow them to become integrated with the local community, while other travelers seek out short-term jobs to finance the next leg of their travels. In Amsterdam, those interested in long-term work are best off seeking employment in larger organizations or through internship programs that are willing to handle the red-tape of work permits. Short term work in Amsterdam largely feeds off the tourism industry. As always, it's important to keep your eyes and ears open for posts available via word-of-mouth. Bulletin boards are also invaluable resources. Be sure to check out postings at the **Openbare Bibliotheek Amsterdam,** Prinsengracht 587, just north of Leidsegracht, the **City Hall Information Center,** Amstel 1, in Waterlooplein, and the **University of Amsterdam.**

VISA INFORMATION

The Dutch Ministry of Justice's Immigration and Naturalization Service runs a helpful website at **www.immigratiedienst.nl.** The full online version (in English and Dutch) offers information on topics from temporary stays to becoming a Dutch citizen to seeking asylum. If you're a citizen of Australia, Canada, Ireland, New Zealand, the UK, the US, or any EU nation, you need only a valid passport to enter and stay in The Netherlands for up to three months on vacation; no entry visa is required. South African citizens need an entry visa just to enter The Netherlands, even for a vacation of less than three months. If you're planning to stay in The Netherlands for more than three months, or intend to work or study for any length of time, you'll need some kind of visa or permit (unless you're an citizen of the EU, in most cases), details of which are outlined below. Beware: these permits are very difficult to obtain.

VISA REQUIREMENTS BY NATIONALITY

EU/EEA

Citizens of the European Union, including Ireland and the UK, as well as citizens of the European Economic Area (that is, Norway and Iceland), do not need student visas or work permits to study or work in The Netherlands. Nor do they officially need residence permits, even for stays of more than three months. However, getting a residence permit even if you are an EU citizen makes sense, as bureaucratic hassles ensue if you don't have one. Even if you are not an EU citizen, you may be able to claim EU work and study status if your parents were born in an EU country.

AUSTRALIA, CANADA, NEW ZEALAND, & THE US

Australian, Canadian, New Zealand, and US citizens need a **work permit** to work in The Netherlands, and unfortunately, these can often be a chore to obtain. For stays of under three months, no residence permit is necessary; for stays over three months, a **residence permit** is required. These can be obtained at Dutch embassies or consulates abroad or at the **Aliens Police Office** in The Netherlands. Australian, Canadian, and New Zealand citizens ages 18-30 can apply to take part in the **Working Holiday Scheme,** which allows you to work in The Netherlands for one year. Applications can be made at Dutch embassies and consulates. For US college students, recent graduates, and young adults, the simplest way to get legal permission to work in The Netherlands is through **Council Exchanges Work Abroad Programs.** Fees are US$300-425. Council Exchanges can help obtain a three- to six-month work permit/visa and also provide assistance finding jobs and housing.

SOUTH AFRICA

For stays of under three months, South African citizens require an entry visa, plus a work permit, if working. Moreover, South Africans need a residence permit plus a **Machtiging tot Voorlopig Verblijf (MVV),** meaning an authorization for temporary stay, for any stay over three months in The Netherlands, including stays for study or work. (The student visa or work permit is also required.) Applications for an MVV can be made to the Dutch consulate or embassy in South Africa, or the applicant's sponsor (that is, an educational institution or employer) in The Netherlands can apply to the Aliens Police. Both methods ordinarily take three to six months; however, many educational institutions, companies, and organizations promoting cultural exchange are allowed to submit MVV applications to the Immigration and Naturalization Service per year under an accelerated schedule. South African citizens may not enter The Netherlands during the application period, not even as tourists. The application fee is €50.

LONG-TERM WORK

Those seeking long-term work in Amsterdam should note that competition increases in the summer, and bureaucratic procedures for visa and work permits are strictly followed by most employers. This may be attributed to attempts during the past decades to curb squatting and drug abuse. All new employes should carry passport or other form of identification to avoid trouble during inspections by tax and social security inspectors and immigration officers. If you're planning on spending more than three months working in Amsterdam, search for a job well in advance. International placement agencies are often the easiest way to find employment abroad, especially for teaching English. Internships, usually for college students, are a good way to segue into working abroad, although they are often unpaid or poorly paid. Be wary of advertisements or companies that claim the ability to get you a job abroad for a fee—the same listings are often available online or in newspapers, or even out of date. Once in The Netherlands, job searches usually begin by inquiring at city employment agencies, called **arbeidsbureaux (AB).** EU Nationals can utilize the ABs only after having the Police grant a "3-month EU job seeker" stamp on their passport and obtain a social security fiscal code (SOFI number) from the local tax office. There are numerous AB offices in Amsterdam. The easiest way to find the address of the nearest one is to check the **Dutch "Yellow Pages" (Gouden Gids).** Another option is to contact the **Head Office of the Dutch employment service** for a list of regional employment offices. Write to the **Central Bureau voor de Arbeidsvoorziening,** Boerhaavelaan 7, Postbus 883, NL-2700 AW Zoetermeer (☎79 371 20 00; fax 79 371 20 99).

International Internships (www.internabroad.com). A search engine for internship postings.

Specialty Travel Index, 305 San Anselmo Ave. #313, San Anselmo, CA 94960, USA (☎888-624-4030 or 415-455-1643; www.specialtytravel.com), has an extensive listing of "off-the-beaten-track" and specialty travel opportunities. US$6.

Transitions Abroad (www.transabroad.com) publishes a bimonthly online newsletter for work, study, and specialized travel abroad.

TEACHING ENGLISH

Teaching jobs abroad are rarely well-paid, and this is nowhere more true than in Amsterdam, where highly skilled English speakers abound. Some elite private American schools can pay somewhat competitive salaries. Volunteering as a teacher in lieu of getting paid is also a popular option; even in those cases, teachers often get some sort of a daily stipend to help with living expenses. In almost all cases, you must have at least a bachelor's degree to be a full-fledged teacher, although college undergraduates can often get summer positions teaching or tutoring. Many schools require teachers to have a **Teaching English as a Foreign Language (TEFL)** certificate. Native English speakers working in private schools are most often hired for English-immersion classrooms where no Dutch is spoken. Those volunteering or teaching in public, poorer schools, are more likely to be working in both English and Dutch. Placement agencies or university fellowship programs are the best resources for finding teaching jobs in Amsterdam. In the case of university fellowships, the best time of the year is several weeks before the start of the school year. The following organizations are extremely helpful in placing teachers in The Netherlands:

International Schools Services (ISS), 15 Roszel Rd., Box 5910, Princeton, NJ 08543-5910, USA (☎609-452-0990; fax 609-452-2690; www.iss.edu), hires teachers for more than 200 overseas schools including some in The Netherlands; candidates should have experience teaching or with international affairs. 2-year commitment expected. US$150 program fee.

European Council of International Schools, 21 Lavant St., Petersfield, Hampshire GU32 3EL, UK (☎+44 1730 268 244; fax +44 1730 267 914; www.ecis.org). An association of over 500 international schools that organizes 4 annual hiring fairs in London, Vancouver, and Melbourne. Website has directory of English-speaking schools in The Netherlands.

Office of Overseas Schools, US Department of State, Room H328, SA-1, Washington, D.C. 20522, USA (☎202-261-8200; fax 202-261-8224; www.state.gov/www/about_state/schools), keeps a comprehensive list of schools abroad and agencies that arrange placement for Americans to teach abroad.

Teach Abroad (www.teachabroad.com) posts listings of available positions for English-speaking instructors.

SCHOOLS IN AMSTERDAM & BEYOND

The Netherlands are home to a large number of English-speaking schools, be they international, American, British, or Dutch. There are also English-speaking schools in Rotterdam, Eindoven, Groningen, and Maastricht. While some schools interview and hire directly, most hire through recruitment fairs (see above).

The International School of Amsterdam, Sportlaan 45, 1185 TB Amstelveen (☎347 11 11; fax 347 12 22; www.isa.nl), in the suburb of Amstelveen.

British School of Amsterdam, Anthonie van Dijckstraat 1 (☎679 78 40; fax 675 83 96).

American School of The Hague, Rijksstraatweg 200, 2241 BX Wassenaar, Den Haag (☎070 512 1060; www.ash.nl).

The British School in The Netherlands, HR Services, The Foundation School, Tarwekamp 3, 2592 XG Den Haag (☎070 315 4063; fax 070 315 4065; www.britishschool.nl).

The International School of The Hague, Theo Mann Bouwmeesterlaan 75, 2597 GV, Den Haag (☎70 328 14 50; fax 70 328 20 49; www.ishthehague.nl).

The Rijnlands Lyceum Oegstgeest, Apollolaan 1, 2341 BA Oestgeest (☎071 519 35 55; fax 071 519 35 50; www.rijnlandslyceum.nl/oegstgeest), between The Hague and Leiden.

AU PAIR WORK

In The Netherlands, au pairs must be between 18 and 25 years of age and are not allowed to work more than 30 hours per week in the household. Au pairs can stay in The Netherlands for a maximum of one year. They must be unmarried, must have no dependents, and must not have been granted a Dutch residence permit previously. Working as an au pair requires a residence permit. Au pairs work as live-in nannies, caring for children and doing light housework in foreign countries in exchange for room, board, and a small spending allowance. Most former au pairs speak favorably of their experience, and of how it allowed them to fully get to know the country and its local culture without the high expenses of traveling. Drawbacks, however, often include long hours of being on-duty and the mediocre pay, roughly €70-90 per week in The Netherlands. Much of the au pair experience depends on the family you end up being placed with.

Accord Cultural Exchange, 750 La Playa, San Francisco, CA 94121, USA (☎415-386-6203; www.cognitext.com/accord).

Activity International, P.O. Box 7097, 9701 JB Groningen (☎050 313 06 66; www.activity.aupair.nl), places au pairs throughout The Netherlands.

Au Pair Homestay, World Learning, Inc., 1015 15th St. NW, Suite 750, Washington, DC 20005, USA (☎800-287-2477; fax 202-408-5397).

Au Pair in Europe, P.O. Box 68056, Blakely Postal Outlet, Hamilton, Ontario, Canada L8M 3M7 (☎905-545-6305; fax 905-544-4121; www.princeent.com), offers programs throughout The Netherlands.

Childcare International, Ltd., Trafalgar House, Grenville Pl., London NW7 3SA, UK (☎44 020 8906 3116; fax 8906-3461; www.childint.co.uk).

InterExchange, 161 Sixth Ave., New York, NY 10013, USA (☎212-924-0446; fax 924-0575; www.interexchange.org), requires a 10-month min. commitment.

SHORT-TERM WORK

Traveling can get expensive; therefore, many travelers try odd jobs to make some extra cash to carry them through another month or two of touring. For several decades now Holland has been a mecca for young, bright-eyed EU nationals seeking short term work. Amsterdam is full of recruitment and temp agencies, called **uitzendbureaux,** though a working knowledge of Dutch is often required. The *Uitzendbureaux* advertise short-term jobs (less than 6 months or 1000 hours), though it is possible to extend a employment up to one year. Jobs offered are usually unskilled and cater to foreigners with little experience. Be aware, however, that these *Uitzendbureaux* often charge a percentage of your wage as a commission.

The **tourism industry** provides a substantial number of jobs to foreigners, who can work and in hotels and hostels year-round. For these jobs it is often best to go through establishment directly rather than through the *uitzendbureaux.* Certain hotels will also hire English speakers to convince tourists in train stations to work at the hotel. Another popular option is to work several hours a day at a hostel in exchange for free or discounted room and/or board. Most often, these short-term jobs are found by word-of-mouth or by talking to the establishment's owner. Another option is to contact the national tourist office **VVV** (www.vvv.nl). Due to the high turnover in the tourism industry, many establishments in Amsterdam and elsewhere, are always eager for help.

Jobs in **agriculture** and the **bulb industry** (processing of flower bulbs and exports) can be grueling, low-paid, and increasingly difficult for foreigners to find. Interested, aggressive EU nationals might want to write to some of the major bulb exporters: **Peter Keur B.V.,** Noorder Leidsevaart 26, 2182 NB Hillegom, and **Van Waveren B.V.,** P.O. Box 10, 2180 AA Hillegom. Be prepared to bring your own tent and bicycle. An avenue for non-EU citizens to explore is **P. Bakker B.V.,** Postbus 601, 2180 AP Hillgom, and **M.G.M. van Haaster,** Lissedk 490a, 2165 AH Lissebroek, or **Frylink & Zonen B.V.,** in Noordwijkerhout. For employment in agriculture generally, particularly between mid-April and October, consider contacting **Eurocom,** Hoboken 213, 4826 EC Breda (☎076 711 468), and **Optima Uitzendbureaux,** Piet Heinstraat 8, 4461 GL Goes (☎0013 211 223). Again, competition is fiercest during the summer.

UITZENDBUREAUX & SEARCH ENGINES

Undutchables, (☎ 623 13 00; fax ☎ 428 17 81; office@amsterdam.undutchables.nl; www.undutchables.nl; mailing address P.O. Box 57204, 1040 BC Amsterdam). The most useful job recruitment agency for foreigners, placing people in jobs that require command of a language other than Dutch. Temporary and permanent jobs available.

Content, Van Baerlestraat 83 (☎ 676 44 41).

Dactylo (www.dactylo.nl).

Manpower (☎ 305 56 55; www.manpower.nl). Numerous branches in Amsterdam, classified by employment sector. See website for the most appropriate address.

Randstad, Dam 4 (☎ 626 22 13; www.randstad.nl).

Vedior Personeelsdiensten (www.vedior.nl).

SETTLING IN

www.undutchables.nl. The website of the Undutchables recruitment agency is full of practical information for foreigners living and working in The Netherlands.

www.howtosurviveholland.nl. Undutchables runs this website, too, which is less practical in nature but contains humorous essays about and introductions to various elements of Dutch culture, written by foreigners.

www.expatica.nl. Devoted to the expatriate community in The Netherlands, this website is geared towards wealthier and older expats but still contains interesting articles.

www.transartists.nl. An information clearinghouse website for artists seeking jobs, lodgings, and studios in The Netherlands. Features classifieds postings and festival and workshop info.

www.fasnrcvg.ie/abroad/netherl.htm. The FAS National Resource Center for Vocational Guidance. Sponsored for Irish citizens wishing to live and work in The Netherlands.

FURTHER READING

Alternatives to the Peace Corps: A Directory of Third World and U.S. Volunteer Opportunities, by Joan Powell. Food First Books, 2000 (US$10).

How to Get a Job in Europe, by Sanborn and Matherly. Surrey Books, 1999 (US$22).

How to Live Your Dream of Volunteering Oversees, by Collins, DeZerega, and Heckscher. Penguin Books, 2002 (US$17).

International Directory of Voluntary Work, by Whetter and Pybus. Peterson's Guides and Vacation Work, 2000 (US$16).

International Jobs, by Kocher and Segal. Perseus Books, 1999 (US$18).

Work Abroad: The Complete Guide to Finding a Job Overseas, by Hubbs, Griffith, and Nolting. Transitions Abroad Publishing, 2000 (US$16).

Work Your Way Around the World, by Susan Griffith. Worldview Publishing, 2001 (US$18).

Invest Yourself: The Catalogue of Volunteer Opportunities, published by the Commission on Voluntary Service and Action (☎ 718-638-8487).

Service Directory

AMERICAN EXPRESS

Damrak 66 (☎504 87 70). Open M-F 9am-5pm, Sa 9am-noon.

BANKS

In general, banking hours in Amsterdam are M, W, F 9am-5pm; Th 9am-7pm.

ABN Amrobank: Branches at Dam 2 and Leidsestraat 1 (☎523 29 00). Open M 11am-5pm, Tu-F 9am-5pm.

GWK: Centraal Station (☎627 27 31). Open M-W and Sa-Su 7am-10:45pm. Julianaplein 1 (☎693 45 45). Open M-Sa 7:30am-8pm, Su 10am-6pm.

Rabobank: Nieuwmarkt 20, Frederiksplein 54, and Dam 16 (☎777 88 99). Open M 1-5pm, Tu-W and F 9:30am-5pm, Th 9:30am-6pm.

BIKE RENTAL

Bike City, 68-70 Bloemgracht (☎626 37 21; www.bikecity.nl), Jordaan. Great rates on 1-, 3-, and 5-speed bikes, from €3.50 for 2hr. to €6.75 for a day or €29,50 for 5 days on the more inexpensive models. Bike rental comes with 2 good locks: use them! Be sure to bring a passport or other government-issued ID. Deposit. €25. Open daily 9am-6pm. AmEx/MC/V with 5% surcharge.

Damstraat Rent-a-Bike, Damstraat 22 (☎625 50 29; www.bikes.nl). Head south down Damrak from Centraal Station until you hit Dam Sq.; from there, go left across the square onto Damstraat. Good deals on all different kinds of bikes. Rentals from €7 per day, €31 per week. Credit card imprint or €25 and an ID required as deposit. Open daily 9am-6pm.

Frederic Rent a Bike, Brouwersgracht 78 (☎62 45 509; www.frederic.nl), in the Shipping Quarter. From Centraal Station, head down Damrak and turn right at Nieuwendijk. Turn left after you cross the Harlemmersluis bridge, and follow along the Brouwersgracht for about 7 blocks; it's on the right. Part bike rental establishment, part tourist office, Fred's is well worth the 10min. walk from Centraal Station. In addition to renting bikes, the friendly and helpful staff provides street maps, cycling know-how, and information suited to customers' particular interests. Bikes €10 per day, which includes lock and theft insurance or €40 per week. Online reservations available. No deposit (though ID or credit card imprint is required). Open daily 9am-6pm. Accepts AmEx/MC/V for deposit, but payment must be in cash.

Holland Rent-a-Bike, Damrak 247 (☎622 32 07), basement of the Beurs de Beurlage. One of the cheapest places around, and right by Centraal Station. Bikes €6.25 per day, €32.50 per week; €100 or €30 plus an ID for deposit. Open M-F 7am-7pm, Sa-Su 8am-6pm, Su 9am-6pm. AmEx/MC/V.

Mac Bike, Marnixstraat 220, Weteringschans 2, Mr. Visserplein 2 (☎626 69 64; www.macbike.nl). This popular chain of bicycle rental stores offers a variety of options, from same-day rentals (€6.50) to 6-day stints (€27.25). Be sure not to rent one of the bikes that has a garish "Mac Bike" logo on the front, lest you brand yourself a tourist. For 50% of the rental price, you can insure your bike against theft and avoid paying the replacement fee of €300-600. Deposit €30. Open daily 9am-6pm. AmEx/MC/V.budget travel agencies

Eurolines, Rokin 10 (☎421 79 51; www.eurolines.nl), will book coach travel throughout Europe. Open M-F 9:30am-5:30pm, Sa 10am-4pm.

CONSULATES & EMBASSIES

Most of the foreign embassies in The Netherlands are in **The Hague,** area code 070:

Australia, Carnegielaan 4, 2517 KH (☎310 82 00). Open M-F 8:30am-4:55pm; visas 10am-12:30pm.

Canada, Sophialaan 7, 2514 JP (☎311 16 00). Open M-F 9am-12:45pm and 1:45-5:30pm.

Ireland, 9 Dr. Kuyperstraat, 2514 BA (☎363 09 93). Open M-F 10am-12:30pm and 2:30-5:00pm.

South Africa, Wassenaarseweg 40, 2596 CJ (☎392 45 01). Open daily 9am-noon.

UK, Lange Voorhout 10 2514 ED (☎427 04 27). Open M-F 9am-noon, 2-5:30pm.

US, Lange Voorhout 102, 2514 EJ (☎310 92 09). Open M-F 8:15am-4pm.

CONSULATES IN AMSTERDAM

American Consulate, Museumplein 19 (☎575 53 09) is open to visitors M-F 8:30am-11:30am

British Consulate, Koningslaan 44 (☎676 43 43). Open M-F 9am-noon, 2-5:30pm.

CURRENCY EXCHANGE

American Express, Damrak 66, offers the best rates, no commission on American Express traveler's cheques, and €4 flat fee for all non-euro cash and non-American Express traveler's checks. Open M-F 9am-5pm, Sa 9am-noon.

GWK, in Centraal Station. Other locations at Damrak 86, Kalverstraat 103, Leidseplein 1-3, and Schiphol Airport, offers good rates, charging €2.25 plus 2.25% commission. Students with ISIC get 25% discount. 3% commission on travelers' cheques. Centraal open Su 9am-11:45pm, M-Sa 7am-11:45pm. Damrak open daily 10am-10pm, Kalverstraat open Su 10:30am-5pm, M-Sa 9am-6pm. Leidseplein open daily 8:30am-10pm, Schiphol open 24hr.

Pott-Change, Damrak 95 (☎626 36 58; open M-F 8am-8pm, Sa-Su 9am-8pm) or Rembrandtplein 10B (☎626 87 68; open M-F 9:15am-4:30pm). No commission on cash; €1.50 flat fee on traveler's checks.

EMERGENCY

See also **Health and Medical Assistance,** p. 322.

Emergencies: ☎112 (police, ambulance, fire brigade), free from all pay phones.

Police: Headquarters, Elandsgracht 117 (☎0800 88 44), at the intersection with Marnixstraat. Call here to get connected to the station nearest you or the rape crisis department.

Crisis Lines: General counseling at **Tele-phone Helpline** (☎675 75 75). Open 24hr. **Rape crisis hotline** (☎612 02 45) staffed M-F 10:30am-11pm, Sa-Su 3:30-11pm. **Drug counseling, Jellinek Clinic** (☎570 22 22). Open M-F 9am-5pm.

AIDS Helpline (☎080 00 22 22 20). Advice and information about AIDS. M-F 2-10pm.

HIV-Plus Line (☎685 00 55). Tu and Th 8-10:30pm and M, W, F 1-4pm.

ENTERTAINMENT INFORMATION

Amsterdams Uit Buro (AUB), Leidseplein 26 (☎621 13 11; open daily 9am-9pm), is stuffed with fliers, pamphlets, and guides to help you sift through theater and music offerings. The AUB also sells tickets and makes reservations for just about any cultural event throughout Holland. Pick up the free monthly *UITKRANT* (in Dutch) or the English-language *Day-by-Day* (€1.50) at any AUB office for a breakdown of what's on. Open M-W and F-Sa 10am-6pm, Th 10am-9pm, Su noon-9pm.

VVV's theater desk, Stationsplein 10. Makes reservations for cultural events. Open M-Sa 10am-5pm.

EXERCISE & ADVENTURE

Squash City, Ketelmakerstraat 6 (☎626 78 83; www.squashcity.com), take bus #18 or 22 to Ketelmakerstraat, dir. Haarlemerplein. About a 5min. bus ride, or 15min. walk west of Centraal Station. Offers squash courts, a gym, and sauna. Gym or aerobics day cards both €8 8:45am-5pm, €9.50 5pm-closing. Squash day card €6.80/€9 per person. Racquet rental €2.50. Sun-tan bed €8 per session. Student discounts available. Open M-F 8:45am-midnight, Sa-Su 8:45am-9pm.

Garden Gym, Jodenbreestraat 158 (☎626 87 72; www.thegarden.nl). Central location in the Jodenbuurt makes working out truly convenient. Day card (€8.50) gets you access to equipment and showers for one full day; equipment and sauna day card €11. See website for aerobics schedules. Open M, W, and F 9am-11pm; Tu, Th noon-10pm; Sa-Su 9am-2pm.

Borchland Sportscentrum, Borchlandweg 6-12 (☎563 33 33). Take Metro #54 to Strandvliet and follow signs to Borchland. This is the city's largest sporting center and a great place to spend a rainy day. Squash €8-18. Racket rental €2.75. Golf 9 holes €10-15, 18 holes €15-21.50, Tennis €15-20. Bowling €15-23. Badminton €10. Located next to the impressive ArenA Amsterdam, the spiffy complex has restaurant and cafe. Open daily 8am-11pm.

De Mirandabad, De Mirandalaan 9 (☎546 44 44; www.zuideramstel.amsterdam.nl), is a waterpark with a wave pool, beach, and indoor and outdoor pools. Admission €3.15, seniors €2.50. Additional charges for some water sports. Open daily 7am-midnight; check website for hours of various facilities.

Avonturenbaai Sloterparkbad, Pres. Allendelaan 3 (☎506 35 06; www.optisport.nl/sloterparkbad/). Take tram #14 to its end. The park contains with indoor and outdoor pools. €3, seniors €2.50. Open M, Th 2-6pm; Tu, F 2-10pm, W 1-10pm; Sa-Su 10am-6pm.

Bungy Jump Holland, Westerdoksdijk 44 (☎419 60 05; www.bungy.nl). Jump from a crane 75m above the Ij canal. You get to choose whether you end up wet or dry. First jump €50, 2nd €40; duo jump €100. Open Apr. Sa-Su noon-6pm; May-June Th-Su noon-7pm; July-Aug. W-Su noon-8pm; Sept.-Oct. Th-Su noon-6pm.

Deco Sauna, Herengracht 115 (☎623 82 15; www.saunadeco.nl). Pamper yourself amidst fabulous 20s art deco surroundings with a massage. €27 for 25min., €44 for 55min. Sauna and Turkish bath also available. Towel rental €2. Open M-Sa noon-11pm, Su 1-6pm. Cash only.

Klimmuur Centruum, De Ruyterkade 160 (☎427 57 77; www.deklimmuur.nl), near Centraal Station; it's the enormous tilted corrugated block. An unsurpassed indoor wall climbing facility. €9 per climb; equipment rental €15. Open M-F 6-10:30pm, Sa 1-7pm, Su 1-10:30pm. Cash only.

GAY & LESBIAN RESOURCES

The monthly *Gay and Night* (€2.25) newspaper provides info on gay venues and events. The fortnightly publications *Gay Krant* (€2.25) and *Shark* (€2.25) also provide excellent and thorough listings of what's going down in queer Amsterdam.

COC, Rozenstraat 14 (☎626 30 87; www.cocamsterdam.nl), exists as a social network and information center. Maps designed specifically for the gay traveler available in the lobby. Office open M-Tu and Th-F 10am-5pm, W 10am-8pm. The cafe on the ground floor turns into a multicultural discotheque on F-Sa nights. Cafe open Th 8pm-midnight, F 8pm-10pm; disco F-Sa 10pm-4am (Sa is women-only).

Gay and Lesbian Switchboard (☎623 65 65) is available to answer questions, suggest events, or listen to personal problems. All switchboard volunteers speak English and some speak other languages. Phone staffed daily 10am-10pm.

Gay Krant Reisservice, Kloveniersburgwal 40 (☎421 00 00; www.gaykrant.nl/reis). A travel service devoted to gay and lesbian travelers. Also features an impressive display of magazines and newspapers for gay travelers. Newsletters available. Open M 2-6pm, Tu-F 10am-6pm, Sa 10am-4pm.

Vrolijk, Paleisstraat 135 (☎623 51 42; www.vrolijk.nu), claims to be the largest gay and lesbian bookstore in Europe. With an excellent selection of literature and periodicals, it's an ideal place to stop in for tips on what's hot and what's not in gay Amsterdam. Various knick-knacks abound; also houses a growing DVD selection. Shop online for books. Open M 11am-6pm; Tu-W, F 10am-6pm; Th 10am-9pm; Sa 10am-5pm.

SAD/Schorerfoundation, P.C. Hoofstraat 5 (☎662 42 06). A counseling center for gay men and women. Open M-F 10am-4pm.

Xantippe Unlimited, Prinsengracht 290 (☎623 58 54; www.xs4all.nl/~xantippe/xantippe_unltd_nl.html). General bookstore, but with a specialization in women's and lesbian issues. Open M 1-7pm, Tu-F 10am-7pm, Sa 10am-6pm, Su noon-5pm.

HEALTH & MEDICAL ASSISTANCE

See also **Emergency,** p. 320.

Academisch Medisch Centrum, Meibergdreef 9 (☎566 91 11), is easily accessible by bus #59, 60, 120, 158 from Centraal (ask the driver to announce the medical center). Arranges for hospital care.

Emergency Medical Hotline, (☎592 33 55). Open 24hr.

Kruispost Medisch Helpcentrum, Oudezijds Voorburgwal 129 (☎624 90 31). From Centraal Station, head out and turn left at the Victoria Hotel, and follow the street until Oudezijds Voorburgwal, on your right. This walk-in clinic offers first aid only to non-insured travelers daily 7am-9pm.

Centrale Doktorsdienst (☎592 34 34). 24hr. medical help. English-speaking service will advise you appropriate treatment.

STD Line, Groenburgwal 44 (☎555 58 22), offers phone counseling and, if you call ahead for an appointment, a free testing clinic. Open for calls M-F 8am-noon, 1-4pm.

INTERNET ACCESS

Internet access is fairly abundant in Amsterdam. There are few copious cyber areas—the best bet may be a cozy coffeeshop with a single computer in the back. The following all have more than five computers and have Internet access as their main attraction.

easyEverything, Reguliersbreestraat 22. (☎320 62 89; www.easyeverything.com). Smaller location at Damrak 34. House hundreds of PCs and webcams on several floors. €1 for 26min., or longer-term deals (24hr. for €5, 1 week for €8, 20 days for €20) using a password given by a machine.

Cyber Cafe Amsterdam, Nieuwendijk 19. From Centraal, turn right at the Victoria Hotel, left at Martelaarsgracht, and right on Nieuwendijk. This is a crowded yet personable cybercafe with Internet at 12 computers (€1 per 30min.). Open Su-Th 10am-1am, F-Sa 10am-3am. Cash only.

Free World, Nieuwendijk 30 (☎620 09 02; http://cafe.euronet.nl). From Centraal Station, turn right at the main street, left at Martelaarsgracht, and right on Nieuwendijk. Quality Internet service (€1 for 30min.) and a slick computer-age interior meet at this dim and smoky cyber coffeeshop. Laptop friendly. Open Su-Th 9am-1am, F-Sa 9am-3am. Cash only.

Internet Cafe, Martelaarsgracht. 11 (627 10 52; www.internetcafe.nl). From Centraal, turn right at the Victoria Hotel and then left on Martelaarsgracht, near the intersection with Nieuwendijk. Very speedy Internet. 20min. half-off with a drink (€1.60-4.90). Otherwise, €1 for 20min. Open Su-Th 9am-1am, F-Sa 9am-2am.

The Mad Processor, Bloemgracht 82 (☎421 1482; mmc@madprocessor.com), in the Jordaan. Tram #10 to Bloemgracht, or any tram to Westermarkt. Open later than most Internet spots in Amsterdam and boasting a beautiful canal-side location, you can count on this spot for the newest computer games plus a hip-hop soundtrack. It's also one of the few spots with floppy disk drive use and capability to plug in your laptop (€4 per hr.). Use of their high-speed-Internet computers €3 per hr. Printing €0.50 per page. Open daily noon-2am. Cash only.

LAUNDRY

If you're running out of clean clothes, you should have no trouble finding a *wasserette* (laundromat) in your area.

Rozengracht Wasserette, Rozengracht 59 (☎638 59 75), in the Jordaan. Go left down Rozengracht from Westermarkt. You can do it yourself (wash €5.50; dry €6 per 5kg load) or have it done for you (€8 for 5kg). Open daily 9am-9pm. Cash only.

Wasserette/Launderette, Oude Doelenstraat 12 (☎624 17 00). From Dam, take Damstraat toward Oude Zijd and the laundromat is on your right just before Oudezijds Achterburgwal; convenient location if staying in the Red Light District, Oude Zijd, or the northern Nieuwe Zijd. Wash and dry a load for €6. Self-service only. Open M-F 8:30am-7pm, Sa 10am-5pm. Cash only.

Aquarette, Oudebrugsteeg 22 (☎ 638 13 97), off Damrak south of Centraal Station. Self-service only. Wash 5kg load for €5, dry €1 per 12min. Go to Continental Hotel across the street for doorkey. Open daily 8am-9:30pm. Cash only.

Wasserette-Stomerij 'De Eland', Elandsgracht 59 (☎625 07 31), in the Jordaan. From the Westermarkt tram stop, turn left at Prinsengracht; after the second bridge, turn right at Elandsgracht. Self-serve only. €4 for 4kg, €6 for 6kg. Open M-Tu and Th-F 8am-8pm, W 8am-6pm, Sa 9am-5pm.

LIBRARY

Openbare Bibliotheek Amsterdam, Prinsengracht 587 (☎523 09 00). The main branch of the city's public library system is the only one in the direct city center. Free Internet access can be reserved for a 30min. slot at the information desk. Check out the reading room and catch up on the latest news from the *Herald Tribune* over a cup of coffee at the inexpensive cafe. Has a fair selection of English magazines and fiction. Open M 1-9pm, Tu-Th 10am-9pm, F-Sa 10am-5pm; Oct.-Mar. Su 1-5pm.

MAIL

Post offices are generally open Monday through Friday 9am-5pm and sometimes Sa 10am-1:30pm. Larger branches may stay open later. Post offices can be recognized by their red and blue signs. For further info, call the information hotline (☎0800 04 17.) For more information on mail rates and delivery, see p. 29.

Main post offices: Singel 250, at Radhuisstraat (open M-W and F 9am-6pm, Th 9am-8pm, Sa 10am-1:30pm); **Oosterdokskade 3,** east of Centraal Station (open M-F 8:30am-9pm, Sa 9am-noon); **St. Antoniebreestraat 16,** near Nieuwmarkt; **Waterlooplein 2,** in Stadhuis (open M-F 9am-6pm, Sa 10am-1:30pm).

PHARMACIES

Look for an *apotheek* sign. Most are open M-F 8:30am-5:30pm. Most pharmacies sell toiletries, first aid supplies, and condoms in addition to filling prescriptions. The city's two major chains are *Nassau Apotheek* and *Da Apotheek*. While no single dedicated 24hr. pharmacy exists in the city, the 24hr. Afgeling Inlichtingen Apotheken hotline (☎694 87 09) will direct you to the nearest pharmacy.

RENTAL AGENCIES

A4U, Internet-based apartments at www.apartments4u.nl.

Accommodation Home Agency BV, Singel 402 (☎422 30 20; www.acc-home-agency.nl).

Amstel Housing, Kostverlorenhof 59, 1183 HG Amstelveen. (☎441 77 75; www.amstel-housing.nl/).

Amsterdam Housing, Slingerbeekstraat 29 (☎671 72 66).

Apartment Services AS, Waalstraat 58 96 (☎672 30 13; fax 676 46 79).

Dutch Housing Centre BV, Valeriusstraat 174 (☎662 12 34; www.apartmentservices.nl).

Horst Housing Service, Elandsgracht 86 (☎627 63 90).

Try the following links for agencies and more information:

www.expatica.com/housing/ Offers extensive information about housing. Specifically geared towards expatriates.

www.housingonline.nl/ An online housing agency with an office at Roelof Hartstraat 23. ☎0800 7356 2283.

www.hakkenbroekhousing.nl Online housing agency. ☎035 628 62 33

www.expatriates.com/classifieds/ Electronic database of classifieds for housing all over the world.

SUPERMARKETS

Albert Heijn supermarkets line the streets in Amsterdam. Check for locations at www.albert.nl

Dirk van den Broek, Big, basic supermarket that's significantly cheaper than Albert Heijn. Many locations throughout Amsterdam. Most open M-Sa 8am-6pm; larger stores open later and on Sun.

TOURIST OFFICES

VVV, Stationsplein 10 (☎0900 400 40 40, €0.55 per min). When exiting Centraal Station, the office is across the tram tracks to the left. Once you make it through the slow-moving lines, get help with hostel/hotel reservations (€3 per person). Buy tickets for museums and canal boat tours or ask for the location of the nearest coffeeshop. Open daily 9am-5pm. Expect a long wait here and at the other offices at platform #2 inside **Centraal Station** (open M-Sa 8am-7:45pm, Su 9am-5pm); **Leidseplein 1,** around the corner on Leidsestraat (open M-Th 9am-6pm, F-Sa 9am-7pm, Su 9am-5pm); **Stationsplein,** Argonautenstraat 98 (Open M-F 9:30am-5:30pm, Sa 10am-4pm).

GVB, across from Centraal Station and to the right of the VVV, with a "Tickets and Service" sign, Specializes in bus, tram, and metro information and has much shorter lines than its neighbor. Buy a *strippenkart* or ask for excursion pamphlets. Open M-F 7am-9pm, Sa-Su 8am-9pm. Info line ☎0900 92 92; €0.30 per min.; M-F 6am-midnight, Sa-Su 7am-midnight.

Eurolines, Rokin 10 (☎560 87 88; www.eurolines.nl), is one of Europe's leading coach services, offering incredibly cheap transport to destinations across Europe. Backpackers often travel on Eurolines, as prices are less than one-third that of train or cheap air transport. Open M-F 9:30am-5:30pm, Sa 10am-4pm. Also purchase tickets at the Eurolines bus depot, at Amstel Station (☎560 87 88 first to ensure availability; take the Metro, any line, to Julianaplein 5; open daily 7am-11:30pm).

Holland Tourist Information at **Schiphol Airport.** Open daily 7am-10pm.

Index

CCR central canal ring **CRW** canal ring west **DP** de pijp **J** jordaan **JP** jodenbuurt & plantage **LP**
leidseplein **MV** museumplein & vondelpark **NZ** nieuwe zijd **OZ** oude zijd **RLD** red light district **RP**
rembrandtplein **SQ** shipping quarter (scheepvaartbuurt) **WO** westerpark & oud-west

CCR central canal ring **CRW** canal ring west **DP** de pijp **J** jordaan **JP** jodenbuurt & plantage **LP** leidseplein **MV** museumplein & vondelpark **NZ** nieuwe zijd **OZ** oude zijd **RLD** red light district **RP** rembrandtplein **SQ** shipping quarter (scheepvaartbuurt) **WO** westerpark & oud-west

327

◙ sights
◙ museums
◘ food & drink
◢ coffeeshops & smartshops
◙ nightlife
◢ arts & entertainment
◘ shopping
◢ accommodations
◢ daytripping
◘ festivals

CCR central canal ring **CRW** canal ring west **DP** de pijp **J** jordaan **JP** jodenbuurt & plantage **LP** leidseplein **MV** museumplein & vondelpark **NZ** nieuwe zijd **OZ** oude zijd **RLD** red light district **RP** rembrandtplein **SQ** shipping quarter (scheepvaartbuurt) **WO** westerpark & oud-west

329

🏛 sights
🏛 museums
🍴 food & drink
🍴 coffeeshops & smartshops
🎵 nightlife
🎭 arts & entertainment
🛍 shopping
🍴 accommodations
🎒 daytripping
🌍 festivals

CCR central canal ring **CRW** canal ring west **DP** de pijp **J** jordaan **JP** jodenbuurt & plantage **LP** leidseplein **MV** museumplein & vondelpark **NZ** nieuwe zijd **OZ** oude zijd **RLD** red light district **RP** rembrandtplein **SQ** shipping quarter (scheepvaartbuurt) **WO** westerpark & oud-west

⬛ sights
⬛ museums
⬛ food & drink
⬛ coffeeshops & smartshops
⬛ nightlife
⬛ arts & entertainment
⬛ shopping
⬛ accommodations
⬛ daytripping
⬛ festivals

T

U

CCR central canal ring **CRW** canal ring west **DP** de pijp **J** jordaan **JP** jodenbuurt & plantage **LP** leidseplein **MV** museumplein & vondelpark **NZ** nieuwe zijd **OZ** oude zijd **RLD** red light district **RP** rembrandtplein **SQ** shipping quarter (scheepvaartbuurt) **WO** westerpark & oud-west

OPENING PHOTOS

Canal Houses, Jodenbuurt	p. 0	Leidseplein	p. 162
Gravenstenenbrug, Haarlem	p. 24	Mozes en Aäronkerk, Waterlooplein	p. 172
Lion Bridge, Rotterdam	p. 36	American Hotel, Leidseplein	p. 182
Westerkerk, Canal Ring West	p. 56	On the road to Edam	p. 206
Tropenmuseum, Jodenbuurt & Plantage	p. 78	Centraal Station, Amsterdam	p. 282
Koninklijk Paleis, Nieuwe Zijd	p. 102	Greenpeace Building, Canal Ring West	p. 302
Casa Rosso, Red Light District	p. 122	Brilmuseum Glasses Shop, Central Canal Ring	p. 318
Heineken Experience Bar, De Pijp	p. 142		

sights · museums · food & drink · coffeeshops & smartshops · nightlife · arts & entertainment · shopping · accommodations · daytripping · festivals

Map Appendix

INSIDE

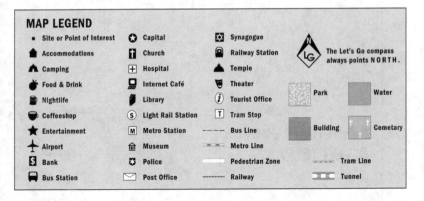

MAP LEGEND

▪ Site or Point of Interest	✪ Capital	✡ Synagogue
♠ Accommodations	🛈 Church	🚂 Railway Station
▲ Camping	✚ Hospital	▲ Temple
🍴 Food & Drink	💻 Internet Café	🎭 Theater
🍷 Nightlife	📖 Library	ⓘ Tourist Office
☕ Coffeeshop	Ⓢ Light Rail Station	T Tram Stop
★ Entertainment	Ⓜ Metro Station	- - - - Bus Line
✈ Airport	🏛 Museum	Metro Line
💲 Bank	🔱 Police	Pedestrian Zone
🚌 Bus Station	✉ Post Office	Railway

The Let's Go compass always points NORTH.

Park   Water

Building   Cemetary

Tram Line

Tunnel

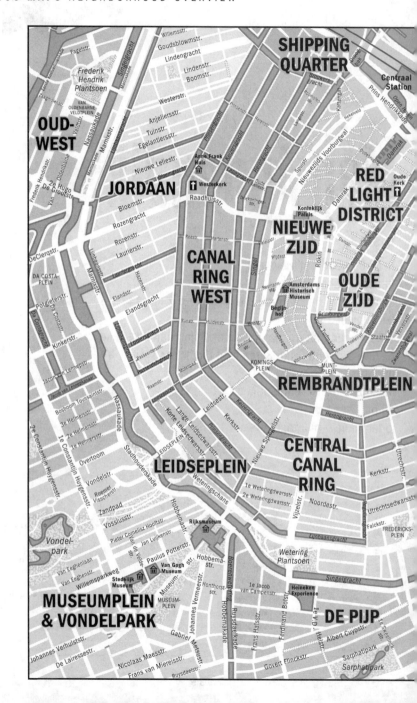

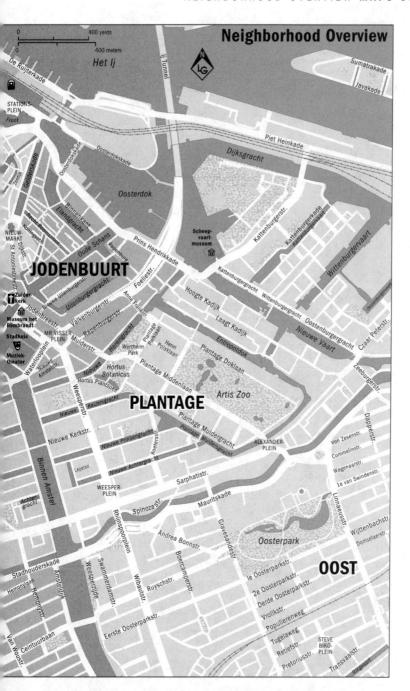

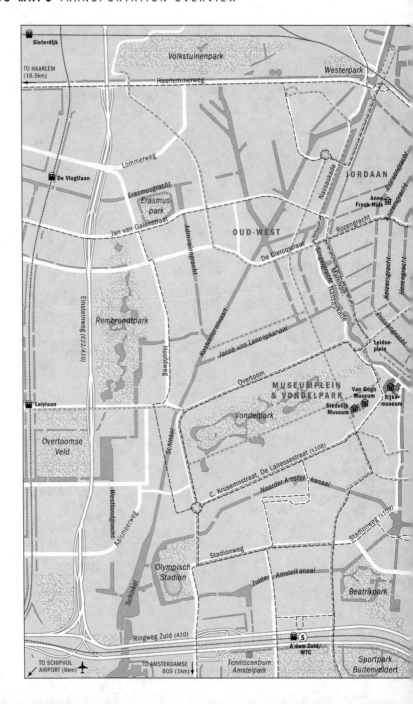

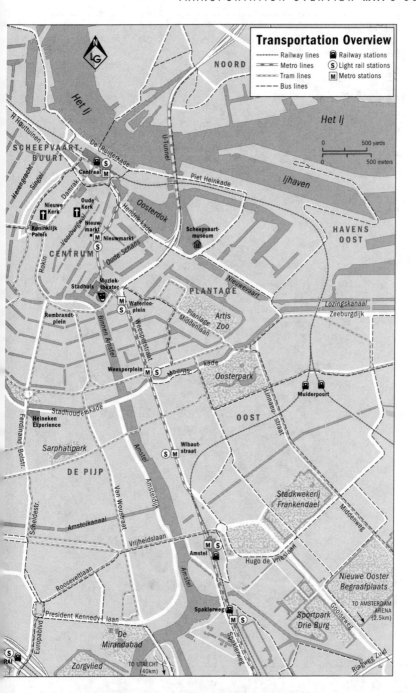

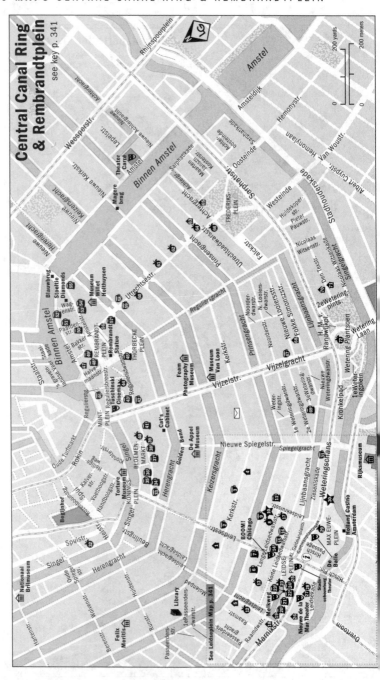

Central Canal Ring & Rembrandtplein

see key p. 341

See Leidseplein Map p. 341

Central Canal Ring & Rembrandtplein

see map p. 340

ACCOMMODATIONS
City Hotel, **56**
Euphemia Budget Hotel, **68**
The Golden Bear, **1**
Hans Brinker Hotel, **4**
Hemp Hotel, **65**
Hotel Asterisk, **71**
Hotel de la Haye, **18**
Hotel de Lantaerne, **19**
Hotel Kap, **70**
Hotel la Boheme, **25**
Hotel Monopole, **47**
Hotel Titus, **26**
International Budget Hostel, **5**
Quentin Hotel, **27**
Radion Inn Youth Hostel, **63**

FOOD & DRINK
Axum, **64**
Bojo, **8**
Bombay Inn, **13**
Carousel Pancake
    House, **72**
Coffee and Jazz, **62**
Eat at Jo's, **23**
Golden Temple, **66**
Kitsch, **60**
La Margarita, **40**
Lanskroon, **32**
NOA, **12**
Rose's Cantina, **39**
Santa Lucia, **17**

FOOD & DRINK (Cont.)
De Smoeshaan, **28**
Tashi Deleg, **61**
Tomo Sushi, **44**
Wagamama, **29**

NIGHTLIFE
Alto, **14**
Arc Bar, **38**
Aroma, **7**
The Back Door, **54**
Bamboo Bar, **6**
De Beetles, **11**
Café April, **36**
Café de Koe, **21**
Café Menschen, **55**
Coco's Outback, **45**
De Duivel, **43**
Escape, **49**
Exit, **41**
The iT, **53**
K2 Apres-Ski Lounge, **51**
Kamer 401, **22**
Lellebel, **57**
Lux, **24**
M Bar, **35**
Mankind, **69**
Melkweg, **23**
Montmartre, **48**
Soho, **37**

NIGHTLIFE (Cont.)
Vive la Vie, **50**
Weber, **20**
You II, **52**

COFFEESHOPS
Coffeeshop Little, **67**
Dreamlounge Smartshop, **3**
Free I, **42**
Global Chillage, **2**
The Noon, **31**
The Other Side, **33**
The Rookies, **15**
The Saint, **46**
Seeds of Passion, **59**
Stix, **58**
Tatanka, **16**
Tops, **9**

ENTERTAINMENT
Bourbon Street Jazz &
    Blues Club, **10**
Paradiso, **30**

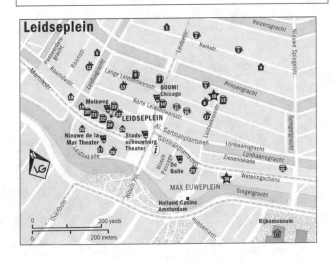

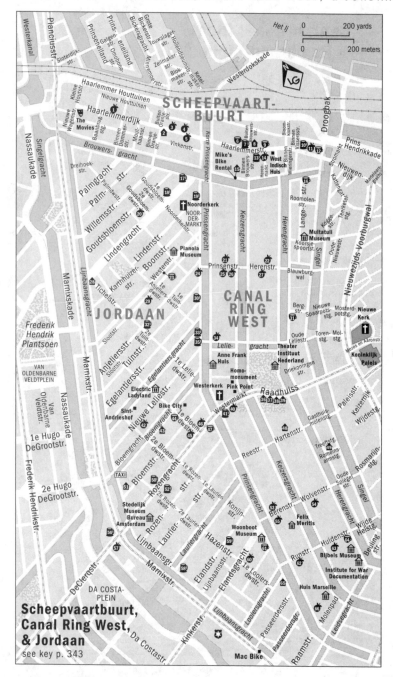

Scheepvaartbuurt,
Canal Ring West,
& Jordaan
see key p. 343

Scheepvaartbuurt, Canal Ring West, & Jordaan

see map p. 342

ACCOMMODATIONS

Frederic Rent-a-Bike, **15**
Hotel Acacia, **28**
Hotel Aspen, **39**
Hotel Belga, **48**
Hotel Clemens, **36**
Hotel Hegra, **49**
Hotel My Home, **8**
Hotel Pax, **37**
Hotel van Onna, **43**
Ramenas Hotel, **2**
The Shelter Jordan, **51**
Westertoren Hotel, **38**
Wiechmann Hotel, **65**

FOOD & DRINK

Bakkerij Paul Année, **62**
Balraj, **4**
Ben Cohen Shawarma, **57**
Bolhoed, **24**
Broodje Mokum, **46**
Cafe de Pels, **63**
Cinema Paradiso, **29**
Dimitri's, **26**
Harlem: Drinks and
  Soul Food, **14**
Hein, **53**
Het Molenpad, **66**
Jay's Juice, **11**
Jordino, **5**
Koh-I-noor, **40**
Lunchcafé Neilsen, **55**
Manzano, **45**
Padi, **3**
Prego, **27**
Rakang, **60**
Rendez-Vous en Afrique, **1**
Ruhe Delicatessen, **25**
Spanjer en Van Twist, **34**
Snackbar Aggie, **20**
Top Thai, **22**
Vennington, **21**
De Vliegende Schotel, **42**
Wolvenstraat 23, **54**

NIGHTLIFE

De Blauwe Druife, **13**
Cafe Thijssen, **17**
Cafe de Tuin, **32**
Cafe de Wilde Zee, **10**
Cafe Kalkhoven, **41**
Cafe P96, **30**
Cafe 't Smalle, **33**
Club More, **52**
Duende, **18**
Dulac, **7**
Korsakoff, **58**
Mazzo, **50**
Proust, **19**
Saarein II, **59**
Sound Garden, **56**
Wil's Cafe, **35**

COFFEESHOPS

Amnesia, **31**
Barney's Coffeeshop, **6**
Black Star Coffeeshop, **47**
Blue Velvet Coffeeshop, **9**
Extreme Amsterdam, **64**
La Tertulia, **61**
Pablow Picasso, **12**
Paradox, **44**
Siberie, **16**
Spirit Coffeeshop, **23**

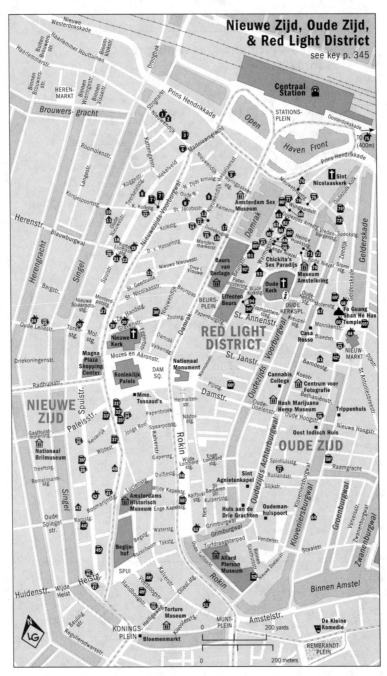

Nieuwe Zijd, Oude Zijd, & Red Light District
see key p. 345

Nieuwe Zijd, Oude Zijd, & Red Light District

see map p. 344

♠ ACCOMMODATIONS

ANCO Hotel, **70**
Anna Youth Hostel, **6**
Bob's Youth Hostel, **22**
Budget Hotel Tamara, **27**
Christian Youth Hostel
"The Shelter", **61**
Durty Nelly's Hostel, **94**
Flying Pig Downtown, **9**
Frisco Inn, **91**
The Greenhouse Effect
Hotel, **88**
Hotel Brian, **10**
Hotel Brouwer, **11**
Hotel Continental, **16**
Hotel Cosmos, **23**
Hotel The Crown, **72**
Hotel Groenendael, **2**
Hotel Hoksbergen, **43**
Hotel Internationaal, **78**
Hotel Nova, **40**
Hotel Rokin, **56**
Hotel Royal Taste, **67**
Hotel Vijaya, **71**
La Canna, **13**
Old Nickel, **76**
Old Quarter, **81**
De Oranje Tulip, **17**
Stablemaster, **80**
Stayokay Amsterdam
Stadsdoelen, **54**
Tourist Inn, **18**
De Witte Tulp Hostel, **93**
Young Budget Hotel
Kabul, **83**

🍎 FOOD & DRINK

Aneka Rasa, **82**
Foodism, **24**
Green Planet, **26**
Hoi Tin, **66**
In de Waag, **64**
La Fruteria, **28**
La Place, **51**
Mister Coco's, **1**
New Season, **84**
Old Highlander, **8**
Pannenkoekenhuis Upstairs, **53**
Ristorante Caprese, **42**
Sea Palace, **75**
Sie Joe, **29**
Taste of Culture, **68**
Tasty and Healthy, **19**
Theehuis Himalaya, **85**
Usama, **21**

🍺 NIGHTLIFE

020, **31**
Absinthe, **35**
Belgique, **30**
Bep, **37**
Blarney Stone, **3**
Blue Boy, **7**
Café de Engelbewaarder, **58**
Café de Jaren, **52**
Cafe de Stevens, **65**
Cafe Heffer, **89**
Casablanca, **73**
Cock and Feathers, **74**
Cockring, **92**
Dansen Bij Jansen, **49**
Durty Nelly's Pub, **94**
The Getaway, **33**
Getto, **86**
Gollem, **44**
Harry's Bar, **45**
Lime, **69**
Lokaal 't Loosje, **62**
Meander, **48**
NL Lounge, **32**
Stablemaster, **80**
The Tara, **55**
Vrankvijk, **38**
Why Not, **7**
Wijnand Fockink, **60**

☕ COFFEESHOPS

420 Cafe (de Kuil), **15**
Abraxas, **34**
Cafe Del Mondo, **63**
Coffeeshop Any Day, **12**
Coffeeshop Goa, **59**
Conscious Dreams
Kokopelli, **77**
Dampkring, **50**
Dutch Flowers, **47**
The Essential Seeds Company
Art and Smart Shop, **4**
Funny People Coffeeshop, **79**
The Greenhouse Effect, **90**
Grey Area, **25**
Hill Street Blues, **87**
Kadinsky, **41**
La Canna, **13**
The Magic Mushroom, **39**
Magic Valley, **20**
Route 99, **5**
Rusland, **57**
Softland, **36**
De Tweede Kamer (The Second
Room), **46**
Wolke Wietje, **14**

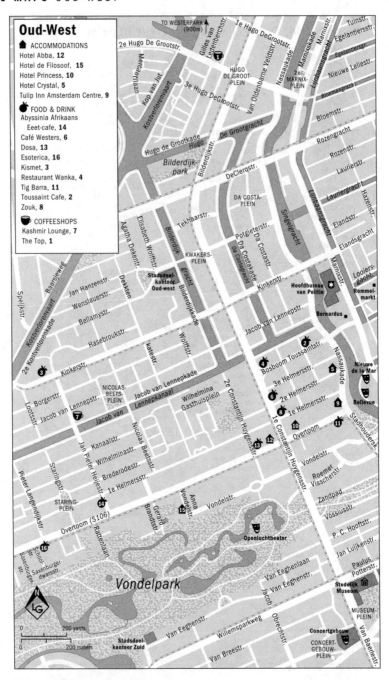

Oud-West

🏠 ACCOMMODATIONS
Hotel Abba, **12**
Hotel de Filosoof, **15**
Hotel Princess, **10**
Hotel Crystal, **5**
Tulip Inn Amsterdam Centre, **9**

🍎 FOOD & DRINK
Abyssinia Afrikaans
  Eeet-cafe, **14**
Café Westers, **6**
Dosa, **13**
Esoterica, **16**
Kismet, **3**
Restaurant Wanka, **4**
Tig Barra, **11**
Toussaint Cafe, **2**
Zouk, **8**

☕ COFFEESHOPS
Kashmir Lounge, **7**
The Top, **1**

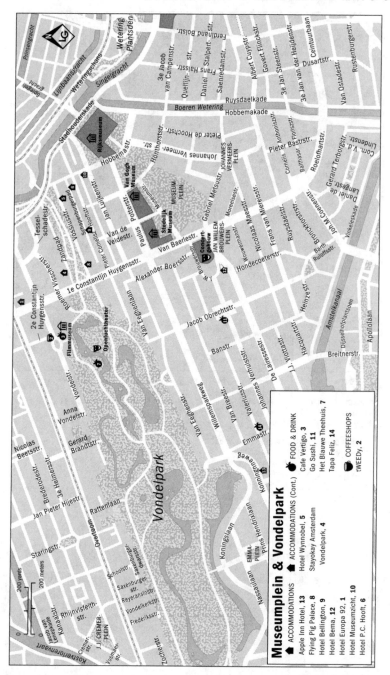

Museumplein & Vondelpark

ACCOMMODATIONS
Apple Inn Hotel, **13**
Flying Pig Palace, **8**
Hotel Bellington, **9**
Hotel Bema, **12**
Hotel Europa 92, **1**
Hotel Museumzicht, **10**
Hotel P. C. Hooft, **6**

ACCOMMODATIONS (Cont.)
Hotel Wynnobel, **5**
Stayokay Amsterdam
Vondelpark, **4**

FOOD & DRINK
Cafe Vertigo, **3**
Go Sushi, **11**
Het Blauwe Theehuis, **7**
Tapa Feliz, **14**

COFFEESHOPS
tWEEDy, **2**

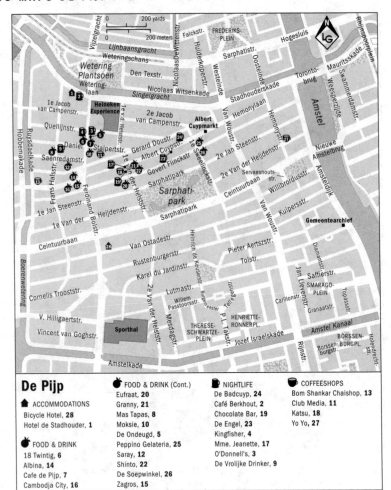

De Pijp

🏠 **ACCOMMODATIONS**
Bicycle Hotel, **28**
Hotel de Stadhouder, **1**

🍅 **FOOD & DRINK**
18 Twintig, **6**
Albina, **14**
Cafe de Pijp, **7**
Cambodja City, **16**

🍅 **FOOD & DRINK (Cont.)**
Eufraat, **20**
Granny, **21**
Mas Tapas, **8**
Moksie, **10**
De Ondeugd, **5**
Peppino Gelateria, **25**
Saray, **12**
Shinto, **22**
De Soepwinkel, **26**
Zagros, **15**

🍸 **NIGHTLIFE**
De Badcuyp, **24**
Café Berkhout, **2**
Chocolate Bar, **19**
De Engel, **23**
Kingfisher, **4**
Mme. Jeanette, **17**
O'Donnell's, **3**
De Vrolijke Drinker, **9**

☕ **COFFEESHOPS**
Bom Shankar Chaishop, **13**
Club Media, **11**
Katsu, **18**
Yo Yo, **27**

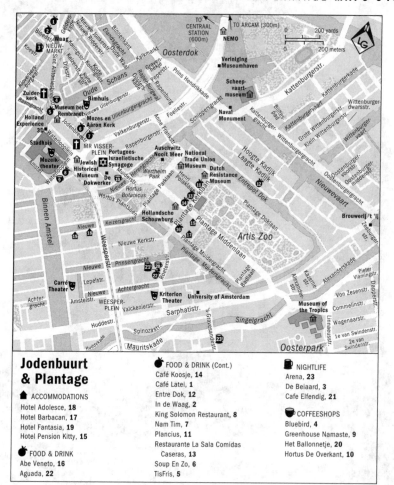

Jodenbuurt & Plantage

🏠 ACCOMMODATIONS
Hotel Adolesce, **18**
Hotel Barbacan, **17**
Hotel Fantasia, **19**
Hotel Pension Kitty, **15**

🍅 FOOD & DRINK
Abe Veneto, **16**
Aguada, **22**

🍅 FOOD & DRINK (Cont.)
Café Koosje, **14**
Café Latei, **1**
Entre Dok, **12**
In de Waag, **2**
King Solomon Restaurant, **8**
Nam Tim, **7**
Plancius, **11**
Restaurante La Sala Comidas
  Caseras, **13**
Soup En Zo, **6**
TisFris, **5**

🍺 NIGHTLIFE
Arena, **23**
De Beiaard, **3**
Cafe Elfendig, **21**

☕ COFFEESHOPS
Bluebird, **4**
Greenhouse Namaste, **9**
Het Ballonnetje, **20**
Hortus De Overkant, **10**

imagine
U in the UK

Travel, Study and Work in the UK.

**The Festivals. The Clubs.
The Sport. The Pubs. The Heritage.
The Cities. The Countryside.**

Come to the UK and access not just one but four different countries all in one destination. Get off the tourist trail, meet the locals and immerse yourself in the local culture – more than the average traveller gets to do. Get the scoop on what's happening in London, working and studying, visas, the hottest clubs, funky shopping, hippest hot spots, great accommodation, a crash course in the culture and much more.

For your survival guide to the UK
www.visitbritain.com/letsgo